COURTS IN FEDERAL COUNTRIES

Federalists or Unitarists?

Courts are key players in the dynamics of federal countries since their rulings have a direct impact on the ability of governments to centralize and decentralize power. *Courts in Federal Countries* examines the role high courts play in thirteen countries, including Australia, Brazil, Canada, Germany, India, Nigeria, Spain, and the United States.

The volume's contributors analyse the centralizing or decentralizing forces at play following a court's ruling on issues such as individual rights, economic affairs, social issues, and other matters. The thirteen substantive chapters have been written to facilitate comparability between the countries. Each chapter outlines a country's federal system, explains the constitutional and institutional status of the court system, and discusses the high court's jurisprudence in light of these features. *Courts in Federal Countries* offers insightful explanations of judicial behaviour in the world's leading federations.

NICHOLAS ARONEY is Professor of Constitutional Law in the School of Law at the University of Queensland.

JOHN KINCAID is the Robert B. and Helen S. Meyner Professor of Government and Public Service as well as the Director of the Robert B. and Helen S. Meyner Center for the Study of State and Local Government at Lafayette College, Easton, Pennsylvania.

Courts in Federal Countries

Federalists or Unitarists?

EDITED BY NICHOLAS ARONEY
AND JOHN KINCAID

UNIVERSITY OF TORONTO PRESS
Toronto Buffalo London

www.utppublishing.com

Reprinted in paperback 2017

ISBN 978-1-4875-0062-7 (cloth) ISBN 978-1-4875-2289-6 (paper)

Library and Archives Canada Cataloguing in Publication

Courts in federal countries : federalists or unitarists?
/ edited by Nicholas Aroney and John Kincaid.

Includes bibliographical references and index.
ISBN 978-1-4875-0062-7 (cloth) ISBN 978-1-4875-2289-6 (softcover)

1. Constitutional courts – Case studies. 2. Federal government – Case studies. I. Kincaid, John, 1946–, author, editor II. Aroney, Nicholas, author, editor

K3370.C69 2017 347′.035 C2016-906227-9

The Forum of Federations, the global network on federalism, supports better governance through learning among federal experts and practitioners. Active on six continents and supported by nine federal countries, it manages programs in established and emerging federations and publishes scholarly and educational materials.

Secrétariat aux affaires intergouvernementales canadiennes
Québec

The Forum of Federations acknowledges the financial support from the Government of Québec.

University of Toronto Press acknowledges the financial assistance to its publishing program of the Canada Council for the Arts and the Ontario Arts Council, an agency of the Government of Ontario.

Canada Council for the Arts
Conseil des Arts du Canada

Funded by the Government of Canada
Financé par le gouvernement du Canada

Contents

A Note from the Forum of Federations

The current volume *Courts in Federal Countries: Federalists or Unitarists?* is part of the Forum of Federations' ongoing commitment to shaping comparative research on federalism. It follows the Forum's work on structural issues of federalism published as a seven-volume set as part of the Global Dialogue Program, as well as multi-country studies on capital cities, oil and gas, internal trade, metropolitan regions, political parties, and intergovernmental relations. Forthcoming volumes with the University of Toronto Press will cover healthcare and public security.

The current volume was financially supported by the Government of Quebec and is possibly the most comprehensive study on courts and judicial systems in federal countries in recent times. Independent courts are an important and essential component of a robust federal system and act as the referee in dynamic and evolving federal systems. The current volume features the experiences and challenges of thirteen federal systems, offering a mix of new and old, as well as examining common law and civil law federations at various levels of development: Australia, Belgium, Brazil, Canada, Ethiopia, Germany, India, Mexico, Nigeria, South Africa, Spain, Switzerland, and the United States. Each country's study presents two case studies that highlight how in practice the judicial systems have acted to preserve federalism. The objective is to share experiences and identify good practices.

This volume represents a continuation of the Forum of Federations' interest in and work on different judicial systems in federal systems. The project follows the Forum's time-tested method for research projects. In consultation with a lead expert, a template was developed that examined the core issues and relevant questions for all contributors to address. Once the topic was defined, the Forum identified leading national experts as country chapter authors. This was followed by workshops at which authors were able to exchange and share ideas while refining the template to ensure that the most pertinent aspects of the topic were included. Some of the larger issues examined include the institutional role of courts compared to that of the executive and legislative process, the contribution of judicial systems to nation building, and the role of the courts in adjudicating disputes regarding federalism.

I am grateful to the individual authors for their contributions, all of which add to the richness of this volume. I would also like to thank editors Nicholas Aroney and John Kincaid for their perseverance in what has been a monumental project. Their dedication and hard work in partnership with the Forum to conceptualize the project, shape the template, and edit this vast piece of research was immeasurable. This volume would not have been possible without financial support from the Secrétariat aux affaires intergouvernementales canadiennes – Québec. We are grateful to Josée Bergeron for her patience and endorsement. I would be remiss if I didn't thank my colleagues at the Forum, Phil Gonzalez, for managing this project from start to finish, and John Light, for overseeing the publication process. Finally, thanks are due to our publisher, the University of Toronto Press, for their tireless work on this exciting volume.

Rupak Chattopadhyay
President and CEO, Forum of Federations

Foreword

A book on courts in federal countries is a welcome addition to the literature on federalism. The judicial dimension of federations is one of the least studied aspects of comparative federal governance. This volume demonstrates that whatever the reason for this neglect, it cannot be the unimportance of the subject. In its role as adjudicator of constitutional disputes, the judicial branch of government in a federation – above all its highest court – can play a crucial role in shaping the balance of power between the orders of government in a federation. It is this aspect of judicial federalism that receives most attention in this volume.

Another aspect of the subject is the organization and structure of courts in federations – the extent to which the division of judicial power parallels the division of legislative and executive power. This aspect of judicial federalism also receives attention in this volume. The only comparative book on court structures in federal countries is W.J. Wagner's *Federal States and Their Judiciaries*, published in 1959. Most of the world's federations did not exist when Wagner wrote his book. We need more systematic comparative study of federal court systems to gain a better understanding of how the organization of courts in federations affects the federal balance of power and the quality of justice.

There is clearly more than one way of properly organizing courts in a federation. Some federal states, such as the United States and some of the Latin American federations, have highly dualistic court systems, while judicial structures are more unitary in Commonwealth federations such as Canada and India, and in civil law federations such as Germany. The way courts are provided for in a constitution and develop over time is shaped by historic circumstances and legal culture. Whereas no particular court structure is essential for a country to qualify as a federation, the same cannot be said about the first dimension of judicial federalism. The judicial umpiring of constitutional disputes about the powers of the constitutional orders of government in a federation would seem to be an essential feature of government in a federation.

In the classical model of a federal state, the powers of its two or three orders of government are constitutionally guaranteed. This volume goes beyond the classical model and includes chapters on the role of the judiciary in devolutionary multinational models of federalism. Disputes about the boundaries of each order of government's competence or jurisdiction are bound to arise, and when they do, an independent judicial tribunal would seem the logical institution for settling the disputes. Switzerland is the one federation in which the highest court, the Federal Tribunal, can declare cantonal laws invalid if they exceed the limits on cantons set by the federal constitution, but it must accept laws of the general legislature as valid. However, any law passed by the federation's legislature can be challenged by referendum at the request of fifty thousand citizens or eight cantons.

This volume shows that there is a great deal of variation among federal countries in the importance of judicial review in settling constitutional disputes about federalism. In some of the older federations, such as Australia, Canada, and the United States, at different times in each country's history, high-court decisions have played a major role in interpreting the federal division of powers. Political leaders in newer federations may be less inclined to allow the judiciary to play a vital role in constitutional development. The question arises of whether excluding the judiciary from the role of arbiter of the constitutional division of power will undermine the integrity of the state's federal character.

There is a natural tendency for the highest courts in federal countries to have a centralist bias. If the judges who serve on these courts live in the national capital (as they usually do) and socialize with federal political leaders who have had an important role in their appointment, they are likely to share the central government's perspective on the powers it needs in order to govern effectively. Most federal constitutions try to offset this tendency by establishing some checks and balances on the central government's appointing power. These range from giving the upper chamber in the federal legislature a major role in selecting judges for the highest court (as with Germany's Bundesrat selecting half the members of the Constitutional Court and the U.S. Senate's advice and consent role in appointing Supreme Court justices), through the inclusion of four members of the Council of States on South Africa's twenty-three-member Judicial Services Commission, and to the legislative requirement in Australia that the federal attorney general consult her state counterparts before filling a vacancy on the country's high court.

It is ironic that in Canada, a relatively decentralized federation, the federal government's power to appoint Supreme Court justices is unencumbered by any obligation to obtain provincial input. But Canada's highest constitutional court until 1949 was the high court of the British Empire, the Judicial Committee of the Privy Council (JCPC), which fashioned a jurisprudence highly supportive of provincial rights. While Canada's Supreme Court, since becoming truly supreme, has not felt bound by the JCPC's legacy, its centralism has been constrained by its justices' concern to retain their legitimacy as a federal arbiter in a country with a very federal political culture.

The Canadian case and accounts of other federations included in this volume suggest that it is the evolving politics of a federal country rather than the intricacies of appointing procedures that have the greatest influence on the role judges perform as arbiters of the federal division of powers. It is easy, for example, to understand why, since the Civil War in the United States, American Supreme Court justices have not shown the respect for states' rights that Canadian Supreme Court justices continue to show for provincial rights. The Spanish Constitutional Court's engagement with the aggressive claims of autonomous communities shows that it is not only in limiting the growth of central government power that the capacity of high courts to resist the tides of federal politics may be tested.

For high courts in countries that adopted federalism at least in part to accommodate regionally based ethnic and/or linguistic minorities, there is a strong rationale for respecting the rights of ethnically distinct sections of the federation. In some of these federations, respect for ethnic and linguistic diversity is built into the structure of their highest court, as with the linguistic requirements of Switzerland's Federal Tribunal and Belgium's Constitutional Court. Similarly, in Canada, a requirement that at least three of its Supreme Court's nine justices must come from Quebec ensures at least minimal representation of jurists nurtured in the distinctive civil-law culture of that province.

High-court justices in federations may find that respecting the cultural distinctiveness of ethnic or linguistic minorities collides with their responsibility for enforcing universal civil rights. In most federations, it is the judiciary's function not only to adjudicate disputes about federal limits on the powers of governments but also limits on legislative and executive powers arising from constitutional guarantees of the fundamental rights of citizens. Indeed, a crucial turning point in American constitutional history was its Supreme Court's rulings that the Bill of Rights in the U.S. Constitution applies to state governments as well as to the federal government. Those decisions and the practice in other federations of applying constitutionally protected citizens' rights against all orders of government should be seen not so much as a centralizing but as a unifying influence on the federal polity, ensuring that its citizens share a common set of civil rights, regardless of the unit of the federal state in which they live.

Ultimately, the most important function of the judicial branch of a federal government is to ensure that the federal state is a constitutional state. Without a judiciary strong enough to protect the powers of governments and the rights of citizens, federalism cannot have much reality. I hope this volume will stimulate scholars and practitioners of federalism to give more attention to how this essential judicial function is performed in federations.

Peter H. Russell

Preface

Courts in Federal Countries: Federalists or Unitarists? is an important addition to the books of comparative scholarship produced by the Forum of Federations that detail many sectoral issues, themes, and practical problems that arise in federal systems around the world.

The Forum of Federations is an international organization and network created by the Government of Canada. It consists of federal partner countries from both mature and developing nations. The forum seeks to strengthen democratic governance by promoting dialogue on, and understanding of, the values, practices, principles, and possibilities of federalism.

Today the work of the Forum of Federations takes the organization to many established and democratizing nations around the globe. It works in these countries sharing the experiences of other federal and decentralized nations that have an interest in shared rule, promoting best practices, and adopting better governance options in the interests of advancing democracy.

The forum's activities in building intellectual capital through projects such as the Courts and Judicial Systems project are a pillar of the organization. These core activities enable it to utilize these experiences around the world with its partners, and in its development assistance programs in countries aspiring to democratic multi-level governance.

A comparison of courts in federal countries has seen little scholarly attention; its vital importance in federations was a compelling reason to investigate this area as part of the Forum of Federations core programming.

In March 2012, the Forum of Federations, in collaboration with the Secrétariat aux affaires intergouvernementales canadiennes,

Government of Quebec, held an international conference titled "Courts and Judicial Systems in Federal Countries." The conference was part of a larger project, generously supported by the Quebec Government, the culmination of which is this volume.

The international conference was organized by volume editors Nicholas Aroney (TC Beirne School of Law, University of Queensland), John Kincaid (Robert B. and Helen S. Meyner Center for the Study of State and Local Government, Lafayette College), Felix Knuepling (Forum of Federations), and Phillip Gonzalez (Forum of Federations). Gonzalez and Knuepling also provided program leadership.

The conference took place in Montreal and was structured to incorporate both an international and a Canadian round table. The meeting brought together country authors and over forty experts, practitioners, and academics. The objective for both meetings was to share experiences, debate issues, and examine practices of federal courts and their judicial systems.

The opening of the conference was complemented by a keynote address by eminent scholar Peter Russell, professor emeritus of political science at the University of Toronto. He offered a brief comparative analysis of the countries under investigation and highlighted some of the challenges and experiences of their courts and judicial systems. His address underlined the importance of the project and this publication.

The international conference presented for discussion the preliminary findings of the experiences of the thirteen federal countries covered by this project: Australia, Belgium, Brazil, Canada, Ethiopia, Germany, India, Mexico, Nigeria, South Africa, Spain, Switzerland, and the United States. This sample of country experiences was selected because it offers a mix of new and old, as well as common-law and civil-law, federations at various levels of development. The round table assembled some of Canada's leading experts, practitioners, and scholars on the subject to debate Canada's courts and judicial system.

During the two days of the conference, country authors presented their case findings based on the template developed by the book editors Nicholas Aroney and John Kincaid. The conference outlined and detailed such national issues as:

- The federal system
- The court system
- Constitutional status of courts and judicial officers
- Institutional role of the courts

- Curial procedures
- Judicial culture
- Federalism jurisprudence

After each country case presentation, subject-matter experts made their own comparative comments. This drove further discussion and provided an additional layer of context and insight for country-chapter authors. A key objective was to analyse underlying trends, and two questions were especially discussed:

- Have courts generally been regarded as institutions that have supported (or alternatively undermined) the values and principles of the federal system?
- What "reforms" or changes are being proposed, or should be considered, for strengthening the role of the courts in supporting or improving the proper operation of the federal system?

A Canadian round table was held on the final day of the conference with about twenty Canadian experts and government representatives. The round table followed a similar approach. Presentations were given by experts reflecting practice, experience, and opinion from across the country. The group discussed a number of issues dealing with jurisprudence specific to Canada and other factors and influences within the Canadian judicial system. The valuable contribution of all participants fed into the research and content being prepared by each country-chapter author.

The editors and the Forum of Federations wish to thank all contributors from the international conference and Canadian round table.

This book, therefore, is the product of many people, most importantly, the editors and contributing authors. The editors and the forum heartily thank the authors for their cooperative participation in seeing this book through several stages and some unexpected turns in development. We enjoyed working with all of them and appreciated their eagerness to produce as comprehensive and up-to-date chapters as possible.

We wish to thank the following people who volunteered their time to review and comment on the first drafts of the book's chapters: Joash Amupitan, University of Jos, Nigeria; A.J. Brown, Griffith University, Brisbane, Australia; Rajeev Dhavan, senior lawyer, Supreme Court of India; Julio Antonio Rios Figueroa, Centro de Investigación y Docencia

Económicas, A.C., Mexico; Alem Habtu, Queens College, City University of New York, United States; Bradley W. Miller, University of Western Ontario and Court of Appeal for Ontario, Canada; Christina Murray, University of Cape Town, South Africa; Johanne Poirier, McGill University, Montreal, Canada; Carles Viver i Pi-Sunyer, Institut d'Estudis Autonòmics, Barcelona, Spain; Cheryl Saunders, University of Melbourne, Australia; Christoph Schönberger, University of Konstanz, Germany; Nicolas Schmitt, Institut du Fédéralisme, Université de Fribourg, Switzerland; Ajay Kumar Singh, Hamdard University, New Delhi, India; Jaap de Visser, University of the Western Cape, Cape Town, South Africa; and Conrad Weiler, Temple University, Philadelphia, United States. Three anonymous reviewers engaged by the University of Toronto Press also provided helpful comments. These individuals, of course, are not responsible for any author's errors of commission or omission, but their observations did help greatly to improve the book.

We thank, as well, Dr John Trone in Brisbane, Australia, who provided professional research assistance, and Terry A. Cooper at the Robert B. and Helen S. Meyner Center for the Study of State and Local Government, who managed many aspects of the book's progress. We would like to acknowledge the support offered by several staff members at the Forum of Federations: Fauziah Pruner and Olu Ayeni. Thanks to Forum CEO and President Rupak Chattopadhyay and Forum Vice-President Charles Cloutier for their input and guidance.

A special note of thanks must be given for the generous financial, intellectual, and logistic support provided by the Secrétariat aux affaires intergouvernementales canadiennes, Government of Quebec. Josée Bergeron has been a wonderful and strong supporter of this project.

The goal of this book is to add greater insight into the role of judicial power in relation to federalism. Given the fundamental role that courts and judicial systems play in most federal systems, the comparative research presented in this volume will add immense value and promote greater research and discussion in this vital area of federal governance. Our aim is to encourage practitioners and scholars to utilize this resource to devise new solutions and to engage with the many active participants around the world in the growing international network on federalism.

Ottawa, May 2016

COURTS IN FEDERAL COUNTRIES

Federalists or Unitarists?

1 Introduction: Courts in Federal Countries

NICHOLAS ARONEY AND JOHN KINCAID

This book examines courts in thirteen federal and quasi-federal countries: Australia, Belgium, Brazil, Canada, Ethiopia, Germany, India, Mexico, Nigeria, South Africa, Spain, Switzerland, and the United States. The book's principal theme is whether the courts, particularly a federation's highest court, lean in a "unitary" direction by fostering or reinforcing centralization, or in a "federalist" direction by fostering or reinforcing powers of the federation's constituent polities (e.g., cantons, Länder, provinces, regions, or states). This theme is important because courts are key players in the dynamics of most federations, and they can affect centralization and decentralization directly by ruling on the constitutional distribution or powers and indirectly by ruling on social issues, individual rights, economic affairs, and other matters. Courts may choose to some extent to be federalist or unitarist, but they also are pushed in one direction or another by the design of the constitution and by uses and abuses of the constitution by political forces.

The book consists of thirteen country chapters written by country experts. Each chapter follows a template which asked authors to (1) outline the main constitutional, structural, and historical features of their federal system; (2) explain the constitutional and institutional status of their country's court system or systems, including organization, judicial selection, degree of independence, curial procedures, judicial culture, and degree of attention to federalism matters; and (3) discuss their high court's federalism jurisprudence in the light of these features. Employing various theoretical perspectives, the book offers possible explanations for the judicial behaviour observed in these countries. Although, because of the diverse conditions in these federations and the exploratory nature of this project, we do not test a specific theory, we hope this work will pave the way for more theory-based research.

Basic characteristics of the thirteen federations are listed in table 1. We classified a federation as "devolutionary" when its origins lie in the devolution of powers from a centralized unitary state or colonial system (e.g., Spain and Nigeria) and as "integrative" when its origins lie in the unification of otherwise actually or potentially independent political communities (e.g., the United States). We classified Canada as devolutionary and integrative, because its foundation involved an imperial division of the unitary Province of Canada into Ontario and Quebec, along with the integration of two maritime provinces, followed by six more provinces from 1870 to 1949. We classified the Federal Republic of Germany similarly, because it was formed from the previously centralized Nazi state, and the boundaries of the Länder were drawn by the Allied military occupiers. However, Länder existed previously and were integrated into a federal arrangement before the Nazi era; then, in 1990, the East German Länder were reconstituted in nearly their historical forms and integrated into a united Germany.

I. Courts and Federalism

Because federalism is a constitutional arrangement in which powers (or competences) are divided and shared between two or three orders of government, courts – as arbiters of constitutional disputes – have a potentially very important role in policing the distribution and sharing of powers. To the extent the courts are independent and vested with a duty to maintain the constitution, they might be expected to uphold the constitutional distribution of powers against political forces bent on altering that distribution in a more centralist or decentralist direction.

Albert Venn Dicey famously claimed that "federalism" necessarily implies "legalism" and the "predominance of the judiciary."[1] He defined federalism as a system in which "the ordinary powers of sovereignty are elaborately divided between the common or national government and the separate states."[2] He believed that proper maintenance of this division of power required a "supreme constitution" with courts having authority to interpret it.[3] Was he right? Partly.

1 Albert Venn Dicey, *Introduction to the Study of the Law of the Constitution*, 8th ed. (London: Macmillan, 1915), 170.

2 Ibid., 139. See also "A true federal government is based on the division of powers" (ibid., lxxvii).

3 Ibid., 140.

Table 1 Basic Information about the Case Federations

Federation	Population 2014 (millions)	GDP per capita (US $)	Date of first federal constitution[a]	Number of constitutions[b]	Number of constituent polities[c]	Integrative/ devolutionary formation	Law tradition[d]	Residual/ reserved powers location[e]	Type of high constitutional court[f]
Australia	23	67,458	1901	1	6	I	Common	CP	Supreme
Belgium	11	46,878	1993	1	6	D	Civil	FED	Constitutional
Brazil	202	11,208	1891	7	26	D	Civil	CP	Supreme
Canada	35	51,958	1867	1	10	DI	Common/civil	FED	Supreme
Ethiopia	97	505	1994	1	9	D	Common/civil	CP	Supreme
Germany	81	42,269	1949	1	16	DI	Civil	CP	Constitutional
India	1,236	1,499	1949	1	28	DI	Common	FED	Supreme
Mexico	120	10,307	1824	9	31	D	Civil	CP	Supreme
Nigeria	177	3,006	1960	6	36	D	Common	CP	Supreme
South Africa	53	6,618	1993	2	9	D	Common	FED	Constitutional
Spain	48	29,863	1978	1	17	D	Civil	FED	Constitutional
Switzerland	8	84,815	1848	3	26	I	Civil	CP	Supreme
United States	318	53,042	1788	1	50	I	Common	CP	Supreme

[a] Excluded are federal-like colonial-era constitutions, post-colonial non-federal constitutions that preceded the first federal constitution, and prior instruments of a confederal nature.

[b] Count includes the first federal constitution and all subsequent constitutions, federal and non-federal.

[c] Excluded are federal districts, territories, and other entities.

[d] Several countries also have customary or religious law systems.

[e] CP = constituent polities; FED = federation.

[f] Some courts classified as "supreme" have more limited jurisdiction than others, and those of Ethiopia and Switzerland lack judicial review authority over federation law.

Sources: Population: U.S. Central Intelligence Agency, *The World Factbook*, https://www.cia.gov/library/publications/the-world-factbook/rankorder/2119rank.html; GDP: The World Bank, "GDP per Capita, PPP," data.worldbank.org/indicator/NY.GDP.PCAP.PP.CD; number of constitutions: Zachary Elkins, Tom Ginsburg, and James Melton, *The Endurance of National Constitutions* (Cambridge: Cambridge University Press, 2009), 215–20.

Dicey's conception of federalism has been criticized as being overly legalistic and excessively influenced by the idea of "sovereignty," which Dicey thought was the prime characteristic of Britain's Parliament. Michael Burgess is scathing: "Dicey's impact and influence upon the British tradition of federalism proved especially damaging," because "it established a narrow legalistic conception of federation that was handed down from one generation to the next in supine fashion."[4] However, Dicey's influence was limited outside of the British tradition, and even Kenneth C. Wheare – an Australian who spent most of his life at Oxford University, and who shared Dicey's view that federalism necessarily involves a division of powers – treated the judicial role as less essential. All that is strictly necessary, he said, is that "some impartial body, independent of the general and regional governments, should decide on the meaning of the division of powers."[5] Wheare, like James Bryce before him,[6] observed that while in the United States, Canada, and Australia this function is performed by the courts, Switzerland is different because the *Tribunal fédéral* lacks authority to determine the constitutionality of federal laws.[7] In 1994, Ethiopia established a high court with no judicial-review authority. However, Wheare still saw that the role of courts in Switzerland, as well as in the other federal systems he examined, is highly significant, and he dedicated several sections of his book to their analysis.[8]

Certainly federalism seems to have had a significant influence on the development of constitutional judicial review. As Andreas Auer observed, federalism "was first in bringing the constitution to the courts, long before civil rights and liberties did the same," and it "has contributed much to the evolution of the constitution from a political recipe to a legal norm."[9] After all, a federal system ordinarily requires

4 Michael Burgess, *Comparative Federalism: Theory and Practice* (New York: Routledge, 2006), 21.

5 Kenneth C. Wheare, *Federal Government*, 1st American ed. (New York: Oxford University Press, 1947), 66.

6 James Bryce, *The American Commonwealth*, 2nd ed. (London: Macmillan, 1889), 1:253–4.

7 Wheare, *Federal Government*, 64–8.

8 E.g., ibid. 72–8 and chap. 4.

9 Andreas Auer, "The Constitutional Scheme of Federalism," *Journal of European Public Policy* 12, no. 3 (2005): 419–31. See also Martin Shapiro, "The Success of Judicial Review," in *Constitutional Dialogues in Comparative Perspective*, ed. Sally J. Kenney, William W. Riesinger, and John C. Reitz, 193–219 (New York: Palgrave Macmillan, 1999).

a written constitution, and a written constitution requires interpretation, usually, though not always exclusively, by judges. The importance of the judiciary was established by most of the pre-federation U.S. state constitutions, such as the Massachusetts Constitution of 1780, the world's oldest written constitution still in effect. The Declaration of Rights of that constitution guarantees all citizens "an impartial interpretation of the laws ... by judges as free, impartial, and independent as the lot of humanity will admit."[10] Given the states' experiences with judicial review before 1788,[11] Alexander Hamilton expressed a widely held view when he wrote in *Federalist* 78 that "whenever a particular statute contravenes the constitution, it will be the duty of the judicial tribunals to adhere to the latter, and disregard the former."[12]

Consequently, judicial review, if it exists in a federal system, is not limited to executive action; it applies also to legislative action that impinges upon federalism, although there may be a judicial presumption of the constitutionality of federal legislation. This power may allow a court to remove a law from the statute books, as can some European courts. Other courts, such as the U.S. Supreme Court, cannot go this far, even though the Court's rulings have the same effect.[13] However, it should be noted that the constitutions of the United States and Australia do not explicitly confer the power of judicial review on the federal supreme court, while some other constitutions (e.g., Germany and India) explicitly authorize it.

The importance of courts also loomed large in the origin of modern federalism because of the fundamental change wrought in the traditional notion of federalism (i.e., confederalism) by the U.S. Constitution. The great innovation of this constitution, said Alexander Hamilton, was the authority of the new "general" government to legislate for individuals, that is, to levy taxes, regulate businesses, conscript men into the military, and prosecute citizens for crimes defined by federal law.

10 Massachusetts Constitution, 1780, Art. XXIX.

11 Julius Goebel, *History of the Supreme Court of the United States*. Vol. 1, *Antecedents and Beginnings to 1801* (New York: Macmillan, 1971); Edward S. Corwin, "The Establishment of Judicial Review I," *Michigan Law Review* 9 (December 1910): 102–5; Corwin, "The Establishment of Judicial Review II," *Michigan Law Review* 9 (February 1911): 283–316.

12 Jacob E. Cooke, ed., *The Federalist* (Middletown, CT: Wesleyan University Press, 1961), 526.

13 Mauro Cappelletti and John Clarke Adams, "Judicial Review of Legislation: European Antecedents and Adaptations," *Harvard Law Review* 79, no. 6 (1966): 1207–24.

The "general" government under the Articles of Confederation had no such authority. The new government's authority to legislate for individuals necessitated establishment of a federal court system, which did not exist under the confederation. Lacking the political ability to displace the states' courts, and recognizing the liabilities of relying only on the states' courts to adjudicate federal matters, the framers of the U.S. Constitution established a separate U.S. Supreme Court and authorized Congress to create lower federal courts.

The power of judicial review, which Alexis de Tocqueville termed "the only power peculiar to an American judge,"[14] is now found in about 83 per cent of the world's constitutions.[15] Multiple explanations have been offered for this diffusion, including the need for coordination in federal systems, elite desires to attract investment for economic growth, a growing worldwide rights consciousness urging courts to restrain intemperate majority rule, diffusion of the principle of judicial review, and desires for political insurance by elites and parties fearing a loss of power after a constitution's founding.[16] Independent judicial review is said to serve "a valuable insurance function for competitors in a stable democracy."[17]

In the U.S. system and others like it (e.g., Canada, Australia, and the Latin American federations), judicial review is non-centralized; ordinary courts at every level of the judiciary can declare a statute unconstitutional, although courts are limited to actual disputes brought to them. In these countries, the highest court is merely the final arbiter in constitutional matters for the whole federation. By contrast, other systems, especially in Europe, employ a centralized system in which a special constitutional court exercises judicial review. This system emerged from the 1920 Federal Constitutional Law of Austria's first republic, which was influenced by Hans Kelsen, who served on Austria's court from 1920 to 1930.[18] The court was established mainly to adjudicate

14 Alexis de Tocqueville, *Democracy in America*, ed. J.P. Mayer, trans. George Lawrence (Garden City, NY: Anchor Books, 1969), 102.

15 Tom Ginsburg and Mila Versteeg, "Why Do Countries Adopt Constitutional Review?" *Journal of Law, Economics, & Organization* 30, no. 3 (2014): 587.

16 Ibid.; and Ran Hirschl, *Toward Juristocracy* (Cambridge, MA: Harvard University Press, 2004).

17 Matthew C. Stephenson, "'When the Devil Turns …': The Political Foundations of Independent Judicial Review," *Journal of Legal Studies* 32, no. 1 (January 2003): 85.

18 See, e.g., Hans Kelsen, "Judicial Review of Legislation: A Comparative Study of the Austrian and American Constitution," *Journal of Politics* 4 (May 1942): 183–200.

constitutional disputes over federalism. Review by a centralized constitutional court is often called "abstract," because the court does not resolve disputes between litigants but resolves constitutional matters referred to it by elected government officers after or before a law's enactment. The Austrian court, for example, addressed challenges to *Land* laws by the federal executive and challenges to federal laws by *Land* governments. Later, Germany authorized citizens to contest the constitutionality of a law or government action with no need to present a specific controversy. A similar process is the writ of *amparo* used in Latin America.

The U.S. non-centralized system of judicial review (with variants), which was the most prevalent system until the end of the twentieth century, was adopted in Argentina, Brazil, and Mexico, among other Latin American countries, as well as in Australia, Canada, India, Nigeria, and Switzerland. Centralized constitutional courts were established in Belgium, Germany, South Africa, and Spain, among many other countries.[19] One cannot, however, make too much of the difference between non-centralized and centralized judicial systems because, as a practical matter, there has been convergence in the operations and effects of both kinds.[20]

Another distinction is between strong and weak judicial review. Under strong judicial review, which exists in Germany and the United States, for example, a court's declaration of unconstitutionality is final until the constitution is amended or the court overrules itself. Indeed, India's Supreme Court has gone so far as to assert authority to invalidate any constitutional amendment that, in the Court's opinion, conflicts with the constitution's "basic structure."[21] Under weak constitutional

---

19 A third system not relevant to this volume is often called the French system, wherein judicial review is exercised by an independent body, the Conseil Constitutionnel, located outside of the regular judicial hierarchy.

20 See, e.g., Mauro Cappelletti, *Judicial Review in the Contemporary World* (Indianapolis: Bobbs-Merrill, 1971); and Louis Favoreu, "Constitutional Review in Europe," in *Constitutionalism and Rights: The Influence of the United States Constitution*, ed. Louis Henkin and Albert J. Rosenthal, 38–62 (New York: Columbia University Press, 1990).

21 *Kesavananda Bharati v. State of Kerala* (1973) 4 SCC 225. See also Sudhir Krishnaswamy, *Democracy and Constitutionalism in India: A Study of the Basic Structure Doctrine* (New Delhi: Oxford University Press, 2009). In Germany, the Basic Law explicitly provides that certain of its most important elements, including the division of the federation into Länder and their participation in the legislative process, cannot be altered by constitutional amendment.

review, a court's declaration of unconstitutionality can be overridden or superseded by an act of the legislature. Weak review is more common in British Commonwealth countries that follow the tradition of parliamentary sovereignty.[22] In Canada, for instance, with respect to certain parts of its 1982 Charter of Rights and Freedoms, the "notwithstanding" clause (*la clause dérogatoire*)[23] allows the federal Parliament or a provincial legislature to validate for five years a statute deemed unconstitutional by the Supreme Court. However, such weak review, to the extent that it exists,[24] usually applies only to the adjudication of rights; in Canada, as in most federal countries, the adjudication of most if not all federalism issues involves the strong form of judicial review.

The relationship between federalism and the courts is basically twofold. First, through the exercise of judicial review, the courts interpret constitutional norms associated with the federal system. These norms most prominently concern the distribution of powers between the federation and its constituent polities, but they also often concern interpretation of the structural features of the federal system, such as the representation of the constituent polities within the federation's political institutions. Courts can shape a federal system through their authoritative interpretation of these and other aspects of the constitution. Second, federalism has certain implications for the judicial system. Given that courts are usually intended to be independent arbiters of constitutional disputes between the federation and the states, they need to be independent of both orders of government. At the least, it is widely thought that judges in federations must have security of tenure, but beyond that, questions are often asked about how judges are appointed and whether they should be, in any sense, representative of the constituent polities, cultural or linguistic groups, or geographic regions. Moreover, because federalism is generally taken to involve a distribution of legislative powers between the federation and the constituent polities, the distribution of judicial power within the federation can itself be shaped by federal ideas, as in the establishment of separate state and federal courts and

22 David Erdos, *Delegating Rights Protection: The Rise of Bills of Rights in the Westminster World* (New York: Oxford University Press, 2010).

23 Canada Constitution, section 33.

24 The Canadian notwithstanding clause is limited in its application and has been used only rarely. See Grant Huscroft, "Rationalizing Judicial Power: The Mischief of Dialogue Theory," in *Contested Constitutionalism: Reflections on the Canadian Charter of Rights and Freedoms*, ed. James B. Kelly and Christopher P. Manfredi, 50–65 (Vancouver: UBC Press, 2009).

the investing of distinct fields of jurisdiction in those courts. Wheare considered that if the federal principle is applied strictly, one would expect a dual judicial system to be established: state courts to apply and interpret state law, and federal courts to apply and interpret federal law. However, of the four countries he examined in the 1940s, only the United States came close to applying this dualist principle. Switzerland and Australia relied extensively on cantonal or state courts to adjudicate disputes concerning both state and federal law, and Canada came close to having a single unified system of courts for the whole country appointed by the dominion government.[25] Wheare concluded that there is "no uniformity among federations in organizing their courts."[26]

II. Legal and Political Perspectives

Lawyers and political scientists tend to adopt different approaches to the analysis and evaluation of the role of courts in adjudicating constitutional disputes. The caricature, which bears some semblance to reality, suggests that lawyers focus on the reasoning used by the courts when they interpret the relevant sources of law (e.g., constitutional text, legislation, and judicial precedents), whereas political scientists focus more on the outcome of a judicial decision in the context of the wider political issues that are at stake and tend to consider the courts as one set of political actors among many. The reality is a complex combination of all these factors.

Gerard Baier argues that there is a sensible middle way between a formal legalistic approach that overemphasizes the stability of legal meaning within constitutional texts and judicial doctrine, and an overreaching political realist approach that reduces legal reasoning to a mere instrument of partisan power and influence.[27] Focusing on the United States, Canada, and Australia, he argues that judicial doctrine operates as an independent variable in judges' decision-making. Drawing on Barry Cushman's account of the U.S. Supreme Court in the New Deal period of the 1930s[28] and on various new institutionalist approaches to

25 Wheare, *Federal Government*, 68–72.

26 Ibid., 71.

27 Gerard Baier, *Courts and Federalism: Judicial Doctrine in the United States, Australia, and Canada* (Vancouver: UBC Press, 2006), 24–9.

28 Barry Cushman, *Rethinking the New Deal Court: The Structure of a Constitutional Revolution* (New York: Oxford University Press, 1998).

the analysis of judicial decision-making,[29] Baier argues that doctrine is a formative influence on judicial decisions, which gain their legitimacy from the traditions and methods of formal legal reasoning. On this view, judicial doctrine is not merely a smokescreen for the real determinants of a decision, nor is it the basis for a formal, almost mechanistic process of reasoning.

One must be alert to the possibility that the conclusions drawn by Baier from three democratic, well-established, common-law federations might not apply to courts in civil-law federations and to courts in countries that do not respect judicial independence. Furthermore, "judicial doctrine" (narrowly conceived) is not the only source or mode of legal reasoning. Philip Bobbitt has proposed six distinct modalities of judicial reasoning in constitutional cases, which he labels textual, structural, historical, doctrinal, ethical, and prudential.[30] Bobbitt contends that courts of final jurisdiction draw on any one or a combination of these modalities of reasoning as seems suitable to the circumstances of the case before them. It is not necessary to accept Bobbitt's pragmatism to recognize that judges frequently use each of these modalities, and constitutional decisions often turn on views about which modalities ought to apply and how they should fit together. This applies just as much to federalism-related cases as it does to other areas of judicial decision-making. A full assessment of the role of courts in interpreting federal constitutions should take account of the role of all of these modalities of reasoning, as well as of how judges select a particular modality to apply to a specific case's circumstances.

It is well known that courts are not fully independent of their political environment.[31] The ways in which politics potentially intersects with judicial reasoning are as diverse as politics itself. To put the matter schematically, politics can be "personal," "partisan," and "ideological." It can be about individuals vying for political power, as was partly the case in

---

29 Howard Gillman and Cornell Clayton, eds., *Supreme Court Decision-Making: New Institutionalist Approaches* (Chicago: University Of Chicago Press, 1999); Rogers Smith, "Political Jurisprudence, the 'New Institutionalism,' and the Future of Public Law," *American Political Science Review* 82 (1998): 89–108; Mark Richards and Herbert Kritzer, "Jurisprudential Regimes in Supreme Court Decision Making," *American Political Science Review* 96 (2002): 305–20.

30 Philip Bobbitt, *Constitutional Fate: Theory of the Constitution* (New York: Oxford University Press, 1982).

31 See, e.g., Robert A. Dahl, *Democracy and Its Critics* (New Haven, CT: Yale University Press, 1991).

Marbury v. Madison,[32] the celebrated 1803 decision of the U.S. Supreme Court to which modern judicial review is routinely traced. Judicial decisions can also have obvious partisan implications, even to the extent of determining the result of a presidential election, as in *Bush v. Gore* (2000).[33] The political background to a constitutional dispute may also be largely ideological, or at least cast in ideological terms;[34] indeed, the very institutions of "judicial review" and "constitutional law" as such can be presented as ideologies and as acts of judicial power,[35] even when they result, paradoxically, in abnegations of judicial jurisdiction or competence, as in *Marbury* or *McCawley v. The King*.[36] The judicial determination of federalism disputes is no exception, although adjudication of demarcations of government power (as in many federalism disputes) and adjudication of human rights occur in very different registers.

What is the underlying federal theory, one might ask, of the courts' determination of federal constitutional issues? Federalism-related political disputes concern a great diversity of issues. Adjudication of the distribution of powers between the federation and its constituent polities is the most prominent example. These cases usually involve questions about the constitutionality of federal or constituent legislation, or of administrative action purportedly authorized by such legislation. The question here can be whether the legislation falls within

---

32 5 U.S. (1 Cranch) 137 (1803). See, e.g., William W. van Alstyne, "A Critical Guide to Marbury v. Madison," *Duke Law Journal* 1 (1969): 1–47; Susan Low Bloch, "The Marbury Mystery: Why Did William Marbury Sue in the Supreme Court?," *Constitutional Commentary* 18 (2001) 607–28.

33 531 U.S. 98 (2000). See, e.g., Cass R. Sunstein, "Of Law and Politics," in *The Vote: Bush, Gore & the Supreme Court*, ed. Cass R. Sunstein and Richard A. Epstein (Chicago: University of Chicago Press, 2001), 1.

34 See, e.g., Bruce Ackerman, "Constitutional Politics/Constitutional Law," *Yale Law Journal* 99, no. 3 (1989): 453–547.

35 Alec Stone Sweet, "The Politics of Constitutional Review in France and Europe," *International Journal of Constitutional Law* 5, no. 1 (2007): 69–92.

36 [1920] AC 691; (1920) 28 CLR 106. See Nicholas Aroney, "Politics, Law and the Constitution in McCawley's Case," *Melbourne University Law Review* 30, no. 3 (2006): 605–56. *McCawley's Case* was a constitutional challenge to the appointment of Thomas McCawley as a judge of the Supreme Court of Queensland by the state's first-ever Labor government. His appointment was opposed with personal, partisan, and ideological motives, and the issues in the case involved the independence of the judiciary, the nature of parliamentary sovereignty, and the bindingness of the Queensland Constitution. His appointment was initially invalidated by the Queensland Supreme Court and the High Court of Australia, but ultimately upheld on appeal by the Privy Council.

a prescribed area of competence, or whether the legislation interferes with the constitutionally guaranteed autonomy of another order of government. Federalism-related issues can be of other kinds as well. There can be disputes between constituent polities over territorial boundaries and other matters, disputes about the representation of the constituent polities in the federation's decision-making institutions, and disputes about the proper way to amend the federal constitution. Moreover, the judicial system or systems within the country are both a reflection and a part of the federal system, and disputes about the jurisdiction of the courts can come before the courts for resolution. Federalism is both shaped by and shapes the judicial system.

As such, the courts, especially a country's highest court, are often objects of political attention and pressure from the federal executive and legislative branches, the constituent polities, and sometimes local governments. Likewise, given the importance of political parties in shaping federal systems,[37] courts are affected by the nature and character of the federal system's political parties. Parties, especially a dominant nationwide party, may even keep certain federalism disputes off the high court's docket by settling them politically.

III. Basic Conceptions of the Federal Polity

One of this book's fundamental questions concerns the underlying conception of the federal polity. Is it conceived – by the courts, by political actors, and by the population generally – in ultimately unitary or federalist terms? In other words, what is the nature of the federal political community? Does it consist of a single demos or plural demoi? Who or what, therefore, is the constituting power – *le pouvoir constituant* – to which courts ultimately owe their own authority? Is it "the people," "the peoples," "the nations"?

Traditional state theory presupposes the unity of the political community, and some writers have sought to interpret federal systems within the parameters of conventional state theory's unitarist assumptions and centralist implications.[38] When Tocqueville studied American federal democracy in the 1830s, he termed the common government created by

37 Klaus Detterbeck, Wolfgang Renzsch, and John Kincaid, eds., *Political Parties and Civil Society in Federal Systems* (Don Mills, ON: Oxford University Press Canada, 2015).

38 E.g., John W. Burgess, *Political Science and Comparative Constitutional Law* (Boston: Ginn, 1890).

the U.S. Constitution "an incomplete national government."[39] By contrast, the authors of *The Federalist* most often referred to the government eventually headquartered in Washington, DC, in non-statist terms as the "general" government, a term used also by the U.S. Supreme Court until the twentieth century, when "federal" and "national" government became common.

Alternative theories stress that federalism needs to be understood as grounded in a covenant, compact, or contract among political communities by which they agree to form a larger political community of which they will become constituent parts, while retaining their discrete and constitutionally protected independent existence.[40] This was the view, for example, that James Bryce took of the American federal system, which he called "a Commonwealth of Commonwealths."[41] Not all federations are integrative in origin or character; some come into being through devolution within a formerly unitary state, although staying together involves some underlying covenantal agreement.

Accounts of the formation, operation, and evolution of federal systems often divide today between those that offer primarily social and cultural explanations and those that emphasize the role of political and legal institutions.[42] By focusing on the way in which the federal polity is conceived, we propose a way of analysing the role of courts in federal countries that mediates between these two approaches. Focusing on the underlying conception of political community can have this synthesizing effect because it simultaneously reflects a certain view of the underlying social and political reality and operates as an effective political principle and legal premise in the formation, design, and interpretation of a federal constitution. This does not mean that only one conception of the federal polity operates in all federations, or in one federation for all time, or that the conception operating in any particular federation is uncontroversial. Rather, there is reason to expect that the underlying conception of the federal polity will be contested, and that this

39 Tocqueville, *Democracy in America*, 157.

40 Daniel J. Elazar, *Exploring Federalism* (Tuscaloosa: University of Alabama Press, 1987); Daniel J. Elazar and John Kincaid, eds., *The Covenant Connection: From Federal Theology to Modern Federalism* (Lanham, MD: Lexington Books, 2000); and Olivier Beaud, *Théorie de la Fédération* (Paris: Presses Universitaires de France, 2009).

41 Bryce, *American Commonwealth*, 1:12–15, 332.

42 Compare Baier, *Courts and Federalism*; and Jan Erk, *Explaining Federalism: State, Society and Congruence in Austria, Belgium, Canada, Germany and Switzerland* (London: Routledge, 2010).

contestation will often lie at the heart of legal controversies about how the federal aspects of the constitution are to be interpreted and applied, whether acknowledged[43] or not.[44]

The terminological history of American federalism illustrates the tension between underlying conceptions of the federal system. Martin Diamond highlighted the different and evolving senses of the term *federal* and its cognates used during the debate over the ratification of the U.S. Constitution.[45] The English word *federal* (and its equivalent in other languages such as French, German, Italian, and Polish) is derived from the Latin, *foedus*, meaning "covenant, compact, or treaty."[46] The term thus carries an original sense of a solemn agreement between parties, whether individuals, groups, or entire nations. The term also has several technical meanings in law, political philosophy, and theology, all of which contributed to debates over the nature of the federal union to be created by the proposed U.S. Constitution in 1787–8.[47] The word *federal* in the 1780s referred to a political system that has, since the 1780s, been termed "confederal." The U.S. Constitution was seen as a novel development because, on James Madison's analysis, it combined both "federal" (i.e., confederal) and "national" features. By *national*, Madison meant "unitary," in the sense of a single location of sovereignty from which the constitution's authority is ultimately derived, in contrast to a "federal" conception, in which the constitution is seen as an agreement between sovereign and independent states.

The common assumption for many (but not all) at the time was that sovereignty had to be located somewhere: either singularly in the unitary

43 As in *McCulloch v. Maryland*, 17 U.S. (4 Wheat.) 316, 435–6; *Lane County v. Oregon*, 74 U.S. (7 Wall.) 71, 77 (1868); *United States v. Curtiss-Wright Export Corporation*, 299 U.S. 304, 316–19 (1936); *Helvering v. Gerhardt*, 304 U.S. 405, 416 (1938); *U.S. Term Limits v. Thornton*, 514 U.S. 779, 801–3, 838–45, 845–9 (1995).

44 See the allusions to the underlying conception of the polity in *National League of Cities v. Usery* 426 U.S. 833, 868–9 (note 9) (1976); *Garcia v. San Antonio Metropolitan Transit Authority*, 469 U.S. 528, 582 (1985); *Printz v. United States*, 521 U.S. 898, 918–19 (1997). For Canadian and Australian cases, see also Nicholas Aroney, "Formation, Representation and Amendment in Federal Constitutions," *American Journal of Comparative Law* 54, no. 1 (2006): 277, 284–305.

45 Martin Diamond, "The Federalist's View of Federalism," in *Essays in Federalism*, ed. George C. S. Benson, 21–64 (Claremont, CA: Institute for Studies in Federalism, 1961).

46 The corresponding Germanic terms *Bund*, *Bundesstaat*, and *Staatenbund* likewise come from roots that convey the sense of binding or being bound by law or covenant.

47 See Daniel J. Elazar and John Kincaid, eds., *The Covenant Connection: From Federal Theology to Modern Federalism* (Lanham, MD: Lexington Books, 2000).

whole, or severally in the federating states. The U.S. Constitution, as a mixture of both national and federal elements, represented a challenge to any extreme view about the necessity to locate sovereignty in either the whole or the parts. All commentators had to recognize the mixed nature of the system, famously expressed by Madison as a "compound republic."[48] Nonetheless, there remained room for debate about its ultimate foundations. The unitarist interpretation tended to locate sovereignty in a singular American people who had decided to form a federal republic under which their "ordinary powers of sovereignty"[49] were distributed among federal and state institutions of government. The federalist interpretation insisted that the federation rested upon the consent of (the peoples of) the federating states, which had agreed to delegate limited powers to the federal institutions of government while retaining for themselves all of the original powers of government they had not transferred. These contending accounts of the federation's foundations led to differing approaches to interpreting the federal constitution.

Although many federal systems, such as those of Switzerland, Germany, and Australia, are largely like the United States in this respect, not all modern federations are. The United States and Switzerland clearly have federative foundations when their origins are compared to the more unitary fundamentals of the constitutions of Belgium, South Africa, and Spain, for instance. The contrast between unitarist and federalist orientations also applies to these countries, but the cultural and historical contexts in which this conceptual scheme operates is significantly different. In Spain, for example, the tension is expressed in the dispute over whether the statutes of autonomy should be interpreted as expressions of self-constitutive authority by the autonomous communities or as ordinary organic laws of the Spanish state.

The various terms used to designate the political communities and governing institutions of a federation are suggestive of this distinction between unitary and federalist orientations. Several federations refer to their constituent polities as *states* (Australia, India, Nigeria, and the United States of America). Other terms include *Länder* (Austria and Germany), *cantons* (Switzerland), *provinces* (Canada), *autonomous communities* (Spain), and *communities* and *regions* (Belgium). Terms used to designate the federation

48 Cooke, *Federalist*, 351 and 416. Hamilton also used the term *compound*, ibid., 149, 553, and 591.

49 As Dicey later put it in his *Introduction to the Study of the Law of the Constitution*, 8th ed. (London: Macmillan, 1915), 139.

also differ: for example, *Union* (India and the United States), *Commonwealth* (Australia), *Dominion* (Canada), *Federation* (Nigeria), and *State* (Belgium and Spain). In some countries, the federation and its institutions are commonly referred to as "federal" or "national" (Australia and the United States). Where there are significant sub-state nations or national movements (Canada, Ethiopia, and Spain), the term *nation* is usually reserved for those entities. The inversion is especially apparent in Spain, where the word *state* is used to designate the general or federal government in Madrid. Each of these terms reflects, to a degree, a view about the status and nature of the federal and constituent polities that make up the federation. The chapters in this book reflect this diversity of terminology and the diversity in federal systems to which the terminology attests.

IV. Potential Explanatory Factors

While this tension between unitary and federalist orientations is of fundamental importance, explaining the behaviour of courts across diverse federal systems must necessarily be multidimensional. We believe that the key explanatory factors concern the federation's (1) federal and pre-federal history, (2) formation by integration or devolution, (3) cultural and political homogeneity or heterogeneity, (4) constitutional and institutional structure, (5) legal traditions and culture, (6) selection of judges and institutional role of courts, and (7) nature of the political party system.

1. Federal and Pre-Federal History

History admittedly covers a broad swathe of explanatory terrain, but salient facets of a federation's history or prehistory can influence both the constitutional design of the federal system and the attitude of the courts towards that design, as well as the extent to which courts are independent and competent. The historical circumstances of each federation are unique, thus ensuring an inherent level of diversity across the country cases. There is, as a consequence, a kind of path dependency at play in many cases,[50] but also a desire to escape path dependency in other cases. One thinks, for example, of the Nazi era that preceded

50 Daniel Ziblatt, *Structuring the State: The Formation of Italy, Germany, and the Puzzle of Federalism* (New Jersey: Princeton University Press, 2006). See, generally, Paul Pierson, "Increasing Returns, Path Dependence, and the Study of Politics," *American Political Science Review* 94 (2000): 251–67.

formation of the Federal Republic of Germany in 1949. Decades of military rule in Nigeria, as well as endemic institutional corruption, warped that country's judiciary. Elements of authoritarian legality persist in Brazil's democratic era from the influence of security courts that operated during prior years of military rule.[51] The United States experienced a bloody civil war in 1861–5 that altered the federal constitution and the behaviour of the U.S. Supreme Court. The Constitutional Court of South Africa operates against a historical backdrop of white minority rule, including the 1948–94 apartheid era. Whether or not courts invoke history explicitly in making decisions, history informs and influences their decision-making, especially when citizens cry, "Never again!"

2. *Homogeneity or Heterogeneity*

Federations are more or less homogeneous or heterogeneous. Some federations are relatively homogeneous (e.g., Germany and Austria), but even among federations with ethno-culturally diverse populations, certain cultural groups within the federation may be concentrated in particular constituent polities (e.g., Belgium, Canada, India, and Switzerland), or they may be dispersed among all of the constituent polities relatively evenly (e.g., Australia and the United States).[52] Especially in multinational or pluri-national federations, the courts may be required or pressured to respond to the country's plural constituencies, and rulings may need to negotiate cleavages produced by this heterogeneity. Depending on the nature of relations among the various cultural or national communities, the federation's high court may lean in a unitarist or federalist direction.

Courts often decide cultural issues that are flashpoints for conflict. In 2013, for example, Canada's Supreme Court struck down three major federal anti-prostitution laws, India's Supreme Court upheld an 1861 colonial-era law that criminalizes gay and lesbian sex nationwide, Australia's High Court held that constituent territories and states cannot legalize same-sex marriage, and the U.S. Supreme Court upheld same-sex marriage in California and struck down a federal law that did not

---

51 Anthony W. Pereira, "Of Judges and Generals: Security Courts under Authoritarian Regimes in Argentina, Brazil, and Chile," in *Rule by Law: The Politics of Courts in Authoritarian Regimes*, ed. Tom Ginsberg and Tamir Moustafa, 23–57 (New York: Cambridge University Press, 2008).

52 Luis Moreno and César Colino, *Diversity and Unity in Federal Countries* (Montreal and Kingston: McGill-Queen's University Press, 2010).

recognize spousal rights under state-authorized same-sex marriages. In making such rulings, courts decide who can and cannot make decisions about cultural matters. In the United States, for example, voters in thirty-one states had amended their state constitution to prohibit gay marriage, while only three states had legalized same-sex marriage by popular vote and eight states by the legislature; yet in 2015, the U.S. Supreme Court struck down all state bans on gay marriage as contrary to the due process and equal protection clauses of the Fourteenth Amendment.[53] In these countries, a key debate has been over who should decide the status of same-sex marriage: voters of the states, voters of the federation as a whole or appointed federal judges? Thus, while rights cases are argued in a register different from that for federalism cases, they can have profound implications for the balance of power within a federation.

In turn, the heterogeneous character of a federal polity will likely influence the composition of its judiciary. In Canada, for instance, the nine-member Supreme Court must include at least three members of the bar or superior judiciary of Quebec, in part because Quebec adheres to civil law while the rest of Canada follows the common law. By convention, the Court also includes three justices from Ontario, two from the western provinces, and one from the Atlantic provinces. Belgium's Constitutional Court consists of six Dutch-speaking and six French-speaking judges. Nigeria's constitution establishes the "federal character" principle by which personnel in all government institutions must adequately reflect all of the country's regional, linguistic, ethnic, and religious groups. Such rules about the composition of courts admit that judicial decision-making is, and should be, influenced by the cultural histories and values that judges bring to the bench.[54] An important question, thus, is the extent to which diversity in judicial appointments affects the way courts approach federalism questions.

3. *Constitutional and Institutional Structure*

The text and structure of the federal constitution are also important. Court decision-making is likely to be influenced by such factors as (1) whether the federal constitution is centralist or decentralist in

---

53 *Obergefell v. Hodges*, 135 S. Ct. 2584; 192 L. Ed. 2d 609; 576 U.S. ___ (2015).

54 Guy Grossman, Oren Gazal-Ayal, Samuel D. Pimentel, and Jeremy M. Weinstein, "Descriptive Representation and Judicial Outcomes in Multiethnic Societies," *American Journal of Political Science* 60, no. 1 (2016): 44–69.

content, nature, or spirit, (2) whether it specifies concurrent powers, (3) where it locates reserved powers (if any), (4) whether the arrangement is dualist (as in the United States) or integrative (as in Germany), (5) whether the specific powers granted to the various orders of government are limited or extensive, (6) whether the constitution recognizes local government as the third order of government, (7) whether the constitution provides for emergency rule or federal intervention into the governance of the constituent polities, and (8) whether certain provisions of the constitution are unamendable or amendable only by special procedures. The extent to which the federal constitution has the character of a general framework or detailed code may also affect judicial decision-making. A highly codified constitution may constrain the interpretative function of a high court.[55]

4. *Selection of Judges and Institutional Role of Courts*

The institutional roles of the courts themselves and modes of judicial selection may also affect court decision-making. Particularly important is the extent to which the constitution and political practices ensure or undermine judicial independence. Can "judges exercise meaningful authority without fear of or manipulation by powerholders"?[56] Each federation places unique expectations on judges and requires them to operate in unique constitutional and political contexts. The manner in which judges are selected, the degree to which appointments are controlled or influenced by the federal and constituent governments, and the extent to which judges are in some sense representative of the federation or the constituent polities all have potential to shape how judges adjudicate federalism-related disputes.

5. *Formation by Integration or Devolution*

A federation formed by the union of previously independent political communities (e.g., the United States and Switzerland) is likely to have structures and to give rise to constitutional issues and pressures that are

55 For a comparison of the high courts of India and South Africa in this respect, see Rosalind Dixon, "Partial Constitutional Codes," University of New South Wales Law Research Paper no. 2014-37, 2014.

56 Peter VonDoepp, *Judicial Politics in New Democracies: Cases from Southern Africa* (Boulder, CO: Lynne Rienner, 2009), 18.

different from those of a federation formed by a devolution of powers from a central state (e.g., Spain and Belgium). Whether a federal system represents a voluntary coming together or an attempt at staying together[57] can have significant jurisprudential implications, because the two modes of formation represent different socio-political agendas. In some federations, there may be a dispute over the nature of formation, as in Canada where the Québécois view the confederation as a compact between two peoples, English and French, while English-speaking Canadians and Aboriginals have different formation beliefs. John C. Calhoun's notion of the U.S. Constitution as a compact among sovereign states[58] was similarly opposed to Daniel Webster's view of it as the "people's Constitution … made for the people, made by the people, and answerable to the people."[59] Even though all modern federal systems were founded during documented historical times, beliefs about the formation of some federal systems have the character of creation myths.

Formation may be overlaid with an ideology or tradition of centralism or decentralism, such as the Iberian tradition of centralism characteristic of most Latin American federations. Although these federations drew heavily on the U.S. Constitution, Simón Bolívar declared that the U.S. Constitution could work only in "a republic of saints" and "that it has never for a moment entered my mind to compare the position and character of two states as dissimilar as the English American and the Spanish American … I am convinced … [Spanish] America can only be ruled by an able despotism,"[60] not federalism.[61]

6. *Legal Traditions and Culture*

Some federations operate within the common-law tradition; others operate within the civil-law tradition. These traditions can lead to

57 Alfred Stepan, "Federalism and Democracy: Beyond the U.S. Model," *Journal of Democracy* 10 (October 1999): 19–34.

58 John C. Calhoun, *A Disquisition on Government, and Selections from the Discourse*, ed. C. Gordon Post (New York: Liberal Arts Press, 1953).

59 Daniel Webster, "Second Reply to Hayne, 1830," in *A Source Book of American Political Theory*, ed. Benjamin Fletcher Wright (New York: Macmillan, 1929), 481.

60 Quoted in Niall Ferguson, *Civilization: The Six Killer Apps of Western Power* (London: Penguin, 2011), 123–4.

61 On the failures of federalism in nineteenth-century Latin America, see also Joshua Simon, "The Americas' More Perfect Unions: New Institutional Insights from Comparative Political Theory," *Perspectives on Politics* 12 (December 2014): 808–28.

different modes of judicial decision-making having jurisprudential consequences affecting a federation's character and internal balance of power. Another important issue is whether a federation has a strong or weak rule-of-law tradition. The developed democratic federations (e.g., Australia) have a robust rule-of-law tradition, but some newer federations in less developed countries (e.g., Nigeria) have weaker traditions, while some federations have elements of authoritarian rule (e.g., Brazil and Ethiopia). Thus, it is important to note that not all the federations examined in this volume are free, rights-respecting democracies. For comparison purposes, table 2 shows rankings of the thirteen case federations on the World Justice Project's rule-of-law index and Freedom House's estimates of freedom and rights protections.

One can also speak of judicial culture, the positive values of which include independence, professionalism, scholarship, and

Table 2 Rankings of Case Federations on Rule-of-Law Index and Freedom House Indices

	Rule of Law*	Freedom	Freedom rating	Political rights	Civil liberties
Germany	.81	Free	1.0	1	1
Australia	.80	Free	1.0	1	1
Canada	.78	Free	1.0	1	1
Belgium	.77	Free	1.0	1	1
United States	.73	Free	1.0	1	1
Spain	.68	Free	1.0	1	1
South Africa	.58	Free	2.0	2	2
Brazil	.54	Free	2.0	2	2
India	.51	Free	2.5	2	3
Mexico	.47	Partly free	3.0	3	3
Ethiopia	.42	Not free	6.0	6	6
Nigeria	.41	Partly free	4.5	4	5
Switzerland	NA	Free	1.0	1	1

* These scores are average scores for the eight index factors provided for each country. The factors are (1) constraints on government powers, (2) absence of corruption, (3) open government, (4) fundamental rights, (5) order and security, (6) regulatory enforcement, (7) civil justice, and (8) criminal justice. The higher the country score, the better the rule of law.

Sources: Column 1: World Justice Project, *The Rule of Law Index 2015*, http://worldjusticeproject.org/sites/default/files/roli_2015_0.pdf; columns 2–5: Freedom House, "Freedom in the World 2015," https://freedomhouse.org.

non-partisanship. While certain global notions of judicial culture have emerged in recent decades, every federation has a judicial culture of its own that is more or less aligned with global values.

Another facet of legal traditions and culture is the late twentieth-century rise of the judicialization of politics, namely, the use of courts to decide important public policy matters, political disputes, and cultural values. Many high courts have narrowed the "political question" doctrine, which holds that courts should not decide political questions or settle issues constitutionally assigned to the legislature or executive. Courts have entered the political thickets of election processes, legislative and executive prerogatives, nation building, and the full range of issues on national policy agendas. In some cases, courts actively seek out political issues; in other cases, political actors prefer to have certain political issues determined by the courts. In emerging democracies, courts can play an important consolidating role by ensuring horizontal accountability, namely, "the controls that state agencies are supposed to exercise over other state agencies."[62] However, if a court becomes too politically aggressive, political forces may corral it.[63]

7. Political Parties

The organization and operation of political parties are important determinants of centralization or decentralization in federal systems.[64] Parties likewise have a substantial influence on the autonomy and operation of courts. Matthew Stephenson argues, "Political competition, a long-term perspective, and a willingness to compromise are fundamental to independent judicial review, and the nature of the political competition and the competitors is largely determinant of the

---

62 Guillermo A. O'Donnell, "Illusions about Consolidation," *Journal of Democracy* 7, no. 2 (April 1999): 44.

63 VonDoepp, *Judicial Politics in New Democracies.*

64 William H. Riker, *Federalism: Origin, Operation, Significance* (Boston: Little, Brown, 1964), 129; Donald V. Smiley, *The Federal Condition in Canada* (Toronto: McGraw-Hill Ryerson, 1987), 103–4; Mikhail Filippov, Peter C. Ordeshook, and Olga Shvestova, *Designing Federalism: A Theory of Self-Sustainable Federal Institutions* (New York: Cambridge University Press. 2004), chap. 6.

conditions, if any, under which judicial independence is viable … [E]fforts to build judicial independence in the absence of genuine and stable political competition will likely founder."[65]

Changes in a country's party system may also affect federalism jurisprudence, as in India where in 1989 the emergence of state-based parties and coalition governments at the centre displaced the monopolistic rule of the Congress Party, which had dominated the country since independence. The new multi-party environment enabled the Supreme Court to become more assertive and sympathetic to state interests. The federations examined in this volume display very different party systems.

V. Selection of Cases

All of these dimensions provide focus for the thirteen federal and quasi-federal countries analysed in this book. In some of these countries, the highest constitutional court plays a significant role in shaping its federal system; in others, this court plays little or no role. We deliberately chose a variety of federal systems. We believed it important to include the major democratic federations (Australia, Canada, Germany, Switzerland, and the United States) that have also historically been models for some other federations, as well as the world's largest democratic federation (India), a sampling of other developed and less developed federal systems (Belgium, Brazil, Ethiopia, Mexico, and Nigeria), and two quasi-federal systems (South Africa and Spain). Some of these federations are very old (Australia, Brazil, Canada, Mexico, Switzerland, and the United States), some younger (Germany, India, and Nigeria), and others comparatively new (Belgium, Ethiopia, South Africa, and Spain). Some of the countries fall within the common-law tradition (Australia, Canada, India, South Africa, and the United States) and some within the civil-law tradition (Belgium, Germany, Spain, and Switzerland), while others have more complex, mixed inheritances (Brazil, Ethiopia, Mexico, and Nigeria). Some of the countries have been stable democracies for a long time (Australia, Belgium, Canada, India, Switzerland, and the United States); others have emerged from, or still struggle with, undemocratic

65 Stephenson, "'When the Devil Turns …,'" 85.

histories and circumstances (Brazil, Ethiopia, Germany, Mexico, Nigeria, South Africa, and Spain).

The countries also vary in degrees of decentralization. Table 3 displays the decentralization rankings among 182 countries of the thirteen federations examined in this volume. The four measures of decentralization were developed by World Bank analysts. On the overall aggregate measure of decentralization, table 3 shows that Switzerland is the third most decentralized country (following Denmark and Sweden) while the United States is the ninth and Mexico is the eighty-first most decentralized country. Consistent with federalism principles, all of the federations rank among the top 45 per cent of most decentralized countries, but inconsistent with federalism principles, many non-federal countries are more decentralized than the thirteen federations examined here. Although it is difficult to measure decentralization empirically, and the data have many limitations, including an inability to measure the centralizing impacts of rights decisions that constrain the federal or constituent governments, the World Bank measures offer

Table 3 Global Rankings of Case Federations on Decentralization Indices

Federation	Decentralization			
	Overall	Political	Administrative	Fiscal
Switzerland	3	2	1	3
United States	9	3	10	4
Canada	12	5	11	6
Brazil	13	4	15	12
Germany	20	15	32	25
Belgium	23	36	25	21
Ethiopia	37	86	59	74
Spain	46	100	67	18
South Africa	47	117	62	30
Nigeria	48	52	98	86
Australia	55	35	40	10
India	76	45	71	47
Mexico	81	8	88	57

Source: Maksym Ivanyna and Anwar Shah, *How Close Is Your Government to Its People? Worldwide Indicators on Localization and Decentralization.* Policy Research Working Paper 6138. The World Bank, March 2012, http://elibrary.worldbank.org/doi/pdf/10.1596/1813-9450-6138.

rough comparative benchmarks for assessing the federalist and unitarist leanings of the high courts of our case federations.[66]

We present the countries alphabetically in this book because it is the most neutral order. The countries might have been ordered thematically, such as heterogeneous versus homogeneous countries, integrative versus devolutionary federations, established versus emerging democracies, or common-law versus civil-law systems, but any of these orders would be an arbitrary pre-judgment that would obscure the important roles of all these classifications in explaining judicial behaviour.

We could not include all of the federal countries or systems that we would have liked. Argentina, Austria, Malaysia, and Russia, for example, are regrettable omissions, although the characteristics of these countries do not substantially differ from countries in our sample except that Russia under Vladimir Putin is arguably no longer federal. The European Union's treaty-based system of supranational governance and the United Kingdom's system of devolution in favour of Scotland, Northern Ireland, and Wales also provide interesting and illuminating points of contrast and comparison with the thirteen federal countries examined here. We draw attention to some of these points in our conclusion to this volume.

VI. Template for Case Analyses

We asked the country experts who contributed to this volume to address structured questions calculated to draw out the various respects in which courts may be asked or required to adjudicate federalism-related issues, as well as the way in which federalism may shape the country's court system. These questions began with the general characteristics of the federation, including how the federal system came into being, how it has evolved over time, and how it is generally regarded within the country. Also of general importance were questions about the degree of ethno-cultural or linguistic diversity in the country and the extent to which this diversity is expressed territorially. Next, we asked the contributors to identify the main structural features of the federal system:

66 Another measure is the regional authority index, but it is not used here because rankings are available for only seven of the thirteen federations. See Liesbet Hooghe, Gary Marks, and Arian H. Schakel, "Operationalizing Regional Authority: A Coding Scheme for 42 Countries, 1950–2006," *Regional and Federal Studies* 18, nos 2–3 (April–June 2008): 123–42, and "Appendix B: Country and Regional Scores," 259–74.

the constituent polities and orders of government; the mode, manner, and extent of the constitutional delineation of legislative, executive, fiscal, and judicial powers or competences; constitutional relationships between federal, constituent, and local orders of government; forms of political representation for constituent polities in the federation's government institutions; and means and mechanisms of constitutional evolution and amendment. Fourth, we asked the authors to describe their country's court system or systems; its broad legal tradition or traditions; the relationships between the courts; the composition of the courts; the manner in which judges are trained, appointed, and dismissed; protections of judicial independence; the extent and nature of court jurisdiction and judicial procedure; and, generally, the influence and importance of the courts within the federation. Finally, authors were asked to explain their court's approaches to interpreting the various federal aspects and dimensions of the federation's constitution, particularly how the court's conceptions of the foundations, nature, and purposes of the federal system are applied to the interpretation of specific constitutional provisions and the resolution of federalism-related disputes. Where, for example, do the courts conceive "sovereignty" to be located within the federation, if anywhere?

The chapters that follow contain the country authors' responses to these questions. Each country is unique; thus, not all of the questions are as apposite to a particular country as others. Each chapter tells its own story about the role of the courts within the country's federal system, and it has not been feasible (or desirable) for each contribution to follow the template slavishly. Nonetheless, the overall structure of each chapter is generically the same, and the questions addressed are as consistent as possible in order to facilitate comparison across the thirteen federal countries.

2 The High Court of Australia: Textual Unitarism vs Structural Federalism

NICHOLAS ARONEY

I. Introduction

The framers of Australia's Constitution expected that the High Court would play a central role in the development of Australian federalism. They were correct, but whether they anticipated that the Court would interpret the Constitution in ways that would enable the powers of the federation ever to wax while allowing those of the states almost always to wane is not clear. The High Court has adopted an approach to constitutional interpretation that is essentially unitarist. It interprets the legislative powers of the federal Parliament in a manner that excludes from consideration a need to reserve any particular powers to the states. The basis for this approach is the view that the Constitution derived its legal force originally from its enactment by the British Parliament and that it obtains its continuing legitimacy from the support of the Australian people considered as an undifferentiated whole.[1] On this view, the Court has held that federal powers are to be interpreted as broadly as the constitutional language can possibly sustain, without imposing any limit on their scope by reference to the merely "residual" capacities of the states, leaving them in an "inherently vulnerable" position.[2]

The Australian states nonetheless play an important role in federal politics and remain vigorous centres of regional and local political engagement. Why is this so? One reason is the sheer size of the country. Another is the continuing attachment to the states as locations of

1 *Amalgamated Society of Engineers v. Adelaide Steamship Co Ltd* (1920) 28 C.L.R. 129, 153.

2 Michael Crommelin, "Federalism," in *Essays on Law and Government*. Vol. 1, *Principles and Values*, ed. Paul D. Finn (Sydney: Law Book, 1995), 168, 172.

political participation and activity. In support of this, although the High Court has denied that the Constitution guarantees to the states any of the particular powers they have exercised historically, it has insisted that they must continue to exist "as separate governments ... exercising independent functions."[3] The status and position of the states within the federation is thus constitutionally entrenched and remains fundamental to Australia's political system, even though their particular functions and roles have been increasingly overridden by the federal government.

II. Federal System

1. *Broad Characteristics*

With a total territory of almost 7.7 million square kilometres, Australia is the sixth-largest country in the world and the only nation state occupying an entire continent.[4] The continent is sparsely populated, with most of its population of approximately twenty-four million concentrated in major urban centres along the eastern, southeastern, and southwestern seaboard.[5] Australia was inhabited by Indigenous peoples for many thousands of years before British settlement in the late eighteenth century. Over the next two centuries, the country was populated by waves of migrants, initially from Britain and Ireland, and later from continental Europe, Asia, Africa, and the Middle East.[6] While the proportion of persons of British or Irish ancestry has declined, English remains the dominant language. The most prominent reported ancestries are Anglo-Celtic, and a significant majority of religious affiliations remain Christian. Australia's different ethno-cultural groups are diffused throughout each of the major cities, regions, and states, so that by international standards, Australia has no strongly pronounced ethno-cultural cleavages

---

3 *Melbourne Corporation v. Commonwealth* (1947) 74 C.L.R. 31, 83.

4 Australian Bureau of Statistics (ABS), *2006 Year Book Australia*, cat. no. 1301.0 (Canberra: ABS, 2006), chap. 1.

5 ABS, *Population Clock*, 10 February 2016, http://www.abs.gov.au. See also Clive Forster, *Australian Cities: Continuity and Change*, 3rd ed. (Oxford: Oxford University Press, 2004), 2–13.

6 ABS, *2006 Census of Population and Housing: Media Releases and Fact Sheets*, cat. no. 2914.0.55.002 (Canberra: ABS, 2000).

that are territorially defined.[7] In 2014, Australia's gross domestic product was US$1,442 billion, the twelfth-largest economy in the world, with a GDP of US$61,066 per person.[8]

The Commonwealth of Australia is a federation of six states formed by an agreement among mutually independent, self-governing British colonies established separately between 1788 and 1859.[9] By the time of federation in 1901, each colony had a bicameral parliament and an operating system of responsible government modelled broadly upon the Westminster system then operating in the United Kingdom. Their reasons for federating included anxiety about European states exercising military power in the region, concerns about unnecessary inter-colonial rivalry and protectionism, and a desire to unite the people of the continent into one political community.[10] A federal form of government was favoured, because there was a widespread desire to preserve the powers of local self-government that five of the six colonies had enjoyed since the 1850s.[11] Throughout the English-speaking world at the time, federalism was seen as the most appropriate structure for governing the vast territories of the New World, as suggested by the prominent examples of the United States and Canada.[12]

At a conference of colonial premiers held in 1890, it was agreed that the colonial parliaments would elect and send delegates to a convention to draft a federal constitution, which would be submitted to the colonies for their consideration. A convention was held in 1891, which drafted a constitution. For various reasons, the proposal lapsed and the federation movement was not reinvigorated until 1895, when it was proposed that

---

7 For more detail, see Nicholas Aroney, "Australia," in *Diversity and Unity in Federal Countries*, ed. Luis Moreno and César Colino, 16–46 (Montreal and Kingston: McGill-Queen's University Press, 2010). For important qualifications, see Nicholas Aroney, Scott Prasser and Alison Taylor, "Federal Diversity in Australia: A Counter Narrative," in *The Future of Australian Federalism: International and Comparative Perspectives*, ed. Gabrielle Appleby, Nicholas Aroney, and Thomas John (Cambridge: Cambridge University Press, 2012), 272.

8 International Monetary Fund, *World Economic Outlook Database*, October 2015, www.imf.org/external/pubs/ft/weo/2015/02/weodata/index.aspx.

9 R.D. Lumb, *The Constitutions of the Australian States*, 5th ed. (Brisbane: University of Queensland Press, 1991), chaps 1–2, 4.

10 Scott Bennett, ed., *The Making of the Commonwealth* (Melbourne: Cassell, 1971), 38–42.

11 Western Australia secured responsible government in the early 1890s.

12 Nicholas Aroney, *The Constitution of a Federal Commonwealth: The Making and Meaning of the Australian Constitution* (Cambridge: Cambridge University Press, 2009), chaps 3–4.

a second convention be elected directly by the voters of each colony. The plan was that the convention would debate and draft a constitution to be submitted to the colonial parliaments for input and then submitted to the voters in each colony for approval by referendum, prior to being submitted to the British Parliament for enactment. The Commonwealth of Australia Constitution Act was accordingly enacted into law by the British Parliament in 1900.[13]

The Constitution attempts to combine the principles of parliamentary responsible government with federalism. In accordance with the conventions of responsible government, Commonwealth executive power, which is formally vested in the Queen and exercised by the governor-general as her appointed representative, is in the ordinary course of events exercised strictly on the advice of a prime minister and other ministers of state who have the confidence and support of the Parliament. In accordance with the federal principles of self-rule and shared rule,[14] not only are the Commonwealth and each of the states constitutionally preserved as self-governing political communities (ss. 106 and 107), but the people of each state are equally represented in one of the houses of Parliament (the Senate), while the people of the Commonwealth as a whole are represented in the lower house (the House of Representatives) (ss. 7 and 24). The combination of these two principles gives rise to tensions concerning the responsibility of the executive to Parliament in the context of the relative powers of the two houses of Parliament over supply bills, as explained below.

The federation has remained constitutionally stable since its inception. No new states have been added to the original six, each of which continues to have the same constitutionally guaranteed status as a self-governing political community. There are now two self-governing territories and several smaller territories, all of which are in principle subject to the authority of the Commonwealth Parliament (s. 122). Only eight of forty-four constitutional amendment proposals have secured the necessary support of a majority of voters in the nation as a whole and a majority in a majority of states (s. 128). This has led some to refer to Australia as the "constitutionally frozen continent."[15] However, the

---

13 Ibid., chap. 6.

14 Daniel J. Elazar, *Exploring Federalism* (Tuscaloosa, AL: University of Alabama Press, 1987), chap. 1.

15 Geoffrey Sawer, *Australian Federalism in the Courts* (Melbourne: Melbourne University Press, 1967), 208.

proposals' failure is not due simply to a supposedly onerous amendment procedure, because most have failed to garner the support of a simple majority of Australian voters. Rather, the proposals have usually involved an increase in federal powers and have not secured bipartisan political support, partly for that reason.[16] The most significant causes of constitutional change have been the tendency of federal governments to press the scope of their powers up to (and arguably beyond) their constitutional limits and High Court decisions which have mostly affirmed those exercises of power, the opposition of the states notwithstanding.

The attitudes of political actors to the federal system have varied. From the time of federation, politicians from states such as Queensland and especially Western Australia have been highly critical of centralization, so much so that in 1933 the government of Western Australia (unsuccessfully) petitioned the British government to allow it to secede.[17] At the federal level, political leaders of the centre-left Labor Party have usually pressed Commonwealth powers as far as politically possible and have been opposed in this endeavour by parties of the centre-right.[18] This general political alignment was partially reversed, however, under the Liberal-National government of Prime Minister John Howard (1996–2007), which initiated numerous programs further expanding federal power, evoking defensive responses from state premiers on both sides of the political spectrum.[19]

According to recent surveys,[20] a very substantial majority of respondents indicated that they considered attributes such as divided power, policy diversity, regional innovation, and intergovernmental collaboration to be desirable features of Australia's political system. At the same

---

16 George Williams and David Hume, *People Power: The History and Future of the Referendum in Australia* (Sydney: UNSW Press, 2010), chap. 4.

17 Gregory Craven, *Secession: The Ultimate States Right* (Melbourne: Melbourne University Press, 1986).

18 Brian Galligan, *A Federal Republic: Australia's Constitutional System of Government* (Cambridge: Cambridge University Press, 1995), chap. 4.

19 Andrew Parkin and Geoff Anderson, "The Howard Government, Regulatory Federalism and the Transformation of Commonwealth-State Relations," *Australian Journal of Political Science* 42, no. 2 (2007): 295.

20 A.J. Brown, "Escaping Purgatory: Public Opinion and the Future of Australia's Federal System," in Appleby, Aroney and John, *Future of Australian Federalism*, 365; Brown, "Measuring the Mysteries of Federal Political Culture in Australia," in *Tomorrow's Federation: Reforming Australian Government*, ed. Paul Kildea, Andrew Lynch, and George Williams (Sydney: Federation, 2012), 310.

time, Australians regard the present system as not being particularly good at securing these benefits. Almost three-quarters of respondents have said that the federal system needs to be restructured, but are split between preferring the abolition of either the Commonwealth, state, or local orders of government, the creation of more states, or the establishment of regional governments.

It is now frequently said that Australia's federal system needs reform, and there have been several recent initiatives directed to this end, including establishment of the Council of Australian Governments Reform Council in 2006 and the Council for the Australian Federation in 2008. Numerous problems are said to exist, including confusion of responsibilities and severe vertical fiscal imbalance between the Commonwealth and the states. But first among the problems identified in the recommendations of the report of the Senate Select Committee on the Reform of the Australian Federation in 2011 was the "tendency towards greater centralisation within the Australian federation resulting from High Court decisions."[21]

The framers of the Constitution intended the High Court to exercise the power of judicial review over both legislation and executive action.[22] This has necessitated the development by the Court of a significant and varied body of federal constitutional law.[23] No other institution has such an important role in laying down the fundamental principles upon which the system must operate, although the Commonwealth, state, and territory governments have played equally important roles in initiating policy, enacting relevant legislation, engaging in intergovernmental negotiations, and constitutionally challenging each other's laws.

2. *Structural Features*

A. DISTRIBUTION OF LEGISLATIVE AND EXECUTIVE POWER

The Constitution guarantees the continuing existence and powers of both the Commonwealth and the states.[24] Although the existence of

---

21 Senate Select Committee on the Reform of the Australian Federation, *Australia's Federation: An Agenda for Reform* (Canberra: Commonwealth of Australia, 2011), xiii.

22 Brian Galligan, *Politics of the High Court* (Brisbane: University of Queensland Press, 1987), chap. 2.

23 Sawer, *Australian Federalism in the Courts*; Leslie Zines, *The High Court and the Constitution*, 4th ed. (Sydney: Butterworths, 1997).

24 *Melbourne Corporation v. Commonwealth* (1947) 74 C.L.R. 31, 82; *Re Australian Education Union; Ex parte Victoria* (1995) 184 C.L.R. 188, 231.

local government is also acknowledged in all of the state constitutions,[25] the state parliaments have the power to subject local government to supervision, control, and fundamental reorganization.[26] A proposal for federal constitutional recognition of local government in the form of a federal power to make financial grants directly to local government was passed by the federal Parliament in 2013, but as the result of an early election called by the prime minister, the necessary referendum could not conveniently be held within the constitutionally required timeframe.[27]

The Constitution distributes legislative, executive, and judicial power between the Commonwealth and the states.[28] The legislative powers of the states are general and plenary (ss. 106 and 107),[29] subject only to the exclusive legislative powers conferred upon the Commonwealth (s. 52) and various general constitutional prohibitions (e.g., ss. 90, 92). By contrast, the legislative powers of the Commonwealth are limited to specific topics (ss. 51, 52).[30] The exclusive Commonwealth legislative powers relate to the Australian Capital Territory, places acquired by the Commonwealth, and the Commonwealth public service (s. 52). The Commonwealth has broad legislative power over its territories generally (s. 122). Concurrent federal legislative powers (s. 51) concern matters such as defence, external affairs, immigration, quarantine, fisheries, interstate trade and commerce, trading and financial corporations, banking, insurance, bills of exchange, bankruptcy, intellectual property, industrial arbitration, postal services and telecommunications, invalid

---

25 Cheryl Saunders, "Constitutional Recognition of Local Government in Australia," in *The Place and Role of Local Government in Federal Systems*, ed. Nico Steytler (Johannesburg: Konrad-Adenauer-Stiftung, 2005), 47, 53–6.

26 Chris Aulich and Rebecca Pietsch, "Left on the Shelf: Local Government and the Australian Constitution," *Australian Journal of Public Administration* 61, no. 4 (2002): 14; Scott Prasser, "Democracy and Local Government: The Queensland Experience," *Sydney Papers* 19, no. 4 (2007): 82.

27 See Expert Panel on Constitutional Recognition of Local Government, *Final Report* (Canberra: Commonwealth of Australia, 2011).

28 John Williams and Clement Macintyre, "Commonwealth of Australia," in *Distribution of Powers and Responsibilities in Federal Countries*, ed. Akhtar Majeed, Ronald Watts, and Douglas Brown, 6–33 (Montreal and Kingston: McGill-Queen's University Press, 2006).

29 Gerard Carney, *The Constitutional Systems of the Australian States and Territories* (Melbourne: Cambridge University Press, 2006), 106–7.

30 *Attorney-General (Cth) v. Colonial Sugar Refining Company Limited* (1913) 17 C.L.R. 644, 651–4.

and old-age pensions, various special allowances and endowments, currency, census statistics, marriage, and divorce. If the Commonwealth cannot show that its legislation is authorized by the Constitution, then it is liable to be held invalid by the courts.

The scope of the executive power of the Commonwealth and the states is less easy to define.[31] As with legislative power, state executive power is not limited to particular topics,[32] whereas the Commonwealth's executive power is constitutionally defined as extending to the "execution and maintenance of [the] Constitution, and of the laws of the Commonwealth" (s. 61). Noting that executive power is formally vested in the reigning British monarch, the executive power includes the common-law prerogatives of the Crown that apply to Australia, as well as specific powers conferred by statute and the Constitution itself. However, the High Court has very recently adopted a narrower view of the scope of executive power than had commonly been assumed, as is explained below.

The Constitution also confers a range of fiscal powers on the Commonwealth, including the powers to borrow money, raise taxes, appropriate public funds for constitutional purposes, and make grants to the states on terms and conditions the Commonwealth thinks fit (ss. 51(ii), (iv), 81, 96). Federal taxes must not be imposed on the property of any state and must not discriminate between states or parts of states (ss. 51(ii), 114). However, the Commonwealth has exclusive power to impose excise and customs duties (s. 90) and, as will be seen, effectively monopolizes the most significant sources of government revenue.

If validly enacted Commonwealth and state laws are inconsistent, the federal law will prevail to the extent of the inconsistency (s. 109). Such inconsistency can be established in at least one of four situations: the two laws impose inconsistent duties so that it is impossible to obey both;[33] one law confers a liberty to act in a certain manner and the other law imposes a duty not to do so;[34] a state law purports to "alter, impair or detract from" the operation of a Commonwealth law;[35] or a Commonwealth law evinces an intention to "cover" a particular "field" or topic

31 The leading account is George Winterton, *Parliament, the Executive and the Governor-General: A Constitutional Analysis* (Melbourne: Melbourne University Press, 1983).

32 Carney, *Constitutional Systems*, chap. 8.

33 *Australian Boot Trade Employees Federation v. Whybrow & Co.* (1910) 10 C.L.R. 266; *R. v. Licensing Court of Brisbane; Ex parte Daniell* (1920) 28 C.L.R. 23.

34 *Clyde Engineering Co Ltd. v. Cowburn* (1926) 37 C.L.R. 466.

35 *Dickson v. The Queen* (2010) 241 C.L.R. 491.

of regulation, thus displacing state law in that field.[36] Such an intention to cover the field can exist explicitly or implicitly, as when a Commonwealth law by virtue of the breadth and depth of its provisions implies an intention to establish a comprehensive and exhaustive regulatory scheme over the entire field in question.[37] The Commonwealth can also explicitly state an intention *not* to cover the field when it wishes state law to continue to operate.[38] However, it cannot do this by retrospective legislation. To do so would undo the effect that the Constitution had in the past, undermining the reliance that citizens place on clear constitutional demarcations of the legislative powers and enactments of the Commonwealth and the states.[39]

Since a body of federal constitutional law has developed around these provisions, the states continue to legislate, regulate, and provide services in important areas such as education, hospitals, policing, and civic infrastructure, but the Commonwealth now exercises substantial regulative control in these fields by placing conditions on financial grants to the states and by enacting overriding legislation. Further adjustments to the federal distribution of power can be achieved in various ways, including formal amendment of the Constitution (s. 128) and state referral of legislative powers to the Commonwealth (s. 51(xxxvii)). Harmonization of law also occurs through the enactment of uniform legislation on the basis of "host" laws enacted in one state and adopted by others, through promulgation of "model" legislative schemes that states and territories "mirror" in their own legislation, and through Commonwealth "framework" laws that operate only in the absence of adequate state or territory laws.[40] Many such "cooperative" arrangements exist in areas of great significance, such as the regulation corporations and securities, employment conditions, consumer protection, and counter-terrorism.[41]

---

36 *Ex parte McLean* (1930) 43 C.L.R. 472.

37 *O'Sullivan v. Noarlunga Meat Ltd.* (1954) 92 C.L.R. 565; *Ansett Transport Industries (Operations) Pty. Ltd. v. Wardley* (1980) 142 C.L.R. 237; *Viskauskas v. Niland* (1983) 153 C.L.R. 280.

38 *R. v. Credit Tribunal; Ex parte General Motors Acceptance Corporation* (1977) 137 C.L.R. 545.

39 *University of Wollongong v. Metwally* (1984) 158 C.L.R. 447.

40 John Wanna, John Phillimore, Alan Fenna, and Jeffrey Harword, *Common Cause: Strengthening Australia's Cooperative Federalism* (Council for the Australian Federation, 2009), 20.

41 Andrew Lynch, "The Reference Power: The Rise and Rise of a Placitum?," in Kildea, Lynch, and Williams, *Tomorrow's Federation*, 193.

Despite these arrangements between the Commonwealth and the states, Australia's Constitution, unlike Germany's Basic Law, for example,[42] does not formally envisage a role for federal framework legislation, partly because the Constitution's framers were influenced by A.V. Dicey's interpretation of federalism as involving a "division" of powers between the federation and the states.[43] This approach was followed by James Bryce – another highly influential figure – who held that federalism distributes powers into separate and "coordinate" federal and state "spheres," each sphere being regulated primarily if not exclusively by the governing institutions of the appropriate order of government.[44] For the Australians, this meant that it was essential that the states continue to exercise full legislative, executive, and judicial powers within their fields of operation and that the Commonwealth, likewise, be granted the constitutional capacity to establish a federal bureaucracy and federal courts to administer and adjudicate laws enacted by a federal legislature. This did not mean, however, that the Constitution was designed to separate the Commonwealth and the states into "watertight" compartments. The decision to confer concurrent powers upon both was deliberate.[45] Nonetheless, Australia's federal system is quite different from that of many of its European counterparts, where the integration of the constituent polities (e.g., Länder and cantons) within the governing institutions of the federation is more far-reaching than in common-law federations such as Australia, Canada, and the United States.[46]

---

42 German Basic Law, Art. 75. See Arthur Gunlicks, "Reforming German Federalism," in Appleby, Aroney, and John, *Future of Australian Federalism*, 115.

43 A.V. Dicey, *Introduction to the Study of the Law of the Constitution*, 5th ed. (London: Macmillan, 1897), 130–55, 410–13.

44 Galligan, *Federal Republic*, 193–4, discussing James Bryce, *The American Commonwealth*, 2nd ed. (London: Macmillan, 1889). See also John Wright, "Anglicizing the United States Constitution: James Bryce's Contribution to Australian Federalism," *Publius: The Journal of Federalism* 31 (2001): 107–31; and Graham Maddox, "James Bryce: Englishness and Federalism in America and Australia," *Publius: The Journal of Federalism* 34 (2004): 53–69.

45 Aroney, *Constitution of a Federal Commonwealth*, chaps 9 and 10; Galligan, *Federal Republic*, chap. 8. The High Court interpreted the Constitution in unnecessarily co-ordinate terms in *Re Wakim; Ex parte McNally* (1999) 198 C.L.R. 511. For a critique, see Nicholas Aroney, "The Constitutional Demise of the Cross-Vesting Scheme," *Insolvency Law Journal* 7 (1999): 116.

46 Thomas Hueglin and Alan Fenna, *Comparative Federalism: A Systematic Inquiry* (Peterborough, ON: Broadview, 2006), 145–78, 235–43.

B. CONSTITUTIONAL JUDICIAL REVIEW

It is generally accepted that the courts and, in particular, the High Court of Australia, have ultimate competence to determine the scope of power possessed by the various institutions of government in the federation.[47] When the High Court decides such matters, although there may be criticism and disagreement, the specific finding and its legal implications are widely adhered to by the other institutions and orders of government. While some scholars have pointed out the difficulties of identifying a textual basis for judicial review in the Constitution[48] and have questioned whether judicial review on federalism grounds can be justified,[49] the Court's decisions are generally accepted as binding and authoritative.

While it is widely acknowledged that the powers conferred upon the Commonwealth were intended to be specific and limited, the High Court has adopted a method of constitutional interpretation that has tended to place the widest possible construction on the scope of those powers, especially since its landmark decision in the *Engineers* case in 1920.[50] Political leaders in the states have frequently expressed grave concern about the centralization of power. These issues have therefore often generated heated disagreement between the two orders of government.[51] Such disagreements often affect the tone and conduct of intergovernmental negotiations concerning the regulation of matters

---

47 See *Australian Communist Party v. Commonwealth* (1951) 83 C.L.R. 1, 262–3, citing *Marbury v. Madison* (1803) 5 U.S. 137; *The Queen v. Kirby; Ex parte Boilermakers' Society of Australia* (1956) 94 C.L.R. 254, 267–68; *Plaintiff S157/2002 v. Commonwealth* (2003) 211 C.L.R. 476, 513–14.

48 James A. Thomson, "Constitutional Authority for Judicial Review: A Contribution from the Framers of the Australian Constitution," in *The Convention Debates 1891–1898: Commentaries, Indices and Guide*, ed. Gregory Craven (Sydney: Law Books, 1986), 6:173.

49 Stephen Gageler, "Foundations of Australian Federalism and the Role of Judicial Review," *Federal Law Review* 17 (1987): 162; Adrienne Stone, "Judicial Review without Rights: Some Problems for the Democratic Legitimacy of Structural Judicial Review," *Oxford Journal of Legal Studies* 28 (2008): 1; Nicholas Aroney, "Reasonable Disagreement, Democracy and the Judicial Safeguards of Federalism," *University of Queensland Law Journal* 27 (2008): 129.

50 George Winterton, "The High Court and Federalism: A Centenary Evaluation," in *Centenary Essays for the High Court of Australia*, ed. Peter Cain (Sydney: LexisNexis Butterworths, 2004), 197; Gregory Craven, "The Crisis of Constitutional Literalism in Australia," in *Australian Constitutional Perspectives*, ed. H. P. Lee and George Winterton (Sydney: Law Book, 1992), 1.

51 E.g., Ted Baillieu, "Speech to the Australia-Israel Chamber of Commerce," Melbourne, 7 August 2012.

ordinarily within state power. They also create incentives for state governments to pool their political resources against the Commonwealth, most recently through the Council for the Australian Federation, a body formed to defend the states in the federal system.[52]

C. DEMOCRATIC REPRESENTATION AND CONSTITUTIONAL CHANGE

The Constitution establishes a system of federal representation of the people of the states in the Commonwealth Parliament, which consists of the Queen and two houses, the Senate and the House of Representatives (s. 1). Each of the six "Original States" is constitutionally entitled to be equally represented in the Senate (s. 7). The House of Representatives is composed of members "directly chosen by the people of the Commonwealth" under a formula that ensures that each state is represented in proportion to its population, but with each state being entitled to a minimum of five members (s. 24). It was envisaged that the House would represent the Australian people as a whole, organized into local electorates.[53] This general principle of constituency electorates with preferential voting is adopted in all but one of the states and territories for the lower house of Parliament.[54] The state and Commonwealth upper houses, by contrast, are generally elected on the basis of a proportional system, based on multiple-member electorates and a single transferable vote. Voting is compulsory in all Australian elections, except local-government elections in some states.[55]

Each state constitution is an ordinary statute of the state parliament, enacted under authority ultimately traceable to Orders in Council or British statutes, the effect of which is continued under the federal Constitution (s. 106). Under these grants of power, the legislative power of each state parliament is "plenary" and extends to the enactment of any law for the state deemed necessary by the parliament.[56] Consequently,

52 Jennifer Menzies, "The Council for the Australian Federation and the Ties That Bind," in Kildea, Lynch, and Williams, *Tomorrow's Federation*, 53. On the general ineffectiveness of the Council, see Shipra Chordia and Andrew Lynch, "Constitutional Incongruence: Explaining the Failure of the Council of the Australian Federation," *Federal Law Review* 43 (2015): 339.

53 Aroney, *Constitution of a Federal Commonwealth*, 224–7.

54 With the exception of Tasmania, where the lower house is elected under a proportional system.

55 Scott Bennett and Rob Lundie, *Australian Electoral Systems*, Research Paper No. 5 (Canberra: Department of the Parliamentary Library, 2007–8).

56 *Clayton v. Heffron* (1960) 105 C.L.R. 214, 249–50.

the general principle is that the state constitutions can be altered by an ordinary statute of the state parliament, either explicitly or by implication.[57] The first qualification is that the state constitutions are "subject to" the federal Constitution (s. 106) and cannot, therefore, contain anything contrary to its relevant requirements, such as the maintenance of state courts meeting the description of "Supreme Courts" (as referred to in s. 73).[58] A second, now far-reaching qualification to this principle is that pursuant to the Australia Acts (1986), whereby the authority of the British Parliament to legislate for Australia was brought to an end, the legislative powers of each state parliament is subject to any "manner and form" requirements that may have been imposed by a predecessor parliament.[59] Pursuant to this, each state has enacted special legislative procedures for amending its constitution in certain important respects, such as the status and role of the Queen and the governor, the composition, procedures, and electoral basis of the parliament, and the independence of the judiciary. The manner and form requirements thus imposed are of varying kinds, such as approval by the voters in a referendum or by a special majority in the parliament.[60] Under the Australia Acts, the subject matter of the law must concern the "constitution, powers or procedure of the Parliament," and so the effectiveness of some manner and form requirements is questionable. There has been some discussion of alternative grounds upon which state constitutional provisions might be entrenched, but the effectiveness of these grounds is subject to serious doubt.[61]

By contrast, the Commonwealth Constitution is fully entrenched and cannot be amended by the Commonwealth Parliament without voter approval in a referendum. In particular, a proposed amendment of the Constitution must be (1) passed by an absolute majority of both houses of the Commonwealth Parliament (or by only one house of the Parliament, if after a period of delay the other house fails or refuses to pass

57 *McCawley v. The King* (1920) 28 C.L.R. 106 (Privy Council), discussed in Nicholas Aroney, "Politics, Law and the Constitution in McCawley's Case," *Melbourne University Law Review* 30, no. 3 (2006): 605.

58 *Kirk v. Industrial Court of New South Wales* (2010) 239 C.L.R. 531, 566, 580–1; *Forge v. Australian Securities and Investments Commission* (2006) 228 C.L.R. 45, 76.

59 Australia Acts, 1986 (Cth) and (UK), s. 6. This limitation was first imposed pursuant to the Colonial Laws Validity Act, 1865 (UK), s. 5.

60 Carney, *Constitutional Systems*, 195–204.

61 *McGinty v. Western Australia* (1996) 186 C.L.R. 140, 296–7; *Attorney-General (W.A.) v. Marquet* (2003) 217 C.L.R. 545.

the proposed law or passes it with amendments with which the first-mentioned house does not agree) and (2) simultaneously approved by a majority of voters in the nation as a whole and by a majority of voters in a majority of states (s. 128). This procedure is competent to amend the Constitution in any respect, except that changes to the territorial limits of a state or its representation in the federal Parliament can be made only with the approval of a majority of voters in the state concerned (s. 128, para. 5). Notably, this procedure concerns only the Constitution itself, and not the preamble and "covering clauses" of the Commonwealth of Australia Constitution Act 1900 (UK), which contains the Constitution. At the time of federation, the British Parliament retained the power to amend the Constitution Act, but since the abdication of its power to legislate for Australia, there is an unanswered question about the location of the residual power to amend the Constitution Act. Various solutions have been proposed, ranging from granting the Commonwealth Parliament the power by ordinary constitutional amendment, to locating it in the peoples and legislatures of the states and Commonwealth acting unanimously.[62] The operative effect of most of the covering clauses is now spent, but the preamble to the Constitution (which significantly recites the "agreement" of the people of the Australian colony-states to be united in a "federal commonwealth under the Crown") is contained in the Constitution Act. When in 1999 an unsuccessful referendum was held on whether Australia would become a republic, there was a second (again unsuccessful) proposal for a new preamble. However, given doubts about the precise mechanism necessary for amending the Constitution Act, the plan was only to insert a second preamble into the Constitution proper, leaving the original preamble in the Constitution Act fully in place.[63]

The ultimate relationship between the Commonwealth and state constitutions has not been entirely resolved. While provisions of the Commonwealth Constitution limit the states' powers (e.g., ss. 90 and 92) and allow appeals to the High Court from state Supreme Courts (s. 73), thus operating in a manner that is paramount to the provisions of the state constitutions, there are isolated judicial dicta that there are limits on the extent to which Commonwealth legislation, although otherwise

62 These views are summarized in Nicholas Aroney, "A Public Choice? Federalism and the Prospects of a Republican Preamble," *University of Queensland Law Journal* 21 (1999): 205.

63 Constitution Alteration (Preamble) 1999 (Cth).

authorized by the Commonwealth Constitution, can alter certain fundamentals of the state constitutions, such as the existence and functioning of state courts.[64]

III. Court System

1. General Features

The Australian judicial system is profoundly shaped by federalism.[65] Prior to federation, each Australian colony had its own court system. Supreme courts of general jurisdiction were established initially in most cases by Imperial authority, together with various inferior courts created by the legislatures.[66] At federation, provision was made in the Commonwealth Constitution for the establishment of the High Court of Australia (s. 71), with general appellate jurisdiction (s. 73) and original jurisdiction in several kinds of matters (ss. 75–6), including the resolution of constitutional disputes. The Constitution also empowers the Commonwealth to confer federal jurisdiction upon state courts (ss. 71, 77(iii)) and to establish other federal courts (ss. 71, 77(i)). The Commonwealth has established the Federal Court of Australia, Family Court of Australia, and Federal Magistrates Court.[67] At federation, the jurisdiction of the Judicial Committee of the Privy Council was also preserved (s. 74), but the High Court soon asserted that it was the final interpreter of the constitutional powers of the Commonwealth and the states ("inter se" matters),[68] and between 1968 and 1986 the Privy Council's jurisdiction to hear appeals from Australian courts was abolished,[69] rendering section 74 "obsolete."[70]

---

64 *Re Tracey; Ex parte Ryan* (1989) 166 C.L.R. 518, 547, 574–5; *Western Australia v. Wilsmore* [1981] W.A.R. 179, 181–3.

65 See James Stellios, *The Federal Judicature – Chapter III of the Constitution: Commentary and Cases* (Sydney: LexisNexis Butterworths, 2010), 1–3, chaps 7–10.

66 James Crawford and Brian Opeskin, *Australian Courts of Law*, 4th ed. (Melbourne: Oxford University Press, 2004), 22–3.

67 Stephen Gageler, "Jurisdiction," in *The Oxford Companion to the High Court of Australia*, ed. Michael Coper, Tony Blackshield, and George Williams, 383–5 (Oxford: Oxford University Press, 2001).

68 *Baxter v. Commissioners of Taxation (N.S.W.)* (1907) 4 C.L.R. 1087.

69 Privy Council (Limitation of Appeals) Act, 1968 (Cth); Privy Council (Appeals from the High Court) Act, 1975 (Cth); Australia Act, 1986 (U.K.) and (Cth), s. 11.

70 *Kirmani v. Captain Cook Cruises Pty. Ltd. (No. 2)* (1985) 159 C.L.R. 461.

The states have their own hierarchies of courts, usually consisting of magistrates courts, district courts, and a supreme court (in some instances including a permanent court of appeal). The two self-governing mainland territories, the Northern Territory and the Australian Capital Territory, have their own supreme courts and systems of magistrates courts. Because the High Court is the general court of appeal from the supreme courts, and those courts are invested with federal jurisdiction, the legal system as a whole has been described as an "integrated system of State and federal courts and organs for the exercise of federal judicial power as well as State judicial power."[71] Because the High Court has general appellate jurisdiction, the theory that there might be different bodies of common law in each state, as in the United States, has been rejected.[72]

2. *Constitutional Status of Courts and Judicial Officers*

The independence of the High Court and other federal courts is guaranteed by the requirement in the Constitution that judges appointed to these courts enjoy tenure to age seventy.[73] The High Court has vigilantly protected its independence, drawing on the separation of powers implied by the distinct investment of legislative, executive, and judicial power in the legislature, executive, and judiciary (ss. 1, 61, and 71), following the U.S. Constitution in this respect.[74] At federation, the independence and tenure of judges of some state courts was also protected,[75] but not through any constitutionally entrenched provisions.[76] Since then, some state constitutions have guaranteed the status and independence of the state supreme courts,[77] and it has been held by the High Court that the general principle of judicial independence

71 *Kable v. Director of Public Prosecutions for N.S.W.* (1996) 189 C.L.R. 51, 114–15.

72 Ibid. See also *Lipohar v. The Queen* (1999) 200 C.L.R. 485, 505.

73 Australian Constitution, s. 72. Such judges can be removed from office only on an address from both houses of Parliament on the ground of proved misbehaviour or incapacity.

74 *R. v. Kirby; Ex parte Boilermakers' Society of Australia* (1956) 94 C.L.R. 254.

75 The protections of judicial tenure contained in the Act of Settlement, 1700 (U.K.) did not apply to colonial judges in Australia until the grant of responsible government in the 1850s: Crawford and Opeskin, *Australian Courts of Law*, 66.

76 *McCawley v. R.* (1918) 26 C.L.R. 9, 58–9.

77 E.g., Constitution Act, 1975 (Vic.), s. 18 and Pt. IIIA; Constitution Act, 1902 (N.S.W.), s. 7B and Pt. 9. Judicial tenure is protected but not entrenched in Queensland: Constitution of Queensland, 2001 (Qld), chap. 4.

required by the Commonwealth Constitution also protects state courts and applies to state judges, because they exercise federal jurisdiction.[78] The tenure of lower court judges is also protected in some instances.[79]

Members of the High Court and Federal Court are appointed by the Governor-General in Council (s. 72(i)) based on a decision made within Cabinet on a recommendation by the attorney-general. The attorney-general is required to consult with the state attorneys-general,[80] but the nature and extent of this consultation is not transparent, and there have been calls for reform. Members of the state courts are correspondingly appointed by the state governors on the advice of the state governments. When conferring federal jurisdiction on state courts, the Commonwealth may regulate the jurisdiction and procedure of such courts, but cannot interfere with their composition and structure, which are matters for each state to determine within the limits prescribed by the federal and state constitutions.[81]

Most individuals appointed to the High Court have had substantial legal and usually judicial experience; relatively few have had political careers.[82] Despite Australia's federal structure and extensive territory, there is no convention that judicial appointments must reflect geographic diversity; indeed, despite a legislative requirement for consultation with the states,[83] the Commonwealth has appointed more than three-quarters of High Court judges from the two largest states, New South Wales and Victoria, and has not yet appointed any High Court judge from the two smallest, South Australia and Tasmania. Persons appointed to the High Court have usually held prior judicial office in either the Federal Court or a state supreme court; occasionally individuals are appointed from the practising bar in one of the states, but this has become increasingly rare.[84] The High Court presently consists of seven judges,[85] and when considering major constitutional cases, the

78 *Kable v. Director of Public Prosecutions for N.S.W.* (1996) 189 C.L.R. 51; *South Australia v. Totani* (2010) 242 C.L.R. 1; *Wainohu v. New South Wales* (2011) 243 C.L.R. 181.

79 Crawford and Opeskin, *Australian Courts of Law*, 68–9.

80 High Court of Australia Act, 1979 (Cth), s. 6.

81 Crawford and Opeskin, *Australian Courts of Law*, 45–6. See *Kirk v. Industrial Court of New South Wales* (2010) 239 C.L.R. 531, 566.

82 Crawford and Opeskin, *Australian Courts of Law*, 191.

83 High Court of Australia Act 1979 (Cth), s. 6.

84 On calls for reform of the appointment process generally, see George Williams, "High Court Appointments: The Need for Reform," *Sydney Law Review* 30, no. 1 (2008): 161.

85 High Court of Australia Act, 1979 (Cth), s. 5.

Court usually sits as a full bench. Only five women have sat on the High Court since its establishment in 1903, three of whom were serving in 2016.

3. *Jurisdiction, Procedure, and Remedies*

Although the High Court's jurisdiction clearly extends to constitutional matters, this arrangement was not entrenched by the Constitution; it had to be affirmed by legislation at the establishment of the Court in 1903.[86] Constitutional jurisdiction is not exclusive to the High Court, however. Any Australian court may consider such questions, on the basis that all courts are responsible to determine what the law is, and such a determination may on occasion involve application of the Constitution.[87] The constitutional jurisdiction of the High Court is enlivened either when its original jurisdiction is directly engaged or when in the course of ordinary litigation, a party raises a constitutional issue and the matter is removed into the Court or comes before it upon appeal. The Federal Court is a superior court of record that likewise has jurisdiction in matters arising under federal laws generally, as well as matters arising under the Constitution or involving its interpretation.[88] The state supreme courts are courts of general jurisdiction in all matters that arise under common law, equity, or statute within the state, which can thus also include constitutional causes. They function as intermediate courts of appeal in state and federal matters and also have general supervisory responsibility for state law, state institutions, and the state's legal profession.[89] The High Court controls its workload by insisting that appeals from state supreme courts and the Federal Court be heard only by special leave,[90] and by remitting matters commenced in its original jurisdiction to federal or state courts.[91]

The High Court's jurisdiction is further limited to "matters" (ss. 75–7). This means that it has no general advisory jurisdiction. As in the United

86 Judiciary Act, 1903 (Cth), s. 30(a); Australian Constitution, s. 76(i).

87 See Judiciary Act, 1903 (Cth), ss. 38 and 39 (re jurisdiction of State courts).

88 Judiciary Act, 1903 (Cth), s. 39B(1A)(b).

89 Crawford and Opeskin, *Australian Courts of Law*, 127.

90 Judiciary Act, 1903 (Cth), s. 35(2); Federal Court of Australia Act, 1976 (Cth), s. 33. Such leave is granted only where it is in the interests of the administration of justice and raises matters of "public importance" or there is a difference of opinion between different courts: Judiciary Act, 1903 (Cth), s. 35A.

91 Judiciary Act, 1903 (Cth), s. 44(1).

States, and unlike Canada, the High Court's jurisdiction is enlivened only when litigants bring a case involving the determination of the particular rights, duties, or liabilities of a person.[92] Further, in order to commence such proceedings, a plaintiff must have standing. While it is clear that an individual will have standing to challenge a law that regulates conduct in which that person has allegedly engaged, the extent to which a person will have standing beyond that is unclear. It is necessary for a plaintiff to show a sufficient "material" or "special" interest in the matter, and thus an interest greater than that of an ordinary member of the public,[93] but what exactly this amounts to has been confused, rather than clarified, by recent High Court cases, partly because the parties have often conceded the issue of standing.[94] However, the Commonwealth and state attorneys-general have standing to challenge the constitutional validity of legislation or executive action of each other,[95] and individuals who lack standing are able to seek the fiat of an attorney-general to bring the action in the attorney-general's name.[96]

When a case involving constitutional issues comes before a court, the court must satisfy itself that notice of the case has been given to the Commonwealth, states, and territories attorneys-general to enable them to consider intervention in the proceedings or seek removal of the cause into the High Court.[97] It is common for attorneys-general to intervene in constitutional cases, especially those involving questions about the distribution of power between the Commonwealth and the states. The Court has only infrequently granted leave to persons and representative groups to appear as amici curiae. At the least, they must demonstrate that their legal interests are liable to be substantially affected by a decision in a case and that the Court would not receive submissions relevant to the matters in issue without their intervention.[98]

---

92 *Re Judiciary and Navigation Acts* (1921) 29 C.L.R. 257.

93 *Australian Conservation Foundation Inc. v. Commonwealth* (1980) 146 C.L.R. 493, 527.

94 Cf. *Croome v. Tasmania* (1997) 191 C.L.R. 119; *Pape v. Commissioner of Taxation* (2009) 238 C.L.R. 1; *Williams v. Commonwealth* (2012) 248 C.L.R. 156.

95 *Attorney-General (Vic); Ex rel. Dale v. Commonwealth* (1945) 71 C.L.R. 237; *Attorney-General (Victoria); Ex rel. Black v. Commonwealth* (1981) 146 C.L.R. 559.

96 E.g., *Attorney-General (Vic); Ex rel. Dale v. Commonwealth* (1945) 71 C.L.R. 237; *Attorney-General (Cth); Ex rel. McKinlay v. Commonwealth* (1975) 135 C.L.R. 1; *Attorney-General (Victoria); Ex rel. Black v. Commonwealth* (1981) 146 C.L.R. 559.

97 Judiciary Act, 1903 (Cth), s. 78B.

98 *Levy v. Victoria* (1997) 189 C.L.R. 579.

Parties alleging a breach of the Constitution may seek several remedies. Three such remedies explicitly recognized by the Constitution are the writs of mandamus, prohibition, and injunction against Commonwealth officers (s. 75(v)). These "constitutional writs" extend to compelling public officials to perform public duties (mandamus) and restraining public officials, especially lower courts or tribunals, from usurping or exceeding jurisdiction (prohibition). The courts can also issue orders quashing decisions of lower courts or tribunals (certiorari), preventing the usurpation of an office (quo warranto), and requiring the liberation of an unlawfully imprisoned person (habeas corpus).[99] In addition, where the aforementioned remedies are not available or inadequate, the courts can issue authoritative declarations as to the legal rights of parties and the true state of the law, including the invalidity of legislation.[100] Although a wide range of remedies is thus available, the High Court has discretion about whether to grant a remedy in any particular case. Nonetheless, in most constitutional cases, declaratory or other orders are readily issued once a finding of invalidity has been made, and it is rare for deserving cases to be without a remedy.[101]

A strict doctrine of precedent applies in Australia; the determinations of all superior courts bind courts lower in the judicial hierarchy.[102] The High Court does not regard itself as being bound by its previous decisions,[103] but only rarely overturns well-established cases, except that it is somewhat more willing to overrule previous decisions in constitutional matters as a result of the entrenched nature of the Constitution, the Court's role as its final interpreter, and the importance of the issues raised in such cases.[104] Under the doctrine of precedent, it is only the decision of the Court and the reasoning necessary for it to arrive at that decision that is binding (the ratio decidendi); all other opinions expressed in

99 High Court Rules, 2004, Pt. 25. See, generally, Leslie Zines, *Cowen and Zines's Federal Jurisdiction in Australia*, 3rd ed. (Sydney: Federation, 2002), 15–16, 46–65.

100 Robert French, "Declarations – Homer Simpson's Remedy – Is There Anything They Cannot Do?" (Paper presented at Faculty of Law, University of Western Australia, 30 November 2007).

101 Garry Downes, "Judicial Review" (Paper presented at the Seminar for the College of Law, Government & Administrative Law, Sydney, 24 March 2011), 4.

102 *Garcia v. National Australia Bank Ltd.* (1998) 194 C.L.R. 395, 403, 418.

103 *Attorney-General for New South Wales v. Perpetual Trustees Company Ltd.* (1952) 85 C.L.R. 237, 244.

104 Zines, *High Court and the Constitution*, 433–4; Michael Kirby, "Precedent Law, Practice and Trends in Australia," *Australian Bar Review* 28 (2007): 243.

a judgment are deemed to be merely obiter dicta – authoritative but not binding. Decisions of Australian courts are usually presented seriatim as the decisions of individual judges. The court's decision is determined by a majority of the judgments, whether agreeing in the reasoning and result or, if necessary, concurring only in the result.[105] Joint judgments (whether forming a majority or a dissenting minority) are common, but in no sense mandatory, although unanimous judgments are often presented per curiam, as a decision of the court as a whole.[106] The ratio decidendi of a case can be very difficult to identify where the majority agrees only about the specific orders to be made by the court, and not on the underlying reasoning.

4. *Institutional Role of the Courts*

Because the Commonwealth and state constitutions do not contain a list of fundamental rights, but only a few scattered guarantees, the vast bulk of the High Court's constitutional jurisprudence has historically concerned federalism-related issues, principally the distribution of power between the Commonwealth and the states.[107] Even the Court's seminal decision on the separation of powers and the independence of the judiciary was theorized in terms of the Court's federal adjudicative role.[108] Since the 1980s, however, an increasing proportion of High Court constitutional cases has concerned other matters, such as judicial independence, the nature and scope of executive power, and implied democratic rights.[109]

The political branches of government generally respect the courts, although in recent years when the High Court has struck down significant legislation, politicians have sometimes criticized such decisions as not being properly grounded in the Constitution.[110] There is a convention that the relevant attorney-general, and not the judges themselves,

105 Andrew Lynch, "Dissent: Towards a Methodology for Measuring Judicial Disagreement in the High Court of Australia," *Sydney Law Review* 24 (2002): 470, 476–8.

106 Ibid., 479.

107 See, generally, Sawer, *Australian Federalism in the Courts*.

108 *R. v. Kirby; Ex parte Boilermakers' Society of Australia* (1956) 94 C.L.R. 254, 267–8; *Forge v. Australian Securities and Investments Commission* (2006) 228 C.L.R. 45, 73. See, further, Stellios, *Federal Judicature*, 96–8.

109 Compare Galligan, *Politics of the High Court*; Haig Patapan, *Judging Democracy: The New Politics of the High Court of Australia* (Melbourne: Cambridge University Press, 2000).

110 Malcolm Fraser, "The Courts Must Rule, above and beyond the Political Fray," *Melbourne Age*, 12 September 2011.

should defend the courts against undue criticism, but this practice has sometimes been placed under pressure, especially when governments contend that the courts have engaged in "judicial activism."[111] This tension between the political and judicial branches has often concerned cases involving implied constitutional rights, but the High Court's federalism jurisprudence has also given rise to political criticism, particularly from the order of government adversely affected by a decision.[112] Another point of occasional tension between the branches of government concerns the financial independence of the courts. The High Court has a significant level of administrative and fiscal autonomy guaranteed under a federal statute,[113] but the independence of state courts is less well protected.[114]

Public confidence in the courts is also complex. While Australians place high value on the courts' importance, they express low confidence in the criminal justice system in particular, both absolutely and relative to other public institutions.[115] Yet judges are frequently called upon in their personal capacity to investigate and report on controversial and sensitive issues, suggesting that they retain a reputation for impartiality, integrity, and good judgment.[116] Nonetheless, with the expansion of the courts' adjudicative role to politically controversial matters, as well as the opportunities for scrutiny made possible by modern communications technology, popular criticism appears to have increased.[117]

---

111 Enid Campbell and H.P. Lee, *The Australian Judiciary* (Melbourne: Cambridge University Press, 2001), 246–59.

112 "Fed-State Powers Need Clarification," *The Age*, 15 November 2006; Chris Merritt, "PM's Attack on High Court Futile and Self-Defeating," *The Australian*, 2 September 2011.

113 High Court of Australia Act, 1979 (Cth), Pts. III–V.

114 Crawford and Opeskin, *Australian Courts of Law*, 129–31.

115 Sharyn Roach Anleu and Kathy Mack, "The Work of the Australian Judiciary: Public and Judicial Attitudes," *Journal of Judicial Administration* 20 (2010): 3, 7.

116 Murray Gleeson, "Public Confidence in the Courts" (Paper presented at the Confidence in the Courts Conference, National Judicial College of Australia, Canberra, 9 February 2007), 10–11. Indeed, the High Court has been vigilant to ensure that such personal appointments do not undermine the independence of the judiciary: *Grollo v. Palmer* (1995) 184 C.L.R. 348.

117 Gerard Brennan, "Judicial Independence" (Paper presented at the Australian Judicial Conference, Australian National University, 2 November 1996); Greg Woods, "Public Confidence in the Judiciary: Some Historical Observations, and a Proposal" (Paper presented at the Confidence in the Courts Conference, National Judicial College of Australia, Canberra, 9 February 2007).

Judges are conscious that confidence in their role and maintenance of their independence depend on the integrity with which they perform their office,[118] and their responses to criticism are rare and usually very circumspect.[119] One of the most influential judicial dictums on the issue was expressed by Sir Owen Dixon upon his appointment as chief justice of the High Court in 1952, when he said, "Close adherence to legal reasoning is the only way to maintain the confidence of all parties in federal conflicts. It may be that the Court is thought to be excessively legalistic. I should be sorry to think that it is anything else. There is no other safe guide to judicial decisions in great conflicts than a strict and complete legalism."[120]

Much of the debate over judicial technique and constitutional interpretation has involved a critique, defence, or adaptation of Dixonian "legalism."[121]

IV. Federalism Jurisprudence

Australia's legal system derives its origins from the English common law.[122] Australian legal reasoning is, for this reason, most comparable to that of other common-law systems, principally the United Kingdom, the United States, and Canada, but also India, South Africa, and other British Commonwealth countries. Following the cessation of appeals to the Privy Council and the termination of the British Parliament's authority to legislate for Australia in 1986,[123] the High Court has sought to reinterpret the conceptual and juridical foundations of the federal Constitution in autochthonous terms[124] and has increasingly taken its

118 Anleu and Mack, "Work of the Australian Judiciary," 14–15.

119 Cf. Michael Kirby, "Attacks on Judges: A Universal Phenomenon," *Judicature* 81 (1997–8): 238.

120 Owen Dixon, *Jesting Pilate and Other Papers and Addresses* (Melbourne: Law Book, 1965), 247. See Philip Ayres, *Owen Dixon* (Melbourne: Miegunyah, 2003), 233–4.

121 Zines, *High Court and the Constitution*, chap. 17; Michael McHugh, "The Constitutional Jurisprudence of the High Court," *Sydney Law Review* 30, no. 1 (2008): 5; Michael Coper, "Court as a Political Institution," in Coper, Blackshield, and Williams, *Oxford Companion to the High Court*, 539–41; Jeffrey Goldsworthy, "Australia: Devolution to Legalism," in *Interpreting Constitutions: A Comparative Study*, ed. Jeffrey Goldswothy, 106–60 (Oxford: Oxford University Press, 2007).

122 Alex Castles, *An Australian Legal History* (Sydney: Law Book, 1982), chap. 17.

123 Australia Act, 1986 (Cth) and (U.K.), s. 1.

124 On autochthony, see Geoffrey Marshall, *Constitutional Theory* (Oxford: Clarendon, 1980), 57–72.

own path in developing the common law of Australia, including constitutional law.[125]

The High Court has at times entertained three fundamental conceptions of the nature of the Constitution: as a British statute, as a federal compact among the Australian states, and as a social contract that derives its authority from the consent of the Australian people as a whole.[126] In addition, the Court uses several modalities of constitutional reasoning, focused variously on text, structure, history, doctrine, political morality, and comparative law.[127] Phases and trends in the High Court's federalism jurisprudence have been shaped by the varied application of these conceptions and modalities to constitutional questions.

1. The Constitution as a Federal Compact

During the first phase of the High Court's federalism jurisprudence (1903–19), a majority of the Court emphasized the Constitution's character as a compact between the Australian states. The Court was at this time composed of judges who had been leading participants at the federal conventions that drafted the Constitution, who interpreted it in the light of the pro-federalist assumptions they believed had animated the vast majority of the framers of the Constitution. As Sir Samuel Griffith, who would be appointed the Court's first chief justice, had put it in 1891, the "essential" condition of federation was that "the separate states are to continue as autonomous bodies, surrendering only so much of their powers as is necessary to the establishment of a general government to do for them collectively what they cannot do individually for themselves, and which they cannot do as a collective body for

125 On Australian constitutional law as a component part of the common law, see Owen Dixon, "The Common Law as an Ultimate Constitutional Foundation," *Australian Law Journal* 31 (1957): 240.

126 James Thomson, "The Australian Constitution: Statute, Fundamental Document or Compact?" *Law Institute Journal* 59 (1985): 1199; for more detail, see Nicholas Aroney, Peter Gerangelos, James Stellios, and Sarah Murray, *The Constitution of the Commonwealth of Australia: History, Principle and Interpretation* (Cambridge: Cambridge University Press, 2015), chaps 3–4.

127 On modalities of constitutional interpretation, see Philip Bobbitt, *Constitutional Fate: Theory of the Constitution* (New York: Oxford University Press, 1982). On their application in Australia, see Nicholas Aroney, "Towards the 'Best Explanation' of the Constitution: Text, Structure, History and Principle in *Roach v. Electoral Commissioner*," *University of Queensland Law Journal* 30 (2011): 145.

themselves."[128] On this view, the legislative powers conferred on the Commonwealth Parliament were intended to be strictly derivative and limited, while the legislative powers retained by the states were to continue as original and plenary.

In accordance with this understanding of the federation, the early High Court read federal legislative powers together in a mutually limiting way, such that deliberate limits placed on the scope of one head of power were seen as relevant to the interpretation of the scope of other heads of power. In particular, the Commonwealth Parliament's power to legislate on *interstate* trade and commerce (s. 51(i)) was understood to imply a limit on the scope of other powers, such that they could not be used to regulate *intra-state* trade and commerce because this fell within the states' "reserved powers."[129] Pursuant to this doctrine, it was held, for example, that a legislative exemption from a federal tax that an employer would enjoy if it engaged employees on certain prescribed conditions could not be characterized as a "tax" (s. 51(ii)) but was rather a regulation of employment relations that fell outside the scope of the Commonwealth's powers and was therefore invalid.[130] Likewise, federal legislation regulating the creation of worker's trademarks was interpreted as not falling within the meaning of the federal trademarks power (s. 51(xviii)) but rather as interfering with matters falling within the states' legislative jurisdiction.[131] Similarly, federal legislation that prohibited trading and financial corporations from engaging in restrictive trade practices was struck down as extending beyond the limits of the Commonwealth's power to legislate with respect to such corporations (s. 51(xx)), which the Court interpreted to extend only to the special kinds of regulatory issues that corporations characteristically pose for a legal system.[132]

---

128 *Official Report of the National Australasian Convention Debates, Sydney* (Sydney: Acting Government Printer, 1891), 31–2; see, likewise, Samuel Griffith, *Notes on Australian Federation: Its Nature and Probable Effects* (Brisbane: Government Printer, 1896), 6–7, 10. On Griffith, see Roger Joyce, *Samuel Walker Griffith* (Brisbane: University of Queensland Press, 1984).

129 Nicholas Aroney, "Constitutional Choices in the Work Choices Case, or What Exactly Is Wrong with the Reserved Powers Doctrine?," *Melbourne University Law Review* 32, no. 1 (2008): 1, 9–18.

130 *R. v. Barger; Commonwealth v. Mackay* (1908) 6 C.L.R. 41.

131 *Attorney-General for New South Wales v. Brewery Employees Union of New South Wales* (1908) 6 C.L.R. 469.

132 *Huddart, Parker & Co. Pty. Ltd. v. Moorehead* (1909) 8 C.L.R. 330. For a discussion, see James Allan and Nicholas Aroney, "An Uncommon Court: How the High Court of Australia Has Undermined Australian Federalism," *Sydney Law Review* 30 (2008): 245, 269–71.

A second characteristic doctrine of the High Court's early federalism jurisprudence concerned a reciprocal immunity enjoyed by both the Commonwealth and the states from interference by the other. This immunity, which prevented any "fetter, control or interference" with an "instrumentality" of the Commonwealth or the states, was said to be an implication of the federal system created by the Constitution, under which each order of government would be "sovereign" within its sphere of operation and, therefore, immune from external interference. As a consequence of this doctrine, state laws purporting to impose taxes on Commonwealth employees, and a Commonwealth law that purported to regulate industrial disputes between state railways and their employees, were deemed unconstitutional.[133]

2. *The Constitution as an Imperial Statute*

In the landmark *Engineers* case (1920), a differently composed High Court abandoned these doctrines in favour of the idea that the Constitution is ultimately to be understood as a statute of the British Parliament, approved by the Australian people as an undifferentiated whole.[134] The Court was now intellectually led by Sir Isaac Isaacs, a frequently dissenting member of the Court since 1906, just as he had been a frequently dissenting member of the federal conventions of the 1890s.[135] Isaacs's vision of the Australian federation had always been highly nationalist and unitarist, but these convictions about Australia's place in the world now shaped the stance taken by the Court as a whole.[136] Isaacs believed that it was the Court's role to look to what he understood to be the interests of the entire nation, rather than the "partial" interests of the states,[137] and he found a way of doing this by interpreting the Constitution in accordance with the ordinary common-law

---

133 *D'Emden v. Pedder* (1904) 1 C.L.R. 91; *Deakin v. Webb* (1904) 1 C.L.R. 585; *Federated Amalgamated Government Railway and Tramway Service Association v. New South Wales Railway Traffic Employees' Association* (1906) 4 C.L.R. 488, following *McCulloch v. Maryland*, 17 U.S. 316 (1819); *Collector v. Day* (1871) 78 U.S. (11 Wall) 113.

134 *Amalgamated Society of Engineers v. Adelaide Steamship Co. Ltd.* (1920) 28 C.L.R. 129, 153.

135 Zelman Cowen, *Isaac Isaacs* (Brisbane: University of Queensland Press, 1993).

136 Cf. R.T.E. Latham, "The Law and the Commonwealth," in *Survey of British Commonwealth Affairs*. Vol. 1, *Problems of Nationality 1918–1936*, ed. W.K. Hancock, 510–630 (Oxford: Oxford University Press, 1937).

137 *Official Record of the National Australasian Convention Debates, Third Session: Melbourne* (Melbourne: Government Printer, 1898), 283.

canons of statutory construction, looking to the actual words of the Constitution, understood in their ordinary and natural meaning.[138] These canons of construction, Isaacs maintained, required that federal grants of power be interpreted with as much liberality as possible.[139] In *Engineers*, it was accordingly held, contrary to previous decisions, that the Commonwealth could indeed regulate the employment conditions of state employees pursuant to its industrial arbitration power (s. 51(xxxv)).[140] Full effect must be given to this grant of power, the Court now said, without considering the "residue" of powers left to the states or any implied "immunities" that might protect the states from interference.[141]

Even though the *Engineers* case has been comprehensively criticized by scholars for its poor organization and suspect reasoning,[142] its fundamental approach to the federal distribution of legislative power has been followed by the Court ever since. The Court has routinely rejected arguments that the interpretation of each federal power must be read in the light of the limited grants of power under other heads or the legislative competence left to the states. For example, the "external affairs" power (s. 51(xxix)) has been interpreted to enable the Commonwealth to legislate to implement international treaties on topics otherwise falling outside the list of section 51 powers.[143] More recently, the Court has interpreted the "corporations" power (s. 51(xx)) as enabling the Commonwealth to regulate any corporate activities, including contracts with employees, notwithstanding the deliberately limited federal power to regulate employment relations through a system of industrial arbitration (s. 51 (xxxv)).[144] In these and other cases, the proposition that the Constitution should be interpreted in a manner that maintains some kind of "federal balance" between the Commonwealth and the

138 *Engineers* (1920) 28 C.L.R. 129, 142, 148–9.

139 Ibid., 153 citing *Hodge v. The Queen* (1883) 9 App. Cas. 117, 132.

140 Ibid., 154.

141 Cf. *Huddart Parker* (1909) 8 C.L.R. 330, 415, per Higgins J: the powers left to the states cannot be determined "until the utmost limits of all the powers conferred on that Parliament by s. 51 have been ascertained."

142 Sawer, *Australian Federalism in the Courts*, 197–201; Zines, *High Court and the Constitution*, 10–14; Geoffrey de Q Walker, "The Seven Pillars of Centralism: Engineers' Case and Federalism," *Australian Law Journal* 76 (2002): 678.

143 *Commonwealth v. Tasmania* (1983) 158 C.L.R. 1.

144 *New South Wales v. Commonwealth* (2006) 229 C.L.R. 1.

states has been rejected as involving a return to the "heretical" reserved powers doctrine said to have been "exploded" in the *Engineers* case.[145]

This clause-bound approach to interpreting Commonwealth powers has had implications for the High Court's approach to the characterization of federal laws for the purpose of determining whether such laws fall within a head of legislative power.[146] Prior to 1920, as a corollary to the reserved powers doctrine, the Court looked for the "true nature or character" of the federal law. This approach was influenced by early Privy Council interpretations of the Canadian British North America Act 1867, where the distribution of legislative power between the dominion and the provinces is determined through two separate lists of powers for each.[147] Although the legislative powers of the dominion are conferred in general terms, the addition of two specific lists suggests that it is necessary to determine the one true character (the "pith and substance") of the law for the purpose of deciding whether it falls within the scope of a particular dominion *or* provincial power.[148] Reserved powers reasoning in Australia required a similar kind of determination; it was necessary to decide whether a law fell within the scope of a particular Commonwealth power *or* a topic reserved to the states. While it took some decades for the implications of the *Engineers* method to be worked out, the High Court eventually abandoned the quest for the "one true character" of the law in a decision upholding a Commonwealth law that deprived superannuation funds of an exemption from income tax unless a proportion of their funds was invested in prescribed public securities. Notwithstanding that the law was substantially concerned with the investment decisions of superannuation funds, it was characterized as a law with respect to "taxation" and therefore upheld.[149] Several subsequent cases have underscored the principle, as one commentator has put it, that "it matters not that a law may properly be characterised as a law with respect to a subject that is not granted to the Commonwealth, provided that it may also be characterised as a law respecting a subject that is within

145 Aroney, "Constitutional Choices in the Work Choices Case," 24–5, 27. See also *Airlines of New South Wales Pty. Ltd. v. New South Wales [No. 2]* (1965) 113 C.L.R. 54, 79; *Melbourne Corporation v. Commonwealth* (1947) 74 C.L.R. 31, 66.

146 Aroney et al., *Constitution of the Commonwealth of Australia*, 136–43.

147 Constitution Act, 1867 (Can.), ss. 91 and 92.

148 See the chapter on Canada in this volume.

149 *Fairfax v. Federal Commissioner of Taxation* (1965) 114 C.L.R. 1

Commonwealth power. The court is not compelled to choose."[150] Such an approach makes it much easier to characterize a federal law as falling within a federal head of legislative power, and therefore as validly enacted.

This expansive attitude towards Commonwealth power has been applied in several other ways. The Court has interpreted the Commonwealth's power to make grants to the states "on the terms and conditions that it thinks fit" (s. 96) to enable the imposition all sorts of conditions for the receipt of grants, even in areas of recognized state jurisdiction, such as roads, education, and health.[151] Although the Commonwealth's power to legislate on taxation is concurrent with the continuing power of the states to levy taxes, the High Court upheld a scheme introduced by the Commonwealth during the Second World War whereby it effectively monopolized the imposition of income taxes.[152] The only explicit prohibition on state taxing powers concerns customs and excise duties (s. 90), a prohibition that the Court has interpreted widely and substantively, so that the states are not able to impose licence fees to conduct business if the fees are in any way referable to the quantity or value of goods or services provided by the business.[153] This particular decision severely restricted a major source of state revenue and was the catalyst for an extensive restructuring of Australia's tax system in 2000. The federal government had for some time wished to introduce a broad-based consumption tax in substitution for a complex and inefficient array of Commonwealth and state taxes, but it faced significant political opposition. The High Court's decision on excise duties enabled the Commonwealth to convince the states to support the introduction of a goods and services tax, the revenue from which is distributed to the states by the Commonwealth on the basis of recommendations of the Commonwealth Grants Commission in order to achieve horizontal

---

150 Zines, *High Court and the Constitution*, 28–9. The cases include *Murphyores Inc. Pty. Ltd. v. Commonwealth* (1976) 136 C.L.R. 1; and *Actors and Announcers Equity Association v. Fontana Films Pty. Ltd.* (1982) 150 C.L.R. 169.

151 *Victoria v. Commonwealth* (1926) 38 C.L.R. 399. The limitations on the terms and conditions that can be stipulated by the Commonwealth concern over-riding constitutional requirements, such as just terms for the acquisition of property (sec. 51(xxxi)) and freedom of religion and the non-establishment of religion (sec. 116): *ICM Agriculture Pty. Ltd. v. Commonwealth* (2009) 240 C.L.R. 140, 164–70.

152 *South Australia v. Commonwealth* (1942) 65 C.L.R. 373; affirmed after the war in *Victoria v. Commonwealth* (1957) 99 C.L.R. 575.

153 *Ha v. New South Wales* (1997) 189 C.L.R. 465

fiscal equalization.[154] Notwithstanding this, Australia's fiscal system involves a severe vertical fiscal imbalance between the Commonwealth and the states, which undermines the political accountability of all orders of government and reduces incentives for competitive innovation.[155]

3. The Constitution as a Fundamental Law

Although the general tendency of the High Court's federalism jurisprudence has been centralizing, several important qualifications need to be noted. From the 1940s in particular, under the emerging intellectual leadership of Sir Owen Dixon,[156] the Court began again to take federal principles into consideration in its interpretation of the Constitution. Recognizing that the Constitution was intended to create a federal system in which both the Commonwealth and the states operate as autonomous political communities, it was held that while they may still make laws that in some respects bind each other, they cannot do so in a manner that prevents the other from functioning as an independent government.[157] Even here, however, an asymmetry remains between the immunities enjoyed by the Commonwealth and the states. On the Court's reasoning in the *Engineers* case, the immunity of federal instrumentalities from state interference could be justified on the basis of the Commonwealth's supposed "supremacy."[158] Somewhat in line with this view, the seminal case redefining the Commonwealth's immunity in the 1960s did so on the basis that the states simply had no power to regulate the Commonwealth, either as colonies before federation or after federation pursuant to the Constitution.[159] Consequently, it has been held that state laws can bind the Commonwealth only through generally applicable laws that regulate the exercise of capacities that the Commonwealth has in common with ordinary persons (such as entering into contracts or dealing with property); and even here the

---

154 A New Tax System (Goods and Services Tax) Act, 1999 (Cth); Intergovernmental Agreement on Federal Financial Relations, 2009, cl. 26.

155 Neil Warren, "Designing Intergovernmental Grants to Facilitate Policy Reform," in Kildea, Lynch, and Williams, *Tomorrow's Federation*, 131.

156 Philip Ayres, *Owen Dixon* (Melbourne: Miegunyah, 2003).

157 *Melbourne Corporation v. Commonwealth* (1947) 74 C.L.R. 31.

158 *Engineers* (1920) 28 C.L.R. 129, 156–60.

159 *Commonwealth v. Cigamatic Pty. Ltd. (In Liquidation)* (1962) 108 C.L.R. 372.

Commonwealth can usually immunize itself by enacting legislation that will prevail over any inconsistent state law.[160] By contrast, the states' immunity is formulated more narrowly. Initially, it was thought to prohibit Commonwealth laws from either discriminating against the states or preventing them from performing their constitutional functions.[161] However, in its most recent decisions, the Court determined that there is only one ground of state immunity – the states' capacity to function as independent governments – so that discrimination is only a factor to be considered, not a ground of invalidity in itself.[162]

One other line of challenge to *Engineers* orthodoxy has emerged from a more recent line of cases in which Court members have suggested that, following the cessation of the British Parliament's power to legislate for Australia, the Constitution now derives its authority from the consent of the Australian people.[163] This idea has laid the foundation for an implied rights jurisprudence inferred from the system of representative and responsible government established by the Constitution.[164] One line of argument here is that the requirement that members of the Commonwealth Parliament be "directly chosen by the people" (ss. 7 and 24) implies that electoral divisions for the House of Representatives ought to contain an equivalent number of voters so as to ensure an "equality of voting power" for all citizens. However, in determining whether this implication follows from the text, structure, and design of the Constitution, members of the Court have drawn attention to "the adaptation of representative democracy to federalism by the framers of the Constitution,"[165] closely examining the way in which federal principles of representation and political participation shaped the formative compact among the people of the states, the representative institutions of the Commonwealth, and the popular procedure for amending the Constitution. While equal citizenship within a national democracy does

---

160 *Re Residential Tenancies Tribunal of NSW; Ex parte Defence Housing Authority* (1997) 190 C.L.R. 410.

161 *Melbourne Corporation v. Commonwealth* (1947) 74 C.L.R. 31; *Queensland Electricity Commission v. Commonwealth* (1985) 159 C.L.R. 192.

162 *Austin v. Commonwealth* (2003) 215 C.L.R. 185; *Clarke v. Commissioner of Taxation* (2009) 240 C.L.R. 272.

163 See Geoffrey Lindell, "Why Is Australia's Constitution Binding? The Reasons in 1900 and Now, and the Effect of Independence," *Federal Law Review* 16 (1986): 29.

164 *Australian Capital Television v. Commonwealth* (1992) 177 C.L.R. 106; *Lange v. Australian Broadcasting Corporation* (1997) 189 C.L.R. 520.

165 *McGinty v. Western Australia* (1996) 186 C.L.R. 140, 274–5.

seem to imply equal voting rights and equality of voting power, federalism involves a plurality of political communities of which citizens are members, making equality of voting power across the entire federation quite beside the point. On this basis, the High Court has departed from the approach to electoral apportionment adopted in the United States and adopted one that is comparable to, although still different from, Canadian jurisprudence.[166]

The principle that the Senate represents the "people of the States" has potential to unsettle other aspects of the High Court's federalism jurisprudence as well.[167] The Constitution provides that the Senate is composed of senators "for each State directly chosen by the people of the State" and guarantees that the six Original States shall be equally represented in the Senate (s. 7). However, the Constitution also grants the Commonwealth Parliament a near plenary power to legislate for federal territories, including power to provide for their representation in the Parliament "to the extent and on the terms which it thinks fit" (s. 122). In exercise of this latter power, the Commonwealth has provided that the two mainland territories are represented in the Senate by two senators each. This provision was challenged in the High Court on the basis that the Senate is to be composed of senators for each state, and if the territories are to be given representation, it must be subject to this fundamental principle. A narrow majority upheld the legislation, but exactly how far the Parliament can constitutionally dilute the character of the Senate as a "States' house" remains an open question.[168]

The powers of the House of Representatives and the Senate are also carefully balanced by the Constitution. The general principle is that the Senate has equal power with the House, subject only to the rule that the Senate may not initiate or amend proposed laws appropriating money or imposing taxation (s. 53). The Constitution's framers were conscious that the Senate's power to refuse or fail to pass an appropriation bill could, under the conventions of parliamentary responsible government, lead to a loss of confidence in the government, with the

166 Nicholas Aroney, "Democracy, Community and Federalism in Electoral Apportionment Cases: The United States, Canada and Australia in Comparative Perspective," *University of Toronto Law Journal* 58, no. 4 (2008): 421.

167 For more detail, see Aroney et al., *Constitution of the Commonwealth of Australia*, 46–61, 89–92.

168 *Western Australia v. Commonwealth* (1975) 134 C.L.R. 201; *Queensland v. Commonwealth* (1977) 139 C.L.R. 585.

implication that the prime minister should resign.[169] This remarkable course of events occurred in 1975, but Prime Minister Gough Whitlam refused to resign. The governor-general controversially exercised his "reserve powers" to dismiss the prime minister and appoint the leader of the opposition as a caretaker prime minister, on condition that a federal election be held as soon as practicable.[170]

The Senate's authority to refuse to pass proposed laws initiated in the House gives rise to the possibility of prolonged deadlocks between the houses. The Constitution provides a complex mechanism for resolving such deadlocks (s. 57). The mechanism comes into play in circumstances where the Senate twice refuses or fails to pass a bill passed by the House, or passes it with amendments to which the House will not agree. In order to allow both houses time to deliberate about the issue, three months must elapse between the Senate's initial response to the proposed law and the second time that the House passes it. In such circumstances, the government is able to call for a dissolution of both houses and a general election. If, following the election, the two houses continue to disagree about the proposed law, the government can advise the governor-general to convene a joint sitting of both houses to determine, by absolute majority, whether to enact the bill. In 1974, several bills were subject to such disagreement between the houses, a general election was held, the houses continued to disagree, and the bills were passed at a joint sitting. In litigation concerning these bills, one question was whether the requisite three months had elapsed between the first failure of the Senate and the House to agree and the second passage of the bill through the House. Because the Senate had in the first instance adjourned debate on the specific bill in question and did not consider it again until four months later, and because the House passed the bill for a second time only days after the Senate had decisively rejected it, the Court had to decide when the requisite three months would commence. The Court held that the Senate had the constitutional right to consider the proposed law, provided it did not put off the debate for an unreasonable period of time, and that the time taken to deal with the bill was not in the circumstances unreasonable.[171]

---

169 Aroney, *Constitution of a Federal Commonwealth*, 359–62.

170 Geoffrey Sawer, *Federation under Strain* (Melbourne: Melbourne University Press, 1977); L.J.M. Cooray, *Conventions, the Australian Constitution and the Future* (Sydney: Legal Books, 1979).

171 *Victoria v. Commonwealth* (1975) 134 C.L.R. 81.

This solicitude for at least some of the federal principles that underwrite the Constitution's system of representative democracy has not generally translated into a more balanced interpretation of the distribution of legislative powers. However, even here there have been some important exceptions.[172] First, where the text of a head of power is expressly limited in some respect, such as section 51(i), which refers to "trade and commerce ... *among the states*," and section 51(xx), which refers to "corporations *formed* within the limits of the Commonwealth" (emphasis added), the Court has insisted that these words of limitation do indeed limit the scope of that particular head of power.[173] Second, in some heads of Commonwealth legislative power the definition of the subject matter is expressed in partly *negative* terms, such as the Commonwealth's power to make laws with respect to "banking, *other than* State banking," and "insurance, *other than* State insurance" (s. 51(xiii), (xiv); emphasis added). On a clause-bound approach, it remains possible to read the negative qualification in these clauses as limiting only the scope of power conferred by each clause, and thus as having no effect on the scope of other heads of power. However, the High Court has read the negative qualification as circumscribing the scope of Commonwealth powers generally, so that, for example, the Commonwealth is not able to legislate with respect to "State banking" by using its power to legislate with respect to "financial corporations" (s. 51(xx)).[174] The High Court has also consistently interpreted the power to legislate with respect to "the acquisition of property on just terms" (s. 51(xxxi)) as limiting the Commonwealth's authority to legislate for the acquisition of property other than "on just terms" pursuant to other heads of power, unless the exercise of such other powers necessarily involves an acquisition of property of some kind, such as "taxation" (s. 51(ii)), the sequestration of the property of a bankrupt person (s. 51(xvii)), or the imposition of financial penalties for breaches of validly enacted federal law.[175]

---

172 For more detail, see Aroney et al., *Constitution of the Commonwealth of Australia*, 157–73.

173 E.g., *Airlines of New South Wales Pty. Ltd. v. New South Wales (No. 2)* (1965) 113 C.L.R. 54, 113–15; *New South Wales v. Commonwealth* (1990) 169 C.L.R. 482.

174 *Bourke v. State Bank of New South Wales* (1990) 170 C.L.R. 276.

175 *Commissioner of Taxation v. Clyne* (1958) 100 C.L.R. 246; *Attorney-General (Cth) v. Schmidt* (1961) 105 C.L.R. 361; *Mutual Pools & Staff Pty. Ltd. v. Commonwealth* (1994) 179 C.L.R. 155.

One final, potentially important development concerns the scope of the Commonwealth's executive power (s. 61). In the 2009 decision of *Pape v. Federal Commissioner of Taxation*,[176] the Court upended the widely held assumption that a parliamentary appropriation of money provided the necessary authority for the expenditure of those funds by the executive. The Constitution provides that no money can be withdrawn from the federal treasury without an appropriation made by law (s. 83) and that such monies are to be appropriated "for the purposes of the Commonwealth" (s. 81). In 1975, the High Court had upheld legislation that appropriated funds to be expended on numerous social welfare programs that otherwise lay beyond the Commonwealth's legislative powers.[177] Although the reasoning of a majority of the judges in that case did not support an unlimited view of the Commonwealth's appropriation and spending powers, over the ensuing years, the Commonwealth appropriated and spent very considerable amounts of money on a wide range of programs falling strictly outside its enumerated legislative powers. It also legislated for the administration of such programs, partly on the ground that such legislation was supported by what came to be called an "implied nationhood power."[178] The finding that such a power exists has been an important part of the centralizing tendencies of the High Court's jurisprudence.[179] However, the Commonwealth's assumptions about the scope of its spending power were profoundly challenged by the High Court when it held in 2009 that a mere appropriation is not sufficient to authorize actual expenditure by the executive. The power to spend, it was said, must be found elsewhere in the Constitution or in statutes validly enacted under the Constitution. While, on the facts of the case, special Commonwealth fiscal stimulus payments made to taxpayers in response to the global financial crisis were upheld by a majority of the Court on the ground that they were authorized by either the implied nationhood or the taxation power, by

---

176 *Pape v. Federal Commissioner of Taxation* (2009) 238 C.L.R. 1.

177 *Victoria v. Commonwealth* (1975) 134 C.L.R. 338. Cf. *Attorney-General for a Victoria; Ex rel. Dale v. Commonwealth* (1945) 71 C.L.R. 237.

178 *Davis v. Commonwealth* (1988) 166 C.L.R. 79. See Cheryl Saunders, "National Implied Power and Implied Restrictions on Commonwealth Power," *Federal Law Review* 14 (1983–4): 267.

179 For a critique, see Anne Twomey, "Pushing the Boundaries of Executive Power: *Pape*, the Prerogative and Nationhood Powers," *Melbourne University Law Review* 34 (2010): 313.

so circumscribing the power to spend, many other items of Commonwealth expenditure were placed in serious doubt.[180]

These doubts were realized in a potentially more significant case, *Williams v. Commonwealth*, decided in 2012.[181] The High Court held that the Commonwealth's executive power does not authorize it to enter contracts and spend money for the provision of chaplaincy services in schools and, because no relevant authorizing legislation had been enacted, such contracts and spending were unconstitutional. Prior to this, most legal experts had assumed that the executive power of the Commonwealth included not only the common-law prerogatives of the Crown, but also the ordinary legal capacities of a natural person, and if there was any further limit to these capacities, it was that executive action must concern matters falling within the Commonwealth's legislative powers pursuant to the Constitution.[182] However, contrary to these assumptions, the High Court held that the Commonwealth does not have the executive capacities of a natural person, that its executive powers do not correspond simply to the scope of its legislative powers, but that they extend in this particular context only to the execution of laws validly enacted by the Parliament. In response, the Parliament passed an omnibus statute purporting to authorize Commonwealth expenditures across the many areas potentially affected by the case.[183] However, there were reasons to doubt the constitutional validity of the law,[184] and in a second case, challenging the application of the statute to the chaplaincy program, the High Court held that the law was relevantly unconstitutional, principally because it was not authorized by the Commonwealth's legislative power with respect to "student benefits."[185]

What is perhaps most remarkable about these recent developments is not only the overturning of widely held assumptions about the scope of the Commonwealth's spending and executive powers, but also the role of the principles of federalism and parliamentary government that informed the Court's reasoning. Chief Justice Robert French began his

180 For more detail, see Aroney et al., *Constitution of the Commonwealth of Australia*, 469–86.

181 *Williams v. Commonwealth* (2012) 248 C.L.R. 156.

182 Winterton, *Parliament, the Executive and the Governor-General*, 44–7.

183 Financial Framework Legislation Amendment Bill (No. 3), 2012 (Cth).

184 Anne Twomey, "Parliament's Abject Surrender to the Executive," *Constitutional Critique* (Sydney: Constitution Reform Unit, 2012); Cheryl Saunders, "The Scope of Executive Power," *Senate Occasional Lecture* (2012): 29.

185 *Williams v. Commonwealth (No. 2)* (2014) 252 C.L.R. 416.

judgment in the first *Williams* case by insisting that the Constitution must be understood as giving effect to "a truly federal government" in which the "preservation of the separate existence and corporate life of each of the component states" is as much an "essential" feature of the Constitution as the establishment of the Commonwealth as an effective government.[186] According to a majority of the Court, the federal principle not only requires that the executive power of the Commonwealth is necessarily limited in scope so as to leave room for the states, but that executive expenditure must ordinarily be authorized by laws enacted by both houses of the Parliament, noting that the Senate represents the people of the states. A parliamentary appropriation is not sufficient, on this view, because the Senate's powers in relation to appropriation bills are limited (see s. 53). To hold that the Commonwealth executive has a general power to deal with matters falling within Commonwealth legislative competence, but without specific legislation, "would undermine parliamentary control of the executive branch and weaken the role of the Senate."[187]

Pape and the first *Williams* case thus suggest the possibility of a renewed interest in preservation of the federal characteristics of the Australian constitutional order. Moreover, the narrow reading of the "student benefits" power in the second *Williams* case suggests, remarkably, that this interest in federalism might even be applied to the scope of the Commonwealth's legislative powers. Whether this does indeed represent a shift in orientation needs to be balanced, however, by a consideration of other recent cases in which a relatively wide view of Commonwealth power has been upheld, such as the High Court's decision in the *Same Sex Marriage* case. In that case, the Court held that a law of the Australian Capital Territory providing for same-sex marriage was inconsistent with the heterosexual definition of marriage in the federal *Marriage Act*. However, it also adopted a relatively very wide reading of the Commonwealth's "marriage" power so that it would enable the Commonwealth to legislate not only for same-sex marriage but also polygamous marriage, provided the union is "consensual."[188]

---

186 *Williams v. Commonwealth* (2012) 248 C.L.R. 156, [1], [61], [83], citing Andrew Inglis Clark, *Studies in Australian Constitutional Law* (Melbourne: Charles F. Maxwell, 1901), 12–13.

187 *Williams v. Commonwealth* (2012) 248 C.L.R. 156, [60].

188 *Commonwealth v. Australian Capital Territory* (2013) 250 C.L.R. 441, discussed in Patrick Parkinson and Nicholas Aroney, "The Territory of Marriage: Constitutional Law, Marriage Law and Family Policy in the Act Same Sex Marriage Case," *Australian Journal of Family Law* 28 (2014): 1.

V. Conclusions

The wider political context in which Australia's High Court has developed its federalism jurisprudence has changed dramatically over time. Australia's evolving political, legal, and constitutional independence from the United Kingdom, while significant for the country's emergence as an independent nation state in international affairs, has tended to bolster the authority and prestige of the Commonwealth at the expense of the states. Harold Laski's view that challenges posed by "modern" economic and social problems made federal systems obsolescent has had influential echoes in Australia, with both political and academic voices calling for an increasing "concentration of political power in the hands of the central parliament."[189] While attempts to amend the Constitution to confer additional powers upon the Commonwealth have almost always failed at referendum,[190] the High Court's expansive interpretations have often been viewed by centralists as making up for the electorate's conservatism.[191]

Those on the other side sometimes suggest that in order to redress the balance, appointments to the High Court should better reflect the federal diversity of the country; but it needs to be recalled that there has been no simple correspondence between a judge's state of origin and his or her federal predilections.[192] More radical surgery is needed, some say, such as fundamental reallocation of legislative and financial powers between the Commonwealth and the states, a Senate that more effectively represents state interests, and measures to increase the accountability and transparency of intergovernmental arrangements.[193] In 2014, the Commonwealth government, following a meeting with the

189 Gordon Greenwood, *The Future of Australian Federalism* (Brisbane: University of Queensland Press, 1946), 340. See Harold Laski, "The Obsolescence of Federalism," *New Republic* 98 (1939): 367.

190 Brian Galligan, "Processes for Reforming Australian Federalism," *University of New South Wales Law Journal* 31 (2008): 617.

191 This was suggested, for example, in former prime minister Gough Whitlam's "The Labor Government and the Constitution," in *Labor and the Constitution 1972–1975*, ed. Gareth Evans (Melbourne: Heinemann, 1977), 305.

192 Allan and Aroney, "Uncommon Court," 290n201.

193 Anne Twomey, "Reforming Australia's Federal System," *Federal Law Review* 36, no. 1 (2008): 57; Cheryl Saunders, "Federalism and Australian Democracy" (Paper presented at the Australian Federalism: Rescue and Reform Conference, Tenterfield, 23–25 October 2008).

states and territories under the auspices of the Council of Australian Governments, issued terms of reference for a White Paper on federalism reform. The terms of reference declared that the federation is not a mere "relic from the past, broken beyond repair and ill-suited to the times," and it was proposed that, "rather than seeking ever greater centralisation of power in the national government as a way of dealing with increasing complexity, now is the time to strengthen the way our federal system works by being clear about who is responsible for what." To these ends, the terms of reference called for a clarification of the "roles and responsibilities" of the states and territories to enable them to become, "as far as possible, sovereign in their own sphere." The terms of reference accordingly call for an inquiry into the "practicality of limiting Commonwealth policies and funding to core national interest matters, as typified by the matters in section 51 of the Constitution."[194]

These are perhaps promising signs, but given the twists and turns that have occurred in the history of the federation, it is difficult to predict where current trends are likely to lead.[195] As far as the High Court's interpretation of the Constitution is concerned, a broad interpretation of the Commonwealth's legislative and financial powers seems firmly entrenched, although there are other aspects of the constitutional system where its federal characteristics appear to be carrying more weight.[196] Indeed, while the High Court has done much to strengthen the Commonwealth, the states are still fundamental to the Constitution.[197] Thus, when the power of the British Parliament to legislate for Australia was ended in 1986, it was of utmost significance that the Australia Act 1986 (Cth) had to be enacted on the basis of a provision in the Constitution that confers upon the federal Parliament the authority to exercise the

---

194 Tony Abbott, "Terms of Reference: White Paper on the Reform of the Federation," 28 June 2014, https://federation.dpmc.gov.au/publications.

195 The White Paper process was abandoned in early 2016 following a change in prime minister. See Nicholas Aroney, "Reforming Australian Federalism: The White Paper Process in Comparative Perspective," in *A People's Federation*, ed. Mark Bruerton, Robyn Hollander, Ron Levy, and Tracey Arklay (Sydney: Federation Press, forthcoming).

196 Cheryl Saunders, "Can Federalism Have Jurisprudential Weight?," in *The Federal Idea: Essays in Honour of Ronald L. Watts*, ed. Thomas J. Courchene, John R. Allan, Christian Leuprecht, and Nadia Verrelli (Montreal and Kingston: McGill-Queen's University Press, 2011), 111, 127.

197 See Nicholas Aroney and Campbell Sharman, "Territorial Politics and the Federal Frame in Australia," in *Handbook of Territorial Politics*, ed. Eve Hepburn and Klaus Detterbeck (Cheltenham: Edward Elgar, 2016).

powers of the British Parliament with respect to Australia, provided that this is done at the request or with the concurrence of the parliaments of all states directly concerned (s. 51(xxxviii)). This provision reflects the underlying principle of the federation, which is the agreement of the states to form themselves into a "federal commonwealth," as recited in the preamble to the Constitution – as a "negotiated federal compact," as Chief Justice French has put it.[198] It is significant that, consistent with this principle, the amendment clause in the Australia Act also requires the unanimous approval of the Australian parliaments. Unanimity among the states is the fundamental decision-making principle of the entire federation.

At the time of federation, one of the leading architects of the Constitution, Sir Samuel Griffith, expressed the hope that one day the constitution of each state would be submitted to its people for their approval, so that the democratic foundations of the Commonwealth Constitution would be extended to those of the constituent states.[199] While the prospects of this happening in the foreseeable future remain rather slim, it is possible to speculate that such a step would contribute to the revitalization of federalism, for it would not only consolidate the authority of the state constitutions over the state governments in a way that would be based on the active participation of their citizens, but it would also give the High Court reason to reconsider its understanding of the fundamental nature of the federal Constitution. It would provide a renewed basis, in other words, for the Court to adopt the view that the Constitution derives its authority, not from the British Parliament, nor from the Australian people as an undifferentiated whole, but from an agreement among the citizens of the several states.[200] A reinvigorated federal system could be the result.

---

198 *Ruddock v. Vadarlis* (2001) 110 FCR 491, 540 (French J., as he then was, of the Federal Court).

199 *Official Report of the National Australasian Convention Debates, Sydney, 2 March to 9 April, 1891* (Sydney: Acting Government Printer, 1891), 490.

200 Queensland Constitutional Review Commission, *Report on the Possible Reform of and Changes to the Acts and Laws that Relate to the Queensland Constitution* (Brisbane: Queensland Constitutional Review Commission, 2000); Nicholas Aroney, "Popular Ratification of the State Constitutions," in Kildea, Lynch, and Williams, *Tomorrow's Federation*, 210.

3 The Constitutional Court of Belgium: Safeguard of the Autonomy of the Communities and Regions

PATRICK PEETERS AND JENS MOSSELMANS

I. Introduction

Belgian federalism is based on a process of devolution. The country has been transformed from a unitary state into a federally structured state through several successive constitutional reforms. The Belgian federal state is composed of three communities and three regions but is basically divided along linguistic lines: Dutch-speaking in the north, French-speaking in the south, and an officially bilingual capital region in the centre. This results in a federal state with strong confederal characteristics.

The transformation into a federal state made it necessary to find an arbitrator to resolve disputes between the legislatures on the division of powers. A central constitutional body was established with judicial authority but separate from the judiciary: the Constitutional Court. The Constitutional Court has played an important role in enforcing the principles governing the relationships between the federal and the federated entities. Reflecting the progressive devolution of legislative powers through successive waves of constitutional reform, the Court has proved to be an important safeguard for the autonomy of the federated entities (the communities and the regions) and has, as such, played a mostly decentralizing role.

II. Federal System

1. *Broad Characteristics*

The population of Belgium is 11,209,044,[1] of which 6.4 million live in Flanders, 3.5 million in Wallonia, and approximately one million in the

1 StatBel, as per 1 January 2016: http://statbel.fgov.be/nl/binaries/NL_kerncijfers_2015_WEB_COMPLET_tcm325-275721.pdf.

Brussels-Capital Region. Belgium has three official languages: Dutch (approximately 60 per cent of the population), French (approximately 40 per cent), and German (74,000 speakers, concentrated in the country's east). In addition, Belgium has about one million foreign residents, including as of 2015 over 159,362 French,156,977 Italians, 149,199 Dutch (from the Netherlands), 82,009 Moroccans, and 68,403 Poles.[2] A majority of Belgium's population is Roman Catholic (57 per cent). Six other recognized religions represent 6 per cent of the population, while 37 per cent profess no religion. The gross domestic product was €400.6 billion in 2014.[3] In the same year, the gross domestic product per inhabitant was €29,200 in the Flemish Region, €21,300 in the Walloon Region, and €55,100 in the Brussels-Capital Region.[4]

Belgium is a federation of three communities (the Flemish Community, the French Community, and the German-speaking Community) and three regions (the Flemish, Walloon, and Brussels-Capital Regions). Both the communities and the regions are territorially based, with an overlap of the Flemish and French Communities in the bilingual Brussels-Capital Region. The autonomy of the federated entities (the communities and the regions) is guaranteed by the Constitution. Each federal and federated entity has its own parliament and government.[5]

The transformation from a unitary into a federally structured state took place in successive phases, mostly by revisions to the Constitution, followed by the dissolution of Parliament, parliamentary elections, and

---

2 Directorate General for Statistics and Economic Information, http://statbel.fgov.be/nl/statistieken/cijfers/.

3 StatBel, as per 1 January 2016.

4 Study centre of the Flemish government, http://www4.vlaanderen.be/sites/svr/cijfers/Exceltabellen/economie/1structuur/ECONECST_001.xls.

5 For more information, see Kris Deschouwer, "Kingdom of Belgium," in *Constitutional Origins, Structure, and Change in Federal Countries*, ed. John Kincaid and G. Alan Tarr, 48–75 (Montreal and Kingston: McGill-Queen's University Press, 2005); Hughes Dumont, Nicolas Lagasse, Marc Van Der Hulst, and Sébastien Van Drooghenbroeck, "Kingdom of Belgium," in *Distribution of Powers and Responsibilities in Federal Countries*, ed. Akhtar Majeed, Ronald L. Watts, and Douglas M. Brown, 34–65 (Montreal and Kingston: McGill-Queen's University Press, 2006); Frank Delmartino, Hughes Dumont, and Sébastien Van Drooghenbroeck, "Kingdom of Belgium," in *Diversity and Unity in Federal Countries*, ed. Luis Moreno and César Colino, 48–74 (Montreal and Kingston: McGill-Queen's University Press, 2010); and Lieven De Winter and Caroline Van Wynsberghe, "Kingdom of Belgium: Partitocracy, Corporatist Society, and Dissociative Federalism," in *Political Parties and Civil Society in Federal Countries*, ed. Klaus Detterbeck, Wolfgang Renzsch, and John Kincaid, 40–69 (Don Mills, ON: Oxford University Press, 2015).

negotiations to form a new government. Indeed, the various political parties tend to make arrangements for state reform during negotiations to form a new government.

The state reforms of 1970–1, 1980, 1988–9, 1993, 2001, and 2011 resulted in the transfer of more powers to the communities and the regions. The division of powers is based on the principle of mutual exclusivity. The federal government, the communities, and the regions are all on an equal footing compared to one another. However, an increasing number of asymmetries can be noted in the institutional development of the communities and the regions. The sixth state reform (2011) reinforced this asymmetry by, for instance, transferring community powers to the Brussels-Capital Region.

Fundamental weaknesses in the Belgian federal model are becoming more apparent. Despite the existence of three communities and three regions, the country is essentially bipolar (Dutch-speaking and French-speaking). In addition, a "centrifugal force" results in a federal state with confederal characteristics. At the federal level, powers must be exercised jointly by the Dutch- and French-speakers, which make it increasingly difficult to form a government. Thus, after the June 2010 federal elections, negotiations to form a government stalled. It took until 11 October 2011 for the eight negotiating political parties to conclude a coalition agreement, including an institutional agreement for the sixth state reform.

The Constitutional Court has exclusive authority to review compliance by the federal, community, and regional legislatures with the allocation of legislative powers provided for by the Constitution. The constitutional provisions on the basis of which the Constitutional Court performs its review are those dealing with the allocation of powers between the federal government, the regions, and the communities, the individual rights and freedoms set out in Part II of the Constitution ("Belgians and Their Rights"), Articles 170, 172, and 191,[6] and the principle of federal loyalty (Art. 143, § 1 Const.). The Constitutional Court has played a significant role in enforcing the division of powers and in interpreting the powers of the regions and the communities.

---

6 Article 170 relates to the principle of legality in tax matters, Article 172 confirms the principle of equal treatment in tax matters, while Article 191 guarantees the equal treatment of foreigners.

2. Structural Features

Belgium's federal structure is mandated by the Constitution. According to Article 1, "Belgium is a federal state composed of three communities and three regions." Articles 2 and 3 refer respectively to the "Flemish, French, and German-Speaking Communities" and to the "Flemish, Walloon and Brussels-Capital Regions." The federal, provincial, and municipal institutions are all recognized by the Constitution (Sections I, II, III, and VIII of Part III of the Constitution).

The division of powers between the federal government, the communities, and the regions is based either directly on the Constitution or on so-called special majority legislation (*bijzondere meerderheidswetgeving; législation à majorité spéciale*) enacted pursuant to the Constitution.[7] The special majority requirement is based on the division of the members of both houses of the federal Parliament (the House of Representatives and the Senate) into a Dutch- and a French-speaking language group. The special majority requirement necessitates a majority of the votes cast in each language group in each house, on condition that a majority of the members of each group is present and provided that the total number of votes in favour that are cast in the two language groups is equal to at least two-thirds of the votes cast. The special majority requirement is intended to neutralize the numerical superiority of Dutch-speakers in Parliament and to prevent the unilateral adoption of legislation on matters pertaining to the autonomous status of the communities and the regions against the will of one linguistic group.

Unlike the federation, the communities and the regions, the provinces and municipalities are merely territorially decentralized entities. Their powers are also enshrined in the Constitution, with reference to the provincial or municipal sphere of interest.[8]

Due to the devolutionary origin of the federation, the default principle has been that the federal government can exercise all residual powers, meaning all powers not expressly assigned by the Constitution to the communities or the regions, while the communities and regions can exercise only those powers expressly allocated to them. Article 35 of the Constitution, which has not yet entered into force, reverses this principle. According to this provision, the federal government will be

7 Arts. 127–30 Const. (communities); Art. 134 Const. (regions).
8 Art. 162 Const.

competent only in relation to those matters expressly assigned to it, while the communities and the regions will become competent to exercise all other powers. However, the coming into force of Article 35 of the Constitution is conditional upon the enactment of a special majority act, which will also determine the date of its entry into force. This is because the exclusive powers of the federal government need to be determined prior to the entry into force of Article 35. Three delicate issues make the implementation of Article 35 particularly difficult. In the first place, Dutch- and French-speakers will have to agree on an exhaustive list of matters that will remain within the federal jurisdiction. Until now, the two sides have been able to agree only upon those matters to be withdrawn from the federation. Second, they will have to determine whether the regions (the general preference of French-speakers) or the communities (the general preference of Dutch-speakers) will take on the residual powers. Finally, the implementation of Article 35 will necessitate a fundamental revision of the financing system of the communities and regions. These difficulties mean that, at this time, Article 35 remains merely symbolic.

The powers of the three communities can be divided into four categories: (1) cultural matters, such as libraries, media, fine arts, physical education, and sports; (2) personal matters, such as preventive health care (but not health care insurance) and social welfare; (3) education (but not the commencement and completion of compulsory education, minimum requirements for the issuance of diplomas and pension arrangements for teachers) (these three matters are reserved to the federal authorities); and (4) the use of languages in administrative matters, education, and industrial relations. The three regions are competent for more territorially based matters, such as urban and country planning, environmental protection and water policy, land use and nature conservation, housing policy, agricultural policy and fisheries, energy policy, employment policy, public works and transport, economic policy, and the rules and regulations governing municipalities and provinces. The federal government's residual powers include monetary policy, justice, social security, safety, defence, civil law, criminal law, commercial and corporate law, and labour law. In addition, the federal government, the communities, and the regions can exercise those legislative and executive powers necessary to execute their constitutionally assigned powers.

The federal authorities as well as the communities and the regions all have the power to conduct international relations. Article 167 of the

Constitution lays down the principle of parallelism between internal and external powers: *in foro interno, in foro externo.* International treaties can thus be concluded by the federal, community, or regional authorities, within the limits of their respective powers.[9]

Legislative powers are divided pursuant to the principle of exclusivity. This means that a given power can be exercised only by one legislature (federal, community, or regional). The principle of exclusivity relates to both the subject matter (*ratione materiae*) and the territorial scope (*ratione loci*) of the legislation. If a given matter falls within the scope of authority of more than one legislature, the Constitutional Court will determine which has jurisdiction, based on where the centre of gravity ("pith and substance") lies. Further, the subject of legislation or regulation must be located within the territory of the legislature in question.

The idea is thus to achieve a closed system of exclusive powers. In principle, there should be no conflicts or antinomies (i.e., the mutual incompatibility of two laws enacted by different legislatures without breaching a rule on the division of powers). It should be noted, however, that the possibility of such conflicts is not completely ruled out. The Constitutional Court indeed has jurisdiction to review conflicts between federal and community or regional legislation, even if there is no violation of the division of powers.[10]

Sometimes other techniques of dividing legislative powers are used, such as framework legislation: the federal government lays down basic rules and the federated entities can either simply apply the rules,[11] or supplement the rules and apply them.[12] This technique has also been developed by case law, in order to reconcile federal policy with the autonomy of the regions and the communities, even in the absence of an explicit legal provision, as explained below.

Belgium has only one constitution, operating at the federal level. This is closely linked to the devolutionary nature of Belgian federalism. The communities and regions are recognized and legally established by

---

9 See also Peter Bursens and Françoise Massart-Piérard, "Kingdom of Belgium," in *Foreign Relations in Federal Countries*, ed. Hans Michelmann, 91–113 (Montreal and Kingston: McGill-Queen's University Press, 2009).

10 Art. 26, para. 1, 2° of the Special Act of 6 January 1989 on the Constitutional Court.

11 See, for instance, Article 6(1)(IX)(4) of the Special Act on Institutional Reform, providing for the application by the regions of federal provisions on labour cards.

12 See, for instance Article 6(1)(VI)(4)(1) of the Special Act on Institutional Reform, providing for the completion and application of the federal rules and ordinances on public tenders.

the federal Constitution, that is, the constitution of the former unitary state. The federated entities therefore do not have constitutional power, although they have been granted a capacity to organize their own institutions, which is commonly called "constitutive autonomy."

Article 195 of the Constitution sets forth the procedure to revise the Constitution, which proceeds in three phases. In the first phase, the three branches of the federal legislature, namely, the House of Representatives, the Senate, and the King (in practice, the federal government), each issue a declaration calling for a revision of the Constitution. These three branches form the Pre-Constituent Assembly. Each branch indicates the provisions it considers necessary to revise. Only those provisions indicated in all three declarations can be revised. The declarations are adopted by a simple majority of votes cast in the two houses of the legislature.

The second phase consists of the publication of the declarations in the *Belgian State Gazette*. This results in the automatic dissolution of both houses of Parliament and the holding of elections within forty days. Within two months after the elections, the newly elected Parliament must be convened. The idea behind the automatic dissolution of Parliament is to give the electorate a say in the proposed constitutional revision. However, in practice, constitutional reform does not normally constitute a major electoral issue.

In the third and final stage, the newly elected Parliament may, together with the King, revise the constitutional provisions indicated in the declarations. The revision must be approved by a double two-thirds majority of both houses. At least two-thirds of the members of each house must be present, and no revision can be adopted unless it is approved by at least two-thirds of the total votes cast in each house. After adoption, the revision must be promulgated by the King, after which it is published in the *Belgian State Gazette*.

The amendment of special majority legislation also requires a majority in each language group and an overall two-thirds majority in each house.

Review of legislative compliance with the Constitution was introduced only with the establishment of the Constitutional Court. Prior to that, state legislation was generally deemed inviolable, except for judicial review of the compliance of a statute, with international laws having direct effect within the country. It was not until the 1980 constitutional reform that the Constitutional Court was entrusted with the power to assess the compliance of legislation with the constitutional provisions on the division of powers and, subsequently, those dealing with fundamental rights and freedoms.

Except where a special majority is required expressly by the Constitution (e.g., a revision to the Constitution [Arts. 195 and 198] and special majority acts [Art. 4(3)]), and certain matters with respect to the monarchy (Arts. 86 and 87), the following decision-making process is applied by Parliament: a majority of the members of the house in question must be present, and the draft bill or proposal must be approved by a majority of the votes cast. Abstentions are taken into account to determine the quorum but not the majority. The same procedure (quorum and majority) applies at the community and regional levels (Arts. 31 to 56 of the Special Act on Institutional Reform).

The sixth state reform thoroughly revised the bicameral system. Both the composition and the legislative powers of the Senate were revised. The representation of the federated entities was deemed too limited to make the Senate function as a chamber of the constituent entities at the federal level. The new Senate is much smaller and it does not sit permanently anymore. There are no longer directly elected senators or senators by right. Only two categories of senators remain: fifty indirectly elected senators appointed by and from the members of the community and regional parliaments (twenty-nine form the Dutch linguistic group, twenty form the French linguistic group, and one is appointed by the German Community Parliament) and ten co-opted senators (six Dutch-speaking and four French-speaking).

The unicameral procedure, in which the legislative power is vested in the House of Representatives and the King without involvement of the Senate, has become the standard legislative procedure. This unicameral procedure applies to all matters for which the optional or full bicameral procedure has not been explicitly prescribed by the Constitution. The remaining powers of the Senate relate mainly to institutional matters such as the revision of the Constitution, the special majority legislation, and other legislation with an institutional character.

It is doubtful whether the Senate will be able to play its role as a safeguard of the interests of the federated entities. It should be noted that, at present, there are other, more efficient guaranties at the federal level to protect the interests of the communities and regions. In this respect, reference can be made to the division of the federal House of Representatives into Dutch and French language groups, the special majority requirements for institutional legislation, and equal representation of Dutch- and French-speakers on the federal Council of Ministers.

III. Court System

1. Court System in General

Belgium's judicial system belongs to the civil law tradition, albeit one traditionally considered to combine elements of the French and English systems.[13] In France, strict application of the principle of separation of powers means the judiciary has no authority when the executive branch is involved in a matter, in which case the matter is dealt with by a distinct administrative court. By contrast, in common law systems, which focus on the protection of individual rights, all disputes are submitted to the general courts, regardless of whether the executive branch is involved. Belgium has opted for a position between these systems by establishing a dual judicial system.[14] All disputes arising from civil rights necessarily fall under the exclusive jurisdiction of the ordinary courts (Art. 144), whereas disputes regarding "political rights"[15] fall under the jurisdiction of the ordinary courts, unless provided otherwise by law (Art. 145). Thus, ordinary Belgian courts usually have jurisdiction, except where administrative courts with assigned powers have been set up by the legislature for cases involving political rights. The federal legislature has indeed set up a number of administrative courts with well-defined tasks. Conflicts of jurisdiction between ordinary and administrative courts are settled by the Court of Cassation.[16]

The judicial review of administrative acts is entrusted to the Council of State, the nation's highest administrative court. The Council of State was established by the Act of 3 December 1946. Its most important power is the ability to suspend and/or set aside unilateral, binding administrative regulations and orders, whether they emanate from a federal or a federated entity. In theory, one might think that this would have a unifying effect across the various orders of government. However, this is not the case, because the Council of State can in principle only suspend or set aside an order or regulation. Since the Council of State reform

13 A. Alen, *Treatise on Belgian Constitutional Law* (Deventer: Kluwer, 1992), 95.

14 A. Alen, *Rechter en bestuur in het Belgische publiekrecht. De grondslagen van een rechterlijke wettigheidscontrole* (Antwerp: Kluwer, 1984), 812–15.

15 Political rights are rights related to taking part in the state-power by the citizen: the *jus sufragii* (the right to vote or to present its candidature for elections), the *jus tribute* (tax rights) or the *jus honorum* (access to public functions).

16 Art. 158 Const.

of 2014, the Council of State can issue an injunction.[17] However, this is limited to exceptional circumstances.

The ordinary judicial system is hierarchical. Cases are first heard by a lower court or tribunal, such as a justice of the peace, police court, court of first instance, labour court, or commercial court. If necessary, a case may be appealed to a higher or appellate court, namely (1) the five courts of appeal listed in Article 156 of the Constitution (situated in Brussels, Antwerp, Ghent, Liège, and Mons); (2) the labour courts of appeal; (3) the Court of Assizes (for major criminal matters); and (4) the Court of Cassation, Belgium's supreme court for civil, criminal, and commercial matters.

By contrast, constitutional and administrative judicial review is not subject to a hierarchical structure. The Council of State is the highest and, in most cases, the only court for disputes between citizens and public authorities or between two public authorities arising from administrative acts. The Constitutional Court has exclusive jurisdiction to determine whether the federal, community, and regional legislatures abide by the allocation of legislative powers laid down in the Constitution.

Courts and tribunals are organized on the basis of the principles of specialization and territorial jurisdiction. The law assigns to each type of court or tribunal a specific subject-matter jurisdiction, which allows the judges to acquire thorough knowledge of the cases entrusted to them.[18]

All the ordinary courts and tribunals, the Council of State, and the Constitutional Court are part of a one (federal) judicial system. The only exceptions to this general rule are a limited number of regional "ad hoc" administrative courts created by regional or community parliaments. Reference can, inter alia, be made to the Flemish Council for Permit Disputes, which is competent for all urban planning, building permits, and zoning disputes in the Flemish Region, while for the Brussels and Walloon regions, the Council of State remains competent.

Since the 2015 judicial reform, cases before the ordinary courts and tribunals are in principle heard by single judge.[19] However, the president of the court or tribunal may ex officio transfer cases to a chamber composed of three judges if he or she decides this is warranted by the complexity

17 Art. 36 of the Act of 3 December 1946 on the Council of State.

18 D. D'hooghe, "The Judiciary," in *The Institutions of Federal Belgium: An Introduction to Belgian Public Law*, ed. G. Craenen, 111–12 (Leuven: Acco, 2001).

19 Art. 91 and 109 bis, § 3 Judicial Code.

or importance of the case, or by special objective circumstances.[20] This exception does not apply to the justice of the peace or the president of the police court, who always sits alone. On the commercial and labour courts, the presiding judge is assisted by two deputy lay judges. The Council of State and the Court of Cassation are composed of chambers of more than one judge (as a general rule, cases are heard by three judges).

The courts and tribunals are divided into two language roles (either the French-speaking or Dutch-speaking language role). A judge belongs to the Dutch-speaking or French-speaking language role, depending on the language of his or her diploma. The language of the proceedings is determined by the residence of the defendant. If the defendant's residence is located in the Flemish Region, proceedings will be initiated in Dutch, while French is chosen if her residence lies in the Walloon Region. If the defendant lives in the bilingual Brussels Capital Region, the language of the proceedings will be determined by the language that the defendant actually speaks (French or Dutch). The Constitutional Court generally hears cases by a panel consisting of the two presidents, one Dutch-speaking and one French-speaking, and five judges. To make up those panels, a list is drawn up by the presidents at the beginning of each annual session. At the request of one of its presidents or any two judges, the Court will hear a case in plenum, that is, with all twelve judges present. In exceptional cases, the Council of State is also composed of a bilingual general assembly of at least eight judges. This will be the case if there is a risk of the Dutch-speaking and French-speaking divisions of the Council of State rendering diverging judgments. All of these arrangements reflect and reinforce the bipolar nature of Belgium's judicial regime.

The judgments of courts and tribunals consisting of more than one judge are taken *per curiam*, with no possibility of dissenting opinions. Together with the secrecy of deliberations, this rule is considered a safeguard against the exertion of undue pressure on the individual members of a court.[21] In the case of the Constitutional Court, which is equally composed of Dutch- and French-speakers, who are selected partly to reflect the spectrum of political trends in the federal Parliament, the fact that all decisions are issued by "the Court" limits the risk of a visible opposition between the two linguistic communities.

---

20 Art. 92, § 1/1, and 109 bis, § 3 Judicial Code.

21 Alen, *Treatise on Belgian Constitutional Law*, 115.

Decisions of the ordinary courts and tribunals are binding only *inter partes* (i.e., on the parties to the proceedings).[22] In contrast to common law countries, the Belgian judicial system does not recognize binding precedents or *stare decisis*. However, in practice, judgments rendered by higher courts do enjoy a considerable degree of moral authority, as most judges do not want their decisions to be set aside on appeal. The Court of Cassation, the nation's highest ordinary court, therefore plays a very powerful role.[23] After setting aside a decision that it considers legally incorrect, the Court of Cassation refers the case to another jurisdiction of the same level as the court from which the annulled decision emanated. This court is not legally obliged to comply with the ruling of the Court of Cassation. If it does, its judgment is final. In the rare case that it does not comply with that ruling, a second (this time binding) ruling is possible, by the Court of Cassation sitting with sections assembled. In that case, the binding effect is limited to the parties involved and to the specific subject matter that has been submitted to the Court.

In contrast to the ordinary courts and tribunals, annulment judgments of the Council of State on acts of government have retroactive effect *erga omnes*. When appropriate, the Council of State can maintain, for a given period of time, the effects of administrative regulations that have been set aside.

The Constitutional Court has exclusive jurisdiction to review cases involving the operation of the federal system and compliance with constitutionally guaranteed individual rights and liberties. It supervises whether the federal, community, and regional legislatures abide by the allocation of legislative powers laid down in the Constitution. The provisions on the basis of which the Constitutional Court performs its review are the constitutional provisions on the division of legislative powers between the federal government, the communities, and the regions, and the provisions on individual rights and freedoms set out in Part II of the Constitution ("Belgians and Their Rights") and Articles 170 (the principle of legality in tax matters), 172 (the principle of equal treatment in tax), and 191 (equal protection of foreigners). The sixth state reform added compliance with the principle of federal loyalty.[24]

---

22 Art. 6 Judicial Code.

23 P. De Vroede and J. Gorus, *Inleiding tot het recht* (Antwerp: Kluwer, 1997), 250–1.

24 Art. 142, 3° Const., and Art. 1, 3° of the Special Majority Act of 6 January 1989 on the Constitutional Court.

The Constitutional Court can set aside and, when appropriate, suspend federal, regional, and community legislation pending annulment proceedings. Annulment judgments rendered by the Constitutional Court are final and binding from the date of their publication in the *Belgian State Gazette*. They operate *erga omnes* and have in principle retroactive effect *ex tunc* or *ab initio*. The Court may, however, limit the effect of the annulment by allowing the consequences of the annulled norm to continue up to a certain time. All courts and tribunals may also ask the Constitutional Court for a preliminary ruling on the compliance of federal, regional, and community legislation with the Constitution. In case of such a preliminary ruling, the judgment of the Court is binding only for the referring court or tribunal and for all other courts or tribunals ruling in the same case. However, a judgment on a preliminary ruling frees the other courts and tribunals from the obligation to refer the same question to the Constitutional Court, provided they comply with the decision of the Court on the same subject matter. If a legislative norm is found unconstitutional further to a preliminary ruling, a new period of six months starts to run to file a request for annulment of the legislative norm in question. Approximately one-third of the Constitutional Court's 200 decisions in each year concern "federal" questions, mostly involving the division of competences and taxes.[25]

2. *Constitutional Status of Courts and Judicial Officers*

The ordinary courts and tribunals exist by force of the Constitution (Arts. 147, 150, 151, 156, and 157), and only the federal legislature has the power to establish courts or tribunals (Art. 146) and to determine and define their procedural rules (pursuant to its residual powers).[26] The communities and regions can also, on the basis of their implied powers, determine the jurisdiction of administrative courts and tribunals, although they have done so only in a very limited fashion. The most recent example is the establishment by the Flemish Parliament of a Flemish Council for Permit Disputes using its implied powers.[27] In contrast

25 Constitutional Court, *Year Report 2012* (Bruges: Die Keure, 2013).

26 Constitutional Court, no. 40/92, 13 May 1992; Constitutional Court, no. 49/93, 24 June 1993.

27 See Article 133(56) of the Flemish Decree of 27 March 2009 on the revision of the Flemish urban code. The Constitutional Court ruled, in judgment no. 8/2011 of 27 January 2011, that the Flemish legislature had complied with the three conditions to have recourse to its implied powers, as laid down in Article 10 of the Special Act on Institutional Reform.

to the constitutional status of ordinary courts and tribunals, administrative courts and tribunals (such as the Flemish Council for Permit Disputes) have a statutory basis. Although the Council of State is mentioned in Article 160 of the Constitution, its rules of procedure and the rules of appointment and qualifications of judges are determined by federal law.[28] The Constitutional Court was established in 1980 pursuant to Article 142 of the Constitution. Its statute of judges and rules of procedure are also determined by federal law (i.e., the Special Majority Act on the Constitutional Court of 6 January 1989).

Pursuant to Article 151(2) of the Constitution, the selection, training, and external audit of judges of the ordinary courts and tribunals are entrusted to the so-called High Council of Justice. The High Council of Justice is an independent authority, not subject to government control. Its members are appointed by the King (i.e., the federal government), who nominates the candidates from a list submitted by the appointments committee of the High Council of Justice.[29]

The Constitutional Court is composed of twelve judges, who are appointed for life by the King from lists of two candidates submitted alternatively by the Senate and the House of Representatives. The lists must be adopted by a two-thirds majority in each house so as to ensure that the Court's composition reflects the political diversity and bipolar structure of the federal state. The Court is thus composed on the basis of language parity: six judges are Dutch-speaking, six are French-speaking. One of the judges must have an adequate knowledge of German (being the third official language besides French and Dutch). Each language group elects its president. The office of chief justice is alternately held for one year by the president of each language group. The language adherence of "judges-lawyers" (see below) is determined by the language of their university diploma, while the language adherence of the "judges-politicians" (see below) is determined by the parliamentary language group of which they were last a member.

In addition to the language parity within the Court, a second balance must be observed, namely, the balance between judges who are former magistrates on the Court of Cassation or Council of State or law professors of a Belgian university (category of judges-lawyers) and judges who are former members of the federal, community, or regional

28 It should be noted that the Council of State was not included in the Constitution until 18 June 1993.

29 See Art. 151(4) Const.

parliaments with at least five years' experience without having necessarily had legal training (category of judges-politicians). Each language group within the Court always comprises three judges-lawyers and three judges-politicians.

The language group of each year's chief justice constitutes a majority (four judges) in each panel of seven judges. If a case is heard *in plenum* by the twelve judges, and in the event of a tied vote, the chief justice's vote is decisive. This system is designed to avoid a structural majority of one language group within the Court, or a permanent deadlock between the language groups. Moreover, the system of alternating language majorities tends to prevent any abuse of the temporary majority situation. Since the office of the chief justice will be held the following year by the president of the other language group, the "ruling" language majority knows that it will become a minority the next year. Finally, the Constitutional Court is composed of members of each gender.[30]

The forty-four judges on the Council of State are appointed by the King from lists of three candidates submitted by the Council of State itself. The Council of State compiles the lists on the basis of interviews with candidates. The Senate and House of Representatives also have a say in the process if the Council of State cannot reach a unanimous decision regarding the nomination of candidates. Thus, while independent, nominations also reflect political affiliations in a rather typical consociative approach.

The High Council of Justice has no authority over the Council of State or the Constitutional Court. However, the Act of 15 September 2006 on the reform of the Council of State provides for an internal evaluation system and the performance assessment of judges, comparable to the powers exercised by the High Council of Justice [31]

Pursuant to Article 100 of the Judicial Code, a judge on a court of first instance, labour court, or commercial court can be appointed to sit on more than one such court. The reform of this article by the Statute of 1 December 2013 aims to improve this mobility. There are no official statistics on the (professional) mobility of judges. In any event, given the fact that the judicial apparatus is almost exclusively under federal

30 See Art. 34, § 5, and Art. 128 of the Special Majority Act of 6 January 1989 on the Constitutional Court.

31 See Arts. 74(7) and 74(8) of the Act of 12 January 1973 on the Council of State.

competence, mobility between courts does not tend to affect judges' conception of federalism.

The impartiality and independence of the judiciary are expressly recognized by Article 151(1) of the Constitution. According to the literature, this provision is considered the cornerstone of the separation of powers between the judiciary and the executive branch.[32] Several guarantees are included in the Constitution in order to safeguard the independence of the judiciary from the executive. Article 152 provides that judges are appointed for life. No judge may be deprived of or suspended from office, except by means of a judgment of the Court of Cassation, which acts as a disciplinary authority. Moreover, pursuant to Article 383 of the Judicial Code, the retirement age and pension of judges are determined by law. Pursuant to Article 152(3) of the Constitution, the transfer of a judge is possible only pursuant to a new appointment and with the judge's express consent.

The members of the judiciary are also financially independent from the executive. Article 154 entrusts the legislature with determining the salaries of judges. Further, Article 155 provides that no judge may accept an ordinarily salaried position from the government unless the judge agrees to exercise the position without remuneration and the position is compatible with the judge's official duties. In this respect, Article 293 of the Judicial Code provides that a judge may not hold a remunerated political office or any administrative position, nor serve as a public notary, bailiff, attorney of law, in the military, or as a member of the clergy.

These constitutional guarantees are applicable only to members of the ordinary courts and tribunals. However, the Special Majority Act on the Constitutional Court and the Coordinated Acts on the Council of State provide similar guarantees,[33] although it should be noted that appointments to the Council of State and the Constitutional Court are more openly dependant on political influence, given the procedure of appointing judges as noted above.

Pursuant to the 1998 judicial reform, the High Council of Justice was established to serve as the supervisor auditor of the judiciary and to train and select judges. In creating the High Council of Justice, the legislature wished to depoliticize the judiciary as much as possible. Although the

32 A. Alen, *Treatise on Belgian Constitutional Law* (Deventer: Kluwer, 1992), 630.
33 Ibid., 632.

judges of the ordinary courts and tribunals are still formally appointed by the King, the executive no longer has discretionary power in this regard, because appointments are now made on the basis of candidate lists submitted by the appointments committee of the High Council of Justice. However, political influence on judicial appointments has not been eliminated altogether. According to recent literature, complete depoliticization can be achieved only once the appointments committee itself is completely free of political influence, which is at present not entirely the case.[34]

Unlike the ordinary courts and tribunals, the Constitutional Court consists of six judges coming from parliamentary circles[35] and six judges from the legal profession, appointed by the King from a list submitted by the Senate and the House of Representatives. Although its judges are impartial and independent, the composition of the Court guarantees that the Court takes into account the political trends and institutional developments in Belgium when rendering decisions on federal matters.

As noted, the organization of courts and tribunals is almost exclusively a federal matter and is based on the principles of specialization and territorial jurisdiction. The federal Judicial Code assigns to each type of court or tribunal a specific subject-matter jurisdiction, which allows the judges to acquire thorough knowledge of the legal issues entrusted to them. It is also possible to increase the number of courts and especially tribunals, more or less based on projected case load. The courts and tribunals are spread across Belgium on the basis of population and the distance litigants have to travel to reach the nearest court or tribunal.[36]

The Court of Cassation is Belgium's highest "ordinary" court, and its principal task is to review the legality of decisions rendered by the judiciary. The Court of Cassation must ensure that decisions rendered by the lower courts do not violate the law or the procedures that must

---

34 M. Storme, *De Hoge Raad voor de Justitie na vier jaar gewogen* (Bruges: Die Keure, 2005), 48–56.

35 The fact that the Court consists of six members of Parliament who do not necessarily have legal training reflects the legislature's innate mistrust of a "government of judges."

36 D'Hooghe, "Judiciary," 111–12; the powers of the Constitutional Court and the Council of State are set out in the Special Acts of 12 January 1973 and 6 January 1989 on the Council of State and Constitutional Court, respectively.

be observed in order not to render a decision null and void, within the meaning of the Judicial Code's Article 608.

3. *Curial Procedures*

A distinction should be drawn between the commencement of proceedings before the ordinary courts and tribunals, the Council of State, and the Constitutional Court. Most claims are initiated before the ordinary courts and tribunals by means of a summons (*citation/dagvaarding*), which is served on the defendant by a bailiff. Civil proceedings can be described as adversarial.

The public prosecutor's office intervenes in some civil proceedings, that is, cases indicated by law[37] or when its involvement is required by public policy.[38] In contrast, the public prosecutor's office does not intervene to help the court to determine whether a preliminary ruling should be requested from the Constitutional Court.

Any interested party can bring an action before the Council of State to set aside or, when appropriate, suspend an administrative act taken by any order of government.[39] Proceedings before the Council of State are essentially written and inquisitorial. The Auditor's Office intervenes in proceedings by drawing up a report on the case and presenting an opinion at the end of the hearing. In almost 90 per cent of cases, the auditor's opinion is followed by the judges. The auditor thus qualifies as a sort of "first judge" of the case.

Proceedings before the Constitutional Court are initiated by means of an application to set aside and, when appropriate, suspend a legislative act (within six months following its publication) or by a request for a preliminary ruling submitted by another court or by the Council of State (at any time).[40] Such proceedings are also inquisitorial. Any natural or legal person having an interest in the eventual annulment of a legislative norm may initiate proceedings for annulment. The petitioner must demonstrate that he or she is directly and unfavourably affected by the

---

37 Art. 764 of the Judicial Code, e.g., when minors are involved in case of forgery of documents, bankruptcy, and other matters.

38 Article 138 bis of the Judicial Code.

39 Proceedings before the Council of State are governed by the Act of 12 January 1973 on the Council of State.

40 Proceedings before the Constitutional Court are regulated by the Special Majority Act of 6 January 1989 on the Constitutional Court.

challenged norm. The federal Council of Ministers, the regional and community governments, and the chairs of the legislative assemblies on request of at least two-thirds of their members are also allowed to file a request for annulment without having to demonstrate their interest.

Given that proceedings before the ordinary courts and tribunals are based on the adversarial principle, the judge can rule only within the limits of the parties' claims, except for grounds based on public policy. The orders and remedies available to the judge vary greatly, depending on the case, and can include an expert's investigation and opinion, interim relief in urgent cases, non-application of unlawful administrative acts (Art. 159 of the Constitution), injunctions, and an award of damages.

In civil matters, there are no official statistics on the effective enforcement of judgments. Enforcement will depend mainly on the nature of the case and the remedy sought by the plaintiff (for instance, an award of damages can be enforced more easily than a court order regarding a neighbour-caused nuisance). Since both law enforcement and justice are federal competencies, this does not really raise federal-type concerns. Divergent cultural and political conceptions of "law and order" in the north and south of the country can nevertheless generate criticism concerning actions by federal authorities (too repressive, too lenient) in this regard.

The Council of State is in principle entitled only to suspend or set aside an unlawful government act. It can only in exceptional cases replace the illegal act and put in place its own decision.[41] According to some scholars,[42] no effective judicial remedy is thus possible before the Council of State, as the government can take exactly the same decision as that set aside by the Council of State. According to recent literature, the legislatures generally comply with the Constitutional Court's judgments.[43]

4. *Judicial Culture*

When Belgium was occupied by French revolutionaries during the ancien régime, Montesquieu's theory of the separation of powers

41 Art 36 of the Act of 3 December 1946 on the Council of State.

42 For example, S. Lust, *Rechtsherstel voor de Raad van State* (Bruges: Die Keure, 2000), 345 a.s.

43 W. Verrijdt, "De plicht tot uitvoering van arresten van het Grondwettelijk Hof door de wetgever," in *Leuvense staatsrechtelijke standpunten* 2, ed. A. Alen, 305–69 (Bruges: Die Keure, 2010).

between the executive, legislative, and judicial branches led to the establishment of an *administration-juge*. This meant that judges were prohibited from reviewing any government act. Only the governments themselves were entitled to review the legality of their acts. When Belgium afterwards became part of the United Kingdom of the Netherlands, King William I continued the *administration-juge* by means of an 1822 decree.

In reaction to abuses under the ancien régime and Dutch occupancy, upon independence in 1831, the Belgian legislature entrusted the protection of all subjective rights to the judiciary.[44] However, as noted earlier, unlike in common law constitutional systems, which focus on effective protection of the rights of the individual and in which all disputes are submitted to the judiciary, regardless of whether an administrative authority is involved, Belgium has a dual judicial system.

Constitutional practice and custom also play an important role in the judicial system. On several occasions, the Council of State has referred to unwritten rules stemming from the principles and objectives underlying the Constitution. Examples are the rules concerning the powers of an outgoing government, which is authorized only to conduct current business, and the rule of constitutional secrecy governing the relations between the King and his ministers.[45]

Three methods and approaches to constitutional interpretation can be distinguished. First, the federal legislature can interpret the Constitution. The Constitution itself often refers to the fact that the legislature can take measures to execute its provisions. The executive and judicial branches are bound by the legislature's interpretation of the Constitution, which is subject to review by the Constitutional Court. Second, when performing its review on the basis of the fundamental rights listed in Part II of the Constitution, the Constitutional Court takes into account the analogous rights and freedoms provided for in international treaties that are binding on Belgium. In doing so, the Constitutional Court undertakes an evolving interpretation of the Constitution.[46] Finally, the *presumption of constitutionality*, introduced by the Court of Cassation in its *Waleffe* judgment of 20 April 1950, is also noteworthy.

---

44 Alen, *Treatise on Belgian Constitutional Law*, 641.

45 Alen, *o.c.*, 42.

46 J. Velaers, "Samenloop van grondrechten: het Arbitragehof, titel II van de Grondwet en de internationale mensenrechtenverdragen," *Tijdschrift voor bestuurswetenschappen en publiekrecht* (2005): 301–4.

When an act is unclear, the court must interpret it, insofar as possible, in conformity with the Constitution. This concept is known as *verfassingskonforme Auslegung*. It also applies to the Council of State and the Constitutional Court.

IV. Federalism Jurisprudence

1. Introduction: Extension of the Constitutional Court's Jurisdiction

The creation of the Constitutional Court is closely linked to Belgium's transformation into a federal state in the 1970s and 1980s. The establishment of the Constitutional Court represented a significant milestone in Belgian public law. Shortly after the establishment of the Kingdom of Belgium in 1830, the Court of Cassation, in a judgment of 23 July 1849, had reiterated the principle that, in view of the trust the constituent assembly had placed in the legislature, it was not up to the courts to review the constitutionality of legislation. Such review should remain a prerogative of the legislature. This ruling set a precedent that would be upheld for more than 130 years. Indeed, this "inviolability of the law" principle would govern relations between the legislative and judicial branches for well over a century.

The "inviolability of the law" principle was partially overruled by the 1971 *Le Ski* case, a landmark decision of the Court of Cassation. The Court held that the lower courts must refuse to enforce legislation that conflicts with provisions of self-executing international treaties. This was the first exception to the "inviolability of the law" principle and led to the rather paradoxical situation that Belgian courts henceforth refused to apply a statute that conflicted with fundamental rights and freedoms guaranteed by self-executing international treaties, such as the European Convention on Human Rights, but, on the other hand, did not have authority to review national legislation for compliance with the fundamental rights and freedoms guaranteed by the Belgian Constitution.

The real breakthrough occurred with the transformation starting in 1970 of the traditional territorially decentralized unitary state into a federal state composed of three communities and three regions. Legislative powers were distributed among the federal, community, and regional parliaments. The equal status of the legislation enacted by these parliaments made it necessary to find an arbitrator to resolve disputes involving conflicting powers. Obviously, it could not be left to each legislature on its own to determine whether its rules complied with the constitutional division of powers. This would have resulted in diverging interpretations of the Constitution, jeopardizing the existence of the state itself.

A solution was instituted by the 1980 constitutional reform, which established the "Court of Arbitration" (*Arbitragehof/Cour d'arbitrage/Schiedshof*), a constitutional body with judicial authority but separate from the judiciary.[47] The court was officially established on 1 October 1984 and heard its first case on 19 March 1985. While the name may appear somewhat misleading, it reflected the first function of the new court as an "arbitrator" between the newly established legislatures, as well as the reluctance in parliament to establish a full-blown constitutional court.

The jurisdiction of the Court of Arbitration was initially limited to conflicts of powers between the legislatures. The Court originally had jurisdiction only to review the compliance of federal, regional, and community law with the constitutional division of legislative powers. However, only five years later, during the 1988–9 state reform, the court's jurisdiction was extended.[48] In addition to its jurisdiction with respect to conflicts of powers, the court acquired jurisdiction to review the compliance of federal, community, and regional legislation with three constitutionally guaranteed fundamental rights, namely, the principles of equal treatment and non-discrimination (Art. 10 and 11) and freedom of education (Art. 24). This extension of the Court's jurisdiction was closely linked to the transfer to the communities of additional legislative powers in the area of education, the court being entrusted with reviewing compliance by the communities with the principle of equal treatment of Catholic and state schools.

According to Article 142 of the Constitution, the court's jurisdiction may be further extended to other constitutional provisions, by means of a special majority act. The legislature made use of this option to extend the jurisdiction of the Court of Arbitration to all articles in Part II of the

---

47 Art. 142, then Art. 107 ter. Article 142 of the Constitution was implemented by the Act of 28 June 1983 on the Court of Arbitration and the Act of 10 May 1985 on the consequences of judgments of the Court of Arbitration setting aside legislation. These acts have since been replaced by the Special Majority Act of 6 January 1989 on the Court of Arbitration, see below.

48 Art. 142 Const. as amended and the Special Majority Act of 6 January 1989 on the Court of Arbitration.

Constitution ("The Belgians and Their Rights") as well as to Articles 170, 172 and 191.[49] Previously, the Court had jurisdiction to review only compliance with Articles 10, 11 and 24. Article 170 relates to the principle of legality in tax matters; Article 172 confirms the principle of equal treatment in tax matters; Article 191 guarantees the equal treatment of foreigners. In 2007, the name "Court of Arbitration" was replaced by "Constitutional Court," reflecting this extended jurisdiction of the court. The jurisdiction of the court was finally extended at the sixth state reform to review compliance of statutory legislation with the constitutional principle of federal loyalty (Art. 143).

2. *Specific Issues regarding the Division of Powers*

A. A BROAD INTERPRETATION OF THE POWERS ALLOCATED TO THE COMMUNITIES AND THE REGIONS

As noted above, the federal government holds residual powers, at least until the entry into force of Article 35 of the Constitution. Until then, the powers of the communities and the regions are limited to those mentioned expressly in the Constitution or in the special majority legislation implementing constitutional provisions. The Constitutional Court nevertheless supports a broad interpretation of the community and regional powers. The Court has put it this way: "Unless indicated otherwise, the Constituent Assembly and Special Majority Legislature should be deemed to have granted to the communities and regions all powers to enact those rules that are proper to their allocated powers, without prejudice to Article 10 of the Special Act of 8 August 1980."[50] In effect, the Constitutional Court takes the autonomy of the communities and the regions as its starting point. Using standard methods to review the division of powers (literal, historic, systematic, or teleological interpretations), and taking into account the extension of the autonomy of the communities and the regions by the 1980 state reform, the Court has thus foregone a restricted interpretation of their powers in favour of a broad-based approach. According to the Court, the powers of the communities and regions should be deemed to have been completely and integrally transferred to them. This also means

---

49 Special Majority Act of 9 March 2003, amending the Special Majority Act of 6 January 1989 on the Court of Arbitration.

50 See, e.g., Constitutional Court, no. 25, 26 June 1986. Article 10 of the Special Act on Institutional Reform provides so-called implied powers to the communities and regions (see below).

that limitations on the allocated powers should be interpreted very narrowly and cannot deprive the communities and regions of their right to exercise those powers.[51]

B. IMPLIED POWERS OF THE COMMUNITIES AND THE REGIONS

As a consequence of the very broad interpretation given to the allocated powers of the communities and regions, it is usually not necessary for them to have recourse to their implied powers. In Belgium, the implied powers of the communities and regions are laid down expressly in Article 10 of the Special Majority Act on Institutional Reform, a provision similar to the "necessary and proper" clause in the U.S. Constitution.[52] Article 10 provides that community and regional legislation "may contain measures relating to matters for which the parliaments of the communities and regions have no authority, provided such provisions are necessary for the exercise of their powers." In other words, Article 10 explicitly recognizes the existence of implied powers in favour of the communities and the regions. Implied powers being basically a rule of interpretation, the Constitutional Court has ruled that despite the absence of a similar explicit recognition, the federal government is also entitled to take measures necessary for the exercise of its powers, even if the matters in question are allocated to the communities and the regions.[53]

The Constitutional Court has made the use of implied powers by the communities and regions subject to the following conditions. First, the envisaged measure must be "necessary" to the useful exercise of powers allocated to the region or community concerned. In other words, there must be a close connection between the allocated power and the measure to be taken on the basis of implied powers. However, recent case law indicates that the Constitutional Court performs only a limited review of this necessity requirement. The Court will uphold the reasons cited by the community or region, unless they are "manifestly erroneous."[54] Second, the matter in which the implied powers are to be

51 See, e.g., Constitutional Court, no. 172/2006, 22 November 2006.

52 Article I, Section 8 of the U.S. Constitution: "To make all laws which shall be necessary and proper for carrying into execution the foregoing powers, and all other powers vested by this Constitution in the Government of the United States, or in any department or officer thereof."

53 Constitutional Court, no. 90/94, 22 December 1994; no. 166/2003, 17 December 2003; no. 49/2008, 13 March 2008.

54 Constitutional Court, no. 189/2002, 19 December 2002; no. 49/2003, 30 April 2003.

exercised must lend itself to diverging regulation.[55] A need to maintain uniformity may, for instance, be derived from European law, Belgian monetary and economic union (see below), or the existence of federal regulation.[56] Third, the concrete measures to be adopted by the communities and regions on the basis of their implied powers cannot have more than a marginal impact on the federal matter in question. This means that no harm may be caused to the essential principles of the (federal) matter in question.[57]

C. EXCLUSIVITY OF POWERS

As pointed out earlier, the prevailing system is one of exclusive powers. This choice is closely connected to the grant of a large degree of autonomy to the communities and regions. Only one authority (the federal government, the communities, or the regions to the exclusion of all the others) is authorized to regulate any given matter. The principle of exclusive powers also reflects the goal of fundamental equality between the federal and federated entities. At least in theory, such a system makes it easier to avoid conflicts of powers.

In most federal states, the residual powers of one government cannot prevent another (federal) government from exercising its expressly allocated powers. In Belgium, however, the (federal) residual powers are considered limits on the expressly allocated powers of the communities and regions. The division of powers is thus based on "spheres of mutually exclusive powers." In other words, the powers of one government delimit the powers of another.

Taken to an extreme, this system recalls the theory of mutual exclusivity used in the United States in the nineteenth century to explain the "dual federalism" of the union and its constituent states: "a great factory wherein two sets of machinery are at work, their revolving wheels apparently intermixed, their bands crossing one another, yet each doing its own work without touching or hampering the other."[58]

---

55 See, e.g., Constitutional Court, no. 6/96, 18 January 1996; no. 68/96, 28 November 1996; no. 105/2000, 25 October 2000.

56 J. Vanpraet, *De latente Staatshervorming: De bevoegdheidsverdeling in de rechtspraak van het Grondwettelijk Hof en de adviespraktijk van de Raad van State* (Bruges: die Keure, 2011), 122.

57 See, e.g., Constitutional Court, no. 67, 9 November 1988; no. 109/2000, 31 October 2000.

58 J. Bryce, *The American Commonwealth* (London: Macmillan, 1888), 1:432, cited in G. Sawer, *Modern Federalism* (Melbourne: Pitman, 1976), 53.

Dual federalism is closely associated with the notion of residual powers, as laid down in the Tenth Amendment to the U.S. Constitution.[59] The amendment was enacted in 1791 at the urging of anti-federalists threatened by the unpredictability and uncertainty surrounding the scope of the states' residual powers. The enumerated powers of the federal government, coupled with the "necessary and proper" clause in Article 1, § 8,[60] and the supremacy clause in Article 6, s 2 of the U.S. Constitution,[61] could lead to a situation whereby each time the federal government succeeds in justifying a provision on the basis of its allocated or implied powers, any conflicting act passed by a constituent state is considered null and void. Under the theory of mutual exclusiveness, the Tenth Amendment would become the basis for the original, sovereign powers of the states. In addition to the Union, the states are also independent, within their respective spheres of authority, and are on an equal footing with one another.

The theory of mutual exclusiveness implies a strict separation of the federal and state spheres of power. In order to prevent overlapping powers, the powers of the federal government and the states must be construed restrictively, in such a way as to render impossible all interference in the other's authority: "a mutual delimitation of the state and federal spheres insofar as [...] the government which acts does not push the outer limit of its own powers."[62] In Belgium, the division of powers on the basis of the principle of mutual exclusivity has never been interpreted in such an extreme way. In Belgium, the notion of exclusivity simply means that every matter or situation can be addressed by one legislature only. Jurisdiction of one legislature excludes jurisdiction of any other legislature.[63] As noted, this principle is applied both *ratione materiae* and *ratione loci*. With respect to subject-matter exclusivity, the

59 10th Amendment to the U.S. Constitution.

60 Article 1, Section 8 of the U.S. Constitution.

61 Article 6 of the U.S. Constitution.

62 K. Lenaerts, "Het leefmilieubeleid in de Verenigde Staten van Amerika: de bevoegdheidsverdeling tussen Unie en Staten," in *De grondwettelijke bevoegdheidsverdeling inzake leefmilieu*, ed. H. Bocken (Brussels: Story-Scientia, 1986), 188–9; see also P. Freund, "Umpiring the Federal System," *Columbia Law Review* 54, no. 4 (1954): 561: "It is the theory of two mutually exclusive, reciprocally limiting fields of powers, the governmental occupants of which confront each other as equals"; see also E.S. Corwin, *The Commerce Power versus the States' Rights: Back to the Constitution* (Princeton: Princeton University Press, 1936), 135.

63 See, for instance, Constitutional Court no. 146/2001, 20 November 2001.

Constitutional Court has ruled that a given matter can be addressed by one legislature only.[64] If a matter falls within the scope of authority of more than one legislature, the Court will decide where the centre of gravity lies.[65] From a territorial point of view, the Court has ruled that the Constitution is based on a system of exclusive territorial powers. This holds true for both the regions and the communities. This means that the subject-matter of a legislator's regulation must be located in the territory for which it is competent, so that in any situation only one legislature will be authorized to act at any given time.[66] The Constitutional Court thus upholds a closed system of exclusive powers. The Court has settled the highly debated question in the case law and literature regarding the possibility of conflicting norms or antinomies (i.e., the mutual incompatibility of two laws enacted by different legislatures without breaching a rule on the division of powers). The chances of the Court finding that such a conflict exists are quite low. It should be noted, though, that the possibility of such conflicts is not ruled out completely. The Constitutional Court has jurisdiction to review such conflicts between federal and community or regional legislation, even if there is no violation of the division of powers.[67]

Contrary to the dual federalism concept, the system of mutually exclusive powers applied in Belgium does not completely rule out the possibility of interference. In this respect, the Constitutional Court applies the proportionality rule. The Court assesses the power of the legislature concerned (federal or federated) both in terms of subject-matter and territory. When exercising its powers, the legislature may not take any measures that would render the policy of another legislature impossible or extremely difficult to execute.[68]

In practice, there are numerous exceptions to the principle of exclusive powers of the federal government, the communities, and the regions.

---

64 See, for instance, Constitutional Court no. 184/2002, 11 December 2002; no. 25/2010, 17 March 2010.

65 Constitutional Court, no. 76/2000, 21 June 2000; no. 184/2002, 11 December 2002; no. 109/2006, 28 June 2006; no. 2/2009, 15 January 2009; no. 87/2009, 28 May 2009.

66 Constitutional Court, nrs. 9 and 10, 30 January 1986; no. 17, 26 March 1986; no. 29, 18 November 1986; no. 56/96, 15 October 1996; no. 51/2006, 19 April 2006, and no. 33/2011, 2 March 2011.

67 Art. 26 (1) (2) of the Special Majority Act of 6 January 1989 on the Constitutional Court.

68 See, for instance, Constitutional Court, no. 54/96, 3 October 1996; no. 109/2006, 28 June 2006; no. 12/2004, 21 January 2004.

The only example of completely concurring power, however, is the general power to tax. The federal government, the communities, and the regions all have the general power to tax. However, a federal act can provide for exceptions to this rule with respect to community and regional taxes, provided it is necessary to do so (Art. 170, § 2(2)). The federal legislature thus has the power to prevent, limit, or repeal certain community or regional taxes. Since the Constitution is silent on the territorial scope of the taxation power of the Flemish and the French Communities, especially in the Brussels-Capital Region, neither the Flemish nor the French Community has exercised its taxation power. When a tax pursues not only financial objectives but also substantive policy (such as an environmental tax), the Constitutional Court reviews whether this non-fiscal aim (the environmental objective) is the primary objective of the tax and, if so, whether the tax does infringe upon the competences of the other authorities in a disproportionate way.[69]

The use of federal framework laws was noted earlier. Pursuant to the case law of the Constitutional Court and the Council of State, this technique can be applied even in cases where no provision has been made expressly to this effect by the special majority legislature. For instance, the communities can complement the federal rules on fire safety in facilities for the elderly.[70] Further, the communities and the regions are entitled to complement and specify the federal legislation on the formal justification of government acts.[71] The communities and regions are entitled only to strengthen the federal rules, not weaken them. This case law illustrates the role of the Constitutional Court in combining the unity of federal policy with the autonomy of the communities and the regions.

The so-called parallel powers are also considered to be exceptions to the principle of exclusivity. Parallel powers can be exercised by several authorities cumulatively and independently. For example, the federal government, the communities, and the regions are, within the framework of their respective powers, each competent for scientific research.[72] Parallel powers can sometimes also be inferred from the Constitutional Court's case law. Indeed, the Constitutional Court has ruled that public

69 Constitutional Court, no. 31/92, 23 April 1992.

70 Constitutional Court, no. 79/92, 23 December 1992; no. 6/96, 18 January 1996.

71 Constitutional Court, no. 55/2001, 8 May 2001; no. 128/2001, 18 October 2001.

72 See Article 6bis(1)(2)(1) of the Special Majority Act on Institutional Reform.

industrial policy is a parallel power of the federal government and the regions, each within its respective sphere of authority, in relation to its respective territory, and with its own means and institutions.[73]

The Constitutional Court seems to accept in recent case law[74] that both the federal and the federated legislatures can sometimes enact the same legal norm. This case law looks similar to what is known as the "double aspect doctrine" in Canada.[75] For instance, the regions can make the export of nuclear material subject to regional licences on the basis of their competence for the import and export of weapons,[76] while the federal authority is empowered to impose a prior federal authorization on the basis of its competence for nuclear infrastructure.[77] Another recent example in the case law of the Constitutional Court[78] is "care insurance" (*zorgverzekering*), which can come under the legislative power of the communities for aid to persons[79] and under the federal legislative power for social security.[80] The double aspect doctrine reinforces the autonomy of the legislatures in their competence spheres. Application of the double aspect doctrine may, however, not result in antinomies (i.e., the mutual incompatibility of two laws enacted by different legislatures without breaching a rule on the division of powers). There is room for double aspect only if the laws enacted by the different legislatures can be applied cumulatively. Otherwise, the Constitutional Court will determine to which competence matter the law in question has the closest link. This will result in the single qualification by the Court of the law in question under this competence matter.[81]

On the other hand, EU law has brought the Constitutional Court to deviate from constitutional power allocation principles. After a

---

73 Constitutional Court, no. 11, 25 February 1986. This case law has been confirmed afterwards by Art. 6(1), VI, (1) of the Special Majority Act on Institutional Reform.

74 Constitutional Court, n° 168/2011, 10 November 2011.

75 Vanpraet, *De latente staatshervorming*, 127; Vanpraet, "Het dogma van de exclusieve bevoegdheden gerelativeerd: de meervoudige bevoegdheidskwalificatie in het federale België," in *België, quo vadis? Waarheen na de zesde staatshervorming?*, ed. P. Popelier, Dave Sardinet, Jan Velaers, and Bea Cantillon (Antwerp: Intersentia, 2012), 209.

76 Art. 6(1), VI, (1), 4° of the Special Majority Act on Institutional Reform.

77 Federal Act of 9 February 1981 on the conditions for export of nuclear material and nuclear infrastructure.

78 Constitutional Court, n° 33/2001, 13 March 2001; n° 51/2006, 19 April 2006; and n° 11/2009, 21 January 2009.

79 Art. 5(1), II of the Special Majority Act on Institutional Reform.

80 Art. 6(1), VI, 5th para., 12° of the Special Majority Act on Institutional Reform.

81 Vanpraet, "Het dogma van de exclusieve bevoegdheden gerelativeerd," 223.

judgment of 1 April 2008 rendered by the European Court of Justice on a request for a preliminary ruling,[82] the Court held that the principle of exclusive territorial jurisdiction of the Flemish Community takes nothing away from the principles of free movement of employees as guaranteed by EU law. Therefore, the Court ruled that the Flemish Community did not legislate ultra vires by extending the territorial scope of its care insurance legislation marginally to persons living in the French- or German-speaking language region in order to guarantee the free movement of employees.[83]

D. ECONOMIC AND MONETARY UNION AS A GENERAL LIMITATION ON THE POWERS OF THE COMMUNITIES AND THE REGIONS

The broad interpretation of the powers of the communities and the regions has not prevented the Constitutional Court from developing a limitation on the exercise of powers by each legislature, namely, economic and monetary union. In a landmark decision of 25 February 1988, the Constitutional Court ruled that it follows from the 1970 and 1980 constitutional reforms that "the new structure of the Belgian state is vested in an economic and monetary union, by which it is meant that the institutional framework of an economy is built on constituent units and is characterised by an integrated monetary union."[84] The Court ruled that the concept of an economic and monetary union limits the constitutional powers of the regions to impose taxes. In economic matters, the regions must exercise their respective powers without hindering the free movement of persons, goods, services, and capital between the federal and federated entities. For example, the Court found that a water tax imposed by a Walloon regional law violated the principle of the free movement of goods.[85] On the occasion of the 1988–9 state reform, the concept of economic and monetary union was officially enacted in the special majority acts on institutional reform. Economic and monetary union (EMU) thus operates as a general limitation on not only the powers of the regions but also those of the other orders of government. The Belgian concept of economic and monetary union refers to the general framework of the economic and monetary union at the European level. The European and Belgian EMUs are not identical, however. National

82 ECJ 1 April 2009, C-212/06.
83 Constitutional Court, no. 11/2009, 21 January 2009.
84 Constitutional Court, no. 47, 25 February 1988.
85 Ibid.

freedom of movement standards may impose stricter restrictions on the jurisdiction of regions and communities than would result from European law. In addition, European rules on the freedom of movement do not necessarily apply to internal national situations.[86]

E. PRINCIPLE OF FEDERAL LOYALTY: FROM A POLITICAL RULE OF CONDUCT TO A RULE OF JURISDICTION

In 1993, a new article was introduced into the Constitution. It reads,

> Article 143, § 1. In order to prevent conflicts of powers, the federal government, the communities, the regions and the joint Community Commission shall take into account federal loyalty when exercising their respective powers.

The principle of federal loyalty was originally meant to clarify the division of powers and counterbalance the intention to transfer the residual powers to the communities and the regions.[87] It was clearly inspired by the case law of Germany's Constitutional Court on the federal comity (*Bundestreue*) principle. This goal was, however, abandoned during the parliamentary debate. As finally enacted, federal loyalty was not meant by the Constituent Assembly to become a criterion for review by the Constitutional Court, the Council of State, or any other judicial body. Some have therefore argued that this principle was merely a "soft form of constitutional law," "a political construction," or a rule of conduct, which, in accordance with the wording of Article 143, § 1, of the Constitution, applies only "for the purpose of preventing conflicts of interests" (i.e., conflicts of a political rather than legal/constitutional nature).

However, more than one decade after the introduction of the constitutional principle of federal loyalty, the Constitutional Court accepted in a decision (no. 119/2004) of 30 June 2004 the principle of federal loyalty as a ground for review, thus manifestly contradicting the express intent of the constitutional assembly. The Court's statement that judicial review on the basis of federal loyalty takes place "in conjunction with the principles of reasonableness and proportionality" does not detract from this conclusion.

---

86 Constitutional Court, no. 11/2009, 21 January 2009.

87 See Art. 35 Const.

The Court has clarified what should be understood by this principle with reference to the legislative history, in the following terms:

> B.3.2. Pursuant to the legislative history to this constitutional provision, the principle of federal loyalty entails an obligation for the federal authority and the federated entities not to disturb the federal structure in its entirety when exercising their powers; it entails more than the mere exercise of powers and indicates the spirit in which this should be done.[88]

In later judgments,[89] the Court expressly reviewed compliance with the principle of federal loyalty, ex officio and without any reservation, when examining contested legislative provisions against the Constitution. This case law of the Constitutional Court was confirmed by the Institutional Agreement on the sixth State Reform of 11 October 2011 and subsequently by an amendment of the Special Majority Act of 6 January 1989 on the Constitutional Court expressly entrusting the Constitutional Court with ensuring oversight of the principle of federal loyalty as an independent norm. An important role is thus reserved for this constitutional provision in the future.

3. *Review with Regard to Fundamental Rights and Freedoms*

The jurisdiction of the Constitutional Court is not limited to review of compliance with provisions on the division of powers, as laid down in the Constitution and the legislation on institutional reform. In the 1988 constitutional reform, the Court was also granted the power to rule on violations by federal, community, and regional legislation of three fundamental rights and freedoms guaranteed by the Constitution, namely, the principle of equal treatment (Art. 10), the prohibition on discrimination (Art. 11), and freedom of education (Art. 24).

The Court has used this extension of its powers to review statutory provisions not only for compliance with Articles 10 and 11 but also with the rights and freedoms guaranteed in other constitutional provisions, international treaties, and general rules of law "read in conjunction with those Articles 10 and 11." In this regard, it should be noted that the Constitutional Court does not limit itself to the self-executing provisions

---

88 *Parliamentary Documents*, Senate, extraordinary session 1991–2, no. 100-29/2.

89 Constitutional Court, no. 95/2010, 29 July 2010, and no. 124/2010, 28 October 2010.

of a treaty. It is sufficient that the rights and freedoms concerned be derived from international treaties that are binding on Belgium.

Since the entry into force on 21 April 2003 of the Special Majority Act of 9 March 2003, the Constitutional Court can directly review the compliance of a statutory provision with all rights and freedoms in Part II of the Constitution and with Articles 170, 172, and 191. Hence, a "detour" via Articles 10 and 11 is no longer required. As a result of the extension of the Court's jurisdiction to compliance with all fundamental rights and freedoms laid down in Part II of the Constitution, the Court is increasingly conducting its review based on analogous guarantees in international treaties. This follows from the Court's case law, which states that, when reviewing compliance with the constitutional rights laid down in Part II of the Constitution, the analogous rights and freedoms laid down in provisions of international treaties that bind Belgium are also taken into account.[90] Hence, the Court considers the case law of the European Court of Human Rights when overseeing compliance with constitutional provisions for which an analogous guarantee exists in the European Convention on Human Rights. In this way, the Constitutional Court guarantees a coherent and evolving interpretation of the Constitution.

In addition to the broad interpretation by the Constitutional Court of the powers allocated to the communities and the regions (see above), the Court has played a major role in upholding community and regional legislation in "reserved matters." The Constitution contains several provisions, especially in the field of fundamental rights and liberties, reserving a regulatory power to the legislator: the matter has to be regulated "by an Act" or "by authority of an Act." Traditionally, this reference to "Act" was understood as a reference to the federal legislator only, excluding community or regional legislation in those matters. The Constitutional Court held that constitutional provisions dating before

90 In a judgment no. 189/2005 of 14 December 2005, the Court found that it "does not have jurisdiction to directly review the compliance of statutory provisions with the ... indicated provisions of the treaty. When a provision of a treaty which is binding on Belgium has a bearing which is analogous to that of a constitutional provision on the basis of which the Constitutional Court is conducting its review and the violation of which is claimed, the guaranties laid down in that treaty provision shall however form an inseparable whole with those laid down in the constitutional provision concerned. It follows that the Court, when supervising compliance with the [...] constitutional provisions mentioned, shall take into account the international provisions guaranteeing analogous rights or freedoms."

the 1970 constitutional reform could not have the meaning of reserving legislative powers to the federal legislator. The reference to "Act" could for these provisions mean only that regulation of the said matters can in principle not be delegated to the executive.[91]

V. Conclusion

Although constitutional change in Belgium is primarily the result of formal changes to the Constitution and special majority legislation, the Constitutional Court has played a decisive role in securing the equilibrium between the federal government and the communities and the regions. The Court has been a safeguard of the autonomy of the communities and regions. Taking into account the devolutionary nature of the Belgian federal state and the ever-increasing powers that were devolved to the communities and regions in successive stages, the Court supports a broad interpretation of community and regional powers. The Court has also upheld a closed system of mutually exclusive powers, while leaving at the same time substantive room for implied powers for the communities and the regions. In addition, recent application of the double aspect doctrine reinforces the autonomy of the community and regional legislatures in their spheres of competence. At the same time, the Constitutional Court has paid attention to the necessary cohesion of the federal state. It has introduced the notion of the economic and monetary union as a general limitation on the powers of the communities and regions. More recently, it has accepted the principle of federal loyalty as a ground for judicial review. This case law was subsequently confirmed expressly by the Special Majority Legislator. The Constitutional Court is also playing a major role in securing individual human rights and liberties. In line with its federalist approach, the Court has limited the scope of the theory of reserved matters, thus upholding community and regional legislation with respect to fundamental rights and liberties contained in constitutional provisions dating before the 1970 constitutional reform. In addition to this, by taking into account case law of the European Court of Human Rights when overseeing compliance with constitutional provisions for which an analogous guarantee exists in the European Convention on Human Rights, the Constitutional Court guarantees a coherent and evolving interpretation of the Constitution.

---

91 Constitutional Court, no. 35/2003, 25 March 2003; no. 115/2004, 30 June 2004 and no. 95/2005, 25 May 2005.

4 The Supreme Federal Court of Brazil: Protecting Democracy and Centralized Power

GILBERTO MARCOS ANTONIO RODRIGUES, MARCO ANTONIO GARCIA LOPES LORENCINI, AND AUGUSTO ZIMMERMANN

I. Introduction

Since enactment of the Constituição da República Federativa do Brasil (Constitution of the Federal Republic of Brazil) on 15 October 1988, judges of the Supremo Tribunal Federal (Supreme Federal Court) and other superior courts have exercised an important role in shaping Brazil's federal system. Remarkably, however, the relationship between federalism and the judiciary rarely enters academic or political debate, or even debates about the judiciary itself. Perhaps this is due to the fact that Brazilian federalism has always been highly centralized, and the contemporary judiciary has largely maintained this centralization.[1] The Supreme Federal Court has not, therefore, articulated any extensive, comprehensive,

1 For a comprehensive analysis of Brazil's federation, see Augusto Zimmermann and Fabio de Macedo Soares P. Condeixa, *Direito Constitucional Brasileiro* (Rio de Janeiro/RJ: Lumen Juris, 2014), 2:577–652. See also Marcelo Piancastelli, "Federal Republic of Brazil," in *Distribution of Powers and Responsibilities in Federal Countries*, ed. Akhtar Majeed, Ronald L. Watts, and Douglas M. Brown, 66–90 (Montreal and Kingston: McGill-Queen's University Press, 2006); and Fernando Rezende, "Federal Republic of Brazil," in *The Practice of Fiscal Federalism: Comparative Perspectives*, ed. Anwar Shah, 73–97 (Montreal and Kingston: McGill-Queen's University Press, 2007); Luis Cesar de Queiroz Ribeiro and Sol Garson, "Federal Republic of Brazil," in *Local Government and Metropolitan Regions in Federal Systems*, ed. Nico Steytler, 75–105 (Montreal and Kingston: McGill-Queen's University Press, 2009); Marcus Faro de Castro and Gilberto Marcos Antonio Rodrigues, "Brazil," in *Diversity and Unity in Federal Countries*, ed. Luis Moreno and César Colino, 76–108 (Montreal and Kingston: McGill-Queen's University Press, 2010); and Marta Arretche, "Intergovernmental Relations in Brazil: An Unequal Federation with Symmetrical Arrangements," in *Intergovernmental Relations in Federal Systems: Comparative Structures and Dynamics*, ed. Johanne Poirier, Cheryl Saunders, and John Kincaid, 108–13 (Don Mills, ON: Oxford University Press, 2015).

or sophisticated federalism jurisprudence. Instead, the federal courts have been more preoccupied with human rights and rule-of-law issues. At the same time, the judiciary suffers from legitimacy deficits due to public concerns about a lack of accountability in the judicial system.

II. Federal System

1. *Broad Characteristics*

Brazil is a vast country consisting of 8,514,876 square kilometres of territory or 47 per cent of South America's landmass. It has a population of approximately 206 million, of which 84 per cent are concentrated in urban zones. The country's population is ethnically diverse, with 50 per cent consisting of Afro-Brazilians (self-declared) and a little less than one per cent consisting of indigenous peoples. Most Brazilians are professed Christians, 60 per cent of whom are Roman Catholics.[2]

Possessing plentiful oil and gas reserves, and marine life, as well as very extensive agricultural lands, Brazil is the world's ninth-largest economy and the biggest in Latin America.[3] Brazil's per capita GDP is about US$12,100. Moreover, economic and political stability during the 2000s enabled the country to undertake an increasing role as a regional leader in South America.

Brazil is one of the four Latin American countries that adopted federalism.[4] Brazilian federalism has passed through five phases: (1) the Old Republic (1889–1930); (2) the authoritarian rule of Getúlio Vargas (1930–45); (3) the Democratic Experiment (1945–64); (4) the Military Regime (1964–1985); and (5) the New Republic (1985 to present).[5] Generally, however,

---

2 The source of the country's data is based on the last national census (2010) conducted and updated by the Brazilian Institute of Geography and Statistics (IBGE). See its website in English, http://www.ibge.gov.br/english/. The IBGE estimates that the population reached 204 million in 2015. See http://www.ibge.gov.br/home/.

3 "Brazil and the IMF," International Monetary Fund, http://www.imf.org/external/country/BRA/.

4 There are four formally federal countries in Latin America and the Caribbean: Argentina, Brazil, Venezuela, and Mexico.

5 For a historical account of Brazilian federalism, see Augusto Zimmermann, *Teoria Geral do Federalismo Democrático*, 2nd ed. (Rio de Janeiro: Lumen Juris, 2005), 289–386. For a critical analysis of Brazilian constitutionalism, see Zimmermann, "Constitutions without Constitutionalism: The Failure of Constitutionalism in Brazil," in *The Rule of Law in Comparative Perspective*, ed. Mortimer Sellers and Tadeusz Tomaszewski, 101–45 (Dordrecht: Springer, 2010).

the country's federal system has always been highly centralized. As Keith S. Rosenn points out,

> Brazilian federalism, like that of the other Latin American federalist nations, is far more centralized than it is in Canada or in the United States. British colonization synthesized Protestantism, Locke's social compact theory, and the natural rights of Englishmen. This North American inheritance of theology and political theory was far more conducive to the structured dispersal of power among many regional centers than Brazil's inheritance of the centralized, hierarchical organization of Roman Catholicism coupled with the absolutism of the Portuguese monarchy.[6]

After independence from Portugal, a constitutional monarchy was established and remained throughout the period of the Brazilian Empire (1822–89). The empire was a unitary state comprising twenty provinces created by the territorial division of the former Portuguese colony.[7] The existence of provinces dates back to the colonial period when the land was divided into many capitainces under the control of a few landowners. Each province was governed by a president chosen and appointed directly by the emperor. The emperor could veto legislative bills passed by the Imperial Parliament, and dissolve the Chamber of Deputies by calling for new elections of its members. An electoral college chosen by citizens appointed members of the Chamber of Deputies (lower house) for a three-year term, while the emperor appointed members of the Senate (upper house) from a list consisting of the names of the three highest-vote winners in each province. These members of the Senate were given life tenure.

The judiciary was constitutionally divided into a Supreme Tribunal of Justice, provincial tribunals, municipal and district judges, and elected judges of the peace with powers limited to the area of municipalities. There were also lay jurors who analysed the facts alleged in lawsuits, although only professional judges were authorized to pass final judgment. Under nomination by the emperor and protected with life tenure, judges could be dismissed only if they were found guilty on formal charges by the higher courts. In contrast, municipal judges were nominated for a fixed term of four years. Overall, the court system was

6 Keith S. Rosenn, "Federalism in Brazil," *Duquesne Law Review* 43 (2005): 579.

7 See Miriam Dolhnikoff, *O Pacto Imperial: Origens do Federalismo no Brasil* (São Paulo: Globo, 2005).

relatively well structured, although the corruption of the judiciary was a "notorious fact, bitterly condemned by many contemporaries."[8]

With the proclamation of the republic on 15 November 1889, the political elite established a federal system out of the existing provinces. The principal leaders of the November coup were army officers backed by disgruntled former slave-owners. As a rule, neither of these groups supported liberal democracy, nor did they have any concern for the welfare of the emancipated black population. As a result, with the establishment of the republic, freed slaves were left to their own fates, and the nation's first president, Field-Marshal Deodoro da Fonseca, nominated army generals to administer the old provinces. He also instituted severe restrictions on speech, forbidding the press to criticize the republican government.

Powerful foreign countries, especially the United Kingdom, were reluctant to recognize the new republican government, thus forcing the military leaders to look for institutional ways to obtain greater international recognition and secure access to foreign credit. In its search for legitimacy, the government convened an Assembléia Constituinte (Constitutional Assembly), and Ruy Barbosa, a renowned lawyer and liberal statesman, was invited to prepare a draft constitution to be used as a model by the members of the Constituent Assembly.[9] The result was a well-advanced federal document by the standards and expectations of the time. Besides establishing a relatively decentralized federal system, the 1891 Constitution declared numerous civil rights, including freedom of expression, natural justice, habeas corpus, due process of law, and a popular jury.

Under the 1891 regime, all federal powers were constitutionalized.[10] The federal legislature was divided into two chambers, the Chamber of Deputies and the Senate, as is common in federations. Senators were directly elected by citizens to represent the new states (former provinces of the old empire) for nine-year terms. The country was the first federation in the world where citizens could vote directly for their senators.

---

8 Victor Nunes Leal, *Coronelismo: The Municipality and Representative Government in Brazil* (Cambridge: Cambridge University Press, 1977), 106.

9 Jordan Young, "Brazil," in *Political Forces in Latin America: Decisions of the Quest for Stability*, ed. B.G. Burnett and K.F. Johnson (Belmont, CA: Wadsworth, 1968), 456.

10 See Celina Souza, "Federative Republic of Brazil," in *Constitutional Origins, Structure and Change in Federal Countries*, ed. John Kincaid and G. Alan Tarr, 77–102 (Montreal and Kingston: McGill-Queen's University Press, 2005).

Furthermore, a presidential system was introduced, and voters could elect the chief executive directly to a four-year mandate. He was not allowed to dissolve the National Congress, and he could be impeached by the Senate after approval of such proceedings by the Chamber of Deputies. The 1891 Constitution also introduced a dual court system made up of federal and state judiciaries. In addition, it provided a general description of the federal judiciary, including procedure and jurisdiction. Federal judges were appointed to life tenure, and only the Senate could impeach the judges on grounds of corruption or poor behaviour. The judges were also protected against reductions in salary. The Supreme Federal Court consisted of fifteen justices appointed by the president following approval by the Senate. The court had powers to invalidate unconstitutional laws and administrative acts. Indeed, at the behest of any litigating party, any judge could review legislation on grounds of unconstitutionality. Moreover, each state had its own court system regulated by state laws and constitutions.

Although state judges were technically granted formal guarantees of life tenure and irreducibility of salary, especially as a consequence of a 1926 amendment to the federal Constitution, in practice state judges remained "at the mercy of the exigencies and seductions of ruling groups and less mindful of the independence and dignity of the judiciary."[11] Indeed, as jurist Victor Nunes Leal observed, "There were various measures taken by state governments to keep the magistrates in a state of submission, such as allocating, altering the boundaries of, or abolishing, judicial territories, withholding salaries, etc. As for the local legal officers, they were generally nominated to their posts and as easily dismissed, so that the prosecutors and their assistants habitually became agents of party politics. Through these large doors the judiciary passed to collaborate unscrupulously in the party politics of the states."[12]

The Constitution of 1891 remained in force for more than forty years. The trouble with the Constitution, although inspired by clauses and ideas from the U.S. Constitution, lay in the fact that it was divorced from the context of Brazil's society.[13] In contrast to the socio-political reality of the United States, Brazil was an illiberal country with no tradition of self-government. Barbosa expected to see his "progressive"

11 Leal, *Coronelismo*, 109.

12 Ibid.

13 Francisco de Oliveira Vianna, *O Idealismo da Constituição* (São Paulo: Cia Editora Nacional, 1939), 93.

liberal constitution change his country's illiberal political culture. However, he was soon confronted by the authoritarian behaviour of elites, consisting largely of landowners, politicians, and army officers who often acted in violation of both the letter and the spirit of the 1891 Constitution.

In a 1938 article, Alvin Martin explained that one of the "most striking shortcomings" of the 1891 Constitution was "the blameworthy intervention of the executive power in the states for the purpose of forcing upon them the rule of factions favored by the authorities in Rio de Janeiro, and the toleration of flagrantly unconstitutional acts by state governments enjoying the favor of the national executive."[14] Another frequent problem was that the presidential system had created "a new kind of centralization of power, infinitely greater than anything existing under the empire."[15] Through the suspension of constitutional guarantees and other means, the president had been able for relatively long periods to arrogate to himself virtually dictatorial power.[16]

The Old Republic was followed by the authoritarian rule of President Getúlio Vargas (1930–45), who strongly centralized power in the federal government. In 1937, Vargas further concentrated power through the *Estado Novo* (new state), which has been broadly described as a form of personal dictatorship in which the states lost their independent bases of taxation and were converted essentially into administrative divisions of a unitary state. Vargas publicly burned the state flags, closed Congress and the state legislatures, and replaced the state governors with intervenors.[17] To give legitimacy to his populist regime, he invited Francisco Campos, a respected lawyer, to write the constitution of the *Estado Novo*. The result of his work was promulgated on 15 November 1937.

The charter of 1937 not only expanded presidential powers dramatically but also outlawed state ensigns, banners, and flags. State constitutions were abolished, and state governors were replaced by federal intervenors. The charter also represented a total eclipse of civil liberties. In a 1938 speech, Vargas openly declared that his dictatorial regime would no longer recognize the individual rights of the citizen against

14 Percy Alvin Martin, "Federalism in Brazil," *Hispanic American Historical Review* 18, no. 2 (1938): 157.

15 Ibid.

16 Ibid.

17 Rosenn, "Federalism in Brazil," 580.

the state because (in his words) "individuals do not have rights; they only have duties. Rights belong to the collective."[18] Nevertheless, contemporary Brazilian historians tend to see the Vargas period through a different lens when looking at rights. As Jose Murilo de Carvalho points out, "The period between 1930 and 1945 was the great momentum for social legislation."[19] In fact, labour and pension rights were strongly developed and represent an important legacy of social rights in Brazil's legal system.

In 1945, a military revolt overthrew the Vargas regime and re-established a federal democracy. With the end of the *Estado Novo*, special legislation in November 1945 conferred on both houses of Congress the power to meet jointly in an *Assembléia Constituinte* (Constituent Assembly), held in 1946 at which a new constitution was drafted. Under the briefly effective 1946 Constitution, the state and local governments received substantial autonomy, state governors were popularly elected, and federal intervention became a rarity. The states were given significant powers, including the power to tax, although they were forced to share tax revenues with the municipalities.[20]

Another coup in 1964, favoured by the anti-communist U.S. foreign policy during the Cold War, produced a further period of strong centralization under a military regime. This regime, which lasted from 1964 to 1985, can be divided into three phases. The first phase, lasting from 1964 to 1968, was a time in which the influence of politicians declined steadily. The second phase, from 1969 to 1978, was the worst in terms of political repression. The final phase, from 1979 to 1985, was a period of transition towards restoration of federal democracy. Unlike Vargas's dictatorship, the military permitted the Congress and state and local governments to function, albeit with restrictions. Presidential elections were formally held, but the franchise was restricted to army generals. State governors were initially appointed by the military, and federal intervention into the states increased significantly.[21] The same happened to some municipalities declared as national security zones (e.g., Santos, a port city).

---

18 See E. Bradford Burns, *A History of Brazil* (New York: Columbia University Press, 1970), 298.

19 Jose Murilo de Carvalho, *Cidadania no Brasil: o longo caminho* (Rio de Janeiro: Civilização Brasileira, 2002), 110.

20 Rosenn, "Federalism in Brazil," 580.

21 Ibid., 581.

In 1984, Brazil elected by indirect means and through the National Congress its first civilian president since 1960, and a new constitution was drafted in 1988. Despite these significant gains, the Constitution of 1988 is a highly centralist document, which confers a vast array of powers on the federal government. Perhaps for this reason, federalism issues have never been in themselves a central theme in Brazil's law schools. Professors of constitutional law devote most of their teaching to the federal Constitution and federal laws.[22] Although each state has its own constitution, very little attention is devoted to state constitutionalism, except for very specific themes such as taxation and environment. Moreover, judges do not share a culture that values the federal system per se. While state autonomy is broadly taken into consideration, there is almost no consideration of the federal-state balance itself. This is largely because Brazil does not have a tradition of states' rights arising out of the state constitutions and laws. Although the people of many Brazilian states are proud of their culture and traditions, there are no calls for further political decentralization.

Indeed, since the 1990s, new federal regulatory bodies and agencies have been established over numerous important fields such as electric power, petroleum, gas and biofuels, telephony, and transportation. Centralization has also occurred in public security and human rights, through the Attorney General's Office for the "federalization" of human rights and the creation of a National Public Security Force.

2. *Structural Features*

Because Brazil has a civil law system that gives primacy to statutory legislation, the federal Constitution is the starting point in legal matters. However, the text is rigid and cannot – at least in theory – be modified easily. Proposals to amend the Constitution must be discussed and voted on twice in each house of Congress and can be approved only if they obtain a three-fifths majority in both rounds of parliamentary discussion. There are also temporal limitations for amending the Constitution. It cannot be done during times of federal intervention

22 Paulo Bonavides is an exception. See Paulo Bonavides, *Curso de Direito Constitucional*, 27th ed. (São Paulo: Malheiros, 2011).

(over any state) or if *estado de sitio* (martial law) is in place; rejected proposals cannot be considered a second time in the same year; and the Constitution forbids any amendment intended to abolish or substantially change the federal system, the system of direct, universal, and periodic elections, the separation of governmental powers, and the protection of individual rights. Over the last twenty-eight years, however, formal rigidity has not been a political obstacle to changing the Constitution. It had been amended ninety-one times as of June 2016.[23]

The document's formal rigidity has done little to prevent the multiplication of constitutional amendments, and nor has the complexity of the amendments helped the Constitution preserve its stability as the basic law. Rather, politicians have been able to change it readily, despite its difficult-to-amend design. In practice, therefore, the Constitution is considerably flexible.[24] It may be possible to point out at least three reasons for the incongruence. First, Brazilians are the heirs of a centralist tradition that lacks a proper understanding of the rule of law and expects too much from the central government. Second, the Constitution's legislators in 1988 were convinced of the need to include as many rights and regulations as possible so as to protect them, under a constitutional shield, against authoritarian usurpations. This necessitated constant changes in order to enable the charter to respond to the demands of Brazil's evolving reality. Third, the Constitution was approved with a clear statist profile just before the beginning of a neoliberal era inaugurated by the Washington Consensus in 1990, which led to major constitutional and legal changes in Latin America to enable state reforms in various areas. This happened in Brazil mainly during President Fernando Henrique Cardoso's years (1995–2002).

Three orders of federative entities are explicitly defined, empowered, and regulated by the Constitution: the union, the states, and the municipalities.[25] The Constitution is, however, highly centralist, providing the federal government with a wide array of general and specific powers, including exclusive, common, and concurrent

---

23 Amendment 91 (February 2016), http://www.planalto.gov.br/ccivil_03/constituicao/Emendas/Emc/emc90.htm.

24 Miguel Schor, "Constitutionalism through the Looking Glass of Latin America," *Texas International Law Journal* 41 (2006): 29.

25 Braz. Const., Art. 1.

competences.[26] The states are left with almost nothing in terms of "reserved powers." Articles 21 and 22 grant the central government a variety of exclusive and concurrent powers, some of which overlap. These include the power to legislate with respect to civil, commercial, criminal, procedural, electoral, agrarian, maritime, aeronautical, space, and labour law; to regulate foreign and interstate commerce, ports, and navigation, the postal service, foreign exchange, expropriation, mining, informatics, national transportation, naturalization, social security, nuclear activities, and commercial advertising. With respect to all these powers, Article 23 stipulates that Congress may adopt complementary laws (approved by an absolute majority) authorizing the states to legislate on specific matters in these areas of exclusive competence.[27]

In regard to concurrent powers, the federal power is limited to establishing general rules.[28] When this occurs, the states can adopt only supplementary legislation. In the absence of federal legislation, the states are in principle free to regulate a subject, although federal law prevails over the state law to the extent of any inconsistency. Like the U.S. Constitution, Brazil's Constitution does not grant exclusive power to the states. Rather, it reserves to the states the powers not forbidden to them by the basic law. This approach was borrowed from the Tenth Amendment to the U.S. Constitution, even though when the Brazilian federation was originally created, the provinces had no powers of their own. However, the powers granted to the central government are so vast and all-encompassing that the states are left with virtually no matters about which they can legislate free from the constraints of federal legislation. Indeed, the supremacy of the federal government is so powerfully

26 Common competences are administrative functions that must be commonly exercised by all the tiers of government (union, states, and municipalities). Such competences are defined in Article 23 and they include, for example, the common administrative power to provide for health and public assistance; to provide the means of access to culture, education, and science; to protect the environment and to fight pollution, etc. By contrast, a competence is constitutionally defined as concurrent when it creates general norms that allow either the union or the states to legislate concurrently on the particular subject-matter. Hence, Article 24 grants the union, the states, and the federal district the concurrent power to legislate on areas such as judicial procedure, education, and sports, as well as taxation, financial and economic law, penal law, urbanistic law, etc.

27 Braz. Const., Art. 23.

28 Braz. Const., Art. 24 (XVI), ¶11.

manifested that the very idea of any legislative power being reserved to the states is effectively meaningless.[29] As Rosenn points out, "Virtually all important legislation in Brazil, such as the civil code, commercial code ... criminal code, procedural codes, labor code, consumer protection code, the corporation law, financial markets law, and electoral law are all federated statutes that apply uniformly throughout Brazil."[30]

The federal parliament is called the Congresso Nacional (National Congress) and is bicameral. By contrast, all the state legislatures are unicameral. These *Assembléias Legislativas* (legislative assemblies) comprise *deputados estaduais* (state deputies) who are directly elected by the citizens. Municipalities are governed by city councils whose *vereadores* (city councillors) are also directly elected. Brazil uses proportional voting systems.

The Federal Senate (Senado Federal) represents Brazil's states symmetrically; three senators per state are chosen through direct election. Formally, the Senate does not represent the municipalities, but some constitutional provisions allow the Senate to approve municipal policies.[31] According to 2013 census data, the state of Roraima had only 488,000 inhabitants, while São Paulo, Brazil's most populous state, had 43.6 million inhabitants. Hence, São Paulo has eighty-nine times as many inhabitants as Roraima, yet each state has three senators. Each senator from São Paulo represents approximately 14.5 million inhabitants; each Roraima senator represents only about 162,666 inhabitants. As Alfred Stepan points out, the result is that small states representing only 13 per cent of the total electorate have 51 per cent of the votes in the Senate, giving them an effective veto over the majority.[32] The House of Representatives (Câmara dos Deputados) represents the people proportionally and by means of direct election. However, the Constitution also requires that smaller states be represented by a minimum of eight deputies, while no state can have more than seventy deputies.[33] As a result,

---

29 See Augusto Zimmermann, *Curso de Direito Constitucional*, 4th ed. (Rio de Janeiro: Lumen Juris, 2006), 415–16.

30 Rosenn, "Federalism in Brazil," 583.

31 Braz. Const., Art. 52.

32 Alfred Stepan, "Toward a New Comparative Politics of Federalism, Multinationalism, and Democracy: Beyond Rikerian Federalism," in *Federalism and Democracy in Latin America*, ed. Edward L. Gibson (Baltimore, MD: Johns Hopkins University Press, 2004), 58.

33 Braz. Const., Art. 45, ¶ 1.

São Paulo, which on a truly proportional system would have 60 times as many representatives as small states like Roraima, Acre, and Amapá, has only 8.75 times as many.

Deputies are elected in each state for a four-year term; senators are elected for an eight-year term. Both deputies and senators enjoy parliamentary immunity, and they have the right to a special trial before the Supreme Federal Court.[34] Their immunities are preserved even during martial law (*estado de sitio*).[35] Parliamentary privileges can be removed only through a two-thirds majority in the legislative chamber to which the parliamentarian belongs.

III. Court System

1. General Features

Brazil belongs to the same tradition of civil law developed by European countries such as Portugal, France, and Italy.[36] However, the constitutional framework based on a combination of federalism and presidentialism is inspired by the United States. The judicial system is divided into regular courts and special courts (the latter being divided into labour, military, and electoral), as well as federal and state Courts of Justice.[37] The various divisions within the court system include a Supreme Federal Court, a Superior Court of Justice, regional federal courts, federal labour courts, electoral courts, military courts, state courts, and federal district courts.[38]

The composition of each court is determined by the federal Constitution. The number of courts and judges varies in each state. The appellate system is divided into ordinary and special courts. In special

---

34 Braz. Const., Art. 53.

35 A new precedent established in 2015 by the Supreme Federal Court was the detention of Senator Delcidio do Amaral, who was caught attempting to obstruct justice.

36 It is important to acknowledge the deep influence exerted by Italian jurists over Brazilian recent law development, e.g., Giuseppe Chiovenda, Piero Calamandrei, Francesco Canelutti, Enrico Tullo Liebman in procedural law; Tullo Ascarelli in commercial law.

37 For a more comprehensive, critical analysis of the judiciary, see Augusto Zimmermann, "How Brazilian Judges Undermine the Rule of Law: A Critical Appraisal," *International Trade and Business Law Review* 11 (2008): 179–217.

38 Braz. Const., Art. 92.

appeals,[39] jurisdiction is vested only in the Superior Court of Justice. The purpose is to render uniform the decisions by lower courts concerning the enforcement of federal laws and the federal Constitution. However, dissenting opinions are published together with the court's official decisions, and in some cases these dissents afford the opportunity of filing additional appeals pursuant to the federal procedural law.

Brazil's courts have authority to construe constitutional and ordinary norms and to order compliance therewith by the executive and legislative branches, in both the state and federal orders of government. In 2004, a constitutional reform vested the Supreme Federal Court with the power to establish binding precedents (*súmulas vinculantes*) by a quorum of eight justices (out of a total of eleven). The contents of such decisions bind all the other federal and state courts and branches of government. Currently, there are fifty-three such binding precedents.[40] Among them, at least twelve are related to, or directly affect, the federal system. For example, Binding Precedent No. 2 restricts the ability of state governments to establish and regulate gambling and lotteries. Similarly, Binding Precedent No. 13 provides that federal legislative rules against nepotism bind all three orders of government. Binding Precedent No. 14 confirms basic elements of due process of law, which affect both federal and state court proceedings.[41]

The country's second-highest court, the Superior Court of Justice (Superior Tribunal de Justiça), was established by the Constitution to enforce federal laws.[42] This is primarily a court with powers of appellate jurisdiction. As a court of appeal, it decides cases in which the final decision of a lower court judge is contested by a litigating party because it is contrary to an international treaty or federal law, it would uphold the validity of state or local law that is inconsistent with federal law, or

39 The special appeal (*recurso especial*) allows applicants to contest before the Superior Court of Justice a decision from a state court or a federal court that (1) is against a treaty or a federal law; (2) supports a local government decision against a federal law; (3) gives an interpretation of a federal law that is different from one already given by another court. Braz. Const., Art. 105, III.

40 Supreme Federal Court, Binding Precedents, http://www.stf.jus.br/portal/jurisprudencia/menuSumario.asp.

41 Binding Precedent 14: The attorney is entitled, in the interests of the litigant, to be allowed full access to the elements of proof that, being already documented at an investigation proceeding conducted by an agency vested with competence of judicial police, relates to the exercise of the right of defence.

42 Braz. Const., Art. 105, I (g).

the decision is based on an interpretation of the federal law that contradicts the court's own precedent.

In relation to constitutional matters, the Supreme Federal Court resolves disputes between branches of the federal or a state government, disputes and conflicts between the federal government and states, disputes between the federal government and the federal district, and disputes between states themselves.[43] The court's primary function is to be a guardian of the federal Constitution. To achieve this, it possesses exclusive jurisdiction over direct actions of unconstitutionality, declaratory actions on the constitutionality of federal and state laws or administrative acts, and actions of unconstitutionality by omission.[44]

2. *Constitutional Status of Courts and Judicial Officers*

Brazil does not have dual jurisdictions (as in the United States). Although judicial organization and the exercise of jurisdictional power are decentralized and exercised under pre-established rules of competence, the judicial branch is regarded as a single body administering a single body of law.

Brazil's courts abide by the liberal-democratic tradition of the rule of law. Central to this tradition is the conviction that a division of government functions constitutes a critical aspect of every system of government that hopes to combine efficiency and the greatest possible protection of individual rights and freedoms. The idea rests on the conception that whenever the power of the state becomes too highly concentrated in the hands of an individual or political agency, the risk of arbitrariness increases accordingly. A truly independent judiciary may, therefore, compel government authorities to respect the proper limits of legality.

Because all courts in Brazil must be independent and impartial, they have acquired administrative autonomy and can also propose their own budgets by submission to the legislative branch (in both the federal and state arenas) for approval prior to the fiscal year. The executive branch does not exercise any direct legal influence on the courts' budgets, although it can impose political pressure regarding the courts' overall impact on the general budget. It is the executive's role to transfer to the

43 Braz. Const., Art. 102, II.
44 Braz. Const., Art. 102, I, a.

judiciary the approved budget resources, a fact that leads to a certain level of operational dependence between the two branches of government.

Were it just a matter of financial resources, Brazil would possess one of the world's best and most efficient court systems. Brazil's judiciary receives more funds as a percentage of the budget than the judiciaries of most developed countries.[45] Prior to Constitutional Amendment No. 45, judges notoriously disrespected their budget limits by claiming that judicial independence gave them the right to do so. This forced the executive to provide supplemental funds to the courts. However, the new amendment requires that during the execution of the budget, there must be no expenditure or assumption of commitments that exceeds the limits established by the law of budgetary directives, except if authorized by special or supplementary credits.[46]

The selection of judges for trial courts is exclusively incumbent upon the respective federal and state judiciaries, whereas the selection of one-fifth of all state and federal judges is determined by the federal executive. The composition of the Superior Court of Justice as well as of the other highest special courts is determined by a formula stated in the Constitution that combines members of state and federal courts and members of the federal and state public prosecution offices and attorneys, whose appointment must be approved by the federal Senate and nominated by the executive.

To enter a judicial career, both the federal and state judiciaries hold periodic competitive examinations and credentials. Examination boards consist primarily of judges, although lawyers, members of the public prosecution office, and legal academics are also members. During these highly competitive examinations, neither the executive nor the legislature participates. Candidates must hold a law degree and possess the minimum background of three years of legal practice. In some states, "schools of magistracy" offer training and continuing education to judges whose appointment is approved in such competitive examinations.

The state justices (*desembargadores*) serving on state courts of appeals (*Tribunais de Justiça*) are selected by the respective courts and pursuant to the criteria of career seniority and merit. However, one-fifth of such

45 William Prillaman, *The Judiciary and Democratic Decay in Latin America: Declining Confidence in the Rule of Law* (London: Praeger, 2000), 170.

46 Braz. Const., Art. 99, ¶ ¶ 3, 4, and 5.

courts consists of members of the public prosecution office and lawyers appointed by state bars. A list of six nominees is initially submitted to the courts, which, in turn, submit to the executive a list of three chosen appointees, whose appointment is ultimately approved by the state legislature. A similar mechanism operates in relation to federal courts.

For special courts, there are specific appointment rules. The Federal Labour Court holds competitive examinations and selects judges for courts pursuant to criteria similar to those of the federal courts. The Federal Electoral Court is permanent – unlike in many countries in which it operates only during the electoral process – and consists of judges from federal and state courts of law, as well as lawyers. The state and federal military courts also have their own career path.

All federal and state judicial officers are constitutionally protected by rights of tenure. They can be removed from office only upon a special judicial order, and their salaries cannot be reduced while in office. All judicial careers, whether state or federal, are well remunerated. Indeed, states have increased their court fees to finance judicial privileges, including special medical benefits for judges and expenses such as weekend retreats for court personnel. Similarly, federal judges receive benefits such as a free apartment, a car with private driver, and a gasoline allowance. While normal workers receive a thirty-day vacation, judges enjoy sixty days of fully paid annual leave.

Members of the judiciary and, indeed, of any other branch of government, may not have earnings higher than those of a Supreme Federal Court justice.[47] Judges, at any level of court, are not allowed to engage in any other paid activity, except for that of professor. In addition, they may not be affiliated with any political party. Nonetheless, taking the Supreme Federal Court as an example, the executive exercises formal power over the nomination of its members and informal power over the acting judges. There is no culture of substantive and strict control by the legislature over the nominations to the Supreme Federal Court. The executive's choice is usually ratified by the Congress. The conditions for eligibility to the Supreme Federal Court are provided by the federal Constitution and are restricted to nationality (i.e., having been born in Brazil or born of a Brazilian parent), age (minimum of thirty-five years, the same criterion as that for a senator), outstanding legal knowledge, and a good reputation. The president of the republic

47 A Supreme Federal Court justice earns an equivalent to US$10,000 per month.

is vested with plenary power in selecting the judges, and there is no further rule or tradition conditioning their eligibility, except that the appointee must be less than sixty-five years old at the time of taking office. Once pre-selected, the executive submits the name to the Senate for the conduct of an oral examination prior to approval. As mentioned, there has been historically a tradition of easy approval by the Senate of appointments by the executive. All federal and state judicial officers, including the Supreme Federal Court justices, are required to retire at the age of seventy-five. This is the compulsory retirement age for all public officers, including federal and state magistrates.[48]

An analysis of the current composition of the Supreme Federal Court suggests some issues related to federalism. There is a prevalence of justices from the southeast, where the three most populated and wealthiest states (São Paulo, Minas Gerais, and Rio de Janeiro) are located. For instance, the State of São Paulo, which is equivalent to the Republic of Argentina in GDP and population, has three judges (i.e., one-fourth of the court's composition). The second-largest representation is that of the southern region, the country's most developed area. The northeast, which comprises the greatest number of states (nine) and the northern region, the largest region in territory and the least populated, have no representatives. That said, although no formal criteria have been instituted in order to create federal symmetry in the selection of Supreme Federal Court justices, there has been a certain balance between federative diversity and population representation in nominations. Rather, the contemporary debate over the selection of judges involves affirmative action on the basis of gender and race. The first woman to be a member of the Supreme Federal Court, Justice Ellen Gracie, was nominated by President Fernando Henrique Cardoso in 2000; the second, Carmem Lúcia, was nominated by President Lula da Silva in 2006; and the third, Rosa Weber, was nominated by President Dilma Roussef in 2011. There are expectations that new nominations may bring more gender balance to the Supreme Court. Regarding affirmative action on grounds of race,[49] Joaquim Barbosa was the first Afro-Brazilian justice

48 Constitutional amendment no. 88 (2015).

49 Although there was no formal rule for affirmative action of race related to the SFC, Lula's government created a federal executive branch – the Presidential Equal Racial Secretary – and new racial public policies were then created. In this federal and public environment, Joaquim Barbosa was chosen, and his credentials also applied the two formal constitutional requirements.

appointed to the Court, on the nomination of President da Silva in 2003. He was chief justice during 2012–14.[50]

There has been ongoing debate over the control and transparency of state and federal courts. Judges acquired from the 1988 Constitution an impressive degree of administrative, financial, and disciplinary independence.[51] They prepare their own budgets, organize their secretariats, and draw up their internal regulations. Since 1988, they have been able to strike down any act of questionable legality enacted by the public authorities. Such independence, however, may paradoxically be seen as having not been altogether beneficial for the rule of law. Indeed, the judiciary is severely affected with corruption, and judges are often accused of crimes that range from diverting funds intended for courthouses to passing lenient sentences on dangerous criminals in return for payment.[52] A question constantly being raised is whether Brazil's judicial elites have become an entrenched and unaccountable "bureaucratic oligarchy."[53]

On the issue of budget, as noted, the federal Constitution gives the judiciary the power to prepare its own budget. But judges have not always administered their funds responsibly. In 1995, for example, the new building of the Superior Court of Justice, a courthouse for just thirty-three magistrates, was finished at a cost of US$170 million. The building has an indoor theatre, exercise rooms, two restaurants, a ballroom, a bar, and even a swimming pool.[54] One might suspect that judges sanction the excessive costs of constructing and furbishing courthouses in order to obtain a share of the proceeds. Indeed, a 1999 fact-finding enquiry carried out by the National Congress found at least two cases supporting such suspicion.[55] Although judges had strongly opposed the congressional inquiry, declaring that elected politicians could not meddle in judicial affairs, the inquiry went ahead and found, among other things, that the Federal Labour Court chief justice in São

50 For a comprehensive analysis of the composition of the Supreme Federal Court, see Fabiana Luci de Oliveira, *Supremo Tribunal Federal: do autoritarismo à democracia* (Rio de Janeiro: Fundação Getúlio Vargas, 2012).

51 Braz. Const., Arts. 96 and 99.

52 For an analysis of judicial corruption, see Zimmermann, "How Brazilian Judges Undermine the Rule of Law," 196–9.

53 Prillaman, *Judiciary and Democratic Decay in Latin America*, 85.

54 Ibid., 88.

55 Ibid.

Paulo state, Nicolau dos Santos Neto, became a multi-millionaire by constructing a new courthouse for his labour-law court. The final cost of the courthouse was at least ten times above market rates. The inquiry also found that the Federal Labour Law Court chief justice in Rio de Janeiro, Mello Porto, had authorized projects at his court at costs that exceeded 340 per cent of market rates.[56]

Judicial corruption, lack of accountability, and arbitrariness are obstacles to realizing the rule of law. In an attempt to improve judicial accountability, a constitutional reform in 2004 (constitutional amendment no. 45, 8 December 2004) led to the creation of a "judicial watchdog" called the National Justice Council (Conselho Nacional de Justiça – CNJ). As justification for its establishment, the government suggested that the courts had become an "impenetrable black box" that resisted social change and were rife with corruption. Advocates of external control argued that the CNJ would be a valid mechanism to monitor judicial performance and discipline wayward judges who otherwise are protected by the corporate interests of other court members. They also argued that judicial independence cannot serve as an excuse for irresponsibility, so that the CNJ can even be seen as a "democratic prerequisite" that would ensure that a judge's misbehaviour will no longer go unpunished. One who enthusiastically supports this view, Professor Dalmo de Abreu Dallari, has argued that the CNJ could somehow "transform the judiciary into a truly democratic power."[57]

The CNJ is conceived as a body external to the court system, with full powers to oversee internal court rules and handle complaints against all members or organs of the judiciary, including its auxiliary services, employees, and agencies rendering notarial and registry services. Under the relevant amendment, Article 93, provision VIII, a judge can be removed, placed on paid availability, or compulsorily retired by the decision of the majority of CNJ members. Article 103-B further states that the CNJ has the power to control the administrative and financial acts of the courts, as well as "the fulfilment of functional duties" by all members and bodies of the judiciary. Chaired by the chief justice of the Supreme Federal Court, the CNJ comprises not just members of the federal and state judiciaries but also members appointed by the Chamber of Deputies and the Federal Senate, as well as representatives of the

56 Ibid.

57 Dalmo de Abreu Dallari, *O Poder dos Juízes* (São Paulo: Saraiva, 1996), 74.

Brazilian Bar Association (OAB) and the Department of Public Prosecution (Ministério Público) from both federal and state levels. Apart from a member of the state judiciary being appointed by the Supreme Federal Court, as well as a member of the state Department of Public Prosecution being appointed by the department, there are no further state representatives on this external body of control over both federal and state judges.

The proper limits of the CNJ's competences are being debated currently, the definition of which will depend on the Supreme Federal Court. There is evident tension between the CNJ and the state courts in relation to administrative control and inspection. One notorious example is the resistance by state courts to being transparent about the cost of state judges' salaries. Using the argument of state autonomy, many state courts have refused to disclose this information upon request by the CNJ. Another important example is the investigation into misconduct by state judges. The CNJ has argued that it has concurrent competence with state courts to investigate state judges, but the state courts deny that. However, the Supreme Federal Court decided that the CNJ has both original and concurrent competence in such matters.

Regarding the influence of public opinion on the courts, with the live television broadcast of trials at superior courts (as of the 2000s), the general public is much more able to know and criticize the judiciary's operation and decisions. With the greater exposure of court operations and methods, as well as through exposure of court rulings themselves, the level of trust in the judiciary has been decreasing. According to a quarterly report produced by the Getulio Vargas Foundation (FGV) in 2013, the judiciary was ranked at the seventh position in terms of the level of trust in Brazilian institutions, with 37 per cent, a result well below the army (71 per cent), the Catholic Church (56 per cent), the Public Prosecution Office (53 per cent), the press (45 per cent), big companies (43 per cent), and the federal government (41 per cent).[58]

The ability of the judiciary to uphold standards of public integrity was recently tested by the controversial decision of the Supreme Federal Court to reopen a notorious corruption scandal that revealed a "voting for money" scheme involving the leaders of the ruling Workers'

58 See Relatório ICJBrasil (São Paulo: Direito FGV, 2013), http://bibliotecadigital.fgv.br/dspace/bitstream/handle/10438/11221/Relat%C3%B3rio%20ICJBrasil%20-%20Ano%204.pdf?sequence=1.

Party (PT) who were caught bribing members of other political parties in return for their votes in Congress. Brought to light in 2005 during the first term of President Lula, the court gave its final verdict in December 2012 after a long deliberation. Of the thirty-seven accused, twenty-five were found guilty of a range of charges including money-laundering, corruption, and accepting bribes. They received penalties of up to forty years in prison. On the occasion, Attorney General Roberto Gurgel described the whole incident as "the most daring and outrageous corruption scheme and embezzlement of public funds ever seen in Brazil."[59]

The landmark decision seemed to mark the end of the country's culture of impunity. As the BBC explained, "This case attracted major coverage as Brazilians watched to see if those found guilty of corruption would be held accountable and the country's long history of impunity ended."[60] The Mensalao Case, as it is popularly known, is considered a turning point by many Brazilian social and legal analysts. The Supreme Federal Court's image benefited from a difficult and complex case, which finally put in jail no less a person than Jose Dirceu, chief of staff of former president Lula da Silva.[61] A strong public expectation arose that the Supreme Federal Court would address similar cases involving major personalities of other political parties, including those of the opposition, with the same fortitude.[62] Conducted by federal judge Sergio Moro and by Justice Teori Zavascki of the Supreme Federal Court, the Lava Jato (car wash) judicial task force opened a new chapter on Brazilian politics regarding the role of the judiciary. A set of arrests and detentions, including high-ranking executives of Petrobras (Brazil's state-owned oil company), as well as many other executives and owners of a contracting firm, brought up allegations of widespread corruption involving almost every political party and politicians from both government and the opposition.

---

59 "Brazil Corruption Trial from Lula Era Starts," BBC, 3 August 2012, http://www.bbc.co.uk/news/world-latin-america-19091137?print=true.

60 "Q&A: Brazil's 'Big Monthly' Corruption Trial," BBC, 16 November 2012, http://www.bbc.co.uk/news/world-latin-america-19081519?print=true.

61 About 700 senior politicians and all 594 members of Congress enjoy special judicial standing.

62 At the conclusion of the Mensalao Case, the Supreme Federal Court included four justices appointed by President da Silva and four justices appointed by President Rousseff, which means two-thirds of the court, showing the actual level of political independence of the court.

3. *Institutional Role of the Courts*

Conceptually, jurisdiction is a power carried out by means of competences established by criteria such as matter, place, and entity. Brazil's judicial system is complex, being divided into ordinary courts and special courts, as well as federal and state courts. In addition, political agents and some administrative agents of the federal government, states, and municipalities have, in some cases, privileges of venue. The determination of competence is determined by both federal law and the federal Constitution.

As a general rule, Brazil's courts do not operate as a consultative agency. They operate only in litigation. The aspect that most resembles a consultative character is the concentrated control of constitutionality actions (such as the Direct Action of Unconstitutionality, the Direct Action of Constitutionality, and the Claim of Breach of Fundamental Precept), in which the Supreme Federal Court and the state courts appraise the law in general terms.[63] In such cases of judicial review of legislation, there is no adverse party, because this model of review rests on the judicial interpretation of legal norms in the abstract. Final decisions on such abstract actions produce *erga omnes* effects and cannot be appealed. To avoid the proliferation of direct actions of unconstitutionality, the Supreme Federal Court adopted the criterion of *pertinência temática* (thematic relevance).[64] Pursuant to this, the Court can refuse to decide cases having no "objective link" between the plaintiff's institutional duties and the content of the challenged legislation. This criterion, however, is not applied to actions filed by the Procurator-General of the Republic, the Bar Association, the Senate, the Chamber of Deputies, and political parties, because these entities are seen as possessing a broader interest in constitutional issues.[65]

4. *Curial Procedures*

In civil jurisdiction, only the holder of a substantive right has standing to sue. Federative entities (e.g., the union, states, or municipalities) may

63 See Gilmar F. Mendes and Paulo G.G. Branco, *Curso de Direito Constitucional*, 7th ed. (São Paulo: Saraiva, 2012).

64 Gilmar Ferreira Mendes, *Jurisdição Constitucional* (São Paulo: Saraiva, 1996), 138.

65 Keith S. Rosenn, "Judicial Review in Brazil: Developments under the 1988 Constitution," *Southwestern Journal of Law and Trade in the Americas* 7 (2000): 301.

be either plaintiffs or defendants to judicial proceedings, and will rely on a body of career lawyers to represent them (such as municipality attorneys, state attorneys, and federal government counsel). As jurisdiction needs to be invoked, the plaintiff will always be required to commence the proceeding.[66]

In addition, Brazil has a highly developed system for protecting trans-individual or collective interests inspired by North American class actions. However, only the Public Prosecution Office, federative entities (the union, states, and municipalities, as well as coalition of municipalities, such as the Municipal National Front – Frente Nacional de Prefeitos), the Brazilian Bar Association, civil associations, and other association bodies have standing to file actions of this kind. In the criminal field, the Public Prosecution Office (federal or state, in accordance with the crime) always has standing to sue. For proceedings against political agents, the attorney general (the ultimate authority of the state or federal public prosecution office) has the prerogative to file the suitable lawsuit.

Whenever the litigation involves an entity of the federal government, the action must be judged by a federal court. In addition to those actions provided in the procedural law for each and every person, the Constitution provides legal remedies for guaranteeing people the protection of fundamental rights (such as writ of mandamus, habeas corpus, habeas data, writ of injunction, and class action). Courts are competent to enforce their decisions and may request support from the state or federal police (a body of the executive branch).

Because all the proceedings held at the three branches are in Portuguese, any document or testimony in a different language must be translated by a sworn translator or official interpreter at the expense of the interested parties in civil cases. In this respect, court communication is homogeneous, although there is the exception of cases in which the parties are indigenous, where anthropologists and interpreters are required in order to guarantee communication with minorities in their own languages. As a general rule, federal courts conduct these cases.[67]

From a procedural perspective, the use of technology by the judiciary has enhanced the quality of access to information, as well as providing

66 See Antonio Carlos de Araújo Cintra, Ada Pellegrini Grinover, and Cândido Rangel Dinamarco, *Teoria Geral do Processo* (São Paulo: Malheiros, 2005).

67 As an exception, when there are no federal judges and federal prosecutors to conduct those cases, state judges.

for transparency of proceedings. All superior federal courts are based in the national capital, Brasília, and receive appeals online from the states, with great autonomy of resources and facilitation of appeal handlings. The same applies to federal and state judicial electronic portals, which allow the parties and their counsel to follow up proceedings from any location, at any time. For a still developing country with "continental" dimensions such as Brazil, the deployment of e-government is a significant factor in democratizing access to the judiciary and improving procedural and cost efficiency.

Other access points to the judiciary are small-claim courts. They were inspired by the small-claims courts of the city of New York; however, they were adapted to Brazilian judicial culture by Law No. 9099/95, which provides the possibility of filing civil judicial actions worth up to forty minimum wages.[68] Among its peculiarities, only individuals and small businesses (*microempresas*) may be the plaintiffs to such claims. It is possible to file a claim without retaining a lawyer. Before trial, an attempt at conciliation must be made so that only a portion of these claims is solved through a judicial ruling.

The same law provides that small-claim courts settle criminal claims of a small offensive character (punishments with imprisonment up to two years). These cases are judged by state judges, although the law provides for the existence of a lay judge. In 2001, a new law was enacted[69] establishing federal small-claim courts to deal with claims worth up to sixty minimum wages to which the defendant is the federal government.[70] Issues involving social security, in particular those regarding the amount of pensions, are the most frequent claims at such federal small-claim courts. More recently, state civil small-claim courts have been created by federal law.[71]

5. *Judicial Culture*

Although Brazil abides by the tradition of civil law (of Romano-Germanic origin) inherited from the Portuguese colonizers, the country's legal system has also been influenced by other Western legal systems. For instance, there is the influence of German and U.S. constitutional

68 Up to US$10,000.
69 Federal Law no. 10.259/2001.
70 Up to US$15,000.
71 Federal Law no. 12.153/2009.

law, French administrative and private law, North American consumer law, and Italian procedural law.

Brazil is a secular state, but its society is deeply religious, and the preamble to the federal Constitution of 1988 explicitly invokes God's protection.[72] The Supreme Court has in its plenary sitting room a crucifix hanging on the wall behind the chief justice's chair, which has raised questions in trials in which the Roman Catholic Church was the interested party, such as the case involving the authorization for stem-cell research in 2008.

The teaching of law in Brazil has been traditionally focused on the theory and practical application of the civil law in litigation. The baccalaureate in law is of five-year duration, and no less than two-thirds of the program is devoted to the study of legislation and court decisions, while very little is dedicated to the study of alternative dispute resolution (ADR). As a consequence of excessively resorting to state court systems to settle all sorts of conflicts, the judiciary faces a huge backlog of cases. A resolution by the National Justice Council has attempted to address the problem by determining the inclusion of subjects that teach ADR in the law schools.[73]

The main mode of judicial reasoning is legal positivist, whereby judges simply apply the black letter of the law, regardless of any possible consequences. The Introductory Law to the Brazilian Legal System, article 4, states, "In the absence of law, judges can apply analogy, customs and general principles of law."[74] This implies that the application of analogy, customs, and general principles occurs only if the written law does not provide a clear answer to the problem. Moreover, the Brazilian Civil Procedure Law Code states in its article 8, "When applying the legal system, the judge should attend the social aims and the needs of the common good, protecting and promoting the dignity of the human beings and taking into account the principles of proportionality, reasonableness, legality, publicity and efficiency."[75]

---

72 The Preamble of the Federal Constitution declares, "We, the representatives of the Brazilian People, convened in the National Constituent Assembly […] promulgate, under the protection of God, this Constitution."

73 CNJ, Resolution N.125, 2010.

74 Introductory Law to Brazilian Legal System (*Lei de Introdução às Normas do Direito Brasileiro*, Decreto-Lei 4657/1942, updated by Lei 12.376/2010). http://www.planalto.gov.br/ccivil_03/decreto-lei/Del4657compilado.htm.

75 Brazilian Civil Procedure Code (*Código de Processo Civil*, Lei n. 13105/2015). http://www.planalto.gov.br/ccivil_03/_ato2015-2018/2015/lei/l13105.htm.

Brazil's judicial culture emphasizes logic, especially syllogism. Logical-systematic, teleological, and grammatical approaches to interpretation tend to prevail, although historical interpretation is used as well. There is also a tendency towards excessive technicality in the teaching of law, reducing the time for humanistic and philosophical subjects. In this regard, there has been an increasing impoverishment of the legal philosophical culture and an increasing prevalence of a more technical or strictly procedural culture.

On the other hand, there has been a considerable proliferation of postgraduate courses in law, which arguably foster greater scientific rigour in the conduct of legal research. These programs are accredited by a special agency of the Ministry of Education called CAPES, and they require faculty and students to publish their research periodically and systematically. Master's and PhD programs in law have been regarded as forms of professional development for judges, public attorneys, and prosecutors. They are also considered important credentials for both entry and advancement in the career path of magistrates and other legal state careers. This of course applies even more strongly to anyone wishing to pursue an academic career in law, because university law programs evaluated by the Ministry of Education take into account the number of academic staff holding a PhD and/or an LLM.

IV. Federalism Jurisprudence

1. General Tendencies

The final arbiter of the meaning of state law can be either a state or federal court, depending on the parties or the matter involved. The basic codes are federal, but whether litigants bring a case in state or federal courts does not depend on the legislation applied. Rather, it depends on the federal government having an interest in the outcome, or if one of its federal agencies is a party in the litigation. In such a case, the matter is brought to the federal court.

If a court decision is alleged to contravene a treaty or federal law, or a court interprets the federal law differently from another court, the decision can be reviewed on special appeal by the Superior Court of Justice, the second-highest federal court. If the decision conflicts with a provision of the federal Constitution, or declares a treaty or federal law unconstitutional, or upholds the constitutionality of a state or local act, then an extraordinary appeal to the Supreme Federal Court may also be taken. The Supreme Federal Court frequently strikes down state and municipal constitutional or statutory provisions because of conflicts with the federal Constitution or federal law, or invasions of powers delegated to the federal government.[76] Curiously, however, one rarely finds any case law invalidating federal legislation for invading powers reserved to the states. As Rosenn explains,

> This is because Brazilian Constitutions have granted far greater powers to the federal government than the U.S. Constitution. In addition, Brazil has no analogue to the Eleventh Amendment to the U.S. Constitution, nor has it had a group of Supreme Court judges who have assumed the role of protecting state's rights from infringement by the federal legislation.[77]

The Supreme Federal Court has selected a set of cases and has called them "historical trials."[78] These cases date back to the colonial period, but include cases decided during the republican and federal eras. The court has identified at least four different cases directly related to federalism. They are (1) the case of the Federalist Revolution (1892–95), which involved two political groups in the State of Rio Grande do Sul and concerned claims for greater state autonomy from the federal government; (2) the case of the Municipal Council of the Federal District (then in Rio de Janeiro) during the presidential term of Nilo Peçanha (1909), which concerned a dispute between two legislatures that had been established for the same purpose; (3) the Contestado War (1900–16), involving a dispute over territorial boundaries between the States of Santa Catarina and Paraná; and (4) President Nilo Peçanha's case on the duplicity of government in Rio de Janeiro in 1914. During these periods, unitarism and centralism prevailed as a result of the increasing role of the federal government in settling such regional conflicts.

More recently, and especially since the 1990s, the theme of state reform has permeated discussion of the country's federal system. Subject matters such as privatization, distribution and transfer of funds to states

---

76 See, e.g., ADI 1472 (D.J. 25 Oct. 2002); ADI 1918 (D.J. 1 Aug 2003); ADI 2487 (D.J. 1 Dec. 2004).

77 Rosenn, "Federalism in Brazil," 585. See also Vanessa Elias de Oliveira, "Poder Judiciário: árbitro dos conflitos constitucionais entre estados e união," Lua Nova, 2009, http://www.scielo.br/scielo.php?pid=S0102-64452009000300011&script=sci_arttext.

78 "Julgamentos Históricos," Supremo Tribunal Federal, http://www.stf.jus.br/portal/cms/verTexto.asp?servico=sobreStfConhecaStfJulgamentoHistorico.

and municipalities, the social security system, fiscal wars between the union and the states and among the states, basic sanitation, transparency and accountability, and assurance of minority rights are examples of some of the leading themes triggering conflicts between the federal government and the states and/or municipalities.[79]

2. *Specific Issues*

There are three critical areas in which the courts, especially the Supreme Federal Court, have shaped Brazil's federal system: (1) human rights, particularly the rights of indigenous minorities; (2) the distribution of gas-and-oil royalties from offshore exploitation; and (3) "fiscal federalism," especially the theme of a "fiscal war" between the union and the states. Other themes involve the coordination of elections and referendums and the control of state court activities.

In relation to fiscal federalism, the Constitution of 1988 increased the revenue capacity of states and municipalities by transferring fiscal resources from the federal government to these orders of government. Yet such a significant transfer of resources to these governments was not followed by a proper redefinition of responsibilities between the different orders of federative power. Indeed, Brazil's federal system remains extremely centralized because the current Constitution did not expand the areas that fell under the responsibility of state and municipal governments in the same proportion that it increased their revenues.

On indigenous rights, the case of Raposa Serra do Sol Indigenous Reserve Demarcation decided in 2009 has set an important precedent in the acknowledgment of an extensive indigenous area in the State of Roraima (northern region of the Amazon), and the legality of its demarcation, performed by the National Indian Foundation and approved by the Ministry of Justice (bodies of the federal executive branch). By means of a class action filed by two senators, the case defined the conflict between the interested parties, the State of Roraima, and the municipalities, on the one part, and the federal government, on the other, abiding by the criterion of the model of continued demarcation of indigenous

79 See Gilberto M.A. Rodrigues, "Impacts of Globalization on Strategies for Competition in Subnational Governments: The Case of Brazil" (Paper presented at Forum of Federations, Federalism in a Globalizing World, New Delhi, 5–6 Aug. 2003), http://www.forumfed.org/libdocs/InFedGlob03/302FGlob0308-Rodrigues.htm.

lands, as adopted by the federal government to the advantage of indigenous peoples.[80]

The decision on indigenous rights preserved the model of continued demarcation and preservation of indigenous lands for indigenous peoples, which is said to be critical to the survival of ethnic groups that historically have been living therein, dismissing state and municipal claims that invoked loss to legal rights in the determination and the use of their territories. But the judgment has gone further and has determined that hereafter the demarcation process of indigenous lands shall require the participation of the affected states and municipalities (principle of participatory federalism). Furthermore, the federal government is authorized to enter the indigenous territory in order to fight organized crime and safeguard national security, as it is located in areas that border neighbouring countries.

Another issue of a federal nature is the "fiscal war" between the union, states, and municipalities. The matter involves several claims that have been filed in the Supreme Federal Court. One of them deserves special attention. It is related to the Direct Action of Unconstitutionality (ADI-875) filed by the governor of the State of Rio Grande do Sul against the president of the republic in order to plead that the criteria for apportionment of the States Participation Fund were unconstitutional. The federal Constitution requires that these criteria be defined by a supplementary law with a view to promoting social-economic balance among the federative entities. In justifying its decision, the Supreme Federal Court declared the unconstitutionality of the acts performed, and defined a period of almost two years (i.e., until 12 December 2012) for the National Congress to reduce conflict between the states and the federal government in relation to the transfer of funds. This mediating conduct adopted by the court denotes, on one hand, respect for the federal legislative branch as the original jurisdiction for settlement of an issue that carries strong political connotation, while it ensures, on the other, compliance with the constitutional provision that defines the criteria to be established for such a theme.[81]

One of the most significant cases in the current debate over federalism involves the distribution of royalties from oil and gas exploitation.

---

80 *Raposa Serra do Sol* (Indigenous Peoples' Land Case), Pet. N. 3.338-RR (D.O.U., 25 September 2009).

81 Supreme Federal Court, ADI-875, http://www.sbdp.org.br/arquivos/material/970_ADI_875_-_Inteiro_teor.pdf.

Pursuant to the federal Constitution and the rules established by ordinary legislation, the states and coastal municipalities were to receive a percentage of such benefits. However, considerable discoveries in 2006 of oil and gas off Brazil's Atlantic coast triggered a legal and political battle between the union, states, and municipalities. Considering the location of those newly discovered reserves, only three states were allowed to enjoy the benefits of royalties arising out of the exploitation of such resources: Rio de Janeiro, Espírito Santo, and São Paulo. As a result, the National Congress passed Federal Law No. 12.734/2012 (on 23 March 2013) amending the former rules of Federal Law No. 9.478/97. This amendment drastically changed the criteria for distributing royalties, with a view to benefiting all the remaining states.

The change has affected not only future exploitation contracts but also those currently in effect. Since the State of Rio de Janeiro was the most adversely affected by the new mode of distribution, it challenged the new rules by means of a Direct Action of Unconstitutionality before the Supreme Federal Court, requesting a provisional remedy in order to invalidate the effects of the law. Reporting on the action, Justice Carmem Lucia commented, "This is an issue whose seriousness is specific to large federative themes." She decided to grant a provisional remedy *ad referendum* to the court in plenary session, but also anticipated her position by criticizing the change to the system in light of federative principles. Justice Lucia stated, "Some federated entities – States and Municipalities – in whose territory there is oil or natural gas exploitation, or which is bordering the exploitation area, have been constitutionally protected in the sharing of resources arising out of such an activity."[82] In May 2015, Justice Carmen Lucia issued another provisional measure to suspend the effects of the equal distribution of royalties amongst the states that had been introduced by the Law of Gas and Oil enacted by President Dilma Roussef. By June 2016, the case had yet to receive a final ruling, but it shows how the interests of states bordering the oil and gas exploitation territory are potentially shaped by the federal system. The case is highly significant in bringing federal issues before the Supreme Federal Court to an extent that has never been seen before in Brazil.

Regarding the organization and coordination of electoral processes, it is important to consider the role played by the Superior Electoral Court

---

82 ADI 4917 (D.J. 18 Mar. 2013).

(Tribunal Superior Eleitoral). The creation of new states, as well as the dismemberment of existing states, can occur only by referendum, which must be organized and coordinated by the Superior Electoral Court. Any conflict involving the boundaries between two or more municipalities, however, is settled by the state courts, not federal courts. In view of the unavoidable political pressures arising out of electoral disputes, the role of the Superior Electoral Court in providing stability, legal security, and reliability in Brazil's elections has been very significant.

Finally, implementation of the National Justice Council (NJC) has caused several federative conflicts concerning the extent of its powers vis-à-vis the autonomy of state courts. In particular, in the Direct Action of Unconstitutionality (ADI-4638) filed by the Brazilian Association of Magistrates against the NJC, a six-to-five majority of the Supreme Federal Court decided, in a plenary judgment delivered in 2012, that the NJC has original and concurrent powers to oversee the activities of both federal and state judges, and therefore the power to establish disciplinary proceedings against any member, federal or state, of the judiciary. This court ruling has obvious federal implications because it reveals that the NJC, in exercising its external control over the activities of state judiciaries, is not restricted to any considerations regarding state autonomy. According to the court, the NJC's Office of the Inspector General may conduct an investigation of a state court whose state inspector's office has not yet concluded an investigation on the same subject. In short, the NJC does not hold only subsidiary powers, but rather holds original and concurrent powers with those of state courts.

V. Conclusion

Because Brazil's federation is highly centralized, federal issues tend to be of lesser importance than issues concerning human rights and the rule of law. Indeed, most of the recent decisions of courts, while reaffirming their commitment to the rule of law and democracy, tend to operate in apparent conflict with the principle of state autonomy. In the field of human rights, advocates of a more centralized state have prevailed over federalists because many violations of human rights have occurred due to omission or action by Brazil's states.

The judiciary, and the Supreme Federal Court as its highest instance, has been a middling actor in shaping federal arrangements. As noted above, its role has been much more effective in empowering the central government and federal policies, purportedly as a guardian of democracy, human rights, and transparency, rather than in protecting states' competences, acts, and interests.

This chapter has addressed some important aspects of the federal tradition in Brazil. It has explained how the country has always possessed a highly centralized federal system. It has also discussed the historical role of the judiciary as a guardian of the federal Constitution. As a constitutional court, the Supreme Federal Court has regularly exercised its basic role as the guardian of a highly centralized constitution that accords virtually all legislative power to the central legislature, either by enforcing constitutional rules (such as in the case of Raposa Serra do Sol) or by paving the way for legislative solutions involving federal-state-municipal conflicts (such as in the case of the "fiscal war"). Faced with the opportunity to decide on the gas-and-oil case, the Supreme Federal Court will be able to deliberate on important federal issues, thus raising the prospect that practical solutions might be presented, which could then be applied to resolve any future conflict between the different orders of government.

5 The Supreme Court of Canada: The Concept of Cooperative Federalism and Its Effect on the Balance of Power

EUGÉNIE BROUILLET

I. Introduction

Canada is one of the world's oldest democratic federations. Its birth in 1867, and its evolution over time, were both marked by the coexistence of communities with distinct languages and cultures, whether Aboriginal, French-speaking, or English-speaking. The federation later accepted immigrants with many ethnic and cultural backgrounds. The country's past as a British colony also left its mark on its institutions, including its constitutional monarchy, parliamentary regime, and system of judicial organization.

Changes to the Canadian federation have been mainly the work of the courts, primarily because of the huge difficulties faced by the federal and provincial governments in formally amending the constitutional texts. The courts of final resort in the constitutional field have, in performing their duties, developed extensive jurisprudence in the area of federative disputes.[1] The dualistic approach to power-sharing promoted by the Judicial Committee of the Privy Council in London (the court of final appeal for Canadian cases until 1949) has been followed by the more cooperative approach to Canadian federalism exemplified in the jurisprudence of the Supreme Court of Canada. The original

* I would like to thank all the participants in the Canadian round table on 28 March 2012 in Montreal that discussed the theme examined in this book. Many of the ideas from the discussion were useful in preparing this chapter.

1 The term *federative disputes* refers here to disputes about sharing legislative powers and disputes that involve a fundamental aspect of the country's federative structure, such as the constitutional amendment procedure, the legal status of the federal and federated entities, or the territory of a federated entity and its authority to secede.

federative system, essentially based on the principle of exclusive powers, has been gradually transformed into a system of overlapping powers. This mutation has had significant consequences for the balance of power between the federal and provincial governments.

II. The Federative System

In this section, we will outline the general and structural characteristics of Canada's federation.

1. General Characteristics of the Federation

Territorially, Canada is the world's second-largest country, with an area of almost 10 million square kilometres. It stretches east to west from the Atlantic to the Pacific coast, and northwards to the Arctic Ocean. In 2011, it had a population of 33.5 million people, concentrated mainly in the south along the U.S. border, and a per-capita gross domestic product of $52,367.[2] Canada, with one of the lowest population densities in the world, is composed of ten provinces and three territories. It has a wealth of natural resources and freshwater reserves, and is one of the world's largest suppliers of agricultural products.

Canada defines itself as a bilingual, multicultural nation. Its official languages are French and English. According to the 2011 census, people having English as their mother tongue constitute 57 per cent of the population, followed by those with French as their mother tongue at 22 per cent, and those with another language as their mother tongue at 19.8 per cent. A total of 90 per cent of Canada's French-speakers live in the province of Quebec, where they make up 79.7 per cent of the population. The country's remaining French-speakers are found mainly in New Brunswick (32.5 per cent of the population), and then in Ontario, which has a French-speaking population of 4.4 per cent. Outside Quebec, 4.2 per cent of the Canadian population speaks French as its mother tongue. According to the 2006 census, Aboriginals make up 3.8 per cent of Canada's population and live mainly in northern and western Canada.[3]

---

2 Statistics Canada, Bank of Canada, "Canada – Economic Indicators," n.d., http://www.international.gc.ca/economist-economiste/assets/pdfs/Data/indicators-indicateurs/Annual_Ec_Indicators-ENG.pdf.

3 Statistics Canada, "2011 Census Program," http://www12.statcan.gc.ca/census-recensement/2011/dp-pd/index-eng.cfm.

During the course of its history, Canada has always welcomed large numbers of immigrants, with each succeeding wave increasing the country's ethnic and cultural diversity. The Canadian population today comprises over 200 different ethnic communities. In 1971, the Canadian government introduced a policy of multiculturalism, first as part of a statute, and then, in 1982, as part of the Canadian Constitution, where it is one of the principles used to interpret the provisions of the Charter of Rights and Freedoms (s. 27).[4]

Prior to French colonization of North America in 1608, the territory of Canada had been occupied for several thousand years by roughly 500,000 Aboriginals from various historical and linguistic nations. The side-by-side presence of French and English communities began when the territory of New France (a French colony from 1608 to 1759) was conquered by the British, a victory consecrated in legal terms by the 1763 Treaty of Paris. The same year, part of the conquered territory became the Province of Quebec under the *Royal Proclamation*. In 1774, the *Quebec Act* extended the boundaries of the province to match those of the former New France. The act also authorized the application of French civil law within the province; hence, Quebec, unlike the other provinces that function under a common-law system, still uses civil law. The years 1776–87 saw the arrival of large numbers of British immigrants, followed by American loyalists fleeing the War of Independence, who settled mainly in the western portion of Quebec. In 1791, the British Parliament passed an act that modified the territorial boundaries of its colony to match the new socio-cultural order. The western part of Quebec was detached to form a new province, Upper Canada, while Quebec became Lower Canada, retaining a large French-speaking, Catholic majority, in contrast to Ontario, which was overwhelmingly English-speaking and Protestant. Each of the two new provinces was given its own legislative assembly (*Constitutional Act, 1791*).

During the 1830s, a broad-based movement to obtain the administrative independence of the colonies from the mother country led to armed popular uprisings that were quickly suppressed by the British army. To quell the calls for autonomy that were far more insistent in Lower Canada (today's Quebec), the British Parliament decided by the *Act of Union* of 1840 to combine Lower and Upper Canada into a single colony, with the avowed intention of assimilating the French-speaking population by

4 *Canadian Charter of Rights and Freedoms*, Part I of Schedule B of the *Constitution Act, 1982*, R.S.C. 1985, App. II, no. 44.

making it the minority in a united parliament. Despite London's plans, however, the united Province of Canada remained composed of two separate groups in sociological, cultural, and political terms. The legislative union was transformed by the facts of the situation into a federative-type regime in which each of the two cultural entities administered its own affairs[5] in the part of the province in which it formed the majority, leading the way to the adoption of a formally federative regime in 1867.

The Canadian federation was created by the *British North America Act, 1867*, a statute of the British Parliament at Westminster enacted after three colonies (the Province of Canada, consisting of present-day Quebec and Ontario, New Brunswick, and Nova Scotia) expressed the wish to join under a federative government.[6] One key factors in the selection of the federative principle as the foundation for the new constitution was the presence within the founding colonies of groups from different cultures as the result of the earlier French and then English colonization.[7]

The federative regime of 1867 represented a compromise between various ideologies and visions for the new country. While many English-speaking political representatives would have preferred the establishment of a legislative union,[8] the French-speaking representatives of Canada East (today's Quebec) made the creation of a federation the condition sine qua non for their support for the project, because it would give them full autonomy in certain matters while allowing them to join the other British colonies in North America in a structure that would lead to the emergence of a shared political nationality.[9] The federative principle was finally chosen as the basis for the new constitution by all its founders. The Preamble to the 1867 Act is unequivocal; it states that "the Provinces … have expressed their Desire to be federally united," although it also states the intention to adopt a "Constitution similar in Principle to that of the United Kingdom." As for the actual shape of the new regime, the act provided for the establishment of a federation in

---

5 Jacques-Yvan Morin and José Woehrling, *Les constitutions du Canada et du Québec du régime français à nos jours* (Montreal: Les Éditions Thémis, 1994), 1:149.

6 Known, since 1982, as the *Constitution Act, 1867*, R.S.C. (1985) App. II, no. 5.

7 Christopher Moore, *1867: How the Fathers Made a Deal* (Toronto: McClelland and Stewart, 1997).

8 *Parliamentary Debates on the Subject of the Confederation of the British North American Provinces*, 3rd Session, 8th Provincial Parliament of Canada. Printed by Order of the Legislature (Quebec: Hunter, Rose, Parliamentary Printers, 1865), 30.

9 Samuel Laselva, *The Moral Foundations of Canadian Federalism* (Montreal and Kingston: McGill-Queen's University Press, 1996).

the legal sense of a distribution of legislative power between two orders of government, each autonomous in its own sphere of jurisdiction.[10]

In the decades following the creation of the federation, six other provinces came into being through an agreement between each province and the federal government and parliament: Manitoba (1870), British Columbia (1871), Prince Edward Island (1873), Alberta (1905), Saskatchewan (1905), and Newfoundland and Labrador (1949). Northern Canada is divided into three federal territories – Northwest Territories, Yukon, and Nunavut – populated mainly by Aboriginal nations. Each territory wields powers delegated by federal legislation, although in practice the powers are similar to those of the provinces.

Formally, the federation is a constitutional monarchy with a parliamentary regime. The head of the Canadian state is Queen Elizabeth II, represented by the governor-general at the federal level and by the lieutenant-governors in the provinces. However, by constitutional convention, the powers of the monarch's representatives must be exercised today as directed by the ministers who are responsible to their respective parliaments.[11]

---

10 Ss. 91–5.

11 For more extensive general information about the Canadian federation, see Rainer Knopff and Anthony Sayers, "Canada," in *Constitutional Origins, Structure, and Change in Federal Countries*, ed. John Kincaid and Alan Tarr, 103–42 (Montreal and Kingston: McGill-Queen's University Press, 2005); Richard Simeon and Martin Papillon, "Canada," in *Distribution of Powers and Responsibilities in Federal Countries*, ed. Akhtar Majeed, Ronald L. Watts, and Douglas M. Brown, 91–122 (Montreal and Kingston: McGill-Queen's University Press, 2006); Thomas O. Hueglin, "Canada," in *Legislative, Executive, and Judicial Governance in Federal Countries*, ed. Katy Le Roy and Cheryl Saunders, 101–34 (Montreal and Kingston: McGill-Queen's University Press, 2006); Robin Badway, "Canada," in *The Practice of Fiscal Federalism: Comparative Perspectives*, ed. Anwar Shah, 98–124 (Montreal and Kingston: McGill-Queen's University Press, 2007); André Lecours, "Canada," in *Foreign Relations in Federal Countries*, ed. Hans Michelmann, 114–40 (Montreal and Kingston: McGill-Queen's University Press, 2009); Robert Young, "Canada," in *Local Government and Metropolitan Regions in Federal Systems*, ed. Nico Steytler, 106–35 (Montreal and Kingston: McGill-Queen's University Press, 2009); Alain-G. Gagnon and Richard Simeon, "Canada," in *Diversity and Unity in Federal Countries*, ed. Luis Moreno and César Colino, 110–38 (Montreal and Kingston: McGill-Queen's University Press, 2010); Marc-Antoine Adam, Josée Bergeron, and Marianne Bonnard, "Intergovernmental Relations in Canada: Competing Visions and Diverse Dynamics," in *Intergovernmental Relations in Federal Systems*, ed. Johanne Poirier, Cheryl Saunders, and John Kincaid, 135–73 (Don Mills, ON: Oxford University Press, 2015); and William Cross, "Canada: A Challenging Landscape for Political Parties and Civil Society in a Fragmented Polity," in *Political Parties and Civil Society in Federal Systems*, ed. Wolfgang Renzsch, Klaus Detterbeck, and John Kincaid, 70–93 (Don Mills, ON: Oxford University Press, 2015).

2. *Structural Characteristics of the Federation*

The Constitution expressly establishes the autonomy of the two orders of government by listing the matters in which they may legislate (opening paragraphs of ss. 91 and 92 of the *Constitution Act, 1867*). Sections 91 to 95 allocate legislative authority over various subjects to each order, and this allocation concerns both legislative and executive authority. Each order of government is responsible for enforcing its own laws. In this respect, the Canadian federation is different from, for example, Germany and Switzerland.

Unlike many other federations, where a list of specific powers is allocated to one order of government and all residual powers remain with the other (such as the United States and Australia), Canada's Constitution contains two lists of matters coming under the exclusive jurisdiction of the federal government (s. 91) and the provincial governments (ss. 92 and 93) respectively. There is also a short list of powers under shared jurisdiction (ss. 92A(3), 94A and 95).[12] The residual power is given to the federal Parliament (opening paragraph of s. 91).[13] The listing of the powers under the jurisdiction of the federal government, in addition to its residual power, apparently resulted from the broad scope of the powers kept by the provinces, especially the jurisdiction over "property and civil rights,"[14] which included some matters that the political representatives of the period wished to assign to the central government (e.g., jurisdiction over trade and commerce, bankruptcy and insolvency, and copyrights). The list of federal powers was therefore designed to remove these powers from provincial jurisdiction.

As in any federation, the distribution of legislative powers was based on a distinction between matters of shared interest and matters of a so-called local nature, reflecting, at least in part, the principle of subsidiarity. Given that the main objective of the federative union was to provide for the economic and military needs of the new federation, legislative authority over these matters was given to the federal Parliament.

---

12 They concern only agriculture and immigration (s. 95), old age pensions and supplementary benefits (s. 94A), interprovincial trade in natural resources (s. 92A(3)).

13 The opening paragraph of section 91 states that the federal Parliament may "make Laws for the Peace, Order, and good Government of Canada, in relation to all Matters not coming within the Classes of Subjects by this Act assigned exclusively to the Legislatures of the Provinces."

14 S. 92(13) of the *Constitution Act, 1867*.

For this reason, the constituent provinces agreed that the federal Parliament would be given exclusive jurisdiction notably to raise money by any mode or system of taxation, and to legislate in order to regulate trade and commerce, banking, legal tender, navigation, militia, military service and defence (s. 91). The federal Parliament also was given the power to create a general court of appeal for Canada (s. 101). We will return to this point below.

The matters under exclusive provincial jurisdiction concerned life in general in each province, that is, all matters connected to the province's lifestyle. Thus, each province retained the exclusive competence to legislate, within its boundaries, in connection notably with the constitution of the province, property and civil rights, education, municipal institutions, the solemnization of marriage, local works and undertakings, the administration of justice, and generally all matters of a merely local or private nature. The provinces also were authorized to raise money by direct taxation for provincial purposes (ss. 92 and 93).

This is the dualistic model that, for the most part, guided the distribution of legislative powers in Canada. However, this legal framework has not prevented the courts from developing doctrines for the implementation of the rules allocating jurisdiction that stem, rather, from a form of cooperative federalism favourable to overlapping powers.

Since the birth of the federation, two main trends can be identified in the approach taken by the courts to the principle of exclusivity. The Judicial Committee of the Privy Council opted for a dualistic approach by seeking to limit overlaps of power between the two orders of government and by preserving each government's sphere of autonomy. The committee used the nautical image of "watertight compartments" to illustrate the need to protect the autonomy of each order of government and balance its powers.[15] Beginning in the mid-twentieth century, however, the Supreme Court of Canada gradually moved away from the dualistic stance of the Judicial Committee to embrace a so-called cooperative approach to federalism, open to overlapping powers. In a number of decisions, it stated that the principle of exclusive powers was not imperative, and that intergovernmental cooperation was the

---

15 *A.-G. for Canada v. A.-G. for Ontario*, [1937] A.C. 326, p. 354, which included Lord Atkin's comment: "While the ship of state now sails on larger ventures and into foreign waters she still retains the watertight compartments which are an essential part of her original structure."

"dominant tide"[16] of modern federalism. The expressions *flexible, cooperative,* and *modern* federalism are used frequently in its jurisprudence, emphasizing the idea that the separation between the orders of government is not absolute. The Court "should favour, where possible, the ordinary operation of statutes enacted by *both* levels of government. In the absence of conflicting enactments of the other level of government, the Court should avoid blocking the application of measures which are taken to be enacted in furtherance of the public interest."[17] The adoption of a cooperative approach has led to an increase in the number of overlaps between equally valid provincial and federal statutes that then trigger the application of the doctrine of federal paramountcy if they prove incompatible. This will be discussed below.

In pursuit of this cooperative approach, the Supreme Court has affirmed the ability of each order of government to incidentally affect matters under the jurisdiction of the other order when both are legislating in their own area of jurisdiction (incidental effects rule).[18] It considers that certain matters may include both federal and provincial aspects, and it upholds legislation by both orders of government in relation to these matters (double aspect doctrine).[19] It also has maintained the constitutional validity of provisions that overlap a matter under the jurisdiction of the other order of government if they are integrated into an otherwise valid legislative whole (ancillary powers doctrine).[20]

With regard to the fiscal relations between the two orders of government, Canadian federalism has, since the late 1950s, been moving away from the dualistic model. Within Canada, as also in many other federative regimes, fiscal powers are becoming increasingly centralized. The Canadian situation is due in part to an agreement temporarily transferring to the federal Parliament the entire sector of personal and corporate income tax during the Second World War. In addition, the

---

16 *Ontario (Attorney General) v. OPSEU*, [1987] 2 S.C.R. 2, par. 27.

17 *Canadian Western Bank v. Alberta*, [2007] 2 S.C.R. 3, par. 37 and 42. See also *Quebec (Attorney General) v. Canada (Attorney General)*, 2015 SCC 14; *Reference re Securities Act*, [2011] 3 S.C.R. 837, pars. 9, 57, 131, 132; *Reference re Assisted Human Reproduction Act*, [2010] 3 S.C.R. 457, pars. 139, 152; *Quebec (Attorney General) v. Lacombe*, [2010] 2 S.C.R. 453, par. 119; *Chatterjee v. Ontario (Attorney General)*, [2009] 1 S.C.R. 624, par. 32.

18 See particularly, *Attorney General (Que.) v. Kellogg's Co. of Canada et al.*, [1978] 2 S.C.R. 211.

19 *British Columbia (Attorney General) v. Lafarge Canada Inc.*, [2007] 2 S.C.R. 86, par. 4.

20 *General Motors of Canada Ltd. v. City National Leasing*, [1989] 1 S.C.R. 641; *Quebec (Attorney General) v. Lacombe*, [2010] 2 S.C.R. 453.

cost of the provinces' constitutional responsibilities (e.g., health care, education, and social services) following the advent of the welfare state continued to rise.

The combined effect of more centralized fiscal powers and the major increase in the cost of provincial responsibilities has led to a vertical imbalance in the practice of Canadian federalism, that is, a gap between the financial resources available to each order of government and the cost of their constitutional responsibilities. The federal government has revenues over and above what it needs to implement its powers, while the provinces face major shortfalls.[21] The federal surplus gives the federal government leeway to spend in areas of provincial jurisdiction and thereby impose its policy preferences.

This "power to spend" refers to the ability of one order of government to spend in areas under the exclusive jurisdiction of the other order of government, "provided it does not, at the same time, legislate with respect to, regulate, or govern such matters."[22] Using its spending power, one order of government can allocate financial resources to certain objectives, whether under its own responsibility or that of the other order of government. This is possible because spending is not subject to the distribution of legislative powers and constitutes a material, rather than a normative, act. Although the Supreme Court of Canada has not yet been asked to rule directly on the constitutionality of conditional spending by the federal government in areas of exclusive provincial jurisdiction, several obiter dicta suggest that it does not consider the spending as a normative act requiring an assessment of constitutionality.[23]

---

21 Quebec, Commission on Fiscal Imbalance, *Report of Commission on Fiscal Imbalance and Supporting Documents*, 2002, http://www.groupes.finances.gouv.qc.ca/desequilibrefiscal/en/document/publication.htm; Conference Board of Canada, *Vertical Fiscal Imbalance: Fiscal Prospects for the Federal and Provincial/Territorial Governments* (Ottawa, 2002, updated February 2004): http://www.conferenceboard.ca/e-library/abstract.aspx?did=413; Alain Noël, "Équilibres et déséquilibres dans le partage des ressources financières," in *Le fédéralisme canadien contemporain, Fondements, traditions, institutions*, ed. Alain-G. Gagnon, 305–38 (Montreal: Les Presses de l'Université de Montréal, 2006).

22 Henri Brun, Guy Tremblay, and Eugénie Brouillet, *Droit constitutionnel*, 6th ed. (Cowansville: Éditions Yvon Blais, 2014), 439 (my translation).

23 *Y.M.H.A. Jewish Center of Winnipeg Inc. v. Brown*, [1989] 1 S.C.R. 1532, 1549; *Reference Re Canada Assistance Plan (B.C.)*, [1991] 2 S.C.R. 525, 567; *Auton (Guardian* ad litem *of) v. British Columbia (Attorney General)*, [2004] 3 S.C.R. 657, Appendix B.

The original division of powers has in practice undergone significant alteration as the decades have passed, even though it can be formally modified only by using a complex amendment procedure. In general, amendments to the federal Constitution require consent from the federal government and from the governments of seven provinces making up 50 per cent of the Canadian population (the so-called general formula) or the unanimous consent of the federal government and all ten provinces (ss. 38, 41, and 42, *Constitution Act, 1982*).[24] In addition to this complex amendment procedure, further constraints have been added since 1982, including the passage by the federal Parliament of the *Act Respecting Constitutional Amendments*,[25] which gives a veto to each of the five Canadian regions[26] over any constitutional amendment that formally requires only the application of the general formula. Several provinces have, in addition, passed laws making consultative referenda necessary before the adoption of resolutions targeting an amendment to the Constitution.[27] All these legal obstacles to constitutional change go a long way towards explaining why only one constitutional reform of any importance has taken place since the birth of the federation in 1867. This reform, in 1982, involved patriating Canada's constituent power, at that time still in the hands of the British Parliament, and incorporating a charter of human rights and freedoms into the Canadian Constitution. Quebec is the only province that has never consented to these constitutional amendments, which nevertheless apply within its territory.

The provinces have the power to amend their own constitutions as they wish, provided they comply with the prescriptions of the Canadian Constitution (*Constitution Act, 1982*, s. 45).[28] The same applies to the

24 *Constitution Act, 1982*, R.S.C. 1985, App. II, no. 44.

25 S.C. 1996, c. 1.

26 Namely Quebec, Ontario, British Columbia, two or more of the Atlantic provinces (having, according to the latest general census, combined populations of at least 50 per cent of the population of all the Atlantic provinces), and two or more of the Prairie provinces (having, according to the latest general census, combined populations of at least 50 per cent of the population of all the Prairie provinces).

27 This is the case in British Columbia and Alberta. Several other provinces have decided to follow this lead by making such referenda possible (but not compulsory); the process has been in place in Quebec since 1978.

28 They do not have formal written constitutions, unlike the states of the United States and Australia; therefore, the "constitutional law" of each province is embodied in nothing more than ordinary statutes of each provincial legislature.

federal Parliament with respect to the rules forming part of the federal Constitution (*Constitution Act, 1982*, s. 44) and that are not subject to a complex amendment procedure, in other words requiring consent from more than one entity. This applies, for example, to any amendment affecting the powers of the Senate and the selection of senators (*Constitution Act, 1982*, s. 42(1)b), which requires the application of the general formula. The provincial and federal constitutions are not, for the most part,[29] independent documents, comparable to American state constitutions. They are formed by a set of scattered rules that govern the organization and functioning of the provincial and federal legislative, executive, and judicial institutions. They must all be compatible to the Canadian Constitution.

The Senate defies all generally admitted notions of what a federative chamber should be. First, the senators are appointed for life by the federal government (s. 24). Second, the composition of Canada's upper house is not based on equal representation of the provinces, but rather on regional parity: Quebec, Ontario, the Maritime provinces, and, later, the Western provinces, are each represented by twenty-four senators (s. 22). The reason most often given by commentators to explain this choice by the original drafters is that the lifetime appointment of members of the Senate allows the upper house to play a temporizing, conservative role with regard to the lower house, whose members are elected by the population; in other words, the Senate is a counterbalance to the democratic element in the government system.[30] Today, although the second federal chamber has, in formal terms, the same powers as the House of Commons (the lower chamber), including the power to pass federal bills, it practically never exercises its right of veto because of its characteristic deficit of democratic and federative legitimacy.

III. The Judicial System

Under the Constitution, both orders of government can legislate with respect to the courts. The provinces have jurisdiction concerning the

29 As an exception, the province of British Columbia: *Constitution Act*, R.S.B.C. 1996, c. 66.

30 The Senate "was intended to provide 'sober second thought' on the legislation adopted by the popular representatives in the House of Commons ... However, it played the additional role of providing a distinct form of representation for the regions that had joined Confederation and ceded a significant portion of their legislative powers to the new federal Parliament": *Reference re Senate Reform*, [2014] 1 S.C.R. 704, par. 15.

administration of justice, extending to the constitution, maintenance and organization of provincial courts of both civil and criminal jurisdiction, and including procedure in civil matters in those courts. The provincial courts divide into two categories: the superior courts and the inferior courts. The superior courts contain a division of first authority (called "Superior Court" in Quebec and "Supreme Court" in a number of the other provinces) and a Court of Appeal. They are courts of inherent jurisdiction.[31] The provinces cannot abolish them either directly or indirectly by withdrawing their inherent jurisdiction. These courts have the jurisdiction to apply both provincial and federal law. The inferior provincial courts have only the jurisdiction conferred by their constitutive law.

Section 101 of the *Constitution Act, 1867*, attributes to the federal Parliament the power to create its own courts and to give them exclusive jurisdiction in certain domains of federal law, which means subtracting these domains from the jurisdiction of provincial courts. The Parliament exercised this power when it created the Federal Court in 1971, which includes a trial division and an appeal division. Article 101 also gives the federal Parliament power to create and to organize a Supreme Court. The existence, the general jurisdiction, the composition, and the other essential features of the Supreme Court of Canada (created by federal statute in 1875) has been constitutionalized (*Constitution Act, 1982*, ss. 41 and 42).[32] The general appellate jurisdiction exercised by the Supreme Court means that, as in Australia but unlike the United States, there is one common law for the whole of Canada, except that the civil law, statutory-based system is preserved in Quebec.

The federal government has the discretion to appoint all the judges of the superior courts, including the Supreme Court (ss. 96 and 101),[33] with no formal participation by the provinces. Several authors have concluded that the lack of provincial involvement in the appointment of judges to the Supreme Court is a major infringement of the federative

31 In other words, the dual jurisdiction recognized under common law: a residual jurisdiction that allows them to hear any matter not assigned exclusively to inferior courts, and the power to scrutinize and control the inferior courts and public administration.

32 This has been recently confirmed by the Supreme Court: *Reference re Supreme Court Act*, ss. 5 and 6, 2014 SCC 21.

33 *Supreme Court Act*, R.S.C. 1985, c. S-26, s. 4(2).

principle.[34] Since the 1960s, reform of the Supreme Court of Canada has been a recurring topic in the legal and political worlds. It has appeared on the agenda of major federal-provincial constitutional conferences, and it has been the focus of numerous reports and White Papers.[35] The effort expended over several decades to consider the status, the role, and the method for appointing the judges of the country's highest court tends to indicate that it faces a legitimacy deficit as a component of the Canadian legal system.[36]

Despite the federative distribution of powers in the field of justice, Canada's judicial system is characterized above all by integration. This can be seen in the lack of watertight distinctions between the constitutional, administrative, criminal, and civil jurisdictions, an approach inherited from the British. Above all, though, in the federative context, it is revealed by the fact that all cases, whether they originate under provincial or federal law, end up in final resort before the same federal court, the Supreme Court of Canada, even if the provincial courts can in principle enforce both federal and provincial laws.[37]

Scrutiny of a provincial and federal law's constitutionality is entrusted to the judicial system as a whole (the judicial-review model). The Supreme Court, placed at the summit of the judicial hierarchy, is

---

34 See, in particular, K.C. Wheare, *Federal Government*, 3rd ed. (London: Oxford University Press, 1947), 55, 56, and 71; Morin and Woehrling, *Les constitutions du Canada et du Québec*, 546.

35 To name but a few, *Final Report of the Special Joint Committee of the Senate and the House of Commons on the Constitution of Canada* (Ottawa: Information Canada, 1972) (referred to as the Molgat-McGuigan Report); Canadian Bar Association Committee on the Constitution, *Towards a New Canada* (Montreal: Canadian Bar Foundation, 1978); Task Force on Canadian Unity, *A Future Together* (Hull: Supply and Services Canada, 1979) (Pepin-Robarts Report); Government of Quebec, *Québec-Canada: A New Deal, The Québec Government Proposal for a New Partnership between Equals: Sovereignty-Association* (Quebec: Official Editor, 1979); Constitutional Committee of the Quebec Liberal Party, *A New Canadian Federation* (Montreal: Quebec Liberal Party, 1980). The issue of the method used to appoint judges was addressed by proposed constitutional amendments in the Meech Lake (1987) and Charlottetown (1992) Accords, which provided for the appointment of Supreme Court judges by the federal government on a proposal by the provincial governments. These two proposals failed.

36 Eugénie Brouillet and Yves Tanguay, "The Legitimacy of the Constitutional Arbitration Process in a Multinational Federative Regime: The Case of the Supreme Court of Canada," *University of British Columbia Law Review* 45 (2012): 47–101.

37 Brun, Tremblay, and Brouillet, *Droit constitutionnel*, 829–50.

the court of final resort for all cases, including federal disputes. Until 1949, however, the Supreme Court's decisions could be appealed to the Judicial Committee of the Privy Council in London. Only when this appeal route was abolished in 1949 did the Supreme Court become the final arbiter of federal disputes.

The Supreme Court can be asked to review constitutionality a posteriori, in a specific case brought to its attention in the form of an appeal from an existing decision, or a priori,[38] in the case of provisions that have not yet been promulgated by the federal or provincial political organs. In the latter case, under the *Supreme Court Act*, the federal government requests the Court's opinion through a reference procedure.[39] The Court is required to respond, unless the question or questions posed are essentially political, in which case it must justify its refusal. Although, in principle, the Court's response is simply an opinion, it is considered to have the same legal force as a decision rendered in a specific case. The dividing line between judicial and political functions in this context is difficult to identify. The reference jurisdiction involves the Court in political decisions, which it would not allow itself to get involved in with respect to individual disputes, because the reference procedure enables the government to request the Supreme Court's opinion concerning the constitutionality of legislative bills and to ask theoretical or politically charged questions. One of the most important examples of this procedure was *Reference re Secession of Quebec*.[40]

The Supreme Court's general appellate jurisdiction requires it to decide cases from two different legal traditions. Canada has a dual legal system for private-law cases; common law is applied in the nine provinces with an English-speaking majority, while civil law is used in Quebec. In 1774, the authorities in Britain expressly maintained the use of French civil law in the territory of the Province of Quebec (*Quebec Act*, s. 8).[41] In 1867, when the federation was created, the recognition given to exclusive provincial jurisdiction over property and

38 Fabien Gélinas, "La primauté du droit et les effets d'une loi inconstitutionnelle," *Revue du Barreau Canada* 57 (1988): 455, 459.

39 *Supreme Court Act*, s. 53. Provincial governments also have a procedure for references to the Court of Appeal (the highest provincial court). Provincial laws provide for the possibility of appealing the court's opinion to the Supreme Court.

40 *Reference re Secession of Quebec*, [1998] 2 S.C.R. 217, 235, and following.

41 R.S.C. 1985, App. II, no. 2, s. 8.

civil rights (s. 92(13)) continued this legal duality. Interaction between the two legal cultures is not always easy, and has given rise, to some extent, to "Canada's dual legal solitudes."[42] To ensure the presence, on the Supreme Court, of judges trained in Quebec's civil law, the *Supreme Court Act* requires the federal government to appoint three judges from Quebec, out of a total of nine.[43] This may also indicate an underlying desire to provide for adequate representation from Quebec because of its distinct culture. The six remaining judges are usually from Ontario (three), the Western provinces (two) and the Atlantic provinces (one). However, except for the rule regarding representation from Quebec, the federal government has no other limits on the exercise of its power to appoint judges. Although the Supreme Court has always, in fact, been made up of both French-speaking and English-speaking judges, bilingualism is not a criterion for appointment to the Supreme Court.

The Supreme Court's decisions are not always unanimous. Dissenting or concurring opinions are expressed frequently. In the area of federal disputes, the years 1970 to 2000 were marked by a movement from decisions expressing a centralizing mindset to those more favourable to provincial autonomy. After a long period of consensus during the early 2000s, recent years have seen the re-emergence of a clear division between two groups of judges, one more centralizing, the other more decentralizing in outlook.[44]

Canadian constitutional law guarantees the independence of the courts and the judiciary from political interference. The constitutional principle of judicial independence is strongly rooted and has several aspects, covering both the independence of the judges themselves (e.g., security of tenure, financial security, immunity, and non-compellability) and that of the courts (i.e., institutional independence).[45]

---

42 Jean-François Gaudreault-Desbiens, *Les solitudes du bijuridisme au Canada* (Montreal: Éditions Thémis, 2007).

43 *Supreme Court Act*, s. 6.

44 Bruce Ryder, "Equal Autonomy in Canadian Federalism: The Continuing Search for Balance in the Interpretation of the Division of Powers," *Supreme Court Law Review* (2d) 54 (2011): 565. Two decisions have been decided unanimously: *Reference re Securities Act*, [2011] 3 S.C.R. 837; *Canada (Attorney General) v. PHS Community Services Society*, [2011] 3 S.C.R. 134.

45 See particularly *Reference re Remuneration of Judges of the Provincial Court (P.E.I.)*, [1997] 3 S.C.R. 3.

IV. Federative Jurisprudence

The enormous difficulty of amending the Constitution has made constitutional jurisprudence the preferred way to modify the regime. It is essentially up to the courts, and ultimately the Supreme Court, to adapt the constitutional texts to new societal conditions. This gradual evolution, less easily perceptible and less spectacular than formal amendments, has nevertheless had a determining influence. Maintaining the federative balance and providing equal protection for the autonomy of each order of government are two tasks that depend especially on the constitutional interpretations of the Supreme Court. Its diktats in federative matters have the same force and the same normative value as the constitutional texts. As a result, they are binding on all federal, provincial, and local political organs and on all other courts.

The question of whether the Supreme Court's federative jurisprudence has a centralizing or decentralizing effect has no unanimous answer in Canada, where different and indeed divergent views exist on what federalism actually is. Two approaches have developed alongside each other. The first, especially noticeable in Canada outside Quebec, is territorial and mono-national in nature; the second, generally prominent in Quebec, is based on a pluri-national view of the country. Superimposed on this divergence is the fact that Canadians outside Quebec have a generally distinct understanding of how the country's political system emerged originally. For the first group, Canada's federation is first and foremost the result of an imperial act; for the second group, it stems from a pact between the three original territorial entities and between separate national communities, which was then ratified by the British authorities. Nor is there a consensus on the nature of the original regime. In general, while Canadians outside Quebec highlight what they perceive to be a highly centralized federative system,[46] Quebecers see it as a genuine federative regime that guarantees protection for the autonomy of each order of government. Furthermore, the English-Canadian literature generally assesses the evolution of the regime from a pragmatic and functional viewpoint based on an analysis of the effectiveness

---

46 Some authors have spoken of a quasi-federation: Wheare, *Federal Government*, 18–20. The two elements most often cited in support of this viewpoint are the power of each lieutenant governor (appointed by the governor general) to reserve provincial legislative bills and the power of the governor general to disallow them. These powers fell into disuse many years ago through the effects of constitutional convention.

of public policy; authors in Quebec are more likely to adopt a normative approach and to measure compliance with the rules governing the allocation of powers in light of the principle of provincial autonomy.[47]

Whatever the truth in each divergent vision, there is broad agreement that Canada is founded on federative principles that require, in normative terms, a division of powers between orders of government that are autonomous but still coordinated. It is therefore important to assess the jurisprudence of the highest court in terms of the essential corollary of federalism, the principle of equal autonomy for each order of government. In the words of Bruno Théret, "An 'authentic' federal system can ... be defined as a system that includes a self-preserving mechanism for the federal principle that permanently regulates the constitutive contradiction between unity and diversity: if unity triumphs over diversity, or if diversity triumphs over unity, the term *federalism* can hardly be seen to apply."[48] The federative nature of Canada's Constitution has been recognized many times by the courts. The Privy Council clearly stated this fact on many occasions, notably in a passage that has since become a classic: "The object of the Act was neither to weld the provinces into one, nor to subordinate provincial governments to a central authority, but to create a federal government in which they should all be represented, entrusted with the exclusive administration of affairs in which they had a common interest, each province retaining its independence and autonomy."[49] The Supreme Court has expressed itself in similar fashion, in particular in *Reference re Secession of Quebec*, in which it states that federalism is one of the constitutional principles underlying the written Constitution, and that "there can be little doubt that the principle of federalism remains a central organizational theme of our Constitution."[50] For this reason, the Court considers that federalism can be used not only to guide the courts in the interpretation and application of the provisions of the constitutional text, but also to fill any gaps.

---

47 On these differences, see François Rocher, "La dynamique Québec-Canada ou le refus de l'idéal fédéral," in Gagnon, *Le fédéralisme canadien contemporain*, 93–146.

48 Bruno Théret, "Du principe fédéral à une typologie des fédérations: quelques propositions," in *Le fédéralisme dans tous ses états: Gouvernance, identité et méthodologie*, ed. Jean-François Gaudreault-Desbiens and Fabien Gélinas (Cowansville: Éditions Yvon Blais, 2005), 128 (my translation).

49 *Liquidators of the Maritime Bank of Canada v. Receiver-General of New Brunswick*, [1892] A.C. 437, 440–2.

50 *Reference re Secession of Quebec*, 250–1.

The jurisprudence from the Supreme Court contains several passages in which it states that the autonomy of each order of government lies at the heart of the federative principle.[51] It also refers, in several places, to the need to preserve a balance between the respective powers of each order.[52] Concerning its role in preserving that balance, the Court considers that it "falls primarily to governments," adding that the way in which powers are shared must, as a result, promote the practice of a type of cooperative federalism open to the overlapping of powers. Its role in maintaining this balance involves, in the Court's view, defining and applying doctrines for the implementation of power-sharing that promote "the legitimate interplay between federal and provincial powers."[53]

However, despite these general statements highlighting the normative implications of the principle of federalism, the jurisprudence of Canada's highest court tends to favour the federal government (see IV, 2). We will look, first, at some specific issues concerning the distribution of legislative powers, before turning to some general trends that can be observed in the Supreme Court's federative jurisprudence.

1. Specific Issues

The Judicial Committee of the Privy Council interpreted the *Constitution Act, 1867*, as an ordinary statute, applying the rules of statutory interpretation. One of the most important is the principle of literal interpretation, which postulates that the constituent power always expresses itself clearly and that the words used match the result sought. The search for legislative or constitutive intent is therefore based primarily on the letter of the law. If the terms used are not clear, or where there may be doubt as to their meaning, they must be interpreted in a manner consistent with the statute as a whole. To put this another way, the provisions must be read one with the other in order to give effect to each. Although the Judicial Committee began to show more openness, beginning in the 1930s, to an evolving or flexible interpretation of the Constitution, it did not, in general, question the application of the rules of statutory interpretation to the *Constitution Act, 1867*.

---

51 For example, *Reference re Secession of Quebec*, par. 58.

52 To list only some recent decisions: *Reference re Securities Act*, [2011] 3 S.C.R. 837, par. 7; *Reference re Assisted Human Reproduction Act*, [2010] 3 S.C.R. 457, par. 43, 74; *Canadian Western Bank*, op. cit., par. 24.

53 *Canadian Western Bank*, par. 24, 36.

From 1970 onwards, the Supreme Court gradually moved away from literal interpretation to embrace the so-called evolving or dynamic method of interpretation. Referring to the famous metaphor comparing the Canadian Constitution to a "a living tree capable of growth and expansion within its natural limits" first expressed by the Judicial Committee,[54] the Court stated that if there is a gap between the constitutional text and the societal conditions to which it is meant to apply, the courts are responsible to adapt its impact accordingly.

In 2005 the Supreme Court had an opportunity to reiterate its preference for the evolving approach in *Reference re Employment Insurance Act (Can.), ss. 22 and 23.*[55] It was asked to examine the constitutional validity of the federal legislative provisions governing parental leave, by determining whether the provisions encroached upon provincial legislative competency over property and civil rights and matters of a merely private or local nature (ss. 92(13) and (16)), or if they came under federal legislative competency over unemployment insurance (s. 91(2A)). The Court used the living tree to identify the extent of federal competence over unemployment insurance and found that it can cover assistance measures. The Quebec Court of Appeal, which had used an approach based on original intent, had concluded that the evidence showed that the constitutional amendment of 1940, which transferred provincial jurisdiction over unemployment insurance to the federal Parliament, was not intended to extend jurisdiction over social security and assistance measures, which remained with the provinces. If this had been the case, the provinces would have refused to agree to the constitutional amendment.[56] According to the Quebec Court of Appeal, the principle of evolutionary interpretation could not be applied if it involved ignoring the intent of the constituent authority in 1940.[57]

As we have seen, the rules governing the division of legislative and executive powers are unusual in that they include two lists, one of

54 *Edward v. A.-G. for Canada*, [1930] A.C. 124, 136: "The British North America Act planted in Canada a living tree capable of growth and expansion within its natural limits." On constitutional interpretation, see Grant Huscroft and Bradley W. Miller, eds., *The Challenge of Originalism: Theories of Constitutional Interpretation* (New York: Cambridge University Press, 2011); and Aileen Kavanagh, "The Idea of a Living Constitution," *Canadian Journal of Law & Jurisprudence* 16 (2003): 55–89.

55 [2005] 2 S.C.R. 669.

56 *Québec (Procureur général) c. Canada (Procureur général)*, (2004) R.J.Q. 399 (C.A.Q), par. 73

57 Ibid., par. 92.

exclusive provincial powers and one of exclusive federal powers, with residual powers being allocated to the federal government. The items in each list have often required interpretation by the Judicial Committee and later by the Supreme Court. Generally speaking, while the Judicial Committee tended to interpret in a restrictive way certain federal powers – which, if interpreted literally, might have emptied some provincial powers of much of their meaning – the Supreme Court has tended to broaden their scope.[58] Examples include the federal government's power to legislate in the fields of trade and commerce, unemployment insurance, and criminal law. The same has applied to the general powers of the federal Parliament.

Concerning trade and commerce (s. 91(2)), the Supreme Court has interpreted the exclusive federal competence as including not only the power to legislate in connection with international and interprovincial trade,[59] but also the right to govern trade in general. On the basis of this latter component, it has recognized the federal government's power to legislate with respect to competition and trademarks.[60] In 2005, it broadened the scope of the federal power to legislate in the area of unemployment insurance beyond what the constituent power had specified, allowing it to legislate not only in connection with jobs lost for economic reasons but also for interruptions of employment for personal reasons, by recognizing a power to legislate with respect to maternity and parental leave.[61] The same result was achieved with respect to federal competence over the criminal law, which now covers not only legislation pursuing a valid criminal law objective by imposing a prohibition,[62] but also regulatory schemes, provided they contribute to the achievement of the law's penal objective.[63]

The *Constitution Act, 1867*, gives the federal Parliament the power to "make Laws for the Peace, Order, and good Government of Canada, in

---

58 As Peter W. Hogg wrote, "Judicial interpretation since the abolition of appeals has permitted some growth of federal power, and this may well continue": Peter W. Hogg, *Constitutional Law of Canada*, loose-leaf edition (Toronto: Thomson Carswell), 5–18.

59 *Citizens Insurance Co. v. Parsons*, (1881) 7 A.C. 96.

60 *General Motors of Canada Ltd. v. City National Leasing*, [1989] 1 S.C.R. 641; *Kirkbi AG v. Gestions Ritvik Inc.*, [2005] 3 S.C.R. 302.

61 *Reference re Employment Insurance Act (Can.), ss. 22 and 23*, op. cit.

62 *Labatt Breweries of Canada Ltd. v. Attorney General of Canada*, [1980] 1 S.C.R. 914.

63 *R. v. Hydro-Québec*, [1997] 3 S.C.R. 213; *RJR-MacDonald Inc. v. Canada*, [1995] 3 S.C.R. 199; *Reference re Assisted Human Reproduction Act*, [2010] 3 S.C.R. 457.

relation to all Matters not coming within the Classes of Subjects by this Act assigned exclusively to the Legislatures of the Provinces" (opening paragraph, s. 91). This formula gives the federal government a residual power concerning anything not awarded exclusively to the provinces. Three categories of federal actions that, today, appear to be completely independent of one another are based on this general federal power: those based on residual power, those based on emergency power, and those based on the power to legislate on matters of national interest.

The residual power itself has been limited by the courts to matters foreseeable in 1867, rather than extended to include all the new legislative fields that have appeared since then. This explains why it has seldom been used as the basis for federal legislation, despite the substantial development of governmental activities. On the basis of the same paragraph, however, the jurisprudence has consistently recognized the federal government's power to deal with emergencies. In these cases, the federal Parliament is allowed to legislate in all areas, including those under the exclusive jurisdiction of the provinces, but only temporarily. Furthermore, the courts recognized at an early date, on the basis of the same paragraph, the federal Parliament's power to legislate on any matter of national importance or presenting a matter of interest for the federation as a whole. This so-called doctrine of national interest had, for more than a century, applied only potentially to distinctive and indivisible matters (as opposed to aggregates of provincial and federal matters) that were not included in any class of subjects assigned to the provinces.[64] Since a 1988 decision by the Supreme Court, the doctrine now applies "to both new matters which did not exist at Confederation and to matters which, although originally matters of a local or private nature in a province, have since, in the absence of national emergency, become matters of national concern."[65] The doctrine operates only centripetally and has permanent effects; the competence acquired by the federal government following a judgment validating its legislative intervention is definitive.

Despite the broadening nature of these interpretations, the courts have, over the decades, confirmed the validity of a number of provincial legislative interventions under the classes listed or related powers, and found certain federal statutes invalid. However, none of these decisions

64 *Re: Anti-Inflation Act*, [1976] 2 S.C.R. 373.
65 *R. v. Crown Zellerbach Canada Ltd.*, [1988] 1 S.C.R. 401.

has led the Supreme Court to extend the jurisdiction of the provinces beyond the parameters traditionally set by the jurisprudence. This asymmetry in the judicial interpretation of the federal and provincial jurisdictions is, in large part, attributable to the omnipresence of the value of efficiency in federative jurisprudence, which favours the federal government to the detriment of regional diversity.[66] Efficiency is at the core of the scope given by the Supreme Court to the doctrine of national interest, the power to encroach, and federal jurisdiction over trade in general. However, in all these cases and in contrast to the European notion of subsidiarity, efficiency has an ascending application only, generates permanent effects, and can apply to matters not placed under the competence of the federal Parliament.[67] The Supreme Court stated that the cooperative approach to Canadian federalism goes hand in hand with the perceived need to promote efficacy over formalism.[68]

2. *Asymmetrical Effects of Cooperative Federalism*

Two different approaches to federalism can be identified in Canadian jurisprudence: the dualist and the cooperative approaches. Dualism is based on the idea that the powers conferred by sections 91 and 92 constitute "watertight compartments" and that, as far as possible, the overlapping of federal and provincial powers must be avoided or limited. As a result, the notion of exclusive legislative jurisdiction plays a key role. In contrast, under cooperative federalism, the principle of exclusive jurisdiction is far more restricted, creating broad areas of concurrent jurisdiction. Overlapping between the two orders of government is considered not only normal but advisable.

In 1867, the dual model was largely followed when legislative powers in Canada were shared out, creating only a few areas of overlapping jurisdiction. This legal situation, however, has not prevented the courts from developing doctrines for the implementation of power-sharing rules that reflect a cooperative approach to federalism and promote overlapping powers.

---

66 Jean Leclair, "The Supreme Court's Understanding of Federalism: Efficiency at the Expense of Diversity," *Queen's Law Journal* 28 (2003): 411–53.

67 Eugénie Brouillet, "Canadian Federalism and the Principle of Subsidiarity: Should We Open Pandora's Box?," *Supreme Court Law Review* (2d) 54 (2011): 601–32.

68 *Quebec (Attorney General) v. Canadian Owners and Pilots Association*, [2010] 2 S.C.R. 536, par. 44.

The Judicial Committee of the Privy Council in London, in its interpretation of the constitutional text, opted clearly for dualism when it sought to limit overlaps in order to preserve the sphere of autonomy of each order of government and a balanced sharing of powers. However, from the second half of the twentieth century, the Supreme Court moved gradually away from the federative jurisprudence established by the Judicial Committee to embrace a cooperative vision of federalism. The adoption of a cooperative or "modern" approach to federalism has led to a multiplication of the number of zones of de facto competition between the federation and the provinces. Even though, in principle, maximizing the number of areas in which each order of government can intervene affords equal protection for their autonomy, the actual situation is different because of various doctrines governing the implementation of the rules for the sharing of legislative powers that undermine this essential corollary of the federative principle.

The rules used to resolve conflicts between laws may have profound implications for the balance of power. According to the doctrine of federal paramountcy, any conflict between a provincial and a federal statute, where both are valid, will see the provincial statute declared inoperative, while the federal statute will alone be applied. The effects of the provincial statute are suspended to the extent that they are incompatible with the federal statute, for as long as they remain incompatible. The doctrine is expressly set out in connection with matters of concurrent jurisdiction (ss. 92A(3) and 95); in only a single case, the advantage is given to the provincial statute (s. 94A). However, the application of the rule of federal paramountcy has been extended by the court's jurisprudence to all conflicts between equally valid statutes.

The effect of this doctrine on the balance of legislative power between the federal and provincial governments depends on the meaning of "conflict" as seen by the courts. For many decades, Canadian courts required proof that it was impossible to comply with both statutes; complying with one meant breaching the other.[69] By applying such a strict test of incompatibility, the Supreme Court attempted to give precedence, as far as was possible, to the regular application of laws passed by both orders of government by preserving the operability of valid provincial statutes. This approach was consistent with the modern conception of power-sharing, which, as mentioned previously,

---

69 *Multiple Access Ltd. v. McCutcheon*, [1982] 2 S.C.R. 161.

supports overlapping laws. However, the jurisprudence today has the effect of making a provincial statute inoperative (of no effect) if it prevents a federal statute from achieving its object or, in other words, if it thwarts the intentions of the federal Parliament. This criterion makes the application of the rule of federal paramountcy conditional simply on the expressed intention of the federal legislator to block a provincial legislative intervention, however valid.[70] The introduction of this criterion is more characteristic of the classical approach to power sharing, which protects the exclusivity of the federal powers alone, than of a modern approach open to overlapping, which is what the Supreme Court claims to support. In an attempt to limit the concern that the frustration of the federal legislative purpose criterion poses a threat to provincial autonomy, the Supreme Court has stated that the paramountcy doctrine should be applied with restraint.[71]

The jurisprudence of the Supreme Court is also at odds with the cooperative approach when it applies the doctrine of interjurisdictional immunity, under which a valid law cannot have an effect on a person, thing, or undertaking under the jurisdiction of the other order of government. The goal is essentially to prevent a valid law from having effects that significantly encroach on the core of a subject under the exclusive jurisdiction of the other order of government.[72] As a result, the doctrine represents an exception to the modern approach to power sharing because it is designed to preserve an area of exclusive jurisdiction in certain circumstances. Until 2007, the courts required proof only of the existence of an effect, regardless of its importance, on an essential element under the jurisdiction of the other order of government in order to conclude that a provincial statute was inoperable. Since 2007, following a shift in the Supreme Court's jurisprudence, the doctrine applies only if there is an impairment of a vital or essential part of the other government's jurisdictional authority.[73]

However, although the doctrine of interjurisdictional immunity may, in theory, be invoked to restrict the application of both provincial and

---

70 *Rothmans, Benson & Hedges Inc. v. Saskatchewan*, [2005] 1 S.C.R. 188, par. 21; *Canadian Western Bank*, op. cit, par. 74. For a criticism of this doctrine, see Peter W. Hogg, "Paramountcy and Tobacco," *Supreme Court Law Review* (2d) 34 (2006): 335–44.

71 *Saskatchewan (Attorney General) v. Lemare Lake Logging Ltd.*, [2015] 3 S.C.R. 419, para. 23–7; *Bank of Montreal v. Marcotte*, [2014] 2 S.C.R. 725, par. 72.

72 Brun, Tremblay, and Brouillet, *Droit constitutionnel*, 472–7.

73 *Canadian Western Bank c. Alberta*, op. cit.

federal statutes, so far it has been used only against provincial laws. Its effect has been asymmetrical, a fact recognized explicitly by the Supreme Court.[74] In addition, even though the introduction of the impairment criterion was intended to re-establish a federative balance, subsequent Supreme Court decisions based on interjurisdictional immunity have not provided concrete examples of this potential rebalancing.[75]

3. *Fundamental Aspects of Federative Life in Canada*

In addition to disputes about the rules governing the sharing of powers between the two orders of government, the Supreme Court has been asked to rule on more unusual questions, touching on fundamental aspects of the country's federative life, that have given it the delicate task of weighing considerations of legality (or constitutionality) against considerations of legitimacy. Examples occurred in 1981 and 1982, in references concerning the patriation of the constituent power, and in 1998, in *Reference re Secession of Quebec*.

Canada's patriation of full sovereignty from Great Britain was the end of a long process. Canada's legal order gradually became detached from the British order, but with no definitive break. Prior to the constitutional reform of 1982, although there was no longer any doubt that Canada was a fully sovereign country both domestically and internationally, the constituent power was still vested in Britain's Parliament. However, there had been an understanding for many years that the British Parliament would legislate on Canadian constitutional matters only in accordance with instructions from Canada.[76]

The project to bring the constituent power back to Canada was frequently discussed by the federal government and the provinces between the 1930s and 1980, but the discussions failed because of a lack of agreement about the amendment procedure to be included in the

74 Ibid., par. 45.

75 *Quebec (Attorney General) v. Canadian Owners and Pilots Association*, [2010] 2 S.C.R. 536; *Quebec (Attorney General) v. Lacombe*, [2010] 2 S.C.R. 453; *Canada (Attorney General) v. PHS Community Services Society*, [2011] 3 S.C.R. 134; *Carter v. Canada (Attorney General)*, [2015] 1 S.C.R. 331, par. 49–53.

76 As early as the 1860s, an imperial policy had developed requiring a degree of consent by a British colony to any constitutional change planned by the mother country. Section 4 of the *Statute of Westminster 1931*, R.S.C. 1985, App. II, no. 27, later confirmed this convention.

constitutional text. In the early 1980s, the federal prime minister, Pierre Trudeau, launched a new project to patriate the constituent power, which would include the insertion of an amendment formula and a charter of human rights and freedoms into the Constitution. These changes were intended to have a significant effect on the powers of the provinces, because they potentially would, on one hand, give the provinces a say in constitutional amendment decisions and, on the other hand, limit the powers of the provinces (and the federal government) by reference to the charter of rights.

The project was initially opposed by eight of the ten provinces. After the federal government had announced that it would still go ahead with the project by submitting a request to the British Parliament, three provinces (Quebec, Manitoba, and Newfoundland) asked their respective courts of appeal to rule on the constitutionality of the government's action, from a strictly legal point of view and also in light of constitutional conventions. The Supreme Court was required to make the final ruling. This was the first time in Canada's constitutional history that the court of final appeal was asked to make such a direct and fundamental decision concerning the actual basis of the constitutional structure of the Canadian state and, more specifically, on its federative nature.

In a majority decision, *Re: Resolution to amend the Constitution*,[77] the Supreme Court ruled that as a matter of law, the federal government could request the patriation of the Constitution and thereby alter the powers of the provinces, despite the opposition of a majority of provinces. The Supreme Court's answer to the question concerning the conventional aspect was, however, completely different. Although the federal Parliament could act legally without consent from the provinces, to do so would be to violate a constitutional convention.[78] On this aspect, the Supreme Court majority considered that Canadian law included a constitutional convention that required the federal Parliament to obtain "a substantial degree of provincial consent"[79] before asking the British

77 [1981] 1 S.C.R. 753.

78 A constitutional convention is a rule defined by agreement between governing authorities or politicians that is not sanctioned by the courts but is applied and complied with by the parties by reason of political necessity. Its existence depends on the answers to three questions: First, what are the precedents? Second, did the actors in the precedents believe that they were bound by a rule? Third, is there a reason for the rule?

79 *Re: Resolution to amend the Constitution*, 905.

Parliament to make a constitutional amendment that would affect the powers of the provinces. The Court stated, "The federal principle cannot be reconciled with a state of affairs where the modification of provincial legislative powers could be obtained by the unilateral action of the federal authorities," and that to admit the contrary would be to allow them to obtain by simple resolution what they could not validly accomplish by statute.[80] In this way, the Supreme Court recognized the principle of equal autonomy of the orders of government, but confined its effects to the conventional dimension of constitutional law.

Following the Supreme Court's decision, the federal government resumed its negotiations with the provinces and, thanks to a small number of changes to the initial project, was able to obtain the consent of the nine provinces with an English-speaking majority, but not of Quebec. The federal government and the signatory provinces to the agreement began the process leading to the patriation and amendment of the Constitution.

Meanwhile, the Quebec government referred a constitutional question to the Court of Appeal of Quebec concerning the existence of a constitutional convention requiring consent from Quebec for amendments to the Constitution that would affect its powers or status within the federation. The Court of Appeal answered the question in the negative, and the decision was upheld by the Supreme Court in *Re: Objection by Quebec to a Resolution to amend the Constitution*[81] eight months after the constitutional amendment came into force. According to the Supreme Court, although an analysis of the precedents showed that all the previous proposed federal changes affecting the rights of the provinces had failed because, in two instances, of opposition from a number of provinces including Quebec and, in two other instances, of opposition from Quebec alone, the Quebec government failed to show that the political actors in those cases felt themselves bound by the need to obtain Quebec's consent.

This decision by Canada's highest court laid to rest the claim, continuously expressed by Quebec governments, that Quebec had a power of veto over amendments that affected its power or position within the federation. It also retired, at least on the legal level, the idea that the Canadian federation was based on an agreement between two equal founding peoples. As a result, although the *Constitution Act, 1982*,

80 Ibid., 905, 906, and 908.

81 [1982] 2 S.C.R. 793.

applies legally to Quebec just as it does to all the other provinces, it suffers from a major lack of political legitimacy from the point of view, at least, of Quebec, for one of the federation's founding provinces, the cradle of French culture in North America, has never consented to the act.

In 1998, the Supreme Court was again asked to rule on a similarly fundamental question, namely the secession of a province. Prior to *Reference re Secession of Quebec*, Canadian constitutional law was silent about this issue. In its decision, the Court first stated that it would limit itself to clarifying the legal framework within which a democratic decision could be taken. The Supreme Court answered the question, whether Quebec could secede unilaterally, in two stages. First, the Court held that Quebec secession is possible within the framework of Canadian constitutional law; that is, a clear majority vote in Quebec on a clear question in favour of sovereignty would create a constitutional obligation on Quebec and Canada to negotiate a constitutional amendment on secession and its possible terms. Second, if the negotiations fail, unilateral secession would be possible outside the scope of the Constitution, supported by recognition from the international community. In other words, Quebec could achieve independence outside the scope of the Canadian Constitution under the aegis of the international community, provided it had previously attempted to negotiate its secession in good faith with Canada. This is not a specific right in either Canadian constitutional law or international law, but a possibility based on the principle of effectivity.

The Supreme Court identified four principles underlying the constitutional texts that, in its opinion, were relevant in answering the question posed: federalism, democracy, constitutionalism (rule of law), and the protection of minorities. On the basis in particular of the principles of federalism and democracy, the Supreme Court attempted to reconcile the considerations of legality and legitimacy by creating a constitutional obligation to negotiate. It was held that Quebec could not invoke the democratic principle in order to secede from Canada unilaterally, and the federal government could not rely on the principles of federalism and constitutionalism to ignore a democratically expressed desire to secede.

V. Conclusion

As a result of their fundamental importance in the normative hierarchy, constitutional texts can be amended only by using a formula that is more stringent than the requirements for amending an ordinary statute. In a federative context, the relative untouchability of the Constitution means that in many federations it evolves mainly through judicial interpretation. This is especially true in Canada because of the huge difficulty of formally amending the constitutional texts. As a result, the Supreme Court has the delicate task of maintaining a balance between the powers of the two orders of government. However, in many respects, the Supreme Court of Canada is an exception among its counterparts in federal states. All its members, like all the judges of the provincial superior courts, are appointed unilaterally by the federal government.[82]

In terms of judicial independence and impartiality, the unilateral appointment process creates problems for the Supreme Court as the "umpire of federalism" because it prevents the judges from being perceived to be independent from the federal government. A reform that would allow the provinces to formally participate would make the Court an institution much more consistent with Canada's federal nature.

Over the decades, the decisions of the Supreme Court in connection with the distribution of powers have created an asymmetric degree of protection for the autonomy of each order of government. While the cooperative approach to federalism has allowed the federal government to maximize, and even extend, its legislative domain, the same cannot be said of the provinces. At a time when state intervention is becoming more widespread and more complex, it is clearly impossible to avoid all overlapping of powers between the two orders of government. However, federalism cannot survive over the long term if legislative powers are completely decompartmentalized.

The trend towards centralization that is generally apparent in the Court's constitutional jurisprudence is, perhaps, a reflection of the natural propensity of all democratic societies to strengthen their centre. However, it constitutes a problem in a multinational federative context. In Canada, the coexistence of two forms of nationalism, one for Canada

82 In most federations, the federal entities are associated to varying degrees with the designation process of the constitutional judges or the members of the Supreme Court, in particular by means of the role recognized by the upper house (or federal chamber). Exceptions are federations whose constitutional law is of British inspiration, such as Canada, India, and Australia, where the federal government has exclusive power to appoint the judges.

and one for Quebec, requires that the balance of power between the federal and provincial governments be preserved. The federative principle and its essential corollary, autonomy for each order of government in the exercise of its legislative powers, is seen in Quebec as more than just a technique for governance; it also is the guarantee that Quebec will be able to take its rightful place as a national group within the Canadian federation.

6 The Supreme Court of Ethiopia: Federalism's Bystander

GEDION T. HESSEBON AND ABDULETIF K. IDRIS

One influential description of federalism is that of a covenant of constituent units that stipulates the terms for self-rule and shared rule.[1] Normally, the terms of a federal covenant are enshrined in a constitution, which is regarded as the supreme law of the land. Furthermore, when disputes arise concerning the meaning and implication of the covenant, courts play the role of an umpire between the parties in dispute.[2] Usually, the highest court of the land or a constitutional court interprets the constitution and adjudicates controversies pertaining to the ambit of self-rule and shared rule. Therefore, in many federal countries, the judiciary plays an important role in delineating the spheres of competence of the different orders of government. The jurisprudence developed in this process is indispensable to understanding the nature of federalism in most countries.

The Federal Democratic Republic of Ethiopia provides an exception to the preceding claim. After more than two decades of federalism, Ethiopia has very little federalism case law, and the federal and state judiciaries have had virtually no role in shaping the development of Ethiopian federalism. In this chapter, an attempt will be made to explain the reasons for this perhaps peculiar state of affairs. To facilitate this discussion and provide some background, the next section will

1 Daniel J. Elazar, *Exploring Federalism* (Tuscaloosa: University of Alabama Press, 1987); Daniel J. Elazar and John Kincaid, eds.,*The Covenant Connection: From Federal Theology to Modern Federalism* (Lanham, MD: Lexington Books, 2000); and Michael Burgess, *Comparative Federalism: Theory and Practice* (Oxon, UK: Routledge, 2006), 49.

2 Ronald L. Watts, *Comparing Federal Systems*, 3rd rev. ed. (Montreal and Kingston: McGill-Queen's University Press, 2008), 159.

describe Ethiopian federalism. That section will be followed by a discussion of the judiciary and of the House of Federation, which is one of the two federal houses and the ultimate authority with the mandate to interpret Ethiopia's Constitution. The final section of the chapter will discuss and analyse the extra-legal explanations for the lack of federalism jurisprudence in Ethiopia.

I. The Ethiopian Federal System

1. Background to Ethiopian Federalism and Country Profile

The population of Ethiopia is more than 96 million, making it Africa's second-most populous country.[3] The latest official census shows considerable diversity in both religion and ethnicity. More than eighty ethnic groups live in Ethiopia, and almost all of them speak their own language.[4] Despite the overwhelming ethnic and linguistic diversity, the four largest ethnic groups make up 73.7 per cent of the total population (the two biggest ethnic groups being the Oromo and the Amhara, constituting 34.5 per cent and 26.9 per cent respectively of the total population). There are only ten ethnic groups with a population exceeding one million.[5] With the exception of major urban centres such as Addis Ababa, there is a high degree of ethnic concentration in the settlement patterns of the population.

Almost half the population adheres to Ethiopian Orthodox Christianity, a third of the population is Muslim (33.9 per cent), and a fifth of the population comprises Protestant Christians (18.6 per cent).[6] These religions crosscut ethnicity, and Orthodox Christianity and Islam have ancient roots in Ethiopia going back to the fourth and seventh centuries, respectively.[7] Although Ethiopia is one of the lowest ranking countries on the UN's Human Development index, during the past decade, its economy has been on the rise. As of 2014, its GDP was US$51 billion,

3 See World Bank, "Ethiopia: Country at a Glance," http://www.worldbank.org/en/country/ethiopia.

4 Federal Democratic Republic of Ethiopia, Population Census Commission, *Summary and Statistical Report of the 2007 Population and Housing Census*, 16–17, http://ecastats.uneca.org/aicmd/Portals/0/Cen2007_firstdraft.pdf.

5 Ibid.

6 Ibid., 17.

7 John S. Trimingham, *Islam in Ethiopia* (Oxford: Oxford University Press, 1952), 38–42.

and its per capita income adjusted for purchasing power parity was about $1,430.[8] Relatively speaking, the disparity in wealth is not substantial among the population at large, but inequality is increasing because of growing urban income inequality.[9] There also is a disparity in the level of development between the more populated central highlands and the peripheral lowlands, which have historically benefited very little from public investment in the provision of social goods and services.

Since 1995, the Ethiopian state has been reconfigured with a federal constitutional dispensation. The Constitution of the Federal Democratic Republic of Ethiopia (FDRE), establishes nine "national regional state" governments and a federal government.[10] The Constitution does not provide for administrative units below the state level but obliges the regional states to establish subregional administrative units with adequate powers to enable the people to participate directly in their own governance.[11] An important and perhaps distinguishing feature of Ethiopia's federal system is that it is established with a view to ensure the right to self-determination of the nations, nationalities, and peoples of Ethiopia.[12] The right to self-determination of the country's ethnolinguistic groups is considered to be the cornerstone of Ethiopia's federal system.[13] Because self-governance is provided as one of the components of the right to self-determination,[14] there has been an attempt to provide each major ethnic group with its own regional state or subregional administrative unit. While six ethnic groups in the country

8 See data from World Bank, https://www.google.nl/publicdata/explore?ds=d5bncppjof8f9_&met_y=ny_gnp_pcap_pp_cd&idim=country:ETH:ERI:KEN&hl=en&dl=en#!ctype=l&strail=false&bcs=d&nselm=h&met_y=ny_gdp_pcap_pp_kd&scale_y=lin&ind_y=false&rdim=region&idim=country:ETH&ifdim=region&hl=en_US&dl=en&ind=false, last updated 2 June 2016; and http://data.worldbank.org/country/ethiopia.

9 See "Global Gini Index (Distribution of Family Income) Ranking by Country," Mongabay.com, 2010, http://data.mongabay.com/reference/stats/rankings/2172.html.

10 FDRE Constitution Articles 47(1) and 50(1).

11 FDRE Constitution Article, 50(4).

12 See Fasil Nahum, *Constitution for a Nation of Nations: The Ethiopian Prospect* (Trenton, NJ: Red Sea, 1997). "Nations, Nationalities, and Peoples" is the phrase used in the Constitution to refer to ethnic groups. No distinction is provided between the three terms.

13 See Assefa Fiseha, *Federalism and the Accommodation of Diversity in Ethiopia: A Comparative Study* (Oisterwijk, Netherlands: Wolf Legal, 2006).

14 FDRE Constitution Article 39(3).

have eponymous national regional states, where in five of which they constitute the overwhelming majority,[15] the other regional states have very diverse ethnic make-ups, necessitating a complex arrangement of special sub-state territorial administrative units.[16]

The Constitution explicitly provides for only two orders of government: the federal or national order and the regional state governments. The *zonal, wereda*, and *kebele* administrations are established by the regional state constitutions. Addis Ababa is accorded a special status in the Constitution as the capital city of the federal government.[17] The Constitution grants residents of Addis Ababa the right to self-governance while recognizing the special interest of the Oromia National Regional State over Addis Ababa.[18] Even though the Constitution does not foresee the establishment of territories to be directly administered by the federal government, the city of Dire Dawa has also, through federal legislation, become a chartered city and federal territory just like Addis Ababa.[19] This arrangement was meant to be provisional resolution of an intractable dispute between Oromia and Somalia regional states, both of which claimed Dire Dawa (an important commercial and industrial hub) as falling within their territory.[20]

The FDRE Constitution was adopted in 1994. The Constitution was drafted and adopted during a three-year transition that started in 1991 at the end of a long civil war that pitted the Marxist-military junta, popularly referred to as the Deurg, against various armed ethno-national political groups.[21] The end of the civil war brought these victorious liberation fronts to power. In particular, the Tigray Peoples' Liberation

---

15 The Harari people make up a minority in the state with the same name.

16 See also Tsegaye Regassa, "Sub-National Constitutions in Ethiopia: Towards Entrenching Constitutionalism at State Level," *Mizan Law Review* 3 (2009): 63; Zemelak Ayitenew Ayele, "The Constitutional Status of Local Government in Federal Systems: The Case of Ethiopia," *Africa Today* 58 (2012): 89–109.

17 FDRE Constitution Article 49.

18 Ibid.

19 See *The Diredawa Administration Charter Proclamation No. 416/2004*.

20 John Markakis, "The Somali in Ethiopia," *Review of African Political Economy* 23 (1996): 567.

21 For an overview of Ethiopia's constitution-making process, see Kifle Wedajo, "The Making of the Ethiopian Constitution," in *The Making of the Ethiopian Constitution*, ed. Göran Hydén, 132–43 (Pretoria: Africa Institute of South Africa, 2001); see also Theodore M. Vestal, "An Analysis of the New Constitution of Ethiopia and the Process of Its Adoption," *Northeast African Studies* 3, no. 2 (1996): 26.

Front (TPLF), which was a principal protagonist of the civil war, and its allies, which together formed the Ethiopian Peoples' Revolutionary Democratic Front (EPRDF),[22] established the new federal system. Arguing that the formation of the modern Ethiopian state at the turn of the twentieth century was an imperial project that had resulted in the subjugation and assimilation of various ethnic groups, the EPRDF championed the right to self-determination up to and including secession and an identity-based federalism as solutions for these historical injustices. The EPRDF argued that while breaking up the Ethiopian state was undesirable, its radical reorganization was necessary to save Ethiopia from dissolution and chaos. The Constitution proclaims the "Nations, Nationalities, and Peoples of Ethiopia" as the sovereign constituent powers who came together to enter into a covenant and form the Federal Democratic Republic of Ethiopia. These legal and political propositions give Ethiopia's federal system the appearance of a *coming together* federalism in which sovereign nations, nationalities, and peoples came together to form the federation while, in reality, federalism was adopted as a means of *holding together* a country that was on the brink of disintegration.[23]

The EPRDF was the major proponent of federalism, contending that it was imperative to adopt federalism and embrace the right to self-determination in order to hold the country together and stave off its disintegration.[24] The option of federalism, particularly its ethnic component as introduced in Ethiopia, was found to be objectionable by those who considered it a harbinger to the total dismemberment of Ethiopia.[25] Traumatized by Eritrea's independence and the breakdown of Yugoslavia, Ethiopian nationalists had a hard time accepting the new federal setup. Nevertheless, the EPRDF, which was leading a transition government until the adoption of the FDRE Constitution, adopted the new Constitution through a constituent assembly in which

22 For a brief description of the party composition of the EPRDF, see below.

23 Fiseha, *Federalism and the Accommodation of Diversity in Ethiopia*, 211.

24 Andreas Eshete, "The Protagonists in Constitution Making in Ethiopia," in *Constitution-Making and Democratization in Africa*, ed. Göran Hydén, 69–78 (Pretoria: Africa Institute of South Africa, 2001).

25 See Minase Haile, "The New Ethiopian Constitution: Its Impact on Unity, Human Rights and Democracy," *Suffolk Transnational Law Review* 20, no. 1 (1996–7): 68. See also John Young, "Regionalism and Democracy in Ethiopia," *Third World Quarterly* 19 (1998): 191, 194.

its dominance was absolute. Although the constituent assembly was popularly elected through first-past-the-post elections conducted in more than 500 single-member district constituencies, and although there were many forums of direct participation in which public opinion was sought, the EPRDF was virtually the only organized political group taking part in the constitution-making process.[26] The assembly deliberated on the draft constitution and adopted its provisions through simple majority votes.[27] All other significant political actors were either in exile or looking from the margins during the adoption of the FDRE Constitution. This was true for groups that opposed and groups that favoured the adoption of a federal system.

Since its adoption, the federal system has undergone no major constitutional, structural, or territorial reforms. Significant political developments have affected federalism in Ethiopia, however. During the early days of the federation, the dominance of the TPLF within the EPRDF as well as that of the federal government over the regional states was very visible and overwhelming.[28] After the TPLF's accumulated experience in the armed struggle against the Deurg, it had the most organized, disciplined, and cohesive leadership among the four members of the EPRDF. Furthermore, the TPLF had firm control over the newly established military and security services, which were formed largely by former TPLF fighters. The TPLF was therefore visibly dominant and played the role of tutor and overseer to the other parties within the EPRDF. Senior TPLF members who were assigned to be informal political advisers in the regional states played a prominent role in running the regional state governments.[29]

Over time, the dominance of a single party within the EPRDF as well as that of the federal government over the regional states has become less

26 See Meaza Ashenafi, "Ethiopia: Process of Democratization and Development," in *Human Rights under African Constitutions: Realizing the Promise for Ourselves*, ed. Abdullahi Ahmed An-Na'im (Philadelphia: University of Pennsylvania Press, 2003), 31–3.

27 Article 11, Transitional Period Charter of Ethiopia No. 1.

28 John Young, "Ethnicity and Power in Ethiopia," *Review of African Political Economy* 23 (1996): 538.

29 International Crisis Group, *Ethiopia: Ethnic Federalism and Its Discontents*, Africa Report no. 153, 4 September 2009, 17, http://www.crisisgroup.org/~/media/Files/africa/horn-of-africa/ethiopia-eritrea/Ethiopia%20Ethnic%20Federalism%20and%20Its%20Discontents.ashx.

visible (although still very much present).[30] This change has been a result of two developments. First, the other parties within the EPRDF recruited members who were more educated and qualified than their original founders. Second and perhaps more important was the split within the TPLF in 2001, which led to the expulsion of many of its senior leaders. Together these developments reduced what had been a lopsided relationship between the TPLF and the other members of the EPRDF and allied parties.

When the FDRE Constitution was adopted, the very idea of a federal system was controversial.[31] Although they were not part of the constitution-making process, there were significant political actors who argued that maintaining a unitary system was essential to ensure the state's territorial integrity. However, over the past two decades, it has become quite clear that federalism will stay, at least as long as the EPRDF is in power. In May 2015, the EPRDF won 500 of the 547 seats in the House of Peoples' Representatives, while EPRDF allies won the other 47 seats. None of the political actors in the mainstream consider a unitary state to be a viable option. In principle, federalism has come to be seen as the most appropriate compromise between Ethiopia's centrifugal and centripetal forces.[32] Almost all major opposition political groups and even the most vehement critics of the EPRDF seem to support the idea of federalism, although they would prefer a federalism with less pronounced or no ethnic component. Some criticize the ethnic dimension of the federal system, the distribution of powers among the different orders of government, as well as the inclusion of a secession right that entitles nations, nationalities, and peoples to secede from the FDRE.[33]

---

30 Jan Záhořík, "Ethiopian Federalism Revisited," in *Africanists on Africa: Current Issues*, ed. Patrick Chabal and Peter Skalník (Berlin: LIT Verlag, 2009), 136. See also Christophe Van der Beken, "Federalism and the Accommodation of Ethnic Diversity: The Case of Ethiopia," in *Proceedings of the 3rd European Conference on African Studies*, 2009, 14; Jon Abbink, "Ethnic-Based Federalism and Ethnicity in Ethiopia: Reassessing the Experiment after 20 Years, "*Journal of Eastern African Studies* 5, no. 4 (2011): 596–618.

31 Aaron Tesfaye, *Political Power and Ethnic Federalism: The Struggle for Democracy in Ethiopia* (Lanham, MD: University Press of America, 2002), 5.

32 All major opposition political groups and even the most vehement critics support the idea of federalism these days, although they would prefer a federalism with less pronounced or no ethnic component.

33 See Assefa Mehretu, "Ethnic Federalism and Its potential to Dismember the Ethiopian State," *Progress in Development Studies* 12 (2012): 113–33; and Alem Habtu, "Multiethnic Federalism in Ethiopia: A Study of the Secession Clause in the Constitution," *Publius: The Journal of Federalism* 35 (2005): 313–35.

However, there are those who are happy with the federal arrangement as it is provided in the Constitution but who criticize the practice on the ground that the system is neither federal nor democratic. These groups contend that behind the rhetoric of federalism and empowerment of hitherto oppressed ethnic groups, the Ethiopian state is still centralized and oppressive.

Ethiopia's federal system is unusual in that the judiciary has no significant role in devising the system's doctrines, principles, and rules. This is so because, as will be discussed below, the Constitution and subsequent laws regarding constitutional interpretation have precluded the judiciary from undertaking constitutional review and interpreting the Constitution.[34] The role of interpreting the Constitution and resolving constitutional disputes has been entrusted to the House of Federation.[35] The House of Federation is a non-legislative federal house with significant powers, particularly over the functioning of the federal system. These powers include the authority to interpret the Constitution, determine the formula for distributing federal transfers to the regional states, resolve disputes between regional states, determine matters of civil law on which there is need for federal legislation, and authorize federal intervention into regional states.[36]

2. *Structural Features of Ethiopian Federalism*

As indicated earlier, the FDRE Constitution provides only for federal and state governments. The Constitution does not provide for a third order of government; it allows the regional states to determine their own subregional administrative structures. The only constitutional obligation the states have in organizing their internal administrative structure is the duty to ensure that "adequate power shall be granted to the lowest units of government to enable the People to participate directly in the administration of such units."[37] Of course, this right is relevant only to ethnic groups constituting a minority in a regional state where another ethnic group constitutes a majority or in regional states

34 See Article 83(1) of the FDRE Constitution. See also "Consolidation of the House of the Federation and Definition of Its Powers and Responsibilities Proclamation No. 251/2001" and "Council of Constitutional Inquiry Proclamation No. 250/2001."

35 FDRE Constitution Article 62(1).

36 See FDRE Constitution Article 62.

37 FDRE Constitution Article 50(4).

constituted by various ethnic groups. Taking their cue from these provisions of the Constitution, the state constitutions guarantee at least a two-tier system of local government.[38] They also provide special local governance units to accommodate minority ethnic groups or different ethnic groups that have no regional state of their own.[39]

The FDRE Constitution allocates legislative, executive, and judicial powers to both orders of government.[40] The allocation of powers is based principally on an extensive list of subject matters designated to fall within the jurisdiction of the federal government.[41] The Constitution also provides concurrent powers mainly with regard to taxation.[42] All powers that are not given expressly to the federal government or designated to be concurrent powers are reserved by the Constitution to the states.[43] Even though all residual powers are allocated to the states, the Constitution, perhaps superfluously or for good measure, still lists some powers belonging to the states. One reading of the list of state powers under Article 52(2) is that it partially fleshes out residual state powers. Furthermore, it is also possible to think of it as fortifying some of the essential powers of the regional states and also providing the states with administrative jurisdiction on matters such as land and natural resources over which the federal government has legislative jurisdiction. Had it not been for Article 52(2), the federal legislature's competence to enact laws on these matters would have given the federal government executive jurisdiction, because, in principle, executive and legislative powers go hand in hand in the Ethiopian federation, just like other countries that have a system of legislative federalism.

The powers given to the federal government include the usual subjects, such as defence, foreign affairs, regulation of interstate and

---

38 See the Revised Constitution of the Oromia National Regional State Constitution, Articles 70–101; the Revised Constitution of the Somali National Regional State, Articles 74–98; the Revised Constitutions of the Southern Nations Nationalities and Peoples' Regional State, Articles 80–114; the Revised Constitution of the Gambella People's National Regional State, Articles 75–109; the Constitution of the National Regional State of Tigray, Articles 68–69; the Revised Constitution of the Amhara National Regional State, Articles 73–107. See also Tsegaye Regassa, "Sub-National Constitutions in Ethiopia: Towards Entrenching Constitutionalism at State Level," *Mizan Law Review* 3 (2009): 61.

39 Fiseha, *Federalism and the Accommodation of Diversity in Ethiopia*, 435.

40 FDRE Constitution, Article 50(2).

41 FDRE Constitution, Articles 51 and 55.

42 FDRE Constitution, Article 98.

43 FDRE Constitution, Article 52(1).

foreign commerce, and transportation.[44] They also include some very broad powers stated in quite general terms, including but not limited to the power to formulate policies for overall economic and social development, draw up and implement plans and strategies of development, and establish national standards and basic criteria for the evaluation of policies in public health, education, science, technology, culture, and the protection and preservation of historical legacies.[45] Even though residual powers belong to the states, given the long list of federal powers and how some of these powers are expressed in broad terms, the balance of power seems to tip to the federal government. This is so particularly when we take into account the fact that most of the lucrative sources of revenue are allocated to the federal government, such as the power to "levy and collect custom duties, taxes and other charges on imports and exports" and to "levy and collect income, profit, sales and excise taxes on enterprises owned by the Federal Government."[46]

The Constitution's division of power allows for some flexibility. In addition to the vague and broad language that lists some of the powers of the federal government, the possibility of delegating federal powers to regional states provides additional flexibility in the distribution of competences between the two orders of government.[47] Although the Constitution provides that federal powers can be delegated to the states, it does not stipulate the procedure through which such delegation is to be made; hence, no formal delegation has been made yet. However, though not formally designated as delegations of federal power, there are some instances in which regional states execute federal legislation. The difficulty is that there is no indication that the states have consented to such arrangements. As such, instead of federal powers being delegated to regional states, it could be seen that regional state structures are being commandeered to execute federal policies and laws. For example, some environmental protection legislation adopted by the federal legislature imposes an obligation on the regional states to establish environmental agencies and enforce environmental standards adopted by the federal government.[48]

44 FDRE Constitution, Articles 51(6, 8, and 12).

45 FDRE Constitution, Articles 51(2 and 3).

46 FDRE Constitution, Article 97(1) and (3).

47 FDRE Constitution, Article 50(9).

48 See Environmental Protection Organs Establishment Proclamation No. 295/2002, Article 25; Environmental Impact Assessment Proclamation No. 299/2002, Article 12; and Environmental Pollution Control Proclamation No.300/2002, Article 7.

Given that the federal legislature unilaterally imposed this duty on the regional states, it is difficult to characterize this as a delegation of powers.

The Constitution is also silent on delegation of state powers to the federal government. However, in practice, the federal government has started to exercise the important power of administering land, which is expressly a power given to the states by the Constitution.[49] The federal government claims that it is exercising this power because it has been delegated authority by the concerned regional states.[50] Unfortunately, this matter has not been brought before the House of Federation; hence, there is no authoritative pronouncement on the constitutionality of federally administered land banks. This and similar practices show that the allocation of power by the Constitution is construed rather loosely, and its interpretation is determined largely by political actors through practice and usage.

What lies beneath is the centralized power structure of the ruling party, which is underpinned by the principle of democratic centralism.[51] This has meant that regardless of the distribution of powers in the Constitution, senior leaders of the ruling party who control the federal government can use the party channel to circumvent or, when necessary, ignore the constitutional allocation of powers. Another important inbuilt flexibility in the Constitution is a provision that empowers the House of Federation to authorize enactment of federal legislation on any civil matter that needs to be regulated by federal legislation in order to foster the creation of one economic community.[52] So far this power has been exercised only once, with regard to urban land registration.[53]

---

49 FDRE Constitution, Article 52(2)(d).

50 Getnet Alemu, *Rural Land Policy, Rural Transformation and Recent Trends In Large-Scale Rural Land Acquisitions In Ethiopia*, European Report on Development, 2012, 15, http://erd-report.eu/erd/report_2011/documents/dev-11-001-11researchpapers_alemu.pdf. See also Alemu, "Understanding Land Investment Deals in Africa Country Report: Ethiopia" (Oakland Institute, 2011), 27. The matter has not been presented to the House of Federation; therefore, the House's position on the issue is not known.

51 Theodore M. Vestal, *Ethiopia: A Post-Cold War African State* (Westport, CT: Greenwood Publishing, 1999), 104.

52 FDRE Constitution, Article 62(2).

53 The House of the Federation was called upon to resolve a dispute among parliamentarians on whether the House of Peoples' Representatives has the power to legislate on nationwide urban land registration. See Getnet Alemu, "Rural Land Policy, Rural Transformation and Recent Trends in Large-scale Rural Land Acquisitions in Ethiopia," https://ec.europa.eu/europeaid/sites/devco/files/erd-consca-dev-researchpapers-alemu-20110101_en.pdf.

An important area on which the Constitution envisions federal legislation and state execution is land. The Constitution empowers the federal government to enact a federal land-law while providing the states the power to administer land and implement that law.[54] Although the constitutional language used does not imply that the law enacted by the federal government should be framework legislation, in practice states have adopted their own land administration law, and the federal land-law is seen as framework legislation.[55] In fact, some states have even adopted land laws on the basis of which they have redistributed land. This issue is of particular importance because all land is publicly owned and agriculture is the mainstay of the country's economy, providing livelihood for nearly 80 per cent of the population.

Another area involving the execution of federal law by the states is criminal law. The Constitution empowers the federal legislature to enact a criminal code and authorizes the states to adopt criminal laws on matters not covered specifically by federal criminal laws.[56] On this basis, the federal government has adopted a comprehensive criminal code. Given that this is federal legislation, one would expect its enforcement to be the task of the federal police, prosecutor, and judiciary. In reality, the Federal Courts Establishment Proclamation has indirectly left the application of a large part of the criminal code to the regional states. The proclamation has designated some crimes as federal crimes, but all other crimes are understood to be non-federal, and their investigation and prosecution are left for the regional states.[57]

Similarly in other areas, such as environmental law, the federal government has enacted laws that are predicated partially on the administrative apparatus of the regional states for their execution.[58] While these practices could be seen as instances of delegation, there is no indication that the consent of the states has been secured in advance or that the federal government provides the financial compensation it is constitutionally required to provide to the states when it delegates its powers

54 FDRE Constitution, Articles 51(5) and 52(2)(d).

55 Abebe Mulatu, *A Review and Analysis of Land Administration & Use Legislation and Applications of Tthe Federal Democratic Republic Ethiopia and the Four Regional States of Amhara, Oromia, SNNPR and Tigrai*, Ethiopian Civil Society Network on Climate Change (2011), 7.

56 FDRE Constitution, Article 55(5).

57 Federal Court Proclamation No. 25/1996, Article 4.

58 See Environmental Pollution Control Proclamation No. 300/2002

and responsibilities.[59] However, such issues do not give rise to public disagreements between the states and the federal government. The ruling party and its affiliates have absolute control over both regional and federal governments, so the trend so far is that neither the states nor the federal government jealously guard their competences and seem to accept in equanimity acts of the other that could be seen as deviations from the constitutional allocation of power.

An interesting aspect of the allocation of power between the states and the federal government is the constitutional delegation of federal judicial powers to the regional states. During the adoption of the Constitution, mindful of the lack of trained legal professionals who could fill parallel federal and state judiciaries, the constitutional drafters delegated the powers of the federal high courts and federal first-instance courts to the regional supreme courts and high courts respectively.[60]

The Constitution does not have a provision equivalent to the U.S. federal supremacy clause and does not clearly say which law will prevail in the case of inconsistency.[61] However, the most convincing view on this question is that federal law should prevail where federal and state powers overlap. In all other cases where the matter falls within the exclusive jurisdiction of the federal or state government, inconsistencies are to be resolved by invalidating the law that was enacted in contravention to the constitutional delineation of powers. This position is supported by the constitutional provision that obliges states and the federal government to respect each other's sphere of competence.[62] Because the power of interpreting the Constitution is vested in the House of Federation, in theory, this house has the ultimate power to decide the competences of the states and the federal government.

II. The Ethiopian Judiciary and the House of Federation

The FDRE Constitution establishes a Federal Supreme Court invested with "supreme federal judicial authority," and it mandates regional states to establish their own supreme, high, and first-instance courts.[63]

---

59 FDRE Constitution, Article 94(1).

60 FDRE Constitution, Article 78(2) and Article 80(2) and (4).

61 Assefa Fiseha, "Federalism and the Adjudication of Constitutional Issues: The Ethiopian Experience," *Netherlands International Law Review* 52 (2005): 1, 10.

62 FDRE Constitution, Article 50(8).

63 FDRE Constitution, Article 78(2) and (3).

The Constitution gives the House of Peoples' Representatives (HPR) the power to establish the federal high court and first-instance courts it deems necessary, either nationwide or in some parts of the country only.[64] Until the establishment of federal high and first-instance courts by the House of Peoples' Representatives, the Constitution provided that the powers of the federal high court and first-instance courts would be exercised by state supreme courts and state high courts respectively.[65] This arrangement was seen as temporary because the Constitution gave the federal legislature the option of establishing federal high and first-instance courts and put an end to the delegation of judicial powers. Accordingly, the federal legislature has established high courts and partially revoked the delegated judicial powers of five of the regional states where the regional judiciaries were deemed lacking in technical competence.[66] The HPR has also established federal courts in the capital city Addis Ababa and in the city of Dire Dawa.[67] The Constitution mandates regional states to establish their own supreme, high, and first-instance courts.[68]

In addition to ordinary state and federal courts, other organs exercise judicial power. In Dire Dawa and Addis Ababa, there are municipal courts with their own first-instance authority and appellate courts established by the respective charters of the cities enacted by the regional House of Representatives.[69] The cities also have their own small-claims social courts as well as a number of quasi-administrative tribunals.[70] Disputes over jurisdiction among federal and municipal courts of the two cities are resolved by the Federal Supreme Court.[71] Furthermore, both the state and federal orders of government include

---

64 Ibid.

65 Ibid.

66 Federal High Court Establishment Proclamation No. 322/2003. This proclamation establishes federal high courts in the states of Afar, Benshangul, Gambella, Somali and Southern Nations Nationalities and Peoples.

67 Federal Court Proclamation No. 25/1996, Article 24(2).

68 FDRE Constitution, Article 78(3).

69 Addis Ababa City Government Revised Charter Proclamation No. 361/2003, Article 43; and the Dire Dawa Administration Charter Proclamation No. 416 12004, Article 35.

70 Addis Ababa City Government Revised Charter Proclamation No. 361/2003, Articles 46–50; and Dire Dawa Administration Charter Proclamation No. 416 12004, Articles 38–41.

71 Addis Ababa City Government Revised Charter Proclamation No. 361/2003, Articles 42(1); and Dire Dawa Administration Charter Proclamation No. 416 12004, Article 34(1).

sharia courts that decide on family and succession disputes among parties who have agreed to settle their disputes in accordance with Islamic law.[72]

In the federal judicial hierarchy, the Federal First Instance court exercises only original jurisdiction, while the Federal High Court has both original and appellate jurisdictions.[73] The Federal Supreme Court has very limited original jurisdiction and serves as the highest court of appeal in the federal judiciary.[74] The cassation division of the Federal Supreme Court exercises the power of cassation review when petitioners contend there has been a fundamental error of law in the final decision of either a federal or state court.[75] The decision of the cassation division, which is decided with a panel of five or more judges, sets a binding precedent both for federal and state courts.[76] The Constitution does not lay down in detail the structure and powers of the judiciary. As a result, the power and the structure of the federal judiciary are provided for largely by a proclamation enacted by the House of Peoples' Representatives.[77] There are many constitutionally problematic issues arising out of this proclamation from the perspective of federalism. One could point to four such issues in particular.

The first problematic aspect of the proclamation is the blurring of the subject-matter jurisdiction of federal and state courts. The Constitution stipulates that the Federal Supreme Court shall have the highest and final judicial power over federal matters and that state supreme courts shall have the highest and final judicial power over state matters.[78] The Constitution does not really say what constitutes state matters or federal matters for the purpose of the judiciary. Logically one would suppose that federal courts will adjudicate disputes arising under federal law, and state courts will adjudicate matters arising under state law. The Federal Courts Establishment Proclamation provides something

72 See Federal Courts of Sharia Consolidation No. 188/1999; see also Mohammed Abdo, "Legal Pluralism, Sharia Courts, and Constitutional Issues in Ethiopia," *Mizan Law Review* 5, no. 1 (2011): 72.

73 Federal Courts Proclamation No. 25/1996, Articles 11–15 as amended by Federal Courts (Amendment) Proclamation No. 138/1998 and Federal Courts Proclamation Re-amendment Proclamation No. 454/2005.

74 Federal Courts Proclamation No. 25/1996, Article 8 and 9.

75 Federal Courts Proclamation No. 25/1996, Article 10.

76 Federal Courts Proclamation Re-amendment Proclamation No. 454/2005, Article 2.

77 Federal High Court Establishment Proclamation No. 322/2003.

78 FDRE Constitution, Article 80(1 and 2).

along these lines in principle.[79] Then, after laying down the principle, the proclamation goes on to enumerate the civil and criminal jurisdiction of federal courts.[80] The enumerated criminal matters leave a significant swathe of the criminal code, which is a federal law, outside the jurisdiction of federal courts. On civil matters, the proclamation provides that depending on who is a party to a civil litigation (e.g., in suits involving a foreign party), federal courts should assume jurisdiction even when the applicable law is a state law. Such allocation of judicial power has not been provided for in the Constitution, and the Federal Courts Establishment Proclamation seems to be an attempt to fill these constitutional gaps.

The second difficult issue is the cassation power of the Federal Supreme Court over the decisions of the state courts on matters that fall squarely within state jurisdiction.[81] This practice is based on the Federal Courts Establishment Proclamation and entitles the federal judiciary not only to interpret state laws but also to set binding precedents that must be followed by state courts in interpreting their own state law.[82] This is so despite the fact that state supreme courts have their own cassation divisions to review basic errors of law, which, according to the FDRE Constitution, have power of cassation "over any final court decision on State matters which contains a basic error of law."[83]

Those who argue in favour of the constitutionality of federal cassation over state matters invoke Article 80(3)(a) of the Constitution, which provides: "The Federal Supreme Court has a power of cassation over *any final court decision* containing a basic error of law."[84] Those in favour of the practice have interpreted "any final court decision" as including decisions by state courts on matters falling within state jurisdiction. Those opposed to this practice argue that the power of cassation of the Federal Supreme Court should not extend beyond decisions of state courts exercising constitutionally delegated federal judicial authority. This practice, in effect, gives an organ of the federal judiciary

79 Federal Courts Proclamation No. 25/1996, Article 3.

80 Ibid., 4 and 5.

81 See Muradu Abdo, "Review of Decisions of State Courts over State Matters by the Federal Supreme Court," *Mizan Law Review* 1, no. 1 (2007): 61–74.

82 Federal Courts Proclamation No. 25/1996, Article 10; and Federal Courts Proclamation Re-amendment Proclamation No. 454/2005, Article 2.

83 FDRE Constitution, Article 80(3)(b) (emphasis added).

84 Emphasis added. See Abdo, "Review of Decisions of State Courts," 68.

the opportunity to have the last say on questions of state law. Taken together with the legally binding precedent-setting power of the cassation division of the Supreme Court, this practice enables the cassation division of the Federal Supreme Court to dictate the interpretation of state law by state courts. This is very problematic and seems to run counter to the spirit and logic of the federal arrangement established in the Constitution.

The third constitutionally problematic issue, from the perspective of federalism, is the language of adjudication in state courts that exercise constitutionally delegated federal judicial authority. Although these courts are applying federal law and acting as federal courts exercising a delegated power, they normally do not use the working language of the federal government; instead, they use the working language of their respective states. This is particularly the case in states and sub-state autonomous administrative units that have working languages different from the federal working language. The matter is further complicated because most of these cases end up before the Federal Supreme Court for appellate or cassation review where Amharic is the working language.

When we come to substantive laws, almost all of the substantive legal codes of Ethiopia are taken from the civil law tradition, while procedural laws are modelled after common law countries. English is the most widely spoken foreign language in Ethiopia and given it is the medium of instruction in higher education, so Ethiopia's legal professionals have very limited access to materials and commentaries from civil law countries. So comparative learning and research as well as legal education are highly influenced by American common law literature, which is relatively more accessible. The influence of the common law is also due to the historical and contemporary links of legal education in Ethiopia with common law countries such as the United States.

Ethiopia's Constitution of 1994 stands apart from most constitutions adopted during the twentieth century in that it does not provide for judicial review or a specialized constitutional court. Some members of the drafting commission proposed the establishment of a constitutional court or decentralized judicial review, but the driving force behind the making of the new constitution, the EPRDF, rejected both proposals.[85]

85 See Minutes of the 94th Regular Session of the Council of Representatives of the Transitional Government of Ethiopia (unpublished), 213–17; and Minutes of the Constitutional Assembly (unpublished) 5:4–19, 1994.

Instead of a constitutional court or constitutional review by the ordinary judiciary, those who adopted and ratified the Constitution provided for a system of constitutional interpretation in which the upper house of parliament (i.e., the House of Federation) with the help of the Council of Constitutional Inquiry (CCI) serves as the authoritative and ultimate interpreter of the Constitution.[86]

The House of Federation is a non-legislative house in which every ethnic group in the country is represented by at least one representative, with one additional representative for every one million of each group's population.[87] Members of the House of Federation can be elected by the state councils of the regional states or be directly elected by members of the ethnic group they represent (the practice so far is election by state councils).[88] Although the House of Federation is supposed to provide the final and authoritative interpretation of the Constitution, the CCI is an auxiliary organ that is supposed to provide expert assistance to the House of Federation on the task of constitutional interpretation. This council is composed largely of lawyers and includes as ex officio members the president and the deputy president of the Federal Supreme Court.[89] Constitutional disputes arising in ordinary courts or raised outside the courts are supposed to be presented to the CCI first, and the council is expected to issue a recommendation that can be adopted or rejected by the House of Federation.[90]

The CCI can also reject a request of constitutional interpretation or a constitutional issue submitted before it if it is of the opinion that the matter does not require constitutional interpretation.[91] In such cases, the petitioner for interpretation or the applicant can appeal to the House of Federation.[92] In practice, most petitions brought before the CCI are rejected as not necessitating constitutional interpretation; so far, therefore, only a few of such appeals have been successful.

The number of petitions submitted before the council is small and many of them are rejected, so the House of Federation has decided only a handful of cases. Such decisions, however, are binding in all similar

86 FDRE Constitution, Articles 62(1), 82 and 83.
87 FDRE Constitution, Articles 61(1) and (2).
88 FDRE Constitution, Article 61.
89 FDRE Constitution, Article 82(2).
90 FDRE Constitution, Article 84(1).
91 Council of Constitutional Inquiry Proclamation No. 250/2001, Article 17(3).
92 Ibid., Article 18.

cases and set a precedent.[93] Unfortunately, the House has so far published only three of its decisions.[94] Apart from constitutional law scholars, the Council of Constitutional Inquiry and the House of Federation receive very little attention from legal practitioners and the media. Members of the CCI engage with the council part-time, and most have full-time jobs. Their meetings are never public and their proceedings are not published. Normally, the House of Federation also meets only twice a year,[95] and the press and the public at large pay very little attention to its activities as the ultimate interpreter of the Constitution. Cognizant of the problems in the institutional set up of constitutional interpretation, a bill to reform the organization of the CCI was adopted in August 2013.[96]

Given that the system of constitutional interpretation described above is unusual, why did the framers of the Constitution adopt this system? In the debates leading up to the Constitution's adoption, proponents of the system presented arguments to reject constitutional review by ordinary courts or a constitutional court. One major argument revolved around the nature of constitutional interpretation. Proponents argued that the power to interpret a constitution is, in effect, the power to amend a constitution in the guise of giving meaning to a constitutional text.[97] They also contended that giving unelected judges such a power over a document that is an expression and embodiment of the sovereignty of the nations, nationalities, and peoples (NNPs) of Ethiopia would be undemocratic.[98] They argued further that the Constitution is not just a legal document but also a pre-eminently political document; hence, its interpretation cannot be considered a mere technical exercise to be left to professionals but a political act in which the nations, nationalities, and peoples of Ethiopia in whom all sovereign power reside should have the final say.[99] So the arguments against constitutional review by judges were rooted in the equation of constitutional interpretation with

93 Consolidation of the House of the Federation and Definition of Its Powers and Responsibilities Proclamation No. 251/200, Article 11(1).

94 See *Journal of Constitutional Decisions* 1, The House of the Federation of the Federal Democratic Republic of Ethiopia 1.2007 (2000 Ethiopian calendar).

95 FDRE Constitution, Article 67(1).

96 Council of Constitutional Inquiry Proclamation No. 798/20, 13.

97 See Minutes of the 94th Regular Session of the Council of Representatives of the Transitional Government of Ethiopia (unpublished) 213–17; and Minutes of the Constitutional Assembly (unpublished), 5:4–19, 1994.

98 Ibid. See also FDRE Constitution, Article 8(1).

99 Ibid.

constitutional amendment, in the nature of the constitution as a political document, the need to maintain the sovereignty of Ethiopia's NNPs, and the perceived undemocratic nature of constitutional review by judges.

Therefore, Ethiopia's constitutional system entrusts a political organ, namely, the House of Federation, not courts, with the task of resolving disputes that might arise in the allocation of powers between the orders of government.[100] While constitutional courts or the ordinary judiciary serve as umpires for these kinds of disputes in most other federal states, in Ethiopia there is neither an ordinary court nor a specialized constitutional court with a mandate to interpret the Constitution in order to resolve federalism-related disputes.

The framers of the Constitution were very suspicious of the judiciary and feared that the new constitutional order could be undermined through the guise of interpretation by judges. To understand this fear, it is important to realize the political and sociological reality of the period in which there was a huge gap between those who were framing the Constitution and those who staffed the judiciary. The political sponsors of the Constitution were mainly ethno-nationalist rebels who had fought for almost two decades to overthrow the Dergue. They viewed those who staffed the judiciary, the bureaucracy, and academia as members or sympathizers of the previous regime. The political forces behind the new Constitution were rebels interested in a complete overhaul of the system; they saw the judiciary as an establishment institution with views that were not aligned with the new federal dispensation.

There has been much controversy among constitutional law scholars regarding whether or not the ordinary judiciary has residual or inherent power to interpret the Constitution. Some have also argued that the drafters of the Constitution did not intend to strip the judiciary of all power to interpret the Constitution. These arguments, though animating and interesting in academia, have not been well received in practice. Not to leave any doubt on the matter, the House of Peoples' Representatives has adopted two proclamations that unequivocally bar the ordinary judiciary from entertaining constitutional disputes.[101] Contrary to some views and even indications from the Council of Constitutional Inquiry that the constitutionality of administrative acts, as

100 Adem Kassie Abebe, "Umpiring Federalism in Africa: Institutional Mosaic and Innovations," *African Studies Quarterly* 13, no. 4 (2013): 65–7.

101 Assefa Fiseha, "Separation of Powers and Its Implications for the Judiciary in Ethiopia," *Journal of Eastern African Studies* 5, no. 4 (2011): 706.

opposed to legislative acts, could be reviewed by ordinary courts, the proclamations clearly provide that all constitutional disputes concerning acts of legislatures (federal and state) or acts of executives (federal and state) are to be decided by the House of Federation.

The courts have shown little inclination to carve out a role for themselves in the interpretation of the Constitution.[102] To avoid the trouble of being referred to the House of Federation, lawyers normally prefer to rely on statutory as opposed to constitutional provisions when they make claims. Courts also are careful not to be seen as usurping the power of the House of Federation; hence, they refrain from expounding on the meaning and implication of constitutional provisions. If and when they do refer to constitutional provisions, it is normally on matters considered to be politically non-sensitive or in perfunctory declarations of the constitutionality of a legislative or executive action in question. Therefore, the ordinary courts have not played a significant role in developing a constitutional jurisprudence.

III. Federalism Jurisprudence

Although it has been more than two decades since the FDRE Constitution came into force, very little constitutional jurisprudence has been developed in Ethiopia. This is particularly true in relation to federalism. The House of Federation has yet to determine a "division of power" dispute in exercising its authority as the final interpreter of the Constitution.[103] The few federalism-related constitutional disputes disposed of by the House were mainly related to the question of self-determination[104] and other parts of the Bill of Rights. The structural

---

102 Takele S. Bulto, "Judicial Referral of Constitutional Disputes in Ethiopia: From Practice to Theory," *African Journal of International and Comparative Law* 19, no. 1 (2011): 100.

103 Though, strictly speaking, we might not call them constitutional disputes, the House has also been called upon to resolve border disputes among the regional states. The most contentious and famous example is the Oromia-Somali Regional States Border case (2002). See *A Decision Rendered Regarding the Identity Claim of the Silte People*. See *Journal of Constitutional Decisions* 1.

104 A good example is the *Silte Case* (2001), which concerned whether the Silte constitute a distinct nation, nationality, and people. Until then, the Silte were regarded as a subgroup of the Gurage ethnic group. Representatives of the Silte successfully petitioned the House of Federation for their right to self-determination and were able to get recognition as a distinct ethnic group. See Ahmed Shide, "Conflicts along Oromia-Somali State Boundaries: The Case of Babile District," in *First National Conference on Federalism, Conflict and Peace Building* (Addis Ababa: United Printers, 2003), 96–112.

parts of the Constitution and those related to the allocation of powers between the federal and state governments have yet to be interpreted by the House. During the early days after the adoption of the Constitution, the CCI was presented with a challenge to the constitutionality of the land redistribution undertaken by the state of Amhara. The petitioners argued that a regional state does not have the power to redistribute land without a federal law authorizing such a measure, because the Constitution allocates the power to enact legislation for the regulation of land to the federal government and assigns to the regional states the power to administer land. The petitioners argued that the land redistribution carried out by the state is inconsistent with the constitutional distribution of competences between the two orders of government. The CCI dismissed the petition because it decided that Amhara was within its power to administer land when it undertook the redistribution of rural land; therefore, there was no need for constitutional interpretation, and it rejected the petition without referring it to the House of Federation.[105] The Council also pointed out that the House of Peoples' Representatives has adopted a land law that retroactively endorses state laws on land administration as long as they are not contrary to the federal Land Administration Proclamation of 89/1989.[106] The House of Federation did not, therefore, need to decide on the petition. The House of Peoples' Representatives followed up this decision by enacting a federal land administration law that retroactively endorsed the land law issued by Amhara and by other regional states as well. In the end, the case was not presented to the House of Federation and was dismissed after review by the CCI.

Although it is not a decision emanating from an adversarial case and is not widely reported, the House of Federation has issued an advisory opinion on the respective competence of the regional states and the federal government to enact legislation on family matters.[107] The advisory opinion was issued on the basis of a request by the Office of the Prime Minister of the FDRE. In its opinion, the House expressed the view that while the federal government can adopt a family law for the two

---

105 *Biyadglegn Meles et al. v. the Amhara National Regional State* (Council of Constitutional Inquiry, 1998); case unpublished, on file with the author.

106 Ibid.

107 Constitutional Inquiry Raised regarding the Promulgation of Family Law and the Decision of the House of Federation (April 2000), unpublished and available on file with the author.

chartered federal cities, the regional states can adopt family laws for the rest of the country on the basis of their residual power. Accordingly, the Federal Family Code adopted by the House of Peoples' Representatives is applicable only in Addis Ababa and Dire Dawa. Meanwhile, all regional states, except Afar and Somali, have adopted their own family laws.

Another recurrent federalism-related case the House of the Federation has to entertain involves to the right to self-determination. Because the Constitution recognizes the right of ethno-linguistic communities to full self-government, including the right to establish their own state within the federation, the petition of a group to be recognized as a separate community is directly related to the federal system. In dealing with these petitions, every group's effort to be recognized as a separate ethnic community necessarily involves the application of the constitutional criterion of peoplehood. However, the House, true to its political nature, has never systematically dealt with the meanings of the criteria laid down in the Constitution. Hence, even in this most recurrent of federalism cases, the House has not developed a meaningful jurisprudence.[108]

As can be seen from this discussion, save for an advisory opinion and a case that could have (perhaps should have) made it to the House of Federation, there is very little federalism case law in Ethiopia. With the enactment of the proclamations consolidating the powers of the House of Federation and the Council of Constitutional Inquiry, the House of Peoples' Representatives unequivocally expressed its view that the judiciary has no power to adjudicate constitutional disputes. While some scholars have argued that these proclamations are of dubious constitutionality, the judiciary has shied away from assuming a substantial role in resolving constitutional disputes. Occasionally the courts interpret some provisions of the constitutional bill of rights they consider to be innocuous, such as those concerning the rights of children,[109] but they have not shown any inclination to invoke other provisions of the Constitution.

---

108 For the most recent of these petitions, see Minutes of the House of the Federation, 4th Parliamentary Period, 5th Year, 2nd Ordinary Session, 24 June 2015.

109 See, for example, *Tsedale Demissie v. Ato Kifle Demissie*, Federal Supreme Court Cassation Division Cassation file no. 23632, 5 October 2007, where the Cassation Division Cassation interpreted and applied the principle of the best interest of the child as enshrined in the FDRE Constitution.

Formally speaking, the House of Federation assisted by the CCI is expected to serve as the constitutional umpire and settle federalism-related disputes. However, the House cannot be said to have discharged this function either. If neither the courts nor the House of Federation are resolving federalism-related disputes, who is resolving disputes? This brings us to another peculiar aspect of the Ethiopian federal system as it has evolved during the last two decades.

Normally, federalism-related disputes arise in either of two scenarios. In the first scenario, the federal government and states disagree about the boundaries of their respective powers. In the second scenario, private entities aggrieved by an act of a federal or state government challenge the constitutional competence of a federal or state government to take the administrative or legislative measure that they are complaining against. In Ethiopia, neither scenario is likely to lead to litigation before a court of law or the House of Federation.

Such disputes are unlikely to end up in courts for the obvious reason that the Constitution and subsequent legislation have denied the courts the power to adjudicate them. These disputes are unlikely to be presented to the House of Federation for several reasons. The most important is that the ruling party, the EPRDF, controls directly or through its affiliates all regional state governments, the House of Federation, and the federal government. Formally, the EPRDF is a coalition of four regional and ethnic parties, each administering a major national regional state. Three of these parties – the TPLF, the Amhara National Democratic Movement, and the Oromo Peoples' Democratic Organization – are supposed to represent the three biggest ethnic groups in Ethiopia. The other member of the coalition is the Southern Ethiopian People's Democratic Movement, which is an amalgam of parties that ostensibly represent the ethnic groups that comprise the Southern Nations Nationalities and Peoples' Regional State. The remaining regional states are administered by other parties that are not formal members of the EPRDF but are affiliated with it in the status of partners. These parties are also included in the federal government, which has been controlled by the EPRDF since the inauguration of the FDRE. Formally, this gives the impression that Ethiopia has a very pluralistic federalism in which no party is administering more than one regional state.

However, despite this appearance of pluralism and decentralization, the EPRDF is a very centralized and hierarchical party. The top leadership of the party controls member organizations of the EPRDF as well as its partner organizations.[110] All major policy decisions and initiatives emanate from the centre or must secure the approval of the central party leaders. Furthermore, in response to the principle of "democratic centralism," which is strictly observed within the EPRDF, despite internal disagreements and debate before decisions are made by the party leadership, once a decision has been adopted, the rank and file as well as the leaders of the party are expected to fully endorse the decision as if they had agreed with it from the beginning. These debates are often concealed from the public and even from ordinary members of the party. Usually only the top party leaders are privy to these debates. Once the debate is over and a decision has been adopted, it is the duty of all party members to implement the decision to the best of their abilities. No dissent or reservation is aired in public. Given this practice and culture of the EPRDF, which is rooted in the ideological views of the party as well as its genesis as an armed group that needed to maintain its cohesiveness for survival, dissent and debate in the party are not encouraged and are hidden from the public whenever possible.

It is unlikely therefore that EPRDF member organizations who control regional states will engage in legal wrangling with the federal government in front of the House of Federation. Any legislation, policy, or measure of the federal government or the regional states is usually sanctioned by the party. Protests and objections to such policies, measures, or legislation are unwelcome and unusual once the party's top leaders have adopted the decision. Democratic centralism leaves little room for second-guessing the party leadership, especially when such second-guessing would challenge the constitutionality of the acts endorsed by the top leaders. Any possible difference that member organizations of the EPRDF might have is addressed inside the party, seldom becomes public, and is not framed as a legal constitutional issue. This is a primary reason that not a single case has been brought before the House of Federation in which the different orders of government were pitted against one another. Furthermore, considering the fact that the EPRDF reigns supreme in the House of Federation, there is little to be gained by the members and partners of the EPRDF to take their disputes to the House of Federation.

---

110 See, for example, Abdi Ismail Samatar, "Ethiopian Ethnic Federalism and Regional Autonomy: The Somali Test," *Bildhaan: An International Journal of Somali Studies* 5, no. 1 (2005), 63–7.

To illustrate how this dynamic works, consider the abortive attempt by Oromia to adopt its own criminal procedure code.[111] The Oromia Regional State drafted a criminal procedure law as part of its judicial reform program. The process of drafting the criminal procedure code was undertaken after regional state authorities reached an understanding with federal authorities that regional states have the constitutional authority to adopt their own criminal procedure code. However, after the draft was complete, the federal government changed its position. The federal minister of justice notified state authorities that the power to adopt a criminal procedure law belongs to the federal government and that the regional state should not adopt its own criminal procedure law. Although the state had expended considerable resources in drafting its criminal procedure law, taking the matter to the House of Federation and challenging the position of the federal government was not a realistic option for the state.

This discussion still leaves unanswered the question of why private actors do not challenge the constitutionality of government actions based on the federal distribution of powers in the Constitution. There are several explanations for the lack of this kind of constitutional case. One is that the House of Federation is not an impartial arbiter of disputes. The House is clearly and by design a political organ, and since its inauguration, it has been controlled by the ruling coalition, whose cohesiveness and strict discipline are the attributes of a single party. As a result, challenging the constitutionality of a government act before this house – which is controlled by the same party that controls both the executive and the legislature in all orders of government in the country – make it a futile exercise. For example, in the general election of May 2015, the EPRDF and its allies won all contested seats at the federal and regional level, enabling it to continue its monopoly of seats in the House of Federation. Hence, almost no one pursues a constitutional case against the regional states or the federal government, because the House of Federation is not seen as an impartial umpire. However, although the House of Federation is not an impartial arbiter, some cases based on the bill of rights of the Constitution are presented to the House, while none based on the federal distribution of powers

111 The information for this paragraph was obtained from a judicial official from the Oromia National Regional State who was involved in the Justice Sector Reform of the state and who wishes to remain anonymous.

have been presented; therefore additional factors might explain the absence of federalism cases decided by the House of Federation.

One reason is the broad nature of federal powers under the Constitution. Many of the provisions that distribute powers between the federal government and the states are vague and general. Although there is an enumerated list of federal and concurrent powers, few matters can be considered federal subjects if the pertinent constitutional provisions are stretched a little. In addition to the reasons discussed above, the chances of any constitutional challenge to the constitutionality of the acts of the federal government on the basis of federalism are very slim.

The lack of real political plurality among the parties that control the orders of government also discourages proceedings on federal aspects of the Constitution. Such challenges are likely to be frustrated because the federal and state governments would stand together and render the case moot. If a third party challenged the actions of regional states, alleging that they had usurped federal powers, the federal government would somehow endorse the act of the regional states. The federal government could easily do so by delegating its power to the regional state. Another avenue to accomplish the same end would be for the federal government to adopt the same law or to take the same administrative measure itself. Any challenge to the actions of the federal government on the basis of the constitutional distribution of powers could be easily frustrated in a similar fashion. Although the Constitution says nothing about the delegation of state powers to the federal government, in practice the federal government has assumed the power of giving land to foreign investors, claiming that this function has been delegated to it by the regional states. Furthermore, the regional states can be counted on to do the bidding of the federal government if need be.

IV. Conclusion

The Constitution presents itself as a covenant among the nations, nationalities, and peoples of Ethiopia. Fearful that the covenant and its objectives would be subverted by professional judges, the Constitution's framers entrusted constitutional interpretation to a political organ in which Ethiopia's nations, nationalities, and peoples are supposed to be represented. This has precluded the judiciary from interpreting the Constitution and delineating the constitutional scope of the powers of the regional states and the federal government. The EPRDF has absolute control of both the federal and state governments, so disputes about the scope of power of the two orders of government have been muted and resolved through the party apparatus. As a result, there is hardly any federalism case law. The centralized party structure in which commands are issued from the top has left little room for pluralistic interaction among orders of government and has obviated the need, as well as the opportunity, to develop a federalist jurisprudence.

Would the current arrangements function properly if the different orders of government were controlled by different political parties? In this eventuality, the absence of an impartial arbiter and the inherently partisan nature of the constitutional interpreter could create serious problems. So long as the same party or coalition of parties controls the House of Federation, intergovernmental disputes between the regional states and the federal government can be solved within the party coalition or settled by the House of Federation (of course, with the assistance of the experts in the Council of Constitutional Inquiry). But if the federal government and one or more regional states were controlled by rival parties, and if one of these parties controlled the House of Federation, it would be very difficult for the House of Federation to settle constitutional disputes among such parties. Given the mistrust and antagonism that characterizes the relationship of political parties in Ethiopia, the House of Federation would easily become entangled in the antagonism between the political parties. This would mean that it would not have the respect and trust of the parties in dispute necessary to resolve their conflict. Therefore, it might be necessary to consider this problem seriously and learn from the experiences of other federal countries before a crisis materializes.

7 The Federal Constitutional Court of Germany: Guardian of Unitarism and Federalism

ARTHUR BENZ

I. Introduction

Powerful federal courts are often assumed to be driving forces towards centralization and unitarism. If this is indeed a tendency observable in many federations, the German Federal Constitutional Court (FCC) is an important exception. In comparative terms, Germany's constitution (the Basic Law) assigns the FCC a very significant role within the political system. Moreover, because redistributive conflicts between governments and party political conflicts are difficult to settle by "joint decision-making" between federal and Land representatives, judgments of the FCC often overcome governance problems. This role of the Court has injected a strong element of legalism into German politics and has made it a key political player. In performing this role, while the FCC has supported unitarism in some respects, in other important respects it has supported federalism. In particular, the Court's rulings on individual and social rights have usually reinforced unitarism while its rulings on most other matters, since about 1980, have usually supported decentralized federalism. The FCC's effect on the operation of German federalism has involved a dynamic interplay between the courts and the political branches of government. This chapter explains the way German courts, especially the FCC, have contributed to the evolution of German federalism with important political consequences in several respects.

A significant feature of German federalism is that the division of powers and intergovernmental relations are regulated by relatively detailed constitutional norms. Because the application of law is often a matter of dispute, one might expect courts to be decisive actors in the operation of German federalism. One also might assume that legalism and powerful courts maintain the status quo and contribute to the rigidity of the federal system.

There is some truth in these assumptions. However, law and courts have not made German federalism especially inflexible. After a period of centralization and the evolution of joint decision-making during the first two decades of the Federal Republic, there has been an incremental but steady trend towards decentralization, especially since the 1980s, either through changes in policymaking or through formal constitutional change. Different forces have contributed to this dynamic, but given the legalist tradition of the German state, the application and interpretation of the law by the courts has been an essential factor. In particular, the powerful FCC has to be taken into account. The Court has supported changes initiated by the federal and Land governments by settling conflicts between them and by interpreting the constitution. Decisions of the Court have also set the agenda for constitutional amendments and have induced the legislature to make statutory changes that have shaped the federal system in important ways.

Although a federal institution, the FCC has never straightforwardly favoured the federal government. Overall, the impact of its decisions has been ambivalent. On one hand, the Court stipulated a clear separation of powers and emphasized the statehood prerogatives of the Länder. Yet it refrained from intervening in allocation-of-powers disputes on the ground that such issues were "political" and thus supported the federal government's attempts to expand its powers. Since 1994, when a constitutional amendment introduced a new procedure compelling the Court to determine intergovernmental competence conflicts, it has followed the opinions prevailing in political debates. Accordingly, the Court has supported decentralization with its decisions on the application of the subsidiarity principle in legislation. On the other hand, the Court has encouraged partnership and solidarity among governments and has clearly favoured unitary solutions by its decisions on human and civil rights. In particular, judgments on the principle of equality have required federation-wide policies. Thus, although the Court seems to have shaped its federalism doctrine generally in favour of the Land governments, it still supports unitary federalism with its decisions on constitutional complaints filed by individual citizens.

Throughout the history of the Federal Republic of Germany, the Constitutional Court has secured ever-increasing power in politics. This power has been challenged by the European Court of Justice (ECJ) since Germany became part of an ever-closer European Union. While the ECJ has strengthened citizen rights and uniform regulation or deregulation, the German Court has defended the integrity of the constitutional foundation of German government, including federalism. The Europeanization of the court system has thus reinforced contradictory dynamics. This ambivalence of court decisions between territorial diversity and uniformity (or equality) reflects contrasting forces currently shaping the dynamics of German federalism. The following sections explain these developments and effects on federalism.

II. Federal System

1. General Characteristics

German federalism emerged from struggles for power among rulers and governments. For centuries the "German Empire" existed as a confederation of states. After the Thirty Years War (1618–48), the states prevailed over the German emperor. In 1806, this construction was formally dissolved and replaced by a weak confederation. A federal state came into being with the unification of Germany in 1871. The constitutional framework of the federal system as it now exists is set forth in the Basic Law, which was established in 1949 in the West German Federal Republic and in 1989 remained the basis of unified Germany without major amendments. Both the ratification of the constitution and the unification process reflected the federal character of the German state. In 1949, the Land parliaments approved the Basic Law. In 1989, the governments of the Länder that were created after the collapse of the centralized communist regime in the German Democratic Republic (GDR) decided to join the Federal Republic. In legal terms, the federal and Land governments constitute the federation, as two orders of "statehood." The constitution recognizes the autonomy of local governments. Although in legal terms, they are administrative units of the Länder, local governments have the right to defend their autonomy by initiating proceedings before the FCC.

Germany's federal system combines a territorial division of powers with a highly uniform legal system operating within a relatively homogeneous society. Deep concern for equality of economic and social conditions is expressed by state-wide parties and interest organizations.[1]

1 Peter J. Katzenstein, *Policy and Politics in West Germany: The Growth of a Semi-Sovereign State* (Philadelphia: Temple University Press, 1987).

Germany's approximately 80 million inhabitants are rather evenly distributed across the country, living mostly in smaller cities and towns developed from the early European "city belt from Italy to the North Sea."[2] There have always been economic disparities between East and West Germany and between the North and the South. These inequalities increased during the forty years of communist rule in the GDR, from which the five eastern Länder are only slowly recovering. Nevertheless, the country is not deeply divided in economic terms. Redistributive welfare policies, made feasible by continuous economic growth, find support in a territorially integrated nation. Wealth inequality, social problems, and immigration are more intense within than between the Länder.

The unitary characteristics of German federalism have their roots in the Reformation and the late nineteenth century. The Reformation produced a confessional division of territories, but also supported a homogenization of the German language through Martin Luther's translation of the Bible. The former caused political decentralization in culturally homogeneous Länder, which later developed into modern states. The German language constituted the basis of social integration across the Länder and the later emergence of German nationalism. For centuries, the German Empire experienced the rise of cultural movements promoting the idea of one nation accompanied by a decline of central rule challenged by powerful administrations among the Länder. Unification of the German nation state was secured under the hegemony of Prussia only in 1871. In those days, centralization was promoted by the economic pressure of industrialization and by emerging "national" parties. However, administrative capacities were retained by the Länder, which maintained those powers pursuant to the federal bargain.[3] Later, a functional division of power developed, which involved centralization of legislation together with decentralization of administration and the participation of the Land governments in federal legislation through the federal council (the Bundesrat). This highly characteristic feature of German federalism requires close cooperation between governments. In many policy fields, federal legislation has to be coordinated with Land governments, and to implement its laws, the federal

2 Stein Rokkan, *State Formation, Nation-Building, and Mass Politics in Europe: The Theory of Stein Rokkan, Based on His Collected Works* (Oxford: Oxford University Press, 1999), 158.

3 Daniel Ziblatt, *Structuring the State: The Formation of Italy and Germany and the Puzzle of Federalism* (Princeton: Princeton University Press, 2006).

government has to rely on Land or local government administration. Cultural diversities among Länder going back to the Reformation and persisting during the nineteenth century[4] were levelled in the course of the twentieth century when two world wars and dictatorships radically transformed society.

How German federalism works is highly influenced by the logic of democracy.[5] During the First World War, Germany evolved from a constitutional monarchy into a parliamentary democracy, which collapsed in 1933 and was restored after 1949 in the West German Republic. Since then, intergovernmental negotiations have usually been shaped by political competition between state-wide parties operating at both levels of the federal system. More often than not, the federal executive and its supporting majority in parliament have been confronted by a Bundesrat in which a majority of votes has been controlled by Land executives supported by the opposition parties. In such cases, political actors representing competing parties have to find agreements and are accountable to their electorates for the result. This particular form of democratic federalism poses a serious dilemma for political actors.[6] They have to choose between competitive and cooperative behaviour without being able to calculate the effects. One way to avoid this dilemma, which is applied more often than not in cases of serious conflict or especially salient issues, is to pass the decision to the Federal Constitutional Court.

2. *Constitutional and Legal Framework*

As in every modern federal system, law is essential to the practical working of German federalism. The particular history of Germany, however, explains why its constitutional and legal framework has been especially important. Drawing on its distinctive legalistic state tradition, the German experience of dictatorship has made the territorial division of

---

4 Derek W. Urwin, "Germany: From Geographical Expression to Regional Accommodation," in *The Politics of Territorial Identity: Studies in European Regionalism*, ed. Stein Rokkan and Derek W. Urwin, 165–249 (London: Sage, 1982).

5 Gerhard Lehmbruch, *Parteienwettbewerb im Bundesstaat: Regelsysteme und Spannungslagen im Institutionengefüge der Bundesrepublik Deutschland*, 3rd ed. (Wiesbaden: Westdeutscher Verlag, 2000).

6 Arthur Benz, "Making Democracy Work in a Federal System," *German Politics* 24, no. 1 (2015): 8–11.

powers and the constitutional guarantee of rights and procedures binding on governments of particular relevance. Accordingly, the division of the federation into Länder and the participation of the Land governments in federal legislation are protected against constitutional amendments (Basic Law, Art. 79 Sec. 3). The rule of law is also constitutionally entrenched as the third fundamental principle of the political system supporting federalism and democracy. All powers are subject to law. Citizens have a right to appeal to courts, which are the guardians of the constitution. As a consequence, law and politics are closely entwined.

The division of powers between the federal, Land, and local governments and procedures of intergovernmental relations are determined by the Basic Law. The principles of subsidiarity, solidarity, and mutual trust among governments ("federal comity") constitute guidelines of the federal order. Uniformity of the law and of public services is also of considerable importance. Constitutional rules providing for the sharing of tax revenues, joint tasks, and fiscal equalization aim to achieve balanced living conditions in all regions of Germany. Although residual powers are located in the Land governments, most areas of legislation are allocated to the federal order and, as a rule, the Land and local governments implement federal law. Thus, cooperative federalism is not an informal practice but is rooted in the constitution. When they believe that their powers are being adversely affected by proposed federal laws, the Land governments have a right to veto the proposed laws through the Bundesrat.

Although federalism might be thought to imply that the federal and Land governments share sovereignty on an equal basis, Germany's legal system, like that of most modern federations, is structured hierarchically insofar as federal law has supremacy over laws passed by Land legislatures (Art. 31). However, a constitutional amendment introduced in 2006 took a step towards greater plurality of law by allowing Land parliaments to pass laws deviating from a federal regulation in enumerated matters of concurrent legislation (Art. 72, sec. 3, as amended). Because Germany is a member of the European Union, federal and Land law is also subject to European law. However, the supremacy of European law introduced by rulings of the European Court of Justice (ECJ) has been disputed by the German FCC. In practice, the hierarchical structure of the legal order clearly outweighs the concurrence of law both in the EU and in German federalism.

Constitutional law and federalism nonetheless remain matters of dispute. Indeed, there is in Germany an increasing tension between uniformity of law or of living conditions on one hand and diversity of policymaking in the Länder on the other. Since the turn of the century, this tension has triggered serious conflicts among governments, and constitutional reforms have so far failed to solve them. This has provided an additional impetus for the FCC to be increasingly involved in adjudicating federalism-related legal issues.

Since coming into force in 1949, the Basic Law has been amended sixty times (as of July 2016) with the required two-thirds majority in the federal parliament and the Bundesrat. Most amendments have concerned the federal order, in particular the allocation of powers and the fiscal relations between the orders of government.[7] However, despite recent attempts to "modernize" German federalism, the basic features of the federal constitution have hardly been transformed. The weighing of votes of individual Land governments in the Bundesrat was modified after German unification, but the institution as such remained intact. With the exception of the creation of Baden-Württemberg, the territory of the Länder was not reorganized as provided in Article 29. Fiscal federalism, which had evolved incrementally into a complex system of sharing revenues and expenditures, was barely modified by the recent reforms. What *have* changed are the conditions affecting how federalism operates. Germany is not only unified, it is also part of the still evolving EU. German society has also developed, one of the consequences being an increasing differentiation of the party system and the increasing tendency of citizens to defend their rights as individuals. Finally, transnational deregulation of the economy has dissolved national coordination in corporatist patterns and given rise to increasing regional differentiation. Constitutional amendments aimed at adjusting federalism to these developments, however, have produced only limited effects.

Because of numerous incremental amendments and compromises between parties, the constitutional framework of the federal system has become burdened with very specific and detailed regulations. This development reveals a tendency to resolve tensions and conflicts by law. The length of the Basic Law has increased significantly as the result of attempts to distribute powers more clearly and to protect the

7 Andreas Busch, "Verfassungspolitik: Stabilität und permanentes Austarieren," in *Regieren in der Bundesrepublik Deutschland*, ed. Manfred G. Schmidt and Reimut Zohlnhöfer, 33–56 (Wiesbaden: VS Verlag für Sozialwissenschaften, 2006).

jurisdiction of Land and local governments against federal encroachment. To an important extent, this "overregulation" of German federalism[8] has been caused by an interchange between politics and court decisions. A detailed account will be provided in the following sections.

III. Court System

Federalism is not only founded on law, it also constitutes a structure supporting the application of law. Both the hierarchy of the legal order and the division of powers in the federal system are reflected in the German court system, which in addition is functionally differentiated. At its centre, the FCC and constitutional courts of the Länder fulfil a special function as guardians of the constitution.

The court hierarchy is intended to guarantee the impartial and consistent application of law to individual cases. In general, plaintiffs have to submit their complaints to a court of first instance, which, depending on the issue at stake, is a local (*Amtsgericht*) or a regional (*Landgericht*) court. Courts of appeal can revise or dismiss decisions of the first instance. Under particular provisions, the issue under dispute can be passed to one of the six supreme courts established for particular fields of law.[9] The federal division of powers serves as an additional device to safeguard the independence of judges. Courts of the first instance and courts of appeal are established by Land governments, which, since 2006, also decide on the payment of their judges. The Land department of justice selects judges of the courts falling under their jurisdiction. The federal government is responsible for the supreme courts. Their judges are selected by a committee of sixteen members of the federal parliament and the sixteen ministers of justice of the Länder and appointed by the federal minister for justice. Courts of both levels form an integrated appellate system that is based on federal statutes. Beyond this vertical differentiation, the court system is divided into specific branches such as civil and criminal law (jurisdiction on "ordinary" matters), labour law, social law, fiscal law, and administrative law ("specific" matters).

---

8 Arthur Benz, "From Joint-Decision Traps to Over-Regulated Federalism: Adverse Effects of a Successful Constitutional Reform," *German Politics* 17, no. 4 (2008): 441–8.

9 *Bundesarbeitsgericht* (labour law) in Erfurt; *Bundesfinanzhof* (financial law) in Munich; *Bundesgerichtshof* (civil and criminal law) in Karlsruhe; *Bundessozialgericht* (social law) in Kassel; *Bundespatentgericht* (law on property rights) in Munich; *Bundesverwaltungsgericht* (administrative law) in Leipzig.

The federal structure and the functional division of power also shapes the system of constitutional courts. They are not part of the ordinary judicial hierarchy and appeal system, but fulfil a particular purpose, as they decide only matters of constitutional law. These matters include conflicts between constitutional bodies or complaints of individuals who claim to be affected in their basic rights by authorities. The responsibilities of the Land constitutional courts vary, depending on the particular regulations of each Land. Not all of them can be addressed by individuals, some decide on conflicts only between public authorities.

According to the constitution, the independence of judges and courts is an essential precondition of the rule of law. The federal organization of the court system is meant to enforce this principle and, in practice, it is strictly respected. Influencing a judge by the executive or by interest groups is not only illegal but also prevented by attentive media. Moreover, judges are embedded in a structure of communication in jurisprudence supported by an association of judges and relations with university law faculties. These relations support an institutional setting providing for a clear separation of powers between courts on one hand and legislative and executive powers of government on the other hand.

With its decisions on individual lawsuits, each court contributes to the interpretation of law, which in most cases is made by the federal legislature. As every single court is independent, its decisions cannot bind other courts in different sectors of the court hierarchy. Therefore, diverging opinions by local or regional courts or by courts in the different sectors cannot be ruled out. Decentralization and differentiation of the court system generates a certain plurality of jurisdiction, while mutual adjustments of decisions and the supremacy of higher courts contribute to coherence. In this way, the law is made sufficiently flexible and can be adjusted to particular cases without becoming subject to arbitrary court decisions.

Thus federalism has an important impact on Germany's court system. Its differentiation allows for flexibility without causing diversity in interpretation or application of the law. The specific content of court decisions can also influence federalism. While lower courts are not in a position to have an impact, higher-court decisions can have consequences for the public expenditures or tax revenues of the federal and Land governments, and the FCC has a very significant capacity to affect the federal system as a whole, particularly through its decisions on the constitutionality of legislation and other governmental acts. In order to understand the role of courts in German federalism, it is therefore necessary to focus in particular on the crucially important functions of the FCC within the German political system as a whole.

1. The Federal Constitutional Court

Like many democracies established after the fall of dictatorships, Germany introduced the institution of a constitutional court to tame executive governments and parliamentary majorities. In accordance with the legalist interpretation of federalism, such courts exist at the federal and the Land levels. In a certain way, Land courts influence the evolution of federalism when they decide matters concerning local government. However, due to the legal superiority of federal constitutional law, the FCC has the final say in cases of conflict between federal and Land law, and it can overrule decisions of constitutional courts of the Länder. As a federal institution, the FCC is responsible to resolve disputes between governments of all levels, while Land courts deal only with conflicts between Land and local governments. The power of the FCC may be constrained by the ECJ when it decides matters concerning the German constitution, except to the extent that the German court insists on its claim to be the final interpreter of the Basic Law. Whatever the case, the judgments shaping German federalism so far have been those of the FCC. It has turned out to be a central player in the federal system.

Inaugurated in 1951 and located in Karlsruhe, at a certain distance from the sites of government and parliament, the FCC soon became a powerful and widely accepted institution. Formally, its powers are limited compared to some other supreme courts, such as those in Canada and Australia, because it does not deal with disputes on the application of normal law. Its sole function is to defend the constitution against infringements by any holder of government power, including parliament, and it decides issues only according to constitutional law.

The organization of the FCC developed during the first two decades of its existence. Since 1971, it has consisted of sixteen judges. Court decisions are prepared and made by one of the two senates, with each assembling eight judges. Most of them are law professors, but three of the eight judges of each senate must have served as judges in the other federal courts. Each senate is responsible for particular matters. In its domain, each senate decides independently from the other and speaks for the whole Court. Only in very rare cases when senates disagree on an issue does a plenary sitting of the Court decide the matter. The plenary

Court also determines the responsibilities of the senates. Usually a senate comes to a unanimous judgment, but majority decisions are possible and individual judges can publish dissenting opinions. The internal organization of the Court does not follow any regional or federalist logic, even though it is the second senate of the Court that usually decides conflicts between constitutional bodies and thus often the fundamental issues of federalism.

Judges are elected by a two-thirds majority of the Bundestag[10] and the Bundesrat for a twelve-year term without the possibility of re-election. In practice, a strict rule of proportionality applies in the selection process. Each house of the legislature elects half of the judges, and both determine the president and the vice-president of the Court. With the Land governments being involved via the Bundesrat, the election of the judges seems to that extent to be guided by territorial criteria. However, there is no empirical evidence that the Land governments aim at regional proportionality, which would be difficult to apply in practice. Neither are judges elected by the Bundesrat prone to represent Land interests, nor are those elected by the federal parliament biased towards the federal level. Conflicts on the nomination of a candidate occur from time to time, but they never concern particular Land interests; instead, they reveal different opinions about the positions, attitudes, or backgrounds of a candidate. Party politics has the most obvious impact on the selection of judges. Yet in order to find a qualified majority, parties have to come to a consensus. Following an informal agreement, the right to fill a vacant Court position is assigned to the party that had nominated the judge who is to be replaced. Nominations may be rejected by other parties, and political disputes have overshadowed some of the recent elections of judges, but this is an exception. All in all, it is the professional reputation of a lawyer that counts,[11] and judges hardly follow the line of a political party or a government.[12]

---

10 For a long time, the Bundestag did not vote on candidates in plenary session, but in a special committee of twelve members elected by the parliament. Since 2015, the plenary votes without debate on the proposal of the committee (Art. 6, Law on the FCC).

11 See Christoph Hönnige, "The Electoral Connection: How the Pivotal Judge Affects Oppositional Success at European Constitutional Courts," *West European Politics* 32, no. 5 (2009): 963–84.

12 Sascha Kneip, *Verfassungsgerichte als demokratische Akteure: Der Beitrag des Bundesverfassungsgerichts zur Qualität der bundesdeutschen Demokratie* (Baden-Baden: Nomos, 2009).

2. *Jurisdiction, Procedure, and Remedies*

The Basic Law defines different areas of jurisdiction of the Court. Depending on the type of conflict, proceedings can be initiated by governments, parliaments, party groups, or citizens who claim to be affected in their fundamental rights. The most important areas are the following.[13]

First, the Court is responsible for constitutional review of laws. "Abstract judicial review" (independent of the application of a law) can be initiated by the federal government, a Land government, or a group of one-third of the members of the Bundestag (Art. 93, sec. 1, no. 2). In addition, all courts can call upon the FCC to decide whether in a specific case the relevant law conforms to the constitution ("concrete judicial review": Art. 100). A dispute on legislative competence may provide reason for instituting these proceedings of constitutional review.

Second, the Court can be called by the federal parliament, the executive, or the federal president or by members of these bodies vested with rights in order to settle conflicts between these constitutional bodies. Issues may concern the law on political parties, electoral law, or parliamentary proceedings. Moreover, in cases of conflict between different orders of government usually concerning the allocation of powers or fiscal equalization, the federal or Land government or a Land parliament can initiate proceedings. Notably, if a body of a Land government feels affected in its constitutional rights, it does not need a majority in the Bundesrat but can act individually. This also applies if the need for a federal law in matters of concurrent legislation is disputed. In this particular case, the Bundesrat also can initiate legal proceedings (Art. 93, sec. 1, no. 2a, and sec. 2). This explains why all important decisions on federal-Land disputes have been initiated by Land governments.

Third, any person alleging that his or her basic rights have been violated has recourse to the Court, provided that he or she has failed in inferior courts responsible for the matter. Introduced in 1951 and entrenched in the Basic Law in 1969, constitutional complaints as of

---

13 Other areas of jurisdiction, not relevant for federalism, aim to maintain democratic procedures and institutions, such as the ban of a political party, the impeachment of the federal president or of judges, and the verification of elections. With the exception of two successful and one failed attempt to ban extremist parties, these procedures have not been of practical relevance.

2014 numbered 207,088 (96.6 per cent of all judicial proceedings).[14] With only 2.34 per cent of all complainants realizing their goals, the success rate is quite low. Issues of federalism can be raised in this context, in particular if the competence of the federal legislature is disputed. Moreover, indirect effects on the federal system can result if the FCC decides in favour of an equal treatment of citizens, especially in matters of taxation.[15]

In principle, the FCC can declare a law invalid if the Court believes it infringes constitutional norms. For this reason, the Court can be characterized as a conditional veto-player in the political process. As it cannot act in its own right, however, its power depends on other actors willing to bring disputes before the Court. The sheer number indicates that citizens address the FCC in relation to many issues. Not unlike in other democratic states, this trend to go to courts reflects a change in relations between politics and citizens and a declining trust in government. For the Court, this extends opportunities not only to settle a legal dispute, but also to check legislative decisions of parliaments. If considered to be particularly relevant, the Court can accept a constitutional appeal before other courts have decided the matter. The Court has thus secured for itself the capacity to define its own jurisdictional agenda.

3. *Institutional Role of the Court*

As mentioned above, government actors often initiate constitutional review of legislation. In a legalist political culture as it has developed in Germany, parties also refer to the constitution when debating on a bill. Consequently, opposition parties in the federal parliament in particular tend to challenge majority decisions in proceedings before the FCC,[16]

---

14 Federal Constitutional Court, "Annual Statistics 2014," http://www.bundesverfassungsgericht.de/SharedDocs/Downloads/EN/Statistik/statistics_2014.pdf?__blob=publicationFile&v=3.

15 Matthias Jestaedt, Oliver Lepsius, Christoph Möllers, and Christoph Schönberger, "Die maßstabsetzende Gewalt," in *Das entgrenzte Gericht: Eine kritische Bilanz nach sechzig Jahren Bundesverfassungsgericht*, ed. Mattias Jestaedt, Oliver Lepsius, Christoph Möllers, and Christoph Schönberger (Frankfurt a.M.: Suhrkamp, 2011), 250–1.

16 The right to initiate an "abstract constitutional review" is a significant right of the opposition parties in parliament. After the 2013 elections, a Grand Coalition formed, with the two opposition parties being left with about 20 per cent of seats. A bill to amend the Constitution, aimed to reduce the existing threshold of one-third of the members, has been rejected by the majority parties.

and more often than not these political conflicts, which sometimes formally involve federal-Land issues, are settled by the Court. In cases of joint decision-making, initiating legal proceedings can allow an executive to signal to its parliament and its citizens that it is seeking to secure their interests by all means at its disposal. Moreover, governments see benefit in shifting responsibility to the Court as final arbiter of contentious political issues. Framing issues as matters of the constitution also suggests that norms rather than interests will guide decisions.

An additional reason explains the powerful position of the FCC in German politics. In its self-perception expressed in a memorandum issued in 1952, the Court defined itself as a constitutional body of equal standing with the federal parliament.[17] Significantly, this interpretation is accepted and enshrined in the law on the FCC. Moreover, the Court has adopted a wide-ranging interpretation of constitutionality. Instead of applying constitutional law to a particular case by context-sensitive balancing of conflicting norms, it derives abstract standards from the constitution and evaluates the law accordingly.[18] As a consequence, the Court does not only decide specific cases but also defines principles that are expressed to be binding on executives and parliaments. More often than not the decisions and reasoning of the Court provide mandatory guidelines for legislation. In this way, the FCC has a profound influence on the agenda of governments and parliaments, including in matters of federalism.

The power and legitimacy of the FCC is debated among law professors and political scientists.[19] However, in public the Court is highly respected. Its reputation is higher than that of other institutions of government, including the federal parliament.[20] Backed by this public

17 Bundesverfassungsgericht, "Denkschrift des Bundesverfassungsgerichts vom 27. Juni 1952. Die Stellung des Bundesverfassungsgerichts," *Jahrbuch des öffentlichen Rechts der Gegenwart* 6 (1957): 144–8.

18 Lepsius, "Die maßstabsetzende Gewalt."

19 Jestaedt et al., *Das entgrenzte Gericht*; Kneip, *Verfassungsgerichte als demokratische Akteure*.

20 Hans Vorländer and André Brodocz, "Das Vertrauen in das Bundesverfassungsgericht: Ergebnisse einer repräsentativen Bevölkerungsumfrage," in *Die Deutungsmacht des Bundesverfassungsgerichts*, ed. Hans Vorländer, 259–96 (Wiesbaden: VS Verlag für Sozialwissenschaften, 2006).

support and as the result of politicians' willingness to accept its decisions, the Court has secured a central position in the political system.

This position has to some extent been challenged by the ECJ. With its interpretation of the principle of non-discrimination derived from the aim to create a common market in Europe, the ECJ has extended its jurisdiction into matters of individual rights and equality.[21] In addition, the ECJ maintains the principle of supremacy of EU law, a principle never explicitly accepted by the German FCC. So far, the courts have pragmatically avoided open conflict by not articulating directly contradicting decisions.[22] However, the German court has transferred its interpretation of federalism and subsidiarity to the European Union. Accordingly, it has tried to define the boundaries of integration and repeatedly threatens to veto European legislation.[23] In addition, it clearly demarcated its domain against an active ECJ. In its famous decision on the Lisbon Treaty, for example, the FCC claimed responsibility for defending the "identity" (i.e., the core rules) of the German constitution:

> If legal protection cannot be obtained at the Union level, the Federal Constitutional Court reviews whether legal instruments of the European institutions and bodies, adhering to the principle of subsidiarity under Community or European law (Article 5.2 ECT; Article 5.1 sentence 2 and 5.3 TEU Lisbon), keep within the boundaries of the sovereign powers accorded to them by way of conferred power ... Furthermore, the Federal Constitutional Court reviews whether the inviolable core content of the

21 Fritz W. Scharpf, "Legitimacy in the Multilevel European Polity," *European Political Science Review* 1, no. 2 (2009): 173–204; Susanne K. Schmidt and R. Daniel Kelemen, eds., *The Power of the European Court of Justice* (Abingdon, Oxon: Routledge, 2013); Alec Stone Sweet, "The European Court of Justice and the Judicialization of EU Governance," *Living Reviews in European Governance* 4 (2010), http://europeangovernance-livingreviews.org/Articles/lreg-2010-2/.

22 Arthur Dyevre, "European Integration and National Courts: Defending Sovereignty under Institutional Constraints?," *European Constitutional Law Review* 9 (2013): 139–68.

23 Monica Claes and Jan-Herman Reestman, "The Protection of National Constitutional Identity and the Limits of European Integration at the Occasion of the Gauweiler Case," *German Law Journal* 16, no. 4 (2015): 917–70; Arthur Dyevre, "The German Federal Constitutional Court and European Judicial Politics," *West European Politics* 34, no. 2 (2011): 346–61; Susanne K. Schmidt, "A Sense of Déjà Vu? The FCC's Preliminary European Stability Mechanism Verdict," *German Law Journal* 14, no. 1 (2013): 1–20.

constitutional identity of the Basic Law pursuant of Article 23.1 sentence 3 in conjunction with Article 79.3 of the Basic Law is respected.[24]

While judicial federalism in Germany is clearly dominated by the FCC, in the EU the relation between courts of the different orders is still in flux. A competition of courts has been prevented by communication among judges in what the president of the FCC recently characterized as a network of constitutional courts.[25] Regarding federalism, judgments of the ECJ may affect Länder governments when they are responsible for implementing European law, but these decisions hardly change the basic structures of German federalism. Moreover, the FCC has safeguarded core principles of the Basic Law in European integration. For these reasons, neither decisions of the ECJ nor its interplay with the FCC have so far had direct repercussions on German federalism, even though the process of European integration has changed the effective structure and operation of the federal system in various respects.

IV. Federalism Jurisprudence

1. General Tendencies

Before unification in 1989, the federal structure of the West German republic was endorsed but hardly shaped by decisions of the FCC. Despite the tradition of state legalism and despite a variety of opportunities for constitutional review, "most federal-state conflicts never reached the Constitutional Court. They [were] usually resolved politically through the mechanisms of collaborative federalism."[26] However, when considering the evolution since unification, this conclusion has to be revised. Various "mechanisms of collaborative federalism" have

---

24 Lisbon Treaty case (2009), BVerfGE 123, 267, headnote 4 (BVerfGE: "Entscheidungen des Bundesverfassungsgerichts," issued by an association of the members of the FCC, Tübingen: Mohr-Siebeck, since 1952. Since 1998, decisions are published on the Court webpage, at http://www.bundesverfassungsgericht.de/EN/Das-Gericht/das-gericht_node.html).

25 Andreas Vosskuhle, "Multilevel Cooperation of the European Constitutional Courts. Der Europäische Verfassungsgerichtsverbund," *European Constitutional Law Review* 6, no. 2 (2010): 175–98.

26 Donald P. Kommers, *The Constitutional Jurisprudence of the Federal Republic of Germany*, 2nd ed. (Durham, NC: Duke University Press, 1997), 87.

in fact been hampered by intense conflicts, and the Court has gained significant influence through its adjudication of disagreements.

During the first three decades after the founding of West German federal republic, continuous economic growth allowed an expansion of welfare services and financial support of less developed regions. Under these conditions, the federal and Land governments were able to settle their conflicts by avoiding redistributive decisions. Legal proceedings having a lasting impact on the political system concerned mainly the protection of democratic institutions and individual rights. The FCC developed its powerful position and gained its legitimacy by its jurisprudence on fundamental rights. It interpreted these rights entrenched in the Basic Law as an objective normative order binding all institutions of government, including the federal and Land legislatures, instead of applying them as rights protecting the freedom and individual rights of citizens against governments.

By this interpretation of the constitution, the Court reinforced the uniformity of law against diversity in federalism. In accordance with this jurisprudence, Konrad Hesse, who later was elected as a judge of the FCC, elaborated his influential theory of unitary federalism.[27] While an integrated nation and equality of public goods and services in the welfare state were unanimously acknowledged as principles guiding governance, principles to which many ascribed a constitutional status, federalism was justified as a device to constrain government by a vertical division of powers. In many proceedings initiated by courts under the concrete judicial review procedure, the FCC took the opportunity to demarcate the powers of the two orders of government, but never tried to modify the basic structure of federalism.[28]

Certainly, federal-Land disputes arose and were brought to the FCC.[29] However, rulings of the FCC generally confirmed the existence

27 Konrad Hesse, *Der unitarische Bundesstaat* (Karlsruhe: C.F. Müller, 1962).

28 Philip M. Blair and Peter Cullen, "Federalism, Legalism and Political Reality: The Record of the Federal Constitutional Court," in *Recasting German Federalism: The Legacies of Unification*, ed. Charlie Jeffery (London: Pinter, 1999), 121–2.

29 Philip M. Blair, *Federalism and Judicial Review in West Germany* (Oxford: Clarendon, 1981); Blair and Cullen, "Federalism, Legalism and Political Reality"; Bert-Sebastian Dörfer, *Bundesverfassungsgericht und Bundesstaat* (Berlin: Duncker & Humblot, 2010); Gunter Kisker, "The West German Federal Constitutional Court," *Publius: The Journal of Federalism* 19, no. 4 (1989): 35–52; Kommers, *Constitutional Jurisprudence of the Federal Republic of Germany*; Stephan Korioth, "Die Rechtsprechung des Bundesverfassungsgerichts zum Bundesstaat," in *Handbuch Bundesverfassungsgericht im politischen System*, 2nd ed., ed. Robert Ch. van Ooyen and Martin H.W. Möllers, 393–412 (Wiesbaden: Springer VS, 2015).

of federalism as it had developed in reality. In its federalism jurisprudence, the Court tried to find a balance between uniformity and diversity by supporting the autonomy of Land governments and also accepting extensive use of concurrent powers by the federal legislature. As a rule, a pragmatic balance of different interests and ideas characterized its decisions. If they revealed a doctrine of federalism, then it resulted from highlighting the idea of partnership or federal comity (*bundestreues Verhalten*)[30] and the division of powers.[31] The first principle expressed political realism, whereas the second followed from a legalist theory of the state defined mainly by territory and sovereignty. With the constitutional entrenchment of federalism, German lawyers had to discard the prevailing view that a state is an integrated legal body and the centre where supreme power is located. They had to accept the idea that sovereignty can be divided.[32] In line with this reasoning, the FCC emphasized the statehood of the Länder and defended an inviolable set of core powers to be assigned to them. Already in those days, the concept of distinct areas of jurisdiction of the federal and the Land governments was formulated. This concept still influences court decisions.

However, although the Court outlined the principle of federalism, it neither unambiguously defended powers of the Länder against centralization nor clearly marked the boundaries of jurisdiction of governments. This does not mean that it failed to safeguard federalism. It has to be noted that representatives of the Land governments in the Bundesrat rarely prevented an extension of federal legislative powers, while the Court, for instance, rejected an attempt by Konrad Adenauer's government to introduce federal television.[33] Yet in cases of conflicts on the application of concurrent powers, the Court refrained from revising political decisions. It declared the principle of subsidiarity expressed in Article 72, sections 1 and 2, as a political norm not to be interpreted by legal reasoning. On the other hand, the Court extended the powers

---

30 Dörfer, *Bundesverfassungsgericht und Bundesstaat*, 68–86.

31 Hans-Hugo Klein, "Der Bundesstaat in der Rechtsprechung des Bundesverfassungsgerichts," in *Handbuch Föderalismus: Föderalismus als demokratische Rechtsordnung und Rechtskultur in Deutschland, Europa und der Welt, Band 3*, ed. Ines Härtel (Berlin: Springer, 2012), 479–86.

32 For a comprehensive discussion of how legal theory on federalism developed in Germany, see Stefan Oeter, *Integration und Subsidiarität im deutschen Bundesstaatsrecht* (Tübingen: Mohr-Siebeck, 1998).

33 Television case (1961), BVerfGE 12, 205.

of the Bundesrat when it endorsed an interpretation implying that if a law affects the Länder in their administrative competences, their right to veto extends to the law as a whole and not only to those parts regulating administrative organization or procedures.[34] Consequently, the FCC reinforced the tendencies towards intense intergovernmental relations and joint decision-making. Until the late 1960s, "cooperative federalism" was considered as a modern form of federalism, in particular among German lawyers. Court decisions reflected this prevailing opinion.[35]

During the 1960s, the apparent conflict between a division of power and cooperation in federalism was debated. A solution was not found by the FCC but by constitutional amendment. In those days, it was not joint decision-making in legislation that was under debate but the informal use of federal funds to subsidize Land policies. This practice was said to be unconstitutional. Notwithstanding the doctrine of a separation of jurisdictions, in 1967 the federal legislature changed the constitution, with the required assent of the Bundesrat, and introduced joint tasks (Art. 91a and b) allowing the federal and Land governments to cooperate in promoting regional policy, agriculture, and research. Federal grants, tax sharing, and fiscal equalization were also extended by the reform. Thus, the concept of cooperative federalism took precedence over the idea of a separation of powers, without any involvement of the FCC.

The Länder soon realized the trap they had run into by legalizing cooperative federalism. While they profited from federal grants, they complained about the loss of autonomy. After German unification, the Länder saw an opportunity to "re-federalize" the political system.[36] Governments of the rich southern Länder took the lead, while other Land governments followed suit: those in West Germany reluctantly and those in East Germany with scepticism. But frustrated by political debates to no avail, they increasingly took recourse to constitutional review. One issue was fiscal equalization, the other the allocation of powers. Faced with an increasing burden in fiscal equalization, Land governments contributing to the equalization fund questioned the

34 Price Act case, BVerfGE 8, 274, 294

35 Kisker, "West German Federal Constitutional Court," 50–2.

36 Hartmut Klatt, "Centralizing Trends in West German Federalism, 1949–1989," in *Recasting German Federalism: The Legacies of Unification*, ed. Charlie Jeffery (London: Pinter, 1999), 47–51.

constitutionality of the law. In 1986, 1992, and 1999, the FCC determined challenges to the law, but without inducing major changes.[37] Against this background, legal action concerning fiscal equalization, initiated in 2013 by the governments of Bavaria and Hesse, appears to be a strategic move by these governments in the current negotiations on a reform of the existing law. In relation to the possible reallocation of powers, the 1994 revision of the constitution, launched in the wake of German unification, ended without the federal and Land governments agreeing on any significant decentralization of legislative powers, a failure due partly to disputes among representatives from rich and poor Länder. However, the Land governments did achieve a constitutional amendment requiring the FCC to determine disputes over the revised rule on concurrent legislative powers of the federal government. What the Court in its earlier rulings had defined as a matter of politics now turned into an issue of law and legal reasoning.

In the newly unified Germany, federalism was burdened by tensions between governments, not the least because of an increase in the economic and social divergences between Länder. Political disputes on the consequences of these disparities gave rise to a growing number of legal proceedings involving the FCC in the form of federal-Land and inter-Land conflicts. Yet characterizing this development as a rise of judicial federalism would be misleading. In fact, what we observe is an interplay between the Court and politics, between interpretation of the constitution and constitutional amendment. Confronted by threatened or actual deadlocks in joint decision-making, both the federal government and many Land governments questioned the existing structures of cooperative federalism and policy uniformity. In order to escape the looming blockades, they discussed an overhaul of the federal system and started a process of "modernizing federalism." At the same time, some Länder tried to achieve more autonomy through proceedings before the FCC, and other Länder aimed at securing more federal support to manage fiscal crises, also through court proceedings. In spite of commitments to solidarity, "the aim of each Land was, on every possible count, to secure a larger slice of the cake for itself and/or to refute the arguments of the other applicant Länder which were trying to do the same."[38]

37 Fiscal Equalization cases I (BVerfGE 72, 330), II (BVerfGE 86, 148), and III (BVerfGE 101, 158).

38 Blair and Cullen, "Federalism, Legalism and Political Reality," 145.

On balance, the jurisdiction of the FCC on federalism remained as ambivalent as ever, as did the evolution of German federalism. On the one hand, the Länder gained more legislative powers. Persuaded by the 1994 constitutional amendment to depart from its former judicial restraint, the Court now defined the conditions allowing the use of concurrent powers by federal legislation in a restrictive way. The practical effect of its judgments was to alter the status quo in favour of the Land governments, all in the context of ongoing negotiations concerning the modernization of German federalism. Following a fourth decision of the FCC on legislative competences in 2004, the federal government, aware of the consequences of this new constitutional environment, conceded a catalogue of legislative competences that were to be transferred to the Land parliaments. A large majority of Land representatives in the Bundesrat accepted the proposal, and the amendment of the Basic Law decentralizing twelve competences was passed by both houses of the federal legislature in 2006.

At the same time, the FCC defended Germany's federal order in the context of European integration, in particular the right of the Bundesrat to participate in European affairs. By acting as a guardian of national statehood against the evolution of a European federal state, the Court emphasized the constitutional framework of German federalism. In its 1993 decision on the Maastricht Treaty, the Court argued that the process of European integration should not weaken basic principles of the German constitution entrenched in Article 79, section 3 of the Basic Law.[39] In this context, the federal and Land governments negotiated a constitutional amendment intended to guarantee the participation of Land governments in European policymaking. In a similar vein, the Court's decision on the Lisbon Treaty in 2009 laid down the constitutional conditions of European integration. The decision stipulated a revision of procedures concerning the role of the federal parliament, and also required the participation of the Bundesrat in particular matters.[40] The federal legislature immediately responded by changing the respective law accordingly.

On the other hand, decisions on fiscal issues came with mixed blessings for the Länder. Regarding fiscal equalization, the Court had limited leeway to adjust the existing law, given the detailed nature of the

39 Maastricht Treaty case (1993), BVerfGE 89, 155.
40 Lisbon Treaty case.

relevant constitutional rules. With its 1999 decision on fiscal equalization, the FCC demanded a more explicit and precise definition of norms of distributive justice in the form of a law setting out these norms explicitly.[41] As a political consequence, this decision launched a debate among governments as to how the level of equalization might be justified. This debate still continues and affects intergovernmental politics significantly. A similar interplay between governments and the Court influenced the agenda of the second Federal Reform Commission established in 2007. This was prompted by the government of Berlin attempting to compel the federal government to bail out the debt-ridden city state. Deviating from an earlier judgment, the FCC ruled against the Land of Berlin and emphasized the responsibility of governments for their own fiscal policies. The Court confirmed the constitutional principles of fiscal equalization and the existing law. However, it called for an improved constitutional regulation to prevent excessive public debt.[42] The commission working on a reform of fiscal federalism reacted to this "clear order of the Federal Constitutional Court"[43] and eventually proposed a new "debt brake," which has been in force since 2009. The new Stability Council supervising the Land budgets can be regarded as an institution conforming to the concept of cooperative federalism.

Moreover, the FCC did not alter its tendency to support uniformity of legislation through its jurisdiction on fundamental rights.[44] In legal disputes concerning the application of the right of equal treatment in social policy and taxation, the Court encouraged harmonized public policies throughout Germany. Moreover, its decisions on cultural disputes such as the exposition of religious symbols in public schools (crucifix in Bavarian schools, headscarves of Muslim teachers) have prevented Land governments from adopting divergent policies. Thus, the integration or harmonization of policy through court decisions, a

---

41 Fiscal Equalization case IV (1999), BVerfGE 101, 156.

42 Budget Crisis Berlin case (2006), BVerfGE 116, 327.

43 Peter Struck and Günter Öttinger, "Eckpunkte zur Modernisierung der Bund-Länder Finanzbeziehungen, Kommission von Bundestag und Bundesrat zur Modernisierung der Bund-Länder-Finanzbeziehungen"; Kommissionsdrucksache 128 (2008): 3, http://webarchiv.bundestag.de/cgi/show.php?fileToLoad=1374&id=1136.

44 Jutta Kramer, "Federal Republic of Germany," in *Constitutional Origins, Structure, and Change in Federal Countries*, ed. John Kincaid and G. Alan Tarr (Montreal and Kingston: McGill-Queen's University Press, 2005), 144, 174.

tendency that scholars have observed within the European Union,[45] is also a driving force in German federalism.

In a nutshell, the FCC has not developed a consistent "doctrine" of federalism in the sense of a "set of standards, maxims, tests, and approaches to the interpretation of the law,"[46] at least insofar as this implies a "model of federalism." Despite the supremacy of the FCC over Land courts, the use of its jurisdiction does not reveal a particular trend in favour of either the federation or the Länder. Rather, the Court seems to be guided by a combination of political realism and legal pragmatism, in accordance to the plurality of its modes of legal reasoning.[47] Judges apply accepted methods of interpretation but also consider political exigency. In general, they tend to follow prevailing discussions in the public sphere.[48] Therefore, after supporting unitary and cooperative federalism until the 1970s, the Court now emphasizes decentralization, the autonomy of governments, and a clear division of powers. It is the interplay between politics and jurisdiction that explains the practical evolution of German federalism. "The rulings of the Court may accelerate or delay a particular development. Sometimes they may even be able to tip the scales, but they can hardly set the trend. As a matter of fact, the power of the Court to act as a kind of co-pilot of the political system is dependent upon the willingness of the judges to adapt to the basic political trend, though certainly not to the surface trends of day-to-day politics."[49]

Despite the important role of courts and a FCC endowed with significant powers to interpret the constitution and constrain political institutions, the evolution of German federalism is not determined by jurisdiction. Compared to the United States or the European Union,[50]

---

45 Karen Alter, *Establishing the Supremacy of European Law* (Oxford: Oxford University Press, 2001); Anne-Marie Burley and Walter Mattli, "Europe before the Court: A Political Theory of Legal Integration," *International Organization* 47, no. 1 (1993): 41–76; Alec Stone Sweet, *The Judicial Construction of Europe* (Oxford: Oxford University Press, 2004).

46 Gerald Baier, *Courts and Federalism, Judicial Doctrine in the United States, Australia and Canada* (Vancouver: UBC Press, 2006), 4.

47 Uwe Kranenpohl, "Die Bedeutung von Interpretationsmethoden und Dogmatik in der Entscheidungspraxis des Bundesverfassungsgerichts," *Der Staat* 48, no. 3 (2009): 387–409.

48 Georg Vanberg, *The Politics of Constitutional Review in Germany* (Cambridge: Cambridge University Press, 2004).

49 Kisker, "West German Federal Constitutional Court," 41.

50 Christopher Banks and John Blakeman, *The U.S. Supreme Court and New Federalism: From the Rehnquist Court to the Roberts Court* (Lantham, MD: Rowman & Littlefield, 2012); Marcus Höreth, *Die Selbstautorisierung des Agenten: Der Europäische Gerichtshof im Vergleich zum U.S. Supreme Court* (Baden-Baden: Nomos, 2008).

judges exert a modest influence on the allocation of powers or on intergovernmental relations in Germany. Here, the dynamics of federalism are driven more by an excessive legalism in politics, for which the Court is only partly responsible. As a consequence, German federalism tends to become more rigid and trapped in constitutional disputes, with the FCC often needed to escape deadlock. The following specific cases tend to illustrate this.

2. *Specific Issues*

In academic discourses on the location of sovereignty in the federal system, German lawyers distinguished two models. According to the first one, federalism constitutes a hierarchical order and the federal government is superior to Land governments. The second model assumes a federation encompassing both the central state and the Länder. On this view, both orders of governments are of an equal footing.[51] The FCC has never unambiguously joined either of these camps. On the one hand, it acknowledged the precedence of the federal government in deciding on the territory of the Länder and in defining constitutional rules of federalism. On the other hand, it has accented the statehood of the Länder and has formulated a theory of separate constitutional spaces. Consequently, in cases of a territorial reorganization of Länder, the Court has required both a federal law and a referendum in the affected territories allowing citizens to express their will.[52] It thus confirmed a principle guiding the procedural rules set down in Article 29 of the Basic Law. Accordingly, any territorial change requires the agreement of both houses of the federal legislature and a majority of the citizens living in the affected territory. The Bundestag and the Bundesrat tried to circumvent these high hurdles for a territorial reorganization by introducing particular procedures for partial territorial reform. Some politicians have proposed the abolition of the obligatory referenda. But apart from a more detailed regulation in Article 29, neither court decisions nor constitutional amendments have resulted in changes of the territorial structure since the creation of Baden-Württemberg in 1952.

51 Kisker, "West German Federal Constitutional Court," 48–50.
52 Citizens Initiative in Baden case (1956), BVerfGE 5, 34.

The FCC and Land constitutional courts were also called to protect the autonomy of local governments.[53] In dialogue with various university professors, the courts formulated different criteria and principles to define the scope of local powers immune from federal or Land intervention. Nevertheless, in particular policy sectors, including both fiscal policies and territorial reforms, conflicts emerged again and again. As a consequence, a constitutional amendment extended the guarantee of local self-government, which now includes a guarantee of the fiscal funds necessary to fulfil local tasks (Art. 28, sec. 2). Moreover, since 2006, the constitution prevents the federal government from delegating tasks to local governments (Art. 84, sec. 1). We can thus observe incremental change in the legal framework. However, neither rulings of courts nor the constitutional amendments have notably improved the status of local governments within the federal system.

Changes in the allocation of legislative powers between the federation and the Länder have revealed similar patterns and effects. As noted above, during the forty years of the West German federal republic, constitutional amendments extended the enumerated powers of the federal government. The 2006 constitutional reform reversed this trend. One of the driving forces of decentralization was the FCC. Its new interpretation of the necessity clause of Article 72, section 2[54] favoured the Länder as the Court allowed the use of concurrent powers by the federal parliament only to avoid the problematic consequences of a fragmentation of the law or if there were considerable disadvantages for the economy and serious disparities between the Länder.[55] These rulings not only put the federal parliament "on a short lead,"[56] they also caused considerable uncertainty

53 Martin Burgi, "Federal Republic of Germany," in *Local Government and Metropolitan Regions in Federal Systems*, ed. Nico Steytler (Montreal and Kingston: McGill-Queen's University Press, 2009), 136–64.

54 Summarized by Dörfer, *Bundesverfassungsgericht und Bundesstaat*, 118–56.

55 Geriatric Nursing Act case (2002), BVerfGE, 106, 62; Fighting Dogs case BVerfGE 110, 141; Junior Professor case (2004), BVerfGE 111, 126; Student Fees case (2005), BVerfGE 112, 226. Following the reasoning applied in these decisions, the FCC recently denied federal legislative power to provide child care allowance intended for parents who raise their children at home (decision of 21 July 2015), 1 BvF 2/13; see "No Federal Legislative Competence for Child Care Allowance," news release, 21 July 2015, http://www.bundesverfassungsgericht.de/SharedDocs/Pressemitteilungen/EN/2015/bvg15-057.html.

56 Markus Rau, "Subsidiarity and Judicial Review in German Federalism: The Decision of the Federal Constitutional Court in the Geriatric Nursing Act Case," *German Law Journal* 4, no. 4 (2003): 223, 234.

about the application of concurrent powers. Politics responded to this situation by changing the wording of the constitution. The compromise between the federal and Land governments implied a differentiation of competence categories and detailed regulation of concurrent powers (Art. 72). In other policy areas, governments also changed the constitution in order to overcome court rulings. When the FCC, following its approach to the division of powers, denied the constitutionality of cooperation between federal and local administrations in employment policy,[57] the federal parliament introduced a new joint task (Art. 91e), discarding all criticism of joint decision-making.

In short, conflicts concerning the application of legislative and administrative powers have occurred regularly in German federalism. However, instead of letting the Constitutional Court make the final decisions, as in the United States, governments in Germany more often than not amend the constitution, sometimes following the guidelines of the Court, sometimes deviating from Court opinions, or overruling constraining interpretations of the Basic Law. Over time, the catalogue of competences became longer and longer. Yet the opportunities for disputes have not decreased.

A difficult problem in federal systems arises in foreign policy, especially when the powers of regional or local governments are affected.[58] In Germany, a first constitutional dispute arose in the 1950s when the federal government asked the FCC to declare unconstitutional the abolition of confessional education by Lower Saxony, which affected an existing contract of the German government with the Vatican. The Court decided in favour of the Land and defended its powers.[59] It pointed to the need of an accommodation between the orders of government.[60] In the course of European integration, constitutional amendments tried to square the circle of interfering foreign and domestic powers. However, by introducing detailed rules on the participation of the Länder in European affairs, they hardly solved the underlying wicked problem of coordinating international and federal-Länder policymaking. In reality, only pragmatic cooperation enabled the federal and Land governments

57 Joint Labour Market Administration case (2007), BVerfGE 119, 331.

58 Hans Michelmann, ed., *Foreign Relations in Federal Countries* (Montreal and Kingston: McGill-Queen's University Press, 2009).

59 Concordat case (1957), BVerfG 6, 309.

60 Blair and Cullen, "Federalism, Legalism and Political Reality," 134.

to find a balance between their legitimate interests. Therefore, they have so far avoided instituting court proceedings on this issue.

A further issue of political dispute concerned the veto rights of the Bundesrat. As mentioned above, the participation of Land representatives in federal legislation is a basic principle protected against constitutional amendments. This does not rule out an institutional change of federal representation, however. This question has never been addressed in court proceedings. However, the FCC has had to determine certain procedural matters related to the issue. One such case concerned voting in the Bundesrat. Representatives from each Land government have to cast their votes unanimously. In very rare cases of divided or unclear voting of a Land, it has been up to the Constitutional Court to decide whether a law was passed according to constitutional provisions or whether it is invalid.[61] More important has been the delimitation of the veto rights of the Bundesrat. With its theory that the substantial and procedural parts of a law cannot be separated,[62] the Court contributed to the fact that more than half of all federal bills needed the assent of the Bundesrat, in most cases because these laws have included regulations on implementation by the Länder. The federal government has tried to reduce the share of these "assent laws" by constitutional amendment. The amendment, which has been in force since 2006, qualifies the veto powers of the Bundesrat, but hardly produced the intended effects.[63] In those matters of legislation where distributive conflicts cause serious problems of joint decision-making, the Länder holding a majority of votes in the Bundesrat can still block a bill passed by the Bundestag.

These examples illustrate how constitutional law and politics are closely coupled in Germany.[64] On the one hand, the FCC is often involved in intergovernmental politics and influences the evolution of federalism. On the other hand, the Basic Law is relatively easy to amend.[65] Together, constitutional review and constitutional politics have led to a rather dense system of rules. As a consequence, the power

61 Immigration Law case (2002), BVerfGE 102, 310.

62 Price Law case (1958), BVerfGE 8, 274.

63 Fritz W. Scharpf, "Community, Diversity and Autonomy: The Challenges of Reforming German Federalism," *German Politics* 17, no. 4 (2008): 509–21.

64 Christoph Möllers, "Legalität, Legitimität und Legitimation des Bundesverfassungsgerichts," in Jestaedt et al., *Das entgrenzte Gericht*, 309–11.

65 Astrid Lorenz, "How to Measure Constitutional Rigidity: Four Concepts and Two Alternatives," *Journal of Theoretical Politics* 17, no. 3 (2005): 339–61.

of the FCC tends to increase since it has become a player in federal politics; with its decisions, the FCC contributes to adjustments of the federal system. But the Court does not determine the evolution of federalism on its own. It fulfils its functions of an impartial "non-political" arbiter, albeit in close relation with politics. Parties and governments use Court proceedings to continue politics by other means. Court rulings and politics mutually constrain each other, but they also enable decisions and policy change in a highly interlocked federal system. Constitutional politics regularly produces formal constitutional amendments but rarely substantial change.

In view of the close interplay between Court rulings and constitutional politics, the problems of practical compliance and of the coherence of the legal order hardly matter. Compliance rests not only on the acceptance of Court rulings but also on the potential to correct them by constitutional amendment. It also rests on institutional conditions of cooperative federalism that make politicians interested in receiving guidance and justification for joint decisions from an independent Court. Coherence is achieved through a hierarchical court structure. Accordingly, "a federal court of last resort always can enforce the federal law against misinterpretation by *Land* judges."[66] This also applies to the relationship between constitutional courts of the Länder and the FCC.

V. Conclusion

In Germany, federalism is reflected in the court system, but the courts in general have a limited impact on federalism. Only the Federal Constitutional Court is a major actor empowered to influence dynamics of federalism. It stabilizes the federal order by maintaining the constitutional framework, but it also induces change by setting the agenda or giving reasons for constitutional amendments. Judicial review "has not assumed the wildcard role it has played in the American, Canadian or Australian systems," as Thomas Hueglin and Alan Fenna correctly observe.[67] But to conclude that federalism does not mean legalism in Germany is misleading. It is the interplay of politics and jurisdiction that shapes and drives German federalism, and the intense interaction

66 Kisker, "West German Federal Constitutional Court," 37.

67 Thomas O. Hueglin and Alan Fenna, *Comparative Federalism: A Systematic Inquiry*, 2nd ed. (Toronto: University of Toronto Press, 2015), 332.

between constitutional review and constitutional policy results in legalism, which is probably more pronounced than in other countries.

The particular effects of court jurisdiction on German federalism and the political consequences caused by them have been ambivalent. The FCC has contributed to an increase in the legitimacy of federalism, in particular during the first two decades after the foundation of the federal republic, when neither the political elite nor the public showed strong interest in decentralization or in accepting regional diversity of public policy. At the same time, Court rulings have shifted the federal balance towards uniformity in policies, despite the FCC's disposition to defend the institutional autonomy of the Länder and local governments. In general, jurisdiction of the Court has contributed to the necessary balance of stability and flexibility and thus has worked as a safeguard of a robust federation.[68] But in close interaction with politics, it has also induced an over-regulation of the constitutional framework of federalism. As a consequence, while federalism and decentralization seem to be widely acknowledged, rigidity of the law might increasingly impede necessary changes.

In order to explain the role and impact of courts in federalism, theories point to two principal causal mechanisms. First, the institutional position of courts in a federal system and the procedures for selecting members of courts are hypothesized to determine the attitudes of judges and, as a consequence, the exercise of judicial power.[69] On this view, the FCC arguably should tend to favour the federal government in conflicts with Land governments. However, the general trend as well as certain recent rulings tend to disconfirm this theory. A second theory seems better to explain the role of the FCC in Germany.[70] This theory states that courts tend to follow general trends in political discussion. In this way, they enhance the likelihood of their decisions being implemented in legislation or constitutional amendments. As outlined above, by emphasizing decentralization, the autonomy of governments or intergovernmental partnership, and uniformity, the FCC has clearly responded to changing trends in public discussion about German federalism.

---

68 Jenna Bednar, *The Robust Federation: Principles of Design* (New York: Cambridge University Press, 2009).

69 E.g., André Bzdera, "Comparative Analysis of Federal High Courts: A Political Theory of Judicial Review," *Canadian Journal of Political Science* 26, no. 1 (1993): 3–29.

70 E.g., Vanberg, *Politics of Constitutional Review in Germany*.

While this second theory better explains decision-making in the Court, it is not sufficient to understand the close interaction of jurisdiction and politics in the evolution of German federalism. At least two further aspects have to be added.

First, the societal foundation of German federalism – a homogeneous, economically well-developed society with increasing, but still moderate, interregional disparities – is the reason why conflicts between governments usually concern the allocation of power and finances, and hardly ever concern fundamental values or identities. Indeed, when it comes to proceedings of the FCC, the general public rarely pays attention. People do not feel immediately affected, and the Court is highly respected as an institution pursuing the common interest. This may explain why in politics the FCC is accepted as an arbiter of conflicts and why it is so frequently called upon to do so.[71] But this also explains why it can engage in highly political disputes without risking its legitimacy.

Second, the institutional structures of German federalism have contributed to make the FCC a central player in politics. Confronted by the apparent contradictions between cooperative federalism and parliamentary democracy, governments tend to refer to the constitution to justify their proposals or decisions. Moreover, when deadlocks in joint decision-making are imminent, governments find an escape route in proceedings of the FCC.

However, while interested in securing support from judges, governments are not willing to abandon power. For this reason, not only does the Court follow political debates, but governments communicate with the Court in order to have their opinions considered by it. This hidden interaction across the boundaries of formally separate institutional arenas generates the particular version of "political legalism" revealed in constitutional jurisdiction or "legalist politics" prevailing in intergovernmental decision-making. Such a close interplay of law and politics increases the rigidity of the federal system, as the result of both the veto power of the FCC and the incremental extension of constitutional regulation. To make federalism work in a flexible way, legal pragmatism in applying the constitution is essential in this context. It characterizes both the judicial culture in the FCC and the political culture in federal politics.

71 Jan Erk, "The Sociology of Constitutional Politics: Demos, Legitimacy and Constitutional Courts in Canada and Germany," *Regional and Federal Studies* 21, nos 4/5 (2011): 523–38.

8 The Supreme Court of India: The Rise of Judicial Power and the Protection of Federalism

MANISH TEWARI AND REKHA SAXENA

I. Introduction

The Indian federation, formed mainly by the division of a centralized unitary state after independence from British rule in 1947, operates under a parliamentary-federal constitution that establishes both the union and the constituent states and makes extensive provision for their respective institutions, powers, and functions within the federation. India's constitutional courts – the Supreme Court and state high courts – play a very important role in defining and developing Indian federalism. They are expressly granted the power of judicial review predicated on the fundamental rights of citizens, federal division of powers in the Constitution, and limited separation of powers consistent with the parliamentary form of government for both the union and state governments. Moreover, extra-constitutional factors like the creation of new states numbering over a dozen since the commencement of the Constitution in 1950 and the rise of approximately a dozen of new regional parties have had significant effects on the workings of the federal system. Arguably, these developments have increased the probability of intergovernmental jurisdictional conflicts creating a fertile ground for adjudication.

While the effect of rights review has generally been to foster nationwide policies and actions, thus reinforcing the parliamentary aspect of the Constitution, federalism adjudication has largely maintained the autonomy of state legislatures and governments, even though the constitutional text contains no explicit theory of strong states' rights. Especially since the emergence of the judicial doctrine of the unamendability of the basic structure of the Constitution in *Keshavananda Bharati v. State of Kerala* (1973),[1] the Supreme Court has extended its power of judicial review beyond legislative and executive acts to include constitutional amendments, arguably making it the most powerful constitutional court in the world.

The pre-eminence of the constitutional courts has also been facilitated by the relative weakening of Parliament and the executive branch of the union government due to the emergence of divided governments produced by India's immense cultural, regional, and social diversities and the rise of a state-based multiparty system since the early 1990s, which necessitates recourse to federal coalition and/or minority governments. Constitutional courts have in this way emerged as a powerful counter-majoritarian institution in an otherwise highly centralized parliamentary federal constitution, including a union executive armed with emergency powers to deal with national, state, and financial emergencies. In the struggle for supremacy between Parliament and the courts, the courts have crafted a system of constitutional supremacy as finally interpreted by them. This has enabled the courts to become a significant factor in engendering a balance between a majoritarian democracy and constitutional and consensual federal governance. Whether the 2014 election, which gave the Bharatiya Janata Party (BJP) control of the union government, will alter this trend remains to be seen.

The constitutional courts in India have, on the whole, gradually moved away from strict legalism and restraint to judicial activism in the post-Nehru era. In adjudication, the courts have, over time, avoided a consistently strict federalist or statist interpretative position. Its judgments reflect a mixed and often non-partisan appraisal of the union that is sensitive partly to the constitutional text and partly to the changing contexts and times. Indeed, one analyst has argued that in the era following the1989 election and the demise of Congress Party dominance, "the Indian Supreme Court has struggled to develop neutral constitutional rules that prevent the conflation of partisan political motivations with constitutionally valid federal interests."[2]

1 *Keshavananda Bharati v. State of Kerala, A.I.R.*, 1973, Supreme Court.

2 Sudhir Krishnaswamy, "Constitutional Federalism in the Indian Supreme Court," in *Unstable Constitutionalism: Law and Politics in South Asia*, ed. Mark Tushnet and Madhav Khosla (Cambridge: Cambridge University Press, 2015), 380.

II. Federal System

1. General Background

The total area of India is 3,287,263 square kilometres with a population of about 1.2 billion. The largest state is Rajasthan, with 342,239 square kilometres; the smallest state is Goa, with 3,702 square kilometres. According to the 2011 census, the most populous state is Uttar Pradesh with 190.9 6million people; the least populated state is Sikkim with a population of 0.67 million. Economic disparity in annual per capita income ranges from Rs. 45,105 in Goa (the highest) to Rs. 5,108 in Bihar (the lowest).[3] Hindus constitute 79.8 per cent of India's population, Muslims 14.23 per cent; Christians 2.3 per cent; Sikhs 1.72 per cent; Jains 0.4 per cent; and Buddhists 0.7 per cent.[4] Ethnic diversity includes Scheduled Castes (SCs) and Scheduled Tribes (STs) with 15 per cent and 7.5 per cent of the population respectively. There are twenty-two official languages in the Eighth Schedule of the Constitution. Hindi and English are the two official languages of the union and state governments (which can also use their regional language for state administration).

Major linguistic communities are regionally concentrated broadly along the lines of various states. Sizeable religious and Hindu castes are generally spread across the board, though Muslims and Sikhs are more densely concentrated in Jammu and Kashmir, and Punjab respectively. The STs have a larger concentration in two the central tribal belt from the Indo-Nepalese border down to the south and in the northeastern states. There are considerable economic disparities along class and regional lines. Major linguistic communities with their own states are Hindi, Bengali, Telugu, Marathi, Tamil, Gujarati, Kannada, Malayalam, Oriya, Punjabi, Assamese, Manipuri, and Kashmiri. However, every state that has a linguistic majority also has significant linguistic minorities. Article 350A of the Constitution expects that every state and local authority will endeavour to provide each linguistic minority with instruction in the mother tongue for its children at the primary stage. The union president may issue directions to this effect to a state government, if deemed necessary. Further, Article 350B provides for the appointment of a special officer for linguistic minorities by the president of India.

---

3 *Census of India*, (State Census) data 2011.

4 *Census of India*, 2001.

India's gross domestic product (GDP) in 2014 at current prices (nominal) was $2.0 trillion; GDP at purchasing power parity (PPP) was $7.3 trillion, the world's third largest; and the per capita GDP (PPP) was $5,777. The growth in per capita income nationally as well as in the states has been impressive since 1980–1. However, India harbours huge income and wealth inequalities in every possible dimension; the same is the case across groups and regions.[5] In mid-2013, Maharashtra had the highest GDP per capita (US$1,496), while Bihar had the lowest (US $346). According to the Tendulkar Committee Report (2009),[6] the Below Poverty Line (BPL) population is 29.8 per cent, with 33 per cent of India's rural population and 20.9 per cent of its urban population being poor. However, the incidence of poverty also declined in all states between 1983 and 2005, with the highest decline recorded in West Bengal, followed by Tamil Nadu and Kerala. The rate of poverty decline has increased especially in the last five years, particularly in the villages. The highest incidence of poverty is found in Orissa, followed by Bihar and Chhattisgarh.[7]

Under the Independence of India Act 1947, the British Parliament transferred power to the Constituent Assembly of India elected indirectly by the provincial legislatures originally established by the Government of India Act 1935. The Indian federal union was formed by federating the British Indian provinces that were obliged under the India Act to be part of the independent Indian state. Under the act, Indian princely states under the suzerainty of the British Crown were granted freedom to stay independent or join either of the two successor states to British India: India or Pakistan. The integration of the 572 princely states posed a serious challenge to India's nationalist leaders during the early stages of constitution-making in 1946–9.

The Constitution drafted by the Constituent Assembly (1950) is the common document for both the union and the states, barring Jammu and Kashmir, which has its own constitution (1957) that broadly conforms to the provisions of the Indian Constitution. There are also several asymmetrical provisions in the Constitution relating to the states

---

5 Satyaki Roy, "Regional Disparities in Growth and Human Development in India," Working Paper no. 2012/05 (New Delhi: Institute for Studies in Industrial Development 2012), 6 and 9.

6 *Report of the Expert Group to Review the Methodology for Estimation of Poverty, Government of India*, chair Suresh D. Tendulkar (New Delhi: Planning Commission, November 2009).

7 Roy, "Regional Disparities in Growth and Human Development in India."

of Nagaland and Mizoram (Article 371 A and G). Acts of Parliament do not automatically apply to these states in certain matters unless endorsed by their legislatures. Further, the Constitution's Fifth and the Sixth Schedules contain special provisions for the administration and protection of scheduled areas and scheduled tribes in some states (Fifth Schedule) and in the states of Assam, Meghalaya, Tripura, and Mizoram (Sixth Schedule) with greater autonomy than elsewhere.[8]

In making the Constitution, the political leaders of the Congress Party in the Constituent Assembly consisting of Jawaharlal Nehru, Vallabhbhai Patel, Maulana Abul Kalam Azad, and Rajendra Prasad gave the political directions; the leading legal luminaries, such as B.R. Ambedkar, Alladi Krishnaawamy Aiyar, K.M. Munshi, and N. Gopalswamy Ayyangar, along with the legal adviser B.N. Rau, translated these ideas into constitutional provisions. The speed and the consensual process that marked India's constitution-making may be attributed to the fact that all the major questions had already been discussed thoroughly during the nationalist movement at various forums in the Indian National Congress (INC) and all-party conferences.

Ethno-linguistic demands became more intense soon after independence, however, and compelled the union government to set up the States Reorganization Commission (SRC) in 1953. Initially, the government resisted demands to create unilingual states, favouring the retention of multilingual states in the interest of promoting national integration. The SRC reflected similar views, conceding such demands only where it was necessary. The 1950s nevertheless saw the reorganization of south India, followed by the reorganization of states in western and northern India in the 1960s and of the northeast in the 1970s by the Parliament of India using its power to redraw the boundaries of the states under Article 3 of the Constitution.

In November 2000, the BJP-led National Democratic Alliance (NDA) government created three new states: Jharkhand, Chhattisgarh, and Uttarakhand. None of these new states follow linguistic or tribal lines per se. Although Jharkhand and Chhattisgarh have substantial tribal populations, the decisive factors in their creation appear to have been regional economic backwardness in their parent state and party political

---

8 Balveer Arora, "Republic of India," in *Diversity and Unity in Federal Countries*, ed. Luis Moreno and César Colino, 201–26 (Montreal and Kingston: McGill-Queen's University Press, 2010); and Rekha Saxena, "Is India a Case of Asymmetrical Federalism?," *Economic and Political Weekly*, 14 January 2012.

considerations. More recently, in 2013, the new state of Telangana was carved out of Andhra Pradesh by the Congress-led United Progressive Alliance (UPA) II government. Telangana, which is Telugu-speaking, is the first non-Hindi-speaking group to be given statehood on the basis of its linguistic identity. It is also unique in that while the region agitated for bifurcation, the parent state opposed the move with equal determination, to the extent of rejecting the proposal by a majority in the state legislature. However, this resolution proved ineffective as the Constitution (Art. 3) requires the Indian Parliament only to *consult* the state and may create a new state *without the consent* of the parent state. In all previous cases, new states were created with the consent of the parent states.[9]

Apart from these far-reaching reorganizations of the states, and despite over 100 amendments to the Constitution, there have been no major structural or constitutional changes in the federal system. Nonetheless, some major politico-economic changes since the early 1990s have considerably enhanced the political autonomy of the state governments and redefined the Hindu communalism of the BJP, which it prefers to call "cultural nationalism" (*Hindutva*). India functioned as a predominantly centralized parliamentary system until 1989, when the one-party dominance under the aegis of the INC was transformed into a multiparty system that produced minority or coalition governments at the national level. The Nehru-Mahalanobis strategy of economic development adopted at the time of the formulation of the second five-year plan allowed the union government to take a prominent role in industrialization and scale the "commanding heights" of the economy. The year 1991 witnessed a paradigm shift from this "socialistic pattern of economy" to business liberalism and globalization. Further, the Mandal Commission Report calling for a 27 per cent reservation in union government services for Other Backward Classes (OBCs) (i.e., castes) in 1990, and the demolition of the Babri Mosque by the *Hindutva* movement in 1992, gave rise to divisive identity politics.

9 *Government of India (Republic), Report of the States Reorganization Commission,* chair Fazal Ali (New Delhi: Ministry of Home Affairs, 1955), 203–4. Also see Ajay Kr. Singh, "Federalism and State Formation: An Appraisal of Indian Practice," in *Indian Federalism in the New Millennium,* ed. B.D. Dua and M.P. Singh, 85–108 (New Delhi: Manohar, 2003); and M.P. Singh, "Borderless Internal Federal Space? Reorganization of States in India," *India Review* 6, no. 4 (2007): 233–50.

All these factors together brought about a major reorientation in Indian political culture and voting behaviour. The national political parties have largely diminished, while regional parties have acquired unprecedented manoeuvrability as balancing or destabilizing forces, not only in state politics but also in federal coalition governments. The net effect has been greater regionalization and religious communal polarization in Indian politics and corresponding greater autonomy and influence of state governments in the federation.

Federalism has come to be generally valued by the political actors and general public as a means of finding a balance between national unity and regional diversity. However, certain insurgent activities aiming at secession have surfaced in some parts of the northeast, northwest, and deep south. In some instances, such as Tamil Nadu, Punjab, and Mizoram, the secession movements abandoned their earlier positions and expressed allegiance to the union. Militancy persists in Jammu and Kashmir and some states of the northeast, though electoral processes and democratic governance have been restored in those areas.[10]

2. *Broad Characteristics*

India has a parliamentary-federal system consisting of twenty-nine states and seven union territories (UTs), including the National Capital Territory of Delhi. The three-tier structure of government includes the

---

10 For more background on Indian federalism, see Akhtar Majeed, "Republic of India," in *Constitutional Origins, Structure, and Change in Federal Countries*, ed. John Kincaid and G. Alan Tarr, 180–207 (Montreal and Kingston: McGill-Queen's University Press, 2005); Govinda Rao, "Republic of India," in *The Practice of Fiscal Federalism: Comparative Perspectives*, ed. Anwar Shah, 151–77 (Montreal and Kingston: McGill-Queen's University Press, 2007); Amitabh Mattoo and Happymon Jacob, "Republic of India," in *Foreign Relations in Federal Countries*, ed. Hans Michelmann, 168–87 (Montreal and Kingston: McGill-Queen's University Press, 2009); George Mathew and Rakesh Hooja, "Republic of India," in *Local Government and Metropolitan Regions in Federal Systems*, ed. Nico Steytler, 166–99 (Montreal and Kingston: McGill-Queen's University Press, 2009); Sandeep Shastri, "Republic of India: Emergence of a Competitive Party System and Civil-Society Space," in *Political Parties and Civil Society in Federal Countries*, ed. Klaus Detterbeck, Wolfgang Renzsch, and John Kincaid, 121–46 (Don Mills, ON: Oxford University Press, 2015); M.P. Singh and Rekha Saxena, "Intergovernmental Relations in India: From Centralization to Decentralization," in *Intergovernmental Relations in Federal Systems: Comparative Structures and Dynamics*, ed. Johanne Poirier, Cheryl Saunders, and John Kincaid, 239–71 (Don Mills, ON: Oxford University Press, 2015).

union and state governments, which is based on the constitutional distribution of power, and local governments, based on a devolutionary model established in state legislation. The 73rd and 74th Amendments to the Constitution in 1992 sanctioned the existence of local governments, but their existence and form depends on state laws, provided they conform to the general requirements of the Union Constitution. The UTs are constitutionally demarcated but lack autonomy, in that they are governed directly by the union through administrators appointed by the union. The president holds diverse residuary powers over the legislative and executive powers of the UTs. Two UTs, Delhi and Puducherry, have semi-state status, with less autonomy than a state and greater autonomy than a UT.[11]

The form of government for the union and the states is parliamentary in the sense that the executive is responsible to the legislature. The Union Parliament consists of two chambers: the Lok Sabha (House of People) and the Rajya Sabha (Council of States). The head of state is the president of India. The head of each constituent state is a governor. The prime minister and the chief ministers of the states with their respective Cabinets are the real executive authorities in the union and the states. The Indian federation is highly unified through a single court hierarchy, an integrated civil service, and a common citizenship. Federal laws and programs are implemented largely by the state governments. In addition, the Election Commission of India administers both union and state elections (Article 324), the comptroller and auditor general of India audit the accounts of both the union and the states (Article 148), and the Finance Commission (Article 280) is appointed to recommend principles and formulas of revenue sharing between the union and the states under the provisions of the Constitution. Intergovernmental relations are conducted largely in such forums as the Inter-State Council (ISC), the National Development Council (NDC), and ad hoc conferences of the prime minister and chief ministers, ministers, and secretaries of the union and state governments.[12]

---

11 Rajeev Dhavan and Rekha Saxena, "Republic of India," in *Legislative, Executive, and Judicial Governance in Federal Countries*, ed. Katy Le Roy and Cheryl Saunders, 165–97 (Montreal and Kingston: McGill-Queen's University Press, 2006); and Rekha Saxena, "Treaty Making Power: A Case for 'Federalisation' and 'Parliamentarisation,'" *Economic and Political Weekly*, 6 January 2007.

12 Rekha Saxena, *Situating Federalism: Mechanisms of Intergovernmental Relations in Canada and India* (New Delhi: Manohar, 2006).

A striking feature of the Constitution is its three types of emergency provisions: a national emergency due to foreign aggression or internal rebellion or both (Article 352); an emergency in a state in the event of the breakdown of the constitutional machinery (Articles 355 and 356); and a financial emergency in the union or a state (Article 360). In 1962, the Sino-Indian war led to the declaration of a national emergency and suspension of liberties. In 1975, an internal emergency was declared in the wake of agitation in the country, but it was later withdrawn and civil liberties restored before the parliamentary elections were called in 1977. In 1978, it was laid down by the 44th Amendment to the Constitution that a general internal emergency can be imposed only if there is "an external aggression or armed rebellion." A financial emergency has never been invoked. A presidential invocation of an emergency must be followed by parliamentary ratification.

The power of the union to take over the administration of a state under Article 356 on the recommendation of the state's governor in the event of the breakdown of the constitutional machinery in a state is the most controversial provision of the Constitution. Minority political parties, especially regional parties, providing parliamentary support to the union government, have often put pressure on union governments to dismiss state governments controlled by parties to which they are opposed. The formation of coalition governments in New Delhi since 1989 added a new dimension to the controversy surrounding president's rule in states. The discordant bicameral political configuration in the Lok Sabha and the Rajya Sabha from 1989 to 2014 brought about a political check on the misuse of president's rule under Article 356, because such an act by the union executive is subject to parliamentary approval by both houses separately. Another constraint was added by the landmark judgment of the Supreme Court in *S.R. Bommai v. Union of India* (1994), in which the Court departed from tradition and made president's rule subject to judicial review. As Justice K. Jayachandra Reddy (speaking for himself) and Justice Rajesh Kumar Agarwal (concurring with Justices P.B. Sawant and Kamal Narain Singh) observed, "The fact that under the scheme of our Constitution, greater power is conferred upon the Centre vis-à-vis the States does not mean that the States are mere appendages of the Centre. Within the sphere allotted to them, States are supreme. The Centre cannot tamper with their powers. More particularly, the courts should not adopt an approach, an interpretation, which has the effect of or tends to have the effect of whittling down the powers reserved to the States."[13] Similar remarks were made by Justice V. Ramaswamy (for himself and concurring with the two others, making it a majority view of five on a nine-judge bench). The Court further reiterated this point in *Rameshwar Prasad v. Union of India* (2006).[14]

Another important area of political contestation is that the union has an executive power to intervene in the legislative process of states by empowering the president to approve or disallow a state legislative bill reserved by the governor of a state for consideration by the union president (Article 201). This presidential veto power has been controversial because presidents can delay approval or withhold assent for a decade or more. The Sarkaria Commission (1978–88) recommended that a governor's discretion to reserve a state bill should be exercised in "rare and exceptional cases" when such a bill is "patently unconstitutional."[15] The commission also recommended that a state bill so reserved should be disposed of within four months from the date of its receipt. This practice of reservation of state bills has continued, with occasional controversies arising when divergent parties are in power in New Delhi and the concerned state. The M.M. Punchhi Commission on Centre-State Relations (2010)[16] recommended disposal of a bill so reserved within six months. Absolute claims to deny federal assent have been curbed by some Supreme Court decisions. Presidential assent will override state legislation only with regard to those provisions of a state statute specifically brought to the president's attention *Kaiser-I-Hind (P) Ltd. v. National Textile Corporation Maharashtra North Ltd* (2002).[17]

3. *Structural Features*

A. DEMARCATION OF POWERS

The demarcation of legislative powers between the union and the states heavily favours the union. Demarcation is set forth in three lists covering

---

13 *S.R. Bommai & others v. Union of India*, 1994, *A.I.R.* 1918, 1994 SCC (3) 1, pp. 146–7, para 276.

14 *Rameshwar Prasad v. Union of India* (2006) 2 SCC 1.

15 Commission on Centre-State Relations, *Report*, Part I (Nasik: Government of India Press, 1988), ch. 5.

16 Commission on Centre-State Relations, *Report: Constitutional Governance and the Management of Centre-State Relations*, chair Justice M.M. Punchhi, vol. 2 (New Delhi: Government of India Press, 2010), paras 7.4.01–02.

17 *Kaiser-I-Hind (P) Ltd. v. National Textile Corporation Maharashtra North Ltd.*, (2002) 8 SCC 182.

exclusive powers of the union, exclusive powers of the states, and concurrent powers. Union laws prevail over state laws unless a state law was enacted with the prior approval of the president of India. Certain subjects in the state list are made subject to those in the union list if the matter is declared to be of national and public interest by a union law. For example, industry and mines are allocated in the first instance to the state legislatures but subject to the regulatory and development powers of Parliament. The original Constitution had ninety-seven items in the union list, sixty-six in the state list, and forty-seven in the concurrent list. The three lists allocate powers of legislation as well as taxation wherever power of legislation is explicitly combined with the power of taxation in the text of the Constitution. In pursuit of an integrated national economy, more flexible and high-yielding taxes payable by mobile persons and corporations are assigned to the union (e.g., income tax, trade and commerce, and welfare). Subjects requiring high investment or technological and scientific skills have also been allotted to the federation. Likewise, matters amenable to territorial nexus and subject to interstate ramifications are assigned to the union or put in the concurrent list. Generally, matters of local import are left to the states, such as agriculture, health, local government, and law and order. The concurrent list typically includes matters like criminal law, preventive detention, family law, contracts, economic and social planning, and legal, medical, and other professions.

A radical departure from the constitutionally prescribed division of powers between the two orders of governments would require a formal constitutional amendment. The amending formula is outlined under Article 368. Citizens have no formal role in amending the Constitution. The courts are the ultimate interpreters or arbiters for determining the powers of the various orders of government. Parliamentary amending powers are, however, limited by the basic-structure doctrine, as mentioned above. This latter theory was invented by the Supreme Court in the context of Parliament's power to amend the Constitution. It limits unrestrained and injudicious alterations to the Constitution by Parliament. This theory was first advanced in *I.C. Golaknath v. State of Punjab* (1967),[18] which was reversed by *Keshavananda Bharati v. State of Kerala* (1973),[19] which held that Parliament can amend any part of the Constitution, including fundamental rights, but in doing so, it cannot destroy the Constitution's basic structure.

18 *Golak Nath v. State of Punjab, A.I.R.*, SC 1967.
19 *Keshavananda Bharati v. State of Kerala, 1973, op. cit.*

The Supreme Court approved the first amendment that added the Ninth Schedule to the Constitution, making parliamentary legislation listed there immune from judicial review. However, since the date of the delivery of the *Keshavananda* judgment, any act in the Ninth Schedule has been open to judicial scrutiny. This position was further fortified by *I.R. Cohelo* (2007),[20] which was a unanimous ruling compared to the *Keshavananda* ruling, which rested on only a 7–6 majority.

During the last half-century, the state list has lost some items to the concurrent and union lists. For example, education and forests, originally on the state list, were transferred to the concurrent list by the 42nd Constitutional Amendment in 1976. Most amendments in the three lists were made during the period of one-party Congress dominance when the party effectively transferred subjects from the state list to the concurrent or union lists. These changes were done because there was a perceived need for socio-economic planning under the directives and resources of the centre. India had also experienced external aggression during those decades, which contributed to centralization. In the phase of multiparty coalition governments from 1989 to 2014, constitutional amendments became extremely difficult to make on account of divided governments in the union and the states.[21]

Another federally relevant provision is Article 275 of the Constitution, which provides for mandatory central grants-in-aid to states that may need assistance. These grants are intended to remove fiscal asymmetry among the states based on the recommendations of the Finance Commission. They may vary from state to state and are in the nature of block grants that are not subject to any conditions. In addition, Article 282 provides for central assistance on a discretionary basis for any specific purpose or subject falling under union, state, or concurrent jurisdiction. A non-statutory Planning Commission was set up in 1950 to advise the centre on these matters.

The 73rd and 74th Amendments to the Constitution gave constitutional footing to village councils and municipal councils and assigned

---

20 *I.R. Coelho v. State of Tamil Nadu, A.I.R.* 2007 SC 580.

21 M.P. Singh, "Federal Division of Responsibilities in India," *Indian Journal of Federal Studies* (January 2004), 1:109; Mahendra Prasad Singh, *Indian Federalism: An Introduction* (New Delhi: National Book Trust, 2011); and George Mathew, "Republic of India," in *Distribution of Powers and Responsibilities in Federal Countries*, ed. Akhtar Majeed, Ronald L. Watts, and Douglas M. Brown, 155–80 (Montreal and Kingston: McGill-Queen's University Press, 2006).

twenty-nine subjects to rural local bodies and eighteen to urban local bodies. These amendments have brought regularity to local government elections conducted by the newly established state election commissions, local planning through the district planning committees and metropolitan planning committees, and regular fiscal transfers through the newly set up state finance commissions from the state governments, besides federal fiscal transfers.

The subjects assigned to the local bodies vary from state to state. Each state has devolved powers to levy certain taxes and fees to the local bodies and also set up a system of sharing their revenues and giving grants to localities. In addition, local bodies implement a number of central-government schemes, and funds earmarked for these purposes are sent to them by the union directly or through state governments.

The Finance Commission of India, being a constitutionally entrenched body, secured greater trust and legitimacy from the state governments than did the Planning Commission, which was established merely by a Cabinet resolution. The Sarkaria Commission had recommended that the Finance Commission be made a permanent body under the Constitution rather than being appointed every five years. It also suggested that the Planning Commission be given a constitutional status. However, these recommendations have not been implemented. Some scholars have suggested that the formation of these bodies should be federalized by giving the state governments some say in their work processes. Soon after the 2014 general elections, the BJP/NDA coalition government announced the government's decision to abolish the Planning Commission. Initially announced as the National Development Reforms Commission in the prime minister's Independence Day Address from the ramparts of the Red Fort in Delhi, it finally came to be called NITI Aayog (National Institution for Transforming India). Established by Cabinet resolution, the policy think tank comprises a civil servant as the chief executive officer, two full-time experts (an economist and a defence research and development expert), six union ministers (three ex-officio and three special invitees), free-market economist Arvind Panagariya as deputy chair, and the prime minister as the chair. Its role is to develop a "national agenda" to be used by the prime minister and the chief ministers to foster a system of "cooperative federalism." Its Governing Council comprises all the chief ministers of the states and lieutenant governors of the union territories, with the prime minister again as chair. A significant method of federal fiscal transfers to states is through the centrally sponsored development schemes under five-year plans initiated by various union ministries in central, state, and concurrent competences.

A number of tax reforms have been on the anvil since the arrival of neoliberal economic reforms in 1991. Among these is a state value-added tax (SVAT) that replaced the states' sales tax. Negotiations were in a very advanced stage to introduce a goods and services tax (GST) by merging a number of central and state taxes. The states were unhappy about the draft constitutional amendments circulated by the union government because the amendments gave veto power to the union finance minister on issues relating to the state GST.[22] Initially mooted and introduced by the Congress-led UPA, the proposal lapsed when the fifteenth Lok Sabha ended. The BJP/NDA government introduced the 122nd Constitutional Amendment bill in the winter session of the Sixteenth Lok Sabha in 2014. It sought to institute a seamless GST across the country by removing the cascading effect of several state and union taxes and levies, including excise duty, service tax, state and central VAT, central sales tax, purchase tax, entertainment and luxury taxes – subsuming them into a single tax. In July 2016, the bill was in limbo for lack of consensus between the federal government and the opposition, the states being divided along similar lines. The Congress, with other opposition parties in the Rajya Sabha, holds a virtual veto over constitutional amendments. It countervailed the BJP/NDA majority in the Lok Sabha. (Constitutional amendments require two-thirds majority separately in both houses of Parliament.) However, by early August the Modi government worked out a consensus with the Congress party and non-Congress opposition. It was a rare moment of bipartisan support between the two major national parties – BJP and Congress – and virtual multipartisan unanimity on GST tax reforms, which promises to transform India into a common national market. India is a member of the WTO and of some free-trading regional blocs, but internal trade across state boundaries in India itself is not yet free, despite there being such an ideal in the Constitution and a provision for an Inter-State Commerce Commission. GST had been on the anvil for about a decade but blocked for lack of consensus between the two major national parties. This consensus saw the constitutional amendment bill first cleared

22 Govinda M. Rao and Nirvikar Singh, *Political Economy of Federalism in India* (New Delhi: Oxford University Press, 2005); and Lawrence Saez, *Federalism without a Centre: The Impact of Political and Economic Reform on India's Federal System* (New Delhi: Sage, 2002).

by the Rajya Sabha itself on 4 August, and also by the Lok Sabha the following day. The conforming parliamentary legislation by simple majority and the ratification of the constitutional amendment by at least 50 per cent of state legislatures by simple majority by the end of 2016 is now only a matter of time. There are a few details, like the rate of the tax, still being worked out, with the Congress and the BJP billing for lower and the state governments for higher rates, but this most significant indirect tax reform since the commencement of the Constitution in 1950 and a fiscal reform in general since the economic liberalisation in 1991 is now well on course, with the union finance minister optimistic about its enforcement from 1 April 2017. A general Inter-State Commerce Commission is, alas, still not in the offing; there is instead a proposed GST Council representing the union and state finance ministers with a two-thirds majority for the state blocs. Another weakness of the GST dispensation is that petroleum products, electricity, and liquor are included in the list of exemptions that reduces the scope of the emerging national common market.

B. REGIONAL REPRESENTATION

Regional representation in Parliament is provided for in the federal second chamber. The Council of States (Rajya Sabha) is indirectly elected by the elected members of the state assemblies in accord with the system of proportional representation by means of a single transferable vote. Regional representation is nominal, however, because states are not represented qua states; they are represented in the Rajya Sabha not on the footing of formal equality, as in the United States of America, but on the basis of their population (Articles 4[1] and 80[2] read with the Fourth Schedule). Thus, Uttar Pradesh has thirty-one seats, whereas northeastern states like Meghalaya, Mizoram, and Manipur as well as Pudicherry and Goa have one seat each in the Rajya Sabha. The popular parliamentary chamber, the Lok Sabha, is elected in territorial constituencies in various states through the plurality or first-past-the-post system of representation. Because both houses are constituted on the basis of state populations, the smaller states are represented by smaller contingents in both houses.[23] The Punchhi Commission on Centre-State Relations (2010)[24] recommended equal representation of states, small or

23 Rekha Saxena, "Role of Rajya Sabha: The Federal Second or Secondary Chamber?" *Indian Journal of Federal Studies* (2007): 75–83.

24 Commission on Centre-State Relations, *Report* (2010), paras 7.4.01 and 02.

large, in the Rajya Sabha in order to bring about a greater federal balance in Parliament.

A constitutional amendment in the Representation of People Act of 1951 was made by the National Democratic Alliance (NDA) government led by the BJP in 2003. It abolished the domiciliary requirement for members of the Rajya Sabha elected from a particular state. Another change required that voting in the Rajya Sabha be done openly rather than by secret ballot so that the party leaders can more effectively ensure that the state legislators do not transgress party lines in voting.

Following this amendment, the Rajya Sabha has often been used as the house to accommodate financiers and loyalists of various parties, even though they may not be residents of the states from where they are elected. Former Rajya Sabha member Kuldip Nayar filed a case in the Supreme Court arguing that this is destructive of the Rajya Sabha's representative credentials as a federal second chamber. The Supreme Court, which in recent years had been exercising its powers of interpretation and review to promote the federal principle, observed that "if the Indian Parliament, in its wisdom has chosen not to require a residential qualification, it would definitely not violate the basic feature of federalism" (*Kuldip Nayar and Others v. Union of India and Others*, 2006).[25]

The National Commission to Review the Working of the Constitution and the M.M. Punchhi Commission Centre-State Relations both recommended that "in order to maintain the basic federal character of the Rajya Sabha, the domiciliary requirement for eligibility to contest elections to the Rayja Sabha from the concerned State is essential."[26]

III. Court System

1. Courts System and Institutional Role of Courts

India's judiciary is an integrated system bound at all levels by the law laid down by the apex court but with administrative autonomy of the high courts and lower courts in the states. The courts play an important role in interpreting the Constitution, which is particularly evident in at least two respects. First, the Supreme Court enunciated the doctrine of

25 *Kuldip Nayar and Others v. Union of India and Others, Supreme Court Cases* (2006), 7 SCC.

26 *Report of the National Commission to Review the Working of the Constitution (NCRWC)* (Delhi: Universal Law Publishing, 2002), 1:100; and Commission on Centre-State Relations, *Report* (2010).

unamendability of the "basic structure" of the Constitution in *Keshavanada Bharati* (1973). Second, the constitutional courts – Supreme Court and state high courts – made the proclamation of president's rule in a state under Article 356 subject to judicial review so as to check the political abuse of this power (e.g., *S.R. Bommai*, 1994, and *Rameshwar Prasad*, 2006).

India is part of the British common law tradition. The Constitution is the longest written text in the world, which is considered to give more latitude to the judiciary in interpreting it and settling federalism disputes. The court system is one integrated judicial structure, as in Canada, rather than a dualist federal-and-state system, as in the United States. The Supreme Court is a branch of the union government; high courts belong to the states, and district courts to the sub-state levels.

The Constitution invests the Supreme Court and high courts with original and appellate jurisdiction under Articles 131 and 131(A), 132, 133, and 134(A). The Supreme Court's original jurisdiction includes union-state and interstate disputes regarding the federal division of powers and fundamental rights of citizens. The Supreme Court's appellate jurisdiction includes appeals from high courts in civil, criminal, and other proceedings, when a high court certifies that the dispute raises substantial questions of law regarding interpretation of the Constitution. The Supreme Court may also grant "special leave to appeal" in "any cause or matter passed or made by any court or tribunal in the territory of India" (Article 136, Clause 1).

Parliament can further enlarge the jurisdiction of the Supreme Court by law vis-à-vis the union list (Article 138, Clause 1). Similarly, the Supreme Court may be invested with new jurisdiction by Parliament in relation to the state and concurrent lists as well as by an agreement between the union and states (Article 138, Clause 2). Further, there is an advisory jurisdiction of the Supreme Court by presidential reference if the union executive considers it "expedient to obtain the opinion of the Supreme Court" (Article 143). Courts at all the levels are bound by the law laid down by the higher courts, though the high courts and lower courts in the states have considerable administrative autonomy. The highest court of appeal is the Supreme Court in constitutional, civil, and criminal cases. The state or local courts, legislatures, or executives cannot deviate, opt out, or refuse to comply with federal court rulings (Article 141).

Only the Supreme Court and the high courts can be called constitutional courts, because they are the only courts that decide legal issues having constitutional implications. In jurisdictional terms at least, the powers of the high courts and the Supreme Court are co-terminus in adjudicating intergovernmental disputes, though as the highest appellate court, the Supreme Court has the last word on any issue relating to interpretation of the law and the Constitution. The question whether the high courts are a major, middling, or minor actor in shaping federal jurisprudence or formal changes to the fundamental law is difficult to answer, for while the sheer corpus of judgments emanating from the high courts exceeds that produced by the Supreme Court, the latter is the highest authority and final arbiter.

India's constitutional courts began more or less with the same powers as such courts in the Commonwealth parliamentary federations of Canada and Australia with judicial review of laws and executive orders. However, since 1973, the Supreme Court created a new power for it to review constitutional amendments in the course of interpreting and adjudicating the power of Parliament to amend the Constitution, as noted above.

A justice of the Supreme Court is appointed by the president of India after consultation with justices of the Supreme Court and the high courts as the president considers necessary for the purpose (Article 124). A high court judge is appointed by the president in consultation with the chief justice of India, the governor of the state, and the chief justice of the state high court (Article 217). Consultation with the chief justice of India has been interpreted as concurrence. In *Supreme Court Advocates-on-Record Association (SCAORA) v. Union of India 1993*,[27] a nine-judge bench of the Supreme Court (with a majority of seven) wrested control of appointments and transfers to the higher judiciary from the executive. The bench ruled that the president can make no appointment to the Supreme Court unless the appointee conforms to the "collective recommendation" of the chief justice of India in due consultation with four of his senior-most colleagues. For a state high court, the "collective recommendation" of the chief justice of the concerned high court in due consultation with two of his senior-most colleagues and endorsed by the "collective recommendation" of the chief justice of India is the basis of high-court appointments by the president.

In 1998, the president made a reference of this matter to the Supreme Court for its advisory opinion under Article 143. A nine-judge bench

27 *Supreme Court Advocates on Record Association v. Union of India*, 1993 (4) SCC 441; *A.I.R.* 1994 SC 268.

clarified that recommendations made by the chief justice of India in the name of the collegium of judges without complying with the "norms and requirements of the consultation process" does not bind the union government. The Supreme Court gave a detailed stipulation of a proper consultation process (*Presidential Reference*, 1999).[28]

For all practical purposes, India's higher judiciary has become self-appointing, even though the president retains the formal appointment power. Parliament has the power to impeach judges of the higher judiciary, but no impeachment has ever been concluded successfully. However, a half-impeached judge of the Calcutta High Court resigned midway through the process in order to escape the ordeal of the entire impeachment process.

Both the Supreme Court and the high courts are empowered to issue writs under Articles 32 and 226 of the Constitution for the protection and enforcement of fundamental rights. A state high court also has the power to issue writs on matters other than fundamental rights. The Supreme Court needs special parliamentary authority to issue writs for a matter other than the enforcement of fundamental rights, but no such parliamentary enactment has been made. India's courts are more or less equally involved in deciding federalism issues along with other issues, such as human rights, separation of powers, and structure of government. Union-state jurisdictional review also forms an important part of the exercise of judicial review, in addition to fundamental rights review and basic-structure-of-the-Constitution review, which applies to all forms of state action to ensure that such action does not "damage or destroy" "basic features of the Constitution."[29]

The Supreme Court operates through three kinds of benches: division benches consisting of two to three judges, a larger three to five judge bench, and a Constitution bench that includes five to seven judges. In exceptional cases, benches have had as many as thirteen judges (*Kesha-vananda Bharati*, 1973) or the entire Supreme Court sitting together, as happened with Prime Minister Indira Gandhi's petition to review the *Keshavanada Bharati* judgment in which Chief Justice A.N. Ray issued notice to convene the entire Court, but dissolved it after two days of hearing. This dissolution followed after the attorney general could

28 *Presidential Reference, A.I.R.* 1999.

29 Sudhir Krishnaswamy, *Democracy and Constitutionalism in India: A Study of the Basic Structure Doctrine* (New Delhi: Oxford University Press, 2009), x.

not produce any satisfactory evidence to establish prima facie that the "basic structure" doctrine would obstruct the country's social progress.

There is no requirement of consensual decision-making. The decision in a case of disagreement is made by majority rule, with dissenting minority opinions recorded. Law declared by the Supreme Court is binding on all courts in the territory of India (Article 141). Moreover, Article 144 obliges all authorities, civil and judicial, to act in aid of the Supreme Court.

2. *Constitutional Status of Courts and Judicial Officers*

The courts are established under the Constitution; supplementary legislation is made by Parliament or state legislatures. The union and state judicial structures are each administered with considerable autonomy. The lower courts are placed under the administrative supervision of the state high courts. In appointments and finances in these matters, the Supreme Court and high courts enjoy considerable freedom from political interference from the respective orders of government.

Judicial officers are recruited by the State Public Service Commission and trained in state academies. Examinations are held for judicial services, senior judicial services, and additional district judges. District judges are appointed by the governor of a state in consultation with the high court of the state. There is career mobility from the district courts to high courts and to the Supreme Court, but such mobility is more frequent from the middle level and the state apex court. In addition to the judicial officers recruited by the foregoing process, high court and Supreme Court judges are more commonly recruited from the bar and the bench.

The Constitution ensures the independence of the judiciary, especially in the cases of the judges of the high courts and the Supreme Court. The salaries of the judges are drawn on the Consolidated Fund of India and those of the high court judges on the Consolidated Fund of each state, which are not subject to legislative vote. Their salaries are not open for parliamentary or legislative sanction or cut, and once appointed, their emoluments and service conditions cannot be altered adversely. A justice of the Supreme Court and of a high court cannot be removed from office except by an order of the president passed after an address by each house of Parliament in the same session by a majority of the total membership of each house and at least a two-thirds majority of members present and voting. An attempt to remove a Supreme Court justice on a charge of misbehaviour in 1993 failed because it fell short of the required majority. The autonomy of lower courts from political interference appears to be somewhat problematic in some states.

Following the 1977 elections, which removed the emergency regime of Prime Minister Indira Gandhi, the higher courts also initiated what has come to be called public interest litigation to bring justice to the poor and underprivileged. The executive and Parliament have often complained about "judicial overreach" in terms of relationships among the three classical organs of the government, but a large constituency of the civil society and media has generally supported the courts.[30]

3. *Curial Procedures*

Procedures before courts are initiated by filing petitions by concerned parties, including governments. This conventional *locus standi* procedure is still the norm, but the higher courts have relaxed it for public interest litigation, which can be initiated by third parties, which may be civic or non-governmental organizations or individuals intervening on behalf of victims suffering injustice. Such proceedings can be started by a postal letter to the court by the victim or by a *suomotu* cognizance of a matter taken by a judge or judges on a bench.

The attorney general or solicitor general has special statutory powers to file contempt or other proceedings on behalf of the executive. The law officers or concerned parties may request to transfer a case from one court to another for specific reasons. In certain cases, a Supreme Court bench can itself amalgamate similar cases to be heard together in the interests of efficiency and uniformity of justice.

Indian courts follow the system of adversarial adjudication prevalent in common law countries as distinguished from the inquisitorial system practised in civil law countries. On complaints filed by appellants to the court, the respondents file their reply. After hearing the parties concerned represented by their advocates and examining witnesses, the court decides a case on its merits. Certain special remedies are used by the courts to resolve litigation or to get it enforced. Amicus curiae are occasionally appointed by the courts on behalf of an exceptionally aggrieved party to help reach a correct decision. The court can also

---

30 B.D. Dua, M.P. Singh, and Rekha Saxena, eds., *Indian Judiciary and Politics: The Changing Landscape* (New Delhi: Manohar Publications, 2006).

appoint commissioners to find the facts on the ground during litigation and report on the implementation of the judgment after its delivery.

India's record on the enforcement of courts' judgments, especially in the post-emergency period, has been generally impressive. The courts are commonly respected by the political class as well as the general public. The constitutional courts exercise their jurisdiction in federal matters, because the Constitution provides for judicial review in most of these concerns. In a few matters, where the courts are supposed to be barred jurisdiction by convention (separation-of-powers matters) or by explicit provisions of the Constitution (president's rule), the courts have been pitch-forked into action by vagaries of excessive political conflicts or abuse of constitutional powers by the executive or legislature.

IV. Federalism Jurisprudence

Judicial interpretation of the Constitution has been generally centralizing. Initially, during the Nehru era, the courts were decidedly centrist. Cases relating to the protection of fundamental rights figured more prominently than protection of the states' rights. The lesser number of states' rights cases pinpoints the reality that union-state relations have been guided primarily by the spirit of "cooperative" federalism, in which the states are constitutionally obliged to conform to the directions of the centre under explicit overriding powers of the centre in certain matters, even during normal non-emergency periods. It is often the constituent units rather than the federal government that question the competence of the government on the other side in constitutional courts.

The superior courts have reconciled the competing claims of Parliament and the state legislatures and sorted out the principles of interpretation of constitutional provisions relating to union-state relations. This trend has been complicated, however, by other developments, resulting in mixed trends when the Court has tried to accommodate states' positions within the framework of the complex intermeshing of powers in the Constitution's union, state, and concurrent lists. In addressing these issues, the judiciary has laid down some guiding principles of adjudication. We will discuss the most important doctrines used in federalism adjudication.

1. Distribution of Legislative Competences

One of the most important federalism-related issues that India's courts are asked to adjudicate involves the distribution of legislative and other powers between the union and the states. Frequently, a law dealing with a topic plainly within a legislature's powers also affects or relates to the subject matter of another legislature. In such situations, the Court examines the substantive character of the impugned law to identify its "pith and substance." P.M. Bakshi observes of this method, "Where the question arises of determining whether a particular subject mentioned is in one list or another, the court looks to the substance of the matter. Thus, if the substance falls within the Union List, then the incidental encroachment by the law on the State List does not make it invalid."[31]

An illustration is *F.N. Balsara* (1951),[32] which concerned the Bombay Prohibition Act 1949. The act antedates the 1950 Constitution of India, and the case was decided on the basis of the Government of India Act 1935. The question raised in the dispute was whether the Bombay Prohibition Act 1949 would fall under entry 31 of the provincial list of powers (production, manufacture, possession, transport, purchase, and sale of intoxicating liquor and narcotics drugs) or entry 19 of the central list (import and export across customs frontiers as defined by the Dominion Government of India). The Court decided that even though the prohibition on liquor may affect its importation, this was incidental to the act's major objective. On the basis of the pith-and-substance doctrine, therefore, the Federal Court of India ruled in favour of the provincial government.[33] A somewhat similar doctrine is that of "colourable legislation." In deciding on the basis of this doctrine, the Court asks what in fact is the basic purpose and consequence of the impugned law rather than its apparent objective and effects.[34]

Judicial decisions reflect the broad principles of interpretation of union-state jurisdictions in such a way as to recognize the exclusivity of the union and state lists. The Constitution stipulates that in matters in the concurrent list, union laws prevail unless the state legislated with the prior consent of the union executive. The courts' approach to interpreting residuary powers of the Union Parliament is to include everything not in the state list falling in this category, in accordance with Article 248, which states, "Parliament has exclusive power to make any

31 P.M. Bakshi, *The Constitution of India*, 12th ed. (New Delhi: Universal Law Publishing, 2013), 246–7.

32 *The State of Bombay and others v. F.N. Balsara*, SC 318: 1951.

33 Madhav Khosla, *Oxford India Short Introduction: The Indian Constitution* (Oxford: Delhi, 2012), 60–1.

34 Ibid.

law with respect to any matter not enumerated in the concurrent list or state list." This is reflected in a unanimous judgment of a nine-judge bench in *Attorney General for India v. Amrat Lal Prajivandas* (1994),[35] which followed the precedent of *Union of India v. H.S. Dhillon* (1971).[36] The Court held that Parliament was competent to enact both of the two impugned laws relating to foreign exchange, smuggling, and security of generic state matters. The interpretative principle laid down by the Court was that where the legislative competence of Parliament is questioned, the Court will examine whether the statute is relatable to any of the entries in the state list. If it is not, no further inquiry is necessary, and it can be held that Parliament is competent to enact that statute by virtue of the entries in the union list and concurrent list under Article 248 of the Constitution.

As mentioned above, several provisions in the state list have been made subject to provisions in the union list. There is no clear and consistent line of interpretation on these matters. The courts have sometimes ruled in favour of the states (e.g., *Tika Ramji v. State of U.P.*, 1956), at times in favour of the Union (e.g., *State of West Bengal v. Union of India*, 1963, and *State of West Bengal v. Kesoram Industries Ltd.*, 2004), and occasionally with mixed results (e.g., *Belsund Sugar Co. Ltd. v. State of Bihar*, 1999).

A law relating to an Utter Pradesh sugar industry was in dispute in *Tika Ramji*.[37] Entry 27 dealing with the production, supply, and distribution of goods such as sugar is within the exclusive sphere of state legislatures in terms of the state list. But it is also subject to entry 33 in the concurrent list, which empowers Parliament to make laws on the same subject if it is considered "expedient in public interest." The Court ruled that the U.P. Sugar Factory Act of 1953 was valid because it confined itself to the regulation and supply of sugarcane required for use in sugar factories; it did not concern itself with controlling and licensing the sugar factories.

In earlier cases such as *West Bengal v. Union of India* (1963),[38] the state challenged the constitutionality of the Coal Bearing Areas (Acquisition and Development) Act enacted by Parliament in 1957. The state contended that ownership of the land was vested in the state government.

---

35 *Attorney General for India v. Amrat Lal Prajivandas* (1994), 5 SCC 54.

36 *S. Dhillon, A.I.R.* 1972 SC 1061: 1972.

37 *Tika Ramji v. State of U.P.A.I.R.* 1956 SC 676.

38 *State of West Bengal v. Union of India* (1963).

The Supreme Court ruled that the state's right in the matter was subject to the union right and national interest under the Constitution. The courts have not generally objected to regulatory measures if they do not obliterate the right of the states to legislate over a primary concern in the field (*Automobile Transport (Rajasthan) Ltd. v. State of Rajasthan*, 1962).[39] The underlying reasons the Court leans on are supposed to be construed harmoniously: (1) the national interest must be given primacy, and (2) the state legislature should not be summarily elbowed out.

The imposition of taxes on goods by states is permitted so long as they do not discriminate against trade and commerce coming from other states and thus do not adversely affect free trade, commerce, and intercourse across the states. The case is relatable to Article 304[a], which provides that restrictions on free trade among states are permissible only if they are non-discriminatory and in the public interest. Any bill proposing to alter the free tax trade regime among states requires prior sanction of the president of India, which in effect means the union executive (Article 304[b]). Several cases have brought to the fore the problem that these provisions constrain states' legislative freedom (e.g., *India Cement v. State of Andhra Pradesh*, 1988, and *Kalyani Stores v. State of Orissa*, 1966).[40] To limit these problems, the Sarkaria Commission recommended that the states' leeway to impose this restriction should be taken away (Sarkaria Commission 1987–8).[41]

Similarly, in *State of West Bengal v. Kesoram Industries* (2004),[42] the matter concerned coal, brick-field, and minor minerals in which entries in the state list are subject to the union's power of regulation and development in the public and national interests. The Court argued, "The Union's power to regulate and control does not result in depriving the States of their power to levy tax or fee within their legislative competence without trenching upon the field of regulation and control." Further, "Every effort should be made as far as possible to reconcile the seeming conflict between the provisions of the state legislation and the union legislation."

Belsund Sugar Co. Ltd. v. State of Bihar (1999)[43] questioned the legality of the levy of market fees under the Bihar Agricultural Produce Market

---

39 *Automobile Transport (Rajasthan Ltd. v. State of Rajasthan)*, *A.I.R.* 1962, SC 1406.

40 *India Cement v. State of Andhra Pradesh* (1988) 1 SCC 743; and *Kalyani Stores v. State of Orissa A.I.R.* 1966 SC 1686.

41 Commission on Centre-State Relations, *Report* (1988), ch. 5.

42 *State of West Bengal v. Kesoram Industries Ltd.* (2004).

43 *Belsund Sugar Co. Ltd. v. State of Bihar* (1999) 9 SCC 620.

Act 1960. The Court reasoned that if the Bihar Produce Market Act had contemplated only the regulation of the location of markets and management of markets and fairs relating to raw material supplied to the sugar factories, the matter would have fallen within the legislative competence of the state legislature under entry 28 of the state list. However, the Market Act dealt with the supply and distribution of sugar products as well as trade and commerce therein, which falls within entry 33 of the concurrent list by virtue of which the union law gets supremacy. Thus, the Court tried to accommodate the state law to a certain extent but declared it invalid beyond that point.

The interstate commerce clauses in the Constitution are union-centric, though they do give some leeway to the states. Article 301 stipulates that trade, commerce, and intercourse throughout the territory of India shall be free, subject to the power of Parliament and state legislatures to impose restrictions in the public interest. A broad judicial view is that restrictions imposed on trade and commerce either by the union or by the states are generally ineffective (*State of Madras v. Nataraja Mudaliar*, 1967).[44] This problem is concerned more with freedom from discriminatory taxation (*India Cement v. State of Andhra Pradesh*, 1988)[45] and not so much with incidental encroachment (*State of Karnataka v. Ranganatha Reddy*, 1977).[46]

2. *Executive Powers Relating to Emergencies and Treaty-Making*

Jurisdictional disputes have arisen over the use of armed forces in troubled areas. The Armed Forces Special Powers Act (1958) was challenged in *Naga Peoples' Movement of Human Rights v. Union of India* (1998).[47] This act conferred special powers on security forces in several northeastern states. The case involved the fundamental rights of the Nagas as well as the federal question relating to the relationship between entry 2A in the union list (deployment of police or military in aid of civil order) and entry 1 of the state list (public order). On the federal question, the relevant point was that entry 2A in the union list – which was added by the 42nd Amendment (1976) and made the police power of the state, earlier an exclusive state jurisdiction, subordinate to the union's power to deploy armed forces or central paramilitary forces in a state – was

44 *State of Madras v. Nataraja Mudaliar, A.I.R.* 1967, SC 147.

45 *India Cement v. State of Andhra Pradesh* (1988) 1 SCC 743.

46 *State of Karnataka v. Ranganatha Reddy* (1977) 4 SCC 471.

47 *Naga Peoples' Movement of Human Rights v. Union of India* (1998), 2 SC 109.

made unilaterally without reference to the state government. This amounted to the use of emergency power governed by a separate part of the Constitution dealing with national, state, and financial emergencies. The Court considered it questionable on the ground that "if the impugned legislation falls within the competence of the state legislature, the question of doing something indirectly which cannot be done directly does not arise."

Another important concern of federalism jurisprudence has been the indiscriminate imposition of emergency rule on states by the union government under Article 356 of the Constitution. In *State of Rajasthan v. Union of India* (1977), the Court viewed the whole question as a "political thicket" left by the Constitution to determination by the union executive. The Court conceded that Article 74(2), relating to the powers of the president, prohibited courts from examining the advice of the council of ministers to the president. However, the Court reasoned that it did not preclude judicial scrutiny of the president's action under Article 356 on the basis of other available information, because it is a constitutional function of the president, which is subject to judicial review. A shift in approach was suggested by *A.K. Roy v. Union of India* (1981), however.[48] The Supreme Court there pointed out that after the repeal of Clause 5 of Article 356 by the 44th Constitutional Amendment, the constitutional theory under which the *Rajasthan* case was decided "cannot any longer hold good." As noted above, *S.R. Bommai v. Union of India* (1994) marked a paradigm shift in judicial interpretation of the power of the union to take over the administration of a state under Article 356.[49] In *Rameshwar Prasad v. Union of India* (2006), the Court extended the reasoning in *S.R. Bommai* and ruled that if a state assembly is unconstitutionally dissolved, the judiciary can revive the dissolved assembly. In this case, the Court restrained itself in view of the fact that the Election Commission had already notified the consequent elections. The use of Article 356 has undergone a marked decline due to factors like fear of judicial scrutiny, transformation of the party system, the advent of coalition and minority governments, and an opposition majority in the federal second chamber.

Many state tax laws have also been scrutinized for purporting to have an extra-territorial operation in other states ("legislative outreach")

48 *A.K. Roy Etc v. Union of India and Anr* 1982 *A.I.R.* 710 1982 SCR (2) 272.
49 *S.R. Bommai and others v. Union of India*, 1994.

(e.g., *Tata Iron & Steel Company v. State of Bihar*, 1958).[50] The Court has said there must be a "*sufficient territorial nexus*" between the legislating state and the extraterritorial matter being regulated. Observing that "the geographical applicability of a law does not by itself illustrate its constitutionality or unconstitutionality," the Court pointed out that "to pronounce on its constitutionality, we must investigate the precise reasons why the law operates extra-territorially."[51] This principle was applied to laws such as the Bihar Hindu Religious Trust Act 1950 in *State of Bihar v. Charusila Dasi* (1959),[52] where the Supreme Court reasoned that even though the trust was registered and had headquarters in Bihar, the act applied to all the properties of the trust in other states as well. The sufficiency of nexus test was restated *in Shrikant Bhalachandran Kurukar v. State of Gujarat* (1994).[53] In a review of important cases decided by the Supreme Court since 1950, M.P. Singh[54] concluded with the view of the Court in a leading case on the topic, *State of Bombay v. M.D. Chamarbaugwala* (1957),[55] that "sufficiency of the territorial connection involves a consideration of two elements, namely i.) the connection must be real and not illusory, and ii.) the liability sought to be imposed must be pertinent to that connection."

Another issue is increasing controversy over the treaty-making power, which is an executive act performed by the government of India on behalf of Parliament. However, Article 253 of the Constitution requires enactment of a law by Parliament to give effect to international agreements. In *Maganbhai Ishwarbhai v. Union of India* (1969), the Court reasoned, "The effect of Article 253 is that if a treaty, agreement or convention with a foreign State deals with a subject within the competence of the State Legislature, the Parliament alone has, notwithstanding Article 246(3), the power to make laws to implement the treaty, agreement or convention or any decision made at any international conference, association, or other body.[56] In *P.B. Samant v. Union of India* (1994),[57] the Court overruled the contention that a treaty relating to GATT's Dunkel

---

50 *The Tata Iron & Steel Co. Ltd. v. The State of Bihar, A.I.R.* 1958 SC 452: 1958.

51 Khosla, *Oxford India Short Introduction.*

52 *The State of Bihar v. Sm. Charusila Dasi, A.I.R.* 1959 SC 1002: 1959.

53 *Shrikant Bhalachandran Kurukar v. State of Gujarat* (1994).

54 M.P. Singh and V.N. Shukla, *Constitution of India*, 10th ed. (Lucknow: Eastern Book, 2001), 631.

55 *The State of Bombay v. R.M.D. Chamarbaugwala, A.I.R.* 1957 SC 699: 1957.

56 *Maganbhai v. Union of India, Hidayatullah CJ, A.I.R.* 1969, Supreme Court: 784.

57 *P.B. Samant v. Union of India, A.I.R.* 1994, Bombay 324.

proposals will affect agricultural products, irrigation facilities, and raw cotton, which fall under the jurisdiction of state legislatures. The Court endorsed the earlier decision of the Supreme Court in the *Maganbhai Patel* case. In *Vishaka v. State of Rajasthan* (1997),[58] the Supreme Court ruled that international conventions signed by the government of India that are consistent with the spirit of the Constitution's fundamental rights, even though not exactly in terms of letters of the Constitution, can be read into the fundamental rights, although the union and state legislatures may not have passed implementing laws to that effect. Thus, by entering into such international conventions, the government of India binds itself as well as the state governments. Similarly when India signed the World Trade Organization treaty, at least three petitions, one each by governments of Tamil Nadu, Rajasthan, and Orissa, were filed in the Supreme Court under Article 131 arguing that they were not consulted in areas that fell in their exclusive jurisdiction. The cases were later withdrawn on the assurance that in the future there will be consultations before entering into such treaties.

Similar state concerns have recurred as, for example, at the signings of the Indo-U.S. Civilian Nuclear Deal (2005), Free Trade Agreement with ASEAN (2012), and Foreign Direct Investment in Multi-Brand Retail (2012). But states' objections could not forestall these agreements.

In the opinion of the Supreme Court, the locus of sovereignty or constitutive authority was exercised by the Constituent Assembly of India and can likewise be exercised by a future Constituent Assembly of India. Parliament and state legislatures can exercise only limited amending power within the parameters of the "basic structure" of the Constitution. This formulation applies to formal constitutional amendments including federalism-related changes such as reallocation of powers and the structures of the various orders of government. However, changes in representation in Parliament and state legislatures, alteration of boundaries of states, and admission of new states are areas in which Parliament can exercise plenary constitutive power subject to judicial review.

There have been some controversies regarding peoples' or states' representation in Parliament. For example, as discussed above, a constitutional amendment that altered the domiciliary requirement for candidates seeking election to the Rajya Sabha was subject to litigation

58 *Vishaka v. State of Rajasthan*, 1997, 6 SCC 241.

on the ground that it affected the regional representative nature of the federal second chamber. However, the Supreme Court validated the impugned amendment.

3. *Institutional Role of the Courts*

Adjudication by the courts has generally made a positive contribution to harmonious functioning of the system of cooperative federalism established under the Constitution. The judicial review powers have been carried to the extent of judicial activism, especially since the emergence of the multiparty system and divided governments where courts' interventions have enabled the system to deal with complex and highly controversial situations. During the 1970s, several decisions of the courts were challenged by the government and Parliament by amending the Constitution itself and curtailing the powers of the courts. The courts, however, defended their review powers, at times with their backs to the wall. But after the party system transformation, a more competitive institutional arena of governance developed, and courts have been able to get away with the kind of activism that was not sustainable earlier. The courts have also been backed by civil-society institutions and the media. A national election survey in the late 1990s found that the Supreme Court and the Election Commission were rated by the respondents as the most legitimate institutions of the federal government.[59]

The constitutional courts have played a significant role in promoting a multicultural and federal conception of nationhood and state. Both community rights and individual rights as well as human rights generally have received a great deal of judicial protection. In a series of recent judgments, the doctrine of the "basic structure" of the Constitution has been elaborated incrementally, and constitutional values and institutions relating to democratically elected governments, secularism, and federalism have been declared to be part of the basic constitutional structure. The "basic structure" doctrine as a construction of the courts is unique to India. It casts a pervasive influence on federal adjudication and has been applied beyond constitutional amendments to other forms of state action, such as the use and abuse of emergency powers

---

59 S.K. Mitra and V.B. Singh, *Democracy and Social Change in India: A Cross Sectional Analysis of the National Electorate* (New Delhi: Sage, 1999).

by the union executive, the conduct of fair and free elections, and denials of secular and cultural constitutional values.

Governments at various levels have generally responded positively to court decisions, though, in a few recent instances, the union government has appealed to the Court for a review of some of the courts' decisions (e.g., the appointment by the Supreme Court of a committee headed by a retired Supreme Court justice to monitor government actions on the stashing of unaccounted money by Indian nationals in foreign banks on the plea that it is the domain of the executive). Various proposals for reform have also been discussed. For example, there has been talk for some time about enhancing the accountability of judges through the establishment of a National Judicial Commission. In 2012, a National Judicial Accountability Bill was introduced into Parliament by the Congress-led UPA-II government.[60] It proposed to set up a panel for preliminary scrutiny of complaints concerning decisions of the Supreme Court and any high court. The panel was to comprise a former chief justice and two sitting judges. The Oversight Committee to which the Scrutiny Committee would refer cases for fuller inquiry was to consist of a retired chief justice of India as the chairperson, a judge of the Supreme Court, a chief justice of a high court, and an eminent person appointed by the president. The bill did not proceed, but soon after coming to power in 2014, the BJP/NDA secured the passage of a constitutional amendment and parliamentary act to establish a National Judicial Appointments Commission (NJAC) to replace the previous system, which had given a judicial collegium consisting of the chief justice of India and four of his or her senior-most colleagues power to recommend judicial appointments, with binding effect on the government.[61] The NJAC comprises the chief justice of India and two of his or her senior-most colleagues, the union minister of law and justice, and two "eminent persons" nominated by a committee consisting of the prime minister, the chief justice of India, and the leaders of the official opposition party or, in its absence, the largest opposition party in the Lok Sabha. The amendment was passed by the requisite two-thirds majorities in each house of Parliament and ratified by at least 50 per cent of the

60 Manish Tewari, speech in the Lok Sabha, 21 May 2012; "Political Prism: NJAC Bill Needs Some introspection," *Mail Today*, 28 August 2014; and "Beware the Tyranny of the Elected," *Asian Age*, 30 October 2015.

61 See *Supreme Court Advocates on Record v. Union of India* (1993) and its elaboration in *Re-presidential Reference* (1998), discussed above.

state legislatures and received the assent of India's president. However, its notification in the *Gazette of India* was postponed on account of a pending public interest litigation challenging its constitutional validity. Subsequently, the Supreme Court declared both the parliamentary act and the constitutional amendment unconstitutional on the ground that they violated the principle of judicial independence, which is part of the "basic structure" of the Constitution and therefore unamendable (*SC Advocates on Record Association v. Union of India*, 2015).[62] The proposed system would have overturned the primacy of the judicial members of the NJAC as any of its two members including the union law minister and two eminent persons nominated by the executive could veto a panel proposed by the judicial members.

V. Conclusion

The courts have generally enjoyed a great deal of legitimacy in the eyes of governments as well as civil society, especially in the post–internal emergency period. The governmental institutional balance has undergone a paradigm shift in the sense that since the 1980s, and especially the 1990s, the governmental system has come to be driven largely by the judiciary, whereas in the Nehru and Indira Gandhi eras, it was driven mostly by the executive and the legislature. The courts have generally supported centralist values, but in recent years, there has been a greater tendency to protect the states, at least in some important fields such as cases related to the exercise of the union's power to take over state administration under emergency provisions of the Constitution.

In the context of the contention between the executive and Parliament, on one hand, and constitutional courts, on the other, on the question of the amending power, Granville Austin figuratively argues that in the "struggle for custody of the Constitution, the Supreme Court has won." He says that "despite occasional self-inflicted wounds, the Court has been the bastion of the Constitution. Parliament enjoys the authority to amend the Constitution. The court has the authority to measure amendments against the basic structure doctrine."[63] Pratap Bhanu

62 *Supreme Court Advocates-on-Record-Association and Another v. Union of India*, 2015.

63 Granville Austin, "The Supreme Court and the Struggle for Custody of the Constitution," in *Supreme But Not Infallible: Essays in Honour of the Supreme Court of India*, ed. B.N. Kripal, Ashok H. Desai, Gopal Subramaniam, Rajeev Dhavan, and Raju Ramachandran (New Delhi: Oxford University Press, 2000), 13.

Mehta concedes the contingent rise of judicial sovereignty but adds that "there is a profound inner conflict at the heart of India's constitutionalism: the question, who is the Constitution's final arbiter, admits no easy answer. The Court has declared itself to be the ultimate judge, and has even assumed the power to override duly enacted constitutional amendments … In India, Parliament and Judiciary have been and are likely to remain competitors when it comes to interpreting the Constitution."[64] This assessment has proved to be prophetic, as corroborated by the NJAC episode narrated above.

64 Pratap Bhanu Mehta, "India's Unlikely Democracy: The Rise of Judicial Sovereignty," *Journal of Democracy* 18, no. 2 (2007): 74–5.

9 The Supreme Court of Mexico: Reconfiguring Federalism through Constitutional Adjudication and Amendment after Single-Party Rule

JOSÉ ANTONIO CABALLERO JUÁREZ

I. Introduction

Approximately twenty-five years ago, Mexico began a dramatic transition in its political system.[1] The transformation included the development of a plural political arena that challenged the single-party rule of the Partido Revolucionario Institucional (PRI), which had governed the country for sixty years. Gradually, politicians from other political parties began to occupy positions in state and municipal governments.[2] In 2000, Mexicans elected a federal president from the Partido Acción Nacional (PAN).[3] These developments significantly altered the relationships between federal, state, and municipal authorities. The PRI's party discipline, which had been one of the main instruments for resolving disputes within the political system, became useless when politicians from other parties assumed power. Eventually, the PRI's internal discipline also weakened.[4]

1 See Rogelio Hernández Rodríguez, "Los gobernadores y el federalismo. La descentralización del poder," in *Una historia contemporánea de México*, vol. 3, *Las Instituciones*, ed. Ilan Bizberg and Lorenzo Meyer, 195–217 (Mexico: Océano-El Colegio de México, 2009); and José Luis Reyna, "El sistema político: cambios y vicisitudes," in ibid., 3:47–89.

2 See Alberto Aziz Nassif, "La construcción de la democracia electoral," in *Una historia contemporánea de México*, vol. 1, *Transformaciones y permanencias*, ed. Ilan Bizberg and Lorenzo Meyer, 367–428 (Mexico: Océano-El Colegio de México, 2009); and María Amparo Casar, "Cien años de política," in *México 2010: El juicio del siglo*, ed. María Amparo Casar and Guadalupe González, 50–62 (Mexico: Taurus, 2010).

3 Vicente Fox, president of Mexico (2000–6), came from the Partido Acción Nacional (PAN).

4 The most compelling example happened when Roberto Madrazo, governor of Tabasco, refused to follow the president's order to step down. They were both from the PRI. See Hernández Rodríguez, "Los gobernadores y el federalismo," 211.

In this context, constitutional provisions that had been overshadowed by politics now became noticed as ways of regulating relationships between the federal, state, and municipal orders of government. Soon litigation was adopted as the solution of choice for these kinds of conflicts.[5] However, in many cases, the constitutional rules regarding intergovernmental relations were considered insufficient or out of date. Every year since the mid-1990s, new constitutional amendments have been passed to rearrange the distribution of power among the three constitutional orders.[6] Many of these amendments have increased the powers of federal authorities.[7] Consequently, constitutional law changed very rapidly during the late 1990s, not only as the result of constitutional amendments but also of new interpretations of the Constitution developed by the Supreme Court. Federalism in Mexico embarked on a new era based on enforcement of the Constitution in and through judicial interpretation.

From a federalism perspective, the role of Mexico's courts has involved two key developments. The first is the growing relevance of judicial decisions concerning the meaning of the Constitution's federal clauses. The second is the influence of federal courts over state courts. These two developments have rather opposite effects on the structure and operation of Mexico's federal institutions. This chapter will explain both. The analysis will show how judicial interpretation, as well as certain constitutional amendments, are closely related in the day-to-day construction of Mexican federalism. The chapter also will show how judicial interpretation provides state and local authorities with new opportunities to exercise their powers. Certain unresolved problems created by the influence of the federal courts over state courts will also

5 The first case that contested state officials' powers to rule over municipal issues arose in 1993 (Controversia Constitucional 1/93 Ayuntamiento de Delicias, Chihuahua). This case was based on a constitutional provision that regulated *controversias constitucionales*, a process mentioned in Article 105 of the Constitution, unregulated by statute and rarely used. Some other cases began immediately afterward. For a list of the cases from 1917 through 1994, see Suprema Corte de Justicia de la Nación, http://www.scjn.gob.mx/pleno/paginas/ControvConsti1917_1994.aspx.

6 The Mexican Constitution has been amended more than seventy times since 1995. For a list of the amendments to the Mexican Constitution, see Biblioteca Jurídica Virtual, http://www.juridicas.unam.mx/infjur/leg/constmex/.

7 In this period, Article 73, which contains the federal legislature's powers, has had more than twenty amendments. These amendments usually give the federal legislature new powers over state and municipal governments. For a list of the amendments, see Biblioteca Jurídica Virtual.

be discussed. It will be seen that the centralism that characterizes Mexico's judicial system may help explain why the development of state courts has been limited.

The chapter approaches these questions beginning with a brief description of Mexico as a federation. It then explains the country's court system, focusing on the centralism that prevails in the court system and describing the problems generated by this centralism. Next, the chapter discusses the way in which the Mexican Supreme Court has interpreted federalism over the last fifteen years, and it concludes with some general remarks on the nature of the Supreme Court's precedents on federalism. It is argued that it is not possible to see a clear pattern in the Court's federalism jurisprudence. Most of the Court's decisions seem to be crafted in response to the circumstances of each case. As a result, the case law provides very little suggestion of an identifiable federalism doctrine. Consequently, Mexican federalism has to be analysed specifically by focusing on particular constitutional provisions and Supreme Court interpretations concerning federal, state, and municipal authorities. If there is one general theme, it is a growing judicial centralism facilitated by the increasing number of federal courts exercising supervisory jurisdiction over state court decisions.

II. Federal System

Mexico has a surface area of 1,964,375 square kilometres.[8] As a federation, it is composed of thirty-one states and Mexico City.[9] In 2012, the GDP was US$1.177 trillion with a GNI per capita of US$9,740.[10] The country has a population of 112 million people, and Spanish is spoken by more than 98 per cent of the population. Approximately 6 per cent of the population belongs to an indigenous ethnic group. These groups, which speak more than twenty-four languages, are distributed

8 Unless otherwise mentioned, general data for Mexico were drawn from the Instituto Nacional de Estadística y Geografía, *Anuario estadístico de los Estados Unidos Mexicanos 2011* (Mexico: INEGI, 2012), http://www.inegi.org.mx/sistemas/productos/default.aspx?c=265&s=inegi&upc=702825042448&pf=prod&ef=&f=2&cl=0&tg=8&pg=0.

9 Constitutional amendment published on the Diario Oficial de la Federación 29 January 2016. Before this amendment the Constitution referred to the area occupied by Mexico City as a federal district.

10 See "Data: Mexico," World Bank, http://data.worldbank.org/country/mexico.

throughout the country.[11] Most of them live in the southern states of Chiapas, Oaxaca, Quintana Roo, and Yucatán.

Mexico became a federation in 1824 after gaining independence from Spain in 1821. The federal system has been governed by three constitutions.[12] The current Constitution, enacted in 1917,[13] establishes a federal system based on five legal orders: constitutional, federal, state, federal district, and municipal.[14]

The constitutional order governs every institution in the country. Article 1 of the Constitution states that every person in the United States of Mexico is entitled to the protection of the human rights recognized therein. Article 133 contains the supremacy clause, which stipulates that every law enacted in the country (by the federal Congress or a state congress) is subject to the Constitution. Every judge in the land also is bound by the Constitution.

The Constitution regulates the powers of the three federal branches of government. Article 40 and the first paragraph of Article 41 define the country's federal system as deriving from the sovereignty of the people, exercised through the governing institutions of the union and the states. The powers of these two orders of government are determined by two articles of the Constitution: Article 73, which specifies the competences of the federal Congress, and Article 124 (the residual clause), which states that any attribution that is expressly granted not to the federation by the Constitution will be deemed to be within the

11 The 2000 census registered eighty-five indigenous languages. Instituto Nacional de Estadística y Geografía, *La población indígena en México* (Mexico: INEGI, 2004), 7. The 2011 national statistical yearbook considers twenty-four languages as the main indigenous languages.

12 Mexico's first Constitution (4 October 1824) stated that Mexico would become a federal state. In 1835 the federal system was substituted for a central system. It was reinstated in 1847 and then replaced by a new federal system based on the 1857 Constitution (5 February 1857). This system was reformed by the 1917 Constitution (5 February 1917).

13 See "The Political Constitution of the Mexican States," http://www.juridicas.unam.mx/infjur/leg/constmex/pdf/consting.pdf.

14 ORDEN JURÍDICO MUNICIPAL. PRINCIPIO DE COMPETENCIA (MUNICIPIOS COMO ÓRGANOS DE GOBIERNO). Controversia constitucional 18/2008. Municipio de Zacatepec de Hidalgo, Estado de Morelos. 18 January 2011. 10a. Época; *SJF y su Gaceta*; Libro I, October 2011, Tomo 1; page 294; Thesis P./J. 44/2011 (9a). For a complete account on Mexican federalism from a legal perspective, see José María Serna de la Garza, *El sistema federal mexicano: Un análisis jurídico* (Mexico: Instituto de Investigaciones Jurídicas, UNAM, 2008).

competence of the states. Article 73 has been amended sixty-five times since 1917, expanding federal powers in several ways.[15] In some cases, federal competence is limited to enacting legislation; in other cases, federal authorities are also responsible for enforcing the law.[16] Other provisions of the Constitution grant to the federal branches of government additional competences, such as Articles 103, 104, and 105, which regulate the federal judiciary.[17] Other provisions establish shared competences in areas such as education (Art. 3), health and environmental protection (Art. 4), public security (Art. 21), and housing and urban development (Art. 27).[18]

Articles 115, 116, 117, and 118 provide specific rules regarding the organization and powers of the state governments. Article 115 requires the states to adopt for their internal government a popular, representative, and republican form of government. Article 116 further requires the public power of the states to be divided among executive, legislative, and judicial organs. Articles 117 and 118 specify limits to state powers, including a prohibition on forming alliances or treaties with other countries. Subject to the limits stated in these articles, the residual powers (Art. 124) of the states are quite extensive, and include, for example, the authority to enact their own criminal and civil codes.[19]

Mexico City is defined in Article 44 and governed by Article 122, which provides the framework for the organization of the City's three branches of government. This framework makes Mexico City's government equivalent to that of a state government. Thus, the City has its own court system; its assembly has vast powers to enact legislation; and its governor is elected by the people in the City.

---

15 Amendments that incorporate sections to Article 73 are common. A clear example may be seen in section XXIX, which is now subdivided into seventeen new sections (XXIX-B to XXIX-Q). Each new section grants additional powers to the federal Congress. See note 8 for a list of the amendments.

16 For example, in labour relations, the federal legislative branch is entitled to enact the labour statute, enforcement is divided between state and federal authorities (Art. 73, sec. X; and 123, part A, sec. XXXI). In some other cases, for instance, gambling, legislation, and enforcement is carried out by federal authorities.

17 See next section.

18 See section III.

19 Since Article 73 does not give the federal Congress the power to enact a uniform civil code or a uniform criminal code, it is understood that under Article 124 that his power is left to state legislatures.

Lastly, the municipal order is regulated by Article 115, sections I–VIII.[20] The intention is to limit state intervention into municipal affairs.[21] Constitutional litigation between states and municipalities over these issues is quite common.

The process to amend the Constitution is contained in Article 135. Amendments must be passed by at least three-quarters of the sitting members of each chamber of the federal Congress (Senate and House of Deputies) and then ratified by more than half of the state legislatures. Despite these apparently rigid requirements, the 1917 Constitution has been revised more than two hundred times.[22]

III. Court System

Mexico has a complex court system that includes thirty-three court subsystems and several other administrative courts.[23] This section will first describe the court system and then explain how the system operates in practice, focusing on the impact of the federal judiciary on the rest of the courts through the use of the *amparo directo* (judicial review).[24]

---

20 The Supreme Court recently recognized the municipal order as it is stated in the precedent cited in note 8: MUNICIPIOS. EL ARTÍCULO 115, FRACCIONES I Y II, DE LA CONSTITUCIÓN FEDERAL RECONOCE LA EXISTENCIA DE UN ORDEN JURÍDICO PROPIO. Controversia constitucional 14/2001. Municipio de Pachuca de Soto, Estado de Hidalgo. 7 July 2005. Novena Época, *SJF y su Gaceta*, XXII, October 2005; page 2070; Thesis P./J. 134/2005. Previous precedents recognized only four orders in the Mexican legal system. See, for example, CONTROVERSIA CONSTITUCIONAL. EL ORDEN JURÍDICO ESTATAL COMPRENDE LAS RELACIONES ENTRE LOS PODERES LOCALES Y SUS MINICIPIOS. Controversia constitucional 31/97. Ayuntamiento de Temixco, Morelos. August 9 1999. Novena Época, *SJF y su Gaceta*, X, September 1999, page 705; Thesis: P./J. 96/99.

21 Article 115 of the Constitution has been recognized as the cornerstone of municipal government in Mexico since 1917. Amendments passed in 1983 and in 1999 strengthened municipal governments, providing further limitations to state governments.

22 See note 7.

23 The system includes the federal judiciary, thirty-one state courts, and the Federal District's courts. For a complete study of Mexico's court system, see Héctor Fix-Zamudio and José Ramón Cossío Díaz, *El poder judicial en el ordenamiento mexicano* (Mexico: Fondo de Cultura Económica, 1999).

24 *Amparo directo* is explained below in this same section. See also note 38.

1. General Features

The Supreme Court heads the federal judiciary. Below it there are three levels of federal courts: collegiate circuit courts, unitary circuit courts, and district courts (Art. 94).[25] The Supreme Court has justices and hears cases *en banc* or in one of its two chambers.[26] The president nominates justices by submitting three candidates to the Senate. The Senate appoints one of the candidates. The federal judiciary is distributed in 32 circuits. There are 239 collegiate circuit courts with three magistrates each, 95 unitary circuit courts, and 391 district courts,[27] each one headed by a judge.[28] Magistrates and judges are appointed thorough a competitive process. Almost all of them have previous experience as clerks in the federal judiciary.

The federal judiciary has jurisdiction to hear constitutional and federal cases (Art. 103, 104, and 105). Federal jurisdiction (Art. 104) includes civil and criminal cases, maritime jurisdiction, controversies to which the federation is party, and conflicts affecting ambassadors and consuls, among others. Federal courts are also competent to hear commercial cases. However, section II of Article 104 mentions that state courts may also hear commercial cases.[29]

Until very recently, the Supreme Court and the federal judiciary were the only courts with jurisdiction to hear constitutional cases.[30]

---

25 The Federal Electoral Court is also part of the federal judiciary. Its organization and jurisdiction are separated from the rest of the federal judiciary (Article 99).

26 Articles 94 through 98 provide several rules on the appointment of justices and the conditions under which they serve.

27 Some of these courts are not called district courts. Still they constitute the first level of the federal and the *amparo* jurisdiction. For example, there are three judges specialized in supervising the inmates who are serving time after being declared guilty.

28 Articles 97 and 100 regulate the appointment of judges and magistrates and service in the judiciary. For the complete list of circuit and district courts, see "Direccíon General de Estadística Judicial," http://www.dgepj.cjf.gob.mx/organosjurisdiccionales/numeroorganos/numorganoscir.asp.

29 State courts hear most of the commercial cases. In fact, a historical claim by state courts is that they should receive federal resources as compensation for their participation in commercial litigation. José Antonio Caballero, Sergio López Ayllón, and Alfonso Oñate Laborde, *Libro Blanco de la reforma judicial* (Mexico: Suprema Corte de Justicia de la Nación, 2006), 183.

30 For a description of the concentrated system of constitutional control, see David García Sarubbi, "Federalism and Constitutional Judicial Review in Mexico and the United States: A Normative Assessment of Two Different Jurisdictional Schemes," *Mexican Law Review* 4, no. 1 (2011): 42–3.

A decision from the Supreme Court[31] delivered in July 2011 opened constitutional control to state courts as well.[32] As a consequence, the current constitutional control system is based on the concentrated jurisdiction of the federal judiciary, which is complemented by limited judicial control carried out by state courts.[33] The federal judiciary exercises constitutional control through three alternative procedures: the *amparo* (Arts. 103 and 107), the *controversias constitucionales* (Art. 105 sec. I), and the *acciones de inconstitucionalidad* (Art. 105 sec. II).[34]

The writ of *amparo* is the most common method of judicial review.[35] The *amparo* may be used to argue against the constitutionality of statutes, administrative decisions, and, generally speaking, any act carried out by an authority, including judicial decisions delivered in federal jurisdiction or in state jurisdiction.[36] District judges or collegiate circuit courts may hear *amparos*. If it is an *amparo*

---

31 Precedents in Mexico are referred to as *jurisprudencia*. *Jurisprudencia* may have a binding character or just an authoritative one. *Jurisprudencia* may refer to the whole text of a decision or to a specific passage that determines the judgment (*ratio decidendi*), or may even refer to passages that provide an opinion on a question that is not strictly related to the case (*dictum*). The most common way of publishing *jurisprudencia* is by selecting passages of decisions. Capital letters are used to give the passage a title. The federal judiciary publishes *jurisprudencia* monthly in the *Semanario Judicial de la Federación y su Gaceta* (*SJF y su Gaceta*), http://ius.scjn.gob.mx/paginas/tesis.aspx. A note on Mexican jurisprudence may be found in José María Serna de la Garza, "The Concept of Jurisprudencia in Mexican Law," *Mexican Law Review* 1, no. 2 (2009): 131–45.

32 SISTEMA DE CONTROL CONSTITUCIONAL EN EL ORDEN JURÍDICO MEXICANO. Varios 912/2010. 14 July 2011. 10a. Época; Pleno; *SJF y su Gaceta*; book III, December 2011, volume 1; page 557; thesis P. LXX/2011 (9a).

33 State judges and courts may exercise constitutional control by refusing to apply a statute that they consider to be unconstitutional. These decisions do not become binding precedents.

34 For an overview of the constitutional control system in Mexico, see José Ramón Cossío Díaz, *Sistemas y modelos de control constitucional en México* (Mexico: Instituto de Investigaciones Jurídicas, UNAM, 2011).

35 A study in English of the *amparo* that is still useful is Richard D. Baker, *Judicial Review in Mexico: A Study of the Amparo Suit* (Austin: University of Texas Press, 1971). A complete overview of the *amparo* appears in Héctor Fix-Zamudio, *Ensayos sobre el derecho de amparo* (Mexico: Porrúa-UNAM, 2003).

36 In these cases it is quite common to see that a federal judge's decision in a federal case may be reviewed by another federal judge via the *amparo* under a constitutional jurisdiction. See subsection 2 *infra*.

directo,[37] it will go to a collegiate circuit court (Art. 107, sec. V). If it is an *amparo indirecto*,[38] it will go to a district judge (Art 107, sec. VII). *Amparo* appeals may go to collegiate circuit courts or to the Supreme Court. The *controversia constitucional* (constitutional controversy) is a procedure designed to solve competence disputes among authorities of different branches or different orders of government.[39] *Controversias* are heard directly by the Supreme Court. *Acciones de inconstitucionalidad* (unconstitutionality actions) are used to challenge the constitutionality of statutes.[40] This method of constitutional control is available only to political parties, congressional minorities (federal or state), the federal attorney general, the national ombudsman, and state ombudsmen. Unlike the *amparo*, which may benefit only the party seeking the remedy (Art. 107, sec. II), the *acción de inconstitucionalidad*, if successful, results in a declaration that the challenged statute is entirely void.

State judiciaries must be organized under the terms stated in section III of Article 116 of the Constitution. Judges and magistrates are required to be independent, their remuneration must be adequate, and it may not be waived nor reduced. State judiciaries are usually divided into three levels: small claims, courts of first instance, and an appeals court. The docket of a state court includes civil, family, criminal, and commercial cases.[41]

In addition to the federal and state judiciaries, there are four other jurisdictions in Mexico. Federal administrative courts are organized under Article 73, section XXIX-H. State administrative courts are organized under Article 116, section V.[42] There are no appeals to the federal administrative court from the decisions of state administrative courts. All of these courts are autonomous bodies that hear complaints filed

---

37 *Amparo directo* is used to challenge decisions delivered by administrative or judicial courts. Procedural or substantive arguments in the *amparo directo* are argued as constitutional violations that affect due process (Art. 14) or regarding the legal reasoning supporting the challenged decision (Art. 16). In some cases, challenges extend to questions regarding the constitutionality of statutes.

38 An *amparo indirecto* is used to challenge the constitutionality of decisions delivered by administrative authorities as well as statutes.

39 For an overview of *controversias constitucionales*, see José Ramón Cossío Díaz, *La controversia constitucional* (Mexico: Porrúa, 2008).

40 For an overview of *acciones de inconstitucionalidad*, see Joaquín Brage Camazano, *La acción de inconstitucionalidad* (Mexico: Instituto de Investigaciones Jurídicas, UNAM, 2000).

41 See note 31.

42 Mexico City's administrative court is organized under article 122, part A, section VIII.

against administrative decisions. Labour conflicts are determined by the Boards of Conciliation and Arbitration mandated by Article 123, section XX, part A. These boards are composed of an equal number of representatives of workers and employers, in addition to one government representative. There is a federal board, thirty-one state boards, and an additional board for Mexico City. Article 123, section XXXI, part A, enunciates the areas and industries where labour conflicts must be reserved to the federal board. State and Federal District boards, subject to their territorial jurisdiction, hear the rest of the conflicts. Labour conflicts between the federal branches of government, as well as Mexico City, and their workers are to be solved in accordance to section XII, part B of Article 123. This section mandates that a Federal Court of Conciliation and Arbitration must hear these cases. States have very similar arrangements concerning bureaucratic labour disputes (Art. 116, sec. VI).

Electoral courts are organized under the terms detailed in Article 99 (Federal Electoral Court) and Article 116, section IV (state electoral courts). General provisions in these articles establish guarantees of the independence of electoral judges for the federation and the states. It is important to note that the Electoral Tribunal of the Federal Judiciary has an autonomous status within the federal judiciary.[43] Article 99 also empowers the Federal Electoral Court to review decisions handed down by state electoral courts. The supreme chamber of the electoral tribunal of the federal judiciary, as well as its regional chambers, publish *jurisprudencia* regularly.[44] According to Article 233 of the Federal Judiciary Act, *jurisprudencia* are binding on federal electoral authorities. In cases where a state electoral issue is addressed, the precedent may also bind electoral authorities in that state.

The Agrarian Superior Court is founded in Article 27, section XIX. Agrarian jurisdiction is also defined in Article 27, section XIX. The agrarian court system hears cases that involve indigenous communities as well as other disputes that involve land rights. Agrarian jurisdiction is federal. Thus, state courts will not hear such disputes. Decisions

---

43 Article 99 provides a framework for the government and administration of the Federal Electoral Court. This framework separates the Electoral Court from the rest of the federal judiciary.

44 Article 232 of the Ley orgánica del Poder Judicial Federal (Federal Judiciary Act) regulates the integration of *jurisprudencia*. *Jurisprudencia* is published online at http://200.23.107.66/siscon/gateway.dll/nJurisprudenciayTesis?f=templates&fn=default.htm. For further information on *jurisprudencia*, see note 33.

handed down by the Agrarian Superior Court prevail over decisions issued by state courts in regard to property rights.[45]

Lastly, the military court system is based on Article 13 of the Constitution. The Code of Military Justice describes the military court system as well as its proceedings. Until very recently, civil courts tended to defer to military courts in almost every case involving a member of the armed forces. In 2009, in light of the *Rosendo Radilla* decision from the Inter-American Court of Human Rights, things began to change.[46] The Supreme Court debated the merits and effects of the Inter-American Court's decision in 2011, and a majority of justices decided that the resolution was binding on Mexican authorities, including judges, and that military jurisdiction had to be reviewed and perhaps limited.[47] In 2012, the Supreme Court heard several new cases on military jurisdiction and concluded that the jurisdiction has to be restricted.[48]

2. *The Amparo Directo and Judicial Centralism*

In the late nineteenth century, the Supreme Court began hearing complaints against decisions delivered by state courts through *amparos*.[49] Lawyers who were not satisfied with a court decision began complaining that judges who drafted it did not apply the law in a proper way

---

45 For example, a piece of land is sold under the Civil Code enacted in the state where the land is located. Any dispute regarding this sale will be heard by a state judge. However, if the said land is considered to be protected by the agrarian property regime under Article 27 of the Constitution, an agrarian court will hear any challenge regarding property rights without taking into account civil law.

46 See Case of Radilla-Pacheco v. Mexico. Preliminary Objections, Merits, Reparations, and Costs. Judgment of 23 November 2009. Series C No. 209.

47 See Expediente Varios 912/2010, Pleno, 14 July 2011.

48 See Amparo en revisión 133/2012, Pleno, 21 August 2012; Conflicto Competencial suscitado entre el Juzgado Séptimo de Distrito en el Estado de Michoacán, y el Juzgado Militar, adscrito a la Quinta Región Militar 60/2012, Pleno, 14 August 2012; and Conflicto Competencial suscitado entre el Juzgado Quinto de Distrito en el Estado de Morelos y el Juzgado Quinto Militar, adscrito a la primera región militar 38/2012, Pleno, 9 August 2012.

49 Lawyers, legislators, and justices debated for several years the convenience of admitting the *amparo* as a means of challenging decisions of state courts. A description of this debate appears in José de Jesús Gudiño Pelayo, "La jurisdicción de amparo y la independencia del juez local," in *Derecho Procesal Constitucional*, ed. Eduardo Ferrer MacGregor, 1:765–88 (Mexico: Porrúa-Colegio de Secretarios de la Suprema Corte de Justicia de la Nación, AC, 2003).

or that their reasoning had erred. These arguments were presented as constitutional violations. A successful complaint meant the Supreme Court had found a constitutional infringement in the decision being reviewed. Successful complaints were remanded to state courts for determination in accordance with the Supreme Court's judgment. Lawyers soon discovered that the *amparo judicial* or *amparo directo,* as it came to be known, could be used as a kind of third instance form of appeal. *Amparos directos* kept arising in the Supreme Court's docket throughout the twentieth century.[50] What began as a discussion over the merits of a constitutional remedy to challenge state court decisions soon evolved into a political discussion. Under these new premises, the *amparo* that challenged state court decisions was understood to be a remedy against unfair and corrupt judges and state courts. The draft 1917 Constitution addressed the *amparo* situation by admitting it as a necessary means to prevent abuses by state judges.[51] This rhetoric is still employed to justify the *amparo directo*.[52]

The increasing use of *amparo directos* forced federal legislators and the Supreme Court to manage the growing caseload. They adopted two main strategies. The first focused on legal adjustments to increase the technical difficulty in having an *amparo* heard by the Supreme Court. The second was to increase the supply of judges available to hear complaints, by increasing the number of justices on the Supreme Court and diverting *amparos* to lower courts. These strategies did not operate harmoniously. Indeed, some reforms, as will be seen, actually increased the demand for the *amparo* procedure.

The Constitution of 1917 incorporated several technical innovations to limit the use of *amparo directo*. Article 107, section III, subsection a requires that the *amparo directo* be admitted only if it is challenging a final decision of a case delivered by a state appeal court.[53] Section III also requires *amparo* challenges to be admitted only against decisions

50 Julio Bustillos published statistics of the *amparos* admitted by the Supreme Court between 1869 and 2006. Julio Bustillos, *El amparo directo en México: Evolución y realidad actual* (Mexico: Porrúa-UNAM, 2008), 197–200.

51 Venustiano Carranza, "Mensaje del primer jefe ante el constituyente: 1° de diciembre de 1916," in *Leyes constitucionales de México, 1808–1998*, ed. Felipe Tena Ramírez (Mexico: Porrúa, 1998), 751.

52 José María Serna de la Garza, "Apuntes sobre el debate relativo al amparo casación en México," *Reforma Judicial: Revista Mexicana de Justicia* 1 (2003): 263–79.

53 This rule was already considered in the 1908 Federal Code of Civil Procedure, article 661.

where the law has been misapplied or where due process infractions have a direct impact on the outcome of a trial. *Amparo* plaintiffs also must prove that they had unsuccessfully sought to challenge the alleged violation through ordinary judicial procedures. In section VIII of Article 107, it is mandated that *amparos* challenging court decisions must be heard directly by the Supreme Court. Until this provision came into force in 1917, these cases were handled by district judges and then would go to the Supreme Court for review.[54]

As noted, one of the first measures to address the demand for the *amparo* procedure was to increase the number of justices on the Supreme Court. According to the 1917 Constitution's original text, the Court had eleven justices (Art. 94). A 1928 amendment increased the number to sixteen. A 1934 amendment further increased the number of justices to twenty-one. Later, in 1951, five auxiliary justices were also appointed.[55]

In 1939, the Amparo Act was amended so that *amparos* could be dismissed for procedural inactivity (lapse of proceedings).[56] This rule was later incorporated into section XIV of Article 107. In 1974, an amendment to Article 79 of the Amparo Act ordered judges to adopt a strict approach to *amparo* suits in civil cases. Their decisions were limited to addressing only what the claimant had specifically argued, and judges could not correct or incorporate new claims to the suit.[57] The amendment to the Amparo Act also enabled judges to impose a fine against litigators who initiated frivolous *amparo* suits (Art. 81). The applicable fine was increased further in 1980 and 1984.

In 1951, the Supreme Court's backlog was estimated to be around 37,000 cases.[58] That same year, sections V and VI of Article 107 were amended to open the way for federal collegiate circuit courts to hear *amparos directos*. However, this provision mandated that collegiate courts hear only

54 Ignacio Burgoa, *El juicio de amparo* (Mexico: Porrúa, 1950), 635–6. Constitutional regulations limiting *amparo* were complemented by the Amparo Act of 1919 and then by the Amparo Act of 1936.

55 See amendments published in the *Diario Oficial de la Federación*, 20 August 1928, 15 December 1934, and 19 February 1951.

56 Article 74, section V. Published in the *Diario Oficial de la Federación*, 30 December 1939. This rule was considered in the 1908 Code of Civil Procedure. It was then removed by the 1919 Amparo Act (Ley Reglamentaria de los Artículos 103 y 104 de la Constitución Federal).

57 Published in the *Diario Oficial de la Federación*, 4 December 1974.

58 Romeo León Orantes, *El juicio de amparo* (Mexico: Editorial José Cajica, Jr, 1957), 90.

amparos where procedural claims were being challenged (*in procedendo*). The Supreme Court would hear *amparos* that challenged the merits of the decision (*in iudicando*). Further reforms in 1967 redistributed the Supreme Court's docket to federal collegiate circuit courts. As a consequence, circuit courts could also hear *amparos* that challenged the merits of decisions. However, circuit courts could only hear cases that involved misdemeanours, agrarian jurisdiction, civil cases depending on the amount being litigated, and family cases.[59] The 1987 constitutional amendment transferred most of the *amparo directo* caseload to federal courts, which left the Supreme Court with a very narrow share of *amparos directos*.

These legal and constitutional reforms had several consequences. The first was a major increase in the number of federal courts.

In 1951 there were five federal circuit courts with three magistrates each. It is reported that in 1951, the Supreme Court transferred 27,000 cases to the new federal collegiate circuit courts. Figure 1 shows how the creation of the new courts (in 1967 and 1987) resulted in a significant transfer cases to them. The increase in the number of courts in the late 1990s is in turn related to the 1994 reform.[60] As of November 2014, there were 246 courts and 738 magistrates. This expansion radically redesigned Mexico's judicial map. In 1951, the federal judiciary was distributed in five circuits.[61] Today, thirty-two circuits are operating. Given that Mexico has thirty-one states as well as the Federal District, the outcome is that every federal entity has its own federal circuit court. Considering the role of the *amparo directo*, every federal entity has some sort of federal court that oversees the state superior court and the rest of

59 Amendments to section V of Article 107 published in the *Diario Oficial de la Federación*, 25 October 1967.

60 The 1994 reform redesigned the federal judiciary. The judiciary council became a key element for the governance of the federal judiciary. Under this role, the federal judiciary became very active in securing resources for the judiciary. Their success opened the door for large investments in justice to fund new courts. See José Antonio Caballero Juárez, "De la marginalidad a los reflectores: El renacimiento de la administración de justicia en México," in *Una historia contemporánea de México*, vol. 3, *Las Instituciones*, ed. Ilan Bizberg and Lorenzo Meyer (Mexico: Océano-El Colegio de México, 2009), 184.

61 José Antonio Caballero Juárez, "Amparos y abogángsters. La justicia en México entre 1940 y 1968," in *Del nacionalismo al neoliberalismo, 1940–1994*, ed. Elisa Servín (Mexico: CIDE, Conaculta, INEHRM, Fundación Cultural de la Ciudad de México, 2010), 150.

Figure 1 Federal Collegiate Circuit Courts (ordinary and auxiliary) 1951–2015

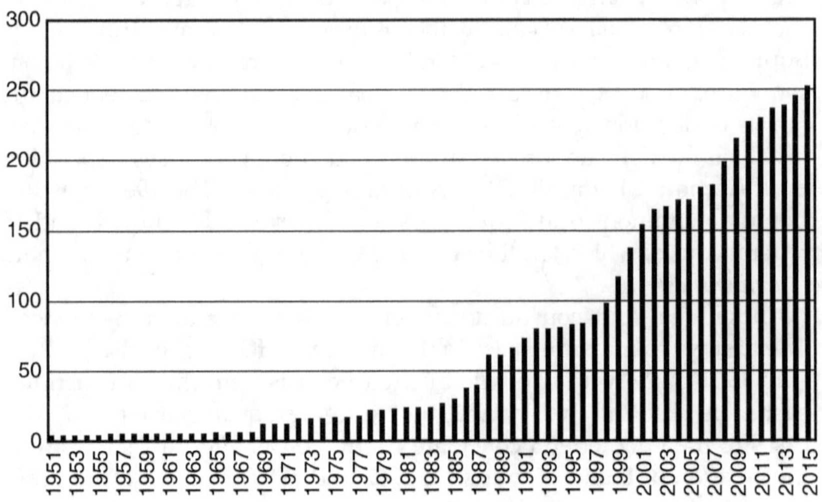

Source: Bustillos, *El amparo directo en México*; and annual reports from the Supreme Court of Justice.

the local judiciary.[62] This means that every single decision handed out by every state court may be reviewed by a federal court that is established in the same state. The practical effect is that Federal Courts have become the final authoritative determination sources for the interpretation of state constitutions and state laws.

A second consequence of the reforms concerns the demand for *amparos*. Constitutional reforms of 1951 and 1967 to relocate *amparos* and reduce the pressure on the Supreme Court's docket had a very limited impact. Each time a constitutional amendment was passed to divert *amparos* to circuit courts, the number of pending *amparos* was reduced immediately, but it did not take long for the numbers to rise again.[63] Despite reforms, the Supreme Court again became unable to process its caseload. The only reform that worked for the Court was the 1987 reform. This reform sent all *amparos* to the circuit courts except those the Supreme Court considers appropriate for its own review.

62 For a map of the current distribution of the federal judiciary, see Direccíon General de Estadística Judicial, http://www.dgepj.cjf.gob.mx/organosjurisdiccionales/ubicacion/ubicacionoj.asp.

63 Bustillos, *El amparo directo.*

However, removing the cases from the Supreme Court and into circuit courts did not solve the problem. The *amparo* caseload in circuit courts has constantly increased since 1951.[64] The federal judiciary's policy to address this phenomenon has been to increase the number of circuit courts (see figure 1). However, it seems that the two variables are linked. This means that increasing the number of circuit courts not only raises the cost of the federal justice system but also seems to be unable to solve the caseload problem. Cases are growing at the same rate as the opening of new federal courts. An additional consequence is the large number of precedents (*jurisprudencia*) published monthly.[65] *Jurisprudencia* published by federal circuit courts are mandatory for every court in the country except for other circuit courts or the Supreme Court.[66] This means that state courts have to follow federal court decisions closely and take them into account when deciding a particular case.[67]

Thus, in 2011 alone, the Supreme Court and federal circuit courts published 206 binding precedents and more than 2,000 authoritative precedents. Even though authoritative precedents are not binding, state courts tend to take them into consideration. They have little option but to do so because the same federal courts that produce the *jurisprudencia* are the ones that will hear, via the *amparo*, any challenges against state court decisions. Indeed, even if a state court follows a federal precedent, this does not mean that the state court decision will be confirmed by a federal circuit court. Because the circuit courts are not bound by other circuit court precedents, if a state court decides to use a precedent issued by one circuit court and the case is reviewed by another circuit court, the latter may nonetheless apply its own criteria and modify the decision subject to review. The question then becomes: to what extent does the Supreme Court provide a unifying function?

---

64 Ibid.; and annual reports from the Supreme Court of Justice. For electronic versions since 2003, see Suprema Corte de Justicia de la Nación, http://www.scjn.gob.mx/Transparencia/Paginas/informe.aspx.

65 See note 33.

66 After the constitutional amendments of 2011, *jurisprudencia* published by a circuit court will be binding only inside the circuit. Only the *jurisprudencia* published by the Supreme Court bind all courts in the country.

67 Although not every precedent that is published is binding, federal circuit courts may consider published precedents when reviewing state court decisions. Therefore, if state courts want to ensure a confirmation, they should consider published precedents.

In 2011 the Supreme Court published more than three hundred opinions resolving divergent precedents,[68] some of which involved divergent precedents published by federal courts even within the *same* circuit. The problem of divergent precedents affects not only state courts but also the construction of legal certainty.[69] An additional consequence is that state courts have almost no incentive to publish their own precedents because they might be modified or overturned by federal circuit courts. Given that every Mexican state has a federal circuit, state courts have de facto lost their status as high courts in their respective states.

The subordination of state courts to federal circuit courts also has an impact on the institutional development of the former.[70] For example, a common way of assessing the performance of state superior court judges is to review their record in *amparo directos* against the cases they have heard.[71] Such an approach assumes that the opinions handed down by federal circuit courts are necessarily better than the decisions delivered by state judges. Federal court judges are all perceived to hold more prestigious positions because their salaries are substantially higher than those of state judges.[72]

68 Section XIII of Article 107 regulates how divergent precedents will be solved by the Supreme Court.

69 The constitutional amendment published on 6 June 2011 provides a new way to solve divergent opinions. Magistrates from every court of the circuit sit *en banc* and solve diverging opinions. See section XIII, Article 107.

70 Baruch Delgado, "Discurso del magistrado Baruch Delgado Carbajal, presidente del Tribunal Superior de Justicia y del Consejo de la Judicatura del Estado de México," *Cuestiones Constitucionales* 24 (2010): 367–71.

71 Sonia Serrano Íñiguez, "Congreso remueve a magistrado por dar información falsa," *Milenio*, Jalisco edition, sec. Cd y Región, 4 May 2012. http://www.milenio.com/cdb/doc/noticias2011/1472005d2d93788edef2f9d906d4e1f5.

72 For a description of the impact of the *amparo directo* over state courts, see Hugo Concha Cantú and José Antonio Caballero, *Diagnóstico de sobre la administración de justicia en las entidades federativas. Un estudio sobre la justicia local en México* (Mexico: Instituto de Investigaciones Jurídicas, UNAM, 2001), 159–66. There is also a perception that litigators abuse in the use of the *amparo directo*: see Silvestre Moreno Cora, *Tratado del Juicio de Amparo conforme a las sentencias de los tribunales federales* (Mexico: Tip y Lit La Europea, de J. Aguilar Vera y Compañía, 1902, reprint Mexico: Supreme Court of Justice, 2008), 639–40; and José Manuel de Alba de Alba, Isidro Pedro Alcántara Valdés, and Mario Alberto Flores García, *Amparo contra resoluciones judiciales: Laberinto procesal* (Mexico: Porrúa, 2006), 93.

IV. Federalism Jurisprudence

1. *Controversias Constitucionales and the Role of the Supreme Court*

In 1995 the Supreme Court of Justice was refounded and new justices were appointed.[73] The eleven new justices were appointed with the nearly unanimous support of all political forces.[74] Most of the appointees were career judges, but some practising lawyers and experienced public servants were appointed as well.[75] Of the eleven justices appointed in 1995, the last two finished their tenure in November 2015. New justices have a profile very similar to that of those they are replacing. They are either career federal judges or lawyers with prestige as litigators, university professors, or public servants. Although a few of the justices have been affiliated with a political party, the appointment process is far from being a quota system in the hands of political parties. Thus, justices are not considered to represent any particular political party. The Court's reform was considered a key part of the agenda of the new political system that arose with the end of the PRI's domination of Mexican politics. Courts before had hardly ever enforced federal clauses because the PRI regime was able to negotiate conflicts through party politics. The new Supreme Court is now recognized as an independent arbitrator and has become a central institution in Mexico's new political system.[76] Citizens as well as political actors have begun employing constitutional litigation as a means of advancing various causes. Some of the most contested cases have involved disputes between branches

---

73 Published in the *Diario Oficial de la Federación*, 31 December 1994. The statute that regulates the *controversias* was published a few months later (*Diario Oficial de la Federación*, 11 May 1995).

74 Senators from the PRI, the PAN, and most senators from the Partido de la Revolución Democrática-Left (PRD) voted in favour of the new justices. See *Diario de los Debates*, Senado de la República, Primer Periodo Extraordinario. LVI Legislatura, 26 January 1995, http://www.senado.gob.mx/index.php?ver=sp&mn=3&sm=3&lg=56&ano=1&id=4474.

75 Seven justices had ample experience as federal judges. For a biographical note on the new justices, see Lucio Cabrera Acevedo, *La Suprema Corte de Justicia durante el gobierno del presidente Ernesto Zedillo Ponce de León (1995–2000)* (Mexico: Suprema Corte de Justicia de la Nación, 2005), 53–77.

76 María Amparo Hernández Chong Cuy, *Suprema Corte y Controversias Constitucionales: Análisis de comportamiento judicial* (Mexico: Porrúa-Instituto Mexicano de Derecho Procesal Constitucional, 2012).

of the federal government or between federal, state, and municipal authorities. These cases have given rise to many significant changes in constitutional law generally, particularly in its federalism-related aspects.

The 1994 constitutional amendment that provided the basis for the Supreme Court's re-establishment also included several new constitutional procedures. The most important one for federalism has been the *controversia constitucional*. The *controversia* is a means to resolve disputes between federal, state, and municipal officials. Since 1995, the Supreme Court has heard an average of ninety such cases each year. Some also involve conflicts between government branches. The 1994 amendment thus gave the Supreme Court a key role in defining the limits of federalism. The *controversia constitucional* in particular became the most common way of making federalism-related claims. In some cases, conflicts of competence also arise in *acciones de inconstitucionalidad*.[77] Some of these actions will receive comment; however, most of the cases included in this section will be *controversias constitucionales*.

The *controversia constitucional* is regulated by Article 105, section I of the Constitution. Additional regulations are included in the *Ley reglamentaria de las fracciones I y II del artículo 105 constitucional* (Law that regulates sections I and II of Article 105). *Controversias* focus on conflicts between branches of government (e.g., Congress against the president) and between orders (e.g., federation against a state or a municipality). A key element in every *controversia* is that plaintiffs need to argue how the application of the act that is being challenged affects them.[78] A *controversia* is essentially a written procedure, with a plaintiff and one or several defendants. Both parties have the opportunity to submit evidence and

---

77 See Acción de Inconstitucionalidad 146/2007 y su acumulada 147/2007, Pleno, 27 May 2010. This case discusses abortion in the Federal District. One of the most important constitutional questions answered in this case was the degree to which the Federal District was bound to follow federal regulations on health. The Supreme Court decided that the Federal District was not bound by such regulation.

78 Unlike *Acciones de inconstitucionalidad, controversias* are not designed to test legislation from an abstract perspective. See CONTROVERSIAS CONSTITUCIONALES Y ACCIONES DE INCONSTITUCIONALIDAD. DIFERENCIAS ENTRE AMBOS MEDIOS DE CONTROL CONSTITUCIONAL. Controversia Constitucional 15/98. Ayuntamiento del Municipio de Río Bravo, Tamaulipas, 11 May 2000. Novena Época; Pleno; *SJF y su Gaceta*, XII, August 2000; page 965; thesis P./J. 71/2000. Also see Hernández Chong Cuy, *Suprema Corte y controversias*, 181–3.

produce allegations.[79] Once allegations are filed, justices will decide on the merits of the case, after debating a draft judgment prepared by one of them. The Supreme Court's debates are public.[80] Article 105, section I includes a list of the entities that may present *controversias* and entities that may be considered defendants. The Supreme Court has adopted a narrow view of legal standing for plaintiffs in *controversias*. Thus, it is not common for the Court to accept a challenge presented by an entity that is not authorized expressly by Article 105, section I.[81] However, the Court is more flexible in the case of defendants, where it tends to accept defendants even if they are not considered expressly by Article 105, section I.[82]

The Supreme Court has resolved 1,283 constitutional controversies since 1995.[83] Most of the caseload comes from municipalities suing a state governor, a state congress, or both.[84] Conflicts between state or federal government branches as well as conflicts between the federal and state or municipal authorities make a up a smaller proportion of the cases. The statistics of *controversias* presented in 2014 provide a good

79 Evidence in *controversias* is usually written. Parties almost never need to present expert witnesses or other sources of evidence that are not based on a document. Allegations are also presented on written documents.

80 Contrary to many other traditions, Mexico's Supreme Court will usually hear oral arguments in chambers, and justices will debate in a public session. These sessions are televised. Transcriptions and videos of these sessions may be accessed in Suprema Corte de Justicia de la Nación, www.scjn.gob.mx.

81 Such is the case that involved the Federal Electoral Institute. In this case the Supreme Court has relied on a literal reading of Article 105, section I to deny standing to the institute as a plaintiff in a *controversia*. See Hernández Chong Cuy, *Suprema Corte y controversias*, 101.

82 CONTROVERSIA CONSTITUCIONAL. LEGITIMACIÓN ACTIVA Y LEGITIMACIÓN PASIVA. Solicitud de revocación por hecho superveniente en el incidente de suspensión relativo a la controversia constitucional 51/96. 16 June 1998. Novena Época; Pleno; *SJF y su Gaceta*, VIII, December 1998; page 790; thesis P. LXXIII/98.

83 These include only cases resolved by the Supreme Court. There are pending cases from these years as well as from 2010 and 2011. Data come from @lex, the statistics website of the Supreme Court of Justice, http://www2.scjn.gob.mx/alex/. See also Hernández Chong Cuy, *Suprema Corte y controversias*, 107.

84 In 2001, more than three hundred municipalities from Oaxaca challenged a constitutional amendment that introduced several rights for indigenous peoples. They claimed that the amendment did not address all the concerns of indigenous peoples in Mexico. However, the Supreme Court declared that municipalities do not have standing to challenge a constitutional amendment. See Controversia constitucional 82/2001. 6 June 2002.

idea of litigation in this area. That year the Court received 121 *controversias.* Eighty-seven were presented by municipalities, twenty-three by states, and eleven by the federation.[85] The most common challenges are against administrative acts, such as inspections, state executive orders, or the distribution of public funds. There are also numerous challenges to laws or regulations.

Despite the number of challenges heard by the Supreme Court between 1995 and 2009, only 12 per cent were successful. Notwithstanding the low rate of success, the 159 cases that obtained a favourable ruling, as well as several other cases where the ruling was against the plaintiff, have made significant contributions to the definition and meaning of Mexican federalism.

2. *Evolving Federalism Jurisprudence*

The Supreme Court's approach to federalism, via the *controversias constitucionales,* has evolved through time. Three key concepts help orient the analysis of federalism: concurrence, coordination, and collaboration. The case law provides several examples of how these concepts are defined and used. It also shows how the *controversia* itself has evolved as a constitutional process used to define the limits of powers and competences.

In a case known as "Temixco" (*controversia constitucional* 31/1997) a municipality challenged a decree passed by a state congress affecting the former's territorial limits.[86] In upholding the municipality's claim, the Supreme Court held that the *controversia* was an appropriate instrument for constitutional control and could be used to review any sort of constitutional violation.[87] The Court reasoned that this interpretation favoured federalism because it provided a remedy for any kind of constitutional grievance concerning an act or a law that might be

---

85 See *Informe Anual de Labores 2014,* ministro presidente Juan N. Silva Meza, https://www.scjn.gob.mx/Transparencia/Docs%20info%20Labores/Informe2014.pdf.

86 Controversia Constitucional 31/97. Pleno. Ayuntamiento de Temixco, Morelos. 9 August 1999.

87 CONTROVERSIA CONSTITUCIONAL. EL CONTROL DE LA REGULARIDAD CONSTITUCIONAL A CARGO DE LA SUPREMA CORTE DE JUSTICIA DE LA NACIÓN, AUTORIZA EL EXAMEN DE TODO TIPO DE VIOLANCIONES A LA CONSTITUCIÓN FEDERAL. Controversia Constitucional 31/97. Ayuntamiento de Temixco, Morelos, 9 August 1999; Novena Época, *SJF y su Gaceta,* X, September 1999, page 703; thesis P./J. 98/99

challenged.[88] This wide and open-ended view of the *controversia* process was challenged, however, in a later case that involved the municipality of Ciudad Juarez against the federal attorney-general (*controversia constitucional* 21/2006). In that case, the Supreme Court limited the use of the *controversia* to cases involving the limits of the powers vested in authorities in light of the five orders recognized by the Mexican Constitution.[89] The federal attorney-general claimed that municipal authorities of Ciudad Juárez had overreached their powers by stipulating the minimum distance between gas stations in their municipality. Because the federal Congress is authorized by the Constitution to regulate energy, the attorney-general argued that municipalities could not regulate where gas stations should be placed. The attorney-general also claimed that such municipal regulation improperly affected landowners' rights to decide the best use of their land. The Supreme Court held, however, that Article 115 expressly grants municipalities the power to regulate public safety and that under that clause municipalities may decide gas station locations. Consequently, the attorney-general's claim that the municipality was invading federal powers to regulate energy did not have any basis. The decision thus provided a strong framework to sustain municipal regulation on public safety grounds notwithstanding federalism-based challenges. The Court did not rule on the merits of the claim regarding the effect on landowners, however, because it was considered that *controversias constitucionales* could be used only to challenge the limits of powers vested in the different orders and could not be used to protect individual rights. This decision narrowed the scope of the *controversia*. Although the decision does not express a clear reason to leave behind the Temixco precedent, it is very likely that justices opted for this new interpretation in an effort to reduce litigation via the *controversia*.

In a later case (*controversia constitucional* 59/2006), the Court confirmed that *controversias* cannot be used to challenge alleged rights violations and extended the principle in relation also to collective rights. Specifically, the Court considered that a municipality cannot use the *controversias* procedure to allege that government acts violate the rights of indigenous peoples, even if they live within the municipality's

88 A brief comment in English to that case with other references can be found in García Sarubbi, *Federalism*, 44.

89 See Controversia Constitucional 21/2006. 24 March 2008, pages 74–80.

boundaries.[90] The *amparo* procedure is considered to be the proper remedy for such challenges.

The Supreme Court's opinions in *controversias constitucionales* offer different solutions to conflicts of competence, depending on the specific issue that is in question. In many cases, the Supreme Court's interpretations determine the boundaries between the five legal orders. For example, in one case (*controversia constitucional* 72/2008), the federal executive branch complained that a municipality was invading federal powers by passing zoning and urban development regulations that extended into a national park. The federal executive branch's claim prevailed and the municipal regulation was declared void.[91] The case involved a national park and an archaeological zone that were created within the territory of a municipality. Some parts of the national park were used for housing and commercial activities. Yet most of them were informal. The municipality decided to enact zoning regulations for an area that included the national park in order to control the expansion of housing and commercial activities. The Supreme Court decided that such regulations could not be enforced on lands considered to be under federal jurisdiction, even if such zones included urban developments. In this case the majority opinion chose to apply a strict reading of the Constitution in order to exclude any municipal intervention in areas considered to be under federal control such as national parks and archaeological zones. Although it was quite clear that the municipality had no competence to unilaterally enact zoning regulations affecting such federal areas, it was also possible to recognize that such regulations could be crafted as a result of collaboration between federal, state, and municipal authorities. Federal laws regulating environment and archaeological sites may be read under this latter interpretation.[92]

---

90 CONTROVERSIA CONSTITUCIONAL. LOS MUNICIPIOS CARECEN DE INTERÉS LEGÍTIMO PARA PROMOVERLA CONTRA DISPOSICIONES GENERALES QUE CONSIDEREN VIOLATORIAS DE DERECHOS DE LOS PUEBLOS Y COMUNIDADES INDÍGENAS QUE HABITEN EN SU TERRITORIO, SI NO GUARDAN RELACIÓN CON LAS ESFERA DE ATRIBUCIONES QUE LA CONSTITUCIÓN POLÍTICA DE LOS ESTADOS UNIDOS MEXICANOS LES CONFIERE. Controversia constitucional 59/2006. Municipio de Coxcatlán, Estado de San Luis Potosí. 15 October 2007. Décima Época, Pleno, *SJF y su Gaceta*, Book III, December 2011, volume 1, page 429. Thesis P./J. 83/2011 (9a).

91 Controversia Constitucional 72/2008. Poder Ejecutivo Federal. 12 May 2011.

92 Justice Salvador Aguirre proposed this interpretation in his dissenting opinion. However, a very similar opinion did obtain a majority a few months earlier. See below on *controversia* 91/2007.

Instead, the majority opted to exclude any sort of municipal participation on a narrow reading of the Constitution and of federal law. Under these terms, justices decided that collaboration may happen only if federal authorities considered it necessary. Justices in the majority probably used this narrow reading to discourage other municipalities from passing zoning regulations that could affect federal zones, thus reducing incentives for the establishment of irregular housing and commercial areas in such zones.

However, other questions are more complex, because the Constitution contains clauses that give the federal Congress power to pass general statutes to regulate a certain topic or entitle authorities from different levels to act on the same subject matter.[93] The first case to review this question was the *amparo en revisión* 120/2002. Here, the Supreme Court decided that general statutes could distribute powers between the federation, states, the Federal District, and municipalities. By acknowledging this, the Court recognized that this was an exception to Article 124 of the Constitution (the residual clause). The only requirement for a general statute to be valid was that it was stated in the Constitution that the federal Congress had the power to pass it.[94] In this case, the majority opinion delivered a new reading of Article 133 of the Constitution (supremacy clause) that recognized a "national order" below the constitutional order but above state and federal legislation.[95] Thus, a general statute became the source for the distribution of powers between federal, state, and municipal authorities on a particular subject area; it also regulated the powers of federal authorities in such a subject area. The drafters of constitutional amendments reacted quickly to this new interpretation. After this decision, Article 73 of the Constitution (which regulates the powers of the federal Congress) was amended several times in order to extend federal powers over states and municipalities, by granting the power to enact general statutes to regulate

---

93 Article 73 of the Constitution states that education, health, and tourism, among several other areas, may be regulated by general statutes. See the discussion on concurrence ahead.

94 LEYES GENERALES. INTERPRETACIÓN DEL ARTÍCULO 133 CONSTITUCIONAL. Amparo en revisión 120/2002. McCain Mexico, SA de CV. 13 February 2007. Novena Época, Pleno, *SJF y su Gaceta*, XXV, April 2007, page 5; thesis P. VII/2007.

95 Justice José Ramón Cossío, in his dissenting opinion, held that general statutes were not part of a new "national order." Instead they were statutes that established rules only to help coordinate the intervention of federal, state, and municipal authorities in a particular area where the constitution gave competence to the three orders.

and distribute powers in many areas.[96] Consequently general statutes became the preferred tool for granting federal government control over state and municipal matters.

Still, according to the Supreme Court (*acción de inconstitucionalidad* 119/2008), general statutes are not the last word concerning the regulation of a particular topic. States may also produce regulations on the same subject matter as long as these new rules do not oppose the standards provided by the general statute.[97] The Court decided (*controversia constitucional* 91/2007) that state rules can even regulate matters that the general statute attributes to federal authorities, provided that enforcement of the federal regulation is given priority over enforcement of the state regulation. This decision was made in the context of a challenge by the federal executive branch against several articles of a forest preservation law enacted by a state. The law contained regulations that were similar to the ones that the forest preservation general statute attributed to federal authorities.[98] The justices held that state legislators are entitled to enact statutes on forest preservation, as long as such statutes do not oppose regulations and competences established in the federal general statute on forest preservation. The decision widens the material authority of states over forest preservation, because it recognizes that states may enact legislation they consider useful to establish

---

96 See, for example, section XXIX-P on the rights of children and adolescents (amendment published on the *Diario Oficial de la Federación*, 12 October 2011), section XXIX-J physical education and sports (amendment published on the *Diario Oficial de la Federación*, 12 October 2011), section XXI General Statute against kidnapping (amendment published on the *Diario Oficial de la Federación*, 4 May 2009), and again section XXI General Statute against human trafficking (amendment published on the *Diario Oficial de la Federación*, 14 July 2011).

97 LEYES EN MATERIAS CONCURRENTES. EN ELLAS SE PUEDEN AUMENTAR LAS PROHIBICIONES O LOS DEBERES IMPUESTOS POR LAS LEYES GENERALES. Acción de inconstitucionalidad 119/2008. Diputados integrantes de la Cuarta Legislatura de la Asamblea Legislativa del Distrito Federal. 3 September 2009. Novena Época, Pleno, *SJF y su Gaceta*, XXXI, February 2010, page 2322, thesis P./J. 5/2010.

98 CONSERVACIÓN Y RESTAURACIÓN DE TIERRAS. LOS ARTÍCULOS 85, FRACCIONES I, II, III Y V, Y 86 DE LA LEY RELATIVA DEL ESTADO MICHOACÁN DE OCAMPO, AL DEFINIR LAS CONDUCTAS QUE SERÁN CONSIDERADAS INFRACCIONES EN MATERIA FORESTAL Y OTORGAR A LA SECRETARÍA DE DESARROLLO RURAL DE LA ENTIDAD LA FACULTAD DE IMPONER SANCIONES POR SU COMISIÓN, NO INVADEN LA COMPETENCIA DE LA FEDERACIÓN. Controversia constitucional 91/2007. Presidente de la República. 28 February 2011. 10a. Época; Pleno; *SJF y su Gaceta*; Libro IX, June 2012, Tomo 1, page 119. Thesis P. IV/2012 (9a).

forest preservation actions and programs. The Supreme Court's decision also recognizes that states may identify and protect lands that are not part of the federal protection programs. Thus, in forest preservation matters there may be two types of protected areas: federal areas and state areas. Lastly the Supreme Court recognized that state and federal authorities may coordinate themselves through formal agreements where they decide who will be responsible to enforce regulations. Justice Aguirre delivered the majority opinion. His approach recognized that the Constitution and the forest preservation general statute grant concurrent powers to the federal, state, and municipal authorities and that coordination of the regulations of all three authorities is therefore needed. Under such an arrangement, if the federal and state authorities agree that the latter would be responsible for enforcing forest preservation regulations, it would be possible for state legislators to enact regulations to complete federal regulations on such matters. Such an approach is more flexible than the one adopted in the *controversia* case 72/2008 mentioned above. While the ruling in *controversia* 72/2008 was based on a strict reading of the Constitution that excludes any sort of municipal participation, *controversia* 91/2007 had accepted the possibility of state intervention in certain circumstances. Neither decision provides an explanation of how the Court's criteria can be regarded as consistent. However, the particular circumstances that arose in each case may help explain why the Supreme Court adopted different approaches. As mentioned above, in *controversia* 72/2008 the justices decided a case that involved the irregular occupation of a national park. In such a case it may have seemed necessary to establish a clear precedent that signalled that irregular occupation of federal land could not be the source of any legitimate claim. In *controversia* 91/2007, however, the justices had to decide if a state regulation concerning authorizations for lumber exploitation invaded an area of federal competence. The case therefore involved only the possibility of granting states the power to regulate areas left behind by the federation, or areas where the federation expressly accepted state intervention.

A similar situation has developed between municipalities and states. In *controversia constitucional* 19/2008, a municipality claimed that a state transportation law violated Article 115 of the Constitution. The Court recognized that regulating public transportation is a power vested in the states. Nevertheless, Article 115 also grants municipalities the power to "participate" in the design of the transportation policy that will be executed in their territories. The Supreme Court stated that the state transportation law did not offer municipalities a true opportunity to exercise their power to participate in drafting the transportation policy.[99] In this case the judges limited the state legislator's power to enact statutes that affected municipalities by requiring consultation as part of the process of enacting a statute. The judges reasoned that the word *participate* in Article 115 means that the municipalities must be enabled to participate in the *drafting* of public transport programs.

3. *Concurrence, Coordination, and Collaboration*

This last example also provides a good introduction to cases dealing with concurrent competences.[100] Mexico's Constitution identifies more than fifteen areas where active collaboration between government orders is meant to occur, including regional development for indigenous peoples (Art. 2); education (Art. 3 and Art. 73); health (Art. 4 and Art. 73); environment (Art. 4 and Art. 73); public security and policing (Art. 21 and Art. 73); planning for development (Art. 26); urban development (Art. 27, Art. 73, and Art. 115); coordination against kidnapping and human trafficking (Art. 73); public safety (Art. 73); physical education and sports (Art. 73); tourism (Art. 73); fishing (Art. 73); promotion and development of cooperative associations (Art. 73); culture (Art. 73); children and adolescents (Art. 73); and intercity coordination (Art. 115).[101] Many of these areas were formerly reserved to the states, but recent changes have expanded federal competence to encompass them. This wide array of areas in which concurrent legislation is possible has made it necessary for the Supreme Court to provide interpretations to help establish the boundaries of concurrence and collaboration.

In a case decided in 2002 (*controversia constitucional* 29/2000), the Supreme Court adopted a relatively broad view of the concurrent

---

99 TRANSPORTE PÚBLICO DE PASAJEROS. AUNQUE EL TITULAR DE LA COMPETENCIA SOBRE LA MATERIA ES EL ESTADO, EL MUNICIPIO DEBE GOZAR DE UNA PARTICIPACIÓN EFECTIVA EN LA FORMULACIÓN Y APLICACIÓN DE LOS PROGRAMAS RELATIVOS EN LO CONCERNIENTE A SU ÁMBITO TERRITORIAL. Controversia constitucional 19/2008. Municipio de Zacatepec, Estado de Morelos. 11 January 2011. 10a. Época; Pleno; *SJF y su Gaceta*; Book I, October 2011, Volume 1, page 308, thesis: P./J. 39/2011 (9a).

100 For a definition of concurrence for Mexico and its differences with other countries, see Serna de la Garza, *El sistema federal*, 105–6.

101 For a study of the Mexican federal models of collaboration, see ibid., 107–70.

powers.[102] Under this approach the Court understood that concurrent powers constituted limits to the residual clause in Article 124 and that the federal Congress can regulate the way in which the federation, states, and municipalities should interact in each concurring competence. In more recent decisions, the Supreme Court has also laid down more specific criteria to determine the scope of concurrent powers, as will be seen. Also important distinctions in doctrine have developed.[103]

In *controversia* 132/2006 on public security and policing, the Supreme Court defined concurrence in terms of the coordination that is between the different orders of government to make policing more effective. The Supreme Court considered that coordination between orders of government can occur not only administratively[104] but also legislatively. With this interpretation the Court created a new source for coordination between federal, state, and municipal authorities. Instead of signing coordination agreements, the federal Congress may enact general statutes that establish jurisdictional boundaries.[105] The justices also considered that the Mexican federal model is to be understood as a cooperative system, and one in which federal competences are to be interpreted widely, thus narrowing the powers of the states (and the municipalities). In the case, Mexico City, in accordance to the current name in the Constitution, had challenged Article 52 of the statute that

---

102 FACULTADES CONCURRENTES EN EL SISTEMA JURÍDICO MEXICANO. SUS CARACTERÍSTICAS GENERALES. Controversia constitucional 29/2000. Poder Ejecutivo Federal. 15 November 2001. Novena Época, Pleno, *SJF y su Gaceta*, XV, January 2002, page 1042; thesis: P./J. 142/2001.

103 For example, concurrence in education is broader than in other fields, since the Constitution contains in Article 3 specific clauses that give Federal Congress a broad power to regulate education. In other fields such as health, the constitutional language is not that specific. Consequently federal and state regulations coexist. See Felipe Tena Ramírez, *Derecho constitucional mexicano* (Mexico: Porrúa, 2000), 119–124; and Serna de la Garza, *El sistema federal*, 116.

104 By administrative coordination the Supreme Court understands that federal, state, and municipal authorities may sign agreements where they decide how to distribute the responsibility to enforce regulation on a particular field. See the comments on the *controversia constitucional* 91/2007.

105 SEGURIDAD PÚBLICA. ES UNA MATERIA CONCURRENTE EN LA QUE TODAS LAS INSTANCIAS DE GOBIERNO DEBEN COORDINAR ESFUERZOS PARA LA CONSECUCIÓN DEL FIN COMÚN DE COMBATE A LA DELINCUENCIA, BAJO UNA LEY GENERAL EXPEDIDA POR EL CONGRESO DE LA UNIÓN. Controversia constitucional 132/2006. Asamblea Legislativa del Distrito Federal. 10 March 2008. 9a. Época; Pleno; *SJF y su Gaceta*; XXIX, April 2009, page 1296; thesis: P. IX/2009.

established the country's national security system, as well as the Private Security Services federal statute, claiming that they invaded the competences of the Federal District provided for in Article 122, which gave the Federal District assembly competence to regulate public security services. The Supreme Court acknowledged that the assembly had such competence, but it decided that there was federal competence in those cases where private security services were offered in more than one state. The Court also recognized that the federal Congress has the power to pass a private security services act. The Court's reasoning began from the premise that Article 21 and Article 73, section XXIII give the federal Congress power to distribute competences among different government orders through a general statute. The general statute that established the national police system stated that when private security services are offered in more than one federal entity, federal authorities will regulate them. The Court considered that the federal Congress does not have an explicit competence to legislate on private security services. However, Article 73, section XXX states that Congress is competent to legislate on all matters where the Constitution implicitly gives it that power. Since the general statute stated that federal authorities have the power to regulate private security services, it must be understood that the federal Congress's power to legislate on that subject matter is included in the implicit cases described in section XXX of Article 73.[106] The decision thus gave effect to a relatively broad interpretation of the concept of concurrence, since its interpretation overruled a competence that was given expressly to the Federal District's assembly.[107] Unlike other cases where the Supreme Court tends to have a very literal approach to the Constitution, in this case the justices decided to open the way for broader federal powers. A possible explanation for this approach is that the justices are recognizing the growing influence

---

106 SERVICIOS DE SEGURIDAD PRESTADOS POR EMPRESAS PRIVADAS. EL ARTÍCULO 52 DE LA LEY GENERAL QUE ESTABLECE LAS BASES DE COORDINACIÓN DEL SISTEMA NACIONAL DE SEGURIDAD PÚBLICA DISPONE UNA DISTRIBUCIÓN IMPLÍCITA DE COMPETENCIAS. Controversia constitucional 132/2006. Asamblea Legislativa del Distrito Federal. 10 March 2008. 9a. Época; Pleno; *SJF y su Gaceta*; XXIX, April 2009; page 1297; thesis: P. XII/2009

107 This is noted by Justice José Ramón Cossío in his dissenting vote. See Controversia constitucional 132/2006. Asamblea Legislativa del Distrito Federal. 10 March 2008. Dissenting vote by Justice José Ramón Cossío, also signed by Justices Margarita Luna Ramos and Olga Sánchez Cordero, pages 9–12. The vote is published together with the majority's decision.

of federal authorities in drafting and executing public security policies nationwide.

In *controversia constitucional* 31/2010, the Supreme Court held that the regulation of environmental protection as well as of urban development are concurrent competences of the three orders of government. According to the Court, the division of competence was to be determined by the environmental protection general statute as well as by the urban development general statute, and the federal, state, and municipal authorities were expected to enforce those general statutes. The question before the Court was how far a state could go in enforcing urban development regulations against a municipality. The case arose when a municipality challenged a state decision to reject an urban development plan drafted by the municipality. The Supreme Court's decision provides guidance about how decisions on urban development have to be analysed under the environmental protection regulations. It also establishes a benchmark for the development of collaboration among federal, state, and municipal authorities. Because in this particular case state regulators proved that the municipality's urban development plan violated environmental protection regulations, the Court decided that the municipality's challenge had no merit.[108] The Supreme Court defined how collaboration is expected to happen, as well as the ways in which each order of government is expected to act. The Court stated that municipalities do have competence to regulate urban development, but such regulations have to be exercised within the boundaries set by state and federal legislation, including environmental protection laws. Still, under these circumstances, the Supreme Court recognizes that municipalities can exercise way their competence autonomously in urban development. Municipalities are entitled to do more than express their opinions on the matter.[109]

The approach in this case illustrates the "collaborative" aspect of Mexican federalism. The decision in this case distinguishes the role that the federal Congress has in distributing competences, but also

108 Controversia constitucional 31/2010. Pleno. Municipio de Benito Juárez, Estado de Quintana Roo. 5 April 2011.

109 ASENTAMIENTOS HUMANOS. LOS MUNICIPIOS GOZAN DE UNA INTERVENCIÓN REAL Y EFECTIVA DENTRO DEL CONTEXTO DE LA NATURALEZA CONSTITUCIONAL CONCURRENTE DE LA MATERIA. Controversia constitucional 94/2009. Municipio de San Pedro Garza García, Estado de Nuevo León. 31 March 2011. 9a. Época; Pleno; *SJF y su Gaceta*; XXXIV, August 2011, page 887; thesis: P./J. 17/2011.

provides rules to determine how some constitutional provisions that give attribution to other orders of government, such as municipalities, may be exercised effectively. On one side, the Supreme Court defined the conditions required to distribute competences through a general statute. On the other, it provided safeguards to ensure collaboration among federal, state, and municipal authorities in the formulation and implementation of policies, when the Constitution requires it.

The regulation of health has also been a contested topic. In *controversia constitucional* 55/2009 a state governor challenged a federal administrative regulation that required hospitals and health centres to offer victims of rape a particular medication that interrupts conception. The state governor claimed that the federal regulation invaded state powers as described in the general health statute.[110] The Court's decision was that even when hospitals and health centres are funded and operated by state governments, they still belong to the national health system, as provided by the general health statute. It was therefore held that the same general health statute empowered the federal administration to pass regulations governing the technical standards and procedures that rule the operation of such state hospitals and health centres.[111]

These cases help us understand the current debate concerning the Supreme Court's federalism decisions. The Supreme Court consistently reasons in terms of two fundamental but distinguishable principles: coordination and concurrence. On the first principle, the Court emphasizes the need to regulate the way in which different government orders collaborate to achieve particular goals where all of them have relevant competences. The solution includes the possibility of signing agreements that will help determine the limits of each party in a specific area. On the second principle, the Court seeks a definition of competences between government orders that can be derived from either the Constitution or a general statute enacted by the federal legislature. The problem here is that, by definition, concurrent competences overlap. To resolve these issues the Supreme Court seeks to identify some topics where collaboration between the orders of government is emphasized, and other areas where constitutional interpretation is used to limit the

110 State powers are usually understood under the residual clause contained in Article 124. Article 13 of the health general statute distributes competence between federal and state authorities.

111 Controversia constitucional 55/2009. Pleno. Gobierno Constitucional del Estado Libre y Soberano de Jalisco.

competence of each government order, usually favouring the federal order. This type of approach is increasing as a consequence of constitutional amendments. The main problem with the approach is that the rules that construct federalism are different for each subject area.

A further important source of litigation is the collaboration clauses that appear expressly in the constitutional text.[112] In these cases the Supreme Court has to determine the meaning of the collaboration clauses and how they should be enforced. It is difficult to enforce constitutional rules that require only the hearing of opinions or that refer to "participation" in broad terms. The Supreme Court usually solves these cases by drafting guidelines that will govern the collaboration that is required by the Constitution.

The Supreme Court also distinguishes between competence and hierarchy as a way to analyse constitutional rules on federalism. In the first case, it is understood that when one order of government has the power to enact a regulation on a subject, the limits of such regulation have to be scrutinized in light of the power of other government orders also to regulate that subject. In the second case, the limits of a specific regulation will be tested in accordance to the limits expressed in the law on which the said regulation is based.

V. Conclusion

Federalism in Mexico, viewed from the court system's perspective, shows a contrasting image. On one hand, the Supreme Court has been very active in producing case law that develops federalism. These opinions have favoured local governments, provided that their competences are clearly stated in the constitutional text. In cases where there is no explicit competence, the Court has enforced, via collaboration clauses, the establishment of formal consultation between federal, state, and municipal authorities for drafting regulations in particular subject areas. In some other cases, the Court has enabled states to exercise their powers in such a way that their development plans are autonomous from the federal plan. Only if a state decides to coordinate with federal authorities on such plans will it do so through a formal agreement. Otherwise, there is no obligation to follow federal guidelines. However, where the rules are less clear, the Court seems to favour federal powers

112 See the public transportation case above: Controversia constitucional 19/2008.

over those of the states and municipalities. A clear example of this trend is the doctrine of the general statute as a law produced by the federal Congress that may distribute competences among federal, state, and municipal governments.

In many cases, the Supreme Court tends to adopt a rather literal interpretation of the Constitution. In those cases where the Supreme Court adopts an interpretation that is less literal, the outcome seems to favour the interests of the federal government. However, thus far it is not possible to establish a clear pattern in the Court's interpretation. Most of its decisions seem to be crafted in response to the particular circumstances of each case. Consequently, there is not one federalism jurisprudence in Mexico but several. Justices tend to balance their decision between constitutional and statutory rules governing the issue at stake on the one hand and the specific problem involved in the case on the other hand. Although the literal approach prevails in many cases, when in doubt regarding the merits or the possible outcome of the case, justices tend to defer to federal order. However, justices do not include arguments in their decisions that justify their preference for the federal order.

A very interesting consequence of the Court's literal approach to the Constitution is its influence over constitutional amendments. The literal approach began by favouring states and municipalities, because the Constitution's structure had in most cases a strict distribution of powers. Under this arrangement the only available way to extend federal powers was through constitutional amendments. When the Supreme Court showed flexibility in its constitutional interpretation and accepted that a general statute was a legitimate source to distribute powers, the drafters of constitutional amendments took note. Accordingly, new constitutional amendments included clauses giving the federal Congress power to enact a general statute to govern the distribution of powers in a particular area. Justices and drafters of constitutional amendments thus seem to be engaged in a constitutional dialogue over federalism.

From a broad perspective, the political transition that Mexico began experiencing in the mid-1990s has had a significant impact on federalism. The new political configuration that arose from the end of the PRI's regime is characterized by a federalism that is continuously redefined through adjudication and constitutional amendments. During the PRI regime, federalism was less visible. Most arrangements took place as a result of internal party negotiations. The weakening of the

PRI's hegemonic position forced actors from every political party to review federal rules and demand their enforcement. The Supreme Court began enforcing articles of the Constitution that had hardly ever been contested before, and new doctrines are being tested. As a whole, this process may be seen as new reconfiguration of Mexican federalism. It is still too early to identify many specific trends in this new process. However, it seems very clear that federalism in Mexico has changed. A few years ago, federalism was discussed mostly in textbooks. Today it is impossible to approach Mexican federalism without taking into consideration the Supreme Court's decisions.

On the other hand, the Supreme Court and the federal judiciary constitute the focal points of the judicial centralism that characterizes Mexico's court system. Every day new examples emerge that illustrate the federal judiciary's intervention to review state court decisions with the argument that their intervention helps correct unfair or poorly crafted judgments. However, this also means that state courts find it very difficult to establish themselves as sources of legal norms that have authority within their respective states. State courts are very substantially subordinated to an overextended federal judiciary. Under these circumstances, the space for the development of independent and accountable state judiciaries remains quite limited.

10 The Supreme Court of Nigeria: An Embattled Judiciary More Centralist Than Federalist

ROTIMI T. SUBERU

I. Introduction

Assessments of Nigeria's judiciary often oscillate between exaggerated criticisms of its fecklessness, dysfunction, and corruption and extravagant celebrations of its principled constitutional activism and bold and balanced interventionism. Such contradictory appraisals are symptomatic of the judiciary's conflicted role in Nigeria's political development and federal evolution. On one hand, the courts have functioned as a vanguard of constitutionalism in a neo-patrimonial post-military authoritarian environment, helping "to roll back abuses of government power more frequently and effectively than any other institution."[1] Indeed, the Supreme Court has played an important role in mediating and moderating Nigeria's overly centralized federal system, helping to arbitrate potentially disruptive conflicts and securing a modicum of sub-national and other constitutional rights, particularly in fostering better sharing of centrally collected oil revenues, scrutinizing the administration of local governance, and resolving partisan and factional contests for political power in the federation. On the other hand, the Supreme Court's arbitrative functions have had to address several difficulties, including an entrenched hyper-centralized constitutional framework, a fraudulent and violent neo-patrimonial political process, and the judiciary's own institutional dysfunction and capacity limitations. Overall, the Court has been more centralist than federalist; it

1 Human Rights Watch, *Corruption on Trial: The Record of Nigeria's Economic and Financial Crimes Commission* (New York: Human Rights Watch, 2011), 36.

has not had a transformational impact on Nigeria's centralized federal system, which remains constitutionally skewed, politically corrupt, ethnically contentious, and, therefore, chronically fragile.

II. Federal System

1. General Characteristics

Nigeria is Africa's most populous country and one of the world's most complex multi-ethnic federations.[2] Its estimated population of 170 million people is divided into three major territorially concentrated ethnic groups (the northern Hausa-Fulani, western Yoruba, and eastern Ibo), hundreds of smaller minority ethnic communities, and roughly equal numbers of Muslims and Christians, making Nigeria the world's largest religiously bi-communal country. The country is also Africa's leading oil producer, and its GDP purchasing power parity (PPP) of $1.053 trillion is the largest on the continent.[3] Despite earning hundreds of billions of dollars in oil revenues since the 1970s, however, Nigeria is ranked low on human development by the United Nations Development Program, with 64.4 per cent of its population living below an estimated poverty line of PPP of US$1.25 per day in 2011. Human

---

2 For analyses of Nigerian federalism, see Ignatius Ayua and Dakas C.J. Dakas, "Federal Republic of Nigeria," in *Constitutional Origins, Structure, and Change in Federal Countries*, ed. John Kincaid and Alan Tarr, 239–75 (Montreal and Kingston: McGill-Queen's University Press, 2005); Isawa Elaigwu, "Federal Republic of Nigeria," in *Distribution of Powers and Responsibilities in Federal Countries*, ed. Akhtar Majeed, Ronald Watts, and Douglas Brown, 207–37 (Montreal and Kingston: McGill-Queen's University Press, 2006); Ebere Osieke, "Federal Republic of Nigeria," in *Legislative, Executive and Judicial Governance in Federal Countries*, ed. Katy Le Roy and Cheryl Saunders, 198–223 (Montreal and Kingston: McGill-Queen's University Press, 2006); Akpan H. Ekpo, "Federal Republic of Nigeria," in *The Practice of Fiscal Federalism*, ed. Anwar Shah, 204–34 (Montreal and Kingston: McGill-Queen's University Press, 2007); Habu Galadima, "Federal Republic of Nigeria," in *Local Government and Metropolitan Regions in Federal Systems*, ed. Nico Steytler, 234–66 (Montreal and Kingston: McGill-Queen's University Press, 2009); Rotimi Suberu, "Nigeria," in *Diversity and Unity in Federal Countries*, ed. Luis Moreno and César Colino, 227–57 (Montreal and Kingston: McGill-Queen's University Press, 2010); and Eghosa E. Osaghae, "Nigeria," in *Intergovernmental Relations in Federal Systems*, ed. Johanne Poirier, Cheryl Saunders, and John Kincaid, 272–304 (Don Mills, ON: Oxford University Press Canada, 2016).

3 See Central Intelligence Agency, "World Fact Book," https://www.cia.gov/library/publications/the-world-factbook/geos/ni.htm.

development indicators are particularly abysmal in the mainly Muslim north, where "the poverty level is between two and three times the rate" in the oil-rich, predominantly Christian, south.[4]

Instituted under British colonial auspices primarily as an ethnic-conflict management device, the federal system is devolutionary in its origins (having evolved from the unitary but decentralized colonial Nigerian state) and symmetrical and highly centralized in its constitutional design. From a relatively decentralized structure of three constituent regions under the quasi-federal Richards Constitution of 1946 and the fully federalist Lyttelton Constitution in 1954, Nigeria's federation now consists of a dominant central government headquartered in the federal capital territory of Abuja, thirty-six states that are distributed into six more or less informal geo-political zones (three each in the north and south), and 774 constitutionally designated local-government areas. This sweeping federal transformation reflects Nigeria's volatile political dynamics, including three failed democratic republics and extended periods of centrist military rule, all of which have affected the evolution of the country's judicial governance.

The First Republic, spanning the period from independence from Britain in 1960 to the first military coup of 1966, juxtaposed Westminster parliamentary institutions with a regionalized federal structure. As underscored by cases such as *Balewa v. Doherty* (1961)[5] and *Adegbenro v. AG Federation* (1962)[6], Nigeria's Supreme Court invariably became embroiled in the polarized ethno-regional conflicts of the First Republic. Its curtailment of federal powers of inquiry over regional institutions in *Balewa v. Doherty*, in particular, provoked strident denunciations of "government by the judiciary" from the federal parliamentary executive.[7] Ultimately, the judiciary was stripped of some of its authority under the revised republican constitution of 1963, which terminated appeals to the British Privy Council and scrapped the judicial service commission in order to enhance direct political control of the courts. Consequently, the Supreme Court began to shy away from "any desire

---

4 Peter Pham, "Boko Haram's Evolving Threat," *Africa Security Brief* no. 20 (Washington, DC: Africa Center for Strategic Studies, 2012), 7.

5 *Balewa v. Doherty* [1961] 1 All NLR 604.

6 *Adegbenro v. AG Federation* [1962] 1 All NLR 431.

7 John P. Mackintosh, *Nigerian Government and Politics* (Evanston, IL: Northwestern University Press, 1966), 42.

to become involved in political issues or to stress federalism in the sense of a division of powers."[8]

Judicial federalism was eviscerated during the two phases of military rule (1966–79 and 1984–99) that followed the collapse of the First Republic (1960–6) and Second Republic (1979–83). The attempted assertion of judicial oversight of the military in *Lakanmi v. AG Western State* (1971)[9] immediately provoked a backlash in the form of a military decree-law, the Constitution (Supremacy and Enforcement of Powers) Decree no. 28 of 1970, which ousted the courts' jurisdiction over the rule and conduct of the soldiers. Meanwhile, the federal division of powers was effectively terminated by the empowerment of the "Federal Military Government" to "make laws for the peace, order and good government of Nigeria or any part thereof with respect to any matter whatsoever."[10] Aided by the rise in the production and international prices of oil, and by its decisive victory in the civil war (1967–70), the military refashioned the country in accord with its own unitary organization and vision. Its political legacies included fragmentation of the regions into smaller and weaker states, centralization of oil revenues, abrogation of separate regional state constitutions, unification of the police and local government structure, and the shift from parliamentary to presidential rule.

Given the subordination of judicial review to parliamentary sovereignty under the First Republic, the abrogation of constitutionalism under military rule, the short duration of the American-styled Second Republic, and the abortion of the Third Nigerian Republic even before its inauguration by the military in 1993, the Fourth Republic (1999 to date) has provided the sole moment of sustained judicial federalism in Nigeria's post-independence history. The republic has witnessed the intensification and amplification of a tradition of federalist judicial review that began in the short-lived Second Republic with cases like *Awolowo v. Shagari & Ors* (1979),[11] *AG Bendel v. AG Federation* (1981),[12] *AG Ogun v. AG Federation* (1982),[13] *and AG Ondo v. AG Federation* (1983),[14]

8 Mackintosh, *Nigerian Government and Politics*, 86.

9 *Lakanmi v. AG Western State* [971] 1 University of Ife Law Reports-UILR 201.

10 Federal Military Government, "Constitution (Suspension and Modification) Decree (1966, no. 1), in *Laws of the Federal Republic of Nigeria, 1966* (Lagos: Government Printer, 1966), A3–A11.

11 *Awolowo v. Shagari & Ors* [1979] All NLR 120.

12 *AG Bendel v. AG Federation* [1981] 10 Supreme Court Cases-SC 1.

13 *AG Ogun v. AG Federation* [1982] 3 Nigeria Constitutional Law Reports-NCLR 166.

14 *AG Ondo v. AG Federation* [1983] 2 Supreme Court of Nigeria Law Reports-SCNLR 269.

which involved constitutional conflicts over electoral governance, revenue allocation, and the centre's policing powers.

2. Structural Features

A major source of inter-governmental conflict and litigation in Nigeria's Fourth Republic is the unitary federalism of the current Constitution of the Federal Republic of Nigeria 1999 (as amended), which concentrates enormous legislative, fiscal, executive, and judicial powers in the central government.[15] Reflecting the legacy of three decades of hyper-centralization under military rule, the Constitution creates an expansive exclusive list of sixty-eight federal legislative powers. Items on the list include arms, aviation, banking, foreign borrowing, currency, customs and excise duties, trade and commerce, taxation of incomes and profits, external affairs, labour and minimum wage, mines and minerals, police and prisons and security services, railways, formation and regulation of political parties, federal and state elections as well as the procedural regulations of local elections, marriages other than customary or Islamic matrimonial causes, and the promotion and enforcement of an omnibus set of fundamental objectives and directive principles of state policy.

Twelve additional items are included within the purview of the federal government by a "concurrent legislative list" that specifies the "extent of federal and state legislative powers" in policy domains like allocation of public revenue, electric power, industrial, commercial, and agricultural development, scientific and technological research, and post-primary education.[16] Under section 4 (5) of the Constitution, if any state law is "inconsistent with any law validly made by the National Assembly," the national law "shall prevail."

These enormous federal legislative powers are vested in a bicameral National Assembly. This consists of a 109-member Senate, including 1 member popularly elected from Abuja and three senators elected from single-member constituencies in each of the thirty-six states, and a 360-member House of Representatives elected from single-member "constituencies of nearly equal population as far as possible, provided that no constituency shall fall within more than one state."[17]

15 See *The Constitution of the Federal Republic of Nigeria 1999* (Lagos: Federal Government, 1999).

16 *The Constitution of the Federal Republic of Nigeria 1999*, Second Schedule, Part II.

17 Ibid., section 49.

The fiscal ramifications of the legislative division of powers are particularly significant. The National Assembly is constitutionally empowered to enact a law for the vertical (federal-state-local) and horizontal (inter-state and inter-local) allocation of centrally collected revenues paid into the Federation Account, on which the three orders of government are dependent for more than 80 per cent of their finances. Currently, the account is distributed vertically in the proportions of 48.50 per cent, 26.72 per cent, 20.60 per cent, and 4.18 per cent to the federal government, states, localities, and centrally controlled special funds, respectively.[18]

Executive powers of the federation are vested in a popularly elected president and commander-in-chief of the armed forces. The president's powers include the appointment (subject to confirmation by the Senate) of the chairman and members of key constitutional or statutory agencies, many of which are designed to operate as independent federal bodies, but almost all of which function as agents of the federal executive. These bodies include the Independent National Electoral Commission (INEC), the Police Service Commission, the National Security Council, the Revenue Mobilization Allocation and Fiscal Commission (RMAFC – a body that determines the salaries of all major public functionaries, including judges), the Economic and Financial Crimes Commission (EFCC), the Independent Corrupt Practices Commission, and the National Boundaries Commission (NBC).

Nigeria's political over-centralization is reinforced by a constitutionally mandated national political party system. This system prohibits sectional parties, vests the conduct of all national and state elections in the INEC, requires the winning candidate for president to obtain broad electoral support from across the federation, and prescribes a uniform electoral cycle for federal and state executives and legislators, with the president and the bicameral National Assembly having the same four-year terms as the state governors and unicameral state assemblies. The presidents and governors are limited constitutionally to a maximum of two terms, while legislative terms are indefinitely renewable.

These electoral regulations have encouraged the development of a dominant national party system, as evident in the rise of the People's Democratic Party (PDP) and, subsequently, the All Progressives

18 See Kalu Idika Kalu, *Fiscal Federalism in Nigeria: Practices and Issues* (Abuja: Revenue Mobilization Allocation and Fiscal Commission, 2011), 14–15.

Congress (APC). Before it succumbed to severe fractionalization and the defection of many of its leaders to the opposition APC in 2013, the PDP controlled the federal presidency, approximately two-thirds of National Assembly seats, and twenty-three (twenty-eight in 2007) of the thirty-six state governorships. Yet such dominance has also often reflected the pathologies of a fraud-riddled authoritarian neo-patrimonial system in which elections have "been stolen more often than won," with the ruling party using the enormous institutional and coercive resources of the central government to tilt the electoral playing field.[19]

Reflecting the hegemony of the central government, the states are relatively weak orders of government, lacking separate constitutions, independent police organizations, significant internal revenue sources, or truly exclusive policy competences. For instance, although some specific concurrent powers (e.g., antiquities, monuments, rural electrification, regulation of cinematography, post-primary education, and industrial, commercial, and agricultural development) and all residual powers are assigned to the states, there are hardly any policy areas that can be described as truly exclusive to the states, given the Constitution's generous construction of federal legislative powers. As the result of the constitutionally mandated redistribution of Federation Account revenues among the three orders of government, however, the states and local governments now account for approximately half of public expenditures and personnel in the federation.

Even more than the states, the local governments constitute a vulnerable component of Nigeria's intergovernmental architecture. The 1999 Constitution incorporates two conflicting visions of the appropriate status of local government in the federal system. The first vision, promoted by the federal government under both military and post-military rule, is that of local government as the third order of the federal system, with an entrenched status under the Constitution, considerable autonomy from state administrations, and direct relations with the federal government, which has a putative responsibility to protect localities from arbitrary interventions or exploitations by the states. Reflecting this vision, the Constitution formally guarantees a "system of local government by democratically elected councils," entrenches the current 774 local government areas, provides for the allocation of Federation Account revenues to the localities, and devotes a whole schedule

19 Human Rights Watch, *Corruption on Trial*, 26.

to the "functions of local government council" (e.g., collection of rates, issuance of licences, provision and maintenance of basic public conveniences and infrastructures, and collaboration with the states in the provision of primary education).[20]

A second vision of the constitutional status of localities, favoured by the states and more or less confirmed by the judiciary since 1999, dismisses the notion of three-tier federalism as anomalous. It conceptualizes the local government system as an inherently sub-national subject, which should be left entirely to the discretion of the states in a proper federal system. This vision is most succinctly captured in section 7 (1) of the Constitution, which gives the states broad powers to legislate for "the establishment, structure, composition, finance and functions" of local councils.

Nigeria's lopsided intergovernmental architecture has engendered intense but mostly southern-based and unfulfilled agitation for the decentralization of the federal system, including proposals for a return to the pre-military regional federalism of the First Republic. A major reason for the abortion of decentralist reform is the absence of the national consensus required to amend the relevant provisions of the 1999 Constitution. The amendment formula, as enshrined in section 9 of the Constitution, requires that a proposal to change the Constitution be approved by not less than two-thirds of all the members of each house of the bicameral National Assembly or by a four-fifths majority of these members if the change concerns the amendment formula itself or the provisions of the Constitution on fundamental human rights, boundary adjustments, and the creation of new states and localities. In both cases, the amendment must be approved by resolutions of the houses of assembly of two-thirds of the states. Although several constitutional provisions were successfully amended in 2011, the changes involved relatively minor institutional adjustments and did not alter the fundamental features of Nigeria's centralized federalism, including the unified judicature.

III. Court System

1. *Judicial Structure*

The Constitution enshrines a tripartite legal tradition consisting of an overarching English common law system complemented by customary

20 *The Constitution of the Federal Republic of Nigeria 1999*, sections 3 (1), 7 (1), 162, First Schedule Part I, and Fourth Schedule.

(tribal) and Islamic legal systems. Chapter 7 of the Constitution establishes and prescribes the composition and jurisdictions of seven federal courts: the Supreme Court, Court of Appeal, Federal High Court, National Industrial Court, High Court of the Federal Capital Territory (FCT, Abuja), Sharia Court of Appeal of the FCT, and Customary Court of Appeal of the FCT. It also provides for three state courts: the High Court of a State, the Sharia Court of Appeal of a State, and the Customary Court of Appeal of a State. The federal and state legislatures are constitutionally empowered to establish additional federal and state courts, respectively, or to confer additional jurisdictions on existing courts, subject to the provisions of the Constitution. The states, in particular, have established several courts (including magistrate, district, area, and/or customary courts) with subordinate jurisdiction to the three constitutionally established state courts.

Despite its formal division into federal and state courts, the judicature functions as a unified structure with common oversight and appointments structures, a pattern of career mobility from state to federal courts (and from the Court of Appeal to the Supreme Court), and a single integrated appellate system atop which sits the Supreme Court, whose decisions are binding on all other courts (federal and state) in accordance with the rules of precedent and hierarchy of courts. The Supreme Court has exclusive original jurisdiction in federal-state, federal executive-legislative, and inter-state conflicts and appellate jurisdiction in decisions emanating from the Court of Appeal. The Court, as stipulated under section 230 of the 1999 Constitution, consists of the "Chief Justice … and such number of Justices … not exceeding twenty-one as may be prescribed by … the National Assembly." Disputes before the Court are determined by a bench of not fewer than five justices or, in constitutional disputes, by seven justices, to be empanelled by the chief justice. The attorneys-general of the federation and each of the states, whose offices are established under sections 150 and 195 of the Constitution respectively, institute intergovernmental disputes before the Court on behalf of the affected governments.

Below the Supreme Court is the Court of Appeal, which is given exclusive original jurisdiction in presidential electoral petitions, as well as appellate jurisdiction over all other courts and tribunals established under the Constitution, including the Code of Conduct Tribunal, and tribunals for gubernatorial and federal and state legislative elections. The Court of Appeal consists of a president of the court and not fewer than forty-nine justices, including at least three justices with learning in Islamic personal law and another three competent in customary law. A panel of not fewer than three justices of the court hears election petition and Islamic and customary cases. The court is administratively divided into judicial divisions that sit in various parts of the country.

The Federal High Court was established in 1973 as a Federal Revenue Court with jurisdiction over causes involving the economic interests of the federal government. Under the 1999 Constitution, the plenary jurisdiction of the federal High Court has been expanded to embrace effectively all federal civil and criminal causes and matters. The court consists of a chief judge and such numbers of judges as the National Assembly may prescribe. The court is duly constituted to exercise its powers if it consists of at least one judge of the court. Like the Court of Appeal, the Federal High Court sits in judicial divisions across the country.

This expansion of the jurisdiction of the Federal High Court has emasculated the state high courts (including the high court of the FCT), which traditionally was the court with the widest original jurisdiction, in both federal and state causes, in Nigeria. Under the current dispensation, the state high courts retain general jurisdiction over civil and criminal causes except causes in respect of which other courts have been vested with exclusive jurisdiction. The high courts are made up of a chief judge and such other number of judges as the state assembly (or the National Assembly in the case of the FCT's high court) may prescribe.

The final tier of superior court of records directly established under the Constitution consists of the customary and sharia courts of appeal in the states and in the FCT. These courts are constitutionally given appellate and supervisory jurisdiction in civil proceedings involving questions of customary and Islamic personal law, respectively. Beginning with Zamfara State in 1999, however, twelve northern Muslim states have controversially and perhaps unconstitutionally conferred general civil and criminal jurisdiction on their sharia courts of appeal. The Sharia Court of Appeal consists of a grand *kadi* (Islamic judge) and such numbers of *kadi*s as a state assembly, or the National Assembly in the case of the Sharia Court of Appeal in the FCT, may prescribe. Similarly, the Customary Court of Appeal consists of the president of the court and such numbers of judges as the relevant governmental legislative authority may prescribe. Panels of at least three judges exercise the jurisdiction of these courts.

2. Judicial Appointments, Tenure, and Functioning

The Constitution prescribes uniform regulations for appointing or removing the various judicial officers in the federal and state courts. Appointments to the federal courts are made by Nigeria's president on the recommendations of the National Judicial Council (NJC), subject to confirmation by the Senate. Appointments to state courts are made by the state governor on the recommendations of the NJC, subject to confirmation by the state house of assembly. In making its recommendations, the NJC receives advice from the Federal Judicial Service Commission in respect of appointments to the four main federal courts (Supreme Court, Court of Appeal, Federal High Court, and National Industrial Court), from the Judicial Service Committee of the FCT in respect of the courts in Abuja, and from state judicial service commissions in respect of the state courts.

In addition to serving as the clearinghouse for judicial appointments, the NJC is charged with disbursing monies appropriated by the National Assembly for the courts established under the Constitution. These monies include the capital and recurrent budgets of the federal courts, as well as the salaries and allowances (recurrent costs) of the judges of the high courts and sharia and customary courts of appeal of the states.

Headed and appointed largely by the chief justice, the twenty-three-member NJC includes some of the most senior jurists in the federation and the states. Although they are smaller in size and less politically insulated than the NJC, the judicial service commissions at federal and state levels also are headed by the chief justice and chief judges, respectively, and comprise mostly senior members of the bench and bar.

The relative non-politicization of judicial appointments through the creation of the NJC and judicial service commissions has not detracted from a long-standing policy to reflect the country's "federal character" or diversity on the courts, especially the Supreme Court. However, whereas it is generally interpreted to require equal representation of the states, the federal character principle has been implemented more judiciously in relation to the Supreme Court, that is, as a rule for the representation of broader geographical identities (e.g., the old regions and current six geopolitical zones). Furthermore, following a succession of southern chief justices during the initial decades of the Supreme Court, the chief justices of the Court since 1987 have been northern Muslims, including Aloma Mukhtar, who was appointed the first female member of the court in June 2005 and served as Nigeria's first female chief justice from July 2012 to November 2014.

Some decisions of the Court, notably *AG Federation v. AG Abia State & Ors* (2001)[21] and *Abacha v. the State* (2002),[22] have highlighted sectional fissures on the bench. However, making the Court substantially politically autonomous and professionally recruited and organized, yet regionally inclusive, has significantly insulated the institution from debilitating sectional bias, fragmentation, or conflict. In addition, the Court has reduced its vulnerability to ethno-politicization through a long-standing aversion to advisory opinions, which is based on a strict reading of section 232 (1) of the Constitution that gives the Court original jurisdiction in any federal-state or inter-state dispute "if and in so far as that dispute involves any question … on which the existence or extent of a legal right depends." The Court has also explicitly evaded some politically sensitive or contentious issues, especially the constitutionality of Islamic sharia law implementation and discrimination on the basis of state of origin. In *Adeyinka A. Badejo v. Federal Minister of Education & Ors* (1996),[23] for instance, the Court ruled that an application filed on behalf of a prospective entrant to a prestigious national unity secondary school scheme to enforce her constitutional right to freedom from discrimination on the basis of state of origin had been overtaken by events (having taken eight years to reach the Supreme Court from the high court) and would amount to a futile academic exercise. Similarly, in *AG Kano v. AG Federation* (2006),[24] the Court argued that Kano's challenge of a federal police ban on the state's sharia-based Hisbah vigilance corps involved a dispute with the inspector general of police (rather than with the federal government), as well as a crime-related cause, both of which are outside the original (as distinct from appellate) jurisdiction of the Court.

Reflecting the Constitution's emphasis on a professionally rather than ethno-politically organized justice sector, judges of the superior courts of record are generally required to have at least ten to fifteen years of experience after qualifying to practise as a legal practitioner. The constitutionally mandated retirement age for judges is seventy years at the Supreme Court, and sixty-five years in all other courts. The heads of federal or

---

21 *AG Federation v. AG Abia & Ors* [2001] 9 Supreme Court Monthly-SCM 45–110.

22 *Abacha v. the State* [2002] 5 Nigeria Weekly Law Reports-NWLR (Part 761) 638.

23 *Badejo v. Federal Minister of Education & Ors* [1996] 8 NWLR (Pt. 464).

24 *AG Kano v. AG Federation* [2007] 6 NWLR (Pt. 1029).

state courts (chief justice, president of the Court of Appeal and Customary Court of Appeal, chief judge, or grand *kadi*) can be removed only by the president or state governor acting on an address supported by a two-thirds majority of the Senate or the House of Assembly. However, on the basis of a holistic reading of the constitutional functions of the NJC, the Supreme Court has affirmed, in *Hon. Justice Raliat Elelu-Habeeb & Anor v. AG Federation & Ors* (2012),[25] that the removal of the head of a court by the political executive and legislature must be predicated on a recommendation to that effect by the NJC. Other judicial officers can be removed directly by the president or the state governor on the recommendation of the NJC that the officer be dismissed on grounds of infirmity, incompetence, or misconduct.

Despite the remarkable provisions written into the Nigerian Constitution to guarantee its political insulation, the judiciary suffers from considerable institutional dysfunction and limitations of human and material capacities. While section 84 (3) of the Constitution provides that "remuneration and salaries" (as proposed by the RMAFC, approved by the National Assembly and administered by the NJC) of judicial officers "shall not be altered to their disadvantage after their appointment," this guarantee explicitly excludes "allowances" (for, among other things, housing, transportation, utilities, and domestic and official aides), which account for approximately 80 per cent of the total pay of judges.[26] More important, because they are only partially funded via the NJC, the state judiciaries are not effectively insulated from financial neglect or manipulation by the state governments, which have mostly ignored constitutional guarantees of budgetary autonomy for courts.

More generally, the NJC has attracted criticisms and even resistance over its centrist influence on judicial appointments at the subnational level, over the overwhelming power of the chief justice on the composition and conduct of the council, and over the failure of the council to eliminate executive interference in budgetary and appropriation processes of the courts. In addition, most Nigerian courts, like courts in many developing African countries, suffer multiple institutional deficiencies, including a deteriorating quality of legal education, poor

25 See *Hon. Justice Raliat Elelu-Habeeb & Anor v. AG Federation & Ors* [2012] Law Pavilion Electronic Law Report-LPELR-SC 281/2010.

26 Nurudeen Abdallah and Adelanwa Bamgboye, "Nigeria: Senior Judges Soak Up N14 Billion Annually," *Daily Trust* (Abuja), 9 December 2013.

physical facilities (e.g., dilapidated courtrooms and absence of standard libraries), outdated legal infrastructure (including procedural and evidentiary rules that have not been reformed since colonial rule), excessive caseload and backlog of appeal cases deriving partly from the abysmal quality of the lower courts, poor assistance for judges, gross abuse (by judges and defence lawyers) of interlocutory appeals or injunctions, and "delays so extreme that they are almost a form of impunity."[27]

Corruption is a particularly pernicious challenge for the judiciary. As claimed by a former president of the Court of Appeal, "There are many lazy, ignorant and dishonest judges in the system."[28] Not surprisingly, successive Afrobarometer surveys suggest that Nigerians do not see effective rule of law in the country and express increasing distrust in law courts, although the courts still evoke relatively greater trust than the notoriously corrupt police.[29] These multiple deficiencies in the justice system are generally more pronounced in the state and local arenas than in the federal arena, although the judiciary in Lagos (the federation's most economically developed and independent state) is considerably better resourced and modernized than in the rest of the federation.[30]

3. *Overview of Judicial Culture*

The aforementioned institutional deficiencies, coupled with the repression of an independent judicial culture during military rule, have undermined the development, professionalism, and sophistication

---

27 Human Rights Watch, *Corruption on Trial*, 34; see also Ameze Guobadia, "Judicial-Executive Relations in Nigeria's Constitutional Development: Clear Patterns or Confusing Signals?," in *Separation of Powers in African Constitutionalism*, ed. Charles Fombad, 239–64 (Oxford: Oxford University Press, 2016) .

28 Ayo Salami, "Eradicating Corruption in the Nigerian Judiciary," Sahara Reporters, 4 December 2015, http://saharareporters.com/2015/12/04/eradicating-corruption-nigerian-judiciary-justice-isa-ayo-salami.

29 Peter Lewis and Michael Bratton, *Attitudes to Democracy and Markets in Nigeria*, Afrobarometer Working Paper no. 3 (2000), 20–1, http://afrobarometer.org/publications/wp3-attitudes-democracy-and-markets-nigeria; Peter Lewis and Etannibi Alemika, *Seeking the Democratic Dividend: Public Attitudes and Attempted Reform in Nigeria*, Afrobarometer Working Paper no. 52 (2005), 39, http://afrobarometer.org/publications/wp52-seeking-democratic-dividend-public-attitudes-and-attempted-reform-nigeria.

30 Human Rights Watch, *Corruption on Trial*, 32, 60.

of the judiciary, including the quality of legal reasoning, which some experts have described as overtly literal, demonstrating "very little intellectual energy," and lacking the sort of investigative depth and rigorous opinion-writing associated with good judicial practice in the common law tradition.[31] Nonetheless, it is possible to discern two broad jurisprudential tendencies: (1) a conservative, passive, and politically restrained approach to judicial reasoning as highlighted, for instance in *Badejo v. Federal Minister of Education & Ors* (1996), and (2) a more progressive, activist, radical, or liberal orientation, as evident in *Lakanmi v. AG Western State* (1971) and *AG Bendel v. AG Federation* (1981). The conservative tendency extols the principle of judicial precedent, upholds very rigid or strict standing rules regarding the right or standing to sue, frowns on attempts to nudge the courts into giving advisory opinions or abstract academic rulings that are not rooted in concrete or "live" contestations, is quite pragmatic in accommodating the exigencies and legacies of military rule, and therefore is generally more centralist in its federalism jurisprudence.

The more progressive orientation interprets the rule of *locus standi* generously in order to expand access to judicial redress, gives the broadest and most liberal construction possible to the jurisdiction of the courts and the provisions of the law, frowns on stultifying narrow legalisms, is intellectually critical of the country's centralizing authoritarian traditions, and consequently is broadly more decentralist in its federalism opinions.[32]

IV. Federalism Jurisprudence

Three specific areas of federalism-related judicial review have featured prominently in the Fourth Republic: revenue allocations, the status of local governments, and the regulation of factional and partisan struggles for national and sub-national power.

---

31 See Tunde Ogowewo, "Self-Inflicted Constraints on Judicial Government in Nigeria," *Journal of African Law* 49, no. 1 (2005): 50; Ben Nwabueze, *The Judiciary as the Third Estate of the Realm* (Ibadan: Gold, 2007), 165–8; Solomon Ukhuegbe, "Jurisdictional Reform and the Role of the Supreme Court of Nigeria: The Path to a Policy Court," 12 April 2012, 80, http://papers.ssrn.com.

32 For a discussion of the two jurisprudential traditions, see Obinna Okere, "Judicial Activism or Passivity in Interpreting the Nigerian Constitution," *International and Comparative Law Quarterly* 36, no. 4 (1987): 788.

1. *Revenue Allocation and Distributive Conflicts*

Reflecting the domination of Nigerian federalism by the redistribution of centrally collected oil revenues lodged in the Federation Account, the Supreme Court has been summoned regularly to arbitrate conflicts over account disbursements. Perhaps the most momentous of these revenue cases was *AG Federation v. AG Abia State & Ors* (2001, 2002),[33] which involved a conflict over the determination of the boundaries of Nigeria's littoral states for the purpose of implementing section 162 (2) of the 1999 Constitution, according to which "the principle of derivation shall be reflected in any approved [revenue allocation] formula as being not less than thirteen percent of the revenue accruing to the Federation Account directly from any natural resources." Designed by the drafters to assuage complaints of economic deprivation in the oil-rich ethnic minority Niger Delta, the so-called 13 per cent derivation principle has been rendered contentious by the chequered political and legislative history of the derivation rule in Nigeria's fiscal federalism, the centrality of oil revenues to the finances of all governments in the federation, and the Constitution's silence on the exact beneficiary of the derivation revenues and its explicit vesting, under section 44 (3), of the proprietorship, control, and management of all "minerals, mineral oils and natural gas … in the Government of the Federation."

The federal government, supported by the non-oil-producing states, conceded the allocation of 13 per cent of onshore oil revenues to the oil-rich states on a derivation basis, but claimed that offshore resources (accounting for about 40 per cent of oil revenues) were exempt from the derivation rule because they belong to the federation as a whole. But the Niger Delta and other southern littoral states (Akwa Ibom, Bayelsa, Cross River, Delta, Rivers, Ondo, and Lagos) insisted on the attribution of offshore resources to the adjoining states and condemned the federal government's initiation of *AG Federation v. AG Abia State & Ors* as politically vexatious, pre-emptive of the National Assembly's revenue allocation powers, and an abuse of judicial process.

In July 2001, a seven-member panel of the Supreme Court, with its sole panellist from the Niger Delta dissenting, decided to exercise jurisdiction in *AG Federation v. AG Abia State & Ors*. In its substantive ruling

33 *AG Federation v. AG Abia State & Ors* [2001] 9 SCM 45–110; *AG Federation v. AG Abia State & Ors* [2002] 6 Supreme Court Monthly-SCM 1–234.

on the suit in April 2002, the Court upheld the federal government's position that the natural resources on Nigeria's continental shelf belong to the federation as a whole and, therefore, cannot be said to be derivable from the adjoining littoral states for revenue-allocation purposes. The southern boundary of the littoral states, the Court argued, is the low-water mark of their land surface or the seaward limit of their internal waters; it does not extend to the country's continental shelf or territorial waters.

According to the Court, Nigeria's southernmost regions (the precursors to the littoral states) were legally defined since British colonial rule as sharing a boundary with the sea, thereby implying that "the sea cannot be a part of the territory of any of the old regions" or their successors. Furthermore, the 1999 Constitution did not include any provision similar to a clause in the 1960 or 1963 constitutions in the First Republic, according to which the "continental shelf of a region shall be deemed to be part of that region" for the purpose of applying the revenue-derivation rule. Finally, the Court held the view that Nigeria's continental shelf is ascribed to the country by virtue of international conventions and concessions that "do not directly apply" to sub-federal units, but are given domestic effect by the exercise of federal legislative competence.[34]

The Supreme Court's blunt affirmation of the fiscal interests of the federal government and the non-oil producing states provoked strident objections from prominent Niger Delta politicians and legal scholars, who disparaged the Court's decision as a "supreme injustice" against the Niger Delta. They faulted the Court for its strained invocations of colonial-era proclamations, disregard of more contemporaneous national and international practices that effaced the dichotomy between onshore and offshore oil resources, conflation of federal jurisdiction over external affairs with the domestic allocation of offshore oil revenues, and contradictory position in pre-empting the allocation of offshore oil revenues while recognizing the broad constitutional mandate of the National Assembly to determine the terms of such allocation.[35]

In response to these resentments, the federal executive brokered a political compromise that culminated in the National Assembly's

---

34 *AG Federation v. AG Abia State & Ors* [2002] 6 SCM 91.

35 See Rotimi T. Suberu, "The Supreme Court and Federalism in Nigeria," *Journal of Modern African Studies* 46, no. 3 (2008): 464.

enactment of the Allocation of Revenue (Abolition of Dichotomy in the Application of the Principle of Derivation) Act of 2004. Under the act, an area of "two hundred meter water depth Isobaths contiguous" to the littoral states is deemed to belong to those states for the purpose of the derivation principle. Although the act failed to satisfy the demands of the Niger Delta states for the complete abrogation of the onshore-offshore oil dichotomy, the act was nonetheless challenged as unconstitutional and contemptuous of the Supreme Court by twenty-two non-littoral/non-oil-producing states, including all nineteen states in the North and Ekiti, Osun, and Oyo in the southwest.

However, the Supreme Court, in *AG Adamawa State & Ors v. AG Federation & Ors* (2005),[36] upheld the counterclaim of the federal government and the littoral states that the Abolition Act was a legitimate law of the National Assembly (including representatives of the non-littoral states) and impugned the plaintiff non-littoral states for failing to "demonstrate sufficiently and effectively how their civil rights ... have been affected by the Act." This finding underscored the Court's willingness to abandon its earlier holding regarding the non-applicability of the derivation rule to offshore oil resources for a more politically judicious approach. This gave recognition to the constitutional powers of the National Assembly to define the parameters of the revenue allocation system or develop the rather incomplete constitutional provisions on derivation in order to accomplish the larger political goals of inter-regional accommodation and the alleviation of ethnic minority grievances in the Niger Delta.

The Supreme Court reaffirmed the federal government's revenue-sharing prerogatives in a series of decisions following *AG Federation v. AG Abia State & Ors* (2001, 2002). In *AG Ogun State & Ors v. AG Federation* (2002),[37] the Supreme Court determined that the federal government cannot be required, as demanded by the five plaintiff southwestern states, to pay all federally collected revenues, net of its own independent revenues, into the general distributable intergovernmental pool or Federation Account, since the government is constitutionally obliged to transfer some portions of federally collected revenues directly to the states on a derivation basis. An inadvertent effect of this ruling was to encourage the federal government to continue to short-change the

36 *AG Adamawa State & Ors v. AG Federation & Ors* [2005] 12 SCM 1–74.

37 *AG Ogun State & Ors v. AG Federation* [2002] 14 SCM 1–32.

sub-national orders by pre-empting considerable amounts of centrally collected revenues from the general distributable pool.

In *AG Abia State & Ors v. AG Federation* (2003),[38] the Court ruled that President Olusẹgun Obasanjo was legally competent to modify the existing revenue-allocation decree-law inherited from the military in order to bring it into conformity with the constitutional provision mandating the allocation of Federation Account revenues among the three orders of government only. This ruling legitimated the president's transfer to the federal government of 7.5 per cent of Federation Account revenues that the decree-law had designated as special funds for purposes like financial stabilization and the development of the FCT. The transfer was unpopular among the state governors who had argued that the president should have prorated the funds to the three orders of government rather than assigning them exclusively to the centre. Although a subsequent political solution reduced the proportion of special funds assigned to the centre to 4.18 per cent, the Supreme Court's ruling underscored the expansive distributive powers of the federal government.

In *AG Abia State v. AG Federation & Ors* (2005),[39] the Supreme Court confirmed the powers of the federal government to make deductions from Abia State's share of the Federation Account in order to service debts incurred by the state, including its obligations for loans incurred by the old Imo State, which was subdivided into Abia and Ebonyi in 1996. The Court ruled that the federal government's role as the guarantor of all external loans incurred by the states entailed a "responsibility to see that repayments for the loans are paid as and when due," which "can only be done by deductions from the states' monies available through the Federal Government, namely, the Federation Account."

In another major decision that ultimately preserved the centre's fiscal hegemony, the Supreme Court declined to exercise jurisdiction in *AG Lagos State v. AG Federation* (2014),[40] involving a challenge to the authority of the Federal Inland Revenue Service (FIRS) to administer the Nigerian Value Added Tax. The Lagos state government contended that activities of the FIRS had impeded the government's efforts to levy and collect taxes within the state on the supply of goods and services,

38 *AG Abia State & Ors v AG Federation* [2003] 1 SCM 1–61.

39 *AG Abia State v. AG Federation & Ors* [2005] 7 SCM 1–70.

40 *AG Lagos State v. AG Federation* [2014] LPELR-SC 20/2008.

which being on neither the concurrent nor exclusive legislative lists, was a residual matter within sub-national jurisdiction. The Court ruled that its original jurisdiction to arbitrate constitutional disputes between the federation and its component units could not properly be invoked in conflicts involving purely administrative or political agents of the federal and/or state governments; moreover, federal government revenue matters were constitutionally within the original jurisdiction of the Federal High Court, from where they would gradually have to ascend the judicial ladder via the Court of Appeal to the Supreme Court.

In *AG Ondo State v. AG Federation & Ors* (2002),[41] the Supreme Court upheld the federal government's authority to enact and administer a federation-wide anti-corruption law designed to ensure transparency in the use of public funds (including Federation Account transfers) by all orders of government. The Court determined that while it contained some irregularities, the national anti-corruption law was consistent with the constitutional powers of the federal government to pursue broad national objectives and directive principles, including the abolition of "all corrupt practices and abuse of power." As a power to legislate generally on corruption was not explicitly on the list of the federal government's exclusive or concurrent legislative powers, the Court's validation of the anti-corruption law relied largely on decisions from common law federal jurisdictions like the United States, Australia, and Canada, including *McCulloch v. Maryland* (1819),[42] *R v. Kidman* (1915),[43] and *Reference re Anti-Inflation Act* (1976),[44] that have given a liberal construction to the centre's authority to promote "peace, order and good government" or to legislate on matters that are "incidental and supplementary" to, or "necessary and proper" for, the furtherance of its express powers.[45]

Yet the Supreme Court has not been simply an instrument for the advancement of the centre's fiscal hegemony. At least three of its revenue-sharing decisions protected the interests of the states under the national revenue-sharing system. First, the Supreme Court invalidated not only the direct allocations of the Federation Account to entities or funds other than the three orders of government, but also upfront

41 *AG Ondo State v. AG Federation & Ors* [2002] 9 SCM 1–70.

42 *McCulloch v. Maryland* 17 US 316 (1819).

43 *R v. Kidman* [1915] 20 CLR 425.

44 *Reference re Anti-inflation Act* [1976] 2 SCR 373.

45 See *AG Ondo State v. AG Federation & Ors* [2002] 9 SCM 61, 70–2.

deductions from centrally collected revenues in the form of first-line charges for such items as external debt payments of the federal government, the NJC, and national priority projects.[46] This potentially expanded the amount of centrally collected revenues available for general intergovernmental redistribution via the Federation Account. This decision, however, weakened the federal government's efforts to save, rather than simply share, windfall oil revenues beyond a federal budgetary benchmark through instruments like the Excess Crude Account, the Sovereign Wealth Fund, and the Fiscal Responsibility Act.

Second, the Court, in *AG Cross River v. AG Federation & Anor* (2005),[47] held that the federal government, as the "trustee in respect of all monies paid into the Federation Account," is obliged to render accurate and regular statements of the account if and when it is clearly requested to do so by the sub-national beneficiaries of the account. The Court also awarded about US$17.1 million verified shortfalls in federal revenue transfers to the Cross River state government.

Finally, the Court has ruled that all monies standing to the credit of the localities in the Federation Account must constitutionally be channelled to the local governments through their respective states rather than transferred directly by the federal government to the local councils.[48]

An important subset of federalism cases arbitrated by the Supreme Court during the Fourth Republic focused on interstate, as distinct from federal-state, conflicts. Many of these conflicts involved disagreements over the location of oil wells in the Niger Delta for revenue-attribution purposes as well as disputes over the boundaries and the sharing of the assets and liabilities of states that were subdivided during the military's state-creation exercises.

In *AG Cross River v. AG Federation & Anor* (2005),[49] for instance, the Supreme Court upheld the legality of the state governor's variation of the internal boundaries of the old Cross River State under the "Local Governments Clans, Villages (Variation) Order No. 1 of 1983." The Court rejected the request by Akwa Ibom State (which was excised from Cross River in 1987) to have the affected clans and villages transferred from Cross River to Akwa Ibom. In a subsequent suit between

46 *AG Federation v. AG Abia & Ors* [2002] 6 SCM 66.

47 *AG Cross River State v. AG Federation & Anor* [2005] 7 SCM 98.

48 *AG Ogun State & Ors v. AG Federation* [2002] 14 SCM 19.

49 *AG Cross River State v. AG Federation & Anor* [2005] 7 SCM 93.

the same parties, *AG Cross River State v. AG Federation & Anor* (2012),[50] the Supreme Court held that Cross River had ceased to be a littoral state following the final implementation of an International Court of Justice decision that handed over Bakassi Peninsula in southern Cross River to the Republic of Cameroon. The Court ruled that the federal government had acted factually, correctly, and legally in transferring derivation revenues in respect of seventy-six offshore oil wells, previously attributed to Cross River, to neighbouring Akwa Ibom.

In *AG Rivers State v. AG Akwa Ibom State & Anor* (2011),[51] the Court ruled that Akwa Ibom could not connive with the NBC and RMAFC to opt out of a "political solution" brokered by the federal president and endorsed by the governors of the two states in October 2006, which shared derivation revenues from 172 disputed oil wells equally between the two states. The Court also ordered the payment to Rivers State by the appropriate federal agencies of all monies, plus interest at the prevailing commercial rate, that had been credited to Akwa Ibom since April 2009 in breach of the political solution.

In *AG Rivers State v. AG Bayelsa State & Anor* (2012),[52] the Supreme Court held that a decision on the appropriate attribution of revenues from the disputed Soku/Oluasiri oilwells would have to await the final demarcation of the boundaries between the two states by the NBC. Berating the NBC for shirking its constitutional responsibilities and for its "lamentable," "reproachable," "technically questionable," and "highly controversial" operations, the Court urged the commission to "give priority" to concluding the boundary demarcation between the two states.

In *AG Plateau State v. AG Nasarawa State* (2005),[53] the Court held Nasarawa liable for debts outstanding on road and water projects executed by the old Plateau state government but located in Nasarawa State, which was excised from Plateau in 1996. In *AG Nasarawa State v. AG Plateau State* (2012),[54] the Court ruled that the Plateau government could not unilaterally rescind the terms of a statutory assets and liabilities sharing process, which had assigned several government buildings, offices, and staff quarters located in Jos (the capital of the old

50 *AG Cross River State v. AG Federation & Anor* [2012] LPELR-SC 250/2009.
51 *AG Rivers State v. AG Akwa Ibom State & Anor* [2011] SC 27/2010.
52 *AG Rivers State v. AG Bayelsa State & Anor* [2012] SC 106/2009.
53 *AG Plateau State v. AG Nasarawa State* [2005] 9 NWLR (Pt. 930).
54 *AG Nasarawa State v. AG Plateau State* [2012] LPELR-SC 214/2007.

and current Plateau State) to Nasarawa. The ruling echoed a previous decision of the Court, in *AG Ondo State v. AG Ekiti State* (2001),[55] that it was not open to any state to seek unilaterally to reject or reinterpret the terms of the assets and liabilities sharing committees established during the military's state-creation exercises.

A theme common to most of the Supreme Court's holdings in interstate distributive disputes is that, in the absence of evidence of fraud or misrepresentation, a state government must, in accordance with the common law principle of estoppel, observe and honour past agreements or contracts no matter how erroneous, contradictory, or undemocratic those pacts may now appear to it to be. As the courts cannot rewrite those contracts, any unilateral attempts to repudiate them would, in the opinion of the Supreme Court, be "reckless with capacity to encourage lawlessness and disobedience to constituted authority and the rule of law, which outcome would not rule out chaos."[56]

2. *Status of Local Government*

The conflicting constitutional visions and provisions regarding the status of local government in the federation have invariably triggered intergovernmental litigation in the Supreme Court. Thus, in the aforementioned case of *AG Ogun & Ors v. AG Federation* (2002),[57] the Supreme Court determined that it is the responsibility of each state government to establish and manage the constitutionally mandated "State Joint Local Government Account" (SJLGA), which is a repository for all allocations to the LGAs of a state from the Federation Account and from the government of the state. The Court accordingly invalidated the establishment of an SJLGA Committee for each state under the subsisting federal revenue decree-law.

Similarly, in its decision in *AG Abia & Ors v. AG Federation* (2002),[58] the Court ruled in favour of a petition by the thirty-six states challenging a 2001 federal Electoral Act that had extended the tenure of local councils from three years, under a 1998 federal military decree-law, to four years. Specifically, the Court confined the applicability of the extension to the six LGAs in the federal capital city of Abuja, restricted

55 *AG Ondo State v. AG Ekiti State* [2001] 17 NWLR (Pt. 743).
56 *AG Nasarawa State v. AG Plateau State* [2012] LPELR-SC 214/2007.
57 *AG Ogun State & Ors v. AG Federation* [2002] 14 SCM 17, 23.
58 *AG Abia & Ors v. AG Federation* [2002] 5 SCM 27–8.

the electoral powers of the National Assembly over local governments nationally to making laws for the registration of voters and the procedural (rather than substantive) regulation of local elections, declared the tenure of local governments to be a residual subject belonging to the states under the practice of the Constitution, and impugned the National Assembly for encroaching on the general powers of the states over their localities.

Yet, while it unanimously held that the National Assembly could not regulate the tenure of local councils, the Court left somewhat unresolved the precise scope of the Assembly's power under item 11 of the concurrent legislative list to make laws "on procedure regulating elections to a local government council." In *AG Abia & Ors v. AG Federation* (2002), the seven-member panel of the Court issued conflicting opinions on the validity of a provision of the 2001 Electoral Act mandating a ninety-day public notice for holding any elections (including local government polls), with four justices (Muhammadu Uwais, Michael Ogundare, Emmanuel Ogwuegbu, and Akintola Ejiwunmi) upholding the validity of this provision, and three justices (Uthman Mohammed, Umaru Kalgo, and Idris Kutigi) invalidating the provision.

In the instructive case of *Osun State Independent Electoral Commission (OSIEC) & Anor v. Action Congress & Ors* (2010),[59] however, the Supreme Court unanimously affirmed the powers of the National Assembly to regulate the length of notifications by the states for local elections. The background to this case was that in November 2007 the opposition Action Congress (AC) party had asked the Osun State High Court to invalidate the Osun State Electoral Law of 2002 on the ground that the 21-day notice provided for holding local government elections under the law was inconsistent with the 2006 federal Electoral Act, which mandated a 150-day notice for holding any elections in Nigeria. Immediately following the rejection of the AC's claim by the high court in December 2007, OSIEC conducted elections in thirty-one local councils, which poll the AC and other opposition parties boycotted. The AC subsequently approached the Court of Appeal, which set aside the 2007 Osun local government elections as illegal and unconstitutional on account of the failure of the OSIEC to provide the federally required 150-day notice of polling. On further appeal to the Supreme Court by

59 *Osun State Independent Electoral Commission (OSIEC) & Anor v. Action Congress & Ors* [2010] LPELR-SC 265/2009.

OSIEC and the Osun government, the apex Court upheld the decision of the Court of Appeal. Invoking the doctrine of covering the field, the Supreme Court affirmed the supremacy of the federal Electoral Act over the Osun law with respect to any provisions "on the procedure regulating elections to a local government council, the issue of notice inclusive." The Court referenced its previous expositions on this doctrine, including *AG Ogun v. AG Federation* (1982) and *AG Abia & Ors v. AG Federation* (2002), which have invoked the position of Justice Owen Dixon of Australia's High Court in *Ex Parte McLean* (1930)[60] that a state law on a concurrent subject is rendered inconsistent and thus invalid or inoperative by a federal statutory scheme intended to "completely, exhaustively or exclusively" cover the same subject.[61]

Essentially, the Supreme Court's decisions, in *AG Abia & Ors v. AG Federation* (2002) and *Osun State Independent Electoral Commission (OSIEC) & Anor v. Action Congress & Ors* (2010), highlighted the conflicted constitutional status of localities by voiding a federal law prescribing the tenure of local councils while upholding another federal act regulating the length of notification for local elections. A further dramatization of this ambivalence was the legal imbroglio between the federal government and Lagos State that followed President Obasanjo's April 2004 directive withholding the payment of local government allocations in the Federation Account to states where elections had been conducted in LGAs created after the 1999 civilian transition. According to Obasanjo, "As the National Assembly is yet to make the necessary consequential provisions in respect of any of the newly created Local Government Areas in the country, conducting any election into them, or funding any of them from the Federation Account, would clearly be a violation of the Constitution."[62]

Unlike the PDP-controlled states of Ebonyi, Katsina, Nasarawa, and Niger, all of which abrogated their new LGAs in order to continue to receive federal transfers to the localities, the opposition-controlled administration of Lagos insisted on its authority to establish local government areas, which the state government had increased from twenty in 1999 to fifty-seven in 2002. Consequently, Lagos approached the Supreme Court for a declaration that it is unlawful and unconstitutional

---

60 *Ex Parte McLean* (1930) 43 CLR 472.

61 *AG Abia & Ors v. AG Federation* [2002] 5 SCM 74.

62 See *AG Lagos State v. AG Federation* [2004] 9–12 SCM 23.

for the federal executive "to suspend or withhold for any period whatsoever the statutory allocation due and payable to the Lagos state government" for the benefit of its localities.[63]

The Supreme Court ruled, in *AG Lagos State v. AG Federation* (2004),[64] that the president had no power to hold back federal transfers meant for the localities in Lagos insofar as the money "applies to the 20 Local Government Councils for the time being recognized by the Constitution and not the new Local Government Areas which are not yet operative." At the same time, the Court did not annul the new Lagos LGAs, which it described as legal but inchoate until their ratification by the National Assembly. The Supreme Court also rejected the federal government's request for the invalidation of the elections into these areas because, according to the Court, the polls involved individuals and groups that were not parties to the suit.

Although celebrated by Lagos State as a judicial vindication of its federalist struggle against an imperial federal presidency, the Supreme Court's decision in *AG Lagos State v. AG Federation* did not resolve the conflict between the state and the federal executive. The federal government continued to withhold the funds for Lagos LGAs on the ground that the creation of new areas had effectively obliterated the legitimate beneficiaries of the funds. As claimed by Ben Nwabueze, "In fairness to the Federal Government ... the contradictory positions of the Supreme Court ... in this case are a contributory factor in [the Government's] refusal to obey the Court's order" regarding the release of the withheld funds.[65]

The Supreme Court, however, issued a more definitive opinion on the constitutional status of localities in *AG Abia & Ors v. AG Federation and Ors* (2006).[66] This suit involved an action by Abia, Delta, and Lagos States challenging the constitutionality of the federal government's Monitoring of Revenue Allocation to Local Government's Act 2005. Drawing on the extensive revenue-sharing powers of the National Assembly, the act required each of the thirty-six states to establish an SJLGA Committee under the chairmanship of the commissioner responsible for local government in the state. The committee's primary function would be

63 *AG Lagos State v. AG Federation* [2004] 9–12 SCM 48.

64 Ibid.

65 Ben Nwabueze, *How President Obasanjo Subverted the Rule of Law and Democracy* (Ibadan: Gold, 2008), 150–1.

66 *AG Abia State & Ors v. AG Federation & Ors* [2006] 10–11 SCM 1–146.

to ensure that all statutory federal and state grants to the localities are "promptly paid into" the SJLGA and distributed among the councils in accordance with the relevant laws of the state legislature. The committee also would render monthly statements of the SJLGA, on the basis of which quarterly reports would be made to the National Assembly through the accountant-general of the federation. Finally, under the act, a state government encroaching on funds due to its localities would have its Federation Account allocations appropriately deducted and credited to the affected local council(s), while a functionary involved in such violation would be "liable on conviction to a fine twice the amount [involved] or imprisonment for a term of five years or to both such fine and imprisonment."[67]

The Supreme Court, by a 5–2 majority, ruled that the Monitoring Act transgressed the states' constitutional autonomy. Specifically, the Court's majority upheld the claims of the plaintiff state governments that the act had usurped the powers of the state legislature to provide for the establishment, composition, and functions of the SJLGA Committee, unlawfully directed the states to include federal appointees (including a commissioner of the RMAFC and a representative of the accountant-general of the federation) on the SJLGA and render reports to the federal government, unconstitutionally conferred on the federal government oversight functions over local administrations within a state, and generally exceeded federal powers to *allocate* revenues to the localities by encroaching on the responsibilities of the states to regulate the *distribution* of such funds to local councils. However, disparaging the majority's attempt to differentiate the federal powers of allocation from the state powers of distribution as a distinction without a difference, the dissenting Justices Idris Legbo Kutigi and Dahiru Musdapher upheld the act as consistent with the integrative orientation of Nigeria's Constitution.

In a comparable decision on the relative powers of the centre and the states over local governance, the Supreme Court, in *AG Lagos State v. AG Federation & Ors* (2003),[68] by a narrow 4–3 majority, invalidated most sections of the Nigerian Urban and Regional Planning Law, enacted under military auspices in 1992. In the opinion of the Court's majority, urban and regional planning is "a residual matter within the exclusive

67 See *AG Abia State & Ors v. AG Federation & Ors* [2006] 10–11 SCM 63.
68 *AG Lagos State v. AG Federation & Ors* [2003] 9 SCM 1–148.

legislative and executive competence" of the states, is conceptually distinct from national environmental policymaking, and is, therefore, beyond the purview of any exclusive, concurrent, or incidental powers assigned to the federal government under the 1999 Constitution. Similarly, in *AG Federation v. AG Lagos State* (2013),[69] the Supreme Court unanimously held that the exclusive legislative powers of the federal government to regulate "tourist traffic," including the movement of foreigners, did not extend to the "regulation, registration, classification and grading of hotels" and other tourism or hospitality establishments, which were "clearly residual matters for the states."

Determined to preserve some measure of local autonomy for state governments in Nigeria's otherwise centralized federation, Justice Uwaifor, speaking for the Court's majority in *AG Lagos State v. AG Federation & Ors* (2003), "completely" and with "great faith" embraced the opinion of Chief Justice William Taft in the American case of *Bailey v. Drexel Furniture Co.* (1922),[70] which rejected the potential use of congressional authority to "breakdown all constitutional limitation of the powers of Congress and completely wipe out the sovereignty of the states."[71] Similarly, Justice Ayoola, while dissenting from the majority's position that urban planning is a residual subject over which the states have exclusive legislative responsibility, argued, citing American case law like *National League of Cities v. Usery* (1976)[72] and *Hodel v. Virginia Surface Mining and Reclamation Association, Inc.* (1981),[73] that any federal government legislation on urban planning must be reasonably related or adapted to national environmental policymaking and exercised in a manner that does not offend or impair the autonomy or sovereignty of the states.[74]

An adverse effect of the Court's holdings on local governance issues, however, was to facilitate the degradations of the putative third order of Nigerian federalism by the state governments, which systematically hijacked and raided local government funds, replaced elected local councils with caretaker committees appointed by the governors, rigged local government elections, or failed to conduct local elections

69 *AG Federation v. AG Lagos State* [2013] LPELR-SC 340/2010.
70 *Bailey v. Drexel Furniture Co.* 259 US 20 (1922).
71 *AG Lagos State v. AG Federation & Ors* [2003] 9 SCM 39.
72 *National League of Cities v. Usery* 426 U.S. 833 (1976).
73 *Hodel v. Virginia Surface Mining and Reclamation Association, Inc* 442 U.S. 264 (1981).
74 *AG Lagos State v. AG Federation & Ors* [2003] 9 SCM 128–31.

altogether. These abuses persist despite the Court's opinion in *Honorable Chigozie Eze & Ors v. Governor of Abia State & Ors* (2014),[75] and a series of decisions of the Court of Appeal, including *AG Plateau State & 3 Ors v. Goyol & 15 Ors* (2007)[76] and *Adamawa State House of Assembly & 2 Ors v. Chubado Batti Tijjani and Ors* (2011),[77] which invalidated attempts by state governments arbitrarily to truncate or terminate the tenures of elected local councils. By August 2012, only thirteen states and the FCT had elected local government chairmen.[78] This crisis of local democracy is emblematic of a broader national debacle of electoral authoritarianism, which poses the most chronic challenge to judicial governance in Nigeria.

3. Restraining Federal Executive and Ruling Party Authoritarianism

A major challenge for constitutionalism in neo-patrimonial African countries is the tendency towards authoritarian "big man," personal, "presidential," and/or single-party rule and the attendant degradation of liberal democratic processes, including the suppression of autonomous pluralistic spheres of political authority outside of the central executive and/or ruling party.[79] In Nigeria, such authoritarianism has included federally backed arbitrary attempts to uproot or overwhelm sub-national governments through stage-managed impeachments or dismissals of governors considered to be partisan or factional "opponents and non-loyalists" of the president, impositions of states of emergency, and manipulations of sub-national and national electoral contests.[80] While states also engage in this kind of unconstitutional behaviour, the abuses by the federal government have been enormously aided and aggravated by presidential control and manipulation of key

75 *Honourable Chigozie Eze & Ors v. Governor of Abia State & Ors* [2014] LPELR-SC 209/2010.

76 *AG Plateau State & 3 Ors v. Goyol & 15 Ors* [2007] 16 NWLR (Pt. 1059).

77 *Adamawa State House of Assembly & 2 Ors v. Chubado Batti Tijjani and Ors* [2011] CA/J/304/2009.

78 See Chuks Okocha, "INEC Directs States with Caretaker Committees to Conduct Council Elections," *This Day* (Lagos), 3 August 2012.

79 See Nicolas van de Walle, "Presidentialism and Clientelism in Africa's Emerging Party Systems," *Journal of Modern African Studies* 41, no. 2 (2003): 297–321.

80 Mamman Lawan, "Abuse of Powers of Impeachment in Nigeria," *Journal of Modern African Studies* 48, no. 2 (2010): 333.

agencies like the anti-corruption bodies, the single national police force, and the national electoral commission.

The Constitution provides guidelines for the impeachment of political executives and presidential proclamations of a state of emergency. The impeachment process for state officials essentially involves four stages: (1) the presentation to the speaker of the state assembly of a written notice signed by at least one-third of the members of the legislature alleging official "gross misconduct" by the executive; (2) a motion, within fourteen days of the presentation (and circulation) of the notice, by at least two-thirds of the legislators supporting the investigation of the alleged misconduct; (3) within seven days of the motion, the appointment by the chief judge on the request of the speaker of an independent seven-member panel to investigate the allegation and submit a report within three months of its appointment; and (4) if the report confirms the allegation, and two-thirds of the legislators adopt the report, the political executive stands removed.[81]

A presidential proclamation of a state of emergency in the federation or any part thereof, which must be approved by a two-thirds majority of all the members of each house of the bicameral National Assembly for a period of only six months at a time, must be predicated on (1) the actual or imminent existence of a dangerous exigency (e.g., war, invasion, breakdown of public order, natural disaster, or threat to the existence of the federation), or (2) a request by the governor of an endangered state, supported by a two-thirds majority of the state assembly, asking the president to proclaim an emergency in the state. During the period of emergency, the federal government may undertake "extraordinary measures" to avert danger or restore peace.[82]

Despite these formal constitutional safeguards, egregious abuses, implicating the federal executive, characterized the invocations of these impeachment or emergency provisions during the Fourth Republic in Anambra, Oyo, and Plateau, among other states. The impeachment processes, in particular, were degraded by numerous interrelated violations of the letter or spirit of the law, including the external initiation or instigation of impeachment processes by the federal executive rather than by the state legislatures; the use of the EFCC, an agency under the president's control and notorious for its politically selective

81 *The Constitution of the Federal Republic of Nigeria 1999*, s. 188.
82 Ibid., s. 305.

anti-corruption program, as the main author or source of the charges of gubernatorial misconduct; the resort to impeachment as a strategy for removing the constitutional immunity of the governors in order to enable their prosecution for corruption by the EFCC; the use of federal security agencies (i.e., the police, state security services, and even the military) to coerce state legislators into endorsing the impeachments; suspensions of recalcitrant legislators in bids to achieve the numbers required for impeachment; the appointment of openly partisan members into, and the unduly hasty conduct of the work of, a panel of investigation; and "tampering with the offices of the speaker of the House of Assembly and of the chief judge, sittings at odd times of the day, acting on an interim report of a panel of investigation, or even acting without a report at all."[83]

The presidential proclamations of emergency, although politically less contentious and procedurally less abusive than the impeachment exercises, were characterized by such questionable processes as "non-compliance with the requirement of an objective factual situation" of a dangerous exigency; "non-compliance with the request requirement"; and use of a constitutionally dubious and arguably moribund law, the Emergency Powers Act of 1961, to suspend the entire executive and legislature of a state during the period of emergency.[84]

The courts were partly reluctant to intervene in these politically fraught impeachment and emergency sagas, especially as the Constitution explicitly prohibits judicial review of impeachment proceedings. Thus, in *AG Anambra State v. AG Federation & Ors* (2005),[85] which was instituted following an attempt by the Nigeria Police Force to force the ouster of Anambra's governor on the basis of a forged or illicitly obtained resignation letter purportedly accepted by the state assembly, the Supreme Court acknowledged the "siege" on the governor, but declined to issue any advisory, "hypothetical," "speculative," or pre-emptive declarations regarding the scope of federal police or emergency powers in the state.

Similarly, in *Plateau State & Anor v. AG Federation & Anor* (2006),[86] the Court struck out a legal challenge to President Obasanjo's suspension of

83 Lawan, "Abuse of Powers of Impeachment in Nigeria," 317–18.

84 Ben Nwabueze, *How President Obasanjo Subverted Nigeria's Federal System* (Ibadan: Gold, 2007), 196–230.

85 *AG Anambra State v. AG Federation & Ors* [2005] 5 SCM 39.

86 *Plateau State & Anor v. AG Federation & Anor* [2006] 1 SCM 163.

the elected executive and legislature of Plateau for six months (18 May–17 November 2004), following an outbreak of ethno-religious violence in the state. The Supreme Court ruled the suit procedurally incompetent because it was instituted during the six-month emergency period by the suspended legislators in the name of Plateau State without the authorization of the centrally imposed administration of the state. That the emergency administration could not possibly have authorized a legal action against its own validity did not stop the Supreme Court from rejecting the action as falling outside its constitutional jurisdiction. The Court also held that the suit involved claims for personal reliefs (or payments of financial compensation for loss of emoluments during the emergency not only to the plaintiff legislators but also to their executive counterparts) that were outside the original, as distinct from appellate, jurisdiction of the Court. It acknowledged that the suit raised "very salient questions" but "founder[ed] on an important procedural point," leading the legal scholar and counsel for the plaintiff, Ben Nwabueze, to conclude that this was "a lamentable instance of the (Court's) policy of avoiding sensitive constitutional or policy issues."[87]

However, in *Hon. Michael Dapianlong & Ors v. Chief (Dr) Joshua Chibi Dariye & Ors* (2007),[88] the Supreme Court affirmed a decision of the Court of Appeal that "held that the jurisdiction of courts is ousted [in impeachment proceedings] only if the procedure outlined in … the constitution is complied with" and therefore voided the removal of the Plateau State governor by only eight members of the twenty-four-member state legislature.[89] Although the eight legislators claimed that fourteen of the state's legislators had effectively vacated the house by decamping from the ruling PDP to the opposition Action Congress, the Supreme Court affirmed that "until the vacancies created by the carpet crossing members are filled by the process of by-election, the Plateau State House of Assembly can only transact such legislative duties that require the participation of less than 2/3 majority of ALL the members of that House, which duties definitely exclude impeachment proceedings."[90]

87 *Plateau State & Anor v. AG Federation & Anor* [2006] 1 SCM 183, 202; Nwabueze, *Judiciary as the Third Estate of the Realm*, 237.

88 *Hon. Michael Dapianlong & Ors v. Chief (Dr) Joshua Chibi Dariye & Ors* [2007] 8 NWLR (Pt. 1036).

89 Lawan, "Abuse of Powers of Impeachment in Nigeria," 317.

90 Ibid., 322 (capitalization in the original).

Similarly, the Supreme Court upheld the Court of Appeal's invalidation of the impeachment of the PDP governor of Oyo State by eighteen of the thirty-two state legislators. Backed openly by the federal attorney general and security agencies, the eighteen members claimed to have suspended seven of their counterparts, thereby reducing the membership of the House to twenty-five and fulfilling the constitutionally mandated two-thirds requirement for the removal of the governor. But in *Hon. Muyiwa Inakoju & Ors v. Hon. Abraham Adeolu Adeleke & Ors* (2007),[91] the Supreme Court affirmed the unconstitutionality of the impeachment proceedings in Oyo and restored the governor to his position as the state's constitutionally elected chief political executive.

Electoral manipulation, along with impeachments and declarations of states of emergency, are key strategies by which the federal executive and its political allies have sought to undermine their sub-national rivals. In Anambra, where the federal executive had sought to employ all three strategies simultaneously, the judiciary made multiple crucial interventions that protected constitutionalism and the state's political autonomy. These included the voiding of the PDP's 2003 gubernatorial victory in March 2006 on account of massive electoral fraud, the invalidation in February 2007 of the procedurally irregular impeachment of the newly installed All Progressives Grand Alliance (APGA) governor by PDP legislators, and the setting aside of the PDP's purported gubernatorial victory in the April 2007 election illegally conducted by INEC when the opposition APGA governor of the state was barely a year into his four-year tenure.

In Anambra, as well as in Edo, Ekiti, Osun, and Ondo, opposition parties were ultimately installed in place of the PDP as state governing parties following active judicial review and annulment of several of the PDP's dubious gubernatorial victories in the massively rigged and heavily litigated 2007 elections. However, the most phenomenal instance of Supreme Court intervention in the elections involved, yet again, a PDP intra-party conflict.

In *Rt Hon. Rotimi Chibuike Amaechi v. INEC & Ors* (2008),[92] the Supreme Court invalidated the electoral victory of Celestine Omehia, the official PDP candidate in the 2007 Rivers gubernatorial election, and instead

91 *Hon. Muyiwa Inakoju & Ors v. Hon. Abraham Adeolu Adeleke & Ors* [2007] 4 NWLR (Pt. 1025).

92 *Rt. Hon. Rotimi Chibuike Amaechi v. INEC & Ors* [2008] 5 NWLR (Pt. 1080).

declared Rotimi Amaechi, who had been prevented by the party from contesting the election, the governor-elect. Amaechi had overwhelmingly won the PDP's Rivers governorship primaries, but his candidacy was surreptitiously substituted by the national-level PDP with Omehia's, who was not even a contestant in the primaries. When Amaechi legally challenged the substitution, the PDP referred to his purported indictment by the EFCC and subsequently expelled him from the party.

Unable to obtain redress in the Federal High Court and the Court of Appeal, Amaechi finally approached the Supreme Court, which held, in an unprecedented but unanimous ruling, that Amaechi, and not Omehia, must be deemed to be the only lawful PDP candidate in, and winner of, the April 2007 Rivers gubernatorial election. The Supreme Court upbraided the Court of Appeal for not following a judicial precedent regarding the unconstitutionality of candidate substitutions that were not based on "cogent and verifiable reasons." It also impugned the attempt to punish Amaechi for an alleged indictment without prosecution in an impartial court of law, and disparaged the federal executive's use of the EFCC and INEC to "politicize the investigation and prosecution of criminal offences." The apex court, however, reserved its harshest words for the PDP for doing "everything possible to subvert the rule of law, frustrate Amaechi and hold the court before the general public as supine and irrelevant."[93]

As underscored by the cases of *Alhaji Atiku Abubakar & Ors v. Alhaji Umaru Musa Yar' Adua & Ors* (2008)[94] and *General Muhammadu Buhari v. INEC & Ors* (2008),[95] however, the Supreme Court was less activist in addressing PDP shenanigans in presidential, as distinct from gubernatorial, elections. In *Alhaji Atiku Abubakar & Ors v. Alhaji Umaru Musa Yar' Adua & Ors*, the Court affirmed the decision of the Court of Appeal rejecting Vice-President Atiku Abubakar's petition that he had been unlawfully excluded from participating in the April 2007 presidential elections. Determined to prevent the allegedly disloyal Abubakar from succeeding to the presidency, the federal executive and the PDP had suspended Abubakar from the party, all but secured his disqualification by INEC from the presidential contest for alleged indictment for corruption, and sought unsuccessfully to remove him as vice-president.

93 Ibid., 321.

94 *Alhaji Atiku Abubakar & Ors v. Alhaji Umaru Musa Yar' Adua & Ors* [2008] 19 NWLR (Pt. 1120).

95 *General Muhammadu Buhari v. INEC & Ors* [2008] 19 NWLR (Pt. 1120).

Forced into protracted legal battles for his political survival, Abubakar got officially on the presidential ballot only on the ticket of the opposition Action Congress just three days before the massively rigged presidential election, coming in a distant third in the election with 7 per cent of the vote. However, the Supreme Court affirmed by a 6–1 majority that, as an official candidate in the presidential election, Abubakar could not claim unlawful exclusion from the election; furthermore, having pleaded unlawful exclusion, Abubakar could not question the election on any other grounds available to a participant in the election.[96]

A similar narrow legalism was evident in *General Muhammadu Buhari v. INEC & Ors*. In this instance, the Court conceded that the conduct of the 2007 elections had been characterized by substantial non-compliance with the provisions of the Electoral Act, including a failure to use serialized ballot papers. But it upheld the results of the elections, by a narrow 4–3 majority, on the ground that Muhammadu Buhari, the runner-up in the elections, had failed to prove that such non-compliance had substantially affected the election's outcome. Yet, as argued by Justice George Oguntade in his dissent, INEC's failure to use serialized ballot papers had made it "impossible to establish [an audit] trail of ballot papers," thereby fundamentally compromising the transparency and validity of the presidential elections. Furthermore, to saddle "a petitioner with the burden of showing non-compliance with the provisions of the Electoral Act and at the same time showing the effect of the alleged non-compliance on the result of election would appear unduly favorable and lenient to the respondent [INEC] who is the perpetrator of disobedience to the law of the land."[97]

The Supreme Court's validation of the universally condemned 2007 presidential election preserved the political hegemony of the PDP and the electoral authoritarianism of the Nigerian federation, while raising serious questions about the Court's credibility and viability as an arbiter. Indeed, the judiciary's interventions in electoral processes have posed the stiffest challenges to the institution's efficacy, authority, and legitimacy.

First, the sheer volume of electoral petitions (1,250 in 2007) strained the judiciary's already overstretched resources, leading to long delays

---

96 *Alhaji Atiku Abubakar & Ors v. Alhaji Umaru Musa Yar' Adua & Ors* [2008] 19 NWLR (Pt. 1120) 215.

97 *General Muhammadu Buhari v. INEC & Ors* [2008] 19 NWLR (Pt. 1120) 452.

in resolving many of the electoral disputes and virtual impunity for election riggers. Second, in inserting the judiciary into high-level political and electoral disputes, Nigeria's system of "democracy by court order" left the institution at the receiving end of politicians' desperate antics, including abuses of court processes and orders, and illicit attempts to influence judges.[98] Third, electoral adjudications have been mired in massive legal contradictions and financial corruption, including credible allegations of huge bribes paid by politicians to judges of election tribunals, the Court of Appeal, and even the Supreme Court. Fourth, the judiciary's immersion in electoral disputes has undermined the institution's internal cohesion. This was evident in 2011–12 when the federation's two highest judicial officers, the chief justice of the Supreme Court and the president of the Court of Appeal, publicly clashed and traded accusations of corruption over electoral adjudication matters.[99] Finally, despite the reining in of some of the worst political excesses of the federal executive and PDP at the sub-national level, judicial interventions in elections failed to end the party's stranglehold on the federal government until the 2015 presidential elections, when the PDP was decisively defeated by the APC. This is partly because the onerous evidentiary burden for electoral petitions is significantly easier to muster in statewide gubernatorial races than in nationwide presidential contests.

V. Conclusion

The judiciary's performance in the development of Nigeria's constitutional federalism has been ambivalent. On the positive side, the Supreme Court has played an important arbitrative role in Nigerian federalism. The Court has been a key mediator of the distributive conflicts that dominate Nigeria's oil-centric federal system, judiciously arbitrating revenue-sharing disputes between the federal government and the states, between the oil-producing and non-oil-producing states, and among the oil-rich states themselves. The Court has adjudicated the conflicted constitutional status of local governments, affirming the broad rights of the states over localities, while seeking to uphold the national framework rules designed to guarantee the integrity of local

98 See "Nigeria: Democracy by Court Order," *Economist* (London), 24 January 2008.
99 Human Rights Watch, *Corruption on Trial*, 36.

government as the putative third order of the federal system. The Court also has helped to strengthen the weak democratic foundations of the federation, restraining political executives' authoritarian attempts to destabilize or remove state and local governments, while curtailing the centre's manipulations of gubernatorial elections.

Less positively, the Supreme Court has played at best a secondary or limited role in the development of Nigerian federalism. Essentially, the Court has seen itself as an interpreter and enforcer of Nigeria's centrist Constitution rather than as a transformational agent for the country's democratic decentralization after years of hyper-centralizing, extra-judicial military rule. As claimed by Justice Niki Tobi in *AG Lagos State v. AG Federation & Ors* (2003), "We may have our own aversions and prejudices on the unitary context of some provisions of our Federal Constitution but there is nothing we can do as judges."[100] Not surprisingly, most of the Court's decisions since 1999 have buttressed federal supremacy by, for instance, affirming federal ownership of oil resources, upholding the federal government's broad revenue-sharing powers, confirming the centre's authority to regulate local government elections and boundaries, and legitimizing the authoritarian electoral control of the PDP at the national level. Furthermore, reflecting the narrow confinement of much of its federalism jurisprudence to concrete intergovernmental disputes, the Supreme Court has remained disengaged from some of the country's major federalist debates and conflicts, including the constitutionality of extensions of sharia law in Muslim states or the legality of discrimination on the basis of state of origin.

The quest for better judicial governance, including a more robust judicial federalism, has produced multiple, often conflicting, proposals for reform.[101] These include the creation of a specialized constitutional court devoted exclusively to the timely arbitration of major political conflicts; the redefinition of the jurisdiction of the Supreme Court to enable it offer advisory constitutional opinions; the evolution of more sensible docket-management doctrines and practices as a way of removing purely practical and procedural causes from the Supreme Court's overloaded docket and, thus, enhancing the quality of the

100 *AG Lagos State v. AG Federation & Ors* [2003] 9 SCM 137.

101 See, for instance, National Political Reform Conference (NPRC), *Report of the Committee on Judiciary and Legal Forms* (Abuja: NPRC, 2005); Adebisi Onanuga, Eric Ikhiale, Joseph Jibueze, and Precious Igbonwelundu, "Will Musdapher's Bill Sail Through?" *Nation* (Lagos), 26 June 2012.

Court's jurisprudence; changes to the composition and qualifications of the Court in order to enhance the professionalism and experience of its justices; the implementation of clean-elections reforms as a means of alleviating the pressures on the courts from electoral petitions; the reconstitution of the NJC in order to enhance its independence from, and oversight of, serving judicial officers, while making it more federal (rather than unitary) in character; the de-politicization of the office of the attorney-general; and strengthening the dignity, quality, and efficiency of lower courts as a way of restoring confidence in these courts and reducing the size of the docket in the appellate courts.

Yet, in the absence of broader changes in the structural foundations and constitutional architecture of Nigeria's semi-democratic and pseudo-federal polity, it is unlikely that the judiciary will be a catalyst for a radically reformed or enhanced democratic federalism.

11 The Constitutional Court of South Africa: Reinforcing an Hourglass System of Multi-Level Government[1]

NICO STEYTLER

I. Introduction

"The supremacy of the constitution and the rule of law" are two foundational values of South Africa's 1996 Constitution (s. 1(c)). An independent judiciary is thus set to play a major role in interpreting and enforcing the Constitution. With some significant federal elements in the Constitution, such as establishing provincial and local orders of government, the courts, with the Constitutional Court at the apex, are bound to give shape and texture to this system of government. Since 1995, the Constitutional Court as well as the Supreme Court of Appeal and High Court have asserted the supremacy of the Constitution and the separation of powers, establishing a jurisprudence that gives effect to the principle of limited government. However, in interpreting the federal arrangements, the Constitutional Court has not given full effect to the self-rule elements of provincial government. Instead, it has more often enforced local government's constitutional "right to govern, on its own initiative, the local government affairs of its community" (s. 151(3)). Furthermore, while soft on the substantive content of provincial self-rule, it has scrupulously policed compliance with the procedural rules of intergovernmental relations. The Court's jurisprudence has given further credence to the hourglass model of multi-level government; provinces are squeezed thin from the top by a dominant national government and from below by powerful metropolitan governments.

1 Helpful suggestions by my colleagues Jaap de Visser, Derek Powell, and the anonymous reviewers are much appreciated. This work is also based is upon research supported by the South African Research Chairs Initiative of the Department of Science and Technology and National Research Foundation.

II. Federal System

1. *The Broad Characteristics*

South Africa's 54 million people are diverse. Africans, comprising nine linguistic communities, constitute 80.2 per cent of the population, followed by Coloureds (a mixed-race category at 8.8 per cent), whites (8.4 per cent), and Indian or Asian (2.5 per cent).[2] A few million undocumented inhabitants (the precise number unknown), originating from neighbouring countries, notably Zimbabwe, should be added to the total. Eleven official languages are constitutionally recognized, and the percentage breakdown of the major language groups is IsiZulu (22.7); IsiXhosa (16); Afrikaans (13.5); English (9.6), Sepedi (9.1); Setswana (8); and Sesotho (7.6).[3] Although the explicit intention was not to create ethnically based provinces, seven of the nine provinces have a linguistic majority. South Africa is regarded as a middle-income country at US$12,900 GDP per capita in 2014; yet it shows one of the highest levels of income disparity (income Gini coefficient 0.69),[4] with nearly half of the population living in poverty spread across urban and rural areas.

Following the demise of apartheid, the interim Constitution of 1993 established two orders of government – the national government and nine provinces. Although local government was recognized in the 1993 Constitution (mainly as a provincial competence), the 1996 Constitution elevated it to a "sphere" of government alongside the national and provincial governments (s. 40(1)).[5]

---

2 Statistics South Africa, *Stats in Brief 2014* (Pretoria: Statistics South Africa, 2014), table 2.3.

3 Statistics South Africa, *Census 2011: Census in Brief* (Pretoria: Statistics South Africa, 2012), 24, figure 2.3.

4 OECD, *OECD Economic Surveys: South Africa 2015*, 7, http://www.treasury.gov.za/publications/other/OECD%20Economic%20Surveys%20South%20Africa%202015.pdf.

5 For further background, see Nico Steytler, "Republic of South Africa," in *Constitutional Origins, Structure, and Change in Federal Countries*, ed. John Kincaid and G. Alan Tarr, 311–46 (Montreal and Kingston: McGill-Queen's University Press, 2005); Christina Murray, "Republic of South Africa," in *Legislative, Executive, and Judicial Governance in Federal Countries*, ed. Katy le Roy and Cheryl Saunders, 258–88 (Montreal and Kingston: McGill-Queen's University Press, 2006); and Jaap de Visser, "Republic of South Africa," in *Local Government and Metropolitan Regions in Federal Systems*, ed. Nico Steytler, 267–97 (Montreal and Kingston: McGill-Queen's University Press, 2009); Chris Tapscott, "Republic of South Africa: An Uncertain Path to Federal Democracy,"

The 1993 Constitution was a peace treaty between the African National Congress (ANC) and the white minority regime. The low-intensity civil war that commenced in 1960 was also taken to the black homeland governments, which were regarded as collaborators of the apartheid government. The formation of the nine provinces was a key compromise between the incumbent white regime and some homeland leaders, notably Chief Mangosuthu Buthelezi from KwaZulu, who championed a strong federal system for ethnic accommodation as well as limiting the power of the centre. However, the ANC demanded a strong centre in order to transform the society after three centuries of racial oppression. The outcome of the "negotiated revolution" was a weak form of federalism, showing strong unitary elements.[6] Although there were four "independent" homelands (recognized as such only by South Africa) and six self-governing territories (giving effect to the grand apartheid design based on ethnicity), the formation of provinces in 1994 was a process of devolution; a largely centralized system, ultimately under the control of the white minority regime, devolved into nine provinces.

The peace negotiations were essentially the business of political parties, most notably the (white) National Party (NP) and the ANC. Because the result was a negotiated constitution, the ANC's demand for a democratically based constitution was met with the undertaking that within two years a final constitution would be drafted by a democratically elected Constitutional Assembly. The NP's fears that the gains it made at the negotiating table would be swept aside by an elected ANC majority were met by the condition that the new constitution had to comply with a number of negotiated constitutional principles, which included protection of the provincial system.

The 1996 Constitution's hybrid federal system, eventually certified by the Constitutional Court as complying with the Constitutional Principles,[7] has been in operation ever since, with no significant changes.

---

in *Political Parties and Civil Society in Federal Countries*, ed. Klaus Detterbeck, Wolfgang Renzsch, and John Kincaid, 199–226 (Don Mills, ON: Oxford University Press, 2015); Derek Powell, "Constructing a Developmental State in South Africa: The Corporatization of Intergovernmental Relations," in *Intergovernmental Relations in Federal Systems: Comparative Structures and Dynamics*, ed. Johanne Poirier, Cheryl Saunders, and John Kincaid, 305–49 (Don Mills, ON: Oxford University Press, 2015).

6 Ronald L. Watts, "Is the New South African Constitution Federal or Unitary?," in *Birth of a Constitution*, ed. Bertus de Villiers (Cape Town: Juta, 1994), 75, 86.

7 In re: Certification of the Constitution of the Republic of South Africa, 1996, 1996 (10) BCLR 1253 (CC) ("First Certification judgment").

Giving effect to the self-rule elements of the hybrid federal system has entailed the subnational governments being responsible for 62 per cent of the total state expenditure; in the 2013/14 financial year, provinces (responsible for the wage bill of teachers and medical staff) expended 36 per cent and municipalities 26 per cent.[8]

Because the ANC never fully embraced the negotiated solution, the system has been under review since 2007.[9] The other two members of the ruling ANC alliance – the Congress of South African Trade Unions (COSATU) and the South African Communist Party (SACP) – are outspoken in criticizing the provinces and advocating their abolition. In contrast, the major opposition party, the Democratic Alliance, which captured the Western Cape province in 2009, and again, with an increased majority, in 2014, is a strong proponent of the provincial system. It not only seeks to exploit the opportunities provided by the current system, but also uses good governance in the Western Cape as the platform for its political campaign to capture other provinces.

Although the high level of maladministration and corruption prevalent in a number of provinces has not endeared them to the public or the national government, strong elites coagulated around such governments, thus making major constitutional reform unlikely.[10] This was reflected in the ANC's 53rd National Conference resolution in December 2012 that effectively retained the provincial system by requiring that "provinces [should] be reformed, reduced and strengthened."[11] What is also on the cards is the continual growth of metropolitan government.[12] The formation in 2000 of six major metropolitan municipalities (increased to eight in 2011) has resulted in ever-increasing demands

8 National Treasury, *Budget Review 2014* (Pretoria: National Treasury, 2014), 93, and table 7.1.

9 ANC, "Legislature and Governance for a National Democratic Society," Policy Discussion Documents, ANC 52nd National Conference 2007, Umrabula Publication (Marshalltown: African National Congress, 2007). See further Nico Steytler "The Politics of Provinces and the Provincialisation of Politics," in *Law, Politics and Rights: Essays in Memory of Kader Asmal*, ed. Tiyanjana Maluwa, 191–214 (Leiden: Martinus Nijhoff, 2014).

10 Steytler, "Politics of Provinces and the Provincialisation of Politics."

11 ANC, Resolutions of 53rd National Conference: Legislatures and Governance, Resolution 4.2.1 (2012).

12 National Planning Commission, *National Development Plan: Our Future – Make It Work* (Pretoria: National Planning Commission, 2012), 435. See also De Visser "Republic of South Africa," 292.

for more functions at the expense of provinces. Over the last few years, the important provincial functions of transport and housing have been slowly assigned to the metropolitan councils.

With constitutional supremacy a core principle of the Constitution,[13] the Constitutional Court's jurisdiction covers all aspects of the federal arrangement. As such, the Court has the power to invalidate legislation and executive action compelling the fulfilment of constitutional obligations (s. 2). Even though the system of multi-level government has operated for two decades, the Constitutional Court has not had a dominant hand in shaping the system; at best, its role can be described as middling.

2. *Structural Features*

The Constitution provides that "government is constituted as national, provincial and local spheres of government which are distinctive, interdependent and interrelated" (s. 40(1)). The "distinctive" characteristic reflects the measure of "self-rule" of provinces and local government; they have entrenched powers and functions and access to revenue sources. The Constitution provides detailed provisions for the functioning of provincial legislative and executive structures and procedures. It also envisages national legislation on provincial administration and financial management.[14] As the constitutional provisions with regard to local government are more schematic, national legislation structures the establishment of municipalities and their internal organizations, functioning, and financial management.[15]

Following an integrative federal approach, the allocation of powers and functions to provinces and municipalities allows for an interwoven and complementary system. First, most provincial functions are

13 The establishment of constitutionalism in South Africa in 1994 finds resonance in the argument of Ran Hirschl (*Towards Juristocracy: The Origins and Consequences of the New Constitutionalism* [Cambridge, MA: Harvard University Press, 2004], 99); judicial empowerment through the constitutionalization of judicial review and a bill of rights is often a "conscious strategy undertaken by threatened political elites seeking to preserve or enhance their hegemony by insulating policy-making from popular political pressures and supported by economic and judicial elites with compatible interests."

14 Inter alia, the Public Service Act, 1994, and the Public Finance Management Act, 1999.

15 See Municipal Structures Act, 1998; Municipal Systems Act, 2000; Municipal Finance Management Act, 2003; Municipal Property Rates Act, 2004; and Municipal Fiscal Powers and Functions Act, 2007.

concurrent with the national government, the principal functions being education, health, social welfare, housing, agriculture, and transport (sch. 4). Much more limited are exclusive provincial powers, which include ambulance services, liquor licences, provincial planning, provincial roads, and traffic control (sch. 5). The adoption of a provincial constitution, although within narrow parameters, is perhaps the only "true" exclusive power. Local government's constitutionally entrenched, but not exclusive, powers include electricity reticulation, water and sanitation, municipal public transport, municipal health services, municipal planning, and municipal roads and traffic (schs. 4B and 5B). The national legislative powers are almost supreme; not only does Parliament have all residual powers, but it may also trump competing concurrent provincial legislation through a qualified override clause (s. 146), as well as exclusive provincial legislation on more limited grounds (s. 44(2)). Both the national and provincial legislatures may regulate the entrenched local government powers (s. 155(7) and schs. 4B and 5B).

In the constitutional scheme, the national Parliament may assign any of its legislative powers (save very specific ones) to provinces and municipalities. Provinces may likewise assign any of their powers to municipalities. Municipalities, on the other hand, may claim the assignment of both national and provincial matters if such matters would most effectively be administered locally (s. 156(4)).

Although the definitions of the various functional areas are often opaque (e.g., the precise differences between national, provincial, and local health services), there is, in the main, agreement on the allocated functions. However, contestation occurs on the cut-off points between functional areas, appropriate allocation of some functions (e.g., housing and transport), and unfunded mandates.

Within the paradigm of constitutional supremacy, the Constitutional Court has the final word on the definition of functional areas. The national Parliament has also on occasion circumscribed the content of broad functional areas by, for example, defining provincial and local health responsibilities in the National Health Act, 2003.

Differing from the German constitutional model on which the South African system of "cooperative government" is based, the Constitution does not prescribe national framework legislation that must be complemented by provincial laws. It does, however, envisage national laws in the terrain of provincial and local governance, as indicated above. In the case of local government, however, both the national and provincial governments may legislate regulatory frameworks for the exercise of local competences (ss. 155(6)(a) and 155(7)).

The Constitution contains specific provisions to deal with conflicting concurrent national and provincial laws by allowing a national law to trump a provincial law if certain broad conditions are met (s. 146). The override sets, however, a low hurdle for national legislation. First, for example, national legislation prevails if a matter "cannot be regulated effectively" by provinces individually (s. 146(2)(a)). Moreover, the interpretational guidance in the Constitution is equally broad. First, courts are guided by the principle that they must always prefer a reasonable interpretation of the conflicting legislation that would avoid the conflict above an interpretation that results in conflict (s. 150). Second, in considering a further override test, namely, whether national legislation is "necessary" to maintain national security, economic unity, and a common economic market, etc., courts must have "due regard to the approval or the rejection of the National Council of Provinces" (s. 146(4)), but there is no indication how such decision is to be used. Third, there is a built-in default position in favour of the national government; if a court cannot resolve the conflict, the national legislation prevails over the provincial legislation (s. 148). In case of a conflict, the law that does not prevail is not invalid but merely becomes inoperative.

Constitutional supremacy is also reflected in the amendment procedures. The Constitution may be amended only by a two-thirds majority of the National Assembly following a special procedure. In the case of the founding values in section 1, a three-quarters majority is required. Depending on the nature of the amendment, the National Council of Provinces (NCOP) (and thus the provinces) has an important veto (s. 74). Any amendment of section 1 and the Bill of Rights requires the consent of at least six of the nine provinces. Also, in respect of any amendment that affects the NCOP, or alters provincial boundaries, powers, functions, or institutions, at least six of the nine provinces must consent. Moreover, if the amendment affects only a specific province or provinces (such as a boundary change), the consent of the legislature(s) of those provinces is required. The two-thirds majority rule also applies to the amendment of provincial constitutions (s. 144).

Although there is no requirement of subjecting amendments to a popular referendum, the Constitutional Court has interpreted the legislative process as requiring adequate public participation. Indeed, the Court has invalidated legislation on the basis of insufficient public participation,[16] including a constitutional amendment that changed the boundaries of the provinces of KwaZulu-Natal and Eastern Cape.[17]

As the upper guardian of the Constitution, the Constitutional Court plays a pivotal role in interpreting the Constitution's federal elements when matters are brought to it. Provincial constitutions do not see the light of day unless the Constitutional Court has certified that they comply with the required constitutional prescripts (s. 144). Given the relative newness of the system and the limited litigation due to the near dominance of the ANC in the provinces, it is premature to map how the Court has altered the operation of the federal system; yet the trend has been favourable to local government but not to the provinces.

The NCOP is one of the pivotal institutions intended to effect an integrative federalism. As the name suggests, it is a council of provinces that participates in the national legislative process. The NCOP is thus described in the Constitution as representing "the provinces to ensure that provincial interests are taken into account in the national sphere of government. It does this mainly by participating in the national legislative process and by providing a national forum for public consideration of issues affecting provinces" (s 42(4)). Owing some dues to its Bundesrat progenitor, each province is represented by a ten-member delegation: four are members of the provincial legislature (with the premier being the leader of the delegation) and six are indirectly elected by the provincial legislatures to serve at the legislatures' pleasure a term of five years. Coming almost as an afterthought, but a logical consequence of the recognition of local government as a sphere of government, organized local government has ten representatives in the NCOP, who may participate in proceedings when the interests of local government are at issue, but may not vote (s. 67).

III. Court System

1. Introduction

Coming from a long tradition of parliamentary supremacy, the advent of democratic rule in 1994 also meant a shift to constitutional

16 Doctors for Life International v. Speaker of the National Assembly and Others, 2006 (12) BCLR 1399 (CC).

17 Matatiele Municipality and Others v. President of the Republic of South Africa and Others, 2007 (1) BCLR 47 (CC).

supremacy and the rule of law. Given that the "revolution" was negotiated, there was no breach of legal continuity; the laws in operation in 1994 continued to apply to the extent that they were compliant with the new constitutional dispensation. This, too, applied to the common law; it had to comply and be developed in conformity with the Bill of Rights.

The 1993 and 1996 Constitutions preserved the distinction between the High Court of general jurisdiction and the lower courts with limited jurisdiction. The Appellate Division, the highest court before 1994, now called the Supreme Court of Appeal (SCA), continued as the highest court in all matters other than constitutional. Final constitutional adjudication was reserved for the newly created Constitutional Court. The separate roles of the SCA and the Constitutional Court were necessitated by the apartheid past. With all judges from the apartheid era continuing in their positions, final interpretation of the new supreme Constitution could not be left in the hands of the SCA. The Constitutional Court was thus established, with only four of the eleven justices drawn from sitting judges. As court of final jurisdiction on constitutional matters, this Court has also the final word on the constitutional framework for multi-level government in South Africa. The Constitution thus makes specific provision that the Constitutional Court is the only court that can "decide disputes between organs of state in the national or provincial sphere concerning the constitutional status, powers and functions of any of those organs of state" (s. 168(4)). The Constitution Seventeenth Amendment Act of 2012 has now unified the appellate structure by making the Constitutional Court the final arbiter also in non-constitutional matters.

The new constitutional order entrenched the judiciary as a national competence. No constitutional provision was made for provincial or local courts. A High Court division has been established for every province, with their jurisdictions coinciding with provincial boundaries. All the courts function in an integrated appellate system. There are appeals from the lower courts to the High Court, from the High Court to the Supreme Court of Appeal, and from there to the Constitutional Court. On constitutional matters, an appeal lies either directly to the Constitutional Court (with leave given in few cases) or via the Supreme Court of Appeal. Where the High Court invalidates a national or provincial law, or presidential conduct, as being unconstitutional, there is an "automatic" review by the Constitutional Court; unless the Court confirms the invalidity, the law or conduct stands (s. 167(5)).

As a trial court, the High Court proceedings are presided over by a single judge. In criminal cases, the judge is joined by two lay assessors. Lower court appeals to the High Court are heard by two or three judges. In the latter case, minority judgments can be delivered. In appeals to the Supreme Court of Appeal, criminal cases are heard by a three-judge bench, while other appeals require a five-judge bench. In the Constitutional Court, a minimum of eight of the eleven justices forms a quorum. All decisions appear under the name of the judges. Only the Constitutional Court has on rare occasions delivered its judgments *en banc*, without reference to the justice who wrote them. Those occasions were of high political significance such as the certifications of the 1996 Constitution[18] and the provincial constitutions of KwaZulu-Natal[19] and the Western Cape.[20] Dissenting judgments are possible and not infrequent. In the Constitutional Court's 2007 term, no fewer than in a third of the twenty-seven judgments contained dissenting opinions,[21] with the percentage in the 2008 term being thirty-nine,[22] remaining the same for the 2012 term.[23] This is a decrease from the 48 per cent of 2006 judgments with dissenting opinions, while the average for the previous decade was only 23 per cent. Judgments of the High Court and appellate courts are published as well as the dissenting opinions.

Rooted in the common-law system, the doctrine of precedent is applied firmly by the courts. The Constitutional Court has asserted this doctrine of *stare decisis* even with regard to judgments originating from the apartheid era, subject, of course, to not being in conflict with the Constitution. The High Court is bound by the decisions of the Supreme Court of Appeal and the Constitutional Court. Even the two appellate courts are bound by their own decisions unless they are satisfied that the previous decision was "clearly wrong."[24]

---

18 In re Certification of the Constitution of the Republic of South Africa, 1996, 1996 (4) SA 744 (CC) para. 287 ("First Certification" judgment).

19 In re: Certification of the Constitution of the Province of KwaZulu-Natal, 1996, 1996 (11) BCLR 1419 (CC) ("KwaZulu-Natal Constitution").

20 In re: Certification of the Constitution of the Western Cape, 1997 (9) BCLR 1167 (CC).

21 Liza Chamberlain and Sha'ista Kazee, "Constitutional Court Statistics for the 2007 Term," *South African Journal on Human Rights* 26 (2010): 571, table 3.

22 Samantha Brener, Michael Eastman, and Jennifer Macleod, "Constitutional Court Statistics for the 2008 Term," *South African Journal on Human Rights* 27 (2011): 566, table 3.

23 Saflii.org.za (analysis of the 34 judgment in the 2012 term).

24 Camps Bay Ratepayers and Residents Association v. Harrison, 2011 (2) BCLR 121 (CC) para. 28. See further, see Jason Brickhill, "Precedent and the Constitutional Court," *Constitutional Court Review* 3 (2010): 79–110.

2. *Constitutional Status of Courts and Judicial Officers*

An entire chapter of the Constitution is devoted to the courts and the administration of justice. Having complied with the Constitutional Principles that there should be "a separation of powers between the legislature, executive and judiciary, with appropriate checks and balances to ensure accountability, responsiveness and openness,"[25] the relationship between the courts and the other branches of government is clearly set.[26] The judicial authority is vested in the courts (s. 165(1)), comprising the courts mentioned above. The Constitution, though, provides for national legislation to further regulate the judicial system. As the judiciary is a national competency, provinces and municipalities play no role in their functioning, bar two exceptions. First, the provinces via the NCOP nominate four of its permanent delegates as members to the Judicial Service Commission (JSC). In addition, the premier of the province is a member of the JSC when it considers a matter relating to the High Court in that province. The second exception is the establishment of a "municipal" court. A municipality may pay for the salary of a nationally appointed magistrate, whose task is then to adjudicate the enforcement of municipal by-laws.

Central to the appointment of judges to the higher courts stands the Judicial Service Commission (JSC). It was created in 1994 as a clear break with the long-standing practice of executive appointments, under which the first black judge was appointed only in 1991.[27] In the new constitutional state, not only is the independence of the judiciary entrenched, but the process of appointment also is more transparent and less controlled by the executive. The JSC's members comprise representatives from the judiciary (three, including the chief justice as chairperson), the minister of justice, the legal profession (four), law schools (one), the National Assembly (six, three of whom must be opposition MPs), NCOP delegates (four), presidential nominees (four),

---

25 Constitutional Principle VI Schedule 4 1993 Constitution.

26 In National Society for the Prevention of Cruelty to Animals v. Minister of Agriculture, Forestry and Fisheries and Others (Licensed Animal Trainers Association and two amici curiae intervening) 2013 (1) BCLR 1159 (CC), the Constitutional Court affirmed the importance of the principle of the separation of powers when it invalidated provisions in a 1935 law that gave magistrates the task of issuing licences for exhibiting and training performing animals, because it was an administrative function totally unrelated to the judicial function.

27 Yvonne Mokgoro, "Judicial Appointments," *Advocate* (December 2010): 44.

and the judge-president and premier of a province where a matter concerns the High Court in that province.

Despite the overhaul of the appointment process, there is still a strong executive hand in appointments to the top curial positions. The president appoints the chief justice and his or her deputy after consultation with the JSC and the leaders of the political parties in the National Assembly. The president needs to consult the JSC with regard to the appointment of the president and deputy president of the Supreme Court of Appeal. When it comes to the nine justices of the Constitutional Court, the president appoints them from a list provided by the JSC (there must be three names more than the vacant positions). For the appointment of all other judges, the president must follow the JSC's advice. Giving effect to the constitutional imprimatur that "the need for the judiciary to reflect broadly the racial and gender composition of South Africa must be considered when judicial officers are appointed" (s. 174(2)), by July 2014 of the 243 judges, 63.4 per cent (147) were black and 32.5 per cent were women.[28] Furthermore, the tradition of appointing judges from the ranks of senior advocates only has been tempered; a number of attorneys (solicitors), magistrates, and a few law professors have been elevated to the bench.

The JSC's conduct has also come under criticism. Given the ANC's strong hand in the JSC's composition (at least twelve of twenty-three would be directly linked to the ruling party through the executive and the legislature), claims of political and biased appointments have been levelled. In 2011, the Cape Bar Council successfully challenged the JSC for not appointing an outstanding white candidate to the Western Cape High Court as being arbitrary and irrational.[29]

The bedrock of the supremacy of the Constitution and the rule of law is the independence of the judiciary. The Constitution thus proclaims, "The courts are independent and subject only to the Constitution and the law, which they must apply impartially and without fear, favour or prejudice" (s. 165(2)). The independence of the judiciary is entrenched through the usual techniques. First, judges have tenure until reaching a specified age.

28 Nomthandazo Ntlama, "The Transformation of the South African Judiciary: A Measure to Weaken Its Capacity?," 9 table 3, New York Law School, http://www.nylslawreview.com/wp-content/uploads/sites/16/2014/10/Ntlama.pdf.

29 Cape Bar Council v. Judicial Service Commission and Another (Centre for Constitutional Rights and Another as Amici Curiae), 2012 (4) BCLR 406 (WC), upheld by the Supreme Court of Appeal in Judicial Service Commission and Another v. Cape Bar Council and Another 2012 (11) BCLR 1239 (SCA).

Before then, their removal requires a finding by the JSC that a judge suffers from incapacity, is grossly incompetent, or is guilty of gross misconduct. This finding must then be supported by a two-thirds vote in the National Assembly. Second, their salaries, allowances, and benefits may not be reduced. Third, after a long wrangle with the executive, the budget of the courts was placed under the control of the chief justice.[30]

The judiciary's independent functioning has not gone uncontested. The first serious volley fired over the bow of the courts was the statement of the secretary-general of the ANC, Gwede Mantashe, that some courts were "counter revolutionaries," stymieing the national democratic revolution.[31] These sentiments were echoed by senior ministers in the national executive. Even President Jacob Zuma weighed in against the Constitutional Court when he ordered a review of the judgments of that Court, stating that the courts cannot be regarded as always right when they produce dissenting opinions. Furthermore, the president's choice of the current chief justice, Mogoeng Mogoeng, was widely criticized because he was the least experienced judge on the Constitutional Court. In each case where the Constitutional Court imposed positive obligations on the state to fulfil socio-economic rights, the complaint by government has been that the judiciary was not respecting the separation of powers. These volleys were, no doubt, instigated by government being on the losing side most often[32] and thus perceiving the Court as an obstacle to its governing.

---

30 Superior Courts Act, 2013.

31 See Sapa, "ANC Defends Mantashe's Remarks on Judges," Polityorg.za, 11 July 2008, http://www.polity.org.za/article/anc-defends-mantashes-remarks-on-judges-2008-07-11.

32 In the Constitutional Court's 2007 term, the Court found in favour of the government only in eight of eighteen cases (47 per cent) (Chamberlain and Kazee, "Constitutional Court Statistics 2007," table 7). The percentage of state success in 2008 was lower at 44 per cent (Brener, Eastman, and Macleod, "Constitutional Court Statistics 2008," 567). In 2011 alone the national executive lost a number of crucial decisions: invalidating the placement a special investigative unit (formerly known as the Directorate of Special Operation, called "the Scorpions," now renamed the Directorate of Priority Crime Investigations, called "the Hawks"), which fell under the jurisdiction of the largely autonomous National Prosecuting Authority, under the South African Police Service (and executive control) (Glenister v. President of the Republic of South Africa and Others, 2011 (7) BCLR 651 (CC)); the unconstitutional extension of Chief Justice Ngcobo's term of office (Justice Alliance of SA v. President of the RSA and Two Similar Applications, 2011 (10) BCLR 1017 (CC)); the invalidation by the SCA of the presidential appointment of the national director of

Matters came to a head when the North Gauteng High Court issued an interim order that the government could not allow the sitting president of Sudan, Omar al-Bashir, who was attending an African Union Summit in Johannesburg in June 2015, to leave South Africa, pending a determination whether South Africa should arrest him and hand him over to the International Criminal Court to face charges of genocide and war crimes. Not only did the government deliberately disobey the court order (see further below), but Cabinet ministers and the ANC unleashed a barrage of criticism against the judiciary.[33] Mantashe proclaimed that the courts were biased against the ruling party and that certain courts had "a negative attitude towards government."[34] At the centre of the complaint was the accusation that the courts did not respect the separation of powers. Instead, they "overreached" into the domain of the executive.

The ANC's attacks on the judiciary have raised grave concerns over the past few years. The first chief justice in the democratic South Africa, Arthur Chaskalson, warned that the attacks against the judiciary coming from senior politicians "undermine the constitutional order and pose a threat to our democracy."[35] He admonished politicians who want to rein in the courts rather to direct their fury to the Constitution, which the courts interpret. Public outcry against political interference has been severe from some legal quarters. For example, a civil-society organization, Freedom under Law, under the leadership of former

public prosecutions (Democratic Alliance v. President of the RSA and Others, 2012 (3) BCLR 291 (SCA)). In 2014 some provisions of the South African Police Services Amendment Act, 2012, which sought to align the Act with the Court's judgment in Glenister (see above), were also invalidated for failing to secure adequate independence for the Hawks (Helen Suzman Foundation v. President of the Republic of South Africa and Others; Glenister v. President of the Republic of South Africa, 2015 (1) BCLR 1 (CC)).

33 Editorial, "This Is a Country of Laws," *City Press*, 21 June 2015.

34 "Gwede Mantashe Criticises Judiciary as Being Problematic," ENCA, 23 June 2015, https://www.enca.com/south-africa/gwede-mantashe-criticises-judiciary-being-problematic.

35 Address on 29 January 2012, University of Cape Town. Arthur Chaskalson, "When Law Irks Power," Times Live, 29 January 2012, http://www.timeslive.co.za/2012/01/29/when-law-irks-power. See also the concerns of former chief justice Sandile Ngcobo, "Sustaining Public Confidence in the Judiciary: An eEssential Condition for Realising the Judicial Role," *South African Law Journal* 128 (2011): 5.

Constitutional Court judge, Johan Kriegler, has sought through legal challenges to overturn the JSC's overtly political decisions.[36]

After the attacks on the judiciary following the al-Bashir debacle, the judiciary responded; under the leadership of the chief justice, senior judges convened in July 2015 and expressed their dismay at what they termed "general gratuitous criticism" by Cabinet ministers and the ANC. Chief Justice Mogoeng and a few senior judges then met in August with President Zuma and a coterie of Cabinet ministers to discuss judicial "overreach" and the separation of powers. From all accounts, the judiciary was not cowed; both sides agreed to respect the separation of powers, exercise caution when criticizing each other, and respect and comply with court orders.[37] This meeting was followed by another in November, this time between Zuma, Mogoeng, and the chairpersons of the two houses of Parliament, in order for the three arms of government to discuss matters of mutual concern. Whether the planned twice-yearly meetings will strengthen the separation of powers or undermine it is too early to tell.

3. *Institutional Role of the Courts*

The organization of the court system shows some specialization. Starting from the top, the Constitutional Court has the final say on constitutional matters and exclusive jurisdiction concerning, among other things, the validity of national legislation and certain intergovernmental disputes. The Supreme Court of Appeal had final appellate jurisdiction on all matters other than constitutional matters. This space was increasingly narrowed as the Constitutional Court decided what is and what is not constitutional. As noted above, the split in jurisdiction has ended; in terms of the Constitution Seventeenth Amendment Act of 2012, the Constitutional Court is also the final appellate court in any non-constitutional matter that "raises an arguable point of law of general importance."[38] The High Court in each province has general

36 Hlope v. Premier of the Western Cape; Hlope v. Freedom under Law and Others (Centre for Applied Legal Studies and Others as Amicus Curiae), 2012 (1) BCLR 1 (CC). A number of civil society organizations successfully challenged the unconstitutional extension of Chief Justice Ngcobo's tenure (Justice Alliance of SA v. President of the RSA and Two Similar Applications, 2011 (10 BCLR 1017 (CC)).

37 "'Historic' Meeting Falters on Separation of Powers," Legalbrief, 31 August 2015, http://legalbrief.co.za/story/historic-meeting-falters-on-separation-of-powers-3/.

38 See Mbata v. University of Zululand 2014 (2) BCLR 123 (CC).

original jurisdiction and appellate jurisdiction from its own ranks as well as from the magistrates' courts. The High Court's jurisdiction is limited by the specific jurisdiction of the Labour Court and the Labour Appeal Court (on labour matters), the Competition Appeal Court (on competition law), the Electoral Court, and the Land Claims Court (on land reform).

In line with common-law jurisdictions, such as the United States and Australia, South African courts, as a rule, entertain live disputes only. The establishment of the Constitutional Court has, however, introduced abstract review. Setting the tone, one of the Court's first tasks was assessing whether the 1996 Constitution complied with the Constitutional Principles set forth in the 1993 Constitution. The 1996 Constitution further embedded abstract review in three instances. First, the president may refuse to sign a bill into law if he or she has doubts about its constitutionality and then refer the matter to the Constitutional Court for an opinion.[39] A similar power is bestowed on premiers of provinces with regard to provincial bills.[40] Second, a third of the members of the National Assembly may place an act assented to by the president before the Constitutional Court to decide on its constitutionality (s. 89). A similar procedure applies to provincial legislatures where the support of only 20 per cent of the members is required (s. 120). The third instance is the duty of the Constitutional Court to certify whether a provincial constitution or amendment thereto complies with the national Constitution (s. 144).

The generous standing rules should also be mentioned. In human rights litigation (as well as other constitutional matters), public interest litigation is encouraged by the Constitution, permitting any person "acting in the public interest" to approach a court (s. 38(d)). Also, as can be gleaned from the case citations in this chapter, civil-society organizations often participate in litigation before the Constitutional Court as friends of the court (amici curiae).

Reflecting on the practice of the Constitutional Court (for the years in which tallies were kept), conflicts relating to governance issues, including disputes between organs of states, constitute a tiny minority of

39 See Ex parte President of the Republic of South Africa: in re: Constitutionality of the Liquor Bill, 2000 (1) BCLR 1 (CC) ("Liquor Bill").

40 See Premier: Limpopo Province v. Speaker: Limpopo Provincial Legislature and Others, 2011 (11) BCLR 1181 ("Limpopo I").

cases. In 2007, only one case dealt with a non–Bill of Rights provision of the Constitution. This pattern is also evident in the preceding years.[41]

4. Curial Procedures

The low number of federalism-related cases can be attributed to two factors. First, with eight of the nine provinces and all but one of the major cities under ANC control, intergovernmental disputes between ANC-controlled organs of state are usually resolved through intra-party directions or mediation. However, a divergent practice has emerged of late; the ANC-controlled Johannesburg Metropolitan Council challenged the ANC-governed Gauteng provincial government over the proper definition of "municipal planning" and won.[42] The second factor is the principle of cooperative government that eschews the solution of intergovernmental disputes through litigation (s. 41(1)(h)(vi)). This obligation has teeth; a court may refer a dispute back to the litigants when it is satisfied that the parties did not make every reasonable effort to settle the dispute by means other than litigation (s. 42(2)).[43] Such other means, including mediation, are provided for, among others, in the Intergovernmental Relations Framework Act, 2005. In a dispute between district municipalities and the National Treasury about the entitlement of the former to an equitable share of the revenue raised nationally, the Court refused to hear the case, because the municipalities had failed to utilize an intergovernmental forum, the Budget Council, to settle the matter.[44] Consequently, federal issues are raised more often than not by private parties when they advance their cause. For example, a community concerned with the substantive issues regulated by the Communal Land Rights Act, 2009, challenged the validity of the law on a procedural ground that reflects a federal element; the correct legislative procedure was not followed in the NCOP, thereby depriving the provinces of their say in the legislative process.[45]

---

41 Chamberlain and Kazee, "Constitutional Court Statistics for the 2007 Term," 571.

42 City of Johannesburg Metropolitan Municipality v. Gauteng Development Tribunal, 2010 (9) BCLR 859 (CC) ("Gauteng Development Tribunal").

43 See, for example, National Gambling Board v. Premier of KwaZulu-Natal, 2002 (2) BCLR 156 (CC) ("National Gambling Board"); Minister of Police and Others v. Premier of the Western Cape and Others, 2013 (12) BCLR 1405 (CC).

44 Uthekela District Municipality and Others v. President of the Republic of South Africa and Others, 2002 (11) BCLR 1220 (CC).

45 Tongoane and Others v. Minister of Agriculture and Land Affairs, 2010 (8) BCLR 741 (CC).

The superior courts are equipped with wide discretion over remedies to enforce the Constitution. A court must declare invalid any law or conduct that is inconsistent with the Constitution. To mitigate the impact of such a declaration, a court has the discretion to "make any order that is just and equitable" (s. 172(1)). Such an order may include limiting the retrospective effect of a declaration of invalidity, or suspending such a declaration for a period of time on conditions it may stipulate. In practice, the Constitutional Court has invalidated a number of laws and in some instances suspended their invalidity for up to eighteen months so as to allow Parliament to remedy the constitutional defect. The courts may also issue a mandamus for the fulfilment of a constitutional obligation.

The courts operate very transparently. Court proceedings are open to the public, and courts are increasingly allowing television cameras into the courtroom, as glaringly illustrated by the 2014 murder trial of para-Olympian Oscar Pistorius, who was convicted of culpable homicide (similar to involuntary manslaughter in the United States). Judgments are delivered in public (and most often within a reasonable time), and those of the Constitutional Court and Supreme Court of Appeal are readily available on these courts' websites.[46] The Constitutional Court also provides media releases on all its judgments. But litigation is, in general, prohibitively expensive. Despite a legal-aid system, which focuses mainly on criminal defence, access to justice is not readily available to the poor or even the middle class.

Former chief justice Ismael Mohamed wrote that in the absence of any physical force at their disposal, the courts' "ultimate power must therefore rest on the esteem in which the judiciary is held within the psyche and soul of the nation."[47] Such esteem has been widespread, as Chief Justice Sandile Ngcobo confirmed: "Enforcement of court decisions and orders has not been an issue in this country."[48] The problem has arisen in some divisions of the High Court where, for example, court orders that pensions should be paid out regularly were not executed, leading

---

46 For judgments of the Constitutional Court and Supreme Court of Appeal, see Constitutional Court of South Africa, www.constitutionalcourt.org.za, and Supreme Court of Appeal of South Africa, http://www.justice.gov.za/sca/judgments/judgem_sca_2012.html.

47 Ismael Mohamed, "The Role of the Judiciary in a Constitutional State," *South African Law Journal* 115 (1999): 111, 112.

48 Ngcobo, "Sustaining Public Confidence in the Judiciary," 5.

to successful class actions.[49] The first open defiance of a court order came, as noted above, when the national government let President al-Bashir leave the country, despite an interim order prohibiting that. In question was whether South Africa was obliged to execute a warrant for his arrest issued by the International Criminal Court on charges of genocide and war crimes. South Africa not only ratified the Rome Statute establishing the court, but it also domesticated the statute in legislation, in terms of which it was bound to execute the court's arrest warrants. A civil society organization obtained an interim order to prevent al-Bashir from leaving the country, but the national government facilitated his escape. The interim order was confirmed by the High Court, finding that the government was indeed obliged to execute the arrest, rejecting the government's argument that it acted in accordance with its diplomatic obligations towards the AU.[50] The circumstances of the case may be unique, but it came on the back of a long-running attack on the alleged "overreach" of the judiciary. The commitment by the president at his August meeting with Chief Justice Mogoeng to respect court orders may be a turning point, but the likely government response will be the appointment of more compliant judges so as to reduce possible conflicts with the executive.

5. *Judicial Culture*

Functioning on a common-law foundation, the judiciary played a major role in developing the legal system within the constraints of the apartheid legal order. In the 1980s, some social critics called for "moral" judges to resign their offices in an act of protest against an abhorrent system, but the dominant liberal view was that judges, given their relative but limited autonomy, could do more to blunt the hard edge of apartheid and repression through the ethical performance of their judicial duties than by resigning. Arguments based on the rule of law and human rights could, unlike in the Nazi courts, be validly raised and were occasionally successful. Former chief justice Ngcobo commented that the tradition of judicial integrity predates 1994.[51] Despite many executive-minded judges, the

---

49 See Jayiya v. MEC Welfare, Eastern Cape and Another, 2004 (2) SA 611 (SCA); MEC, Department of Welfare, Eastern Cape v. Kate, 2006 (4) SA 478 (SCA).

50 Southern Africa Litigation Centre v. Minister of Justice and Constitutional Affairs, 2015 (9) BLCR 108 (GP).

51 Ngcobo, "Sustaining Public Confidence in the Judiciary," 7. A fellow constitutional court judge, Yvonne Mokgoro, is less charitable and refers to the "few maverick" judges who used the law to restrain the apartheid state (Mokgoro, "Appointment of Judges," 44).

integrity of the bench as a whole made legal continuity with respect to the judiciary not a bridge too far in the post-apartheid South Africa. Legal continuity also pertained to pre-1994 laws; they continued to apply, provided they were compatible with the Constitution. In the common-law tradition, most judgments were carefully reasoned. The Constitutional Court has continued to excel in providing path-breaking judgments on the Bill of Rights that have been celebrated across the legal world, albeit not without criticism.

The role of the judiciary increased substantially under the Constitution. With the supremacy of a broadly worded constitution firmly entrenched, the post-1994 courts have become a significant check and balance on the executive and the legislature. Moreover, it has become the institution of last resort when politics fail. For example, when the opposition parties failed to get a motion of no confidence in the president tabled in the National Assembly, the Constitutional Court, by a vote of five to four, held that the rules of the National Assembly were inconsistent with the Constitution to the extent that they did not allow a political party or a member to enforce the right to table such a motion.[52] While this leads to the judicialization of politics, it has also resulted in the politicization of the judiciary.[53] Within this environment, as Heinz Klug argues, the Constitutional Court has managed reasonably well the tension between "principled" reasoning on one hand and "institutional pragmatism" on the other.[54]

The Constitutional Court as final interpreter of the Constitution has followed a purposive approach to interpretation. The purpose of a provision is gleaned from a number of sources, mainly from the language used and the context or scheme of the Constitution, with historical

52 Masibuko v. Sisulu and Another, 2013 (11) BCLR 1297 (CC). See also Oriani-Ambrosini, MP v. Sisulu, MP, Speaker of the National Assembly, 2013 (1) BCLR 14 (CC).

53 Herschl, *Towards Juristocracy*, 203. See C. Neal Tate and Torbjorn Vallinder, eds., *The Global Expansion of Judicial Power* (New York: New York University Press, 1995).

54 Heinz Klug, "Finding the Constitutional Court's Place in South Africa's Democracy: The Interaction of Principle and Institutional Pragmatism in the Court's Decision Making," *Constitutional Court Review* 3 (2010): 1–33. For a critique of the Court's approach to one party dominance with respect to democracy, which has had a negative impact on "real" federalism emerging, see Sujit Choudhry, "'He had a mandate': The South African Constitutional Court and the African National Congress in a Dominant Party Democracy," *Constitutional Court Review* 2 (2009): 1–86. For a challenge on the premises of Choudhry's argument, see Jonathan Klaaren, "Dominant Democracy in South Africa? A Response to Choudhry," *Constitutional Court Review* 2 (2009): 87–96.

context being of subsidiary value. Consistent with this hermeneutical approach, the Constitutional Court viewed its task of interpreting the federal elements in a purposive manner; there were no different or additional, subject-specific principles of interpretation. In a decision dealing with the appropriate assignment of functions to provinces in terms of the interim Constitution, the Court said, in response to an argument that provincial powers should be construed restrictively, "In the interpretation of those schedules [listing provincial powers] there is no presumption in favour of either the national legislature or the provincial legislatures. The functional areas must be purposively interpreted in a manner which will enable the national parliament and the provincial legislatures to exercise their respective legislative powers fully and effectively."[55]

The Court's view that by such a purposeful reading (without any underlying presumption) the constitutional text will reveal itself, has resulted in a series of decisions that did not facilitate the ability of provinces to exercise a measure of self-governance.

IV. Federalism Jurisprudence

1. Introduction

In an assessment in 2005 of judicial behaviour in the context of the federal elements of the Constitution, I argued elsewhere that the Constitutional Court exhibited a pro-centre stance in the majority of cases that came before it, emphasizing the unitary language in the Constitution.[56] The explanation offered was that the Court's stance was driven primarily by two factors. First, the Court was concerned about national unity. After decades of the pernicious divide-and-rule of ethnic and racial groups, the first task was to forge a new nation through its state institutions. The second factor was the need for order. Where the provinces in particular proved to be singularly inept to provide services effectively and efficiently, the Court stepped in as the bulwark of order. In the sea of provincial ineptitude, favouring the centre was inevitable.

---

55 DVB Behuising (Pty) Limited v. North West Provincial Government and Another, 2000 (4) BCLR 347 (CC), para. 17.

56 Nico Steytler, "Judicial Neutrality in the Face of Ineptitude: The Constitutional Court and Multi-Level Government in South Africa," in *Judge Made Federalism*, ed. H.-P. Schneider, J. Kramer, and B. Caravito (Baden: Nomos Verlag, 2009), 27.

Since 2005, the Constitutional Court has not changed its tune appreciably, although the record is not always centre-prone. What has changed is that local government has come off the better in its scraps with provinces and the national government. Whether there is a decidedly pro-local and anti-provincial attitude is too early to say, but the complexity of overseeing a multi-level system is now coming to the fore, and the balancing of the powers of the three spheres of government is that much more challenging.

Regarding these centre-prone decisions, the Court's justification could be traced to a fundamental conception of the nature of the South African state. First, the proclamation in section 1 that South Africa is "one sovereign, democratic state" gives the Constitution a "unitary emphasis," the Court has said.[57] Yet the Constitution contains very definite federal elements of local and provincial self-rule, which the Court has sought to harmonize with the unitary emphasis through the notion of "cooperative government." In the words of the Constitutional Court, the Constitution embodies not "competitive federalism" but rather a "new philosophy" of "co-operative government."[58]

In interpreting the Constitution's federal features, the Court's departure point is that provinces derive their powers and functions exclusively from the Constitution. In the first case on the exercise of concurrent powers (education) under the interim Constitution, minority political parties and the KwaZulu-Natal provincial government challenged the constitutionality of the National Education Policy Bill, 1995, on the ground that it would oblige provinces to adhere to national education policy.[59] The applicants placed much reliance on the U.S. Supreme Court majority opinion in *New York v. United States*,[60] which held that the U.S. Constitution did not confer on Congress the power to compel states to take particular actions. The Constitutional Court found this decision not relevant because of the differences in history and language of the two constitutions. In the United States, several sovereign states where brought together in a federation, surrendering only a part of their sovereignty to the federal government and retaining the remainder. In South Africa, on the other hand, the provinces were not sovereign states: "They were created by the Constitution and have only

57 First Certification, para. 287. See also Liquor Bill, para. 41.

58 Ibid., para. 469.

59 In re: The National Educational Policy Bill, No. 83 of 1995, 1996 (4) BCLR 518 (CC).

60 New York v. United States 505 US 144 (1992).

those powers that are specifically conferred on them under the Constitution."[61] Furthermore, the powers conferred on provinces were not exclusive but held concurrently with the national Parliament. The process of state formation through devolution of powers to provinces thus produced a result that was significantly different from what prevails in the United States.

Within the limited parameters set by the Constitution, a measure of self-rule is permissible. Although the Bill of Rights may impose uniform standards, total uniformity is not required. The Court thus rejected a claim that differing provincial legislation could give rise to an anti-discrimination challenge.[62] A bookie taking bets at horse racing complained that he was discriminated against in KwaZulu-Natal because, in that province's gambling law, only a person in his or her personal capacity could obtain a betting licence, contrary to the position in all other provinces, where both a natural and a juridical person could ply the bookmaking trade. The Court found that because the gambling law was within the province's competence, it did not offend the right against unfair discrimination. Provincial differences were legitimate differentiation.

Provincial experimentation and innovation have not, however, been articulated expressly as a value worth pursuing. No reference has yet been made to the celebrated dictum of Justice Louis Brandeis in *New State Ice Co. v. Liebmann*: "It is one of the happy incidents of the federal system that a single courageous state may, if its citizens choose, serve as a laboratory, and try novel social and economic experiments without risk to the rest of the country."[63] One exception has been, but only so by implication, the *Treatment Action Campaign* case,[64] where provincial differences were used in legal reasoning without highlighting the value added of such experimentation. The Treatment Action Campaign (TAC), a civil-society organization, challenged the decision of the national government and eight provinces to limit access to an anti-HIV drug to prevent mother-to-baby infection to two pilot sites per province. TAC argued that this measure was inconsistent with the socio-economic right of access to health services (s. 26), because it was

61 National Educational Policy Bill, para. 23.

62 Weare and Another v. Ndebele and Others, 2009 (4) BCLR 370 (CC), para. 70.

63 285 U.S. 262, 311 (1932).

64 Minister of Health and Others v. Treatment Action Campaign and Others (1), 2002 (10) BCLR 1033 (CC), para. 93 ("Treatment Action Campaign").

unreasonable and the roll-out of the treatment to all clinics in provinces was within the provinces' available resources – the conditions on which the fulfilment of this right are predicated. Their argument was based principally on the conduct of one province (the Western Cape), which, within the same budget as the other provinces, provided the medicine in all its clinics. The Constitutional Court (and the High Court more explicitly[65]) accepted the argument and found that the national government's efforts fell short of a reasonable standard and the province could afford to fulfil the positive obligation imposed by the right.[66]

In shaping the Constitutional Court's federalism jurisprudence, supranational bodies have played no part. The Court has, more often in the earlier years, referred to American,[67] Canadian,[68] Indian,[69] German,[70] and Australian[71] cases, but has emphasized the unique history and language of South Africa's constitutions. For example, in *The National Education Policy Bill* decision, referred to above, the Court thus cautioned, "Decisions of the courts of the United States dealing with state rights are not a safe guide as to how our courts should address problems that may arise in relation to the rights of provinces under our Constitution."[72]

2. *Specific Issues*

Since the creation of South Africa's hybrid federal system, the Constitutional Court's point of departure is that the provinces' only source of authority is the Constitution. In the KwaZulu-Natal Provincial

65 Minister of Health and Others v. Treatment Action Campaign and Others, 2002 (4) BCLR 356 (T).

66 Nico Steytler, "Federal Homogeneity from the Bottom Up: Provincial Shaping of National HIV/AIDS Policy in South Africa," *Publius: The Journal of Federalism* 33, no. 1 (2003): 59–74.

67 KwaZulu-Natal Constitution, para. 24; Constitution of the Western Cape, para. 28; Treatment Action Campaign, para. 107; Matatiele Municipality and Others v. President of the Republic of South Africa and Others, 2007 (1) BCLR 47 (CC) para. 79 ("Matatiele Municipality") .

68 Liquor Bill, para. 62; DVB Behuising, para. 36; Treatment Action Campaign, para. 110; Matatiele Municipality, para. 66.

69 DVB Behuising, para. 36; Treatment Action Campaign, para. 108.

70 Treatment Action Campaign, para. 109; Matatiele Municipality, para. 36.

71 KwaZulu-Natal Constitution, para. 24; DVB Behuising, para. 36;

72 National Educational Policy Bill, para. 23.

Constitution Certification case, that constitution was rejected because it gave the province powers not found in the Constitution. The Court described it as a case where the province sought to pull itself up by its own federal bootstraps. Any power or function has thus to be located within the four corners of the Constitution, which, of course, requires an interpretation of the broad constitutional language.

Arguably the most important exclusive provincial power is the adoption and amendment of a provincial constitution, the scope of which was forged in the last months before the first democratic election of 1994.[73] To bring the Inkatha Freedom Party into the negotiating process, a provision was inserted in the interim Constitution that a provincial constitution could be different from the national Constitution with regard to "legislative and executive structures and procedures."[74] While the first provincial constitution drafted by the KwaZulu-Natal Legislature never attempted to comply with the provisions of the interim Constitution, and was easily rejected by the Constitutional Court, the Western Cape sought to remain within the parameters of the Constitution, even though it, too, pushed the constitutional envelope. The Western Cape's draft constitution floundered principally on the interpretation of the elusive terms *legislative structures and procedures*. It not only set the number of seats of the provincial legislature but also established an electoral system that incorporated both a party list system and constituency-based presentation to produce proportional representation (the national Constitution, although it stipulates that the system should "result, in general in proportional representation" [s. 105(1)(d)], prescribes a pure party list electoral system). Averse to the idea that a province could establish its own form of PR, the Constitutional Court gave a restricted interpretation of "legislative structures and procedures" by confining them to "no more than a difference regarding the nature and the number of the elements constituting the legislative structure."[75] The Court thus accepted the setting of the number of seats in the provincial legislature (as opposed to the constitutional requirement that the number must be set in terms of a formula prescribed by national legislation), but rejected the different electoral system. The latter conclusion,

---

73 See Nico Steytler and Johann Mettler, "Federalism and Peacemaking: A South African Case Study," *Publius: The Journal of Federalism* 31 (2001): 93–106.

74 Section 143(1)(a) of the 1996 Constitution is a similar provision.

75 Western Cape Constitution, para. 48.

commentators argued, was not the only credible one the Court could have reached.[76]

The interpretation of provinces' other "exclusive" competences (those listed in Schedule 5A) received equally parsimonious treatment. At issue was the functional area of "liquor licences" and a national Liquor Bill that sought to control the liquor industry, including providing for the national issuing of licences for manufacturing, distribution, and local retail. The national Parliament may intrude on "exclusive" provincial powers, provided that certain qualifications are met, such as if it is "necessary," inter alia, "to maintain national security, economic unity and essential national standards" (s. 44(2)). The question that the Court had to confront was whether all or any of the licences listed above fell in the provincial exclusive zone. The Court adopted a restrictive interpretation; any aspect of the liquor trade that had an extra-provincial dimension fell outside the ambit of provincial competences. Provincial exclusive powers apply "primarily to matters which may appropriately be regulated intra-provincially."[77] Intra-provincial matters are concerned with "activities that take place within or can be regulated in a manner that has a direct effect upon the inhabitants of the province alone."[78] Excluded thus are matters with "a national dimension,"[79] which included all licences for manufacturing liquor (including all wine estates in the Western Cape), because such liquor may be destined to cross a provincial boundary. Only licences dealing with consumption within a province can be an exclusively provincial. The Court's reasoning was based on the need for "economic unity,"[80] which disallowed any regulatory spillage over a provincial boundary.

Other constitutional sources of provincial competences, apart from concurrent and exclusive powers, have also been met with a tight-fisted

---

76 Rassie Malherbe, "The Role of the Constitutional Court in the Development of Provincial Autonomy," *SA Public Law* 16, no. 2 (2001): 255; Christina Murray, "Provincial Constitution-Making in South Africa: The (Non)example of the Western Cape," *Jahrbuch des Őffentlichen Rechts der Gegenwart* 49 (2001): 481–512; Robert F. Williams, "Comparative Subnational Constitutional Law: South Africa's Provincial Constitutional Experiments," *South Texas Law Review* 40 (1999): 625; Stu Woolman, "Provincial Constitutions," in *Constitutional Law of South Africa*, ed. Stuart Woolman and Michael Bishop, 21-1–21-25 (Cape Town: Juta).

77 Liquor Bill, para. 53.

78 Ibid., para. 72.

79 Ibid., para. 75.

80 Ibid., para. 76.

Court, but dissenting voices are beginning to emerge.[81] In *Premier: Limpopo Province v. Speaker: Limpopo Provincial Legislature and Others I*,[82] the issue was the constitutionality of a provincial bill to regulate the provincial legislature's financial management. The bill would pass constitutional muster if the subject matter was "expressly assigned to the province by national legislation" or if it was a "matter for which a provision of the Constitution envisages the enactment of provincial legislation" (s. 104(1)(b)(iii) & (iv)). The provincial legislature maintained that the power was "expressly assigned" to provinces by the national Financial Management of Parliament Act, 2009, although the reference to provincial legislation was only in a schedule.[83] Focusing on the word *expressly*, the Court held that it "intended to remove any doubt about the nature and the extent of the powers of the provinces."[84] The Court maintained that "the constitutional scheme shows that the legislative authority of the provinces must be conveyed in clear terms."[85] In the Court's opinion, the provincial bill did not have a firm constitutional footing because the national act did not expressly assign the power to

81 In the early decision of Executive Council of the Western Cape v. Minister for Provincial Affairs and Constitutional Development of the Republic of South Africa; Executive Council of KwaZulu-Natal v. President of the Republic of South Africa and Others, 1999 (12) BCLR 1360 (CC) the Constitutional Court did not support a generous interpretation of provincial powers over local government. The Western Cape and KwaZulu-Natal, both in opposition hands, contested the constitutionality of a national law, the Municipal Structures Act, 1998, which gave to the national government the power to establish metropolitan areas and district management areas, a power the two provinces claimed belonged to them in terms of section 155. The Court agreed that this power did not fall in the domain of the national government, but neither did it resort under provinces. The power should be exercised by the Municipal Demarcation Board, an independent constitutional institution. The Court found in favour of a provincial power only on a minor point. In terms of section 155(5), provinces determine the types of municipalities and not the national government, as the Act provided. See Jaap de Visser, "Provinces v Structures Act: Demarcation Board Walks Off with Spoils," *Local Government Law Bulletin* 1, no. 4 (1999): 1–3.

82 2011 (11) BCLR 1181 (CC) ("Limpopo I").

83 Six provinces drafted and adopted such legislation with the guidance of the National Treasury. That it was the intention of Parliament to assign such a power was also evident from the submission of the Speaker of Parliament to the Court (Premier: Limpopo Province v. Speaker: Limpopo Provincial Legislature and Others, 2012 (6) BCLR 583 (CC) ("Limpopo II").

84 Limpopo I, para. 23.

85 Ibid., para. 35.

the provinces (despite the fact that there was a direct reference to provincial legislation in the act).[86]

The same quest for clarity was applied to the second source of provincial powers, namely where legislation was "envisaged" by the Constitution. Although the Constitution does not use the word *expressly*, the majority, nevertheless, imposed such a requirement. Speaking for the Court, Chief Justice Ngcobo held, "Our constitutional scheme does not permit legislative powers of the provincial legislatures to be implied. Were it to be otherwise, the constitutional scheme for the allocation of legislative power would be undermined. The careful delineation between the legislative competence of Parliament and that of provincial legislatures would be blurred. This may very well result in uncertainty about the limits of the legislative powers of the provinces ... This is not what the drafters of our Constitution had in mind."[87] This "clear line" scheme of the Constitution was contested in two dissenting opinions. Justice Edwin Cameron remarked that by the very nature of the Constitution's drafting, clarity will remain "a chimera."[88] Moreover, he continued, "as a matter of fundamental outlook, it would seem to me surprising if the Constitution did not envisage that provinces may legislate for the financial management of their own legislatures."[89] The difference in judicial opinion was one of "fundamental outlook"; the majority adopted a parsimonious view of provincial space, while the dissents sought to breathe some life into "legitimate provincial autonomy."

The Court's parsimonious approach to provincial powers is perhaps explained by its experience of provincial dysfunctionality. In 2002, it took Mr Mashavha, who was entitled to a disability grant from the provincial government of Limpopo, more than two years to receive some but not all that was owed to him. His wife's disability grant as well as his daughter's child-support grant also were outstanding. He and his family, the Constitutional Court noted, were reliant on "the proper administration of the disability grant for their daily sustenance and wellbeing."[90] Although "social

---

86 See Robert Williams and Nico Steytler, "Squeezing Out Provinces' Legislative Competence in Premier: Limpopo Province v Speaker: Limpopo Provincial Legislature and Others I and II," *South African Law Journal* 129, no. 4 (2012): 621–37.

87 Limpopo I, para. 52.

88 Ibid., para. 121.

89 Ibid., para. 124.

90 Mashavha v. President of the Republic of South Africa and Others, 2004 (12) BCLR 1243 (CC) para. 9.

welfare" is a national and provincial concurrent competency, Mashavha argued that the administration of the Social Security Act, 1992, in terms of which disability grants were dispensed, should never have been assigned to provinces when they were established in 1994 because such assignment could be done only if the provinces had the capacity to administer it. The argument was thus that if the administration of the Social Security Act was not assigned to the provinces, Mashavha would have received his grant from a more competent national department. The Constitutional Court agreed and invalidated the assignment of the Social Assistance Act to provinces ten years after the assignment. Before the fifteen-month period of suspension of invalidity lapsed, the South African Social Security Agency was established with the mandate to distribute all social grants. As the administration of grants was, along with education and health, the major expenditure item of provinces, the impact of the shift in responsibility on provinces was a massive loss in national transfers.

In 2013, a charge of incompetence was levelled against the national government. Civil society organizations requested the premier of the Western Cape to appoint a commission of inquiry into the abject failure of the national police (SAPS) to provide safety and security in Khayalitsha, a large black township of Cape Town. The Constitution provides for the appointment of such a provincial commission of inquiry into "any complaints of police inefficiency or a breakdown in relations between the police and any community" (s. 206(5)). When Premier Helen Zille, who is also the leader of the opposition Democratic Alliance, appointed a commission, the national minister of police contested her constitutional power to do so in a rare occurrence that the national government questioned a provincial competence largely because of provincial inactivity. Before the Constitutional Court, the national minister conceded the existence of such a power, but nevertheless contended that such a commission could not subpoena police officers because that would constitute controlling the national police force, a power that falls outside provincial competence. The Court first asserted a province's right to oversee the SAPS's activities in a province and then made short shrift of the minister's contention, finding that without subpoenaing powers, a commission of inquiry would not be able to fulfil its mandate.[91] Because the case was driven largely by a political agenda against an

---

91 Minister of Police and Others v. Premier of the Western Cape and Others, 2013 (12) BCLR 1405 (CC) ("Minister of Police") para. 50.

opposition-held province rather than by a contested legal principle, the judgment does not signal a fundamental shift in the Court's approach to provincial powers. However, its significance lies in the fact that it was the province that sought to do something to ameliorate national government failure. The Court thus found that it was the duty of the premier to take reasonable steps "to shield the residents of Khayalitsha from an unrelenting invasion of their fundamental rights because of police inefficiency in combatting crime and the breakdown of relations between the police and the community."[92] As "there is much to worry about when the [national] institutions that are meant to protect vulnerable residents fail, or are perceived to be failing," it was appropriate for the province to exact accountability in terms of its constitutional powers.[93] As will be argued below, the Court's positive approach to the province's efforts to assist in providing safety and security came in the face of national failure, a reversal of roles from the Mashavha case where the focus was on provincial failure.

When it came to interpreting local government's powers, the Constitutional Court showed a generosity of spirit at the expense of provincial powers. Contrary to the view of the majority in the *Limpopo* judgment, the Constitution is not a model of clarity when cut-off points between provincial and local government powers are in issue.[94] The local government's functional areas of health, roads, traffic, tourism, airports, and abattoirs are distinguished from similar provincial functional areas by the addition of the qualifier *local* to the former (e.g., *local tourism* vis-à-vis *provincial tourism*). Furthermore, many provincial functional areas are inclusive of a local government functional area. For example, included in the provincial power of "pollution control" is the local functional area of "air pollution." How are cut-off points to be determined?

The City of Johannesburg argued that the Gauteng provincial government had no final decision-making powers on matters related to land-use planning because this functional area fell in the local competence of "municipal planning." Gauteng replied that its Development Tribunal could decide matters of land use because it fell within the provincial functional areas of "regional planning" and "urban and rural development." The Constitutional Court sided firmly with the city, reiterating

92 Ibid., para 51.

93 Ibid., para 52.

94 See Nico Steytler and Yonatan Fessha, "Defining Local Government Powers and Functions," *South African Law Journal* 124 (2007): 320–38.

its view that competences must enable local government to exercise its functions "fully and effectively."[95] As most local government functions could be included in the broader powers of national and provincial government, the Constitutional Court implicitly adopted the view that local government functions should be defined first, with the residue falling in the provincial or national domain.[96] Consequently, "municipal planning," which includes all questions relating to the zoning of land and the establishment of townships, are to be decided by the municipality.[97]

With "municipal planning" entrenched against provincial incursion, it could not be trumped by national legislation either. The fact that mining is an exclusive national competence does not mean, the Constitutional Court held, that a national mining licence trumps municipal land-use permission. Rather, dual approvals are required; without such land-use permission from a municipality, the mining licence cannot be exercised.[98]

The Constitutional Court has also not hesitated to expand local government's remit beyond what the Constitution prescribes. In a number of judgments on the state's obligation to positively fulfil the implementation of socio-economic rights, the Court imposed duties on municipalities in areas falling outside their constitutional competences. In the area of housing (a concurrent national and provincial function), municipalities were ordered to assist national and provincial governments with the provision of emergency housing for the homeless[99] and

95 City of Johannesburg Metropolitan Municipality v. Gauteng Development Tribunal, 2010 (9) BCLR 859 (CC) para. 49. See further Nico Steytler and Jaap de Visser, *Local Government Law of South Africa*, 4th update (Durban: LexisNexis Butterworth, 2011), 5–19.

96 This view was clearly expressed by the Supreme Court of Appeal in City of Johannesburg Metropolitan Municipality v. Gauteng Development Tribunal, 2010 (2) BCLR 157 (SCA) paras 35–6.

97 See also Minister of Local Government, Environmental Affairs and Development Planning of the Western Cape v. Lagoonbay Lifestyle Estate (Pty) Ltd and Others, 2014 (2) BCLR 182 (CC); Minister of Local Government, Environmental Affairs and Development Planning, Western Cape v. Habitat Council and Others (City of Johannesburg Metropolitan Municipality as *Amicus Curiae*), 2014 (5) BCLR 591 (CC).

98 Maccsands (Pty) Ltd v. City of Cape Town and Others (Chamber of Mines of South Africa and Another as Amici Curiae), 2012 (7) BCLR 690 (CC); Minister of Mineral Resources v. Swartland Municipality and Others, 2012 (7) BCLR 690 (CC).

99 Government of the RSA and Others v. Grootboom and Others, 2000 (11) BCLR 1169 (CC).

the vulnerable after eviction from state or private property.[100] These decisions were based on the constitutional obligation that rests on all spheres of government to realize the right of access to adequate housing (s. 26) and not on the listed municipal competences.

The other side of the parsimonious attitude toward provincial treatment is the generous approach to national competences in respect to national legislation that covers both the national and provincial governments. One such law is on the single public service for the national and provincial administrations (s. 197(1)). The Western Cape objected when the national Public Service Act, 1994, was amended in 1998 because it removed provincial discretion on creating new departments. While the province could not challenge the national competence to make a law on the provincial public service, it argued that such a power should be exercised in the light of the principles of cooperative government, including the principle that "all spheres of government must exercise their powers and perform their functions in a manner that does not encroach on the geographical, functional or institutional integrity of the government of another sphere" (s. 41(1)(g)). The Constitutional Court accepted this principle as judicially enforceable but found that the very intrusive provisions complained of did not offend this principle.[101]

In contrast to the Court's stinginess with respect to the substance of provincial powers, it has given full effect to the provinces' procedural rights to shared rule institutions. As noted above, the provinces through their representation in the NCOP form part of the national Parliament and have, although not an absolute veto, a significant voice in the passage of national legislation affecting provinces (s. 76). Further, a constitutional amendment that effects boundary changes must be passed by six of the nine provinces in the NCOP as well as with the consent of the affected provincial legislatures. The first notable case dealt with the latter issue. In order to eliminate municipalities that crossed provincial boundaries (because the latter followed apartheid-drawn magisterial districts), boundaries of seven provinces were amended by the Constitution Twelfth Amendment Act of 2005. Although the KwaZulu-Natal and Eastern Cape provincial legislatures voted for the amendment, the

100 City of Johannesburg Metropolitan Municipality v. Blue Moonlight Properties 39 (Pty) Ltd and Another (Lawyers for Human Rights as Amicus Curiae), 2012 (2) BCLR 150 (CC).

101 Premier of the Province of the Western Cape v. President of the RSA, 1999 (4) BCLR 382 (CC).

community of Matatiele (which was to be moved from KwaZulu-Natal to the Eastern Cape without its consent) contested the legitimacy of the vote because Matatiele was not properly consulted by the provincial legislature. The Constitutional Court agreed by asserting, first, the need for provincial consent for a boundary change and, second, the need for proper consultation on the basis of the constitutional principle of participatory democracy.[102] The provisions of the constitutional amendment affecting KwaZulu-Natal and the Eastern Cape were thus declared invalid, because a procedural requirement for passing a valid law (proper public participation) was not complied with. However, Parliament and the two provinces were given eighteen months to rectify the legislative process. After due consultation with Matatiele, the KwaZulu-Natal legislature again voted for the boundary change, and the Constitution Thirteenth Amendment Act was validly passed in 2007 effecting the change.

The Court has also protected the provinces' procedural rights when Parliament considers legislation affecting provinces, by insisting that the correct legislative procedure be followed in the NCOP. Parliament regarded the Communal Land Rights Bill as a bill that did not affect provincial interests, a "tagging" decision made by the Speaker of the National Assembly and the chairperson of the NCOP.[103] Parliament argued that the bill dealt with "land," which is a national residual power, despite the fact that communal land rights by their every essence affect the provinces' concurrent function of "traditional leadership." As a result, the bill was passed following the so-called section 75 procedure. The NCOP delegates voted as individual members (not as provincial blocs), with a vote rejecting the bill having only delaying effect. If the bill was regarded as affecting provincial interests, then the provinces had to vote as provincial blocs, and a negative vote could be overcome only by a two-thirds majority in the National Assembly. The community of Tongoana, disapproving of the substance of the act, attacked the bill's procedural route, contending it affected the provinces. The Constitutional Court agreed with a generous interpretation of "provincial interests." It rejected the argument that provincial interests were synonymous with provincial competences and held that the test is more broadly drawn: "Any Bill whose provisions substantially

---

102 Matatiele Municipality and Others v. President of the Republic of South Africa and Others, 2007 (1) BCLR 47 (CC).

103 Christina Murray and Richard Simeon, "'Tagging' Bills in Parliament: Section 75 or Section 76?," *South African Law Journal* 123 (2006): 232.

affect the interests of provinces must be enacted in accordance with the procedure stipulated in section 76."[104] Following the wrong route that undermined provincial participation in the law-making process rendered the law invalid.

Outside the legislative arena, the courts also safeguarded a province's right to participate in the Judicial Service Commission's proceedings where it affected a judge of the High Court in that province (s. 178(1)(k)). The premier of the Western Cape objected for not having been invited to participate in the proceedings of the JSC when it had to consider impeachment proceedings against the judge-president of the Western Cape High Court for allegedly trying improperly to influence two Constitutional Court justices. The Supreme Court sustained a High Court decision that set aside the relevant JSC proceedings, because a premier's right to participate was not confined to judicial appointments but extended to the conduct of judges of the High Court in that province.[105]

The procedural requirement of cooperative government that all organs of state should "avoid legal proceedings against one another" (s. 41(1)(h)(iv)) was enforced against the national government when it sought to interdict the KwaZulu-Natal government from establishing a gambling monitoring regime in competition with a national system (gambling being a concurrent function). The Constitutional Court refused to entertain the application, because the parties displayed no effort to settle the matter amicably.[106]

In summary, the Constitutional Court has confined provincial powers, to the clearest expressions in the Constitution. Provincial competences also are squeezed from below by an expansive view of municipalities' functions. Consequently, the Court has given further impetus to the construction of an hourglass federation, where provinces are squeezed thin between the national and local governments. At the same time, procedural rights have received full protection from the Court. It may well be that the courts are more comfortable enforcing procedural rules

---

104 Tongoane v. Minister of Agriculture and Land Affairs, 2010 (8) BCLR 741 (CC) para. 72.

105 Hlophe v. Premier of the Western Cape Province; Hlophe v. Freedom Under Law and Other 2012 (6) BCLR 567 (CC), read with Democratic Alliance v. President of the RSA and Others, 2012 (3) BCLR 291 (SCA). Because a number of Constitutional Court judges were involved in the complaint against the judge-president and could therefore not hear the case, the decision of the SCA was the final word on the matter.

106 National Gambling Board.

than dealing with substantive matters, particularly the complex issue of carving out a space for provincial self-government.

These developments have hardly raised a public eyebrow. With most provinces not fulfilling their constitutional mandate of service delivery of education, health, and housing, more public trust is placed in the national government to remedy the ills of the provinces. In most provinces, the public may well support the ANC's call for an overhaul of the provincial system and a reduction in the number of provinces.

3. *Significance of the Courts*

In assessing the courts' role in securing federally relevant goals and objectives, it should be borne in mind that the federal elements in South Africa's Constitution are not confined to the provincial institutions of self-rule and the shared rule in the National Council of Provinces. The Constitution establishes a system of multi-level government where local governments, and the large metropolitan governments in particular, play a major role in governance. The courts' performance should thus be assessed on how they have dealt with the entire system of multi-level government. On the positive side, the Constitutional Court has strengthened the hand of municipalities by interpreting their powers generously, not only vis-à-vis the provincial sphere of government, but also in competition with the national government. The latter government in exercising its broad residual powers cannot automatically override local autonomy. The supportive approach towards local government has not been apparent with respect to provincial self-rule. Although the Constitutional Court professed to be neither for nor against provinces, it did not assert provincial constitutional space when it could reasonably have done so. The niggardly approach to provinces has of late, however, prompted some dissenting voices seeking to give some flesh to the original Constitutional Principle of "legitimate provincial autonomy." Overall, the Court has supported the hourglass model of multi-level government: a strong supervisory national government, a development-oriented local government at the bottom, and, in the middle, a provincial order of government providing ever fewer services. But the hourglass is kept functioning by allowing the intergovernmental sands of procedural compliance to flow freely.

The Court's concern in the early years was, no doubt, with building a nation from the fractured past. It emphasized the unitary vision of the country when it rejected in 1996 the wayward attempt in the

KwaZulu-Natal provincial constitution to clamour for more federalism. It may also have been less than charitable to the Western Cape constitution with the province then under the hand of the New National Party exhibiting much of the old National Party in attitude. These isolationist forces no longer threaten the united vision of the South African nation, and the main opposition party has national ambitions. The second reason for a pro-centre stance was the perilous state of provincial governance. Little improvement on this score has been witnessed; some provinces have retrogressed, as indicated by the national interventions in Limpopo and other provinces in 2012.

Why then the support of local municipalities? First, local government as a necessity of government poses no centrifugal threat to the nation; to the contrary, the cities have been the melting pot where the new South African nation is taking shape. Second, despite the failure of many municipalities, particularly in rural areas, the large metros and cities are reasonably well governed; Johannesburg, Cape Town, Ethekwini (Durban), and Tshwane (Pretoria) are functioning adequately and hold the key to economic growth and poverty reduction. As to the question of why the judiciary supports procedural compliance, the answer may lie in the pragmatics of the judicial function, as suggested above.

The judicial contribution to multi-level government has to some degree supported federal objectives and goals. As the original purpose of ethnic/nationalist accommodation is no longer an overt concern, the focus shifts to development goals and limiting the centre's monopoly on power. Support for local government, particularly for the major metros having budgets in excess of the smaller provinces, contributes to development goals. Collectively provinces and local government (again with metros in the forefront) pose a counterweight to central dominance.

The Court's hourglass approach fits snuggly with the national government and ANC policy. The ANC never embraced provinces, although it may now find it very difficult to unmake the provinces. Over the past five years, the debate has moved from the premise that provinces have served their initial purpose[107] and are therefore now expendable, to a more focused concern for greater functionality of perhaps fewer provinces. In the ANC's Policy Document of March 2012, there is a call "to reform, rationalize and strengthen provinces" by, among other

107 ANC, "Legislature and Governance for a National Democratic Society," 2007.

things, having "fewer provinces which are functional, effective, economically sustainable, integrate communities on a non-racial basis and do away with ethnic boundaries."[108] As noted above, the outcome of the ANC National Conference in December 2012 was a cryptic statement: "Provinces [should] be reformed, reduced and strengthened."[109] The conference further recommended the devolution of certain provincial functions to stronger municipalities (which include the metros). This reflects much of the national government's view, articulated in the National Planning Commission's *National Development Plan: Our Future – Make It Work.*[110] Provinces are there to stay, but they must become part of the "capable state" that can tackle poverty and inequality, while an enhanced role is to be accorded to metros. This would include the devolution of more provincial powers to metros in the areas of housing, transport, and planning.

Although the Constitutional Court may be *ad idem* with the government on multi-level government, its independent stance and exercise of judicial powers in other areas of the Constitution do not always sit comfortably with the government. Although there are no moves afoot to clip the wings of the Constitutional Court (its powers have been enhanced when it assumed the function of the court of final appeal in all matters), changes to the bench may see judges being more deferential to Parliament and the executive. However, the Court's value as an independent and fearless guardian of the Constitution is widely appreciated both inside and outside of government. Changes will not come easily.

To return to the initial question – does South Africa have a unitarist court in a hybrid federal system? – the answer is nuanced. In terms of a narrow conception of federalism, focusing alone on the provincial order of government, the Constitutional Court has certainly been unitarist. Using a broader definition of federalism that encompasses multi-level government, the answer is different, even though it may result in an hourglass federation. The Court's strengthening of local government and procedural intergovernmental relations counterbalances its narrow "fundamental outlook" on the role of provinces. However, the consequence of this approach is that the Constitutional

---

108 ANC, Policy Discussion Document, March 2012, Legislature and Governance, 12.

109 ANC, Resolutions of 53rd National Conference: Legislatures and Governance, Resolution 4.2.1 (2012).

110 National Planning Commission, *Development Plan: Our Future*, 434–5.

Court has not breathed life into the constitutional space for provincial self-governance.

Given the looming reform of provinces and local government, the Court is bound in the short term to play at the side lines of the main game. The main actors shaping the system are the ANC (determining policy on provinces and local government), the government implementing the structure and the National Treasury giving budget effect to policy (and at times determining policy through budget choices). The Constitutional Court will, however, play a decisive role in changing the number and boundaries of provinces, demanding scrupulous compliance with procedures.

What would strengthen the courts' role in supporting or improving the functioning of multi-level government? Ironically, the provinces themselves could be the most important actors in contributing to a more sympathetic court. Although nation building is stumbling along, territorially based centrifugal and isolationist tendencies have evaporated. The capturing of the Western Cape by the DA in 2009 was not an attempt at isolation, but a platform for expansion to other provinces.[111] Nation building per se may thus no longer be a burning concern for the Court. The other ostensible reason for the Court's apathy towards provinces could be the continued poor performance of seven out of the nine provinces. Yet, in many instances, national departments fare no better than provincial ones. The South African Social Security Agency, which took over the distribution of social grants from provinces, has not been a shining example of efficiency and financial rectitude.[112] Yet the assumption remains that the national government does better. Although poor administration is a legitimate concern, it could also hide a deeper, underlying ideological view that sees centralization and uniformity as values in themselves and preferable to regional experimentation and innovation.

111 In the May 2014 national and provincial elections, the DA increased its percentage of the vote from 17 to 23 per cent nationally. More importantly, the ANC retained the most populous and wealthiest province, Gauteng, with a slender margin of 53 per cent. In the 2016 local government elections it may lose its majority in Gauteng's three metropolitan municipalities.

112 For example, in AllPay Consolidated Investment Holdings (Pty) Ltd and Others v. Chief Executive Officer of the South African Social Security Agency and Others (Corruption Watch and Another as *Amici Curiae*), 2014 (1) BCLR 1 (CC), the Constitutional Court set aside a massive tender award for the distribution of grants because of the defective management of the tender process.

The answer to both impediments lies with provinces themselves. If provinces show themselves not as dens of patronage and maladministration but as capable and effective instruments of governance and development, and if they add value through diversity, the courts might see the advantage of expanding the provinces' constitutional space. This is best illustrated in the contested appointment of the provincial commission of inquiry in the Western Cape to investigate the failure of the South African Police Service (SAPS) to provide safety and security in Khayalitsha,[113] Given this failure, the Court asserted and protected the province's right (and duty) to call the SAPS to account in order to better protect its residents. The same argument applies to municipalities. A virtuous circle may then emerge: better subnational governance makes for better judgments.

113 Minister of Police and Others v. Premier of the Western Cape.

12 The Constitutional Court of Spain: From System Balancer to Polarizing Centralist

ELISENDA CASANAS ADAM

I. Introduction

Spain's Constitutional Court has played an important role in establishing the Spanish "state of the autonomies," a concept largely undefined by the Constitution.[1] In the extensive litigation that has occurred between the Spanish state (i.e., the central government) and the autonomous communities (ACs) since the inauguration of the 1978 democratic Constitution, the Court's case law is generally perceived as having been fairly balanced between the state and the ACs. Although the Court has validated expansive interpretations of the central state's competences, it has made some important decisions defending the ACs. However, the recent wave of reforms of the ACs' statutes of autonomy, and particularly the constitutional challenge to the Statute of Catalonia, have put the Court at the forefront of the political conflict over the territorial organization of the state. The Court's 2010 decision in the Catalonia case strongly divided scholars, institutions, and public opinion, leaving the future of the system at a crossroads and undermining the Court's legitimacy in the eyes of some people in Spain. Since then, the Spanish government's insistent use of the Court to block attempts to hold an independence referendum in Catalonia threatens to further compromise the Court's position.

1 *State of the autonomies* (or *autonomic state*) is the term generally used to refer the Spanish federal or quasi-federal model of territorial organization of the state.

II. The State of the Autonomies

1. *Broad Characteristics*

Spain has 46,449,565 inhabitants, the vast majority of whom are indigenous.[2] Spain is not ethnically or racially diverse. In recent years, though, Spain has become home to a growing number of immigrants who are changing the population's profile. The country's gross domestic product is US$1.38 trillion.[3] The sovereign Spanish state was constructed through the union of independent crowns, dating back to the fifteenth century, and the territorial organization of the state has been the source of ongoing conflict in Spanish constitutional history. Today, it is generally acknowledged that Spain is a pluri-national state. The current territorial model was established to accommodate the nationalist claims of Catalonia, the Basque Country, and, to a lesser degree, Galicia. The 1978 Constitution is "based on the indissoluble unity of the Spanish nation," but it also "recognizes and guarantees the right to self-government of the nationalities and regions of which it is composed" (Art. 2). The term *nationality* was a compromise term used to give some recognition to the minority nations in the Constitution. The common official language, Spanish, coexists with other languages such as Catalan, *Euskera,* and Galician, which have a co-official status in the territories where they are spoken, when so provided. The Constitution also recognizes other asymmetrical particularities for certain ACs, known as "differential elements" (e.g., a special historical private law or tax and financing system). The Spanish state is organized into seventeen autonomous communities, two autonomous cities (Ceuta and Melilla), and a strong level of local government organized in provinces and municipalities.

A specific feature of the Spanish model is that the Constitution does not define the system of territorial organization or contain a list of ACs. The Constitution was the result of a consensus between different political forces in a peaceful transition to democracy after forty years of dictatorship. At the same time, the regulation of some of the more controversial elements was left largely open and undefined. As regards political decentralization, the constitutional provisions established

2 Data for 1 January 2015. Instituto Nacional de Estadística, http://www.ine.es/inebaseDYN/cp30321/cp_inicio.htm.

3 Data for 2014. World Development Indicators, World Bank, http://data.worldbank.org/country/spain.

a wide framework within which the nationalities and regions could constitute themselves as autonomous communities.[4] This framework included the identification of those territories that could access self-government; the necessary procedure for doing so, namely, the elaboration of a statute of autonomy of each AC; and the minimum content required for these statutes, including a list of competences the AC could assume. The initiative was left to the territories to proceed towards autonomy and complete the model's design. It was therefore initially unclear exactly how the state of the autonomies would develop.

The terminology of "nationalities" and "regions" used in the Constitution was meant to establish a distinction between those ACs constituted by national minorities that had a previous experience of autonomy (i.e., Catalonia, the Basque Country, and Galicia) and those that could be constituted in the rest of Spain's territory. The Constitution also included two different procedures for elaborating the statutes of autonomy. First, a more complex yet faster procedure enabled ACs to secure a higher level of self-government. This was included specifically for the historic nationalities where support for self-government was very strong. Second, a less complex and slower procedure resulted in an initially inferior level of autonomy for some ACs, at least for the first five years. This was meant for the rest of the Spanish territories, where it was unclear if such a process would take place. After 1978, all the territories progressively initiated a procedure towards self-government, culminating in the establishment of a fully decentralized state consisting of seventeen ACs by 1983. Andalusia followed Catalonia, the Basque Country, and Galicia in adopting the faster process and assuming also the maximum level of competences; the slower procedure was used by all the rest.

The trend has been to move towards an equalization and symmetry between the different ACs; hence, the initial distinction between two types or levels has been blurred. Part of this is the result of intentional action of the two main statewide political parties – the Union of the Democratic Centre/People's Party (UCD/PP) and Spanish Socialist Workers' Party (PSOE) – manifested in two sets of agreements. The first "autonomic agreements," signed in 1981, established a fully decentralized state, extending autonomy to those territories where there was initially no strong desire for self-government. The second, signed in 1992,

4 See generally, Eliseo Aja, *El Estado Autonómico: Federalismo y Hechos Diferenciales* (Madrid: Alianza, 2003).

levelled the scope of competences of all the ACs. However, an attempt by the two statewide parties to recentralize the system in 1982 was challenged and invalidated by the Constitutional Court, which had been established in 1978 as, among other things, an arbiter between the two orders of government. Another important feature of the development of the state of the autonomies has been the high levels of conflict between the ACs and the state, which has resulted in substantial interventions by the Court.

Spain's accession to the European Union (then European Community – EC) in 1986 posed a new set of challenges to the newly created state of the autonomies. As the Constitution was silent on the issue of implementation and application of EC law, which extended to both areas of Spanish state and AC competence, there was an initial debate over the level at which these functions should be carried out. Despite claims by the state institutions that these were now encompassed within their more general competence over "international relations" (Art. 149.1.3) or "external commerce" (Art. 149.1.10), the Constitutional Court ruled that European integration did not alter the distribution of competences between the Spanish state and the ACs. Any related functions must be distributed in accordance with pre-existing criteria.[5] The ACs were also the most affected by the transfer to, and progressive expansion of, competences at the European level, as the state could still continue to participate in European law-making through their representation in the Council of the EC/EU. Following the model of the German Länder, the ACs progressively secured different modes of participation in European law-making in areas of AC competence, initially in the development of the Spanish state's position in the Council, then in the Council's working groups, and finally in the Spanish representation in the Council itself.[6]

Overall, the development of the state of the autonomies so far has largely been considered a success, as it has allowed for transformation of a unitary system into a fully functioning territorially decentralized state. As for the system's future, there is a diversity of opinions across the academic, political, and wider public spheres. Some favour a degree of recentralization, particularly as a result of

5 Constitutional Court Decision 252/1988.

6 See Agustin Ruiz, "Spanish Autonomous Communities and EU Policies," *Perspectives on Federalism* 5, no. 2 (2013), 29–50.

the post-2007 economic recession. Others favour the status quo, considering that the overall model has now been completed. And some favour increasing the self-government of some or all the ACs, in certain cases, to reach full independence from the state (mainly in the Basque Country and Catalonia). The party in government at the state level from 2011 to 2015, the PP, is notably more centralist than its predecessor, the PSOE, which was in government from 2004 to 2011. Indeed, the election of the PSOE's Jose Luis Zapatero in 2004 spurred a generalized wave of reform of the statutes of autonomy, attempting a bottom-up reform that was described as a "refounding of the state of the autonomies."[7] However, as these reforms proceeded, they became more controversial and ended up being challenged and largely deactivated by the Constitutional Court in 2010. As will be seen below, this resulted in the most significant crisis for the system since its establishment.

The PP won the 2015 general elections again but by a much smaller margin (123 seats). The irruption of two new parties onto the Spanish political landscape, *Podemos* and *Ciudadanos*, with 69 and 40 seats respectively, has for the first time overthrown the traditional two-party system (the PSOE gained 90 seats). The tensions within the state of autonomies are central to the positions of these two new parties. *Ciudadanos* was born as a regional party to counter Catalan nationalism and is strongly centralist. *Podemos* is an anti-austerity party that defends the need for asymmetry between the different ACs and a much more robust articulation of Spain as a pluri-national state, including the right of Catalonia and the other minority nations to hold an independence referendum. How the significant presence of these two new parties in the Spanish parliament will affect the development of the state of autonomies remains to be seen.

2. *Structural Features*

The Constitution safeguards the "indissoluble unity of the Spanish nation" and "guarantees the right to self-government of the nationalities and regions" (Art. 2). The autonomy of the ACs is also protected by their statutes of autonomy, which the Constitution provides are

7 Pedro Cruz, "La Reforma del Estado de las Autonomías," *Revista d'Estudis Federals i Autonòmics* 2 (2006): 84.

the "basic institutional rule of each autonomous community," and which the state is obliged to "recognize and protect … as an integral part of its legal system" (Art. 147, Sec. 1). Because the constitutional provisions are so open, the most distinctive aspect of Spain's system is the importance of the statutes of autonomy in completing the content of the Constitution and rendering more complete the general aspects of the territorial power structure.[8] The margin conferred on the regional assemblies (and now the self-governing parliaments) to design their corresponding AC in their statute is known as the "dispositive principle." It is also a fundamental feature of the system.[9] As a result, the territorial organization of the state cannot be understood without considering both the constitutional provisions and the different statutes of autonomy that constitute part of what is known as the "block of constitutionality." From a legal perspective, the statutes of autonomy are negotiated norms that are, at the same time, state laws and the basic institutional laws of the ACs, and are finally formally enacted by the state. But once in force, they cannot be amended unilaterally or abolished by the state parliament, and any initiative for their reform must come from the autonomous community itself. The autonomy of local municipalities is also guaranteed in the Constitution (Art. 140), and all three orders of government are provided with a direct appeal to the Constitutional Court if they believe their autonomy is infringed.

The distribution of competences is not specifically established by the Constitution but is based on a system of double lists, one with the competences that may be assumed by the ACs in their statutes of autonomy (Art. 148) and one setting out the competences that are reserved to the state (Art. 149). In these lists, the Constitution establishes a clear preeminence of the state, which is responsible for the competences typical of the central government of a federal state (e.g., defence, international relations, immigration, and currency), the main branches of the law (i.e., criminal, procedural, commercial, and labour), and the main economic and social sectors (e.g., social security, health, the environment,

8 Carles Viver, "Spain's Constitution and the Statutes of Autonomy: Explaining the Evolution and Political Decentralisation," in *Constitutional Dynamics in Federal Systems: Sub-national Perspectives*, ed. Michael Burgess and G. Alan Tarr, 218–37 (Montreal and Kingston: McGill-Queen's University Press, 2012).

9 Enric Fossas, *El principio dispositivo en el Estado Autonómico* (Barcelona: IVAP / Marcial Pons, 2007).

education, and public safety).[10] Yet in many of these areas, the state is not invested with all the functions in relation to a specific field, and the ACs can intervene also. Thus, for example, in some areas, the basic legislation and their coordination are the responsibility of the state, and the ACs can legislate within this framework. In others, the ACs are granted executive power to implement legislation enacted by the state. These areas, then, require the cooperation of both orders of government in the exercise of their powers. Within this framework, the ACs have significant competences in areas such as internal transport and tourism, urbanism, and agriculture; they also provide many public services, such as education, health, and social assistance. All matters not conferred explicitly by the Constitution on the central institutions can be assumed by the ACs by virtue of their statutes of autonomy. From among those open to them, matters not assumed by statutes of autonomy belong to the state, whose norms prevail in case of conflict over those of the ACs in everything that is not attributed to their exclusive competence (Art. 149(3)). Finally, two additional mechanisms allow for some flexibility of the system. The state may pass harmonization laws in matters of AC competence (Art. 150, Secs. 1 and 2). It can also delegate or transfer the exercise of its competences to the ACs (Art. 149(3)).[11]

The Constitution provides for a central bicameral parliament (Congress and Senate), where the Senate is the house of territorial representation. The Senate currently represents the fifty provinces (the historical model of territorial subdivision of the unitary Spanish state, which was retained with the establishment of the ACs), however, rather than the seventeen ACs, whose parliaments appoint only a small number of senators (1 each, and another for every million inhabitants, out of a total of 266). It is generally accepted that with its current composition, the Senate is of little utility because it is largely a duplicate of the Congress. On many occasions, it simply validates its decisions. The Senate's functions

10 Carles Viver, "Centralization and Decentralization in Trends in Spain: An Assessment of the Present Allocation of Competences between the State and the Autonomous Communities," in *Decentralizing and Re-Centralizing Trends in the Distribution of Powers within Federal Countries*, ed. Institut d'Estudis Autonòmics, 155–79 (Barcelona: Generalitat de Catalunya, 2010); and Enric Argullol and Xavier Bernadi, "Spain," in *Distribution of Powers and Responsibilities in Federal Countries*, ed. Akthar Majeed, Ronald L. Watts, and Douglas M. Brown, 238–65 (Montreal and Kingston: McGill-Queen's University Press, 2006).

11 Article 155 of the Constitution also confers extraordinary or emergency powers on the state, which have never been used.

are also largely similar to those of the Congress; it can present bills, and it considers and votes on any proposed bills after the Congress has considered them. However, any amendments voted by the Senate can be overruled by a simple majority in the Congress, and if the Senate votes to veto a bill, this can also be overruled by an absolute majority in the Congress, or a simple majority after a period of two months. In practice, this makes the Senate's veto power ineffective. There have been failed attempts to convert this chamber into an institution that would effectively represent the ACs at the state level. Apart from their very minimal representation in the Senate, there is no representation of the ACs in the other institutions and bodies of the state. This also is considered by many to be an important deficiency of the system.

The Constitution provides two different procedures for its amendment, which depend on the object and scope of the proposed reform. The more rigid procedure, which applies to a total revision (the drafting of a new Constitution) and to revisions of the preliminary title (this contains the fundamental principles of the constitutional system), the charter of fundamental rights, and the provisions on the monarchy, requires the approval by two-thirds of both chambers of the state parliament in two successive parliaments (the first must be dissolved after the vote and new elections held) and ratification by referendum (Art. 168). Amendment of the rest of the Constitution's provisions, including those relating to the state of the autonomies, requires a majority of three-fifths of each chamber and, if one-tenth of the members of one chamber requests it, ratification by referendum (Art. 167). The ACs' participation in the process is limited to being able to propose a reform of the Constitution, either by filing a bill directly to the central parliament or by requesting the central government to do so (Arts. 167 and 87). While there is again a common agreement that certain reforms of the fundamental norm would be advisable, it is also generally acknowledged that, at least until very recently, it was impossible for lack of the minimum consensus between the two main statewide parties required to reach the necessary majority. The only two reforms since the Constitution's enactment have been due to requirements imposed by the European Union.[12] As noted above, the irruption of two new parties

12 Article 13.2 was amended in 1992 in order to allow EU nationals to vote in local elections. Article 135 was amended in 2011 to introduce the principle of "budgetary stability."

with a significant number of seats in the 2015 general elections may open new possibilities for change. Two aspects where a reform is considered particularly advisable are the composition and functions of the Senate and an update and systemization of the provisions on the state of the autonomies, which in its development has become largely "de-constitutionalized."[13] The impossibility of reforming the Constitution in this final aspect was one factor that initiated the 2004 wave of reforms of the statutes of autonomy.

The procedures for amending the statutes of autonomy are included in the statutes themselves. These are initiated and drafted by the parliament of the autonomous community and require a strong majority to pass this initial stage (e.g., two-thirds in Catalonia or three-fifths in Murcia). By specific mandate of the Constitution, they then require the approval of the Spanish parliament through a special strengthened procedure known as an "organic law" (in practice, this requires an absolute majority in the Congress). The ACs that attained their autonomy through the faster process prescribed more complex procedures for the reform of their statutes, which include a binding referendum in the AC. As the majority for approving a reformed statute of autonomy in the Spanish parliament is less strict than for a reform of the Constitution, an important difference is that they can be reformed with the consent of only one of the two main statewide parties. Since their initial enactment, different statutes have been subject to various reforms to update or amend specific aspects. These reforms, with the exception of the more recent ones, have been driven by the state or by statewide parties.

The generalized wave of reform of the statutes of autonomy of the ACs initiated in 2004 was broad and encompassing. It was directed to updating these norms and maximizing their scope of competences and self-government within the framework of the Constitution, while resolving some of the main deficiencies of the system. Between 2004 and early 2013, eight ACs reformed their statutes, although the scope and intensity of the reforms varied. The first was Valencia in April 2006. The drafting and enactment of its new statute of autonomy was largely unproblematic. However, two other ACs challenged one of its provisions, which included a right to water resources and to the

13 Eliseo Aja and Carles Viver, "Valoración de 25 Años de Autonomía," *Revista Española de Derecho Constitucional* 69 (2003): 69–113.

transfer of surplus water from other basins. (This was seen as threat to resources on which the other ACs depended.) The challenge was unsuccessful, but the case prepared the ground for the Court's later decision on the challenge to the controversial new Statute of Catalonia. The Catalan statute, enacted in August 2006, was highly innovative and was seen as the leading model for the reforms, including, among other aspects, a full charter of rights and an extensive chapter on the judicial branch. In addition, it included a series of largely symbolic provisions to strengthen recognition of the history and identity of Catalonia as a minority nation within the constitutional framework. These provisions included references, for example, to the symbols and historical rights of Catalonia, and, most controversially, a reference to Catalonia as a "nation" in the preamble. Because of all the above, the statute was very strongly opposed from the drafting of the initial proposal by the centralist PP, which considered it to be a violation of the Constitution and a threat to the unity of Spain. However, as a minority in the Catalan parliament, the PP could not stop it.[14] The PP also strongly opposed and campaigned against the new statute during the debates and amendments in the Spanish parliament, but the support of the PSOE and the nationalist parties again secured the necessary majority for it to be enacted. Once in force, the PP then challenged a substantive part of the outcome in the Constitutional Court. The extent and nature of the challenge was received with outrage by supporters of the statute and by the Catalan people more generally, as it had been negotiated and agreed to by both the Catalan and state parliament and ratified by referendum in Catalonia. The political conflict was therefore laid before the Court, and the intense pressure from both sides continued throughout the proceedings. Finally, after a drawn-out consideration, in 2010 the Court deactivated many of the new reforms and the process was brought to an abrupt end, resulting in significant difference between ACs that had reformed their statutes and those that had not.

---

14 The Catalan group of the PP in the Catalan parliament voted against the approval of the proposal in response to the content and extent of the proposed reforms, and the representatives of the party again voted against its enactment in the Congress. Their challenge then included 136 provisions of the total of 223 articles, as well as additional and final provisions. They were then joined by the ombudsman and five autonomous communities.

III. Court System

1. Ordinary Court System

The court system, which is based on civil law, is organized along four main jurisdictions: civil (for civil and commercial matters), criminal, administrative, and labour (for employment and social security matters).[15] The Constitutional Court is considered separate from the courts of ordinary jurisdiction and is invested with final jurisdiction concerning the interpretation of the Constitution. Within each ordinary jurisdiction, the different courts are located at municipal, district, provincial, autonomous-community, and state levels and are organized hierarchically so that appeals can be made against the judgments of the lower courts. A distinction is made between the *juzgados*, composed of a single judge, and the *tribunales*, which are collegiate bodies composed of a panel of judges. At the municipal level, the peace courts (*Juzgados de Paz*) operate in municipalities that have no district-level courts. At the district level, there are courts of first instance (*Juzgados de Primera Instancia*) and criminal investigation courts (*Juzgados de Instrucción*); some major cities also have specific courts to fight violence against women (*Juzgados de Violencia sobre la Mujer*). At the provincial level, there are different *Juzgados* for criminal, administrative, social, juvenile, prison vigilance, and commercial matters, as well as collegiate provincial courts (*Audiencias Provinciales*) that hear civil and criminal cases. At the AC level, the higher courts of justice (*Tribunales Superiores de Justicia*) hear civil, criminal, administrative, and social cases. At the central level, the National Court (*Audiencia Nacional*) hears cases that affect the whole state, and the Supreme Court (*Tribunal Supremo*) is the final court of appeal in all jurisdictions.

The Constitution states that "the principle of jurisdictional unity is the basis for the organization and functioning of the courts" and that "the highest judicial body in all jurisdictions" shall be the Supreme Court (Art. 117(5)). For lack of further definition in the constitutional text, this principle has been given several meanings, among which is a principle of territorial jurisdictional unity that precludes the ACs from

---

15 The organization of the Spanish court system is regulated in the "Organic Law 6/1985, of 1 July, of the Judicial Power," which has been reformed on numerous occasions. This is then complemented by the specific procedural norms enacted for each of the jurisdictions.

having their own court systems.[16] In this respect, Spain's Constitutional Court has stated that "the judicial power established by our fundamental norm requires that the different courts in which the exercise of the jurisdictional powers is vested be integrated in one single jurisdictional organisation."[17] At the same time, in its provisions regarding the state of the autonomies, the Constitution establishes the higher courts of justice as bodies that "culminate the jurisdictional organization in the territory of the Autonomous Communities" (Art. 153(1)). There is a higher court of justice in each of the seventeen ACs, constituting a distinct level within the unitary judicial system. It is generally accepted that these courts are the instrument through which the judicial branch adapts its organization and functioning to reflect the existence of the ACs as an autonomous order of government with the capacity to create their own laws.

The above duality is not, however, present in the distribution of competences; the Constitution confers exclusive competence on the Spanish state over the "administration of justice" (Art. 149.1.5). The specific content of this provision has been determined by the Constitutional Court in various decisions as extending only to "the essential nucleus of the administration of justice."[18] In practice, this has allowed the ACs to participate in what the Court has also defined as "the administration of the administration of justice," consisting of the provision of personal and material resources to the judicial offices and some other limited functions. The Constitution also confers exclusive competence on the Spanish parliament to enact procedural legislation, although "taking into account the necessary specialities derived from particularities of the substantive law of the autonomous communities" (Art. 149.1.6). This final provision, however, has been construed in such a way as to deprive it of content, as the Court has adopted an extremely restrictive interpretation of when such particularities would arise, giving a clear pre-eminence to safeguarding the uniformity of procedural rules and instruments across the state.[19]

---

16 Miguel Ángel Cabellos, "La adecuación del Poder Judicial al modelo de Estado," *Revista Vasca de Administración Publica* 68 (2004): 77–95.

17 Constitutional Court Decision 254/1994.

18 Constitutional Court Decisions 56/1990 and 106/2000.

19 Miguel Ángel Cabellos, "En torno a la práctica desaparición de una competencia. El art. 149.1.6 CE y las especialidades procesales autonómicas," *Revista Vasca de Administración Publica* 93 (2012): 103–23.

The Supreme Court in Spain is the *Tribunal Supremo*, based in Madrid. The origin of this Court can be traced to 1812. With the establishment of the state of autonomies in 1978, its functions have been progressively adapted to the state's composite nature.[20] It is a Continental-style *cour de cassation*, structured in five divisions (i.e., civil, criminal, administrative, labour, and military) and hears a substantial number of cases each year. As the highest court in the single judicial system, with jurisdiction over the territory of the whole state, the position and functions of the Supreme Court are strongly linked to the principle of unity of the judicial branch established by the Constitution. On the basis of the different procedural instruments, either in original or appellate jurisdiction, it renders the final decision of the ordinary judicial branch on all ordinary questions of law. The only exceptions are constitutional issues, where the Constitutional Court takes the final decision, and issues involving exclusive law of the ACs, where the final decision is taken by their respective higher courts of justice. Although these latter courts are fully integrated into the single judicial system of Spain as a whole, the higher courts of justice function as "supreme courts" for their corresponding autonomous community, and are responsible for the final appeals (*cassation*) in issues of their own civil and administrative law under the general procedural legislation.[21] In addition, in coordination with the statutes of autonomy, this legislation provides that they hear cases of judicial review of the decisions of, and civil and criminal liability cases against, their highest institutions of government. Their functions therefore largely reproduce those of the Supreme Court within their sphere of jurisdiction. In ACs that have a co-official language, proceedings can also be held in that language.

The Constitution states that the judicial branch will be "integrated by career judges," establishing a Continental-style judiciary "forming a single body" (Art.122(1)). Again, the result of the interpretation of this provision has been that the ACs cannot have their own judiciaries. The Constitution also establishes a governing body for the judiciary, the General Council of the Judiciary, in order to guarantee the

20 Manuel Gerpe, coord., *La posición del Tribunal Supremo en el Estado Autonómico* (Barcelona: Institut d'Estudis Autonòmics, 2008).

21 Manuel Gerpe Landin, coord., *Posición y funciones de los Tribunales Superiores de Justicia* (Barcelona: Institut d'Estudis Autonòmics, 2008).

independence of the judicial branch.[22] Its functions include judicial appointments, promotion, and discipline. Judges are classified into three categories, from the lowest to the highest: judge, magistrate, and magistrate of the Supreme Court. As a general rule, all candidates enter the judicial system as ordinary judges after passing a selection exam. They can then move up to the higher categories through a ranking system based on a combination of years of experience in the post and activities related to the judicial function or competitive specialization exams when a vacancy appears. In the case of the judges of the Supreme Court, the General Council of the Judiciary has greater discretion in selecting among the candidates who fulfil the requirements for the post and, as an exception to the general rule above, one of every five judges appointed is selected from outside the pool of judicial candidates among lawyers and other jurists of recognized competence. The appointment of judges of the higher courts of justice of the ACs follows the general system, although the ranking method provides that for the appointment of judges in ACs with a co-official language or a special historical civil law, knowledge of these is considered a merit (but not a requirement) and therefore results in additional points. Moreover, in the civil and criminal sections of these courts, one in every three vacancies is filled by a legal professional of recognized standing with more than ten years of experience within the respective AC, appointed from a list presented by the parliament of the relevant AC.

In order to guarantee their independence, all judges enjoy security of tenure and cannot be removed, suspended, transferred, or retired from their position without their consent. While in office, they cannot hold or run for public office, belong to political parties or trade unions, or carry out any remunerated work except teaching, legal research, and creative work. The judges have therefore established their separate judicial associations to defend their interests. These associations play an important role in the appointment of the judicial representatives on the General Council of the Judiciary and are also strongly politicized. The age of compulsory retirement is seventy-five; until then, judges can

22 Article 122, Section 3, of the Constitution provides it will be composed of the president of the Supreme Court, who presides, and twenty members, twelve of whom must be judges and magistrates. The other eight are appointed by the Congress and the Senate, elected by three-fifths, among lawyers and other jurists of recognized competence with more than fifteen years of professional practice.

be dismissed only according to the rules provided by law and in compliance with the necessary guarantees.

The lack of real participation of the ACs in the organization and functioning of the judicial branch has been a matter of ongoing of debate and one of the main areas where further autonomy is claimed by the ACs.[23] Recent discussions have centred on strengthening the role of the higher courts of justice to unburden the Supreme Court, and on the decentralization of the some of the functions of the General Council of the Judiciary to new judicial councils of the ACs, over which their institutions would have certain competences. As a result, the recently reformed statutes of autonomy contained more extensive provisions concerning the courts in their territory, in particular their corresponding higher courts of justice, and provided for the creation of new judicial councils in coordination with the required legislation by the Spanish parliament.[24] These were challenged in the case of the Catalan statute, and the Constitutional Court, emphasizing again its restrictive interpretation of the principle of unity, declared that "the territorial organization of the state is of no relevance, as a matter of principle, to the judicial branch as a power of the state."[25]

2. *The Constitutional Court*

The Constitutional Court was established by the 1978 Constitution and started functioning in 1980.[26] It has a precedent in Spanish constitutional history, which is the *Tribunal de Garantías Constitucionales* of 1931.[27] The basic regulation of the Court can be found in the constitutional provisions that define it as a court of extraordinary jurisdiction and separate from the ordinary court system. Further regulation is conferred in an Organic Law on the Constitutional Court, enacted by the

23 Manuel Gerpe and Miguel Ángel Cabellos, coords., *Poder Judicial y Modelo de Estado* (Barcelona: Institut d'Estudis Autonòmics, 2013).

24 Miguel Ángel Cabellos, "Los Consejos de Justicia en el actual proceso de reformas estatutarias y sus perspectivas de futuro," *Revista de Derecho Publico* 80 (2011): 89–116.

25 Constitutional Court Decision 31/2010.

26 José A. Marín, *Naturaleza Jurídica del Tribunal Constitucional* (Barcelona: Ariel, 1998).

27 This was established in the Constitution of 1931 and existed during the Second Spanish Republic. See Francisco Rubio, "Del Tribunal de Garantías al Tribunal Constitucional," *Revista de Derecho Político* 16 (1982–3): 27–37.

state parliament.[28] The Court is composed of twelve judges appointed by the king, four at the proposal of the Congress (by three-fifths of its members), four proposed by the Senate (by the same majority), two proposed by the government, and two proposed by the General Council of the Judiciary. Possible candidates include ordinary judges, prosecutors, university lecturers, public officials, and lawyers, all of whom must have a recognized standing with at least fifteen years of professional practice. The composition of the Court has generally presented a balance between members of judicial origin and of non-judicial origin, with a strong presence of academics; therefore, the Court has a profile that is different from that of the courts in the ordinary judicial branch.[29] Constitutional Court judges are appointed for nine years and are renewed by thirds (four judges) every three years in order to ensure some continuity for the Court's composition and work. The president of the Court is appointed by the king from among its members on the proposal of the Court itself, for a period of three years, and has a casting vote. One major problem has been delays in selecting new candidates by the political institutions, particularly the Congress and the Senate, when political parties try to ensure appointments in accordance with their ideological viewpoints.[30]

Members of the Court must be independent and enjoy security of tenure during their term in office. By specific constitutional mandate, membership of the Constitutional Court is incompatible with any position of a representative nature, any political or administrative office, employment in a political party or trade union, active service as an ordinary judge or prosecutor, or any professional or business activity. Incompatibilities for the members of the ordinary judicial branch also apply to the members of the Constitutional Court. Here again, the practice established by political parties in the appointment process has led to a perception of the Court being politicized, with judges being linked to a specific party, accused of voting accordingly, and divided into a "conservative" and a "progressive" group. The large majorities

28 "Organic Law 2/1979, of 3 October, of the Constitutional Court," which has been reformed on various occasions.

29 Javier García, "La experiencia de veinticinco años de jurisdicción constitucional en España," in *La Reforma del Tribunal Constitucional: actas del V Congreso de la Asociación de Constitucionalistas de España*, coord. Pablo Pérez 17–120 (Valencia: Tirant Blanch, 2007).

30 Francisco Rubio, "El Tribunal Constitucional," *Revista Española de Derecho Constitucional* 71 (2004): 11–33.

required to select a judge, aimed at securing a strong cross-party support for the appointments, have led to the practice of political parties distributing the vacancies arising among themselves (sometimes this includes the appointments conferred on more than one institution, producing the long delays referred to above), and where then each party agrees to vote for the others' candidates. This leads to the appointments being divided largely between the two main statewide parties and clearly violates the intention behind the constitutional provisions on the appointment system. This view of the Court being politicized also affects the disputes regarding the territorial organization of the state, where the "conservative" judges are perceived as favouring a stronger central state, while the "progressive" judges are perceived as being more sensitive to the claims of the ACs.

The conferral of the appointment of two of judges of the Constitutional Court on the Senate highlights the fact that the territorial perspective was taken into account in designing the Court. However, as seen above, the Senate does not represent the interests of the ACs, and their participation in the appointment of the jurisdictional body conferred with the task of resolving disputes between both orders of government has also been one of their ongoing claims. A recent reform strengthened their participation in these appointments by establishing that those judges appointed by the Senate be selected among candidates presented by the parliaments of the ACs.[31] This controversial reform was rejected by the opposition in the Spanish parliament (PP) and had to be validated by the Constitutional Court itself, which ruled that it is constitutional insofar as the Senate is still free to select candidates in addition to those nominated by the ACs.[32] In practice, this rendered the reform meaningless. Moreover, the first Senate appointment after the reform highlighted again the pre-eminence of party interests, as all the AC parliaments governed by one of the two main parties (again, PP) proposed the same two candidates, which were, in effect, the party's chosen candidates for the posts.[33]

The Constitutional Court is the final interpreter of the Constitution. As such, it is independent of the other constitutional bodies of the state

31 This was introduced in the "Organic Law 6/2007, of 24 May, for the Reform of the Organic Law of the Constitutional Court."

32 Constitutional Court Decisions 49/2008 and 101/2008.

33 "El Senado sortea la estrategia del PP contra la renovación del Constitucional," *El País*, 1 July 2010.

and subject only to the Constitution and its own governing statute.[34] The decisions of the Constitutional Court have the force of *res judicata* from the day following their publication and are fully binding on all institutions and bodies of both the central state and ACs. The Constitutional Court hears cases concerning conflicts of jurisdiction between the Spanish state and the ACs or between particular ACs themselves, conflicts between different constitutional bodies of the state (including the central government, the Congress, the Senate, and the General Council of the Judiciary), challenges against statutes for violating the Constitution, appeals in defence of local autonomy, declarations of the constitutionality of international treaties, and extraordinary appeals to protect fundamental rights. Cases concerning conflicts of jurisdiction (*conflictos de competencia*) may be lodged by the government of the central state or by the executives of the ACs against regulations (secondary legislation) of the other order of government (positive conflicts), or a failure to act in a specific area (negative conflicts). Many conflicts between the state and the ACs are also lodged via the "appeal of unconstitutionality" (*recurso de inconstitucionalidad*), which allows the Court to carry out an abstract review of statutes at the request of the president of the government, fifty members of the Congress, fifty members of the Senate, the AC executives and parliaments, or the ombudsman, during the three months after their publication. Once the three-month post-publication period is over, all statutes can be referred to the Constitutional Court by the ordinary courts in relation to a specific controversy through the procedure of "question of unconstitutionality" (*questión de inconstitucionalidad*), for which there is no time limit. An essential function of the Court and the largest number of cases it hears are the "extraordinary appeals for protection against violations of fundamental rights" (*recurso de amparo*), which can be lodged by the directly affected party, the ombudsman, or the prosecution, when all other judicial remedies have been exhausted. Finally, and as a result of the controversial case of the reformed Catalan statute, as of 2015 the Court can also hear challenges against proposals for the enactment or amendment of statutes of autonomy.[35]

---

34 "Organic Law of the Constitutional Court," Art. 1.

35 "Organic Law 12/2015, of 22 September, for the amendment of the Organic Law of the Constitutional Court, for the establishment of the pre-enactment appeal of unconstitutionality for proposals for the enactment or amendment of statutes of autonomy."

As noted above, as a general rule, only privileged applicants can lodge appeals against either the Spanish state or an AC for violating the constitutional provisions on the state of the autonomies. Individuals may not, therefore, do so, with the exception of a negative conflict of jurisdiction when their interests are affected. The most common case is that the state challenges statutes or regulations of the ACs or that ACs challenge statutes or regulations of the state. When there is a conflict of jurisdiction, before the appeal can be lodged, the relevant provisions provide that there must be an initial attempt to negotiate a solution (this is not binding for the state).[36] Similarly, in order to try to reduce the number of "appeals of unconstitutionality" lodged against statutes by both orders of government, a reform introduced in 2000 allows for the extension of the period to appeal from three to nine months when there is an agreement to negotiate to try to resolve the discrepancies, and this is notified to the Court.[37] If the challenges go ahead, various scholars have highlighted that the state and the ACs are in an asymmetrical position with regard to their initial effects.[38] If the state challenges an AC regulation directly before the Court, on competence grounds or not, it will result in the automatic suspension of the norm for a period of five months, after which the Court must decide if it will maintain the suspension until the final decision on the case.[39] The ACs can obtain the suspension of a regulation of the state only when the challenge is on competence grounds and if they can prove it could cause irreparable damage.[40] In addition, as a general norm, an "appeal of unconstitutionality" does not result in the suspension of the validity of the statute, but in the cases where the Spanish government challenges the constitutionality of a statute enacted by an AC, this will be suspended automatically up to a period of five months, and if ratified by the Court, until there is a final decision. The significant differences in the effects of these challenges highlight a presumption in favour of the state.

36 "Organic Law of the Constitutional Court," Arts. 62–3.

37 Ibid., Art. 33, as amended by the "Organic Law 1/2000, of 7 January."

38 Enoch Alberti, "La intervención del Tribunal Constitucional en la construcción del Estado Autonómico español," in *50 años de Corte Constitucional Italiana, 25 años de Tribunal Constitucional español*, coords. Miguel Revenga, Emilio Pajares, and Juan Ramón Rodríguez, 193–212 (Madrid: Ministerio de Justicia, 2007).

39 Spanish Constitution, Art. 161, Sec. 2.

40 "Organic Law of the Constitutional Court," Art. 64, Sec. 3.

In exercising its functions, the Court is described as carrying out the role of a "negative legislator," analysing the initiatives of both the state and AC legislators, when challenged, and invalidating those that do not comply with the Constitution. Because the constitutional provisions are open to interpretation in many aspects, scholars have highlighted the importance of the Court's self-restraint and of a strong presumption of the constitutionality of legislation. In the area of the territorial organization of the state, its governing statute provides specifically that when analysing conformity with the Constitution of a state or AC statute, the Court will take into consideration not only the constitutional provisions but also other statutes enacted within the framework of the Constitution to delimit or harmonize the competences of the state and the different autonomous communities.[41] As a result, the Court has engaged in an ongoing and evolving dialogue with both the central state and AC legislatures. Some scholars highlight the fact that the Court has extended its role further than a simple veto ("negative legislator"). The Court has contributed, for example, its own doctrines and principles to the interpretation and development of the Constitution. It also makes use of the technique of "interpretative opinions," reconstruing challenged provisions to make them compatible with the Constitution, which are more activist than simply invalidating them.[42] The style of its opinions has been characterized as "professorial," because they tend to be long and discursive, with arguments constructed on the basis of previous decisions and showing an engagement with specialized legal scholarship, even if not referring to it specifically. Dissenting opinions are common and are published together with the majority opinion. In cases where the Court is divided, dissenting opinions are considered very important, because in many cases they can signal a future change in the Court's position.

IV. Federalism Jurisprudence

1. General Tendencies

Within the largely open model outlined in the Constitution, the Constitutional Court has a fundamental role in contributing to the construction of the state of the autonomies. Many of the different constitutional

41 Ibid., Art. 28.

42 See García, "La experiencia de veinticinco años de jurisdicción constitucional en España."

provisions concerning the territorial organization of the Spanish state, especially the competence provisions, have been developed and fleshed out by hundreds of decisions. It is impossible, therefore, to understand the functioning of the state of the autonomies without taking the Court's case law into consideration.[43] Litigation during the first years of the state of the autonomies was especially intense, with a large number of challenges brought by both the ACs and the state (an average of 100 challenges per year in 1984–8). Since then, the number of challenges has decreased, and the role of the Court has become more one of fine-tuning in specific cases, although the number of competence challenges is still notably high. The reasons proffered for this include the openness of the constitutional provisions as well as the use of constitutional challenges by government institutions and political parties to obtain short-term political goals, knowing that the over-burdened Court and the long delay in resolving challenges (in some cases, currently, up to ten years), may not produce a final decision until two parliamentary sessions later. Also a significant number of challenges are subsequently withdrawn as a result of political negotiations or changes in the governing majorities at the state and AC levels. On the other hand, the number of challenges between ACs has been very limited and has not had a significant effect on the development of the system, although they have recently gained prominence in the challenges against the newly reformed statutes of autonomy.

Development of the state of the autonomies within the possibilities provided by the Constitution has been notably centralizing through an extensive interpretation of the functional and substantive competences of the state, thus limiting the ACs' scope of self-government. The Constitutional Court has contributed to this process by validating many of the expansive statutes and decisions adopted by the central-state legislature, which has defined the model largely through the coordinated action of the two dominant statewide parties. Therefore the Court has helped consolidate a notably centralized interpretation of the constitutional provisions on the territorial organization of the state, foreclosing other possible interpretations that would have been much more favourable to the ACs. At the same time, however, in certain crucial

43 For a detailed commentary, see Gerard Martin, "La jurisprudència constitucional sobre l'organització territorial de l'Estat Autonòmic i bibliografia sobre la incidència d'aquesta jurisprudència," *Revista Catalana de Dret Públic* 43 (2011): 221–76.

cases, the Court has made important decisions defending the ACs. It is precisely because on these occasions the Court limited the centralizing tendencies of the state institutions that – until recent decisions on the reformed Statute of Autonomy of Valencia and, in particular, on the Statute of Autonomy of Catalonia – it was generally accepted that its intervention had been fairly balanced overall.[44] These two decisions of 2007 and 2010 were notably controversial and for the first time very strongly split academic and more general political, institutional, and public opinion on the Court.[45] As will be seen, for the supporters of the new statutes, in making these decisions, the Constitutional Court had bowed to the pressure of those opposing the reforms, and in order to do so had reversed much of its previous case law on the state of the autonomies, adopting a much more restrictive interpretation of the role of the ACs and their statutes of autonomy within the system. The Court was also accused of reinforcing its own position, to the extent that it conferred on itself the role of "prorogued constituent power" with the authority to further define or limit what the Constitution purposely left open.[46] For those opposing the reforms, however, the Court was simply safeguarding the model established by the Constitution, a model that was violated by a pact between the state and self-governing legislatures aimed at an "undercover" reform of the Constitution through the statutes of autonomy.[47]

These two controversial decisions also highlighted the division of the Court into two blocks with radically opposite understandings of the Constitution's provisions on the territorial organization of the state.

---

44 Among others, German Fernández, *La Contribución del Tribunal Constitucional al Estado Autonómico* (Madrid: Iustel, 2005).

45 The Valencian decision was seen largely as setting the groundwork for the Catalan case, in which many of the provisions challenged had been reproduced in other statutes and approved by the members of the challenging party. By the time the Catalan decision was finally adopted (four years after the challenge), one judge had died and three of the judges' mandates had expired, with the filling of the four vacancies being postponed in order to avoid altering the majorities on the Court, and leading to allegations of it being adopted by an "illegal court."

46 Paloma Requejo Rodriguez, "La posición del Tribunal Constitucional Español tras su Sentencia 31/2010," *Revista Catalana de Dret Públic* 43 (2011): 317–41.

47 As an example, see the following monographic issues: "Justícia constitucional i estats compostos: reflexions a partir de la sentència del Tribunal Constitucional sobre l'Estatut d'Autonomia de Catalunya," *Revista Catalana de Dret Públic* 43 (2011); "Monográfico: STC 31/2010," *Teoría y Realidad Constitucional* 27 (2011); and "El Tribunal Constitucional y el Estatut," *El Cronista del Estado Democrático de Derecho* 15 (2010).

The Valencian decision was adopted by a very tight majority (7–5), and part of the reason for the long delay in the Catalan decision was the lack of a minimum consensus among the Court's members, a fact that was continuously leaked to the press. An example of the depth of this division was that in order to obtain the final Catalan opinion, the ten judges (one was ruled to have a disqualifying interest and one had died without being replaced) had to vote on different blocks of challenged provisions separately, with different judges voting in favour and against each block. A first block included the preamble and the reference to Catalonia as a nation (6–4); a second block concerned the challenged provisions declared unconstitutional (8–2); a third block dealt with the challenged provisions declared constitutional (6–4); and a fourth block concerned the provisions that had to be reconstrued in order to be constitutional. The decision was also accompanied by four dissenting opinions, three from "conservative" judges and one from a "progressive" judge.

2. *Specific Issues*

The Constitutional Court's explicit understanding of the Constitution's provisions on the state of the autonomies is that they are very open and allow for the inclusion of very different political options pertaining to the design of the territorial organization of the state.[48] In this sense, the Court has always been careful to refer to the Spanish polity as a "composite state" (*Estado compuesto*), safeguarding the autonomy of the ACs, but at the same time avoiding commitment to a more specific characterization. In the 2007 decision on the Statute of Autonomy of Valencia, the Court summarized its conception of the territorial organization of the state as resting on five fundamental principles.[49] First, the Court stated that the system rests on the adequate integration of the principle of unity, translated into the existence of one organization – the state – for the whole of the Spanish territory, with the principle of autonomy of the nationalities and regions. According to the Court, the principle of autonomy, which ensures a sphere of self-government for the ACs, is not opposed to the principle of unity, but encompassed by and attains its true meaning within the latter. These are then complemented by the

48 Constitutional Court Decisions 76/1983 and 247/2007.
49 Constitutional Court Decision 247/2007.

principle of solidarity, which applies to the state and the ACs and also to the different ACs among themselves, the principle of the equality of citizens, which ensures the common basic conditions in the exercise of their rights, and the more general principle of loyalty to the Constitution. This final principle, which is not expressly included in the Constitution, requires that all decisions adopted by the different orders of government are in the general public interest.

As regards the locus of constitutive authority upon which the system is legally founded, the Court has declared that national sovereignty, which the Constitution says belongs to the Spanish people, is not the result of a pact between historical territorial entities that retain rights going back to before the Constitution, but is a provision emanating from the constituent power with general binding force.[50] The Court reiterated this idea in its decision on the Statute of Catalonia, declaring that the references to Catalonia as "nation" or a "national reality" in the preamble do not have any interpretative legal effect and that the references to "the historical rights of the Catalan people" had to be interpreted as the rights the Constitution itself provides with regard to, for example, their distinct private law or minority languages, and not as a separate foundation of the self-government of Catalonia.[51] Similarly, it has declared that statutes of autonomy are not the expression of a sovereign power, but of autonomy founded in the Constitution. However, while thus distinguishing autonomy from sovereignty, the Court has stated that the political nature of the autonomy of the ACs means that they should have the capacity to establish their own public policies in the areas of their competence.[52] Further, a necessary consequence of the political autonomy of the ACs is that citizens living in different parts of the state can be subject to different legal rules and thus have different rights without violating the general principle of equality of rights across the state.[53]

A large part of the constitutional litigation on the territorial organization of the state has centred on the distribution of competences between both orders of government. Using a diversity of techniques, the Court has defined in detail the functional and substantive content of the different competences reserved as "exclusive" to the Spanish state.[54] This has

---

50 Constitutional Court Decisions 4/1981 and 247/2007.

51 Constitutional Court Decision 31/2010.

52 Constitutional Court Decisions 4/1981 and 25/1981.

53 Constitutional Court Decisions 37/1981 and 247/2007.

54 Fernández, *La Contribución del Tribunal Constitucional al Estado Autonómico.*

also required it to define the different concepts used in the Constitution when doing this in each specific area, which in turn also delimited the scope of intervention of the ACs: where the competence over the "bases" or "basic legislation" is conferred on the central state, the ACs can enact more detailed legislation within the basic state legislative framework; where the competence to enact "legislation" is conferred on the central state, the ACs are granted executive powers to implement it; and the more general conferral of competence over "coordination" on the central state means it is granted powers to coordinate a specific field, notwithstanding the related competences of the ACs. As part of this process, the Court has allowed for an expansive interpretation of the central state's competences, with two headings that have become known as "horizontal clauses." These as well as "basic legislation" have been particularly invasive. The Court has adopted a more restrictive approach to those headings assumed as exclusive AC competences in their statutes of autonomy, stating that in these cases, exclusivity does not mean that ACs are granted all functions pertaining to a particular field.[55] In some of its first decisions, the Court already established that the term "exclusive" was not absolute when used in a statute of autonomy to refer to competences assumed by an AC because the statutes cannot impede the central state from exercising its exclusive competences, which may result in an intervention in those fields.[56] As the statutes of autonomy have tended to occupy all the areas left open by the Constitution, the Court has hardly ever applied the residual clause, and it has not conferred additional competences on the central state.

The two central competence headings that have become known as "horizontal clauses" are the provision of the "basic rules and coordination of the general planning of economic activity" (Art. 14, Sec 1.13) and the regulation of "the basic conditions that guarantee the equality of all Spanish citizens in the exercise of their rights and in the fulfilment of their constitutional duties" (Art. 149(1.1)). In both cases, the Court has established a more limiting initial definition, but has then allowed for a wide variety of exceptions that have largely expanded their application. In the first, which has been the object of notable conflicts and a high number of decisions, the Court has established that this provision cannot be interpreted to annul the competences of the ACs that happen

55 Constitutional Court Decision 56/1986.
56 Constitutional Court Decision 3/1981.

to have certain economic aspects, and that it can authorize only those measures that concern matters having a direct and significant impact on general economic activity.[57] Yet the Court has validated numerous exceptions to these rules to cover individual measures, which the state argued were necessary to attain particular important objectives.[58] Similarly, regarding the equality of all Spanish citizens in the exercise of their rights and fulfilment of their duties, the Court has again held that the provision covers only the conditions that have a direct and immediate relation to basic constitutional rights in a strict sense, and that a regulation must still leave scope for the ACs to exercise their competences in the relevant field, but has then permitted much more detailed and expansive central regulations to stand.[59]

The Court's definition of "basic laws" (framework laws) has followed a pattern similar to the cases above. In its initial decisions, it established that the "basic" content must be included in a statute and that it must provide the minimum normative common denominator on the basis of which each AC can build and establish its own particular legislative policies.[60] However, since then, the Court has allowed for exceptions to the above rules, including the use of secondary legislation and even an administrative act, along with detailed regulations in particular fields and variations in their general application across all ACs.[61] The Court has also established that the specific content of the "basis" of a basic law is mutable. It can be amended over time; consequently, changes by the central legislator can result in previously valid AC statutes becoming unconstitutional.[62] The Court has been similarly flexible about the powers of coordination conferred on the central state, allowing their use to be extended farther than the specific competence headings that provide for them, with the objective of the integration of the global system.[63]

In some cases, the Court has defended the autonomy of the ACs and adopted an open and flexible interpretation of their competences in areas that are included in the central state's exclusive competences. A fundamental decision from the viewpoint of the ACs was invalidation

57 Constitutional Court Decisions 125/1984 and 76/1991.
58 As an example, Constitutional Court Decision 95/1986.
59 Constitutional Court Decisions 61/1997 and 164/2001.
60 Constitutional Court Decisions 32/1981 and 1/1882.
61 Constitutional Court Decisions 49/1988, 50/1999, and 109/1988.
62 Constitutional Court Decisions 1/1982 and 2/1989.
63 Constitutional Court Decisions 32/1983 and 104/1988.

of the state "Organic Law for the Harmonization of the Process of Self-Government" (known as LOAPA), enacted in 1982 as an attempt to re-centralize powers and stall the "autonomic process." The Court declared that the state's harmonization power was restricted to the special circumstances provided for in the Constitution, and that the public interest did not allow it to infringe or take over competences that had been assumed by the ACs.[64] Some examples of the Court carrying out an extensive interpretation of the competences of the ACs include the field of "administration of justice," discussed above, and the development by the ACs of their special historical civil law, where the Court has allowed them to regulate institutions connected to those in their compilations, without strictly binding them to their original content.[65] Other decisions favouring the ACs include accepting their international activity, validating the Catalan language policy, impeding the central state from using funding to invade areas of AC competence, and allowing ACs to open offices in Brussels to facilitate their contacts with EU institutions and bodies.[66] As seen above, the Court also has stated that integration and implementation of EU law does not alter the distribution of competences between the Spanish state and the ACs, and that any related functions must be distributed in accordance with pre-existing criteria.

As part of the above decisions, the Court has developed interpretative principles and criteria for resolving inconsistencies or contradictions between state and AC laws. Notably, the Court has not made significant use of the "prevalence clause," which favours the law of the state in these cases, and has usually resolved conflicts on the basis of the principle of competence.[67] Additional principles include the "irrenounceability" and "unavailability" of AC competences, meaning that once assumed by an AC in its statute of autonomy, they cannot be returned to or taken back by the central state; and the principle of "specificity," where the most generic competence must give way to the more specific.[68] The Court also has stated that implicit in the system is a general principle of collaboration between the Spanish state and the ACs.[69]

---

64 Constitutional Court Decision 76/1983.

65 Constitutional Court Decision 88/1993.

66 Constitutional Court Decisions 153/1989, 165/1994, 82, 83, 84/1986, 337/1994, and 179/1985.

67 Constitutional Court Decision 163/1995.

68 Constitutional Court Decisions 87/1993 and 71/1982.

69 Constitutional Court Decision 18/1982.

In its Valencian and Catalan decisions, the Court issued a series of general propositions about the role and functions of the statutes of autonomy. These propositions have been objects of much controversy. The reformed AC statutes contained several novelties, including detailed delimitation of the competence categories and fields to safeguard the ACs against the expansiveness of central-state competences, and the representation of the ACs in certain state and EU bodies and institutions, following and building on the court's own case-law. As seen above, until then, it was generally accepted that the statutes of autonomy had a fundamental role in completing the constitutional design of the state of the autonomies and were a central part of the "block of constitutionality." However, while in the initial Valencian decision the Court seemed to accept this role of the statutes, in the Catalan decision it declared that any understanding of these norms as being "constitutional in substance" was merely academic and gave them no added legal value or force.[70] Disregarding their negotiated nature, and the fact that the Constitution itself provides that they are "the basic institutional norm of each AC" (Art. 147.1), the Court went on to state that the statutes of autonomy are simply "organic laws," the formal category under which they are finally enacted in the Spanish parliament.[71] On this basis, the court then declared that the statutes of autonomy could describe the functional and substantive content of competences, but that only the Court itself could carry out a "genuine and unchallengeable interpretation of the principles and categories in the Constitution."[72] In a similar sense, the Court ruled that the provisions regarding AC participation in state and EU institutions and bodies were void of any normative content and depended on being provided for in state legislation, which the state has absolute freedom to enact or not. In a final decision of nearly 900 pages, it deactivated most of the reforms included in the statute, in many cases by re-construing them in a way that went against their original meaning and left them with no legal effect. The Court, however, did not openly acknowledge or explain this change in its case law, and the reasons for it therefore are not fully clear. As noted above, this challenge was the result of a political rather than

70 Constitutional Court Decision 31/2010.

71 The court equated the statutes with the rest of organic laws that regulate specific areas when so provided by the Constitution, and which can be freely enacted and amended at the state level (Art. 81.1).

72 Constitutional Court Decision 31/2010.

a strictly legal conflict, and the Court was under substantial pressure from both sides. In this context, and after an extensive and complex deliberation, a majority of the judges decided to block the new reforms. Possible reasons for this decision are that some judges considered the reforms to be a threat to the unity of Spain; some believed that reforms of this nature should be carried out through the constitutional amendment process; and others thought that they could not be enacted in such a controversial climate or without wider consensus at the central level.

As noted above, the Constitutional Court's decisions are fully binding on all ordinary courts, legislatures, and executives. These institutions cannot deviate from, opt out of, or refuse to comply with the Court's doctrines and rulings. The Court's decisions have, however, been contested by nationalist politicians and governments. The Court was even the object of a boycott by the Basque Country, which for years refused to present any challenges to the Court after a decision on justice matters in 1990. These criticisms reached their highest point in the Barcelona Declaration, signed in 1998 by *Convergència i Unió* (a federation of two Catalan nationalist parties), *Partido Nacionalista Vasco* (Basque Nationalist Party), and *Bloque Nacionalista Galego* (Galician Nationalist Coalition). The declaration described the Court as an instrument for centralism and accused it of formulating a unitary reading of the Constitution.[73] A notable precedent to the Catalan statute conflict was the Basque proposal for a "freely associated state" (also known as the "Ibarretxe plan"), approved by the Basque parliament in 2004 as a reform of its statute of autonomy, which was later declared invalid by the central state parliament. Both sides of the conflict required the intervention of the Constitutional Court, which finally validated the state parliament's decision, resulting in strong criticism from the nationalist parties and institutions.[74] The reaction against its decision on Catalonia's statute of autonomy was unprecedented and included a joint editorial by twelve Catalan newspapers (entitled "The dignity of Catalonia") some months before and a massive protest march headed by civil-society organizations and all political parties except the PP, which had presented the

73 Signed on 16 July 1988, it requested a redefinition of the state as a multinational and multilingual nation.

74 Constitutional Court Decrees 135/2004, 44 and 45/2005. The Court declared invalid a challenge by the state government to the Basque government's initial agreement, as well as two individual challenges to the state Congress's refusal to consider the proposal.

challenge.[75] Immediate academic criticisms also were published within and outside Catalonia, directed at both the content and form of the decision.[76] Criticisms were centred, first, on the fact that the Court went back on a substantial part of its previous case law on the state of the autonomies, and it did so without putting forward clear reasons for such a change. Second, the decision was criticized for its harshness and apodictic tone, particularly as the Court was considering a statute that had been negotiated by both orders of government and ratified by referendum. Finally, the decision was strongly criticized for its extensive use of the technique of stating the "constitutionally compatible interpretation" of the challenged provisions, and for re-construing them in such a way that it converted them into a set of general programmatic provisions. At the same time, however, strong voices were raised in defence of the Court and its decision.[77]

V. Conclusion

The role of the Constitutional Court in enabling the ACs to exercise significant levels of political autonomy and self-determination has been important, particularly during the first years of the Constitution and the initial construction of the state of the autonomies. In the development of the system, the expansive interpretation of the competences of the Spanish state and the resulting restriction of the sphere of self-government of the ACs cannot be attributed directly to the Court, as it has simply validated the initiatives of the state legislator within the open provisions of the Constitution. Its recent intervention in the new wave of reform of the statutes of autonomy has proved much more problematic. The principal objectives of this bottom-up constitutional initiative to develop the state of the autonomies were to expand the self-government of the ACs to the maximum within the Constitution and to resolve some of the system's ongoing problems. In order to do so, the required procedures were followed and the required majorities in both the self-governing AC parliaments and the state parliament were obtained, constituting

75 26 November 2009. For example, "La dignidad de Catalunya," La Vanguardia, http://www.lavanguardia.com/politica/20091126/53831123016/la-dignidad-de-catalunya.html.

76 See *Revista Catalana de Dret Public* 43 (2011): 44.

77 For example, Francesc de Carreras, Catalunya tras la Sentencia del Estatuto, *Letras Libres* (September 2010): 32–7.

an exercise of "self-rule" combined with "shared-rule."[78] As part of this process, the statutes were subject to scrutiny by constitutional experts and amended, following deliberation, by both orders of government; so it is arguable that they were in accordance with at least one possible and plausible interpretation of the Constitution. However, the Court deactivated most of these reforms, devalued the legal status of the statutes of autonomy, and left them with a large number of programmatic provisions having no normative content. By expunging the statutes of autonomy from the "block of constitutionality," the Court also left key elements of the autonomy of the ACs to the discretion of the state parliament. As a result, the state of the autonomies is at a crossroads, with the only option for the ACs to improve their self-government and resolve some of the deficiencies of the system being reform of the Constitution itself, which, at least until very recently, has been highly unlikely.

Further, the Court has played a fundamental role in securing individual rights and liberties as part of a transition to a fully constitutional system, in particular by incorporating the case-law of the European Court of Human Rights as well as other international human-rights treaties and decisions. The Court has, at the same time, been more restrictive in allowing the development of a multi-level system of rights protection in accordance with the principles of unity and autonomy on which the system is based. Another of the new aspects in the reformed statutes was the inclusion of a charter of rights; yet it was also part of the provisions challenged in both cases.[79] In the Valencian decision, the Court stated that there are no constitutional impediments for the statutes of autonomy to include "statutory rights," but in the Catalan case, the Court declared that these are in reality not individual rights but simply mandates to the AC legislator, binding within their sphere of competences. Of particular significance, the Court also invalidated the conferral on the Council of Statutory Guarantees of Catalonia – an expert advisory body on constitutional and statutory matters – of the power to give a binding opinion on the compatibility of bills presented in the Catalan parliament with the rights included in the statute. In practice, this would have allowed the council to block those bills considered in violation of the statutory rights, and part of the grounds for

78 Daniel Elazar, *Exploring Federalism* (Tuscaloosa: University of Alabama Press, 1987), 5.

79 Enriqueta Expósito, "La regulación de los derechos en los nuevos estatutos de autonomía," *Revista d'Estudis Federals i Autonòmics* 5 (2007): 147–202.

the Court's decision were that it would confer on the council a role too similar to its own.

Within the above framework, one still largely unresolved issue in the state of the autonomies is the "national question," particularly with respect to the Basque Country and Catalonia. After the conflict surrounding the Basque proposal for a "freely associated state," which was blocked because it was considered too much of a fundamental challenge to the constitutional framework, the Catalan proposal was clearly and carefully drafted to fit within the constitutional provisions. Together with maximizing self-government, parts of the provisions of the new statute were directed at introducing elements that recognized the identity of Catalonia as a minority nation within the state, including references to its history and cultural heritage. As seen above, in many cases these provisions had no direct legal effect on the organization and functioning of the system, and, again, their scrutiny by constitutional experts meant that they were arguably also compatible with at least one possible interpretation of the Constitution. When considering these provisions, however, the Court was particularly harsh in its tone and wording, showing a lack of sensitivity to the situation of national pluralism, which is clearly recognized in the Constitution, thereby increasing the feeling of alienation and support for independence in Catalonia. For example, the Court stated that "the Constitution doesn't recognize any other nation than the Spanish nation."[80] With such an approach, the Court missed an opportunity to set out an authoritative interpretation of the constitutional use of the terms *nationalities* and *nation*, which could have allowed for an inclusive understanding of the constitutional framework in a way that could accommodate both the minority and majority nations in recognition of Spain's pluri-national reality.

Until the 2010 decision on the Statute of Autonomy of Catalonia, the Constitutional Court was generally regarded as an institution that supported the state of the autonomies and contributed to its development in a generally balanced fashion. The decision on the Statute of Autonomy of Catalonia put the Court at the forefront of the political conflict on the territorial organization of the state and for the first time very strongly divided specialized scholars, political parties, institutions, and public opinion more generally on its role in the system. Of particular gravity, the division not only concerned the specific content of the decision, but

80 Constitutional Court Decision 31/2010.

also how the Court exercised its jurisdiction, with it being accused of establishing itself as an extension of the constituent power and breaching its constitutional limits. Moreover, while the criticism was strongest in Catalonia and among the defenders of the Catalan statute, some of those who supported the general outcome of the Court's decision were also critical of its quality and of its impact on the Court's previous case law on the state of the autonomies. Most critics and defenders of the Court agree that this decision has come at a high cost for the Court in its prestige and perceived legitimacy, and polls show that the public's trust in the Court has dropped significantly since.[81] Proposals to reform the system, especially to reduce the delays and backlogs of cases, and also to avoid political malpractice in appointing the judges, have been ongoing and have increased since the decision. As noted above, a pre-enactment review for reforms of statutes of autonomy was introduced in 2015 in order to prevent situations like the Catalan case from arising again.

More generally, the Court's decision on the Statute of Autonomy of Catalonia has increased support for independence in the region, and with it, the uncertainty regarding the future of the overall model. The decision was followed by a victory of the PP, responsible for the challenge, in the elections at the state level in November 2011, fuelling tensions in Catalonia further. On the celebration of the Diada (the national holiday of Catalonia, which commemorates the fight for Barcelona in 1714) on 11 September 2012, 1.5 million Catalan citizens participated in a march in favour of independence from Spain. This led to the holding of elections in Catalonia two months later and to a parliamentary majority in favour of holding a referendum on independence. Despite the central government stating that such a referendum is not possible within the constitutional framework, the Catalan government began a process of national transition to the Catalans' "own state," the first step of which was adoption of a "Declaration of Sovereignty and Right to Decide of

81 The decline in the perception of the legitimacy of the Constitutional Court can be seen in the CIS statewide polls on the public's trust in institutions for 1998, 2011, 2013, 2014, and 2015 respectively, where the results for high and low trust in the Court have been as follows: 1998 – high (23 per cent) and low (11 per cent) of responses; 2011 – high (18 per cent) and low (20 per cent; and 2013 – high (10 per cent) and low (38 per cent). The average overall rating of the court from 1 to 10 has also decreased across the three years considered: 5.53 (1998), 4.71 (2011) 3.51 (2013), 3.35 (2014), and 3.40 (2015). Sources: CIS Barometers 2039, 2861 2984, 3021, and 3080.

the People of Catalonia" by the Catalan parliament.[82] The preamble of the declaration refers to "impediments and refusals by the institutions of the Spanish state" in relation to measures to transform the political and legal framework, "among which Sentence 31/2010 passed by the Spanish Constitutional Court deserves particular emphasis."[83] The Court's decision is still at the centre of the conflict; as a result, in Catalonia, it is not perceived as an impartial arbiter able to mediate between both orders of government to help resolve it. This was put clearly into words before the Catalan parliament by Miquel Roca, a leading Catalan advocate and one of the drafters of the 1978 Constitution, who stated that "the opinion of Constitutional Court does not deserve any respect."[84]

To end this chapter on a more positive note regarding the Court's case law, a recent carefully drafted unanimous decision cast a ray of hope on the current situation and can be interpreted as a first step in the Court reconsidering its fundamental constitutional position and role as a mediator in a complex pluri-national state. This decision resolved a constitutional challenge by the Spanish government to the "Declaration of Sovereignty and of the Right to Decide of the People of Catalonia" adopted by the Catalan parliament.[85] When considering the different grounds of the challenge, the Court ruled, first, that the "declaration of sovereignty" of the people of Catalonia was incompatible with the constitutional provision, stating that sovereignty belongs to the "Spanish people" (Art. 1.1.). However, the Court then argued that the references to the initiation of a process to exercise "the right to decide of the Catalan people" could be interpreted as the expression of a political aspiration susceptible to being defended within the constitutional framework. More importantly, it stressed problems such as those deriving from one part of the state wanting to alter its legal status could

---

82 Available at http://www.catdem.org/cat/downloads2/declaration-of-sovereignty.pdf.

83 Ibid.

84 As reported in "Miquel Roca: 'El TC no me merece ningún respeto desde la sentencia del Estatut,'" La Vanguardia, 30 July 2013, http://www.lavanguardia.com/politica/20130730/54378991824/miquel-roca-el-tc-no-me-merece-ningun-respeto-desde-la-sentencia-del-estatut.html.

85 Constitutional Court Decision 42/2014. Interestingly, a first issue the Court had to consider was if it could actually review the political declaration, which the Catalan parliament argued had no real and concrete legal effects. The Court decided that, despite its prominently political nature, the resolution was also susceptible to producing legal effects, as it conferred attributes of sovereignty on the Catalan people, and initiated a process directed at enabling their exercise of the right to decide.

not be resolved by the Court, whose function is to safeguard the strict observance of the Constitution, and must be resolved through dialogue and cooperation between the different political institutions within the state of the autonomies. The Court seemed to point to the option of constitutional reform as a solution to the current conflict, stating that if an AC parliament initiated such a process, the Spanish parliament would be bound to consider its proposals under the general principle of loyalty to the Constitution. The decision was largely well received in Catalonia and interpreted as recognizing the legitimacy of Catalonia's claims and the process of constitutional reform currently underway.[86]

However, since the Constitutional Court's call for dialogue and for a political resolution of the conflict, Spain's government has refused to engage with the Catalan process, which has continued regardless. Of particular concern for the issues considered in this chapter, the Spanish government's response has been to use the Constitutional Court to block the different legal avenues the Catalan authorities have sought to pursue to allow their citizens to vote on the constitutional future of Catalonia, thus placing the responsibility for stopping the Catalan process on the Court. Following the "Declaration of Sovereignty," they challenged the "Catalan Statute on Popular Consultations" (enacted to provide an alternative to a referendum, which requires authorization of the Spanish government under the Constitution), the Catalan decree providing for holding such a consultation on independence (both were invalidated by the Court for providing for what it considered to be an undercover referendum), and even the Catalan government's involvement in what ultimately became a citizens' participation event on the set date.[87] Finally, in response to the Catalan government's announcement that it would then hold plebiscitary elections on independence, the Spanish government enacted emergency legislation giving the Constitutional Court new powers to impose sanctions and suspend public authorities that do not comply with its judgments.[88] The reason for this

86 As an example, see the Catalan government's report on the decision, available at http://presidencia.gencat.cat/web/.content/ambits_actuacio/transicio_nacional/iea/observatori_autogovern/autogovern/arxius/informe_sentencia_tc_sobirania_parlament_vesp.pdf.

87 Constitutional Court Decisions 31/2015, 32/2015, and 138/2015.

88 "Organic Law 15/2015, of 16 October, for the reform of the Organic Law of the Constitutional Court, for the enforcement of the decisions of the Constitutional Court as a safeguard for the rule of law."

reform is to enable the Constitutional Court to suspend the Catalan authorities if they take any actions seen as leading to a process of unilateral independence, despite the Spanish government having its own powers to take "all measures necessary" to make an AC comply with its obligations under the Constitution (Art 155). This has not only placed further responsibility on the Court, but has effectively converted it into the Spanish government's enforcer.

In the "plebiscitary" elections to the Catalan parliament, held on 27 September 2015, the pro-independence parties gained a majority of seats (72 out of 135), with 48 per cent of votes, and announced the start of a "process of the creation of an independent Catalan state in the form of a republic."[89] Catalonia's parliament voted in favour of starting this process on 9 November 2015 in a resolution that includes refusal to continue compliance with decisions of Spanish state institutions, among them, the Constitutional Court.[90] The resolution was again challenged by the Spanish government before the Court, which declared its provisional suspension. For the first time, and at the request of the state government, the Court's order included a personal notification with a specific warning to leaders of the Catalan parliament and provisional Catalan government of the consequences of non-compliance. Less than a month after, the Court ruled unanimously that the resolution was in violation of the Constitution.[91]

Whatever the final outcome of this conflict, the Court's call for negotiation and for a political solution has so far been ignored, and the Court has been forced to remain a central player in blocking the Catalan process. The extensive use of the Court and the establishment of its new powers of enforcement have therefore so far thwarted its attempt to regain some of its lost legitimacy and reinstate itself as an effective mediator between both orders of government; they have simply reinforced the perception in Catalonia that the Court is the enforcing arm of the Spanish government. Overall, this ongoing conflict between Catalonia and the state authorities is a consequence of the long-standing

---

89 See, for example, M. Colomer, O. Maarch, and R. Tugas, "Principi d'acord per a la declaració rupturista del Parlament," Política, 23 October 2015, http://www.ara.cat/politica/Principi-dacord-declaracio-rupturista-Parlament_0_1454254647.html.

90 "El Parlament declara l'inici del procés de creació de l'estat català independent en forma de república," Parlament de Catalunya, 9 November 2015, http://www.parlament.cat/web/actualitat/noticies/index.html?p_format=D&p_id=176474300.

91 Constitutional Court Decision 259/2015.

problems and tensions within the state of the autonomies that have been highlighted in this chapter. These problems need to be urgently and comprehensively addressed by the relevant political institutions; hopefully recent changes in the composition of the state parliament will help facilitate this. However, until this happens, the Constitutional Court cannot resolve them alone. Continuously placing the Court at the forefront of the political conflicts that arise within the state of the autonomies only further compromises its position and legitimacy.

13 The Federal Supreme Court of Switzerland: Judicial Balancing of Federalism without Judicial Review

ANDREAS LIENHARD, DANIEL KETTIGER, JACQUES BÜHLER, LORANNE MÉRILLAT, AND DANIELA WINKLER

I. Introduction

This chapter gives an overview of the structure of Switzerland as a federal state and the organization of its judicial system and judicial proceedings. It also analyses the rulings of the highest judicial body, the Federal Supreme Court, in terms of its influence in the federal sphere.

The Swiss state is highly federalist. The state is structured on three levels: the confederation, the twenty-six cantons, and around 2,324[1] municipalities. Subsidiarity is the defining principle in the division of powers among these orders of government. The confederation may assume a function only if that function exceeds cantonal powers or uniform regulation is required. Although a certain centralization trend may be observed, responsibility for executing federal law essentially remains with the cantons (commonly known as executive or administrative federalism). Within this structure, the cantons are largely autonomous both organizationally and financially. Moreover, the Federal Constitution (FC) expressly guarantees municipal autonomy under cantonal law. Despite this underlying federal structure, the functions of government and administration are increasingly being fulfilled through vertical and horizontal alliances (cooperative federalism) and the use of (financial) balancing mechanisms.

The judicial system also follows a federal pattern. The cantons have their own higher and lower courts with both criminal and civil

1 1 January 2015 (Swiss Federal Statistical Office). The number of municipalities is decreasing every year.

jurisdiction. Cases involving administrative decisions are often determined by cantonal administrative judicial authorities as courts of first instance below the upper courts, but the constitutional guarantee of legal recourse generally means that these decisions can be appealed to the Federal Supreme Court. There are also lower federal courts, whose decisions can generally also be appealed to the Federal Supreme Court. While codes of procedure for civil and criminal action were harmonized across all cantons in 2011, administrative proceedings are still subject to twenty-six separate cantonal ordinances, although these are becoming increasingly aligned. Each federal court has its own code of procedure. In contrast to most other European countries, the Federal Supreme Court does not exercise judicial review over federal legislation. Judges are generally appointed by the parliaments for a defined period of office, with party membership taken into account alongside professional capabilities. Switzerland attaches great importance to the independence of judges and the institutions they serve, even though the judiciary and the courts are also subject to democratic systems of checks and balances.

Complementing the regular legislative processes of the parliaments and the electorate, the Federal Supreme Court is the only court whose rulings shape the general development of Swiss law. This is illustrated clearly by the charter of fundamental rights that gradually came into being over several decades before being incorporated into the Federal Constitution when the latter underwent comprehensive revision in 1999. The Federal Supreme Court nonetheless respects the discretionary powers of the cantons as far as is possible. For example, it will declare cantonal norms to be unconstitutional only if it appears genuinely impossible to apply them in conformity with the Federal Constitution. Another illustration of the limited influence of the Federal Supreme Court on the application of law by the cantons is that the highest court in the land is essentially bound by facts established by the lower courts. Furthermore, where the interpretation and application of cantonal statute law are concerned, the Federal Supreme Court has the power only to sanction the arbitrary application of law by a canton. However, where federal or international law sets out clear (harmonization) requirements for the cantons, the Court unequivocally imposes these requirements. In the separation of powers that exists under the Swiss system, (federal) jurisdiction therefore also has an important function in the modern evolution of the balance between federalism and centralism. Yet a generalization of the impact is not possible. There is a slight unitarist tendency in the decisions of the Federal Supreme Court. But this might well be the result of a tendency to unitarism in federal legislation.

II. Federal System

1. Broad Characteristics

Some 8.24 million people live in Switzerland.[2] At 24.3 per cent, the country is home to one of the highest proportions of foreign nationals anywhere in Europe. Switzerland has four official national languages: 63.5 per cent of the population speaks German, 22.5 per cent French, 8.1 per cent Italian, and 0.5 per cent Romansh. The remaining 5.4 per cent of the Swiss population speaks a language other than these four. The four national languages are not distributed evenly across Switzerland, but instead form four distinct language regions, each with its own dominant language. Where religion is concerned, 38.2 per cent of the population is Roman Catholic and 26.9 per cent Protestant. The remainder of the population belongs to another religion (12.2 per cent) or to no religion (21.4 per cent). These religious differences were once closely linked to particular territories within Switzerland but are no longer especially significant.

GDP per capita was estimated at US$88,746 for 2015; based on purchasing power parity, the figure was put at US$49,497.[3] Among Western industrialized countries, Switzerland has one of the most uneven distributions of income and wealth, with tax on the assets held by the richest 3 per cent of the population equalling that paid on the assets belonging to the other 97 per cent.[4] In 2011, the wealthiest 20 per cent of society enjoyed incomes that were an average of 4.3 times higher than those of the lowest-income 20 per cent.[5] The Gini coefficient is 28.5.[6]

---

2 These statistics on population, language, and religion, as well as those given below, can be accessed at "Population," Swiss Federal Statistical Office, http://www.bfs.admin.ch/bfs/portal/en/index/themen/01.html.

3 International Monetary Fund, "World Economic Outlook Database," http://www.imf.org/external/pubs/ft/weo/2014/01/weodata/index.aspx.

4 See Ueli Mäder, Ganga Jay Aratnam, and Sarah Schilliger, *Wie Reiche denken und lenken. Reichtum in der Schweiz: Geschichte, Fakten, Gespräche* (Zurich: Rotpunktverlag, 2010).

5 For further information, see "Wirtschaftliche und soziale Situation der Bevölkerung," Panorama, http://www.bfs.admin.ch/bfs/portal/de/index/themen/20/01/pan.html.

6 Based on 2013 (Swiss Federal Statistical Office).

The federal system[7] consists of three orders of government, each with its own institutions. These are the confederation, the twenty-six cantons,[8] and 2,324 municipalities.[9] At each level, powers are generally divided among executive, legislative, and judicial bodies.[10] All cantons enjoy the same constitutional status, even though there are major differences in number of inhabitants, size of territory, and economic significance.[11] Each canton has its own constitution. The structure of the municipalities, which also vary significantly in size and population, differs from canton to canton and is governed by cantonal law.

The modern Swiss Confederation[12] was founded with the first federal constitution of 1848. It was based on a political compromise between the largely Protestant Liberals and the rural and largely Roman Catholic Conservatives. The confederation came about as a union of sovereign cantons, although the process of integration took several hundred years. Switzerland is not a nation in the conventional sense, but rather a nation forged by the Federal Constitution as an expression of political

---

7 For a summary of the federal system in Switzerland, see Adrian Vatter, "Föderalismus," in *Handbuch der Schweizer Politik*, ed. Peter Knoepfel, Yannis Papadopoulos, Pascal Sciarini, Adrian Vatter, and Silja Häusermann, 5th ed., 119–44 (Zürich: Neue Zürcher Zeitung, 2014); see also Adrian Vatter, *Das politische System der Schweiz* (Baden-Baden: Nomos, 2014), 427–75.

8 The confederation consists of twenty-three full cantons and six "half" cantons (Basel-Stadt, Basel-Land, Appenzell Ausserrhoden, Appenzell Innerrhoden, Obwalden, and Nidwalden). For historical reasons, the half-cantons' votes are only counted for half, and they have only one representative in the Council of States.

9 1 January 2015 (Swiss Federal Statistical Office); the number of municipalities is decreasing every year.

10 For a detailed description of Switzerland's federal institutions, see Wolf Linder and Isabelle Steffen, "Swiss Confederation," in *Legislative, Executive, and Judicial Governance in Federal Countries*, ed. Katy Le Roy and Cheryl Saunders, 298–315 (Montreal and Kingston: McGill-Queen's University Press, 2006).

11 For example, the population of Canton Zurich is 100 times that of Appenzell-Innerrhoden. In land area, the largest canton is Graubünden (Grisons), while the smallest is Basel-Stadt. Where economic differences are concerned, the urban cantons of Geneva and Basel, combined with the Zurich region, wield more financial power than the rest of Switzerland put together. Some rural and mountain regions are relatively poor by comparison.

12 Despite its official name, Switzerland is not a confederation but a classical federal state; see Thomas Fleiner, Alexander Misic, and Nicole Toepperwien, *Constitutional Law in Switzerland* (Alphen aan den Rijn: Kluwer Law International, 2012), 27. The old name "Confederation" has been preserved by the founders in 1848 in order not to destabilize voters who had to adopt the new constitution in a popular vote.

will (*Willensnation*) – albeit one that still insists that cultural, linguistic, and religious diversity be upheld.[13] Within a highly decentralized federal system, the cantons – as the constituent units of the confederation – have been able to maintain their original autonomy and their own constitutions, as well as to a large extent also their identities and differences. Furthermore, the constitutional power-sharing concept reflects a "bottom-up" approach to the structure of the confederation, which rests on the residual powers of the cantons and, in some cases, even those of the municipalities.[14]

Since modern Switzerland was founded, the Federal Constitution has undergone comprehensive revision only twice, in 1874 and 1999. The comprehensive revision of 1874, which did not fundamentally alter the Swiss system, was followed by more than 100 partial revisions, most of which were intended to strengthen the powers of the confederation. The latest Federal Constitution was approved by the Swiss people on 18 April 1999 and entered into force on 1 January 2000.[15] This version is essentially an update,[16] which contains no underlying changes. One significant amendment, however, was the inclusion in the new Federal Constitution of the comprehensive charter of fundamental rights (Arts. 7 to 34). This charter was shaped to a considerable extent by the practices of the Federal Supreme Court. Furthermore, the new Federal Constitution marked a shift from "self-rule" towards the principle of "shared rule."[17] It centralized a variety of originally cantonal powers and strengthened those of the confederation, yet offered the cantons greater opportunities to participate in confederation decision-making

---

13 Nicolas Schmitt, "Swiss Confederation," in *Constitutional Origins, Structure, and Change in Federal Countries*, ed. John Kincaid and G. Alan Tarr (Montreal and Kingston: McGill-Queen's University Press, 2005), 376. For further information on diversity in Switzerland, see Thomas Fleiner, *The Current Situation of Federalism in Switzerland*, REAF, no. 9 (2009), 51–90 and Thomas Fleiner and Maya Hertig, "Swiss Confederation," in *Diversity and Unity in Federal Countries*, ed. Luis Moreno and Cesar Colino, 320–48 (Montreal and Kingston: McGill-Queen's University Press, 2010).

14 Thomas Fleiner, "Swiss Confederation," in *Distribution of Powers and Responsibilities in Federal Countries*, ed. Akhtar Majeed, Ronald L. Watts, and Douglas M. Brown (Montreal and Kingston: McGill-Queen's University Press, 2006), 267.

15 The Swiss Federal Constitution can be accessed at https://www.admin.ch/opc/en/classified-compilation/19995395/index.html. Unless stated otherwise, "Art." references in this chapter refer to articles in the Federal Constitution of 1999.

16 See Fleiner, Misic, and Toepperwien, *Constitutional Law in Switzerland*, 31.

17 Fleiner, *Current Situation of Federalism in Switzerland*, 82–3.

processes (such as those concerning foreign policy matters).[18] The Swiss political system has thus remained largely unaltered since 1848. However, there has been one important territorial change since then: 1979 saw the foundation of Canton Jura when the French-speaking Catholic part of Canton Bern broke away from the largely German-speaking Protestant part.[19] Furthermore, it is worth mentioning the partial revision concerning the restructuring of the financial equalization system between the cantons, and the distribution of functions between the confederation and the cantons. This revision, which entered into force on 1 January 2008, represents real reform in the federal system.[20] One of its central elements is fiscal equivalence, in which the purposes, costs, and benefits of policies must be aligned in the way in which the tasks of government are financed.[21] It is also worth mentioning the trend in recent years towards municipalities merging into larger units to enable them to perform their functions more effectively.

Federalism is an important element of consensus (or concordance) democracy in Switzerland, which is characterized by political power-sharing.[22] Direct democracy is another central feature. In addition to appointing their representatives in regular elections, the people play a direct part in political decision-making through referenda and popular initiatives. As such, the people are part of the legislative process in the federal system. It is the people – and not parliament or the courts – who make the most important decisions.[23]

The Swiss people are proud of their political institutions. Federalism is seen as one of Switzerland's strongest symbolic values. The federal system has made it possible peacefully to bridge the country's cultural, religious, and linguistic divides. There is criticism from some quarters

---

18 Ibid., 83.

19 For more detail, see Wolf Linder, *Swiss Democracy: Possible Solutions to Conflict in Multicultural Societies*, 3rd ed. (New York: Palgrave Macmillan, 2010), 72; Andreas Kley, *Geschichte des öffentlichen Rechts der Schweiz* (Zurich: Dike, 2011).

20 In detail, "Grundlagen," https://www.efv.admin.ch/efv/de/home/themen/finanzausgleich/uebersicht.html.

21 Andreas Lienhard and Agata Zielniewicz, "Finanzverfassung," in *Schweizerisches Bundesverwaltungsrecht (SBVR)* (Basel: Helbling Lichtenhahn, 2011), 10:1, 30–1.

22 See Linder, *Swiss Democracy*, 128.

23 Linder and Steffen, "Swiss Confederation," 291. See also, in general, Arnold Koller, Daniel Thürer, Bernard Dafflon, Bernhard Ehrenzeller, Thomas Pfisterer, and Bernhard Waldmann, *Principles of Federalism, Guidelines for Good Federal Practices: A Swiss Contribution, Swiss Law in a Nutshell* (Zurich: Dike, 2012).

that the cantons are too small to be efficient service-providers, but the proposal to reduce the number of cantons is unlikely to succeed. Cantonal autonomy and self-determination are much-vaunted principles and would prove a significant obstacle to any such institutional reforms.

2. *Structural Features*

The Federal Constitution guarantees the existence of the cantons in Article 1 of the Federal Constitution, which lists the cantons, and Article 53, according to which the confederation must protect both the existence and the territory of the cantons.[24] In addition, Article 3 guarantees cantonal sovereignty to the extent that it is not limited by the Federal Constitution. Legislation and administration are the responsibility of the confederation only where it is granted such powers by the Federal Constitution; otherwise they fall within the competence of the cantons (Art. 3 and Arts. 42–43a). The division of powers between the confederation and the cantons is laid down by area under the third title of the Federal Constitution (Arts. 54–124). Furthermore, the Federal Constitution contains general rules on cooperation between the confederation and the cantons (Arts. 42–53, 126–35) and guarantees to the cantons, among other things, a high degree of organizational autonomy (Art. 46, para. 2, and Art. 47, para. 2). The cantons enjoy considerable legislative, organizational, and financial autonomy and have the right to their own systems of democracy, government, and justice. Their constitutions must nonetheless be guaranteed by the confederation (i.e., they must be approved by the United Federal Assembly[25] if the cantonal constitution is not contrary to federal law[26]) and must thus uphold federal law and democracy (Art. 51). The confederation must also protect the constitutional order of the cantons (Art. 52).

Because the cantons have the authority to organize themselves, there are significant differences in the scope of municipal powers from canton to canton. Article 50, paragraph 1 guarantees the autonomy of the municipalities, but this guarantee is contingent upon the autonomy that those municipalities are granted by their individual cantonal

---

24 See Walter Haller, *The Swiss Constitution in a Comparative Context* (Zurich: Dike, 2009), 50.

25 The joint meetings of the National Council and the Council of State are named the United Federal Assembly.

26 See Fleiner, Misic, and Toepperwien, *Constitutional Law in Switzerland*, 166; see also n95.

constitutions.[27] Article 50 also states that the confederation must take account of the possible consequences of its policies for municipalities, as well as for cities, conurbations, and mountain regions. An infringement of municipal autonomy may ultimately be taken before the Federal Supreme Court as the court of last instance (Art. 198, para. 1).

The high degree of autonomy enjoyed by the cantons and localities places a practical and effective limit on the extension of confederation powers.[28] As mentioned earlier, the principle of subsidiarity dictates that the confederation should fulfil only those functions that cannot be performed effectively by the cantons or municipalities (Art. 5a, 43a, para. 1).

The confederation's powers are specified by the Federal Constitution. All residual powers remain with the cantons. According to Article 3, the cantons exercise all rights that are not vested explicitly in the Confederation. Depending on the density of regulation, this covers different types of power – exclusive, parallel, and partial.[29] There are no generally valid criteria for drawing the line between federal and cantonal powers. In many areas, power is exercised in a form of alliances between the confederation, the cantons, and the local authorities (see in particular Art. 48 and Art. 48a).[30]

Foreign affairs are the responsibility of the confederation (Art. 54). However, the cantons can participate in foreign policy decisions where these affect their own powers or essential interests. The confederation must also inform the cantons in good time and consult with them (Art. 55). Indeed, according to Article 56, the cantons may conclude treaties with foreign states on matters that lie within their powers.

---

27 See Haller, *Swiss Constitution in a Comparative Context*, 48.

28 Linder, *Swiss Democracy*, 47.

29 See Haller, *Swiss Constitution in a Comparative Context*, 59-60. Exclusive competencies of the confederation mean that only the federal parliament may legislate, and the execution is with the federal administration. With partial competencies the cantons may legislate as far as the federal parliament does not do this. As to parallel competencies, there is a complete separation of jurisdiction, and the confederation and the cantons are independent in legislation in their jurisdiction (e.g., legislation on the organization of the administration).

30 The following summarizes the allocation of powers in certain areas. For a detailed and comprehensive description of the allocation of powers, see Haller, *Swiss Constitution in a Comparative Context*, 65; for a table listing how powers are distributed, see also Linder, *Swiss Democracy*, 46; Fleiner, "Swiss Confederation," 288; Fleiner, Misic, and Toepperwien, *Constitutional Law in Switzerland*, 131.

The confederation and the cantons together are responsible for national security and for protecting the population (Arts. 57–61). The specific responsibilities of the confederation include external security (the armed forces), while large parts of the internal security remit (the police) fall within the authority of the cantons.

All three orders of government (confederation, cantons, and municipalities) may levy taxes, but the confederation's tax powers are limited under the Constitution. The authority to levy taxes is an important power for the cantons and the municipalities, as they determine more than two-thirds of their own income and expenditure. Nonetheless, the confederation must promote financial equalization between the cantons (Art. 128).[31]

Basic schooling falls within the authority of the cantons, while vocational training is governed by the confederation, and higher education is the joint responsibility of the confederation and cantons.[32] Culture and language are cantonal matters, but the confederation must support cultural activities that are in the national interest and also help to preserve Switzerland's linguistic diversity. The Federal Constitution also guarantees religious freedom, but the cantons may decide independently on the relationship between church and state (Art. 72). The cantons many also exercise broad discretion in health care.

The examples given above illustrate the close cooperation among the three levels of the federal system. This is sometimes referred to as "cooperative federalism."[33] Article 44, paragraph 1 requires the confederation and the cantons to support each other in fulfilling their duties and generally to cooperate with each other. Disputes between cantons, as well as between cantons and the confederation should, where possible, be resolved by negotiation and mediation (Art. 44, para. 3). The Federal Supreme Court makes any judicial decisions that may be required (Art. 189, para. 2). In contrast to other federal states, however, disputes between cantons and the confederation are rarely resolved through the courts, but rather by negotiation or by amendments to laws and constitutions.[34] In this sense, the federal government must consult the cantonal governments on all important matters and, in particular, on proposed legislative decisions (Art. 45).

31 Lienhard and Zielniewicz, "Finanzverfassung," 10:38.
32 Fleiner, "Current Situation of Federalism in Switzerland," 57.
33 Lienhard and Zielniewicz, "Finanzverfassung," 10:33.
34 Fleiner, "Swiss Confederation," 276.

Federal law is implemented largely by the cantons ("executive federalism"[35]) (Art. 46). Within this system, the confederation allows the cantons the greatest possible freedom of action, supports them financially, and respects their individuality. The implementation of federal law by the cantons therefore relies to a considerable extent on the cantons' political will. Furthermore, Article 47 requires the confederation to respect the autonomy of the cantons. Article 49 is also important here, in that it determines that every type or form of federal law takes precedence over any conflicting provision in cantonal law; even the statutory instruments of the Federal Council take precedence over cantonal law. The confederation is also responsible for ensuring that the cantons comply with federal law.

The allocation of powers laid down in the Constitution is conclusive.[36] Cantonal powers are guaranteed by the Constitution to the extent that they cannot simply be transferred by law to the Confederation. New powers for the confederation can be conferred only by means of a formal constitutional amendment. Such an amendment requires both a majority in both chambers of the federal parliament (National Council and Council of States) and the approval of the majority of the people and the cantons (i.e., the majority of the electorate in at least twelve cantons). Constitutional amendments may be initiated by members of the Federal Assembly (parliament), the Federal Council (executive), the cantons (cantonal initiative), or by 100,000 members of the electorate (popular initiative). The processes of direct democracy lend broad legitimacy to such changes and ensure widespread acceptance of their implementation. In contrast to other federal states, the courts do not play a significant role in decisions on the distribution of power based on how the Constitution is interpreted.[37]

The Council of States is an important institution that allows the cantons to represent their interests and influence the decisions of the confederation.[38] Alongside the National Council, which represents the people, the Council of States is the second chamber of the United Federal Assembly. Both chambers hold the same status. With the exception

---

35 With regard to executive federalism, see also Haller, *Swiss Constitution in a Comparative Context* 57; and Fleiner, "Swiss Confederation," 278–9.

36 Haller, *Swiss Constitution in a Comparative Context*, 60.

37 Fleiner, "Swiss Confederation," 267–8.

38 With regard to the organization of confederation authorities, see also Axel Tschentscher and Andreas Lienhard, *Öffentliches Recht: Ein Grundriss* (Zurich: Dike, 2011).

of the six "half cantons," each canton is represented equally in the Council of States, irrespective of its size and population. The council comprises two members from each full canton and one member from each half canton (i.e., forty-six members in total). Because all parliamentary decisions require a majority in both chambers, the small and generally rural cantons have a strong voice. Each canton determines its own procedure for elections to the Council of States. Members of the council are elected directly by the people in all cantons, usually by the majority first-past-the-post system. The Conference of Cantonal Governments (KdK)[39] and the various conferences of cantonal directors also play an important role in the federal system.[40]

III. Court System

1. General Features

The court system reflects the federal structure of the state and has a distinct hierarchy.[41] The cantonal lower and upper courts (first and second instance) usually enforce both cantonal and federal law. In line with this structure, a judgment by one of the cantonal courts may generally be taken before the Federal Supreme Court, as the highest judicial authority in the land.[42] This system is flanked by the Federal Administrative Court, the Federal Criminal Court, and the Federal Patent Court. These three Courts are generally responsible as courts of first instance in their particular fields for hearing legal disputes under federal law, which is

---

39 The Conference of Cantonal Governments (KdK) was created only in 1993 and plays an important role for the lobbying of cantonal interests. As far as federalism is concerned, it is the symbol of a certain "rebirth" of the cantons at the turn of the century, because the Council of State does not play its role very well. The KdK also plays a certain role in preserving the coherence of the cantonal politics and preventing the mighty sectoral politics of the huge number of sectoral cantonal conferences.

40 See Haller, *Swiss Constitution in a Comparative Context*, 84.

41 For a summary of the Swiss judicial system, see Christine Rothmayr Allison and Frederic Varone, "Justiz," in *Handbuch der Schweizer Politik*, ed. Peter Knoepfel, Yannis Papadopoulos, Pascal Sciarini, Adrian Vatter, and Silja Häusermann, 5th ed., 219–41 (Zürich: Verlag Neue Zürcher Zeitung, 2014); Vatter, *Das politische System der Schweiz* (Baden-Baden: Nomos, 2014), 477–517.

42 With regard to the Federal Supreme Court, see Alain Wurzburger, *Le Tribunal fédéral: Comprendre son fonctionnement, agir devant ses juges* (Geneva: Schulthess, 2011).

applied directly by federal authorities.[43] An important element of the federal state is the option under the Constitution for disputes between the different levels of the state, as well as between the constituent states, to be heard before a court. The Swiss Federal Constitution provides explicitly that the Federal Supreme Court may rule directly on disputes between the confederation and cantons or between cantons (Art. 189, para. 2).[44] Municipalities are also able to take violations of their constitutionally guaranteed autonomy before the Federal Supreme Court by lodging an official, authority-level complaint.[45]

The system of law is based essentially on the laws enacted by federal, cantonal, and municipal legislators. The principal task of the courts is therefore to interpret the law as it relates to individual cases. Most courts sit as a bench of three or five judges, although certain legal proceedings are often heard by a single judge. Usually the bench passes judgment according to the majority principle. It sets out its decision in writing, supported by a legal argument. The formal written judgments of the courts usually do not include dissenting opinions,[46] what are subject to an actual debate.[47] The central role and sometimes significant responsibility of the legally trained clerks of the court are important. Clerks of the court support the judges in their judgments. In contrast to the majority of other countries, their function extends beyond

---

43 The courts of first instance at the federal level were established with the justice reform adopted in 2007. For an evaluation of the new legal system's effectiveness, see Andreas Lienhard, Stefan Rieder, Martin Killias, Christof Schwenkel, Sophie Nunweiler, and Andreas Müller, *Evaluation der Wirksamkeit der neuen Bundesrechtspflege* (Bern: KPM/Interface/Universität Zürich, 2012).

44 See also 2.2 above.

45 This right is laid down in Article 189 paragraph 1e of the Swiss Federal Constitution of 18 April 1999 (FC, SR 101); see also Linder, *Swiss Democracy*, 57–8; Haller, *Swiss Constitution in a Comparative Context*, 48.

46 However, academic opinion in some quarters advocates the introduction of such "dissenting opinions," at least at the highest judicial level. See also Peter Studer, "Medien, Gerichte und Kritik an Gerichten," in *Akteure der Gerichtsbarkeit*, ed. Benjamin Schindler and Patrick Sutter (Zurich: Dike, 2007), 361, with reference to Rainer J. Schweizer and Patrick Sutter, "Das Institut der abweichenden oder zustimmenden Richtermeinung im System der EMRK," in *Strafrecht, Strafprozessrecht und Menschenrechte*, ed. Andreas Donatsch, Marc Forster, and Christian Schwarzenegger (Zurich: Schulthess, 2002), 107.

47 See Arnold Marti, "Offenlegen von Minderheitsmeinungen [dissenting opinion] – eine Forderung von Transparenz und Fairness im gerichtlichen Verfahren," *Justice – Justiz – Giustizia* 4 (2012).

administrative tasks. As a rule, they draft the judgments, are consulted in an advisory capacity, and it is often they, not the judges, who produce or finalize the written judgment.[48]

In principle, the courts are bound by their own decisions and the decisions and legal analysis of superior courts if a case is referred back to them for re-evaluation. The findings established in court judgments – especially those of the Federal Supreme Court – are usually taken into account in subsequent cases. However, the courts are not bound by prior judgments, and past judicial practices may be amended by rulings made in contradiction of set precedents.[49]

2. *Constitutional Status of Courts and Judicial Officers*

The Federal Constitution provides the foundation and legitimation for the Federal Supreme Court and the confederation's judicial authorities of first instance. The Constitution obliges the cantons to set up courts to determine disputes under civil and public law, as well as in criminal cases. As part of their organizational autonomy, the cantons can make provision concerning their own cantonal courts.[50] However, authority to make laws with respect to civil and criminal procedure passed from the cantons to the confederation in 2011, and corresponding codes now prescribe norms of procedure for all cantons.[51]

A peculiarity of the Swiss system is the absence of any judicial review of the constitutionality of federal laws. As a result, the Federal Supreme Court must apply federal laws even if it judges them to be

---

48 See Peter Uebersax, "Stellung der Gerichtsschreiberinnen und Gerichtsschreiber in der Gerichtsverfassung," in *Akteure der Gerichtsbarkeit*, ed. Benjamin Schindler and Patrick Sutter, 77–114 (Zurich: Dike, 2007).

49 In contrast to the common law context, in Switzerland the word *precedent* does not mean a previous decision, which is strictly binding. Precedents are court decisions that are considered by the courts as important "landmarks" and are usually published in a particular manner (the precedents of the Federal Supreme Court are labelled as "BGE").

50 See also Andreas Lienhard, Daniel Kettiger, and Daniela Winkler, "Status of Court Management in Switzerland," *International Journal for Court Administration*, Special Issue December 2012, 4. For an overview of the Swiss courts, see Peter Bieri, "Die Gerichte der Schweiz: Eine Übersicht," *Justice – Justiz – Giustizia* 2 (2014).

51 The Federal Codes of Civil Procedure and Criminal Procedure entered into force on 1 January 2011. They are based on the judicial reform of 8 October 1999, which was adopted by the Swiss people and the cantons on 12 March 2000. By contrast, no standardization is planned in the laws on administrative procedure.

unconstitutional. The same applies to Federal Council ordinances, as well as to cantonal decrees issued on the basis of authority granted by unconstitutional federal legislation. This limitation on the courts is laid down in the Federal Constitution (Art. 190). It is founded on the fear that the rescission of parliamentary decrees by the Federal Supreme Court might turn the latter into a political body and is therefore legitimized by the separation of powers.[52] Consistent with this view is the fact that Switzerland does not have a federal-level constitutional court either.[53] The Federal Supreme Court is nonetheless permitted to examine the constitutionality of cantonal laws and ordinances, both in specific cases (i.e., relating to individual elements of law in their application to particular cases) and in relation to abstract judicial review (i.e., relating to procedure).[54] However, the Court will declare cantonal norms to be unconstitutional only if it appears impossible to apply them in conformity with the Federal Constitution.

The way in which judges are appointed is another unique characteristic of the Swiss court system. At the federal level, and in the cantons to some extent, any member of the electorate is eligible in principle to be appointed as a judge. This makes possible the appointment to judicial office of lay people without any form of legal training. In practice, lay judges are usually appointed only to courts of first instance. Also in contrast to other European states, Switzerland has no form of systematic judicial training. In the cantons, judges are generally elected by the people or by the cantonal parliament respecting the principle of proportional representation (i.e., all major political parties represented in the parliament shall be represented in the same way, at least in the courts of appeal). The judges of the Federal Supreme Court and of the three other confederation courts are appointed by the federal parliament. This makes it almost impossible to be elected as a judge without the support of a political party, and party membership is virtually a prerequisite. In view of this electoral system and the

---

52 See Art. 189, para. 4, and Art. 190.

53 See Haller, *Swiss Constitution in a Comparative Context*, 245–6. A recent attempt to introduce a review of constitutional jurisdiction as part of parliamentary consultations has not been supported by the parliament (see Parliamentary Initiatives 07.476 and 05.445). This was not the first attempt to introduce constitutional jurisdiction; see W.J. Wagner, *The Federal State and Their Judiciaries* (Gravenhage: Mouton, 1959), 105–6.

54 See Haller, *Swiss Constitution in a Comparative Context*, 247.

requirements for election, political criteria play the decisive role in the appointment of judges.[55] Sex, language, origin, and religion, in addition to legal expertise and party allegiance are considered when a judge is proposed for election. As long as their personal independence remains assured, nothing bars the election of these candidates progressing up to a higher court. Realistically, however, the career paths of lay judges are limited by the fact that upper cantonal and federal courts increasingly employ trained lawyers. Furthermore, a move to a court in another canton or promotion to the Federal Supreme Court may be hampered by the need to secure the party support that is essential for appointment.

The guarantee that the courts and the judges who sit in them are independent is nonetheless one of the fundamental constitutional principles of the rule of law in Switzerland.[56] This principle encompasses the functional, personal, and organizational independence of the courts.[57] It also includes the budgetary autonomy that applies to federal and cantonal courts – albeit to differing degrees. For example, the Federal Supreme Court benefits from a global budget and has the competence to prepare and to apply it to parliament directly.[58] Judicial independence also means the independence of the courts and their judges from external influences such as pressure from other authorities or the media. If just and fair proceedings are rendered impossible by such impairments to judicial independence (e.g., by the media, the government, or the parliament), they may be challenged by those concerned. The influence that the political parties wield over the electoral system for judges in Switzerland should also be mentioned in

---

55 For more details, see Martin Ziegler, "Laienrichterinnen und -richter," in *Akteure der Gerichtsbarkeit*, ed. Benjamin Schindler and Patrick Sutter (Zurich: Dike, 2007), 65; Rainer Klopfer, "Management in der Justiz: Richterbild im Wandel," *Justice – Justiz – Giustizia*, 2007/2; Walter Bosshart, *Die Wählbarkeit zum Richter im Bund und in den Kantonen* (Zurich: Schellenberg, 1961).

56 On judicial independence, see Regina Kiener, *Richterliche Unabhängigkeit, Verfassungsrechtliche Anforderungen an Richter und Gerichte* (Bern: Stämpfli, 2001).

57 Art. 30, para. 1, and Art. 191c.

58 With regard to judicial independence, see Andreas Lienhard, "Die Bernische Gerichtsbarkeit auf dem Weg zur Selbstverwaltung," in *Bernische Verwaltungsgerichtsbarkeit in Geschichte und Gegenwart, 100 Jahre Verwaltungsgericht des Kantons Bern*, ed. Ruth Herzog and Reto Feller (Bern: Geiger, 2010), 401; Hans Wipfli, "Justizielle Selbstverwaltung," in *Akteure der Gerichtsbarkeit*, ed. Benjamin Schindler and Patrick Sutter (Zurich: Dike, 2007), 116.

relation with the independence of judges. Unlike the United States, judges in Switzerland are not, in principle, appointed for life. Most of the cantons and the confederation provide for a limited term of office, and judges have to be reappointed if their official position is to continue. A political party that disagrees with decisions of a judge they have supported can threaten the judge with withdrawal of support.[59] Once a judge is elected, however, party politics usually cease to be a major issue. Furthermore, the public perception is that judges are independent.

In addition to the division of powers, the judiciary has a system of checks and balances to prevent the abuse of judicial power. The supervisory body overseeing the courts of first instance in the cantons is often the cantonal court or the upper court, with the court of second instance itself supervised by the cantonal parliament. Responsibility for the overall supervision of the Federal Supreme Court and the other judicial authorities of the confederation lies with the national parliament. In view of the institutional autonomy of the justice system, this supervision is administrative and does not permit the supervisory authorities to rescind or amend court judgments.[60]

3. *Institutional Role of the Courts*

In the cantons, the district courts (*Bezirksgerichte*, or *Kreisgerichte* in the case of cities) are competent to rule as the body of first instance on civil and criminal matters, while the governments or governmental authorities are responsible as the body of first instance in the administrative judicature. In addition to the court of first instance, the cantons are obliged by federal law to constitute a court of second instance, or upper court, for all civil and criminal matters. In the public law arena, the cantonal administrative courts and social insurance courts serve as the courts of lower instance before recourse to the Federal Supreme Court is sought. However, in most cantons, this structure is supported by a number of specialist judicial tribunals such as the commercial courts,

---

59 Martin Kayser, "Richterwahlen: Unabhängigkeit im Spannungsfeld von Rechtsstaatlichkeit und Demokratie," in *Akteure der Gerichtsbarkeit*, ed. Benjamin Schindler and Patrick Sutter (Zurich: Dike, 2007), 46.

60 Andreas Lienhard, "Supervisory Control and Court Management," *International Journal for Court Administration* 3 (August 2009): 30–45; Kiener, *Richterliche Unabhängigkeit*, 296–7, 299.

juvenile courts, financial courts, and family courts.[61] It is mandatory for civil cases to be heard by an arbitration body before action is taken before the court of first instance. In recent years, the confederation has set up its own specialist judicial authorities with the Federal Administrative Court (2007), the Federal Criminal Court (2004), and the Federal Patent Court (2012).

Unlike the cantonal courts and the federal courts of first instance, the Federal Supreme Court, as the highest court, does not usually re-establish the facts of a given case. As an appellate court, the Federal Supreme Court is limited to examining questions of law.[62] In addition to examining specific cases, the Federal Supreme Court and other relevant federal judicial authorities may state their position in hearings and consultations on federal parliament bills that concern proceedings before the Federal Supreme Court or other federal judicial authorities, as well as the status, organization, and administration of these bodies. As long as they do not prejudice an ongoing case, judges are also entitled to exercise their right to freedom of speech by offering academic opinions on legal or judicial policy issues.

The courts must observe the principles laid down in the Federal Constitution, such as democracy, federalism, and fundamental rights. The confederation and the cantons also must respect international law (Art. 5, para. 4, Art. 190). The Constitution does not explicitly govern the relationship between federal and international law in the event of conflicting provisions. According to Federal Supreme Court precedent, however, provisions under international law that protect human rights, at least, must be given precedence on a case-by-case basis over provisions of federal law.[63] That said, even if a federal law is found to infringe the principle of federalism, it must still be applied by the court, despite its unconstitutionality (see 3.2).[64] With respect to the federal system, mention should be made of the judicial restraint exercised in the

---

61 Further information in Raphaël Arn, Nicole Saurer, and André Kuhn, eds., *Organisation der kantonalen und eidgenössischen Strafbehörden und strafrechtliche Ausführungsbestimmungen* (Basel: Helbing Lichtenhahn, 2011); René A. Rhinow, *Öffentliches Prozessrecht* (Basel: Helbing Lichtenhahn, 2010); Thomas Sutter-Somm, Franz Hasenböhler, and Christoph Leuenberger, eds., *Kommentar zur Schweizerischen Zivilprozessordnung (ZPO)* (Zurich: Schulthess, 2010).

62 See also Tschentscher and Lienhard, *Öffentliches Recht*, 295–6.

63 See Alexander R. Ziegler, *Einführung in das Völkerrecht*, 3rd ed. (Bern: Stämpfli, 2015), 122.

64 See Haller, *Swiss Constitution in a Comparative Context*, 245.

examination by appellate bodies of decisions made by courts of lower instance where such decisions concern cantonal autonomy. It is deemed appropriate, in the event of doubt, for the appellate body to uphold the opinion and conclusions of the highest cantonal court in matters that fall within the scope of cantonal autonomy.[65]

4. Curial Procedures

Procedures and procedural requirements differ across the fields of law. In civil law, the parties themselves decide whether they wish to take their dispute to court; in public law, the decision on whether to prosecute lies with the public prosecuting authorities.

The Swiss courts act only when the individuals or authorities concerned demand judicial examination of a particular matter. This also applies to disputes between the different orders of government, which may be heard before the Federal Supreme Court. Such disputes often concern conflicts relating specifically to law-making authority and to the application of the law, as well as disputes under civil or public law. The latter include boundary disputes, breaches of the guarantee of existence and territory, conflicts relating to loyalty to the confederation, disputes arising from inter-cantonal agreements or treaties between the confederation and the cantons (Art. 48, Abs. 2). Action may be brought by cantonal or federal authorities. Consequently, private individuals and political parties may not institute such proceedings, although their participation is not ruled out.[66]

Depending on the nature of the decision, a number of instruments are available to authorities to enforce a final court ruling. Decisions relating to payments may be enforced by a compulsory order under

---

65 See also Yvo Hangartner, "Behördenrechtliche Kognitionsbeschränkung in der Verwaltungsrechtspflege," in *Mélanges en l'honneur de Pierre Moor, Théorie du droit – Droit administratif – Organisation du territoire*, ed. Bovay Benoît and Minh Son Nguyen (Bern: Stämpfli, 2005), 319, 328–9.

66 Hansjörg Seiler, Nicolas von Werdt, and Andreas Güngerich, *Bundesgerichtsgesetz (BGG), Bundesgesetz über das Bundesgericht* (Bern: Stämpfli, 2007), Art. 120; Marcel Alexander Niggli, Peter Uebersax, and Hans Wiprächtiger, *Bundesgerichtsgesetz, Basler Kommentar*, 2nd ed. (Basel: Helbing & Lichtenhahn, 2011), Art. 120. See also Heinz Aemisegger and André Jomini, "Der Föderalismus in der Rechtsprechung des Bundesgerichts," in *1. Nationale Föderalismuskonferenz, Der kooperative Föderalismus vor neuen Herausforderungen*, ed. Bernhard Waldmann, Institute of Federalism (Basel: Helbing & Lichtenhahn, 2005), 173.

debt and insolvency law. The cantons determine the procedures for enforcing penalties and measures, as does the confederation within the particular scope of its authority.

The Federal Constitution guarantees that court proceedings and written judgments are public, although legislators may provide for exceptions to this rule (Art. 30, para. 3). The public and the media may be excluded from court hearings where necessitated by overriding interests, such as public order and safety or the protection of an individual's privacy. Judgments must be made public in all cases without exception, however. The decisions of the Federal Supreme Court, as well as many of those handed down by cantonal courts – at least of second instance – are available on the Internet.

5. *Judicial Culture*

Statute law – which provides the foundation of the Swiss system of law – takes precedence, even if the wording of the law is not entirely clear and the sense of the norm requires interpretation. If no rule can be inferred from the interpretation of the written statutes, then this legal loophole must be closed by invoking common (customary) law. The courts themselves have only a subsidiary role in the development of law. Compared with countries with a common-law system, case law in Switzerland is much less significant in the law's evolution.

When establishing the meaning of a legal norm, the courts pay particular attention to its grammatical, systematic, historical, and teleological interpretation. These four methods of interpretation are not applied according to a fixed order of precedence but, in keeping with the plurality approach, will be more or less relevant to the meaning of the norm, depending on the situation. The various methods of interpretation must therefore be applied in a careful balance. This limits interpretive inventiveness. Moreover, the constitutionality of the resulting interpretation must also be taken into account. This interpretive process must be applied to all fields of law, even to legal action before the Federal Supreme Court in disputes over authority between the confederation and the cantons. However, in areas in which the Federal Supreme Court has a consistent, published practice, it will no longer interpret the law in individual cases, but instead be guided by its prior landmark rulings.[67]

---

67 See Hansjörg Seiler, *Praktische Rechtsanwendung* (Bern: Stämpfli, 2009), 4.

III. Jurisprudence under Federalism

1. *General Tendencies*

The structure of the federal state is deeply rooted in the Federal Constitution (see II.2). Alongside the parliament, which must respect the constitutional framework when enacting new federal legislation, the Federal Supreme Court plays in a historical context a central role as the guardian of federalism: since 1874 the adjudication of disputes between the federation and the cantons has always been a primary duty of the court (Art. 189, para. 2).[68] The importance of the Federal Supreme Court is all the greater because its rulings display a high degree of consistency. In the federal context, the rulings of the lower Federal Administrative Court, Federal Criminal Court, and Federal Patent Court tend to be of lesser importance. Indeed, as relatively recent additions to the judicial system, their practices have yet to become properly established. The rulings of the cantonal courts have also had little impact on federalism.[69] That said, the judgments of the cantonal courts of highest instance may have had some bearing on

---

68 See Haller, *Swiss Constitution in a Comparative Context*, 141. This role of the Federal Supreme Court has to be seen in a historical context; see Jakob Dubs, *Das öffentliche Recht der Schweizerischen Eidgenossenschaft*, Zweiter Teil (Zurich: Orell Füssli, 1878), 72. In Article 113 of the old Federal Constitution of 1874 the adjudication of disputes between the federation and the cantons ranks number 1, the adjudication of conflicts among the cantons number 2, all before the ruling over violation of constitutional rights. See also Walter Burckhardt, *Kommentar der schweizerischen Bundesverfassung vom 29. Mai 1874*, 3rd ed. (Bern: Stämpfli, 1931), Art. 113, 771; Zaccaria Giacometti and Fritz Fleiner, *Schweizerisches Bundesstaatsrecht* (Zurich: Polygraphischer Verlag, 1949), 834–5: "So erscheint es naheliegend, dass das Bundesgericht die mit der bundesstaatlichen Struktur des Landes im Zusammenhang stehenden Streitigkeiten, d.h. Kompetenzkonflikte zwischen Bundesbehörden und kantonalen Behörden sowie Streitigkeiten zwischen Kantonen zu beurteilen hat" (Therefore it seems obvious that the Federal Supreme Court has to adjudicate the disputes related to the federal structure of the country, such as conflicts of competence between the federal authorities and cantonal authorities or disputes between cantons; translation by authors).

69 See also Arnold Marti, "Die Bedeutung der EMRK in der Rechtsprechung der kantonalen Gerichte – am Beispiel des Kantons Schaffhausen," in *Die Europäische Menschenrechtskonvention und die Kantone*, ed. Samantha Besson and Eva Maria Belser (Genf: Schulthess, 2014), 95.

municipal autonomy, in particular with regard to the delineation of responsibilities between the local and cantonal authorities.[70]

2. *Specific Issues*

A. FUNDAMENTAL PRINCIPLES OF FEDERALISM

Article 3 of the Federal Constitution states that the cantons are sovereign to the extent that their sovereignty is not limited by the Federal Constitution.[71] They exercise all rights that are not vested in the confederation. The cantons decide on the duties that they must fulfil within the scope of their powers (Art. 43). The Federal Supreme Court invokes this particular article only in rare cases, even though it regularly examines whether the confederation or the cantons have authority over a specific area, and whether they have exercised the powers incumbent upon them (this does not interfere with the principle that the court does not exercise constitutional judicial review over federal laws). Numerous examples can be given.[72]

For instance, the Federal Supreme Court has decided that federal legislation on animal welfare does not prevent the cantons from issuing police

70 For example, in its judgment B 2010/45 of 14 October 2010, the Administrative Court of St Gallen examined whether and to what extent the Cantonal Works Department may issue instructions to the municipalities, which are responsible for building inspectors, on enforcement of planning permission. In this case, it held that municipal autonomy had not been infringed. Meanwhile, in case B 2011/9, the same court held, "Municipal autonomy, in the form of the issue of a municipal schedule of criteria, is restricted to third-class municipal roads which serve fewer than ten permanently inhabited residential units, provided the requirements of the Roads Act and the Circular on the Enforcement of the Roads Act of 22 November 1988 are observed." In a judgment related to the law of administrative procedure, which falls within cantonal jurisdiction, the Administrative Court of Aarau determined that a referral back to the municipality with strict and specific instructions to make revisions was not consistent with cantonal buildings legislation because the local authorities' decision-making freedom must be maintained even where an application is rejected (AGVE 72 278).

71 BGE 2C_76/2015 E. 3.2.2 (foreseen for publication in the official compilation of the decisions of the Federal Supreme Court); BGE 140 I 176 E. 7.1; BGE 140 I 218 E. 5.4; BGE 138 I 435 E. 3.4.1: General reminder of the principle of Art. 3 Federal Constitution in recent cases regarding tax law, public health.

72 These examples are all drawn from the official compilation of the decisions of the Federal Supreme Court (BGE). These can be accessed at www.bger.ch, under "Rechtsprechung"). For further detail, see also Heinz Aemisegger and André Jomini, "Le fédéralisme dans la jurisprudence du Tribunal fédéral," in Waldmann, *1. Nationale Föderalismuskonferenz*, 193–212. The authors are grateful to the documents service of the Federal Supreme Court, and to Ms Geneviève Rod in particular, for research conducted in the Federal Supreme Court's database of case law.

guidelines to prevent dog attacks on humans. Geneva and Zurich have instituted measures such as a ban on breeding dangerous dogs, the obligation to obtain a permit to own such dogs, and bans on doing so. Citing Article 3 specifically, the Federal Supreme Court deemed these measures to be constitutional.[73] A similar conclusion was reached even in the case of the absolute ban imposed by Valais on certain breeds of dog, which in effect covered less than 1.7 per cent of all dogs in the canton.[74]

Article 3 was also cited in a Federal Supreme Court ruling in connection with the fiscal sovereignty of the cantons, with particular regard to patents. In a case from Solothurn, the Federal Supreme Court determined that the levy of patent fees cannot be ruled out solely by the fact that the new Federal Constitution no longer makes explicit provision for commercial levies by the cantons, as was the case in Article 31, paragraph 2 of the previous Constitution.[75] The Court reasoned that by virtue of Article 3 the fact that the Federal Constitution no longer rules about such cantonal patent fees or taxes does not mean that the cantonal legislators commit an infraction of the Constitution by fixing such patent fees.

Article 3 was also referred to explicitly in a case relating to land law in Valais. The Federal Supreme Court ruled that the key factor was whether, and to what extent, the federal parliament as legislator had made use of its power to enact (framework) legislation, as granted to it in the amendment of land law. If the confederation has not exercised its legislative powers, ruled the Court, then the cantons are not only responsible for issuing regulations guaranteeing property rights in greater detail, but are also free under Articles 3, 42, and 43a to grant those whose property was expropriated the right to make a claim for damages, with such rights extending beyond the guarantee laid down in Article 22ter, paragraph 3 of the old Federal Constitution.[76]

Spatial planning is an area governed by federal legislation. The cantons and local authorities are responsible for its application. The Federal Supreme Court has had the opportunity to clarify the interpretation of the law in this field in many of its judgments. In doing so, the Court, on one hand, respects the considerable planning freedom that the cantons and the local authorities enjoy within building zones, but on the other hand enforces the strict and directly applicable rules of federal

---

73 BGE 133 I 172 E. 2; BGE 136 I 1 E. 3–5.

74 BGE 133 I 249 E. 3–4.

75 BGE 128 I 102 E. 5.

76 BGE 127 I 185 E. 4.

legislation concerning construction outside building zones[77] and with respect to environmental conservation.[78]

According to Article 42 of the Federal Constitution, the confederation fulfils the duties that are assigned to it by the Constitution. This principle has been applied by the Federal Supreme Court on a number of occasions, including a judgment concerning common public procurement (i.e., relating to a joint venture project of the confederation and the cantons). The Court determined that in cases of parallel competencies of the confederation and the cantons, the confederation must issue a conflict of laws rule on the applicable law and responsible authority.[79]

Article 44 contains the principles of cooperation between the confederation and the cantons, including mutual support and cooperation in fulfilling tasks and duties of mutual consideration and assistance.[80] Article 46 states that the cantons implement federal law in accord with the Federal Constitution and federal legislation, and that the confederation must uphold the independence of the cantons. This has been applied, for example, in the following areas:

- *Spatial planning:* The Federal Supreme Court has held that, by setting up twenty-six different offices instead of one single competent authority, the canton of Bern failed to meet the requirements of federal legislation (see the more detailed explanation of the spatial planning case below).
- *Aliens law:* Because the Federal Constitution does not address the matter in Article 121 (authority of the confederation to legislate on the residence and permanent settlement of foreign nationals), in view of the principle laid down in Article 46, paragraph 1 it is the federal legislators who must determine the extent to which the cantons should be entrusted with the enforcement of federal law as it relates to foreign nationals (see also Art. 164, para. 1f).[81]
- *Validity of a cantonal initiative:* See the example below of the Geneva peace initiative as examined under Article 52.[82]

---

77 BGE 137 II 338, 136 II 359.

78 BGE 138 II 23.

79 BGE 130 I 156 E. 2.

80 See, for example, BGE 139 I 195 E. 4 concerning proportional representation in the cantonal law, which does not respect the principle of collaboration between the confederation and the concerned canton (here canton Zug).

81 BGE 127 II 49 E. 3.

82 BGE 125 I 227.

The cantons may conclude agreements between each other and may also set up joint organizations and institutions (inter-cantonal agreements). The confederation may participate in such agreements within the scope of its authority (Art. 48). For example, the Federal Supreme Court has determined that confederation gaming and lottery law[83] does not preclude an inter-cantonal process that transfers licensing decisions to a common body.[84]

Article 49, which provides that federal law will prevail over inconsistent cantonal law, is one of the fundamental provisions of the federal system, and it has been subject to more Federal Supreme Court rulings than most. The actual rulings on the precedence of and compliance with federal law are given here:

- The Federal Supreme Court confirmed that Zurich's regulations on criminal prosecution powers conformed to federal law. It found that the cantonal provision did not contradict the Swiss Code of Criminal Procedure.[85]
- The Federal Supreme Court declared as part of its judgment that a flat-rate fee charged, irrespective of the volume of waste accrued, was incompatible with federal law.[86]
- The Federal Supreme Court established a breach of the power of derogation of federal law. A cantonal law on the construction of social housing, which included buildings that did not receive any federal aid, could not permit the landlord (on the grounds of the corresponding provisions in the Swiss Code of Obligations) to invoice expenditure associated with the existence of the rental property itself as ancillary costs.[87]

---

83 Federal Lotteries and Commercial Betting Act, SR 935.51.

84 BGE 135 II 338. Opposite decision concerning an inter-cantonal agreement about culture of hemp, in BGE 138 I 435.

85 BGE 137 IV 269.

86 BGE 137 I 257.

87 BGE 137 I 135; see also BGE 5A_948/2015 (foreseen for publication in the official compilation of the decisions of the Federal Supreme Court): non-admissibility of cantonal civil procedure rules regarding the recent Swiss Civil Procedure Code; BGE 142 I 16: admissibility of specific cantonal names for high school institutions regarding the Federal regulation; BGE 139 I 195 about proportional representation in the cantonal law, which does not respect the principles of the Federal Constitution; BGE 139 I 242 about admissibility, regarding the federal rules, of cantonal law concerning no smoking areas in restaurants.

Under Article 51, cantonal constitutions require the guarantee of the confederation, which must be given, provided the constitution does not contradict federal law. The meaning of this confederation guarantee was rendered more precise in a recent judgment by the Federal Supreme Court on a provision in the constitution of Vaud concerning a mandatory referendum on measures to restructure the cantonal budget. The provision in the cantonal constitution was deemed to be insufficiently clear to commit the cantonal electorate to a decision between a restructuring measure and a corresponding increase in the cantonal tax rate. The Court ruled that such a specific referendum process must be set out in detail in advance at statute level.[88] Otherwise it will foster infractions of the guarantee of political rights of the Constitution (Art. 34).

Article 52 states that the confederation must protect the constitutional order of the cantons. The confederation will intervene when public order in a canton is disrupted or under threat and the canton is unable to maintain order alone or with the aid of other cantons. A cantonal initiative to support military measures that promote peace is lawful in principle, provided the initiative furthers action such as participation of the canton in international institutions, endeavours to reduce the military budget, repurposing of military sites for civilian use, shift of business activities connected with the military to the civilian sector, or protection of victims of violence and promotion of community service in the context of an objective information policy and an appropriate infrastructure. By contrast, it would be unlawful for a canton to decide that military personnel may not be used under any circumstances to maintain peace and public order on cantonal territory or to ensure the safety of international conferences. The Federal Supreme Court therefore ruled the Geneva popular peace initiative (based on political rights of the cantonal constitution) to be invalid.[89]

Article 53 states that the confederation must protect the existence and the territory of the cantons. A popular initiative (the "Unir" initiative) submitted in Canton Jura, which would have obliged the cantonal authorities to work unilaterally and consistently towards the incorporation of certain districts of Canton Bern, was declared invalid by the

88 BGE 131 I 126; see also BGE 140 I 394 about election rules on the cantonal level; BGE 140 I 58 about referendum rules on the local level.
89 BGE 125 I 227.

Federal Supreme Court because of the danger of disrupting peaceful relations between the two cantons.[90]

B. DISTRIBUTION OF POWERS BETWEEN THE CONFEDERATION AND THE CANTONS

Legislative power is one of the most important components of federalism. The way in which such powers are distributed between the confederation and the cantons may vary.

Confederation holds exclusive powers (legislative and executive): If the confederation holds exclusive legislative powers in respect of civil law, this includes the exclusive competencies of ruling about the personal effects of marriage. A canton may therefore not issue regulations about the retention or loss of a woman's cantonal or local citizenship when she marries.[91]

Confederation holds exclusive legislative power – executive power lies with the cantons: The confederation is responsible for spatial planning legislation (Art. 75) and has enacted a corresponding law.[92] This law (Art. 25, para. 2 Spatial Planning Act) requires, among other things, that all applications for building projects outside building zones be examined by a single authority of the canton for reasons of an equal treatment all over the territory of the canton. One canton had set up twenty-six local administrative offices, because this better accommodated the actual organizational structure of the administration and led to shorter procedures. The Federal Supreme Court ruled this arrangement inadmissible.[93]

Powers shared between confederation and cantons or inter-cantonal bodies: Federal lotteries and gaming legislation[94] do not preclude an inter-cantonal process that transfers licensing decisions to a common body.[95]

The measures provided for in the inter-cantonal concordat on action against violence at sporting events (e.g., travel bans, regular "checking in" with the authorities, and police custody) are deemed compatible with federal law.[96]

---

90 BGE 118 Ia 195.
91 BGE 108 Ib 392.
92 Federal Spatial Planning Act, SR 700.
93 BGE 128 I 254 E. 4.
94 Federal Lotteries and Commercial Betting Act, SR 935.51.
95 BGE 128 I 254 E. 4.
96 BGE 137 I 31 E. 4.

Cantons hold exclusive powers: According to Article 39, paragraph 1, the cantons have exclusive authority over the exercise of political rights in cantonal and municipal matters. In cantonal legislation relating to elections to the cantonal parliament, the electoral process and the rules that apply to proportional representation must respect the principles of the Federal Constitution. Specifically, cantonal electoral processes must be compatible with principles of proportional representation and with the corresponding distribution of seats. This does not rule out recognition by federal authorities of cantonal customary law (i.e., unwritten cantonal constitutional law historically practised by the cantonal authorities), which gives even the smallest municipality the right to a minimum of two seats in the cantonal parliament.[97] This adjudication of the Federal Supreme Court gave rise to something that is very rare (it happens two to three times in a century). The Federal Council asked the Federal Assembly not to approve section 48 of the new constitution of Canton Schwyz because this new cantonal regulation is not compatible with principles of proportional representation.[98] A canton may also not use this exclusive authority to forbid women exercising political rights in cantonal and municipal affairs. The constitutional principle of gender equality (Art. 8, para. 3) takes precedence over cantonal autonomy.[99]

Despite their inherent shortcomings, cantons may hold a cantonal referendum in the form of a public meeting, or *Landsgemeinde*, because voting with a show of hands at such a meeting does not constitute a breach of electoral freedom.[100]

C. AUTONOMY OF THE CANTONS AND MUNICIPALITIES

The municipalities are independent with regard to their public procurement. In public votes, interested citizens select their preferred project from a range of studies that have been open to public inspection. In one particular case, the project concerned the construction of new local authority offices. The Federal Supreme Court held that the "public voting" (a rather informal instrument of public participation to select the

---

97 BGE 136 I 376 E. 4–5,BGE 136 I 352 E. 2–5; and BGE 139 I 195.

98 FF 2012 7331; according to Art. 51 par. 2 FC the Federal Assembly has to approve the cantonal constitutions and their amendments to guarantee that the cantonal constitution is not contrary to federal law; see Haller, *Swiss Constitution in a Comparative Context*, 54–5; see also also 2.2.

99 BGE 116 Ia 359.

100 BGE 121 I 138 E. 5.

best among several projects) cannot be equated with a referendum, and provides only a rough estimate of the acceptance of a project among the population. It would nonetheless be appropriate for an authority to take due account of the will of the people even at the preliminary project stage. It would be a violation of municipal autonomy if a cantonal appeal body were to declare public voting to be fundamentally unlawful in the award of a public procurement contract.[101]

Cantonal and federal authorities apply restraint when managing disputes about municipal autonomy. In the naturalization process for foreign nationals, the grant of citizenship is one area in which local authorities can act independently. In this regard, the Federal Supreme Court has ruled that the cantonal court that is called upon to rule on rejected applications for citizenship is free in its consideration of the facts of the case and the application of the law. It must nonetheless respect the scope of the local authority's powers. In effect, this means that the cantonal court may examine whether or not the minimum procedural requirements for determining, such as language skills, have been met. It may not conduct its own investigations, however.[102]

Under certain circumstances, cantonal authorities may order the compulsory merger of local authorities. These circumstances include the existence of cantonal parliamentary powers to order compulsory mergers, a specific legal base, hearings among the populations of the local authorities concerned, and the appropriateness of such a move in view of the prevailing general and financial situation.[103]

D. CONFLICTS BETWEEN CONSTITUENT STATES

The Federal Supreme Court is the only body competent to hear disputes between cantons (Art. 189, para. 2). Such disputes are very uncommon (three in twenty years), but have involved a range of issues.

Inter-cantonal conflicts may concern the precise location of boundaries. One case concerned the boundary between Bern and Valais at the Plaine-Morte glacier. Canton Bern had recognized the boundary as drawn on the map of 1863, making the Plaine-Morte fall within Valais. However, improved geographical knowledge about the course of the water divide between the two cantons meant that later federal maps showed a different path for the cantonal boundary. This was adopted

101 BGE 138 I 143.

102 BGE 137 I 235 E. 2–3, BGE 138 I 242; and BGE 139 I 169.

103 BGE 131 I 91 E 2–3.

in the overview land survey drawn up by Valais. The Court held that the tacit recognition of the adjustment to the boundary would be held against Canton Bern's claim in favour of the earlier boundary. The Plaine-Morte glacier thus now forms part of the territory of Bern.[104]

Disputes between cantons may also concern voting rights. A number of referenda were held in Bern to determine the precise boundary of Canton Jura, which was formed from a part of Bern. Jura took the matter to the Federal Supreme Court, claiming that the boundaries of its territory had been drawn too narrowly because of defects in the conduct of a referendum. The Federal Supreme Court refused to admit the constitutional claim. It found that Jura did not have the authority to challenge any errors in the referendum because it was not itself entitled to vote in that referendum, neither could it invoke any special norm that might have been enacted in its favour.[105]

Where tax law is concerned, the principle outlawing double taxation prevents a canton from taxing commuters from a neighbouring canton. With the exception of certain special cases, attempts by Geneva's tax authorities to tax the incomes of commuters from Vaud was held to infringe Vaud's fiscal sovereignty.[106]

The Federal Supreme Court is also competent to adjudicate cases concerning a conflict of competences between the adult protection authorities of two cantons.[107]

E. DEVELOPMENT OF FUNDAMENTAL RIGHTS IN THE SWISS FEDERAL STATE

The first Federal Constitution of 1848 and the second Federal Constitution of 1874, which remained in effect until 1999, contained only a few specific guarantees of fundamental rights; only those that appeared insufficiently assured by cantonal constitutional law were incorporated into the Constitution.[108] Before they were codified in the Federal Constitution of 1999, today's guarantees of fundamental rights evolved from the interplay of fundamental rights in the cantonal constitutions on one

104 BGE 120 Ib 512.

105 BGE 117 Ia 233.

106 BGE 125 I 458; see also BGE 139 II 373 regarding a conflict between tax authorities of the cantons Zürich and Aargau.

107 BGE 141 III 84 E 1 to 4.

108 See Haller, *Swiss Constitution in a Comparative Context*, 149; Regina Kiener and Walter Kälin, *Grundrechte*, 2nd ed. (Bern: Stämpfli, 2011), 5–6.

hand, and the extraordinarily comprehensive body of case law from the Federal Supreme Court on the other.[109] This was guided to some extent by the development of human rights legislation in Europe (see 4.2.6) and the precedent set by the Supreme Court in the United States (the American Supreme Court has had a very significant influence on the development of human rights in Switzerland, but there is no discernible influence concerning federalist matters).

F. THE LEGAL QUESTION OF LANGUAGES

Switzerland traditionally is a multilingual country. The Constitution declares German, French, Italian, and partly Romansh (only concerning relations with the Romansh population) as official languages for the use by authorities of the confederation (Art. 70). Each canton can define its official languages. Twenty-two of the twenty-six cantons are monolingual. The cantons of Bern, Fribourg, and Valais are bilingual, where the official languages are German and French. The only trilingual canton is Graubünden, with German, Romansh, and Italian as its official languages.

The Federal Supreme Court played an important role in defining the linguistic rights at a time where there were no regulations in the Constitution.[110] The Court originally adopted a very strict application of the principle of territoriality in a famous case, "Association de l'Ecole française."[111] It prevented a private French-speaking school from teaching in Zurich in order to protect the traditional German-speaking linguistic zone. Since then, and especially taking into account three important decisions, the Court has shifted from strict implementation of territoriality towards a certain degree of recognition of freedom of language, as granted by the Constitution (Art. 18).[112] On closer examination, the legal question of languages in Switzerland – reflected by the decisions of the Federal Supreme Court – is not a federal question in a strict sense

---

109 See Haller, *Swiss Constitution in a Comparative Context*, 19–20, 149; Kiener and Kälin, *Grundrechte*, 5–6; Wurzburger, *Le Tribunal fédéral*, 37–8.

110 See *in extenso* Nicolas Schmitt, "Principles and Criteria of the Jurisprudence of the Swiss Federal Tribunal concerning Linguistic Questions," in *Jurisprudències constitucionals en matèria lingüística: principis i criteri*, eds. Institut d'Estudis Autonòmics, dir. (Barcelona: Institut d'Estudis Autonòmics, 2011), 11.

111 BGE 91 I 480.

112 See Schmitt, "Principles and Criteria," 24; Fleiner, Misic, and Toepperwien, *Constitutional Law in Switzerland*, 268–9.

but rather "a struggle between the freedom of language and the principle of territoriality."[113]

G. ENFORCEMENT OF THE EUROPEAN CONVENTION ON HUMAN RIGHTS AGAINST FEDERAL INTERESTS

In the past, the Federal Supreme Court has upheld enforcement of the fundamental freedoms of the European Convention on Human Rights against federal interests. In doing so, it has also intervened in the organizational autonomy of the cantons. This is illustrated clearly by the example of judicial independence, where the Federal Supreme Court – adopting the practices of the Strasbourg authorities – determined institutional inconsistences, which resulted in costly reorganizations and legislative amendments in the cantons concerned:[114] a person may be both a public prosecutor and a presiding criminal judge;[115] a person may be both an investigating magistrate and a presiding criminal judge;[116] a person may be both a sentencing judge and a presiding criminal judge if a sentencing order is appealed and court proceedings thus instituted;[117] and a person may be both a magistrate and a presiding criminal judge.[118]

H. COMPLIANCE WITH FEDERAL COURT DOCTRINES OR RULINGS

Although the Federal Supreme Court issues rulings on individual cases that are binding on the courts of lower instance only in the case at hand, it is rare for the cantonal courts not to respect the case law of the Federal Supreme Court, and especially its landmark rulings.[119] The reason for this probably has less to do with the obedience of the cantonal courts than with the fact that the great majority of Federal Supreme Court rulings become the accepted doctrine in the form of textbooks and commentaries, and that the courts of first and second instance also tend to follow this doctrine in their own decisions. Another factor may be that

---

113 Schmitt, "Principles and Criteria," 12.

114 See also Jörg Paul Müller and Markus Schefer, *Grundrechte in der Schweiz*, 4th ed. (Bern: Stämpfli, 2008), 943.

115 BGE 117 Ia 159 E. 2, following Piersack c. Belgium, EuGRZ 1985, 301.

116 E.g., BGE 111 Ia 290; BGE 113 Ia 72; BGE 117 Ib 64, following De Cubber c. Belgium, EuGRZ 1985, 407.

117 BGE 114 Ia 143.

118 BGE 115 Ia 180; BGE 121 II 53, following Hauschildt c. Denmark, Series A No. 154.

119 See Wurzburger, *Le Tribunal fédéral*, 35.

many court decisions are prepared by the clerks of the court (see 3.1 above), who are often younger and less experienced lawyers.

Furthermore, in the few cases in which the Federal Supreme Court has declared a cantonal norm as unconstitutional in the context of an abstract review, the competent authorities have also tended to comply with the Federal Supreme Court ruling. In such cases, cantonal legislators have amended the norm in question at the next opportunity.

Finally, it should be pointed out that cantonal legislators may deviate from the Federal Constitution where fundamental rights are concerned if the cantonal constitution extends the protection of fundamental rights beyond the guarantees that are laid down in the Federal Constitution. For example, the constitution of Canton Bern grants an individual constitutional right to inspect official records (the principle of public access). This is similar to what has been called the "new judicial federalism" in the United States.[120]

I. OUTLOOK

The introduction of standard codes of civil and criminal procedure for the whole of Switzerland on 1 January 2011 was – together with the corresponding amendments of the Constitution (Art. 29a, Art. 121, Art. 122) – the greatest intervention in the federal structure of the justice system since the beginning of the nineteenth century. It remains to be seen precisely what the effects on federalism will be. Many cantons have used the introduction of the new codes of procedure as an opportunity to reform their own judicial structures. Exercising the organizational autonomy granted to them in respect of their court systems (Art. 122, para. 2, and Art. 123, para. 2), and taking their different sizes and structures into account, the cantons have chosen a variety of organizational models.[121] Indeed, the diversity in cantonal judicial systems would appear to be even greater today than it was before the reforms. The criminal prosecution authorities are an exception.[122] In view of the sequence of steps in criminal proceedings, the new Swiss Code of Criminal Procedure prescribes a particular model of public prosecution, although the cantons retain a degree of organizational scope even here.

---

120 See, for example, John Kincaid, "State Court Protections of Individual Rights under State Constitutions: The New Judicial Federalism," *Journal of State Government* 61 (September/October 1988): 163–9.

121 See Fleiner, Misic, and Toepperwien, *Constitutional Law in Switzerland*, 113.

122 See ibid., 116–17.

To date, the Federal Supreme Court has rejected individual cantons' challenges to this new public prosecution model.[123]

As mentioned above, there is no constitutional jurisdiction at the national level.[124] In 2012, the question of introducing a federal constitutional court was debated by parliament once again.[125] It might have a positive effect on federalism as a whole in Switzerland, however, if the Federal Supreme Court were able to examine the constitutionality of federal legislation. The Federal Supreme Court would then also be able to examine whether and to what extent federal legislators were at all authorized to issue a particular norm that formed the basis for the decision of the cantonal courts in an individual case. The parliament decided against a constitutional jurisdiction. It is difficult to get clear reasons out of the debate, yet federalism was not an issue in the discussion.

3. *Securing Federally Relevant Goals and Objectives*

The Federal Supreme Court plays an important role in promoting the universal application of federal legislation in the interests of the federal state overall. In this regard, the Federal Supreme Court has had a particular effect in several areas over the past twenty years.

Social insurance law: Traditionally, the Federal Supreme Court (from 1917 onwards, up to just a few years ago, an independent federal court in Lucerne) played a very important part in ensuring the standard application of federal legislation on social insurance (e.g., old-age and survivors' insurance, disability insurance, and occupational pension provision).[126]

---

123 For example, in implementing the public prosecution model II, some cantons have reorganized the public prosecutor's office as part of the independent justice system, subject to the supervision of the upper court. In its judgment 1B_320/2009 on 5 July 2010, the Federal Supreme Court held that judicial independence was not biased or infringed if the upper court or its administrative board appoint public prosecutors, on the one hand, and, on the other, the same members of the upper court rule in appeal proceedings on a refusal to enter into or suspension of criminal prosecutions of those public prosecutors. See Daniel Kettiger, "Zur Unabhängigkeit der Staatsanwaltschaft in der Justizorganisation," *Justice – Justiz – Giustizia* 4 (2010).

124 See Haller, *Swiss Constitution in a Comparative Context*, 245-246.

125 See Parliamentary Initiatives 07.476 and 05.445. This is not the first attempt to introduce constitutional jurisdiction; see Wagner, *Federal State and Their Judiciaries*, 105–6.

126 See Wurzburger, *Le Tribunal fédéral*, 14–15.

Tax harmonization: The cantons enjoy fiscal sovereignty, as well as independent legislative authority to enact norms relating specifically to income and wealth taxes (direct taxes). Legislative diversity between the cantons is thus correspondingly broad. With an amendment of the Constitution (Art. 129) and its Tax Harmonization Act,[127] the confederation brought about a degree of formal standardization in areas such as liability to tax, taxable incomes, and capital gains, as well as assets and capital, tax assessment periods, the procedures to be followed, and criminal tax law, in particular. This harmonization did not, however, include tax rates. In this sense, there is no material harmonization of the tax system. The Federal Supreme Court has since had a number of opportunities to support these harmonization efforts.[128] For example, it held that new income tax rates imposed by Obwalden were inconsistent with the general tenet of equality before the law and the principle of taxation on the basis of ability to pay (Art. 127). The Court further ruled that neither tax competition grounds nor other fiscal or non-fiscal objectives justified this incompatibility with federal law.[129]

Unified economic area: A unified economic area forms an integral part of Switzerland's economic constitution (Art. 27, Art. 94). The Domestic Market Act[130] is intended to give persons who are permanently settled or domiciled in Switzerland free and equal access to the market to pursue employment throughout the whole of Swiss territory. The Federal Supreme Court has applied this principle in greater detail in a broad body of case law.[131]

Enforcement of guarantees of fundamental rights under international law (see 4.2.5) and harmonization of legislation on spatial planning (see 4.2.2) also illustrate the role of the courts in securing federally relevant goals and objectives.

---

127 Federal Act of 14 December 1990 on the Harmonization of Direct Taxes Levied by Cantons and Local Authorities (StHG; SR 642.14).

128 See also Ulrich Cavelty, "Schranken des Steuerföderalismus," *Rechtliche Rahmenbedingungen des Wirtschaftsstandortes Schweiz*, ed. Department of Law at the University of St Gallen (St Gallen: Dike, 2007), 367.

129 BGE 133 I 206.

130 Federal Act of 6 October 1995 on the Domestic Market (Domestic Market Act, BGBM, SR943.02).

131 For an overview of the relevant case law, see Giovanni Biaggini, Andreas Lienhard, Paul Richli, and Felix Uhlmann, *Wirtschaftsverwaltungsrecht des Bundes*, 5th ed. (Basel: Helbling Lichtenhahn, 2009), 40.

V. Conclusion

As noted above, only the rulings of the Federal Supreme Court have any bearing on federalism in Switzerland. The rulings of the cantonal courts and other federal courts are of negligible importance. Since its foundation in 1848, the Federal Supreme Court has played the very role in the federalist structure of the Swiss state that, with regard to federalism, it was designed to play.[132] It has struck a balance between the necessary degree of legislative harmonization in a federal state, and the legal and organizational independence of the cantons, as is their due according to the principles of federalism. In more than 150 years, the jurisdiction of the Federal Supreme Court does not show any clear tendency towards unitarism or federalism. There has been a slight unitarist tendency in the decisions of the Federal Supreme Court in the last twenty years. But this might as well be the result of a tendency to unitarism in federal legislation. Concerning federal matters, no justifiable generalizations can be made about the attitude and outlook of the Court. However, there is one exception. When the Federal Supreme Court has to decide whether a paragraph of a cantonal law is compatible with the Federal Constitution, the Court clearly follows a federalist view. In respect of decisions made by a cantonal parliament or even by a canton's voters, it declares such a paragraph non-constitutional (with the effect it is declared null) only if there is no possible way to apply the paragraph in a constitutional way.

Jurisdiction is just one of several aspects in the evolution of Swiss federalism, however. The principal role is taken by the legislators (i.e., the federal parliament and the electorate), which have laid down the principles of the federalist division of power between the confederation and the cantons. In comparison to the legislator, the Federal Supreme Court is only a middling actor in shaping the Swiss federal arrangement. The reshaping of this arrangements take place mostly by modifications of federal laws (and seldom by partial revisions of the Constitution). These principles continue to be refined, particularly with the restructuring of the financial equalization system and the distribution of functions between the confederation and cantons in 2008. The executive government of the confederation plays an important role in preparing the implementation of laws and in enforcing them. That said,

---

132 See note 68.

Swiss federalism rests on the cantons themselves. On the basis of their general subsidiary powers and the associated financial autonomy, they form the federal state. This remains true despite an emerging shift in power from the cantons to the confederation, and the increasing importance of alliances between the cantons and the confederation. In this delicate interplay, the court system – and the Federal Supreme Court particularly – is called upon to support an appropriate balance between federalism and centralism.

14 The Supreme Court of the United States: Promoting Centralization More Than State Autonomy

ILYA SOMIN

I. Introduction

The relative scope of federal and state power under the U.S. Constitution has been a major bone of contention for over two hundred years. Federal courts have often intervened both for and against assertions of federal authority. Judicial review has sometimes enforced substantial limits on federal authority by striking down federal laws deemed to be outside the scope of Congress's enumerated powers under Article I of the Constitution. At the same time, federal courts have often constrained state power by invalidating state laws as violations of constitutional rights.

While judicial review has therefore promoted both centralization and state autonomy at different times, on balance it has strengthened the former at the expense of the latter. This pattern has been especially prevalent since the 1930s, as the U.S. Supreme Court largely abandoned earlier efforts to police limits on congressional power, while simultaneously enforcing a growing array of individual rights against state and local governments.

This chapter does not consider the extent to which the federal courts' decisions on federalism and individual rights questions have been correct; instead, it examines the impact of judicial review on American federalism without attempting a normative judgment. I briefly outline the structure of American federalism and judicial review, and then describe the history of judicial review of structural limits on federal power. In the nineteenth and early twentieth centuries, the Supreme Court engaged in limited but significant efforts to constrain congressional power. These efforts were to a large extent abandoned after the constitutional revolution of the New Deal period in the 1930s. Beginning in the early 1990s, the Supreme Court attempted to revive judicial enforcement of limits on federal power. So far, these efforts have had only a limited effect.

The chapter then summarizes the history of judicial review of state laws. The range of issues on which federal courts have invalidated state laws is so broad that it is impossible to consider it in more than a general way here. But that in itself is a strong indication of the extent to which state policymaking authority has been curbed by the courts. Overall, the impact of these rulings in restricting state autonomy significantly exceeds the effects of the courts' more limited efforts to constrain federal power. However, they have promoted a kind of decentralization by increasing the freedom of individual citizens and private organizations.

The last part of the chapter briefly explains why the centralizing effect of judicial review was not accidental. Because federal judges are appointed by the president and confirmed by the Senate, the chance that they will resist the political agenda of the dominant political coalition in the federal government is reduced. Even when federal judges would like to invalidate federal legislation, they may hesitate to do so when the result might create a political confrontation that the courts are likely to lose. Federal judges face fewer political risks when they strike down state legislation.

I. The American System of Federalism

The United States is one of the world's largest and most diverse federal systems, second only to India in population size. The nation also boasts enormous ethnic and religious diversity. As of 2010, the U.S. population was about 308 million people.[1] That includes about 65 per cent who describe themselves as "white," 12 per cent black or African-American, and almost 16 per cent Hispanic (including some black Hispanics).[2] There are also many smaller minority groups, most notably Asian-Americans and Native American descendants of the aboriginal population. The United States has by far the world's largest economy

1 U.S. Census Bureau, *Statistical Abstract of the United States* (Washington, DC: U.S. Government Printing Office, 2012), 8. The constantly updated Census Bureau Population Clock estimates it at about 322 million in December 2015. U.S. Census Bureau, U.S. and World Population Clock, 12 December 2015, available at http://www.census.gov/popclock/.

2 Data calculated from figures in U.S. Census Bureau, *Statistical Abstract of the United States*, 10.

and is also among the world's wealthiest nations in terms of per capita income.

The U.S. federal system includes fifty state governments, all of which have legally equal standing under the Constitution, as well as six associated territories such as Puerto Rico, American Samoa, and the U.S. Virgin Islands. The District of Columbia, which includes the capital of Washington, DC, is a special territory controlled directly by the federal government. Aboriginal Native American tribal governments have a complex quasi-autonomous status that has been a focus of much controversy and is difficult to classify precisely.[3]

There are also over 89,000 local governments of various types, including counties, towns, and cities.[4] As far as the federal Constitution is concerned, local political entities are under the complete control of state governments; however, many of them are granted a measure of autonomy or home rule under state constitutional or statutory law.

As discussed later, the power of the federal government relative to the states has greatly increased over time. The federal government has come to play a much larger role in economic and social policy, and in protecting a variety of individual rights. Today, as in many previous periods in American history, the scope of federal power is a major focus of political controversy. Generally speaking, most political liberals believe that the role of the federal government should be as great as or even greater than it is today, while most conservatives and libertarians argue that it should be reduced. At the same time, neither side of the political spectrum is consistent in its attitude towards federal power; conservatives sometimes favour expansions of federal power that seem in tension with their ideology, while liberals sometimes favour state autonomy. Overall, there is no consensus on where the boundary between state and federal authority should lie. But few Americans want to transform the nation into a completely unitary polity.

---

3 For overviews of Indian tribal governments' relationship with American federalism, see, e.g., Vine DeLoria Jr and Clifford M. Lytle, *The Nations Within: The Past and Future of American Indian Sovereignty* (Austin: University of Texas Press, 1998); David E. Wilkins and Heidi Kiiwetinepinesiik Stark, *American Indian Politics and the American Political System*, 3rd ed. (New York: Rowman & Littlefield, 2010); Harvard Project on American Indian Economic Development, *The State of the Native Nations: Conditions under US Policies of Self-Determination* (New York: Oxford University Press, 2007), section 1.

4 U.S. Census Bureau, 2012 Census of Governments, table 2, http://www2.census.gov/govs/cog/2012/formatted_prelim_counts_23jul2012_2.pdf.

As compared with most other federal systems, the United States is unusual in that there are almost no states where an ethnic, religious, linguistic, or racial group that is in the minority nationally is the majority within the state. In many other federal nations, the existence of national minorities that are regional majorities was one of the main justifications for the establishment of a federal system in the first place.[5] The one partial exception to the U.S. pattern is the state of Utah, where adherents of the Mormon religion – a minority faith that was persecuted by national and state governments in the nineteenth century – are in the majority.[6] External possessions such as Puerto Rico and the U.S. Virgin Islands also have majority populations that differ in ethnicity from that of the United States. But they, like Utah, have had only marginal influence on the development of American federalism as a whole.

The United States emerged from a rebellion against British rule by thirteen previously separate colonies on the east coast of North America. In 1776, the colonies joined together in a Declaration of Independence, and Britain recognized the new nation after an eight-year conflict that Americans commonly call the Revolutionary War.

The U.S. Constitution was drafted in 1787 and is the oldest continuously functioning written national constitution in the world. It replaced the earlier Articles of Confederation, established in 1781, under which the powers of the federal government were significantly weaker.[7] Many political leaders, including George Washington, commander of the Continental Army that won the Revolutionary War, Alexander Hamilton, and James Madison, the eventual "father of the Constitution," believed that the federal government created by the Articles was too weak, and tolerated far too much abusive behaviour by the states. During the 1780s, political support for the establishment of a stronger

5 For an overview covering many such cases, see Luis Moreno and César Colino, eds., *Diversity and Unity in Federal Countries* (Montreal and Kingston: McGill-Queen's University Press, 2010); see also Dawn Brancati, *Peace by Design: Managing Intrastate Conflict through Decentralization* (New York: Oxford University Press, 2009).

6 For a survey of the issues raised by Utah and the Mormons' confrontations with the federal government, see Sarah Barringer Gordon, *The Mormon Question: Polygamy and Constitutional Conflict in Nineteenth-Century America* (Chapel Hill: University of North Carolina Press, 2002).

7 For a helpful summary of the origin and development of the Constitution, see G. Alan Tarr, "The United States of America," in *Constitutional Origin, Structure, and Change in Federal Countries*, ed. John Kincaid and G. Alan Tarr (Montreal and Kingston: McGill-Queen's University Press, 2005), 381–8.

federal government gradually increased, until a new constitution was drafted in 1787 by a convention of state delegates originally called to revise the Articles of Confederation.

The new Constitution was approved by specially elected ratifying conventions within the states. Article VII of the Constitution stipulated that the Constitution would come into force once ratified by nine of the thirteen states. Many prominent politicians and Revolutionary War leaders supported the Constitution. These included Madison, Hamilton, and John Jay, who wrote the famous *Federalist Papers* in an attempt to promote ratification. But others, including George Mason and Patrick Henry, opposed the Constitution because they believed it concentrated too much power in the federal government.

The Constitution establishes a system of separation of powers within the federal government, with an elected executive (the president, Article II), a bicameral legislature (Article I), and an independent judiciary (Article III). The upper house of Congress, the Senate, has two senators for every state; originally they were chosen by state legislatures, but they have been popularly elected since enactment of the Seventeenth Amendment in 1913. The House of Representatives, the lower house, is chosen by plurality voting in single-member districts allocated to the states based on population.

Federal judges serve for life and are appointed by the president, subject to confirmation by a majority of the Senate. The judicial system is hierarchical, with a Supreme Court composed of nine justices at the top.[8] Unlike in some other nations, there is no separate constitutional court. Most significant cases are decided through publicly available written opinions signed by the judge who writes them. Since at least the early nineteenth century, the federal judiciary – particularly the Supreme Court – has been a major player in the political and legal system, imposing constraints on the powers of both the states and the other two branches of the federal government.

In addition to the Supreme Court, there are two lower levels of generalist federal judges – district court judges (who hear trials) and court of appeals judges (who hear appeals from the district courts). There are also a number of specialized courts, such as those that consider tax cases, bankruptcy cases, and cases arising in the military justice system.

8 Before 1869, the Supreme Court often had six, seven, or ten justices rather than nine. The present number was set by Congress in 1869, and has remained the same ever since.

Article III gives federal courts jurisdiction over all "cases" and "controversies" arising under the Constitution and other federal law. Over time, the Supreme Court has interpreted this to forbid the issuing of "advisory" opinions and to limit federal litigation to cases involving parties that can obtain "standing" by having suffered at least some form of tangible harm through violations of the law.

Each state has its own courts, including a state supreme court, which are independent of the federal courts and hear cases addressing issues of both state and federal law. Each also has its own state constitution, many of which contain guarantees of rights that differ from or go beyond those protected by the federal Constitution.[9] State courts must follow federal appellate court precedent on issues involving the federal Constitution and federal law. But they exercise considerable independent authority when they interpret state constitutional law, often in ways that restrict the authority of the other branches of their state governments. Some federal judges are former state judges appointed to the federal judiciary, though most are not.

The United States is a common law nation with a legal culture heavily influenced by its British origins.[10] In interpreting the Constitution, federal judges have resorted to a wide range of methodologies, including textualism, originalism, reliance on precedent, and a variety of "living constitution" theories that allow for changing interpretation in response to economic and social developments. Both within and outside the judiciary, there is an active debate between supporters of different theories of interpretation – particularly between originalists and living constitution advocates – with no definitive resolution in sight.

One issue that has often been the focus of conflict between interpreters of the Constitution over the last two centuries is the question of whether the Constitution was established by the people of the United States as a whole, or is instead a compact created by state governments.[11]

---

9 For useful surveys of state constitutional law and its history, see John J. Dinan, *The American State Constitutional Tradition* (Lawrence: University Press of Kansas, 2006); and G. Alan Tarr, *Understanding State Constitutions* (Princeton: Princeton University Press, 2000).

10 The one exception to this generalization is Louisiana, which maintains a civil law system inherited from its days as a French and Spanish colony prior to its transfer to the United States in 1803.

11 For helpful statements of the arguments on each side with citations to various historical sources and earlier debates on the issue, see the majority and dissenting opinions in *US Term Limits v. Thornton*, 514 U.S. 779 (1995).

Advocates on both sides have usually assumed that the latter theory implies a narrower scope for federal authority than the former. This is not necessarily true. Even if an undifferentiated people created the Constitution, they could still have chosen to put strict limits on federal power. Conversely, even if the Constitution was established by the states, they could have chosen to delegate very broad authority to the federal government. Even so, the issue continues to be the subject of considerable debate.

Until recently, judicial decisions on federalism issues have not been much influenced by international treaties and international law. Over the last fifteen years, a few Supreme Court decisions have cited such sources, and some scholars advocate greater reliance on them. But the practice remains rare and controversial.

Article I, Section 8 of the Constitution gives Congress a variety of powers, most notably the power to declare war, raise and support armies, mint money, impose taxes, and regulate interstate and foreign commerce. There is also a Necessary and Proper Clause (Article I, Section 8, Clause 18), which gives Congress the power to adopt legislation that is "necessary and proper" for "carrying into execution" the other powers granted to the federal government in the Constitution. The Constitution also grants a number of powers to the president, most notably the power to command the armed forces, make treaties subject to ratification by two-thirds of the Senate, and veto legislation adopted by Congress, subject to override by a two-thirds majority in each house. The Supremacy Clause of Article VI of the Constitution specifies that the Constitution, international treaties signed and ratified by the United States, and federal statutory law are all "the supreme Law of the Land" and trump state law when they conflict with it. The extent to which federal statutes "pre-empt" state laws that do not directly violate federal law but may go against it indirectly, has long been a focus of extensive debate.[12]

The Constitution does not contain a specified list of state powers. The implicit assumption is that states retain all powers not granted to the federal government or explicitly prohibited to the states by the Constitution. There are only a few examples of the latter, such as the

---

12 For detailed discussion, see, e.g., Richard Epstein and Michael Greve, eds., *Federal Preemption: States' Powers, National Interests* (Washington, DC: AEI, 2007); and Christopher R. Drahozal, *The Supremacy Clause* (Westport, CT: Praeger, 2004), 89–126.

prohibition on states' issuing their own currency or signing treaties with foreign powers (Article I, Section 10, Clause 1). States can also legislate on many matters on which the federal government can enact laws, so long as state laws do not conflict with federal ones. This has meant that states retain broad authority to legislate on a wide range of issues, even as the scope of federal power has expanded, especially since the 1930s. Still, state policies are increasingly subject to overriding or modification by federal legislation.

A wide range of individual rights provisions constrain both federal and state power, including amendments protecting freedom of speech and religion, property rights, and the rights of criminal defendants. All of the former are part of the Bill of Rights, the first ten amendments to the U.S. Constitution enacted simultaneously in 1791. The Thirteenth, Fourteenth, and Fifteenth Amendments, enacted in the late 1860s shortly after the Civil War, forbid slavery and restrict racial and ethnic discrimination by state governments. Various provisions of the Fourteenth Amendment have long been interpreted to protect other individual rights as well.

As discussed more fully below, the federal courts have often enforced constitutional limits on both federal and state authority. Issues related to the proper scope of state and federal power have always been among the most important on the federal courts' agenda. At the same time, Congress, the president, public opinion, and a variety of political and economic factors have had major effects as well. Judicial review has influenced the development of American federalism, but it has never been the only influence and rarely the most important.

Article V of the Constitution sets out multiple mechanisms for enacting constitutional amendments. The only one that has ever been used in practice requires the support of a two-thirds majority in both houses of Congress, followed by ratification by three-quarters of the state legislatures. This amendment process is one of the most difficult in the world, and only twenty-seven amendments have been adopted in the 230-year history of the Constitution, including just seventeen since the adoption of the Bill of Rights in 1791. In practice, constitutional change has more often arisen through changing interpretations of the constitutional text than through formal amendment. Many state constitutions are much easier to amend, and some have been amended numerous times.

II. Judicial Enforcement of Limits on Federal Government Power

1. *The Early Republic and Antebellum Eras*

Efforts at judicial enforcement of limits on federal power date back to the early republic. Their successes and failures have waxed and waned at different times. Many of the Founding Fathers envisioned the judiciary as an adjudicator of the boundary between federal and state power. In the *Federalist Papers*, Madison wrote that the Supreme Court would decide "controversies relating to the boundary between the two jurisdictions."[13]

In the 1790s, the rival parties debated the constitutionality of federal legislation such as the federally chartered Bank of the United States, a federal government–created corporation that sought to attract private depositors and make it easier for the federal government to obtain credit. Critics of the bank in the nascent Democratic-Republican Party, including future presidents Thomas Jefferson and James Madison, argued that its creation exceeded Congress's enumerated powers under Article I of the Constitution.[14] Federalist Party defenders of the bank, led by Secretary of the Treasury Alexander Hamilton, contended that the Necessary and Proper Clause was broad enough to authorize it.[15] The parties also clashed over the constitutionality of other elements of Hamilton's economic policy program, such as the assumption of state debts by the federal government.[16]

The first Bank of the United States' charter was allowed to expire after Jefferson won the presidency in 1800 and his party took control of Congress. But in 1819 the Supreme Court decided the crucial case of *McCulloch v. Maryland*,[17] which involved a challenge to the constitutionality of a Maryland tax imposed on the second Bank of the United

---

13 James Madison, "Federalist 39," in *The Federalist Papers*, ed. Clinton Rossiter (New York: Mentor, 1961).

14 See, e.g., James Madison, "Speech on the Bank Bill," House of Representatives, 2 February 1791, in James Madison, *Writings*, ed. Jack N. Rakove (New York: Vintage, 1999), 480.

15 See, e.g., Alexander Hamilton, "Opinion on the Constitutionality of the Bank," 23 February 1791, in *The Founders' Constitution*, ed. Philip B. Kurland and Ralph Lerner (Chicago: University of Chicago Press, 1987), 3:247–9.

16 See David Currie, *The Constitution in Congress: The Federalist Period 1789–1801* (Chicago: University of Chicago Press, 1997), 76–7.

17 17 U.S. (4 Wheat.) 316 (1819).

States, which had been created in 1816. In the process of addressing the constitutionality of Maryland's tax, the Court also had to consider Maryland's argument that the Bank of the United States itself was unconstitutional. In a landmark opinion written by Chief Justice John Marshall, himself a Federalist, the Court not only upheld the constitutionality of the bank, but also endorsed Hamilton's argument that the word *necessary* in the Necessary and Proper Clause could be interpreted to allow Congress to enact any legislation that was merely "useful" or "convenient" as a tool for executing one of Congress's other enumerated powers.[18]

McCulloch is traditionally seen as an endorsement of extremely broad congressional power, and this conventional wisdom is supported at least partly by the Court's broad interpretation of the meaning of *necessary*. While the Court interpreted *necessary* very loosely, it did not give Congress a blank check to enact virtually any legislation it might want. Marshall's opinion indicated that the clause authorizes legislation only with a "legitimate" purpose that is "within the scope of the constitution," and uses "means which are appropriate, which are plainly adapted to that end, which are not prohibited, but consist with the letter and spirit of the constitution."[19] This passage suggests four constraints on the scope of congressional power authorized by the clause: (1) the "end" pursued must be "legitimate" and "within the scope of the constitution"; (2) the means must be "appropriate" and "plainly adapted to that end"; (3) the means must "not [be] prohibited" elsewhere in the Constitution; and (4) the means must be "consist[ent] with the letter and spirit of the Constitution." Marshall also emphasized that "should Congress, under the pretext of executing its powers, pass laws for the accomplishment of objects not intrusted to the Government, it would become the painful duty of this tribunal, should a case requiring such a decision come before it, to say that such an act was not the law of the land."[20]

In *Gibbons v. Ogden* (1824),[21] Marshall issued the Court's first major opinion addressing the scope of congressional authority to regulate "commerce ... among the several States."[22] *Gibbons* upheld the

---

18 Ibid., 413–15.
19 McCulloch. 17 U.S. (4. Wheat), at 421.
20 Ibid., 423.
21 22 U.S. (9 Wheat.) 1 (1824).
22 U.S. Constitution, Art. I, § 8, cl. 3.

constitutionality of a federal law granting navigation licences to ships engaged in "the coasting trade," and barred the State of New York from granting a monopoly of navigation on the Hudson River, the lower part of which runs between New Jersey and New York.[23]

Marshall defined *commerce* relatively broadly as "intercourse."[24] But he also emphasized that the commerce power has significant limits, listing "inspection laws, quarantine laws, health laws of every description, as well as laws for regulating the internal commerce of a State, and those which respect turnpike roads, ferries," as part of the great "mass" of issues that federal power under the Commerce Clause does not cover.[25] Unlike modern Commerce Clause jurisprudence, Marshall's theory of the clause specifically did not include everything that "may have a remote and considerable influence on commerce."[26]

Although relatively supportive of federal power, the pre–Civil War Supreme Court did issue two major opinions constraining it: *Marbury v. Madison*[27] and *Dred Scott v. Sandford*.[28] The former is most famous for its role in helping to establish the power of judicial review.[29] It also represented an early case where the Court enforced constitutional limits on the powers of the federal government. But its actual impact in constraining federal power was extremely limited because it invalidated only a relatively minor provision of the Judiciary Act of 1789.

Dred Scott was far more consequential. For decades, one of the biggest issues in nineteenth-century American politics was whether to permit slavery in the nation's extensive western territories. Under the Constitution, these territories were controlled by the federal government until they could be formed into states. In legislating for them, Congress was not limited by the enumerated powers constraints that applied in established states. Southern supporters of slavery sought to ensure that as much territory as possible would be open to slave-owners; most

---

23 *Gibbons*, 22 U.S. (9 Wheat.) at 1–2.
24 *Gibbons*, 22 U.S. at 189.
25 Ibid., 203.
26 Ibid.
27 5 U.S. (1 Cranch) 137 (1803).
28 60 U.S. (19 How.) 393 (1857).
29 Historical evidence indicates that the idea of judicial review was widely accepted in American legal thought and practice well before *Marbury*. See, e.g., Philip Hamburger, *Law and Judicial Duty* (Cambridge: Harvard University Press, 2008); and Scott Gerber, *A Distinct Judicial Power: The Origins of an Independent Judiciary, 1606–1787* (New York: Oxford University Press, 2011).

northerners preferred that slavery be banned in the federal territories. Both sides knew that a territory where slavery was legal would likely become a slave state, while a free territory would probably be a free state, thereby affecting the balance of power in Congress.

In two major political bargains – the Missouri Compromise of 1820 and the Compromise of 1850 – northerners and southerners agreed to ban slavery in some western territories, while allowing it in others. In *Dred Scott,* the Supreme Court upended this delicate balancing act by ruling that Congress lacked the power to ban slavery in the federal territories, thereby invalidating key parts of the two grand bargains; the Court also ruled that the Constitution did not permit even those blacks who were not slaves to become citizens.[30] The 7–2 decision, written by pro-slavery Chief Justice Roger B. Taney, was legally dubious and politically explosive.[31]

The resulting furore undermined northern moderates who sought to compromise with the South, and helped lead to the election of Abraham Lincoln to the presidency in 1860, on a platform that took a hard line against the expansion of slavery. That, in turn, precipitated the secession of the southern states and the bloody Civil War of 1861–5 that ultimately led to the abolition of slavery by the enactment of the Thirteenth Amendment in 1865. Other key aspects of *Dred Scott,* including the ban on black citizenship, were overturned by the enactment of the Fourteenth Amendment in 1868, which, among other things, guaranteed citizenship to "all persons born or naturalized in the United States, and subject to the jurisdiction thereof."[32]

2. The Post–Civil War Period

After the Civil War, the Supreme Court entered a seventy-year period during which it enforced significant limits on federal powers and issued a number of notable decisions constraining congressional authority under the Commerce Clause and other parts of the Constitution. In *Paul*

---

30 For a discussion of *Dred Scott* and its impact, see Don Fehrenbacher, *The Dred Scott Case: Its Significance in American Law and Politics* (New York: Oxford University Press, 1978).

31 For a good summary of the legal weaknesses in Taney's opinion, see David Currie, *The Constitution in the Supreme Court: The First Hundred Years, 1789–1888* (Chicago: University of Chicago Press, 1985), 264–73.

32 U.S. Const. Amend. XIV, Section 1.

v. Virginia (1869), the Court ruled that the commerce power did not cover regulation of insurance contracts because the latter were not "articles in commerce."[33] In *United States v. E.C. Knight* (1895), the Court invalidated the application of federal antitrust laws to a manufacturing firm as beyond the commerce power because there is a distinction between interstate commerce and manufacturing that takes place within the boundaries of a single state.[34]

The late nineteenth-century Court also limited federal power under Section 5 of the Fourteenth Amendment, which gave Congress the authority to adopt "appropriate" legislation enforcing that amendment's various provisions protecting the rights of recently freed slaves and others, against state governments. In the *Civil Rights Cases* of 1883,[35] the Court struck down the Civil Rights Act of 1875, which banned racial discrimination by private businesses operating places of public accommodation; the Court ruled that Congress could not use Section 5 in this way, because the amendment prohibits only discrimination by state governments, not private entities.

The Court's most widely reviled decision limiting federal power was *Hammer v. Dagenhart* (1918), which struck down a law that banned the interstate transportation of manufactured goods produced by children under the age of sixteen.[36] Over time, this ruling came to symbolize the supposed excesses of the pre–New Deal Court.[37]

The Court also issued a controversial decision limiting Congress's power to impose taxes, holding that an income tax qualified as a "direct tax" that must be apportioned among the states in proportion to population, as required by the Constitution's Direct Tax Clause.[38] This decision was negated by the ratification of the Sixteenth Amendment in 1913, which gave Congress the power to adopt income taxes without apportionment.

---

33 75 U.S. (8 Wall.) 168, 183 (1869).

34 156 U.S. 1 (1895). The distinction between commerce and manufacturing echoed Chief Justice Marshall's distinction between commerce and activities that merely "have a remote and considerable influence on commerce." *Gibbons*, 22 U.S. at 203.

35 109 U.S. 3 (1883).

36 247 U.S. 251 (1918).

37 For a recent discussion and critical evaluation of *Hammer*'s negative historical reputation, see Logan Everett Sawyer, III, "Creating *Hammer v. Dagenhart*," *William and Mary Bill of Rights Journal* 21 (2012): 67–122.

38 *Pollock v. Farmers' Loan & Trust Company*, 157 U.S. 429 (1895).

While the pre–New Deal Court enforced some significant limits on the powers of the federal government, it also often upheld federal economic regulations against potentially plausible challenges. These included laws banning the transportation of lottery tickets across state lines,[39] federal regulation of railroad rates on lines that do not cross state borders,[40] the "White Slave Act" forbidding interstate transportation of women for prostitution or other "immoral" purposes,[41] and the Pure Food and Drug Act forbidding interstate transportation of "adulterated" food.[42]

In two consolidated 1923 decisions addressing the scope of Congress's power to spend for the "General Welfare," the Court made it very difficult for states to challenge the constitutionality of conditions attached to federal spending grants to state and local governments and almost impossible for most individual citizens to do so.[43]

Even when the pre–New Deal Supreme Court imposed significant limits on federal power, it did so supported by a political consensus in favour of constitutional constraints on federal authority. The Supreme Court sometimes bucked majority public opinion, most notably in *Hammer v. Dagenhart*. But although nineteenth- and early twentieth-century public and elite opinion was characterized by numerous disputes about the scope of federal authority, there was broad agreement that there should be some strong constitutional limits.[44] Long-standing regional rivalries between the North and the South also helped limit federal power by making it more difficult to build a consensus in favour of broad new federal legislation. These ideological and political foundations for limits on federal power deteriorated only slowly during the early twentieth century.

---

39 *Champion v. Ames*, 188 U.S. 321 (1903).

40 *Shreveport Rates Case*, 234 U.S. 342 (1914).

41 *Hoke v. United States*, 227 U.S. 308 (1913).

42 *Hipolite Egg Co. v. United States*, 220 U.S. 45 (1911).

43 See *Massachusetts v. Mellon* and *Frothingham v. Mellon*, 262 U.S. 447 (1923).

44 For summaries of this broadly held view, see Robert Higgs, *Crisis and Leviathan: Critical Episodes in the Growth of American Government* (New York: Oxford University Press, 1987), 78–84; and Barry Weingast, "The Economic Role of Political Institutions: Market-Preserving Federalism and Economic Development," *Journal of Law, Economics, and Organization* 11 (1995): 1–31.

3. *The New Deal Transformation*

Although many on the political left had criticized the Supreme Court's decisions limiting federal power – especially over economic issues – for years, these attacks gained added momentum from the Great Depression that began in 1929.[45] The federal government, led after 1933 by President Franklin D. Roosevelt, began to enact a wide range of "New Deal" interventionist policies intended to alleviate the crisis and, more generally, regulate the economy in unprecedented ways.[46]

At first, the Supreme Court resisted many of the new policies. Most of the justices on the Court in the mid-1930s had been appointed by pre–New Deal presidents, and they supported judicial enforcement of limits on federal power. Between 1935 and 1937, the Court invalidated several major New Deal policies, including the National Recovery Act (NRA) of 1933, the centrepiece of Roosevelt's First New Deal, and arguably the most sweeping regulatory legislation in American history.[47] The NRA established a system of wage and price controls and cartels that encompassed nearly the entire non-agricultural economy.[48] The unanimous decision striking down the law was joined by progressive justices such as Louis Brandeis and Benjamin Cardozo, as well as the Court's conservatives. This line-up indicates both the NRA's radical nature and the extent to which judicial enforcement of limits on federal power commanded widespread support among pre–New Deal jurists.

The Court also invalidated other important New Deal laws, such as laws restricting agricultural production in order to raise prices,[49] regulating wages, prices, and production of coal,[50] and constraining the sale

45 For discussions of constitutional change during this period, see, e.g., Barry Cushman, *Rethinking the New Deal Court: The Structure of a Constitutional Revolution* (New York: Oxford University Press, 1998); and William Leuchtenburg, *The Supreme Court Reborn* (New York: Oxford University Press, 1995).

46 For a survey of the different New Deal interventions, see Higgs, *Crisis and Leviathan,* 159–95. Many New Deal policies actually had their origins in the initiatives of the previous administration of Herbert Hoover, who was a convinced interventionist, not an advocate of laissez-faire. See Joan Hoff Wilson, *Herbert Hoover: Forgotten Progressive* (Boston: Little Brown, 1975).

47 *A.L.A. Schechter Poultry Corp. v. United States,* 295 U.S. 495 (1935).

48 See Michael Weinstein, *Recovery and Redistribution under the NIRA* (New York: North-Holland, 1981).

49 *United States v. Butler,* 297 U.S. 1 (1936).

50 *Carter v. Carter Coal Company,* 298 U.S. 238 (1936).

of oil produced in excess of quotas established by the federal government.[51] But even during the early New Deal period, the Court did not strike down all major new regulatory legislation.[52]

In 1937, the Court largely stopped resisting the expansion of Congress's powers. The shift in the Court's position coincided with President Roosevelt's effort to "pack" the Court by enacting a law that would allow him to add a new justice for every current justice over the age of seventy who chose not to resign. Since many of the justices who voted to strike down New Deal laws were over age seventy, the effect would have been to allow Roosevelt to create a new majority more amenable to his preferences. Controversy still rages over whether the Court's change of course was a "switch in time that saved nine" motivated by a desire to forestall the court-packing plan, which was eventually defeated in Congress.[53] Whatever the reason, the majority of the Court gradually gave up its resistance to New Deal legislation. In *United States v. Jones & Laughlin Steel* (1937)[54] and *United States v. Darby* (1941),[55] the Court repudiated most of the pre–New Deal restrictions on Congress's Commerce Clause authority.

In Steward Machine Co. v. Davis (1937)[56] and *Helvering v. Davis*,[57] the Supreme Court upheld the constitutionality of the Social Security Act, which created federal and cooperative intergovernmental programs for unemployment insurance, retirement pensions, and welfare for single mothers. *Davis* and the Court's earlier decision in *Butler* also endorsed the theory that Congress's power to spend money for the "General Welfare" allows it to spend for nearly any purpose.[58]

---

51 *Panama Refining Co. v. Ryan*, 293 U.S. 388 (1935).

52 For example, in 1935, the Court narrowly upheld the constitutionality of sweeping new federal regulations requiring private individuals to turn in all gold coins and gold bullion they owned to the government. See *United States v. Bankers Trust Co.*, 294 U.S. 240 (1935); *Nortz v. United States*, 294 U.S. 317 (1935); *Perry v. United States*, 294 U.S. 330 (1935).

53 For recent accounts, see, e.g., Burt Solomon, *FDR v. the Constitution: The Court-Packing Fight and the Triumph of Democracy* (New York: Walker, 2009); and Jeff Shesol, *Supreme Power: Franklin Roosevelt vs. the Supreme Court* (New York: Norton, 2010). For an influential account suggesting that the Court's shift was not motivated by political considerations, see Cushman, *Rethinking the New Deal Court*, 20–32.

54 301 U.S. 1 (1937).

55 312 U.S. 100 (1941).

56 301 U.S. 548 (1937).

57 301 U.S. 619 (1937).

58 Ibid., 640–41; *Butler*, 297 U.S. at 65. *Butler* had nonetheless invalidated part of the Agricultural Adjustment Act on other grounds.

The Supreme Court's broadest New Deal–era interpretation of federal power came in *Wickard v. Filburn* (1942).[59] The Court ruled that the Commerce Clause authorized a provision of the 1938 Agricultural Adjustment Act that required a wheat farmer to limit his production of wheat, even though none of that wheat was ever sold in interstate commerce or crossed state lines. This decision went beyond previous cases such as *Darby*, which had all involved regulation of commercial employment relationships or the production of goods for sale in the market. It suggested that Congress had the power to regulate almost any activity that, in the aggregate, has a significant effect on commerce. In the modern world, that could mean almost any activity of any kind.

By 1942, all but one of the nine Supreme Court justices had been appointed by Franklin D. Roosevelt. Even if the swing voter justices on the old Court had held firm, they could not have continued to resist for long. The president, backed by a Democratic majority in the Senate, could eventually get what he wanted by appointing justices willing to uphold it. This was a nearly inevitable result of the Democratic Party's long string of electoral victories in the 1930s and early 1940s, which allowed it to dominate both Congress and the presidency.

4. The Partial Revival of Judicial Enforcement of Limits on Federal Power

After the New Deal transformation of constitutional law, few structural limits on federal power remained. Between 1937 and 1995, the Supreme Court did not invalidate a single federal law as beyond Congress's Commerce Clause authority. The Court issued noteworthy unanimous decisions holding that the clause authorized Title II of the Civil Rights Act of 1964, which banned racial discrimination in places of public accommodation, such as hotels and restaurants.[60] One of them justified the application of the law to a local restaurant that served almost exclusively in-state residents.[61] The Court concluded that the clause authorized congressional regulation of any activity that Congress had a "rational basis" for believing might have an effect on interstate commerce.[62]

---

59 317 U.S. 111 (1942).

60 *Katzenbach v. McClung*, 379 U.S. 294 (1964); *Heart of Atlanta Motel, Inc. v. United States*, 379 U.S. 241 (1964).

61 *McClung*, 379 U.S. at 300–4.

62 Ibid. at 304.

A 1971 decision reinforced the point by upholding a federal law banning loan-sharking, even though it applied mostly to small-time local loan sharks.[63] In dissent, Justice Potter Stewart lamented that "under the statute before us, a man can be convicted without any proof of interstate movement, of the use of the facilities of interstate commerce, or of facts showing that his conduct affected interstate commerce."[64] The Warren Court of the 1960s, led by liberal Chief Justice Earl Warren, also took a permissive approach to the scope of Congress's enforcement powers under Section 5 of the Fourteenth Amendment, largely deferring to congressional judgments of what qualified as "appropriate" enforcement legislation.[65]

In *National League of Cities v. Usery* (1976),[66] the Court offered a ray of hope to advocates of judicial limits on federal power when it struck down a federal law requiring state governments to comply with the federal Fair Labor Standards Act in their dealings with their own employees. The Court ruled that, although Congress had broad power to regulate private economic activity under the Commerce Clause, the Tenth Amendment restricts such regulation when applied against state governments. The Amendment states that "powers not delegated to the United States by the Constitution, nor prohibited by it to the States, are reserved to the States respectively, or to the people"; in the majority's judgment, this language limited direct federal control of "the states as states."[67] *National League of Cities* contrasts with the New Deal Court's dismissal of the Tenth Amendment as "but a truism" that imposes little if any constraint on the scope of Congressional authority.[68]

National League of Cities was, however, overruled in 1985 in *Garcia v. San Antonio Metropolitan Transit Authority*.[69] The majority came close to endorsing the notion that the constitutional division of authority between the federal and state governments should be determined entirely by the political process, because state governments can

---

63 *Perez v. United States*, 402 U.S. 146 (1971).
64 Ibid., 157, (Stewart, J., dissenting).
65 See, e.g., *Katzenbach v. Morgan*, 384 U.S. 641 (1966).
66 426 U.S. 833 (1976).
67 Ibid., 837.
68 *Darby*, 312 U.S. at 124.
69 469 U.S. 528 (1985).

effectively look after their own interests without assistance from the courts.[70]

By the 1970s, the dominant view among legal elites was that judicial review would not and should not significantly constrain the scope of federal power. This belief was buttressed both by the idea that broad federal power is necessary to deal with the complexity of the modern economy and by the association between federalism and racism that had arisen thanks to southern state governments' attempts to use "states' rights" to oppose federal intervention against racial discrimination by state and local governments.

Beginning in the early 1990s, however, judicial enforcement of limits on federal power was partially revived under Chief Justice William Rehnquist, who was appointed to that position by President Ronald Reagan in 1986. The Rehnquist revival had several causes. In the 1980s and 1990s, the resurgent Republican Party claimed that federal power had grown too great and advocated allowing the states greater autonomy. Reagan and his successor, President George H.W. Bush, appointed several Supreme Court justices committed to reinvigorating judicial enforcement of federalism, including Sandra Day O'Connor, Antonin Scalia, and Clarence Thomas.

Just as the earlier collapse of judicial review of federalism had its roots in the triumph of the New Deal coalition that dominated American politics for several decades, so the Rehnquist revival would not have been possible without the rise of more conservative political forces in the 1980s.[71] In addition, a new generation of conservative and libertarian legal scholars began to challenge the previous intellectual consensus against judicial review of federalism.[72] Finally, as time passed since the

---

70 The idea that federalism issues should be left to the political process enjoyed wide support among legal academics during this period. For leading statements of that view, see, e.g., Jesse H. Choper, *Judicial Review and the National Political Process* (Chicago: University of Chicago Press, 1980); and Herbert J. Wechsler, "The Political Safeguards of Federalism: The Role of the States in the Composition and Selection of the Federal Government," *Columbia Law Review* 54 (1954): 543–64.

71 For a well-known work defending the theory that judicial review generally follows the dictates of dominant political coalitions at the federal level, see Jack M. Balkin and Sanford Levinson, "Understanding the Constitutional Revolution," *Virginia Law Review* 87 (2001): 1045–1109.

72 See Steven Teles, *The Rise of the Conservative Legal Movement* (Princeton: Princeton University Press, 2008).

Civil Rights revolution of the 1960s, the association of federalism with racism diminished in the public mind.

The 1990s revival of judicial review of federalism proceeded along several fronts. In *United States v. Lopez* (1995),[73] the Court issued its first decision constraining congressional power under the Commerce Clause since the 1930s. Five years later, the Court invalidated another law as beyond the commerce power in *United States v. Morrison*.[74]

In interpreting the scope of Section 5 of the Fourteenth Amendment, the Rehnquist Court was less deferential than its predecessor in the 1960s. It ruled that Section 5 legislation must be "congruent and proportional" to the unconstitutional state action it seeks to remedy and cannot forbid too much state activity that is not unconstitutional in and of itself.[75] In its 2013 ruling in *Shelby County v. Holder*,[76] the Roberts Court similarly limited the scope of Congress's powers under Section 2 of the Fifteenth Amendment, which authorizes it to pass "appropriate" legislation to implement the amendment's ban on racial discrimination in voting.

In response to massive long-standing discrimination against African-American voters in the southern states, Congress had enacted the Voting Rights Act of 1965, which included a provision requiring many state and local government in the South (and a few elsewhere) to "pre-clear" any changes to their voting laws with the federal Justice Department. While few today doubt that this sweeping measure was "appropriate" in 1965, the issue confronting the Court in *Shelby County* was whether the application of pre-clearance to these same jurisdictions was still appropriate after nearly fifty years of extensive political change, during which minority participation in elections has greatly increased, to the point where it is often no worse in the covered jurisdictions than elsewhere.

Because "things have changed [so] dramatically," a narrow 5–4 majority ruled that Congress's 2006 reauthorization of the list of jurisdictions subject to pre-clearance was unconstitutional because there is no longer a close enough fit between the list of covered jurisdictions

73 514 U.S. 549 (1995).

74 529 U.S. 598 (2000).

75 See *City of Boerne v. Flores*, 521 U.S. 507 (1997). *Morrison* also applied this principle in ruling that a provision of the Violence against Women Act was not narrowly enough targeted against actual state government discrimination against women.

76 133 S.Ct. 2612 (2013).

and the prevalence of discrimination against minority voters.[77] Both the justices and outside commentators were sharply divided between those (mostly on the right) who believed that the Court's decision was a justifiable response to changing historical circumstances, and those (mostly on the left) who argued that it showed insufficient deference to Congress and opened the door to future racial discrimination in election law.[78]

The Rehnquist Court also issued a series of decisions ruling that the Tenth Amendment bars federal "commandeering" of state officials for the purpose of using them to enforce federal law.[79] In the 2013 case of *Windsor v. United States*, the Roberts Court built on the Rehnquist Court's emphasis on respect for state prerogatives by striking down Section 3 of the Federal Defense of Marriage Act, which denied federal marriage benefits to same-sex couples who had entered into marriages in states that permit gay marriage under their state law.[80] The Court invalidated the law in part because it intruded into a field normally left to the states.[81]

Finally, the Court began to enforce more vigorously the theory that the Eleventh Amendment, which bars suits against non-consenting state governments "by Citizens of another State, or by Citizens or Subjects of any Foreign State,"[82] also implicitly forbids the federal government from authorizing private lawsuits against states even by their own citizens.[83]

The Rehnquist "federalism revolution" was an important jurisprudential development. But its impact on the scope of federal power has so far been limited. In the Commerce Clause field, the Court struck down only relatively minor laws in *Lopez* and *Morrison*: the Gun Free School Zones Act barring gun possession near a school zone, and a provision of the Violence against Women Act giving victims of gender-motivated

---

77 Ibid. at 2625–31.

78 For the latter view, see ibid. at 2636–51 (Ginsburg, J., dissenting).

79 See *New York v. United States*, 505 U.S. 144, 166 (1992); and *Printz v. United States*, 521 U.S. 898, 923 (1997).

80 *United States v. Windsor*, 133 S.Ct. 2675 (2013).

81 Because of its significant implications for individual rights, this case is discussed in greater detail in part III of this chapter.

82 U.S. Constitution, Amendment XI.

83 See *Seminole Tribe of Florida v. Florida*, 517 U.S. 44 (1996), applying this principle to lawsuits in federal courts; and *Alden v. Maine*, 527 U.S. 706, 733 (1999), which extended it to bar congressional authorization of lawsuits in state court.

violence the right to sue their alleged assailants in federal court. Both were invalidated because they did not regulate any kind of "economic activity" and were not an "essential" part of any broader economic regulatory scheme.[84] This leaves plenty of room for Congress to continue to regulate economic transactions and even any "non-economic" activities that it seeks to control as part of a broader system of economic regulation. Moreover, any restrictive impact that *Lopez* and *Morrison* might have had was seriously undermined by the Court's next Commerce Clause decision, *Gonzales v. Raich* (2005).[85]

The 6–3 majority in *Raich* ruled that the Commerce Clause allows Congress to ban the possession and production of medical marijuana, even when the drug in question has never crossed state lines or been sold in any market. Unlike the farmer in *Wickard*, who used his wheat to feed his own cows as part of a commercial farming operation,[86] Angel Raich's marijuana production was not part of any commercial enterprise. The Court nonetheless ruled that Congress's power extends to this case because Raich's actions qualified as "economic activity," which it defined broadly as any activity that involves "the production, distribution, and consumption of commodities,"[87] and also because it was "rationally" connected to a broader regulatory effort to suppress the national market in marijuana. By defining "economic activity" so broadly and taking a deferential stance on the issue of whether even non-economic activity can be regulated, *Raich* diminished the likelihood that *Lopez* and *Morrison* would lead to significant constraints on federal power.[88] Importantly, the *Raich* majority included key conservative justices Anthony Kennedy and Antonin Scalia, who had voted to limit federal authority in *Lopez* and *Morrison*.

Similar, though less severe, constraints limit the impact of the Court's other recent decisions restraining federal power. The commandeering cases can be circumvented to a large extent by tying mandates imposed on state governments to federal grants as conditions that the recipients must meet. Conditional grants can also be used to get around the

---

84 *Lopez*, 514 U.S. at 558–64; *Morrison*, 529 U.S. at 610–14.

85 545 U.S. 1 (2005).

86 *Wickard*, 317 U.S. at 114.

87 *Raich*, 545 U.S. at 25–6.

88 For a more detailed analysis of *Raich*, see Ilya Somin, "Gonzales v. Raich: Federalism as a Casualty of the War on Drugs," *Cornell Journal of Law and Public Policy* 15 (2006): 507–50.

Court's Eleventh Amendment jurisprudence. States can be induced to consent to allow themselves to be sued as a condition of receiving federal funds. In addition, the Court has ruled that the Eleventh Amendment does not bar lawsuits authorized by Congress's enforcement powers under the Fourteenth Amendment, which the Court still sometimes defines broadly.[89]

Finally, until very recently, the Court made no effort to limit Congress's powers under the Spending Clause. The 1987 case of *South Dakota v. Dole* reiterated the rule that Congress's power to spend money for the General Welfare encompasses almost any objective the legislature might choose, and also gives it broad power to make conditional grants to state governments.[90]

It is probably still too early to fully assess the potential effects of *NFIB v. Sebelius*,[91] the Court's blockbuster 2012 ruling on constitutional challenges to the Affordable Care Act, President Barack Obama's 2010 health-care law.[92] In *NFIB*, twenty-six state governments and various private parties challenged the constitutionality of a central provision of the ACA, the mandate requiring most Americans to purchase government-approved health insurance by 2014. The challengers argued that the mandate was different from previous federal regulations approved under the Commerce Clause, because it did not regulate any pre-existing economic activity, even under the broad definition of such endorsed by the Court in *Raich*. Instead, it forced people to buy insurance even if they had been inactive.

A 5–4 majority accepted this argument, concluding, as Chief Justice Roberts put it, that Congress does not have the power to "regulate individuals precisely *because* they are doing nothing."[93] A majority of the Court also ruled that the mandate is not authorized by the Necessary

89 See, e.g. *Nevada Department of Human Resources v. Hibbs*, 538 U.S. 721 (2003), which upheld the application of the U.S. Family and Medical Leave Act to state governments, despite the relative weakness of evidence that the absence of mandated family leave in some states was a result of unconstitutional sex discrimination.

90 483 U.S. 203 (1987).

91 132 S.Ct. 2566 (2012).

92 For a variety of perspectives on the health-care decision, see Gillian Metzger, Trevor Morrison, and Nathaniel Persily, eds., *The Health Care Case: The Supreme Court Decision and Its Implications* (New York: Oxford University Press, 2013). For my own tentative early assessment, see Ilya Somin, "A Taxing, but Potentially Hopeful Decision," SCOTUSblog, 28 June 2012, http://www.scotusblog.com/2012/06/a-taxing-but-potentially-hopeful-decision.

93 *NFIB*, 132 S.Ct. at 2587 (Roberts, C.J.).

and Proper Clause, holding that the mandate is not "proper," even if it is necessary.[94]

However, Roberts broke with the Court's other four conservatives and upheld the mandate on the basis that it could be interpreted as a tax authorized by Congress's power to impose taxes.[95] He claimed that the mandate might be considered a tax because an individual's failure to purchase insurance (1) triggered a relatively small monetary fine collected by the Internal Revenue Service, (2) does not qualify as a crime if the fine is paid, and (3) does not require a showing of criminal intent.[96] Thus, he avoided striking down what would have been the most important federal law invalidated by the Court as beyond the scope of federal power since the 1930s.

The twenty-six state governments challenging the ACA also argued that its requirement that states greatly expand the scope of their Medicaid programs (i.e., health insurance for the poor), or else lose all of their federal Medicaid money, was unconstitutional. Surprisingly, they prevailed. Chief Justice Roberts and six other justices voted to partially strike down the Medicaid expansion because it was unconstitutionally "coercive," acting as a "gun to the head" of the states, which stood to lose federal Medicaid subsidies equal to as much as 10 to 16 per cent or more of their total state budgets, unless they accepted the expansion.[97] While previous decisions had noted that "coercive" grants were unconstitutional, this was the first use of the spending power that the Supreme Court invalidated as unconstitutional since the 1930s.

Whether *NFIB* has any major impact on future cases remains to be seen. The ruling that the Commerce Clause and Necessary and Proper Clause do not authorize federal regulation of people who are "doing nothing" might limit future federal mandates.[98] But such mandates

---

94 Ibid., 2591–3.

95 Ibid., 2594–2600.

96 Ibid.

97 Ibid., 2601–7. The Court did, however, allow the federal government to offer the states new subsidies in exchange for expanding Medicaid, even though it eliminated the threat to cut the states' massive pre-existing Medicaid grants. Ibid.

98 Some contend that this ruling is not part of the Court's holding, since it was not necessary to reach the ultimate result that the mandate is constitutional. In a section of his opinion joined by the four liberal justices who also voted to uphold the mandate, the Court specifically states that the Commerce Clause ruling is part of the holding. Ibid., 2593. Whether future Supreme Court decisions accept this characterization of the holding remains to be seen.

could be structured to fit Roberts's definition of a tax, though the penalties for violation would have to be limited to monetary fines similar to those embedded in the ACA.

The Spending Clause ruling could limit future conditions attached to federal grants to state governments. But it is hard to say whether any such conditions will be deemed by courts to be so coercive as to amount to a "gun to the head." The ruling has, however, already had an important effect on the ACA itself. As of late 2015, twenty-two state governments had rejected the Medicaid expansion, including such major states as Texas and Florida.[99] They would not have been able to do so if the Supreme Court had upheld this part of the ACA.

The Supreme Court might also consider additional federalism-based challenges to the Affordable Care Act. For example, lawsuits currently in the lower courts contend that, if the individual mandate is a tax, as the Court concluded in *NFIB*, then the mandate violates the Constitution's requirement that revenue bills originate in the House of Representatives rather than the Senate, where the final version of the ACA was first adopted.[100] If this argument prevails, it could invalidate major portions of the ACA.

Shelby County v. Holder, discussed above, may also have significant real-world effects. The pre-clearance system invalidated by the Court had a major effect on politics in the covered states. However, the long-term effects of the ruling are difficult to predict. Congress remains free to design new criteria for selecting jurisdictions for pre-clearance, and the Voting Rights Act includes other tools for combating racial discrimination in voting.

It is important to emphasize that most of the recent decisions striking down federal laws as beyond the scope of congressional power were

---

99 Nick Madigan, "Health Care Expansion Is Rejected in Florida," *New York Times*, 5 June 2015.

100 See *Sissel v. Department of Health and Human Services*, 760 F. 3d 1 (D.C. Cir. 2014). The first federal appellate court to have considered this issue ruled in favour of the federal government. It is possible to argue that the Origination Clause is not really a limit on the scope of federal power, as such, because it merely allocates power between the two houses of Congress. However, the purpose of requiring revenue bills to originate in the House was probably to make it more difficult for the federal government to raise taxes without strong popular support. See James V. Saturno, "The Origination Clause of the U.S. Constitution: Interpretation and Enforcement," Congressional Research Service, 15 March 2011, http://fas.org/sgp/crs/misc/RL31399.pdf; and J. Michael Medina, "The Origination Clause in the American Constitution: A Comparative Survey," *Tulsa Law Journal* 23 (1987): 165–234.

5–4 rulings pitting the Court's five conservatives against its four liberals.[101] Although there are some signs that this may be changing,[102] most liberal judges and legal scholars continue to oppose anything more than minimal judicial enforcement of limits on federal power. As evidenced by the *Raich* case, among others, conservative jurists have not been completely consistent in their support of limits on federal power. But many of them do favour enforcement of at least some substantial constraints. Whether the federalism revival of the last twenty years has any long-term staying power is likely to depend on which party makes future Supreme Court appointments, and also on whether advocates of judicial enforcement of federalism are able to attract more liberal support.[103] The unexpected recent death of Justice Antonin Scalia – a key supporter of most pro-federalism rulings of the last twenty-five years – raises questions about the future of the Court's revival of judicial constraints on federal power.

III. Judicial Enforcement of Limits on State Power

In contrast to the Supreme Court's equivocal record of enforcing limits on federal power, it has historically enforced a variety of limits on state power. Even as judicial enforcement of the former waned after the 1930s, the exercise of judicial power against state governments greatly expanded and shows few signs of abating. The federal courts' restrictions on state laws have been so many and varied that it is impossible to give more than a general summary. There has never been a prolonged period when the federal courts did *not* use judicial review to impose substantial restrictions on state governments.

1. The Nineteenth and Early Twentieth Centuries

The period before the Civil War of 1861–5 and the enactment of the Fourteenth Amendment in 1868 is sometimes seen as a time when the judiciary did little to constrain the states. During this era, the Court

---

101 *NFIB* was a rare exception, in that two liberal justices joined the five conservatives in striking down part of the law's expansion of Medicaid.

102 I discuss some indications that this may be the case in Ilya Somin, "Federalism and the Roberts Court," *Publius: The Journal of Federalism* 46 (2016): 1–22.

103 For a more detailed assessment of the Supreme Court's recent federalism jurisprudence and prospects for the future, see ibid.

did not apply the Bill of Rights – the individual rights protected by the first ten amendments of the U.S. Constitution – to state governments.[104] Even after enactment of the Fourteenth Amendment, the Court did not apply the Bill of Rights to the states for many years. Nonetheless, pre–Civil War federal courts restricted state governments in other ways.

Several important early Supreme Court decisions overturned state laws that set aside contractual obligations, as violating the Contract Clause of the Constitution, which forbids states from impairing the obligation of contracts.[105] The nineteenth-century federal courts also enforced the "Dormant Commerce Clause" against the states, interpreting the Commerce Clause's grant of power to regulate interstate commerce as an implicit prohibition on state legislation that restricted interstate trade and commercial enterprise, even in the absence of contrary federal legislation.[106] *Gibbons v. Ogden* and *McCulloch v. Maryland* both invalidated state laws interfering with interstate commercial enterprises, as well as upholding federal laws.[107] The Supreme Court also acted to curb some northern states' efforts to protect free blacks and escaped slaves from the onerous federal Fugitive Slave Acts.[108]

After the Civil War, the Court applied the newly enacted Thirteenth, Fourteenth, and Fifteenth Amendments, which abolished slavery and protected a variety of individual rights, against infringement by state governments. In the Court's first major case involving the Fourteenth Amendment, the *Slaughterhouse Cases* (1873),[109] it took a narrow view of the amendment's Privileges or Immunities Clause, which bars states from infringing on the "Privileges or Immunities" of American citizens. The Court interpreted the clause as primarily a protection for existing federal rights, rather than one that protected a variety of economic and

---

104 In 1833, the Court ruled that the Bill of Rights applied only against the federal government. See *Barron v. Mayor of Baltimore*, 32 U.S. (7 Pet.) 243 (1833).

105 See, e.g., *Fletcher v. Peck*, 10 U.S. (6 Cranch) 87 (1810).

106 For a review of these cases and their impact, see Michael S. Greve, *The Upside-Down Constitution* (Cambridge, MA: Harvard University Press, 2012), chap. 4.

107 See discussion of these cases in part II.

108 See, e.g., *Prigg v. Pennsylvania*, 41 U.S. (16 Pet.) 539 (1842), which ruled that the act and the Fugitive Slave Clause of the Constitution negated Pennsylvania's "personal liberty law," which sought to protect blacks against "self-help" kidnapping by slavecatchers. See also *Ableman v. Booth*, 62 U.S. (21 How.) 506 (1859), which overruled Wisconsin's efforts to free an abolitionist imprisoned for trying to help blacks resist the Fugitive Slave Act.

109 83 U.S. (16 Wall.) 36 (1873).

personal liberties. This decision largely gutted what many of the amendment's framers had considered to be its most important provision.[110]

The late nineteenth-century Court did, however, make some efforts to enforce the amendment's protections against racial discrimination, most notably in *Strauder v. West Virginia*, which struck down a state law banning African-Americans from juries.[111] In *Yick Wo v. Hopkins* (1886),[112] the Court established the important principle that even a law that does not discriminate on its face might be struck down if strong evidence suggests that it was enacted for the purpose of disadvantaging a racial minority.

These decisions, however, had only a limited impact. As Reconstruction ended in the late 1870s and early 1880s, and northern whites became less interested in protecting the rights of African-Americans in the South, the Court's efforts to enforce those rights waned. In 1896, the Court decided *Plessy v. Ferguson*,[113] a ruling that upheld the constitutionality of a state law mandating segregation in railroad cars and generally gave states wide latitude to adopt racially discriminatory legislation. *Plessy* ultimately became one of the most reviled decisions in Supreme Court history. It inaugurated an era where the courts tolerated extensive racial discrimination against blacks and other minorities.

Some scholars argue that, so long as public and elite opinion was largely supportive or at least indifferent to such discrimination, the courts did little or nothing to protect minorities against it.[114] But even during the height of Jim Crow segregation, the Supreme Court issued important decisions ameliorating the plight of African-Americans – most notably

---

110 On the centrality of the Privileges or Immunities Clause to the framers of the amendment and its undermining by the *Slaughterhouse Cases*, see, e.g., Michael Kent Curtis, *No State Shall Abridge: The Fourteenth Amendment and the Bill of Rights* (Durham: Duke University Press, 1986), 161–7, 174–7; Randy E. Barnett, *Restoring the Lost Constitution: The Presumption of Liberty* (Princeton: Princeton University Press, 2004), 195–203.

111 100 U.S. 303 (1880).

112 118 U.S. 356 (1886).

113 163 U.S. 537 (1896). On *Plessy* and its significance, see Charles Lofgren, *The Plessy Case: A Legal-Historical Interpretation* (New York: Oxford University Press, 1988).

114 For the most thorough defence of this position, see Michael Klarman, *From Jim Crow to Civil Rights: The Supreme Court and the Struggle for Racial Equality* (New York: Oxford University Press, 2004); see also Gerald N. Rosenberg, *The Hollow Hope*, rev. ed. (Chicago: University of Chicago Press, 2008).

the peonage cases,[115] which struck down state laws limiting the ability of black workers to leave their jobs, and *Buchanan v. Warley*, a 1917 decision striking down residential segregation laws.[116]

Judicial review of state laws in the nineteenth and early twentieth centuries is perhaps best known for the "*Lochner* era" of invalidation of state economic regulations, named after *Lochner v. New York*,[117] a 1905 case striking down a New York law imposing maximum hours for bakers under the Due Process Clause of the Fourteenth Amendment, which forbids states from depriving people of life, liberty, or property without "due process of law." Like *Plessy*, *Lochner* has become one of the Court's most denounced rulings, often disparaged as "judicial activism" intended to benefit the wealthy at the expense of the poor.[118] Many critics have also attacked what they consider to be *Lochner*'s oxymoronic use of "substantive due process." By definition, they argue, "due process" cannot include any protection for substantive rights.

Revisionist scholars have pointed out that the *Lochner*-era Supreme Court upheld far more state regulatory laws than it struck down – invalidating only those that seemed clearly driven by interest-group lobbying rather than genuine efforts to protect public health or safety. Revisionists also contend that judicial review of economic regulations had greater basis in precedent and original meaning than conventional wisdom suggests.[119] Although the extent of its "activism" is sometimes exaggerated, the early twentieth-century Court did impose some meaningful constraints on state economic regulation.[120]

Lochner-era Due Process Clause review of state laws protected what we today would call civil liberties, as well as economic freedoms. For example, it led the Court to strike down state laws forbidding foreign-language instruction for students[121] and mandating that children attend

---

115 *Bailey v. Alabama*, 219 U.S. 219 (1911); *United States v. Reynolds*, 235 U.S. 133 (1914).

116 245 U.S. 60 (1917). For a detailed discussion of the important real-world effects of these cases, see David E. Bernstein and Ilya Somin, "Judicial Power and Civil Rights Reconsidered," *Yale Law Journal* 114 (2004): 593–657.

117 198 U.S. 45 (1905).

118 For a modern defence of this conventional wisdom, see Paul Kens, *Lochner v. New York: Economic Regulation on Trial* (Lawrence: University of Kansas Press, 1998).

119 See, e.g., David E. Bernstein, *Rehabilitating Lochner* (Chicago: University of Chicago Press, 2011).

120 For other notable cases striking down economic regulations, see, e.g., *Adkins v. Children's Hospital*, 261 U.S. 525 (1923) (striking down a minimum wage law for women); and *Allgeyer v. Louisiana*, 165 U.S. 578 (1897).

121 *Meyer v. Nebraska*, 262 U.S. 390 (1923).

public schools instead of private religious schools.[122] "Substantive" due process also contributed to the Court's crucial decision striking down residential segregation laws in *Buchanan v. Warley*.[123] Although *Buchanan* did not end residential segregation, it played an important role in enabling African-Americans to move into many areas otherwise barred to them.[124]

2. The Modern "Rights Revolution"

The New Deal transformation of the 1930s that undermined judicial review of federalism issues also reversed *Lochner* and other cases that used the Due Process Clause to protect economic liberty against state governments.[125] By 1955, the Court ruled that "economic" regulations could be invalidated only if there was no conceivable "rational basis" for them, even one that the state legislature did not consider when it adopted the law.[126] The New Deal–era Court also undermined previously strong judicial enforcement of contractual rights under the Contracts Clause, thereby increasing state autonomy.[127] As with the decline of judicial enforcement of federalism, declining judicial protection of economic liberties was caused in large part by changing public and elite opinion, and the appointment of new Supreme Court justices in line with prevailing sentiment.

But the post–New Deal Court continued and greatly expanded judicial review of state laws infringing a variety of non-economic rights. The period since the Second World War witnessed a "rights revolution" that led to the growth of judicial enforcement of numerous rights provisions against state governments.[128]

Perhaps the most important expansion of judicial review during this period was the Court's effort to curb racial discrimination by state governments. *Brown v. Board of Education* (1954),[129] which

---

122 *Pierce v. Society of Sisters*, 268 U.S. 510 (1925). For the connection between *Meyer* and *Pierce* and *Lochner*, see Bernstein, *Rehabilitating Lochner*, 93–6.

123 Bernstein, *Rehabilitating Lochner*, 78–86.

124 For a detailed discussion of *Buchanan*'s effects, see Bernstein and Somin, "Judicial Power and Civil Rights Reconsidered," 631–40.

125 See, e.g., *West Coast Hotel v. Parrish*, 300 U.S. 379 (1937).

126 *Williamson v. Lee Optical Co.*, 348 U.S. 483 (1955).

127 *Home Bldg. & Loan Association v. Blaisdell*, 290 U.S. 398 (1934).

128 See Charles Epp, *The Rights Revolution* (Chicago: University of Chicago Press, 1998).

129 347 U.S. 54 (1954).

struck down racial segregation in public schools, is probably the most iconic decision in Supreme Court history. Although *Brown* built on earlier precedents, including some from before the New Deal, it would not have been possible in the absence of outside political changes, including liberalization of northern white opinion on racial issues, the increasing political power of African-Americans in the North, and the slowly rising social and economic status of non-whites.[130]

Even so, *Brown* represented a major judicial effort to curb racial discrimination by state governments at a time when the president and Congress were not yet ready to act on the issue in a significant way. Over the next twenty years, the Supreme Court and lower courts issued many decisions following up on *Brown* and also striking down other types of state discrimination against racial minorities.[131]

The conventional wisdom holds that these decisions played a key role in revolutionizing American race relations and ensuring greater equality for racial minorities.[132] Revisionist scholars, however, argue that they had little effect until Congress and the president began their own efforts to enforce black civil rights in the mid-1960s.[133] It is true that there was little school desegregation in most of the South until Congress intervened. But *Brown* and its progeny played a key role in promoting desegregation in other ways, including by raising the political and economic costs of maintaining Jim Crow policies for state governments.[134]

The fight against racial discrimination also stimulated efforts by various social movements to persuade the judiciary to interpret the Equal Protection Clause to constrain discrimination against other groups. Beginning in the 1970s, the Supreme Court issued a series of decisions

---

130 For a review of these points, see Klarman, *From Jim Crow to Civil Rights.*

131 See, e.g., *Brown v. Board of Education II*, 349 U.S. 294 (1955) (following up on *Brown*); *Swann v. Charlotte-Mecklenburg Board of Education*, 402 U.S. 1 (1971) (enforcing desegregation orders); *Loving v. Virginia*, 388 U.S. 1 (1967) (striking down laws banning interracial marriage).

132 See, e.g., Richard Kluger, *Simple Justice: The History of Brown v. Board of Education and Black America's Struggle for Equality* (New York: Vintage, 1976).

133 See, e.g., Rosenberg, *The Hollow Hope,* chaps 2–5.

134 For a critique of the revisionist literature, see Bernstein and Somin, "Judicial Power and Civil Rights Reconsidered," 645–56.

imposing heightened "intermediate" scrutiny of laws that discriminate on the basis of gender.[135]

Starting in the 1990s, the Court began to limit laws discriminating against gays and lesbians.[136] In 2013, the Court struck down Section 3 of the Defense of Marriage Act (DOMA), a federal law that denied federal marriage benefits to people who entered into same-sex marriages in the twelve states that permitted them at the time.[137] The decision was based partly on federalism considerations. Because of "DOMA's unusual deviation from the usual tradition of recognizing and accepting state definitions of marriage," Section 3 was subject to a higher level of judicial scrutiny than would otherwise have applied.[138] But the Court also emphasized that DOMA's discrimination against same-sex marriage was unconstitutional because the law was based on "animus" against gays and lesbians and intended to "have the purpose and effect" of signalling "disapproval" of same-sex couples.[139] For this reason, the Court concluded that DOMA "violates basic due process and equal protection principles applicable to the federal government."[140] Indeed, federalism considerations were relevant precisely because Congress's intrusion into an area usually left to the states created a "discrimination of an unusual character" that required added judicial scrutiny to determine if it was adopted for an illicit purpose.[141]

Obviously, the "due process and equal protection principles" applicable to the federal government also apply to the states, as a result of the Fourteenth Amendment. This suggested that *Windsor* might eventually lead to a Supreme Court decision striking down state laws banning gay marriage. Over the next two years, numerous state and lower

---

135 See *Craig v. Boren*, 429 U.S. 190 (1976), the decision that first adopted that standard; and *United States v. Virginia*, 518 U.S. 515 (1996), a key case restricting single-sex education at state universities.

136 See *Romer v. Evans*, 517 U.S. 620 (1996), which struck down a law based on "animus" against gays; and *Lawrence v. Texas*, 539 U.S. 558 (2003) (striking down anti-sodomy laws).

137 *United States v. Windsor*, 133 S.Ct. 2675 (2013).

138 Ibid. at 2693. For a more detailed discussion of the federalism issues in the Windsor case, see Ilya Somin, "The DOMA Decision and Federalism," Volokh Conspiracy, 26 June 2013, http://volokh.com/2013/06/26/the-doma-decision-and-federalism/.

139 *Windsor*, 133 S.Ct. at 2693.

140 Ibid.

141 Ibid.

federal courts invalidated laws banning same-sex marriage, with only one appellate court reaching the opposite result.[142]

In June 2015, the Supreme Court ruled 5–4 in *Obergefell v. Snyder* that state laws banning same-sex marriage violate the Fourteenth Amendment.[143] The majority relied on a combination of the Due Process and Equal Protection Clauses of the amendment to reach this decision, although its rationale did not clearly endorse any of the specific theories commonly advanced by advocates of same-sex marriage and relied on by lower court decisions that reached the same result as *Obergefell*.[144]

As in *Windsor*, the majority consisted of the four most liberal justices and Justice Anthony Kennedy, while the four most conservative justices dissented. The Court's ruling is highly controversial. It was met with bitter dissents by the four justices in the minority, and angry denunciations by social conservatives outside the judiciary. Some who supported the decision – myself included – would have preferred that the Court rely on a different and clearer rationale for it.[145]

For present purposes, the key point is that *Obergefell* represents a decision where the Court resolved an important issue in a way that

---

142 See, e.g., *Latta v. Otter*, 771 F.3d 459 (9th Cir. 2014); *Baskin v. Bogan*, 776 F.3d 648 (7th Cir. 2014); *Bostic v. Schaefer*, 760 F.3d 352 (4th Cir. 2014); *Kitchen v. Herbert*, 961 F.Supp. 2d 1181 (D. Utah 2013); *Bishop v. United States*, 962 F.Supp.2d 1252 (N.D. Okla. 2014); *Bostic v. Rainey*, 970 F.Supp.2d 456 (E.D. Va. 2014); *McGee v. Cole*, 2014 WL 321122 (S.D. W.Va. Jan. 29, 2014); *Bourke v. Beshear*, 2014 WL556729 (W.D. Ky. 12 Feb. 2014); *De Leon v. Perry*, 2014 WL 715741 (W.D. Tex. 26 Feb. 2014); *DeBoer v. Snyder*, 2014 WL 1100794 (E.D. Mich. Mar. 21, 2014); *Latta v. Otter*, 2014 WL 1909999 (D. Idaho, 13 May 2014); *Geiger v. Kitzhaber*, 2014 WL 2054264 (D. Ore. 19 May 2014); *Griego v. Oliver*, 316 P.3d 865 (N.M. 2013). The one major exception was *DeBoer v. Snyder*, 772 F.3d 388, 395 (6th Cir. 2014), which was eventually overruled by the Supreme Court.

143 135 S.Ct. 2071 (2015).

144 These include claims that these laws fail even minimal "rational basis" review, claims that they engage in unconstitutional discrimination on the basis of sexual orientation or gender, the argument that they violate a "fundamental" right to marry under the Due Process Clause, and others. For a summary of these arguments, see Ilya Somin, "Implications of Alternative Rationales for Striking Down Laws Banning Same-Sex Marriage," Volokh Conspiracy blog, *Washington Post*, 27 February 2014, https://www.washingtonpost.com/news/volokh-conspiracy/wp/2014/02/27/implications-of-alternative-rationales-for-striking-down-laws-banning-same-sex-marriage/.

145 See Ilya Somin, "A Great Decision on Same-Sex Marriage – But Based on Dubious Reasoning," Volokh Conspiracy blog, *Washington Post*, 26 June 2015, https://www.washingtonpost.com/news/volokh-conspiracy/wp/2015/06/26/a-great-decision-on-same-sex-marriage-but-based-on-dubious-reasoning/.

went against the preferences of many state governments. While public opinion was rapidly moving in favour of same-sex marriage in the years before *Obergefell*,[146] it is likely that some conservative states would have continued to ban it for a considerable length of time, if not for the Supreme Court's intervention.

Over the last sixty years, the Supreme Court has gradually adopted the view that the Fourteenth Amendment "incorporates" all or most of the U.S. Bill of Rights against state governments through the Due Process Clause.[147] After the Court's 2010 decision incorporating the Second Amendment right to "keep and bear arms,"[148] only the Third Amendment right not to have troops quartered in private homes, the Fifth Amendment right to an indictment by a grand jury in criminal cases, and the Seventh Amendment guarantee of a jury trial in civil cases remain unincorporated.

The cumulative impact of these incorporation decisions has been extremely broad, forcing states to adhere to unitary national standards in a wide range of areas. The incorporation of the First Amendment's Free Speech Clause has resulted in stringent limits on censorship of most types of speech,[149] including tight restrictions on state regulation of pornography and obscenity.[150] Application of the First Amendment's ban on the establishment of religion has led to strict limits on the ability of government to endorse religions, require prayer in public schools,[151] and display religious symbols on public property.[152] These decisions

---

146 According to surveys conducted by Gallup, public support for same-sex marriage rose from 37 per cent in 2005 to a record 60 per cent in May 2015, just before *Obergefell*. Justin McCarthy, "Record-High 60% of Americans Support Same-Sex Marriage," Gallup.com, 19 May 2015, http://www.gallup.com/poll/183272/record-high-americans-support-sex-marriage.aspx.

147 The prevailing legal standard is that these rights will be incorporated if they are considered "fundamental" and "deeply rooted in American history and tradition." See, e.g., *Duncan v. Louisiana*, 391 U.S. 145 (1968). For arguments that incorporation is consistent with the original meaning of the Fourteenth Amendment, see, e.g., Akhil Reed Amar, *The Bill of Rights* (New Haven, CT: Yale University Press, 1998); and Michael Kent Curtis, *No State Shall Abridge: The Fourteenth Amendment and the Bill of Rights* (Durham, NC: Duke University Press, 1986).

148 *McDonald v. City of Chicago*, 561 U.S. 3025 (2010).

149 See *Brandenburg v. Ohio*, 395 U.S. 444 (1969), which established the highly restrictive modern standard for speech restrictions.

150 See, e.g., *Miller v. California*, 413 U.S. 15 (1973).

151 *Abington School District v. Schempp*, 374 U.S. 203 (1963).

152 E.g., *Allegheny County v. ACLU*, 492 U.S. 573 (1989).

remain profoundly controversial, especially in socially conservative areas of the country where local public opinion prefers greater integration of religion into public education and civic life. Since education policy in the United States has historically been controlled largely by local governments, there is sometimes considerable resentment over federal court intervention in this field.

Incorporation of the First Amendment's Free Exercise of Religion clause has prevented states from targeting unpopular religious minorities.[153] The incorporation of the Eighth Amendment's ban on "cruel and unusual punishment" has resulted in numerous court decisions regulating the treatment of prisoners,[154] and several decisions restricting the application of the death penalty.[155]

One of the most extensive effects of incorporation has been in the field of criminal procedure, where the incorporation of rights such as the Sixth Amendment right to counsel and to a jury trial,[156] the Fourth Amendment protection against unreasonable searches and seizures, including the "exclusionary rule" requiring exclusion of illegally seized evidence from trials,[157] and the Fifth Amendment's right against self-incrimination have led to a profound transformation in state criminal procedure, as well as in police and court practices. This is so large a topic that covering it would require an article of its own.[158] But it is worth noting that the famous *Miranda* warning familiar to television and movie audiences around the world is a requirement imposed on states by a 1966 Supreme Court decision.[159] Because of its widespread

---

153 See, e.g., *Church of Lukumi Babalu Aye v. City of Hialeah*, 508 U.S. 520 (1993), an important Supreme Court decision protecting practitioners of Vodun, popularly known as "Voodoo" from laws banning their animal sacrifices.

154 See Malcolm Feeley and Edward Rubin, *Judicial Policy Making and the Modern State: How the Courts Reformed America's Prisons* (New York: Oxford University Press, 1998).

155 See, e.g., *Coker v. Georgia*, 433 U.S. 584 (1977) (banning imposition of the death penalty for rape); *Atkins v. Virginia*, 536 U.S. 304 (2002) (banning the death penalty for the mentally ill); *Roper v. Simmons*, 543 U.S. 551 (2005) (forbidding imposition of the death penalty on minors).

156 *Gideon v. Wainwright*, 372 U.S. 335 (1963).

157 *Mapp v. Ohio*, 367 U.S. 643 (1961).

158 For a helpful overview, see Yale Kamisar, "The Warren Court and Criminal Justice," in *The Warren Court: A Retrospective*, ed. Bernard Schwartz, 116–58 (New York: Oxford University Press, 1996). For an interesting evaluation of the Supreme Court's jurisprudence in this field, see Akhil Reed Amar, *The Constitution and Criminal Procedure* (New Haven, CT: Yale University Press, 1997).

159 *Miranda v. Arizona*, 384 U.S. 436 (1966).

and highly visible effects, this form of judicial intervention against the states has probably had a greater impact on popular consciousness than almost any other. The trend towards incorporation of these provisions was motivated partly by a sense that it was required by the text and history of the Fourteenth Amendment, but also partly by a desire to curb the abusive treatment of African-American and other minority defendants by state and local authorities, particularly in the South.[160]

The end of economic "substantive due process" after the demise of *Lochner* emphatically did not put an end to the use of the Due Process Clause to protect other, "non-economic" rights. The scope of such judicially enforced rights has expanded over the last fifty years. In addition to the incorporation of most of the Bill of Rights, "substantive due process" has also been used to protect a wide range of "unenumerated" rights that are not specifically listed in the Constitution.

The most controversial of the new Due Process Clause rights protected by the Court in this way are those considered to be part of the right to "privacy." The Court first addressed privacy explicitly in a 1965 decision that struck down the only remaining state law banning possession of contraceptives even by married people.[161] From this modest beginning, the right to privacy expanded to cover other issues,[162] most notably in *Roe v. Wade* (1973),[163] the Supreme Court's controversial decision establishing a right to abortion. Even forty years later, *Roe* remains a focus of bitter political conflict, especially in conservative states that would like to establish significantly tighter restrictions on abortion than allowed by the Court's jurisprudence.

During the 1960s and 1970s, judicial protection of rights against state governments was seen as a largely liberal cause. Conservatives

---

160 On this aspect of the incorporation of protections for criminal defendants, see, e.g., Lucas Powe Jr, *The Warren Court and American Politics* (Cambridge, MA: Harvard University Press, 2000), chaps 15–16; and William Stuntz, *The Collapse of the American Criminal Justice System* (Cambridge, MA: Harvard University Press, 2011), chaps 7–8.

161 *Griswold v. Connecticut*, 381 U.S. 479 (1965).

162 For a detailed and generally sympathetic overview of the Court's decisions in this area, see David Garrow, *Liberty and Sexuality: The Right to Privacy and the Making of Roe v. Wade* (New York: Macmillan, 1998). The Court modified *Roe* significantly, but reaffirmed its central premises in *Planned Parenthood of Pennsylvania v. Casey*, 505 U.S. 833 (1992). In a very recent decision, the Court took a strong line against state regulations that restrict abortion in the name of health and safety regulation. See *Whole Women's Health v. Hellerstedt*, 2016 WL 3461560 (U.S. Sup. Ct., 27 June 2016).

163 410 U.S. 113 (1973).

routinely denounced the Court for its "activism." As the Court's composition became more conservative over the last thirty years, however, conservatives and libertarians have sought to use judicial review to protect rights they value. The Court's recent incorporation of the Second Amendment right to keep and bear arms is the culmination of a long-standing effort by advocates of gun rights.

Conservative opponents of preferences for racial minorities have persuaded the Court to rule that its earlier precedents banning racial discrimination by state governments also require "strict scrutiny" of preferences intended to benefit historically disadvantaged minorities.[164] Conservatives and libertarians have also sought – with mixed success – to persuade the courts to provide stronger protection for property rights under the Fifth Amendment's Takings Clause, which requires that private property be "taken" only for a "public use" and with "just compensation."[165]

Judicial review has also had a substantial effect on state political processes. The Court's 1964 decision in *Reynolds v. Sims* interpreted the Fourteenth Amendment as requiring states to have election districts of equal population size for their state legislatures, ending the widespread practice of giving "extra" representation to rural districts and others.[166] A 1995 decision invalidated state laws limiting the number of terms to which members of Congress can be elected.[167]

---

164 See, e.g., *City of Richmond v. Croson*, 88 U.S. 469 (1989), the case that first applied strict scrutiny to affirmative action programs. The court recently reiterated the view that judicial scrutiny of state affirmative action programs must be rigorous and non-deferential in *Fisher v. University of Texas*, 133 S.Ct. 2411 (2013), in the process modifying an earlier 2003 ruling that had given greater deference to state officials seeking to use affirmative action to promote "diversity" in higher education. For the earlier decision, see *Grutter v. Bollinger*, 539 U.S. 306 (2003).

165 For an overview, see Ilya Somin, "Taking Property Rights Seriously? The Supreme Court and the 'Poor Relation' of Constitutional Law," George Mason Law & Economics Research Paper no. 08-53 (2008), http://papers.ssrn.com/sol3/papers.cfm?abstract_id=1247854. For an analysis of the most famous and controversial decision arising from these efforts, see Ilya Somin, *The Grasping Hand:* Kelo v. City New London *and the Limits of Eminent Domain* (Chicago: University of Chicago Press, 2015).

166 377 U.S. 533 (1964).

167 *US Term Limits v. Thornton*, 514 U.S. 779 (1995). Unlike *Reynolds*, this ruling invalidated a state election law because the majority concluded that it violated the Constitution's implicit requirement that states cannot limit the range of people eligible to run for federal offices, rather than because it violated individual rights.

Some of the Court's decisions enforcing individual constitutional rights restrict the federal government as well as states, and a few have invalidated significant federal laws.[168] But historically the federal courts have invalidated many fewer federal laws than state laws. And even when they strike down federal laws, the result does not necessarily promote state autonomy, because the relevant legal norm is still defined and enforced by a federal institution.

In sum, the Court has a long history of enforcing a wide range of constraints on state governments, a trend that shows little sign of abating. The net effect of this tendency is to substantially restrict the power of state and local governments. In that sense, it tends to promote political centralization at the expense of regional autonomy.

Nonetheless, judicial protection of individual rights against state governments does promote decentralization in another important sense; it devolves more decision-making power to individual citizens and private organizations, which often means an even greater extent of decentralization than would regulation by state and local governments.[169] If, for example, federal courts prevent state governments from censoring speech, regulating religion, restricting marriage rights, or overriding private property rights, power over these aspects of society is transferred to a lower, more decentralized level than the state government or even a local one. As a result, individual citizens are now more free to speak as they wish, use their property as they see fit, or marry the partner of their choice.

IV. Why Judicial Review Promotes Unitarism More Than Federalism

Although judicial review has limited both federal and state power at different times, it has constrained the states far more. Especially since the late 1930s, federal courts have imposed only modest constraints on the federal government, even as they enforce far greater restrictions on

---

168 See, e.g., *Bolling v. Sharpe*, 347 U.S. 497 (1954) (ruling that the Fourteenth Amendment's restrictions on racial discrimination apply to the federal government); *Citizens United v. Federal Election Commission*, 558 U.S. 50 (2010) (striking down a significant federal campaign finance law as violating the First Amendment).

169 On devolution to individual choice as the ultimate form of decentralization, see Ilya Somin, "Foot Voting, Federalism, and Political Freedom," in *Nomos LV: Federalism and Subsidiarity*, ed. James Fleming and Jacob S. Levy, 83–122 (New York: New York University Press, 2014).

state government autonomy. Today, the courts enforce an extraordinarily wide range of rights against state governments, most of them tending to force the states to adhere to relatively uniform, federally imposed standards.

This pattern is not accidental. Judicial action against federal laws is hampered by several structural constraints. Most importantly, federal judges are appointed by the president and confirmed by the Senate, limiting the extent to which there is likely to be a Supreme Court majority that diverges greatly from the preferences of the federal government's political branches. When the Court substantially deviates from the latter's views, it is often brought into line by new judicial appointments. Historically, presidents have usually sought to appoint judges supportive of their party's agenda, which often coincides with that of majority public opinion.

Even when justices wish to restrict federal power, they are careful not to offend majority public opinion and the national political branches too much, because they depend on the latter to enforce their decisions. Congress also has the power to limit the courts' appellate jurisdiction, increase (but not decrease) judicial pay, and create new judicial positions to be filled by appointees potentially more amenable to the wishes of the dominant political coalition in the federal government.

Flouting national public opinion can create a damaging political backlash that leads to the Court's defeat.[170] In the most dramatic such case, the Court's efforts to protect slavery in *Dred Scott* backfired so completely that it helped bring on the early abolition of the institution Chief Justice Taney hoped to defend. While both state and federal officials usually comply with judicial rulings, and the institution of judicial review enjoys broad public support,[171] the justices know that both compliance and support could erode if they make too many unpopular decisions.

---

170 For the argument that the courts have been increasingly attentive to majority opinion over time, see Barry Friedman, *The Will of the People: How Public Opinion Has Influenced the Supreme Court and Shaped the Meaning of the Constitution* (New York: Farrar, Straus & Giroux, 2009).

171 The Supreme Court typically enjoys much higher public approval ratings than the other branches of government. Even when public approval of the Court was unusually low in early 2013, 52 per cent of Americans still approved of its performance, compared to only 31 per cent who disapproved. See Pew Research Foundation, "Supreme Court's Favorable Rating Still at Historic Low," 25 March 2013, http://www.people-press.org/2013/03/25/supreme-courts-favorable-rating-still-at-historic-low/. Since 1985, the Court's approval rating has usually ranged from 60 to 75 per cent. Ibid.

In some federal systems, efforts to limit federal power are buttressed by the reality that subnational governments are bulwarks for national ethnic minorities that are majorities within a particular region.[172] In the United States, however, the most important national minorities are also minorities within the states. As a result, minority groups usually do not view state governments as their protectors, and – at least for a long time – American federalism was tainted by its association with racial discrimination against African-Americans.[173]

Even state governments often have an interest in promoting expanded federal power, because they want more federal subsidies and often also support federal laws that limit economic competition between state governments.[174] *NFIB v. Sebelius* was thus an unusual case because twenty-eight state governments had filed lawsuits against a major new federal program.[175]

Courts face much weaker constraints when they strike down state legislation, especially state laws that are disapproved of by national political majorities. In such situations, dissenting states can do little to retaliate against the judges. The federal government and sympathetic state governments elsewhere in the country may even support such judicial intervention.

This is not to suggest that the courts can never impose significant limits on federal power. The Supreme Court often enforced such limits during the country's first 150 years. Also, judicial enforcement of limits on federal power has experienced a modest revival over the last twenty-five years. In both instances, however, judicial intervention was effective in part because external political forces backed it.

The fact that federal judges serve until they die, resign, or (in rare cases) are impeached and removed from office also creates opportunities for the judiciary to check the other branches of government. In

---

172 See works cited in note 4.

173 This may be changing in recent years, as minority groups have gained greater power in state and local governments and in some cases have achieved greater influence over them than over the federal government. For an argument along these lines, see Heather K. Gerken, "A New Progressive Federalism," *Democracy* 24 (Spring 2012), http://democracyjournal.org/magazine/24/a-new-progressive-federalism/.

174 John McGinnis and Ilya Somin, "Federalism v. States' Rights: The Case for Judicial Review in a Federal System," *Northwestern University Law Review* 99 (2004): 89–130.

175 In addition to the twenty-six states involved in the case that reached the Supreme Court, two other states, Virginia and Oklahoma, filed separate lawsuits challenging the law.

some cases, the incumbent justices were appointed by previous presidents whose ideological orientation may be very different from that of their newer colleagues. Democrats Franklin Roosevelt in the 1930s and Barack Obama since 2009 both had to cope with ideologically inimical justices appointed by their predecessors. Republican presidents sometimes face similar problems, as did Richard Nixon, for example. Judicial autonomy is also reinforced by widespread political ignorance, which ensures that most voters are often unaware of all but the most controversial Supreme Court decisions.[176] This sometimes enables the courts to strike down even relatively popular laws without suffering a major political backlash.

V. Conclusion

Overall, American judicial review has done far more to promote centralization than to limit the power of the federal government. This pattern is unlikely to change in the foreseeable future. However, the extent to which the courts are willing and able to limit federal power has varied widely over the course of American history.

Currently, there is sharp conflict between those who want much more aggressive judicial enforcement of limits on federal power and those who believe that this type of judicial review should be cut back or even abolished. The deep disagreement over *NFIB v. Sebelius* (2012) and *Shelby County v. Holder* (2013) reflects this division. It is not clear which side will ultimately prevail. Perhaps neither will for a long time to come.

In recent decades, the debate over federalism and judicial review has become connected to debates over interpretive methodology. Many conservative jurists, such as the late Justice Antonin Scalia and Clarence Thomas, argue that the Constitution should be interpreted in accordance with its original meaning, which they argue justifies stronger judicial enforcement of limits on federal power.[177] Liberals such as Justice Stephen Breyer tend to support "living Constitution" theories of interpretation that justify reinterpreting the text in light of contemporary

---

176 See Ilya Somin, "Political Ignorance and the Countermajoritarian Difficulty: A New Perspective on the 'Central Obsession' of Constitutional Theory," *Iowa Law Review* 90 (2004): 1287–371.

177 See, e.g., Thomas's concurring opinions in *Lopez* and *Morrison* and the joint dissenting opinion authored by four conservative justices in *NFIB v. Sebelius*.

needs, which they contend require broad federal power.[178] The overlap between conflicts over federalism and debates over interpretive methodology makes consensus in this field even more difficult to achieve.[179]

Some conservatives still criticize the federal courts for what they regard as excessive limits on state-government powers in the name of enforcing individual rights. At the same time, many liberals and libertarians argue that the courts should enforce a broader menu of individual rights against the states. While federal judicial enforcement of individual rights against state governments is often associated with political liberals, in recent decades conservatives also have advocated increased judicial intervention to protect some rights, particularly property rights and the rights of gun owners. It seems unlikely that we will see a major rollback of the use of judicial review to protect individual rights against state governments. But it is difficult to say how many additional constraints courts will impose on the states in the future.

In contrast to widespread criticism of the federal courts' role in interpreting the Constitution, there have been few serious recent efforts to restructure the federal system by constitutional amendment. Some scholars have argued for significantly restructuring the Constitution in various ways.[180] But such ideas have gained little political traction. In 1995, Congress came close to passing an amendment requiring the federal government to balance its budget. But it is doubtful that it would have been ratified by the necessary three-quarters of the states, even if it had passed Congress. Various other federalism-related amendment proposals have had even less success. The extraordinary difficulty of amending the Constitution has probably reduced the attractiveness of this strategy for change.

The federal courts play a complex dual role in the federal system, protecting the states in some ways while restricting their power in others. Federal judges are always likely to impose substantial constraints on state governments, especially when their policies diverge greatly from the views of national political majorities. In the right circumstances, however, the courts can also impose meaningful restraints on Washington.

---

178 See Stephen Breyer, *Active Liberty: Interpreting Our Democratic Constitution* (New York: Knopf, 2005); Stephen Breyer, *Making Our Democracy Work: A Judge's View* (New York: Vintage, 2011), chap. 10.

179 Recently, some liberal constitutional law scholars have embraced originalism and argued that it justifies an expansive interpretation of federal power. See, e.g., Jack Balkin, *Living Originalism* (Cambridge, MA: Harvard University Press, 2011).

180 See, e.g., Sanford Levinson, *Our Undemocratic Constitution* (Princeton: Princeton University Press, 2006).

15 Comparative Observations and Conclusions

NICHOLAS ARONEY AND JOHN KINCAID

In one of several essays published in the *New York Journal* in 1787 and 1788, Anti-Federalist[1] author "Brutus"[2] predicted that the Supreme Court of the United States would "lean strongly in favour of the general government." He emphasized two reasons. First, the provisions of the U.S. Constitution are expressed in "general and indefinite terms" that invite a nationalist interpretation. Second, members of the Court would be motivated to "extend their power and increase their rights" both directly by expanding their own jurisdiction and indirectly by allowing the general government to enlarge its authority.[3] In response, Alexander Hamilton famously proclaimed that the judiciary "will always be the least dangerous" branch of the federal government.[4]

Later, Brutus expressed concern that the Court, as an "independent authority," would be "exalted above all other power in the government."[5] Extremely sceptical about the neutral role of this high court in the world's first modern federation, he observed, "Had the construction of the constitution been left with the legislature, they would have

1 Anti-Federalists opposed the proposed U.S. Constitution in 1787–8. The name "Anti-Federalist" was a term of opprobrium fastened on them by supporters of the proposed constitution who seized the rhetorical high ground by calling themselves "Federalists."

2 Brutus was probably Robert Yates, a New York judge, delegate to the 1787 Constitutional Convention, and friend of New York's Anti-Federalist governor, George Clinton.

3 Brutus XI (31 January 1788) in Herbert J. Storing, ed., *The Complete Anti-Federalist* (Chicago: University of Chicago Press, 1981), 2:420–1.

4 Jacob E. Cooke, ed., *The Federalist* (Middletown, CT: Wesleyan University Press, 1961), 522.

5 Brutus XV (20 March 1788), in *The Complete Anti-Federalist*, 437.

explained it at their peril; if they exceed their powers, or sought to find, in the spirit of the constitution, more than was expressed in the letter, the people from whom they derived their power could remove them, and do themselves right." But when the ultimate power is "lodged in the hands of men independent of the people ... no way is left to control them but *with a high hand and an outstretched arm.*"[6]

Was Brutus prophetic? Do high courts in federal countries generally interpret their constitutions so as to "extend the powers of the general government"? Are they federalists or unitarists? The evidence presented in this volume is mixed, though leaning in Brutus's direction.

I. General Findings

1. Centralizing and Decentralizing Trends

In some countries, the federation courts have contributed to a gradual centralization of power. Ilya Somin concludes in this volume, for example, that while the U.S. Supreme Court has promoted both centralization and state autonomy at different times, on balance it has strengthened the power of the federal government, including the power of the federal courts, at the expense of the states' powers – a pattern unlikely to change in the foreseeable future. Nicholas Aroney likewise argues that, despite occasional variations, a centralizing pattern has been evident in Australia for almost a century. These findings confirm Daniel J. Elazar's observation that the U.S. Supreme Court and the Australian High Court stand out as centralizers among the courts of federal countries.[7]

Some other federal countries suggest a similar story, especially where the constitution, although federal in form, is relatively centralist in substance. Rotimi Suberu concludes in this volume that the Nigerian Supreme Court, while playing a role in moderating Nigeria's "overly centralized federal system" and helping to arbitrate conflicts, has had only limited impact on the federal system, which remains "constitutionally skewed, politically corrupt, ethnically contentious, and, therefore, chronically fragile." Rodrigues, Lorencini, and Zimmermann note, "Brazilian federalism has always been highly centralized," and "the

6 Ibid., 442.

7 Daniel J. Elazar, *Exploring Federalism* (Tuscaloosa: University of Alabama Press, 1987), 214–26. See also John Kincaid, "From Cooperative to Coercive Federalism," *Annals of the American Academy of Political and Social Science* 509 (1990): 139–52.

contemporary judiciary has largely maintained this centralization."[8] Although Canada is usually seen as having been transformed from a centralized federal system into a much more decentralized one,[9] Eugénie Brouillet points to recent shifts towards more unitarist jurisprudence by Canada's Supreme Court.[10] Elisenda Casanas Adam describes Spain's Constitutional Court as having been, until recently, "fairly balanced" between expansive interpretations of the central state's competences, and rulings defending powers of the autonomous communities. More lately, the Court has become a "polarizing centralist."

Whether centralization is a general or necessary tendency may certainly be questioned, however, if the conclusions of the other contributors to this volume are taken into account. Arthur Benz depicts the German Constitutional Court's "balanced" approach as a clear exception to any general inclination of federal courts to foster centralization. A similar role of securing an "equilibrium" between the orders of government and protecting constituent-government powers is ascribed to Belgium's Supreme Court by Patrick Peeters and Jens Mosselmans. José Caballero Juárez concludes that Mexico's Supreme Court has played a varied role, on one hand interpreting the Constitution in ways that provide state and local authorities with new opportunities to exercise their powers, while, on the other hand, standing at the apex of an integrated judicial system that prevents state courts from establishing themselves as sources of legal norms having authority within their states.

Complex pictures are presented for other countries. Nico Steytler points out that while South Africa's constitutional court has tended to support the constitutional rights of local government, it has not given full effect to the corresponding rights of provincial governments under the national Constitution, resulting in "hourglass" federalism in which the provinces are squeezed by both a dominant national government

---

8 See, similarly, Jacob Dolinger and Luís Roberto Barroso, "Federalism and Legal Unification in Brazil," in *Federalism and Legal Unification: A Comparative Empirical Investigation of Twenty Systems*, ed. Daniel Halberstam and Mathias Reimann, 153–67 (Dordrecht: Springer, 2014).

9 See Alan Cairns, "The Judicial Committee and Its Critics," *Canadian Journal of Political Science* 4 (1971): 301–45; Peter W. Hogg, "Is the Supreme Court of Canada Biased in Constitutional Cases?," *Canadian Bar Review* 57 (1979): 721–39; Katherine E. Swinton, "Federalism under Fire: The Role of the Supreme Court of Canada," *Law and Contemporary Problems* 55 (1992): 121–45.

10 See also Emmanuelle Richez, "Losing Relevance: Quebec and the Constitutional Politics of Language," *Osgoode Hall Law Journal* 52, no. 1 (2014): 191–233.

"above" and powerful local and metropolitan governments "below." Manish Tewari and Rekha Saxena note that while India's Supreme Court was apparently unitarist for much of its history, the Court has shown signs of a somewhat more federalist orientation since the early 1990s, albeit against the weight of a Constitution that is mostly centralist in design and purpose.

India and South Africa also highlight a relatively new development in which local governments have been constitutionally recognized as the third order of government, as is true in Brazil, Mexico, and Nigeria.[11] Some other constitutions, such as those of Germany, Spain, and Switzerland, contain provisions guaranteeing local self-government. Aside from the "hourglass" outcome in South Africa, the constitutional recognition of local government has not yet had significant impacts on the federalist or unitarist leanings of high courts.

Andreas Lienhard and his colleagues recognize that Switzerland is a distinct case, especially because the federal Supreme Court does not exercise judicial review over federal legislation. Nonetheless, they point to its tendency to avoid finding cantonal legislation unconstitutional wherever possible. The general effect of the Court's judgments has been to strike a "balance" between centralization and decentralization. Another exceptional case is Ethiopia, where, according to Gedion Hessebon and Abduletif Idris, there is very little federalism-related case law, principally because the Constitution prevents the courts from playing such a role. They conclude that neither the federal nor the state judiciaries have had any significant role in shaping the development of the federal system because the House of Federation is charged with deciding constitutional disputes between the central government and the states.

Although the variations noted above inhibit easy generalization, the predominant leaning of nine of the eleven high courts that exercise judicial review over federation law has been unitarist. Five of these courts – Australia, Brazil, Mexico, Nigeria, and the United States – have a marked unitarist orientation. Mixed cases are Canada, where the court was generally province-friendly but recently took a more centralist tack; India, where the court long had a centralist orientation but issued more decentralist rulings after 1989; South Africa, where the constitutional court has been centralist with respect to the provinces but somewhat decentralist with respect to local governments; and Spain, where the court has often

11 Nico Steytler, ed., *Local Government and Metropolitan Regions in Federal Systems* (Montreal and Kingston: McGill-Queen's University Press, 2009).

balanced the powers of the centre and the autonomous communities but issued a notably centralist ruling in 2010 on Catalonia's statute of autonomy. The Basque Country, moreover, boycotted the court for many years. The only high courts described as being consistently balanced between unitarism and federalism are those of Belgium and Germany. Strikingly, no contributor to this volume describes his or her federation's high court as leaning regularly in a federalist direction or as favouring decentralization, although Belgium's court is a candidate for this category. On balance, Brutus was perhaps more prescient than Hamilton about the long-term impacts of high courts on federal systems.

To the extent that any of these courts are politically independent, they have some choice as to whether to lean in a federalist or unitarist direction, but such choices are constrained by often powerful constitutional, institutional, and political forces that impel them to list in one or another direction. Independent courts are not insulated from political processes, and they are obliged to interpret a constitution that is more or less federalist in substance. Similarly, these same forces play an important role in whether a federation's high court performs a major, minor, or no role in shaping a federal system's arrangements.

2. *Importance of Internal and External Vantage Points*

These findings might seem to be at odds with the decentralization indices presented in table 3 in the Introduction. Despite the centralist orientations of the high courts of Brazil, Canada, and the United States, these federations are among the top thirteen most decentralized countries globally, according to the World Bank's indices. The high courts of Australia and the United States have long been seen by many observers as being among the most centralizing of federal high courts, but Australia is the fifty-fifth most decentralized country, while the United States is the ninth most decentralized. Furthermore, no European country has apparently become more centralized since 1980; devolution has been more common.[12] Indeed, about 95 per cent of democracies worldwide now have some type of elected subnational government.[13]

12 Gary Marks and Liesbet Hooghe, "Contrasting Visions of Multi-level Governance," in *Multi-level Governance*, ed. Ian Bache and Matthew Flinders, 15–30 (Oxford: Oxford University Press, 2004).

13 World Bank, *World Development Report 1999/2000* (New York: Oxford University Press, 1999), 107.

There is, we believe, no contradiction. The decentralization indices, while rough, provide a useful two-dimensional benchmark for understanding the impacts of the courts examined in this volume, namely, (1) centralization or decentralization trends relative to each federation's past, and (2) centralization and decentralization trends relative to other countries. For example, while the U.S. federal government is vastly more powerful relative to the states than it was in the past, in part because the U.S. Supreme Court has been significantly centralist since 1937, this centralization has occurred in a system that was substantially non-centralized at its founding, and it remains, relative to most countries, comparatively non-centralized today. The enumeration of limited powers in the federal Constitution, the Anti-Federalist tradition of opposition to centralization, and the dualistic character of U.S. federalism with non-delegated powers reserved to the states or the people, as well as other factors, allow the states to continue being significant polities. Compared to other countries, moreover, they are huge polities. The GDP of the United States is of course comparatively gargantuan, but just as remarkable is the fact that, in 2014, the GDP of California equalled that of Brazil; Texas equalled Canada; New York, Spain; Ohio, Nigeria; Maryland, South Africa; and Pennsylvania, Switzerland.[14] The U.S. states, while individually small compared to the United States, do not suffer from puny governance capacities.

The centralizing leanings of recent Canadian Supreme Court rulings likewise occur within a system that was and remains comparatively non-centralized in practice. What is surprising about the World Bank indices is that many observers have long regarded Canada as more decentralized than the United States.[15] Likewise, the World Bank's index ranks Brazil as more decentralized than thought by most scholars, while Australia's fifty-fifth-place ranking more closely matches scholars' qualitative rankings.

Devolution trends evident in Europe since 1980 help to explain the findings that all three European constitutional courts examined in this

---

14 Steven Perlberg, "This Brilliant Map Renames Each US State with a Country Generating the Same GDP," Business Insider, 12 February 2014, http://www.businessinsider.com/countries-vs-us-states-gdp-map-2014-2.

15 E.g., Ronald L. Watts, *Comparing Federal Systems*, 3rd ed. (Montreal and Kingston: McGill-Queen's University Press, 2008), 177; and Thomas O. Hueglin and Alan Fenna, *Comparative Federalism: A Systematic Inquiry*, 2nd ed. (Toronto: University of Toronto Press, 2015), 22 and 110.

volume – Belgium, Germany, and Spain – have been comparatively balanced between unitarism and federalism, although recently the Belgian court has moved in a more decentralist direction while the Spanish court has put some brakes on devolution.

How one assesses the federalist or unitarist impacts of a federation's high court depends partly, therefore, on where one stands. Inside a federation, the high court can appear to have had substantial unitarist impacts; from a comparative perspective, the high court's unitarist impacts can appear less substantial.

3. *Relevance of Exceptional Cases Having No Judicial Umpire*

It is also important to consider the significance of two federations that have no high court authorized to invalidate federation laws. These federations, Switzerland and Ethiopia, challenge notions of judicial supremacy and offer important lessons. First, a federation can endure and function democratically without such a court. Whether this requires special circumstances is uncertain. Swiss federalism in its various incarnations is more than seven hundred years old. The customary and traditional modes of mutual accommodation built up over centuries likely obviated the need to institute a U.S.-style supreme court in 1848. The United States had no such history in the 1780s, nor did any other federation examined in this book. The litmus test of this proposition is whether Ethiopia can endure as a federation and become democratic without a high court empowered to engage in constitutional review, challenge a monopolistic party system, and ensure more rights protections.

Second, these cases partly reflect the kind of view held by American Anti-Federalists like Brutus, namely, that a federation's high court is inevitably a creature of the federation government. It is not a true third party neutrally umpiring disputes between the federation and its constituent polities. The Swiss, therefore, leave this power in the hands of the sovereign people construed as both a single national people and as multiple peoples. A constitutional amendment requires a double majority of the people of the country and of the peoples of a majority of the cantons. Whether this approach requires special circumstances also is uncertain. Switzerland is a small country with a population equal to that of New York City. Ethiopia's House of Federation is a variation on the Anti-Federalist view because it consists of representatives chosen through the constituent state councils, and each nation, nationality, and people is guaranteed at least one representative, with another representative provided for each additional one million population of each nation and nationality. The paucity of cases in Ethiopia prohibits any firm conclusion, but given the dominance of a single party coalition nationwide, one suspects that the House of Federation is a creature of the party controlling the federation government. By contrast, Belgium's constitutional court may be the only example in this volume of a court being almost a creature of the constituent polities.

Third, the Ethiopian and Swiss exceptions acknowledge that interpreting a constitution and umpiring relations between a federation government and its constituent polities are ultimately political acts that significantly affect the balance of power and, thereby, the well-being of different citizens and communities. Establishment of an independent constitutional or supreme court creates an appearance of legalistic non-political decision-making, the symbolism of which may be important for the life of a federation, but it does not alter the fact that such a court is a political actor and, moreover, an actor usually independent of the people and their elected representatives. This undemocratic and counter-majoritarian character of high courts sometimes elicits attacks on the legitimacy of their exercise of judicial review.[16] Some critics suggest that the political process, not the courts, should determine the balance of power between the federation and its constituent polities.[17] Although these debates are not the focus of this volume, the analyses of judicial behaviour undertaken in this the book are very relevant to such questions.

4. Relevance of the Constituent Power

A fundamental question faced by courts in federal countries concerns the conception of the political community underlying the federal polity. Is it conceived ultimately in singular unitary terms or plural federal terms? This question can be interrogated from social, political, and legal perspectives.

---

16 E.g., Jeremy Waldron, "The Core of the Case against Judicial Review," *Yale Law Journal* 115, no. 6 (April 2006): 1346–1406; and Alexander M. Bickel, *The Least Dangerous Branch*, 2nd ed. (New Haven, CT: Yale University Press, 1986).

17 E.g., Jesse H. Choper, *Judicial Review and the National Political Process: A Functional Reconsideration of the Role of the Supreme Court* (Chicago: University of Chicago Press, 1980), but see Nicholas Aroney, "Reasonable Disagreement, Democracy and the Judicial Safeguards of Federalism," *University of Queensland Law Journal* 27, no. 1 (2008): 137–43.

Most federal constitutions refer to the constitutive authority by which the federation was legally constituted. Some, for example, appeal to "the people"; others appeal to "the states"; and yet others to some combination of "the people" and "the states." Many textual features and structural relationships established by federal constitutions are shaped by conceptions of the constitutive authority (*le pouvoir constituant*) upon which they are based, and much judicial reasoning and interpretation of such constitutions proceeds, explicitly or implicitly, on a certain view of the location and nature of that constitutive authority. The conception of constitutive authority presupposed by a court may or may not be altogether consistent with what the constitution declares that authority to be, but either way, the underlying conception influences the way in which the court interprets the constitution. As such, ideas about the underlying constitutive demos or demoi can be a focus point for both the social and political context in which the federation operates and the constitutional rules and principles applied by the courts.

Determining whether a federal constitution's foundations are federalist or unitarist in this sense is important but complex. Not only are there no ideal types, but the relevant data and ways of analysing the question are diverse. Many federal constitutions expressly attribute originating or ultimate sovereignty to the "people," the "nation" or the "state" in the singular (e.g., Belgium, Brazil, India, Mexico, Nigeria, and Spain); some, however, attribute it to a plurality of "peoples," "nations," and "states" (e.g., Ethiopia); others use more ambiguous formulas, such as where the singular "people" is used together with a reference to a plurality of constituent polities (e.g., Australia, Germany, Switzerland, and the United States). These statements as to originating or ultimate sovereignty may or may not be entirely consistent with a federation's actual historical origin. Despite the reference to "the people" in Australia, Germany, and the United States, for example, all three constitutions were ratified or approved by all of the constituent polities as expressed by their respective parliaments, special conventions, or popular referendums.

In such federations, the underlying juridical question concerns the location or identity of the "constituent power." However, identifying this power, because it has to do with what Hans Kelsen called the *Grundnorm*[18] or what H.L.A. Hart called the "rule of

18 Hans Kelsen, *General Theory of Law and State* (Cambridge, MA: Harvard University Press, 1949).

recognition,"[19] is a matter not only of law but also of normative presuppositions and political effectiveness (Kelsen) or social fact (Hart). The location and nature of this constituent power can therefore be assessed both before and after the federation has come into being. Thus, it can be asked: (1) what was the effective legal-political authority by which the content of the federal constitution was then determined, and (2) to what legal-political authority is its validity now ascribed? Judicial assumptions about these matters can shape courts' approaches to their interpretation of the constitution.

This is especially so when courts face novel questions about the scope of federal and state power where the text is silent or ambiguous. The Canadian *Patriation Reference* is an example. The Supreme Court was asked whether a Canadian request for British legislation to amend the Constitution could be made unilaterally by the federal Parliament or whether a "sufficient" degree of agreement from the provinces would also be necessary.[20] While a majority of the Court held that as a matter of law the federation could request an act of patriation without reference to the provinces,[21] a differently composed majority held that a constitutional convention[22] constrained the federation from doing so without a sufficiently representative (but not necessarily unanimous) degree of provincial consent.[23] Because the texts of the relevant constitutional instruments do not address this question explicitly, the Court reasoned on the basis of a particular theory of the fundamental grounds and nature of Canada's federation.[24]

Another example is *U.S. Term Limits v. Thornton*, which asked whether the people of Arkansas could amend their state constitution to impose term limits on their representatives in the federal

---

19 H.L.A. Hart, *The Concept of Law*, 3rd ed. (Oxford: Oxford University Press, 2012), chap. 5.

20 *Patriation Reference* [1981] 1 S.C.R. 753.

21 Ibid., 762–809 (Laskin, C.J., Dickson, Beetz, Estey, McIntyre, Chouinard, and Lamer JJ.). This involved a rejection of the "confederal" arguments accepted by the minority: ibid., 809–48 (Martland and Ritchie JJ.).

22 According to Peter W. Hogg, conventions "are rules of the constitution that are not enforced by the law courts," but they "regulate the working of the constitution" and "prescribe the way in which legal powers shall be exercised." *Constitutional Law of Canada*, 4th ed. (Scarborough, ON: Carswell, 1997), 19.

23 Ibid., 874–910 (Martland, Ritchie, Dickson, Beetz, Chouinard, and Lamer JJ.).

24 Similar reasoning occurred in the *Quebec Veto Reference* [1982] 2 S.C.R. 793; and the *Quebec Secession Reference* [1998] 2 S.C.R. 217.

Congress.[25] The Constitution does not provide explicit guidance on the question, so the Supreme Court sought to resolve it by asking whether members of Congress are to be conceived as representatives of their respective states or of the people of the United States as a whole, and whether the Constitution itself derives from the people of the states or the people of the nation. Four members of the Court maintained that the "ultimate source of the Constitution's authority" is "the consent of the people of each individual State, not the consent of the undifferentiated people of the Nation as a whole" and that it remains within the reserved powers of the states to impose term limits on their representatives in the federal Congress.[26] However, a majority of the Court considered that the qualifications laid down in the Constitution are "fixed and unalterable," and that the Constitution gives effect to the principle that "sovereignty is vested in the people" and that this confers on the people "the right to choose freely their representatives" in the Congress.[27] The states do retain a significant array of powers under the Constitution, but the power to add qualifications is not part of those powers and, even if they were, the Constitution removed such powers from the states.[28] According to the majority, this is because the states are not a collection of "independent nations bound together only by treaties"; rather, the Constitution created a national government that owes its allegiance to the people of the nation as a whole.[29] As Justice Anthony Kennedy put it, "The whole people of the United States asserted their political identity and unity of purpose when they created the federal system."[30] The fact that the Supreme Court split 5–4 in favour of a nationalist interpretation that struck down congressional term-limits laws in twenty-three states shows that this question of the ultimate grounds of the Constitution remains alive in the United States.

The jurisprudence of Australia's High Court offers a third example. In its early decisions, it proceeded on the view that the Constitution embodied a compact between independent states, interpreting federal

---

25 Cynthia L. Cates, "Splitting the Atom of Sovereignty: Term Limits, Inc.'s Conflicting Views of Popular Autonomy in a Federal Republic," *Publius: The Journal of Federalism* 26, no. 3 (Spring 1996): 127–40.

26 *U.S. Term Limits v. Thornton*, 514 U.S. 779, 846–50 (1995).

27 Ibid., 514 U.S. 779, 791, 794–5 (1995), relying on *Powell v. McCormack*, 395 U.S. 486 (1969).

28 *U.S. Term Limits v. Thornton*, 514 U.S. 779, 801–2, 806 (1995).

29 Ibid., 514 U.S. 779, 803 (1995).

30 Ibid., 514 U.S. 779, 838 (1995).

power narrowly and constructing a strong doctrine of intergovernmental immunities on that basis. However, since its landmark decision in 1920 in the *Engineers Case*,[31] premised on a view of the Constitution as an act of the British Parliament that gave effect to the will of the Australian people, it has interpreted federal power very widely and limited the intergovernmental immunity doctrine to preserving state government "autonomy."

Even though the latter two cases reflect the way in which the American and Australian courts have, often by close majorities, tended towards centralizing interpretations of their respective constitutions, these shifts are relative to the constitutive foundations of each system. In the aftermath of the Civil War, for example, the U.S. Supreme Court described the U.S. Constitution as establishing "an indestructible Union, composed of indestructible States."[32] Not only is the union indissoluble, but the states are permanent, constituent members of the federation. While much the same could be said of Australia's states, this is not the case in India, where the federal authorities can overrule the distribution of powers by a two-thirds resolution of the Council of States,[33] require state governments to implement federal laws and policies,[34] intervene in the affairs of the states in cases of "emergency,"[35] and make alterations to the territories of the states and create new states by amalgamating or dividing the territories of existing states.[36] As India's Supreme Court has observed, "There is no warrant for the assumption that the Provinces were sovereign, autonomous units which had parted with such power as they considered reasonable or proper for enabling the Central Government to function for the common good. The legal theory on which the Constitution was based was the withdrawal or resumption of all the powers of sovereignty into the people of this country and the distribution of these powers … between the Union and

31 *Amalgamated Society of Engineers v. Adelaide Steamship Co Ltd*, (1920) 28 C.L.R. 129.

32 *Texas v. White*, 74 U.S. 700, 725 (1869).

33 Indian Constitution, Art. 149; see also Art. 150.

34 Indian Constitution, Arts. 256, 257.

35 Indian Constitution, Pt. XVIII.

36 Indian Constitution, Arts. 3, 4. An amendment to the Constitution in 1955 stipulated that such proposals must first be recommended by the president and be referred to the legislature of any affected state for the expression of its views, but the power to make the change remains vested in the Union Parliament acting by simple majority. The States Reorganisation Act 1956, enacted in this way, implemented a far-reaching reorganization of the states along linguistic lines.

the States."[37] The Constituent Assembly that established the Constitution, purporting to act in the name of the people of India as a whole, deliberately constructed a constitution that could be either "unitary" or "federal," as "time and circumstances" required.[38]

South Africa and Spain are similar to India in this respect. In South Africa's *Education Policy Case*, for example, the Constitutional Court held that the merely derivative status of the provinces means that there can be no room in South Africa for a version of the "anti-commandeering" doctrine developed in the United States whereby the federal Congress cannot require state officials to enact or administer federal law.[39] Likewise, in its decision on the revised statute of autonomy enacted by Catalonia in 2006, Spain's Constitutional Court deliberately read down those aspects of the autonomy statute that appeared to assert a kind of constitutive power in the Catalan people, reasoning that sovereignty is vested in the entire Spanish people and that the statute of autonomy is strictly subordinate to the Constitution as authoritatively interpreted by the central court.[40]

Each of these cases underscores the importance of attending to (the often contested) conceptions of the basic constitutional foundations of each country's federal system. While the jurisprudence of each country develops dynamically in response to changes in that country's social and political conditions, conceptions of the federation as being founded on an agreement among "sovereign" states or on the consent of the people of the "nation" as a whole play an important role in shaping the court's jurisprudence. Conceptions of the nature of the political community underlying the federal polity are important in shaping the orientation of the court in a relatively federalist or unitarist direction. These conceptions, in turn, are influenced by an array of factors identified in the Introduction to this volume, and discussed in detail in the remainder of this chapter.

II. Possible Explanatory Factors

Ambiguities in constitutional provisions on federalism create opportunities for courts to intervene and expand their power and to forge

37 *West Bengal v. India*, AIR 1963 SC 1241; 1964 SCR (1) 371, 396.

38 India, *Constituent Assembly Debates* (New Delhi, 1951), (13 December 1946; 22 January 1947), "Objectives Resolutions 1 and 4," (4 November 1948), "Motion re. Draft Constitution."

39 See *In re: The National Educational Policy Bill, No. 83 of 1995*, 1996 (4) BCLR 518 (CC); *New York v. United States*, 505 US 144 (1992).

40 Constitutional Court Decision 247/2007.

jurisprudential approaches to federalism that reflect the court's conceptions of the federation's foundations, structure, and raison d'être. The variety of approaches to federalism displayed by federal high courts is cause for much reflection. As Cheryl Saunders argues, federalism is routinely defined as involving a constitutional distribution of powers; yet, in some federations, there has been an inexorable expansion of central power to the point that the courts are close to abandoning the task of enforcing the distribution of powers.[41] However, as noted above, in a few countries, the courts appear to have adopted a more balanced approach.

What accounts for this variation? There are a number of possible explanations, some interrelated. One general explanation is that a federal system, like any system of government, evolves in response to influential social and political pressures. It may be that the tendency to centralization or non-centralization is determined primarily by the federation's underlying socio-political reality. On this account, a decisive question is whether the federation is territorially homogeneous or heterogeneous in its ethno-linguistic and religious make-up.[42] Alternative explanations are more institutional. Here, relevant questions concern the way in which the constitution distributes and allocates responsibilities, the structural relationships between the federation and the constituent polities, and the assumptions, methods, and values embedded in the judicial process itself.[43] Other explanations lie in the organization and operation of political parties, which substantially determine the extent of government centralization or non-centralization in a federation,[44] and the influence of history on the founding and operation of a federal system.

---

41 Cheryl Saunders, "Can Federalism Have Jurisprudential Weight?," in *The Federal Idea: Essays in Honour of Ronald L. Watts*, ed. Thomas J. Courchene, John R. Allan, Christian Leuprecht, and Nadia Verrelli (Montreal and Kingston: McGill-Queen's University Press, 2011), 111.

42 Jan Erk, *Explaining Federalism: State, Society and Congruence in Austria, Belgium, Canada, Germany and Switzerland* (London: Routledge, 2010).

43 See Gerard Baier, *Courts and Federalism: Judicial Doctrine in the United States, Australia, and Canada* (Vancouver: UBC Press, 2006).

44 William H. Riker, *Federalism: Origin, Operation, Significance* (Boston: Little, Brown, 1964), 129; Donald V. Smiley, *The Federal Condition in Canada* (Toronto: McGraw-Hill Ryerson, 1987), 103–4; Mikhail Filippov, Peter C. Ordeshook, and Olga Shvestova, *Designing Federalism: A Theory of Self-Sustainable Federal Institutions* (New York: Cambridge University Press, 2004), chap. 6; Klaus Detterbeck, Wolfgang Renzsch, and John Kincaid, eds., *Political Parties and Civil Society in Federal Countries* (Don Mills, ON: Oxford University Press, 2015).

The questions we posed to the contributors to this volume were intended to elicit information relevant to answering explanatory questions such as these. In what follows, we offer tentative answers, while recognizing the need for more research. The sections below generally follow but expand upon the explanatory factors set out in the Introduction to this volume.

1. Federal and Pre-Federal History

The impacts of history on the formation and operation of federations and their courts are evident in the case studies. All of the devolutionary federations reflect responses to centralized, authoritarian pasts. Belgium's system reflects, in part, reactions to abuses that occurred under long periods of rule by the Dutch, Austrians, and French. The judiciary was elevated to a prominent position at independence in 1831. By contrast, the framers of Ethiopia's 1994 Constitution were suspicious of the judiciary because judges were seen as sympathizers with the brutal Marxist Derg regime of 1974–87. Federal Nigeria reflects, in part, reactions to centralized colonial pasts, while South Africa and Spain represent reactions to domestic authoritarianism – Francoism in Spain and apartheid in South Africa – and Brazil and Mexico had prior centralized and authoritarian regimes.

Of the federations we have labelled as both devolutionary and integrative, Germany had prior centralized and authoritarian periods, and Canada and India had colonial pasts with considerable power centred in London. In Canada, moreover, Québécois desires for autonomy and even independence need to be understood in the context of Canada's British colonial history and continuing English-speaking majority in the country as a whole.

Of the three integrative federations, Australia and the United States also had British colonial histories, but the individual colonies enjoyed measurable degrees of self-government and semi-independent courts that were well-established and largely retained at the time of federation. The Swiss, who have no colonial or authoritarian past (except for the brief and unpopular Helvetic Republic imposed by Napoleon between 1798 and 1803), forged the most non-centralized federation of all and saw no need to vest their federal high court with judicial review authority over federal law. It exercises this authority only over cantonal law.

Other historical circumstances also contributed to differential responses to centralized, authoritarian pasts. In South Africa, where the ruling African National Congress (ANC) views the polity as a single national community, the Constitutional Court has been accorded considerable respect as an independent guardian of human rights, but its federalism jurisprudence is less independent of the ANC line. In plural Canada and Spain, certain constituent polities exhibit more restrained support for the high court, because it can weaken the cultural identity and self-government of those polities by its rulings on both human rights and the balance of power within the federation.

Path dependence produced by history can cast a long arc over high-court jurisprudence. For example, the constitutional development of the United States and the federalism jurisprudence of its Supreme Court cannot be properly understood without appreciating their entanglement with the consequences of the country's 246-year history of black slavery. This legacy is reflected in, among other things, the Court's numerous nationalizing rulings based on the Fourteenth Amendment (1868) of the U.S. Constitution and its controversial rulings on the federal Voting Rights Act of 1965.[45]

Historical influences are also durable for institutional reasons, including the legal system. In common-law federations, history endures through the body of precedents that have been built up over time. Although courts in civil-law systems do not rely on precedents in the same way, the civil law reflects historical influences and is usually slow to change. A considerable amount of custom and tradition can be codified and locked into civil law for generations.

However, courts occasionally make dramatic turnabouts, as in the famous "switch in time that saved nine" in the United States in 1937. Facing considerable Democratic political pressure from the White House and Congress, the Supreme Court reversed course on its commerce-clause jurisprudence. Australia's High Court took a significant change in course in its landmark *Engineers Case* in 1920. Germany's Constitutional Court turned towards more Land-friendly decisions during the 1980s. Mexico's Supreme Court inaugurated a new era of constitutional enforcement in the late 1990s. Nigeria's Supreme Court reduced its federalism decision-making after 2007. Spain's Constitutional Court took a big step away from precedent in its 2010 ruling on Catalonia's statute of autonomy, a ruling that provoked massive public

45 *Shelby County v. Holder*, 570 U.S. ___, 133 S.Ct. 1236 (2013); and *Northwest Austin Municipal Utility District No. 1 v. Holder*, 557 U.S. 193 (2009).

protests in Catalonia. Courts, therefore, also overrule themselves. In early 2015, Canada's Supreme Court, responding to its conception of changing cultural norms, overturned a 1993 precedent by ruling that physician-assisted suicide is a fundamental right.[46] This controversial decision invalidated a federal law banning such suicide; as a result, it let stand a 2014 Quebec law allowing it.

Finally, an important aspect of history we could not adequately incorporate in this volume concerns the conquests of indigenous peoples that occurred in Australia and all the western hemisphere federations. The peoples who survived the conquests were marginalized, and credible efforts to redress injustices did not begin until the 1960s. One trend has been to facilitate reassertions of territorial self-government while also protecting individual rights. The Constitution of Brazil provides for the recognition of the rights of indigenous peoples to their traditional lands,[47] and a decision of 2009 upheld the legality of a federal demarcation and preservation of indigenous land.[48] In Mexico, a constitutional amendment of 2001 went farther by recognising the right to self-determination of indigenous peoples, to be implemented by the states in a manner consistent with "national unity."[49] In the United States, the federal executive branch treats tribal governments on a government-to-government basis, but the U.S. Supreme Court has not befriended tribal sovereignty.[50] Canada established the self-governing territory of Nunavut in 1999, and its Supreme Court issued a landmark ruling expanding First Nations' land rights in 2014.[51] The ruling will substantially affect certain powers of both the federal and provincial governments. Similarly, Australia's High Court issued two groundbreaking rulings expanding Aboriginal land rights,[52] but the decisions provoked legislation that restricted the rulings' reach. Whether

---

46 *Carter v. Canada* 2015 SCC 5.

47 Constitution of Brazil, Art. 231.

48 *Raposa Serra do Sol*, Pet. N. 3.338-RR (D.O.U., 25 September 2009).

49 Constitution of Mexico, Art. 2.4. See Guillermo de la Peña, "A New Mexican Nationalism? Indigenous Rights, Constitutional Reform and the Conflicting Meanings of Multiculturalism," *Nations and Nationalism* 12, no. 2 (2006): 291–2.

50 David E. Wilkins and Keith Richotte, "The Rehnquist Court and Indigenous Rights: The Expedited Diminution of Native Powers of Governance," *Publius: The Journal of Federalism* 33, no. 3 (Summer 2003): 83–110.

51 *Tsilhqot'in Nation v. British Columbia* 2014 SCC 44.

52 *Mabo v. Queensland (No. 2)* (1992) 175 C.L.R. 1; and *The Wik Peoples v. Queensland* (1996) 187 C.L.R. 1.

indigenous governments will become constituent polities within these federations or occupy some asymmetric or junior position remains to be seen.

In summary, courts operate within the constraints and traditions of their federation's history while also helping to shape that history to the extent they make independent rulings of political and socioeconomic import. These decisions, in turn, often affect the balance of power between the federation and the constituent states. However, as the case studies in this volume demonstrate, high courts vary in their willingness or ability to shape history.

2. *One People or Many Peoples?*

As noted above, the conception of political community underlying a federal polity serves as a focal point for both the social and political context in which the federation operates and the constitutional rules and principles that are interpreted and applied by the courts. Whether a federal country consists of a single ethno-linguistic or religious community or incorporates several such communities, especially territorially located communities such as the peoples of the Basque Country and Catalonia in Spain, can have a long-term association with the evolution of the federal system towards more or less decentralization. Ethno-linguistic or religious communities may advocate for national policies that benefit them and preserve their distinctiveness. These communities, especially territorially concentrated ones, constitute multiple demoi who may not regard themselves as part of one demos. Additional challenges arise when some constituent polities representing discrete ethno-linguistic or religious groupings have not ratified the federal constitution, such as Quebec, which has not ratified the Constitution Act, 1982, and six Swiss cantons that never ratified any of Switzerland's three modern federal constitutions. Where, then, lies *le pouvoir constituant*? If there is a single demos, the pressure may be towards formulating uniform policies across the country, as in Germany, but if there are several demoi, political outcomes, especially on issues of salience to particular cultural identities, will often be implemented in ways shaped by those identities, as in Belgium, Canada, and Spain.[53]

53 Erk, *Explaining Federalism*, 7–10.

The latter three countries, although devolutionary or mixed in origin, have undergone significant transformation in a federalizing direction as a result of both formal changes to their constitutions and judicial interpretation. The impact in Canada of the *Patriation Reference* on the formal process by which the Canadian Constitution was patriated has been noted. In Belgium, a succession of formal changes introduced since 1970–1 have resulted in the conferral of substantial powers on the communities and regions, and the Belgian Constitutional Court has engaged in a relatively broad approach to interpreting those powers, taking the autonomy of the communities and regions as its starting point. Moreover, the new Article 35 proposes to reverse the basic logic of the system from the devolutionary principle that the federation retains all residual powers to the federative principle that the federation will be limited to matters expressly assigned to it. In Spain, the historic nations and geographic regions have taken advantage of their capacity to initiate statutes of autonomy, thus exercising a kind of semi-constitutive power in the context of a formerly unitary constitution and devolutionary system. The role of Spain's Constitutional Court is said to have been generally balanced, although its decisions to limit the scope of the reformed statutes of autonomy of Valencia and Catalonia have elicited considerable criticism and heightened secessionist sentiment in Catalonia.

Belgium, Canada, and Spain demonstrate how an originally devolutionary and relatively centralized constitution can, under conditions of territorial heterogeneity, be federalized over time, just as Australia and the United States illustrate how the reverse can occur under conditions of relative territorial homogeneity. However, this pattern does not always obtain. The Constitutional Court of relatively homogeneous Germany and the Constitutional Court of heterogeneous Belgium are both described in this volume as relatively "balanced." In heterogeneous Canada, the Supreme Court has moved from a generally decentralist to a slightly more centralist orientation, while the Supreme Court of heterogeneous India has done the reverse. Seeking to hold heterogeneous regions together, courts sometimes respond by tightening central control and sometimes by strengthening regional autonomy. Indeed, the decision may depend on the gravity of the case at hand. As in India, it seems, Spain's Constitutional Court, rightly or wrongly, deemed Catalonia's 2006 statute of autonomy to be the camel's nose in the tent that posed an existential threat to the Spanish state.

Courts in multilingual federations face special interpretative challenges when their federal constitution is officially rendered in multiple languages, such as English and Hindi in India. In Canada, the English and French versions of the Constitution Act, 1982 and amendments are equally authoritative, although interpretive problems may arise when the versions are not clearly harmonious. Usually, when one version is clearer on a point than the other, the courts favour the clearer version. Courts may also prefer the version that best protects a right, construes it more liberally, or best effectuates the purpose of a right. However, some contend that proper interpretation requires compatibility between both language versions.[54] Linguistic diversity within a federation can contribute to deep cleavages that doubly complicate the contested nature of constitutional interpretation.

Nonetheless, despite the importance of managing multinational conflict in territorially heterogeneous Belgium, Canada, Ethiopia, India, Nigeria, Spain, and Switzerland, we do not find high courts being major direct players in managing such conflict; conflict is managed (or mismanaged) mainly through political processes. In Ethiopia and Switzerland, the courts are sidelined from such management. In the other federations, high courts help set some of the rules of multinational coexistence (e.g., Canada's secession reference case[55]) and enforce the constitutional choices made by the political process, but high courts are not superior participants or even equal co-participants with other political actors in such conflict management. Furthermore, the composition of the high courts in most heterogeneous federations mirrors to some extent the multinational composition of the federation, thereby sensitizing these courts to the political interests of the federation's constituent communities. Only in Spain has the Constitutional Court arguably aggravated multinational conflict since 2010. When high courts do enter the political thicket of multicultural conflict management, it is often at the request of political forces, as in Canada's secession case, or the insistence of political forces, as in the Spanish Court's rulings on Catalonia.

3. *Constitutional and Institutional Structure*

The above considerations do not mean that constitutions are entirely malleable in the hands of the courts, but they do mean that underlying

54 Hugo Cyr and Monica Popescu, "Constitutional Reasoning in the Supreme Court of Canada," draft, 3 August 2014, 20, Social Science Research Network, http://papers.ssrn.com/sol3/papers.cfm?abstract_id=2475709.

55 *Reference Re Secession of Quebec*, [1998] 2 S.C.R. 217.

conceptions of the purpose, foundations, and nature of the federation can influence the outcome in borderline cases. The texts and structures of constitutions are meant to impose constraints on judicial discretion. To some extent, they do, although more so in some countries than in others.[56] Consider the distribution of legislative competences. The allocation of powers in a federal constitution can be more or less generous to the federation or the constituent polities, and the logic and structure of the distribution can vary. Areas of competence can be distributed specifically between the federation and the constituent polities, or specific competences can be given to one and the residue assigned to the other. Some competences may be exclusive, others concurrent. Sometimes framework powers are conferred on the federation, leaving the states to enact more detailed and specific laws within the parameters determined by federal law. The formal logic of a federal constitution can thus be to distribute legislative competences into "coordinate" spheres of law and administration, with strict constitutional rules for resolving conflicts and inconsistencies between federal law and laws of the constituent polities, or it can envisage a more cooperative framework where, for example, general laws are enacted by the federal legislature but implemented by the executive authorities of the constituent polities. All of these "technical" differences in constitutional language and logic make a difference, not only to the forms of argument that can sensibly be advanced by lawyers, but also to the interpretations of the constitution that are reasonably open to the courts. It is important to identify the "margin of decisional freedom" available to the courts in any particular context.[57]

As noted, an important distinction is between federations established through the integration of previously independent political communities and those that emerged through constitutional devolution of responsibilities to sub-state political communities (see table 1 in the Introduction).[58] This is a significant distinction, although its sharpness

56 Jeffrey Goldsworthy, *Interpreting Constitutions: A Comparative Study* (New York: Oxford University Press, 2006), 3–4, chap. 7.

57 André Bzdera, "Comparative Analysis of Federal High Courts: A Political Theory of Judicial Review," *Canadian Journal of Political Science* 26 (1993): 7.

58 Carl Joachim Friedrich, *Trends of Federalism in Theory and Practice* (New York: Praeger, 1968), 177; Ivo D. Duchacek, *Comparative Federalism: The Territorial Dimension of Politics* (New York: Holt, Rinehart and Winston, 1970), 113–15, 120–8; Koen Lenaerts, "Constitutionalism and the Many Faces of Federalism," *American Journal of Comparative Law* 38 (1990): 205, 206–7; Alfred Stepan, *Arguing Comparative Politics* (Oxford: Oxford University Press, 2001), 320–3.

is not always easy to maintain.[59] The clearest cases of integration, such as the United States and Switzerland, are, for different reasons, not quite pure instances,[60] and the clearest cases of devolution, such as Spain and Belgium, involve the recognition of very old, once independent sub-state nations.[61] Cases that fall between these two poles, such as Australia and Canada, display features of both, the former tending more towards the integration end of the spectrum, the latter towards the devolution end. But despite the difficulty of finding a pure type, the distinction between integration and devolution has explanatory power, at least in relation to how the constitutive foundations of a federal system are understood, and how this understanding tends to shape the way in which government powers are distributed among the orders of government, how the federation's governing institutions are constructed, and the prescribed means by which the federal constitution can be amended in the future.[62] An assessment of the role of the courts in each country must consider these basic facts about the constitutive origin of the system and the terms of the federative settlement expressed in the constitution's text and structure. These features often shape the composition and jurisdiction of the courts themselves, and they constitute the very substance of the constitution the courts are called upon to interpret and apply.

The constitutional logic of the distribution of powers is thus related to the underlying conception of the federation. Integrative federations presuppose the prior existence of the constituent polities as self-governing political communities. Their constitutions, therefore, usually take the existence, nature, and scope of the constituent political institutions and competences for granted, and provide only for the establishment of the governing institutions of the federation, including its legislative competences. Moreover, in strongly integrative systems (e.g., United States,

59 See Watts, *Comparing Federal Systems*, 65.

60 Richard Kay, "The Illegality of the Constitution," *Constitutional Commentary* 4 (1987): 57–80; Jean-François Aubert, *Traité de Droit Constitutionnel Suisse* (Neuchâtel: Ides et Calendes, 1967), 30–2.

61 Frank Delmartino, Hugues Dumont, and Sebastien van Drooghenbroeck, "Kingdom of Belgium," and Luis Moreno and César Colino, "Kingdom of Spain," in *Diversity and Unity in Federal Countries*, ed. Luis Moreno and César Colino, 48–74 and 289–319 (Montreal and Kingston: McGill-Queen's University Press, 2010).

62 John Kincaid and G. Alan Tarr, eds., *Constitutional Origins, Structure, and Change in Federal Countries* (Montreal and Kingston: McGill-Queen's University Press, 2005); Nicholas Aroney, "Formation, Representation and Amendment in Federal Constitutions," *American Journal of Comparative Law* 54, no. 1 (2006): 277–336.

Switzerland, and Australia), the premise is that the powers of the constituent polities were originally plenary or general and were qualified or limited under the constitution only in the specific ways agreed upon as a condition of federation. In all the integrative federations, residual or "reserved" powers lie with the constituent polities. In strongly devolutionary systems that emerged from a unitary state (e.g., Belgium and Spain), the federative logic usually goes in the opposite direction; the competences of the federation are originally general and continuing, subject to the grant of specific powers to the constituent polities.[63] In systems that fall roughly between these two poles, the competences are often specifically distributed between both the federation and the constituent polities, albeit sometimes supplemented by a "catch-all" residuary clause (e.g., Canada and India). In some devolutionary states that had at least rudiments of constituent polities before federation (e.g., Brazil and Ethiopia), the residual power may lie with the constituent polities.

The critically important question in distribution-of-powers cases concerns the relationship between the scope of federal power and the scope of the constituent polities' power. Even though the presupposition of integrative and devolutionary systems is to accord a certain logical priority to the competences of the *original* political unit (in devolutionary systems) or units (in integrative systems), the *specificity* of the powers conferred on the *derivative* political unit (in integrative systems) or units (in devolutionary systems) can advantage those derivative units. This is because the powers can be interpreted in essentially two ways: either solely by reference to the positive language in which they are conferred (on the derivative unit or units) or by keeping also in mind the powers that are reserved (to the original unit or units). If these putatively "reserved" powers are not spelt out in the constitution, the courts have to infer them from the intentions, structures, or purposes of the constitution. But because this can be a controversial judicial method, courts often prefer to focus on the words used by the constitution; thus, the

---

63 Devolution within the United Kingdom is a partial exception. There, the distribution of powers is exceptionally complex and asymmetrical. However, the whole scheme is founded on the assumption of British parliamentary sovereignty. See Alan Trench, "The Framework of Devolution: The Formal Structure of Devolved Power," in *Devolution and Power in the United Kingdom*, ed. Alan Trench (Manchester: Manchester University Press, 2007), 48.

specificity of the powers conferred on the derivative unit of government garners for them a kind of interpretive priority.

In integrative systems that specify only the federation's powers, the result of this kind of reasoning tends to favour the authority of the whole over the parts. This is apparent even in the distribution of competences within the European Union. According to the president of the European Court of Justice, Koen Lenaerts, "The residual powers of the Member States have no reserved status. The Community may indeed exercise its specific, implied or non-specific powers in the fullest way possible, without running into any inherent limitation set to these powers as a result of the sovereignty which the Member States retain as subjects of international law. There simply is no nucleus of sovereignty that the Member States can invoke, as such, against the Community."[64] While the constitutional courts of many of the EU's member states have maintained that the member states retain certain fundamental constitutional prerogatives, it is widely recognized that the European Court of Justice almost always upholds EU laws against challenges.[65]

Much the same outlook has been adopted by the U.S. Supreme Court in its interpretation of the Tenth Amendment of the U.S. Constitution, which guarantees that "the powers not delegated to the United States by the Constitution, nor prohibited by it to the States, are reserved to the States respectively, or to the people." Rather than treating this principle as a factor that shapes the interpretation of federal powers, it has been termed merely a "truism that all is retained which has not been surrendered."[66] Accordingly, the Court has held that the power of Congress over interstate commerce, for example, "is complete in itself, may be exercised to its utmost extent, and acknowledges no limitations other than are prescribed in the Constitution"[67] and that it is a power that "can neither be enlarged nor diminished by the exercise or non-exercise of state power."[68] It took some time, as Somin shows, for this

64 Lenaerts, "Constitutionalism and the Many Faces of Federalism," 220.

65 Joseph Weiler, "The Transformation of Europe," *Yale Law Journal* 100 (1991): 2403–83. Although see Alan Dashwood, "The Limits of European Community Powers," *European Law Review* 21 (1996): 113–28; Renaud Dehousse, "Community Competences: Are There Limits to Growth?," in *Europe after Maastricht: An Ever Closer Union?*, ed. Renaud Dehousse, 103–25 (Munich: Law Books in Europe, 1994).

66 *United States v. Darby*, 312 U.S. 100, 124 (1941).

67 Ibid., 114, citing *Gibbons v. Ogden*, 22 U.S. (9 Wheat.) 1 (1824), 196.

68 Ibid.

principle to work itself out in the United States,[69] but it ultimately contributed to the expansive commerce-clause jurisprudence that is now U.S. Supreme Court orthodoxy.[70] That said, the Court still endorses the principle of enumeration and on some (limited) occasions has deployed it to impose some restraints on federal power.[71]

In Australia, similarly, the constitutional guarantee of the continuing existence of state powers and state constitutions[72] has been treated as irrelevant to determining the scope of federal legislative powers, which are interpreted as widely as the language used can sustain, without consideration of the powers reserved to the states or with a view to maintaining a "federal balance."[73] Perhaps more so in the United States, the principle of enumeration has been applied by the High Court to strike down federal laws,[74] but the general trend has been to read federal powers as widely as possible. The only substantial limit on federal power in these countries concerns cases where federal law is deemed to interfere excessively with the functioning of the constituent polities themselves, which in Australia means interfering with their capacity to function as independent governments,[75] and in the United States means that congressional legislation cannot "commandeer" the states[76] and cannot unduly interfere with the "special and specific position" that the states occupy in the constitutional system.[77]

69 See also John Kincaid, "The Rise of Coercive Federalism in the United States: Dynamic Change with Little Formal Reform," in *The Future of Australian Federalism: Comparative and Interdisciplinary Perspectives*, ed. Gabrielle Appleby, Nicholas Aroney, and Thomas John (Cambridge: Cambridge University Press, 2012), 157.

70 E.g., *Wickard v. Filburn*, 317 U.S. 111 (1942).

71 E.g., *United States v. Lopez*, 514 U.S. 549 (1995); *United States v. Morrison*, 529 U.S. 598 (2000); and *National Federation of Independent Business v. Sebelius*, 132 S.Ct 2566 (2012).

72 Australia Constitution, ss. 106 and 107.

73 E.g., *New South Wales v. Commonwealth* (2006) 229 C.L.R. 1.

74 Especially in relation to the "commerce" power, which the High Court has insisted is limited to the regulation of *interstate* trade and commerce: e.g., *Airlines of New South Wales Pty Ltd v. New South Wales (No. 2)* (1965) 113 C.L.R. 54.

75 *Melbourne Corporation v. Commonwealth*, (1947) 74 C.L.R. 31; *Austin v. Commonwealth*, (2003) 215 C.L.R. 185.

76 *New York v. United States*, 505 U.S. 144 (1992); and *Printz v. United States*, 521 U.S. 898 (1997).

77 *Garcia v. San Antonio Metropolitan Transit Authority*, 469 U.S. 528, 556 (1985). See also *National League of Cities v. Usery*, 426 U.S. 833, 842–4 (1976), which was overruled by *Garcia*.

It would be tempting to conclude, as Malcolm Feeley and Edward Rubin argue, that when the court's jurisprudence fails to identify a core set of issues over which the states retain exclusive and constitutionally guaranteed authority, this is evidence that a genuinely federal system does not exist anymore.[78] However, such a conclusion rests on an unduly stringent definition of federalism; it requires a core set of constitutionally reserved state competences that can be *positively identified* prior to the interpretation of the powers of the federation – a condition that no integrative federation that is silent about the powers reserved to the states can satisfy short of judicial construction of a list of reserved powers by implication.[79] Because the competences of the constituent polities are undefined in such systems, there is nothing specific in the constitution's text to help the courts identify a core set of issues over which the constituent polities retain exclusive authority. This contrasts markedly with such devolutionary federal systems as Belgium and Spain and with mixed systems (e.g., Canada and India) in which the competences available to the general and regional orders of government are both specified in the constitution. In the former, there is a clear textual basis for identifying the devolved powers of the constituent polities; in the latter, the courts have to determine how the two lists of powers are to be understood together.

In Canada, the dual list of competences has made it relatively easier for the courts to maintain a kind of balance between the respective powers of the dominion and the provinces. In the early interpretation of the *British North America Act, 1867* (UK), the prevailing view of the Judicial Committee of the Privy Council was that the explicit competences granted to both orders of government must be taken into consideration when interpreting the scope of power granted to either. Adopting the nautical image of "watertight compartments," the Judicial Committee embraced a dualistic approach that avoided overlaps of power between the exclusive powers granted to the two orders of government.[80] In recent years, Canada's Supreme Court has adopted a more dynamic or evolutionary (i.e., "living tree") approach to interpreting the Constitution[81] in which the possibility of concurrent legislative competence is

78 Malcolm M. Feeley and Edward L. Rubin, *Federalism: Political Identity and Tragic Compromise* (Ann Arbor, MI: University of Michigan Press, 2009), chap. 5.

79 It also overlooks the many other characteristic elements of these political systems that are recognizably federal: see Watts, *Comparing Federal Systems*.

80 *A.-G. for Canada v. A.-G. for Ontario*, [1937] A.C. 326, 354.

81 The metaphor can be traced to *Edward v. A.-G. for Canada*, [1930] A.C. 124, 136.

made possible through, among other things, a "double aspect" doctrine that enables both orders of government to legislate in a way that relates to the same subject matter.[82] Nonetheless, when the interpretative approaches of the closely related federations of Canada and Australia are compared, it is evident that the Canadian Court's approach to the grant of specific exclusive powers to the provinces results in a relatively more balanced approach than occurs in Australia.[83]

Belgium offers another instructive example. Its Constitutional Court regards the powers specifically conferred upon the communities and regions as having been completely and integrally transferred to them; hence, limitations on those powers are interpreted narrowly. As Peeters and Mosselmans observe, because the powers granted respectively to the federation, the communities, and the regions are exclusive, the Constitutional Court considers it necessary to determine "where the centre of gravity lies" in each case and to attribute authority to the appropriate order of government. A "double aspect" doctrine, similar to that applied in Canada, marks a limited exception to this approach by allowing federal and regional legislation to regulate the same subject, provided there is no incompatibility between the two laws. However, in relation to the concurrent power over taxation, for example, when a tax law is primarily a non-fiscal policy instrument, the Court asks whether the law infringes on the competences of the other authorities in a disproportionate manner. The constitutional principle of "federal loyalty" (similar to the German concept of *Bundestreue*, discussed below) has also been interpreted by the Belgian Constitutional Court as a ground for review of legislation, even though the probable intent of the constitutional provision was that it be applied politically rather than enforced judicially. In the 2012–14 state reform, the Special Majority legislator extended the Constitutional Court's jurisdiction in order to confirm this case law of the Court.

Spain's quasi-federalism also proceeds on the basis of two sets of powers: competences reserved to the central state and competences that may be assumed by the autonomous communities through their statutes of autonomy. This constitutional capacity of the autonomous communities

---

82 *British Columbia (Attorney General) v. Lafarge Canada Inc.*, [2007] 2 S.C.R. 86, para. 4.

83 Compare Leslie Zines, *The High Court and the Constitution*, 4th ed. (Sydney: Butterworths, 1997), 28–9; Bruce Ryder, "The Demise and Rise of the Classical Paradigm," *McGill Law Journal* 36 (1991): 308–81; Nicholas Aroney, "Reserved Matters, Legislative Purpose and the Referendum on Scottish Independence," *Public Law* (2014): 421–45.

to exercise the power to define, within limits, their own competences has been moderated, however, by the Constitutional Court's insistence that sovereignty remains located in the Spanish people as a whole, and that the powers exercised by the autonomous communities are conferred by the Constitution rather than deriving independently from the sovereign rights of the people of each autonomous community. Consistent with this outlook, the Court has tended to interpret the competences of the Spanish state expansively, while adopting a more restrictive approach to the competences of the autonomous communities, reasoning that their "exclusive" powers must not prevent the central state from exercising its exclusive powers. Especially in relation to the powers of the central state over such matters as economic planning and equality of individual rights, Adam points out that while the Court has maintained that room must be left for the autonomous communities to exercise powers that affect these matters, it has nonetheless formulated numerous exceptions for measures that the Spanish state argues are necessary to attain important central-state objectives. Similarly, in relation to "framework" laws, while the Court has affirmed that it should articulate minimum standards on the basis of which the autonomous communities can enact particular legislative policies, the Court has subsequently allowed the central state to enact a whole range of secondary laws, administrative acts, and detailed regulations in particular fields. This has been "balanced" by decisions that have interpreted autonomous-community competences flexibly and protected them from efforts by the central state to usurp recognized competences of the autonomous communities, but as the Court's decision concerning Catalonia's 2006 statute of autonomy demonstrates, the devolutionary nature of Spain's system provides the Court with a basis for reading statutes of autonomy, not as expressions of self-constitutive authority but as ordinary organic laws of the Spanish state.

Similar observations can be made about the Indian Supreme Court's approach to the federal distribution of power in that country. When a law enacted within a particular legislature's powers also affects or relates to the subject matter of another legislature, the Court examines the substantive character of the impugned law to identify its "pith and substance."[84]

84 The "pith and substance" doctrine can be traced to decisions of the Privy Council interpreting several "federal" arrangements and constitutions within the British Empire, including those in Canada and Northern Ireland. See, e.g., *Union Colliery Co. of British Columbia Ltd v. Bryden* [1899] A.C. 580, 587; and *Gallagher v. Lynn* [1937] A.C. 863, 869–70.

Such an approach can be used to support and protect the exclusivity of both state and union competences, but given the very large array of powers conferred upon the union, it tends to favour the central authority. As one constitutional authority cited by Tewari and Saxena observes, "Where the question arises of determining whether a particular subject mentioned is in one list or another, the court looks to the substance of the matter. Thus, if the substance falls within the Union List, then the incidental encroachment by the law on the State List does not make it invalid."[85] Nonetheless, the existence of the union, state, and concurrent lists of powers obligates the Court to consider whether a union law unconstitutionally enters a field of exclusive state power. Tewari and Saxena explain that when undertaking this inquiry, the Court seeks to give effect to two principles, which are supposed to be construed harmoniously, namely, that the national interest must be given primacy, and state legislatures should not be summarily excluded from legislating.

Over time, of course, the distribution of powers in a federation may be altered by constitutional amendments, giving rise to an interplay between those amendments and the high court's interpretation of the distribution of powers. Brouillet notes that Canada's Supreme Court has had a substantial impact on federalism because the federal and provincial governments have been unable to amend the Constitution. Somin makes a similar point about the United States because of the difficulty of amending the U.S. Constitution. Benz argues that in Germany, constitutional amendments, which are common, enhanced federal power until 2006 when constitutional reform reversed the centralization trend. In turn, he reports that the Constitutional Court has become more Land friendly. In Belgium, constitutional change has given more powers to the regions and communities, and the constitutional court has followed suit. In Mexico, amendments have increased federal power and constrained judicial sympathies for decentralization. In Switzerland, constitutional change, as well as the introduction of uniform codes of civil and criminal procedure in 2011, have had centralizing effects, although cantons have been given more avenues to participate in federation decision-making. Swiss federalism, argue

85 P.M. Bakshi, *The Constitution of India*, 12th ed. (New Delhi: Universal Law Publishing, 2013), 246–7.

Lienhard and colleagues, has moved from an emphasis on self-rule to an emphasis on shared rule.[86]

4. *Legal Traditions and Culture*

The way in which a constitution distributes competences cannot explain all the variations in approach displayed by courts in federal countries. Another significant explanatory factor concerns the courts' legal and institutional context. There are important differences in judicial appointment processes and legal procedures, as well as in conceptual assumptions and methods of reasoning, that tend to be displayed by the constitutional courts of most civil-law federations and the supreme courts of many common-law federations. Although there are risks in over-estimating differences between the common-law and civil-law traditions, as well as in failing to recognize important differences among specific legal systems within each tradition, certain distinctive features of the two traditions appear to be significant for the way in which the courts understand and interpret their federal constitution.[87]

One way to put the distinction is that in civil-law systems, the tendency is to assume that law is essentially statutory, that it consists of deliberately enacted legal codes that lay down the structure of the entire

86 A further consideration is asymmetric federalism (see Watts, *Comparing Federal Systems*, 125–30). Belgium, Canada, India, and Spain are examples of constitutional asymmetry, where the constitution itself accords more powers to some constituent polities than others. Except for the Spanish Constitutional Court's 2010 ruling on Catalonia's statute of autonomy, which constrained asymmetry, this matter has not been prominent on high court dockets. Political asymmetry refers to differential powers of constituent polities that arise from demographic and socio-economic factors. All federations display this kind of asymmetry, although the extent of it varies. The effect can be considerable, as when the U.S. state of California introduced a law requiring all eggs sold in the state to come from chickens kept in coops large enough for them to stand up and extend their wings. A challenge to the law, on the basis that it violated the federal commerce clause because it imposed costly regulations on out-of-state egg producers, failed, but the affected states plan to appeal the decision. See *Florida Lime & Avocado Growers, Inc. v. Paul*, 373 U.S. 132 (1963), in which the court rejected a challenge by Florida farmers to a California law that set a standard of ripeness for avocados sold in the state.

87 See Konrad Zweigert and Hein Kötz, *Introduction to Comparative Law*, 3rd ed. (Oxford: Clarendon, 1998), 1:68–70; Mirjan Damaška, "The Common Law/Civil Law Divide: Residual Truth of a Misleading Distinction," *Supreme Court Law Review (Canada) (2d)* 49 (2010): 3–21.

body of law conceived as a comprehensive, rationally organized system of norms. In common-law systems, the tendency is to assume that law is essentially decisional, that it consists of a body of judicial decisions made in response to specific cases initiated by parties to particular legal disputes. It is true that, notwithstanding these tendencies, judicial decisions in civil-law systems play a significant role in determining the exact meaning and application of codified law, while statutory law plays an increasingly important role in common-law countries. But the underlying conceptual orientation exerts a powerful influence. At the risk of over-simplification, in the civil-law tradition, law tends to be conceived as an entire systematic whole, whereas in the common-law tradition, it is generally conceived as a collection of discrete judicial decisions made in the particular circumstances of each case. As Daniel Halberstam and Mathias Reimann have suggested, these kinds of differences seem to be associated with the extent to which a legal system is substantively unified in terms of the content of its applicable rules of law.[88]

A written constitution has a moderating influence in common-law countries, because it transforms a legal system constituted fundamentally by "unwritten" common law into a system based ultimately on a written document.[89] Nonetheless, the exact relationship between the written constitution and the common law remains controversial. Some argue that the common law continues to be the fundamental context in which the constitution operates;[90] others maintain that the constitutional law of the country remains ultimately "judge-made."[91] As Justice Oliver Wendell Holmes famously remarked in relation to American common law, "The life of the law has not been logic, it has been experience."[92] This general outlook is especially influential in

88 Daniel Halberstam and Mathias Reimann, "Federalism and Legal Unification: Comparing Methods, Results, and Explanations across 20 Systems," in *Federalism and Legal Unification: A Comparative Empirical Investigation of Twenty Systems*, ed. Daniel Halberstam and Mathias Reimann (Dordrecht: Springer, 2014), 3, 41–5.

89 In relation to the United States, see, e.g., Antonin Scalia, *A Matter of Interpretation: Federal Courts and the Law* (Princeton: Princeton University Press, 1997).

90 Owen Dixon, "The Common Law as an Ultimate Constitutional Foundation," *Australian Law Journal* 31 (1957): 240.

91 David A. Strauss, "Common Law Constitutional Interpretation," *University of Chicago Law Review* 63 (1996): 877–935. Indeed, it is consistent with such views to defend federalism in the language of Burkean conservatism: Ernest A. Young, "The Conservative Case for Federalism," *George Washington Law Review* 74 (2006): 874–87.

92 Oliver Wendell Holmes, *The Common Law* (Boston: Little, Brown, 1881), 1.

federal countries like Canada and Australia, which were formed in a manner that maintained legal continuity with British law and the traditional English conventions of the Westminster version of parliamentary responsible government. In Canada and Australia, the federation's body of constitutional law is not contained in a single constitutional document but in several constitutional enactments.[93] In the interstices between these documents, judge-made law and Westminster conventions sometimes play decisive roles, with very important implications for the federal system.[94] By contrast, in common-law countries that came into being through revolutionary assertions of independence, such as the United States and India, it is easier to identify a discrete "founding moment" for the polity, and the sources of fundamental constitutional law are less complex and fragmented. Although the United States and India are within the common-law tradition, their constitutional jurisprudence has developed away from its original, English moorings more than is evident in Canada and Australia.[95]

Related to these differences in the underlying conception of law are important differences in curial procedure in constitutional cases. In common-law countries, judicial review is usually exercised by any court when litigating parties raise constitutional issues. In civil-law countries, normally only constitutional courts exercise judicial review, typically either in the form of "abstract" review initiated by political actors and government institutions, "concrete" or "incidental" review initiated by ordinary judges when constitutional issues arise in particular cases, or "constitutional complaints" when individual litigants seek constitutional relief from the application of a law to their circumstances, usually when all other legal remedies have been exhausted, such as the

93 In addition to the federal constitutions of each country, these enactments include the *Statute of Westminster 1931* (UK); the *Canada Act 1982* (UK); and the *Australia Acts 1986* (UK and Aust.).

94 E.g., *Patriation Reference* [1981] 1 S.C.R. 753; United Kingdom, "Report by the Joint Committee of the House of Lords and the House of Commons Appointed to Consider the Petition of the State of Western Australia" (1934–44).

95 See, generally, Leslie Zines, *Constitutional Change in the Commonwealth* (Cambridge: Cambridge University Press, 1991); Peter C. Oliver, *The Constitution of Independence: The Development of Constitutional Theory in Australia, Canada, and New Zealand* (Oxford: Oxford University Press, 2005); Bruce McPherson, *The Reception of English Law Abroad* (Brisbane: Supreme Court of Queensland Library, 2007).

recurso de amparo in Spain.[96] Thus, although constitutional courts may be called upon to exercise judicial review in the context of the specifics of a particular case, they often exercise the power in the abstract and upon the initiative of political actors and institutions, such as governments, members of the legislature, or representatives of constituent polities. In common-law countries, this function is usually undertaken in the context of a specific case, initiated by the affected party or parties, and exercisable by any court.

The federal jurisprudence of Germany's Constitutional Court provides an important illustration of a civil-law approach to constitutional adjudication. As Donald Kommers explained, the style and content of the Court's judgments give the impression of a jurisprudence "based on reason and logic" rather than "experience," an approach that reflects a conception of law as a "self-contained, rational, deductive system of rules and norms" rather than a pragmatic response to context and social realities.[97] In the *Southwest State* case, for instance, the Court in its first major decision began its substantive reasoning by emphasizing the "internal coherence and structural unity" of the Basic Law, stating that "no single constitutional provision may be taken out of its context and interpreted by itself" but must be interpreted "in such a way as to render it compatible with the fundamental principles of the Constitution and the intentions of its authors."[98] Emphasizing the "unity of the Constitution as a logical-teleological entity,"[99] the Court often says that it aims to maintain a "practical concordance" of the constitution's

---

96 See Alec Stone Sweet, "Constitutional Courts," in *The Oxford Handbook of Comparative Constitutional Law*, ed. Michel Rosenfeld and András Sajó (Oxford: Oxford University Press, 2012), 816. The distinction between abstract and concrete review is not quite as clear as this in practice. See David Feldman, "Judicial Review of Legislation" (paper presented at the Anglo-Israeli Judicial Workshop, Jerusalem, 2007). A partial exception is the availability in Canada of abstract review of legislation through the "reference" jurisdiction of the Supreme Court: *Supreme Court Act*, R.S.C., 1985, c. S-26 (Can), s. 53. Another is the combination of both decentralized-incidental and centralized-abstract review available in Brazil: Keith S. Rosenn, "Judicial Review in Brazil: Developments under the 1988 Constitution," *Southwestern Journal of Law and Trade in the Americas* 7 (2000): 293.

97 Donald Kommers, *The Constitutional Jurisprudence of the Federal Republic of Germany*, 2nd ed. (Durham, NC: Duke University Press, 1997), 40–1.

98 *Southwest State* case, 1 BVerfGE 14, 32 (1951), reproduced in Kommers, *Constitutional Jurisprudence of the Federal Republic of Germany*, 62–6.

99 *Church Construction Tax* case, 19 BVerfGE 206, 220 (1965), cited in Donald Kommers, "German Constitutionalism: A Prolegomenon," *Emory Law Journal* 40 (1991): 837–51.

basic principles by which apparently conflicting values are brought into "harmony."[100]

Numerous textual and structural features of Germany's Basic Law encourage this outlook. Thus, while the range of exclusive and concurrent powers conferred on the federal legislature is very extensive,[101] unlike most other federations, the Land governments participate directly in the formation of federal policy and legislation through the Bundesrat.[102] Germany's system of "administrative federalism" also requires the cooperation of the Länder in the administration of federal legislation.[103] The capacity of the federation to exercise several of its concurrent legislative powers is restricted to circumstances where it is necessary to establish "equivalent living conditions" throughout Germany or to maintain "legal or economic unity."[104] Moreover, the federation and the Länder are bound to a highly integrated financial system that closely regulates their powers to impose taxes and apportions tax revenues among them.[105] Consistent with these features, the Constitutional Court has developed the principle of "federal comity" or *Bundestreue*, by which the federation and the Länder must exercise their respective powers in a pro-federal manner that respects each other's authority.[106] The Court also has applied the principle of subsidiarity to control the exercise of federal concurrent powers,[107] a development that led to a constitutional amendment in 2006 to restrict the operation of the principle to only some of the concurrent powers.[108]

As Benz points out, aspects of the Court's jurisprudence have sometimes favoured "federal unity"[109] and at other times "Länder autonomy."[110] But when placed in comparative perspective, what is perhaps

---

100 Kommers, *Constitutional Jurisprudence of the Federal Republic of Germany*, 46–7.

101 Basic Law, Arts. 73–4.

102 Ibid., Arts. 50–1.

103 Ibid., Arts. 83–5.

104 Ibid., Art. 72(2), amended in 2006.

105 Ibid., Arts. 105–8.

106 *Television I* case, 12 BVerfGE 205 (1961). See also Fabian Wittreck, "Die Bundestreue," in *Handbuch Föderalismus*, ed. Ines Härtel (Berlin: Springer, 2012), 1:497–525.

107 Greg Taylor, "Germany: The Subsidiarity Principle," *International Journal of Constitutional Law* 4 (2006): 115–30.

108 Greg Taylor, "Germany: A Slow Death for Subsidiarity?," *International Journal of Constitutional Law* 7 (2009): 139–54.

109 E.g., *Atomic Weapons Referenda I* case, 8 BVerfGE 104 (1958).

110 See the attempt to harmonize these principles in the *Southwest State* case, 1 BVerfGE 14 (1951).

most remarkable is the Court's willingness to narrow its interpretation of federal powers on the ground that the scheme of the Basic Law is to confer only specific and limited powers on the federation with the intention that the Länder retain power to legislate in relation to all matters not specifically allocated to the federation, even though (and possibly because) the number of these "reserved" powers is not comparatively large.[111] Such an approach to federal and state power is strikingly different from what occurs in the United States and Australia, where the courts do not generally reason in terms of competences reserved to the states.

Switzerland presents another important illustration. As in Germany, Swiss federalism is predicated on a "cooperative" relationship between the federation and the cantons,[112] including the principle that federal law is implemented largely by the cantons.[113] The federation is also constitutionally required to respect the autonomy of the cantons,[114] and the constitutional principle of subsidiarity authorizes the federation to act only when the cantons or municipalities are unable to do so effectively.[115] Moreover, disputes between the federation and the cantons are usually resolved by negotiation, and sometimes by a popularly initiated constitutional referendum rather than by judicial action. In this context, even though the *Tribunal fédéral* does not exercise judicial review over federal legislation, the court has drawn on the principle of cantonal sovereignty to uphold cantonal legislation in the face of allegedly inconsistent federal laws. This has extended to the finding that the general reservation of cantonal sovereignty supports the retention of very specific powers, even where an amendment to the constitution has removed explicit reference to those powers.

Mexico presents another illustration. Its Constitution adopts the same pattern of distribution of legislative competences as in the United States, Germany, and Australia. The competences of the federal Congress are specified, and those powers not expressly granted to the federation by the Constitution are deemed to be within the competence of the states. However, as José Caballero Juárez points out, since 1995, the

111 E.g., *Concordat* case, 6 BVerfGE 309 (1957); *Television I* case, 12 BVerfGE 205 (1961); *Explosives Control* case, 13 BVerfGE 367 (1962); *Engineers* case, 26 BVerfGE 246 (1969).

112 Swiss Constitution, Art. 44.

113 Ibid., Art. 46.

114 Ibid., Art. 47.

115 Ibid., Art. 5a, 43a para. 1.

Supreme Court, particularly through the *controversias constitucionales* procedure, has used its powers of review to protect the "five orders" recognized by the Constitution.[116] While Mexico's federal system has a highly centralized background, rooted in its Aztec, colonial, and post-colonial history,[117] the Supreme Court has recognized, as Juárez puts it, that when one order of government has the power to regulate a certain topic, the limits of such regulation have to be scrutinized in light of the power of other government orders also to regulate that topic.

The situation in Brazil appears to be very different. As Rodrigues, Lorencini, and Zimmermann point out, while the Constitution reserves to the states the powers not conferred upon the federation, the powers granted to the central government are so vast that the states are left with virtually no matters about which they can legislate free from the constraints of federal legislation. Consequently, the idea of any legislative power being reserved to the states is effectively meaningless. While many court decisions have struck down state and municipal laws in response to conflicts with the federal Constitution or federal law, very few decisions have invalidated federal laws on federalism grounds.

Another relevant dimension of domestic legal cultures is the growing influence of foreign and international law. This is most evident in the federal member-states (as well as Switzerland) of the European Union where treaties, community law, and decisions of the European Court of Justice have affected the distribution of powers within those federations. This has been of such major concern that all these countries have amended their constitutions or revised laws to allow their constituent polities a sizable voice in EU decision-making that affects their powers. Consequently, the EU establishes both constraints and opportunities for decision-making by the constitutional courts of these federations. Foreign-law influences are evident to varying degrees in nearly all the high courts examined in this volume, but those influences appear to have had little impact on the courts' federalism jurisprudence. These influences have more impacts on other areas of law, such as human rights, environmental protection, and economic development. However, insofar as international law and foreign law emphasize legal uniformity in many areas such as rights protection, labour regulation,

116 Namely, constitutional, federal, state, federal district, and municipal.

117 Victoria E. Rodríguez, "Recasting Federalism in Mexico," *Publius: The Journal of Federalism* 28, no. 1 (1998): 235–54.

and environmental protection, then those influences will push federal courts and legislatures in a unitarist direction.

A further factor in a federation's legal traditions and culture is the extent to which federalism is a value. Many observers have argued that a federal system requires, among other supports, a federal political culture to sustain it.[118] A notable finding of our comparative analysis is that, except for Switzerland, where federalism is an important value, federalism is not deemed an especially important or intrinsic value by the courts in most of the federations. It may be a given value insofar as it is entrenched in each country's constitution (except South Africa and Spain), but federalism is often little more than an instrumental value. Halberstam observes, "Rarely do courts consciously consider calibrating the degree of integration in the light of principles of federalism."[119]

Germany and India appear to have accepted federalism as a generally worthwhile value, and to protect that value, each country's constitution ensures it against majoritarian erosion. The eternity clause in Germany's Basic Law[120] protects the country's federal features against amendment, and the federal features of India's Constitution are the most difficult to amend. Such amendment requires a majority vote of all members of each house of Parliament, a two-thirds majority of all members present and voting, and ratification by at least half the states. Brazil's Constitution forbids amendments that would abolish or debilitate the federal system, but federalism nonetheless competes with a unitarist culture, and federalism has never been a prominent theme in Brazil's law schools. Ethiopia's political leaders do not believe a unitary system would be viable, but federalism seems to be regarded mainly as an expedient strategic balance of centrifugal and centripetal forces. Likewise in Canada, Nigeria, and Spain, federalism seems to be seen as the best option for holding these heterogeneous countries together. Australians see their federalism as desirable, but want to restructure it, although there is no agreement on how to do so. While few Americans would support a unitary system, most Americans treat federalism as an instrumental value and have supported expansions of federal power

---

118 Elazar, *Exploring Federalism*, 192–7; and Jenna Bednar, *The Robust Federation: Principles of Design* (Cambridge: Cambridge University Press, 2007), 187–8.

119 Daniel Halberstam, "Comparative Federalism and the Role of the Judiciary," in *The Oxford Handbook of Law and Politics*, ed. Gregory A. Caldeira, R. Daniel Kelemen, and Keith E. Whittington (Oxford: Oxford University Press, 2008), 157.

120 Art. 73(3).

that produce outcomes they like. In Mexico and South Africa, federalism is perhaps little more than a necessary evil. Mexico has had a history of centralized governance, and some important political groups in South Africa want to abolish the provinces. In Belgium, despite the "federal loyalty" provision contained in its Constitution, it is not clear that the two major linguistic groups wish to maintain a long-term federal marriage. Meanwhile, the Constitution stipulates procedural rules intended to protect each group from undesirable autonomy dilutions.

Only some of the courts examined in this volume have a developed federalism jurisprudence (i.e., Australia, Canada, Germany, and the United States) or appear to be developing one (i.e., Belgium and India). However, with the partial exception of the German Court's embrace of *Bundestreue*, no court has formulated a consistent and coherent long-term doctrine of federalism or treated federalism as an especially important value. The only country where federalism appears to be such a value, namely, Switzerland, has no high court authorized to tamper with it.

5. Selection of Judges and Institutional Roles of Courts

Another approach to explaining how courts interpret their federal constitution is the institutional position of courts in the federal system and the procedures for selecting judges. Most federations not only rely on the institution of judicial review to regulate the distribution of authority within the federation, but also confer final authority to do so on a court of ultimate constitutional jurisdiction. Although the structure of the court may differ as between the broad models of a constitutional court established separately from the general system of courts or a supreme court that operates at the apex of the court hierarchy,[121] the capacity of the court to determine constitutional matters is essentially very similar. Conferring such power on a single court in a federation tends to align the court with the governing institutions of the federation as a whole, even though a court's composition, jurisdiction, and institutional setting may ameliorate this to some extent. Are such courts

121 Mauro Cappelletti and William Cohen, *Comparative Constitutional Law: Cases and Materials* (Indianapolis: Bobbs-Merrill, 1979), 76–83; and Alan R. Brewer-Carias, *Judicial Review in Comparative Law* (Cambridge: Cambridge University Press, 1989), 128–31.

independent arbiters of federal disputes, or are they "device[s] of centralized policymaking"?[122]

The way in which constitutional courts and supreme courts are constituted varies considerably. Judges of federation supreme courts are typically appointed by the federal government, often with only minimal consultation with leaders of opposition parties or representatives of the constituent polities, and they are usually chosen from the ranks of lower court judges or very senior legal practitioners. The membership of constitutional courts often consists not only of sitting judges and senior practitioners but also law professors and former politicians, usually appointed through deliberative parliamentary processes that involve significant political negotiation and compromise over candidates and often give the political representatives of the constituent polities substantial opportunity to influence appointments.

In this respect, the countries examined in this book can be placed roughly on a spectrum. At one end is the High Court of Australia – a court strongly aligned with the federation as a whole. First, the Court sits atop an integrated hierarchy of federal, state, and territory courts over which it exercises both general appellate jurisdiction and special constitutional jurisdiction. Second, members of the Court are appointed by the federal government with only nominal consultation by the federal attorney-general with his or her state counterparts. Third, the Court is not especially representative of the various states; more than three-quarters of all its appointees have come from the two largest states and none yet from the two smallest ones. These factors combine to suggest an important explanatory factor for the High Court's strongly centralist orientation.[123]

A similar explanation of judicial centralism seems possible for India. Until recently, members of India's Supreme Court were appointed by the president in consultation with the Supreme Court, but the Court interpreted this as requiring the Court itself to concur in the appointment.[124]

---

122 Martin Shapiro, *Courts: A Comparative and Political Analysis* (Chicago: University of Chicago Press, 1981), 55; André Bzdera, "Comparative Analysis of Federal High Courts: A Political Theory of Judicial Review," *Canadian Journal of Political Science* 26 (1993): 3–29.

123 James Allan and Nicholas Aroney, "An Uncommon Court: How the High Court of Australia Has Undermined Australian Federalism," *Sydney Law Review* 30 (2008): 290–1.

124 *Supreme Court Advocates-on-Record Association v. Union of India*, 1993 (4) SCC 441; AIR 1994 SC 268.

This stance reflects the exceptionally powerful and unifying role the Court has played in India's legal and political system and the breadth of its original, appellate, and advisory jurisdiction across all areas of law, including constitutional, statutory, and common law. It remains to be seen what difference will be made by the new National Judicial Appointments Commission (NJAC), which, pursuant to the 121st Constitutional Amendment Act, 2014, provides binding advice to the president on judicial appointments.[125] The Supreme Federal Court of Brazil is likewise oriented to the federation as a whole. Although appointments to the Court proposed by the federal president must be ratified by the Senate, this usually occurs as a matter of course, and most appointees have been drawn from the three most populous and wealthy states.

Judges of the U.S. Supreme Court and other federal courts are appointed by the president subject to confirmation by the U.S. Senate.[126] This process has produced different results at various times in American history. Famous among them is the confrontation between the Court and President Franklin D. Roosevelt over "New Deal" legislation during the 1930s, which was eventually resolved through the threat of the president's "court packing" plan and the fact that the Democratic Party's electoral victories enabled it to dominate both Congress and the presidency. Likewise, the partial revival of judicial enforcement of federal limits on congressional power from the mid-1990s can be traced to appointments to the Court made by Republican Presidents Richard M. Nixon, Ronald Reagan, George H.W. Bush, and George W. Bush. In the past, non-judges such as former governors, members of Congress, a former president, and law professors were appointed to the Court, but politicization of the Senate's confirmation process in recent decades has led presidents to nominate judges from lower federal courts. President Barack Obama deviated from this pattern in 2010 when he nominated Elena Kagan, who had no prior judicial service, but in 2016, he nominated an appeals court judge to replace the late Antonin Scalia.

---

125 The NJAC consists of the chief justice of India, two other senior-most Supreme Court judges, the union minister of law, and two "eminent persons" nominated by a committee consisting of the prime minister, the chief justice of India, and the leader of the opposition or of the largest opposition party in the Lok Sabha. One of the two "eminent persons" is to be nominated from among scheduled castes, scheduled tribes, minorities, or women. Its advice, if not vetoed by any two of its members, is binding on the president, subject to only one request for reconsideration by the commission.

126 US Constitution, Art. II, Sec. 2.

During vacancies on the high court, appeals court judges desiring elevation to the Supreme Court are more likely to vote in harmony with the president's ideology, vote for the United States as a party, and write more dissenting opinions in which they can articulate their views more clearly for the president's advisers.[127]

Canada presents a complex picture, too. All judicial appointments of superior courts, even at the provincial level, are made by the federal government, but the Supreme Court Act requires that three judges of the high court be from Quebec.[128] The history of Canadian federal jurisprudence needs also to be assessed in the light of the important early role of the Judicial Committee of the Privy Council. The movement in Canadian doctrine from an emphasis on a dualistic system of exclusive powers under the Judicial Committee to a cooperative system of overlapping powers under the Supreme Court marks a movement towards centralization, though not so far as exists in Australia, India, and the United States.

The appointment of constitutional judges in Belgium, Germany, Spain, and Switzerland is more federalistic than in the above common-law federations. Judges of the two senates of Germany's Constitutional Court are elected by a two-thirds majority of the Bundestag and the Bundesrat according to a rule that requires each house to elect half of the judges, while the appointment of the Court's president and the vice-president alternates between the two chambers. Appointment to Belgium's Constitutional Court is especially adjusted to that country's bipolar federalism. Members of the Court are appointed by the king from lists of two candidates submitted alternatively by the Senate and the House of Representatives, having first been adopted by a two-thirds majority, and subject also to the requirement that the Court be composed of six Dutch-speaking and six French-speaking judges. Spain's Constitutional Court consists of twelve judges appointed by the king from four proposed by the Congress, four by the Senate, two by the federal government, and two by the General Council of the Judiciary, but without explicit regard to linguistic or regional representation. In Switzerland, judges of the *Tribunal fédéral* and other federal courts are appointed by the federal parliament, and appointments are made by

---

127 Ryan C. Black and Ryan J. Owens, "Courting the President: How Circuit Court Judges Alter Their Behavior for Promotion to the Supreme Court," *American Journal of Political Science* 60, no. 1 (2016): 30–43.

128 In addition, there is a convention that three judges will come from Ontario, two from the western provinces, and one from the Atlantic provinces.

consensus in a way that preserves a high level of diversity in language, religion, cantonal origin, and party allegiance.

As Arthur Benz and César Colino have pointed out, constitutional change in a federation is a "multi-dimensional process" that cannot be reduced to any one factor.[129] It is thus generally not possible to draw direct lines between particular judicial decisions and the composition of the courts that make the decisions. A wide variety of factors may influence judges in one direction or the other.[130] But when the overall tendencies of the federal jurisprudence of the supreme courts of Australia, India, and the United States are compared with those of the constitutional courts of Belgium, Germany, and Spain, a general pattern seems to emerge in which a more federalist mode of judicial appointment is associated with a more federalist, or at least "balanced," jurisprudence, while centralized modes of appointment are associated with unitarist tendencies in constitutional interpretation. An exception to this generalization is Nigeria. Appointments to the federal courts are made by the president on the recommendation of the National Judicial Council, subject to confirmation by the Senate, and there is a policy of ensuring that judicial appointments broadly reflect the country's diverse federal and geographical identities. In that country's troubled circumstances, however, the Supreme Court has played an ambivalent role, at times effectively arbitrating revenue-sharing disputes among the federal government and the states, but in the main seeing itself as "an interpreter and enforcer of Nigeria's centrist Constitution." Mexico's Supreme Court is appointed by the Senate from three candidates nominated by the federal president, but the Court only recently began interpreting the Constitution's federal clauses in a significant way.

The notion that courts should in some sense be representative of the various political and regional identities within the country cuts against the account of them as independent of politics and impartial as between the interests of the federation and the constituent polities. Furthest along the spectrum in this respect are the systems of Switzerland and Ethiopia, where deliberate decisions have been taken to reduce or eliminate the role of judicial review in federalism disputes and to place greater emphasis on "federal-democratic" participation in the political system.

129 Arthur Benz and César Colino, "Constitutional Change in Federations: A Framework for Analysis," *Regional & Federal Studies* 21 (2011): 381–406.

130 Halberstam, "Comparative Federalism and the Role of the Judiciary." Several of the factors cited by Halberstam are, however, neutral in relation to federalism issues.

The reasons for this, however, differ in the two countries. The Swiss have a long-standing tradition of governance by consensus, democratically expressed through the representative institutions of the federation and, ultimately, the popular referendum. In Ethiopia, there is concern that the dominance of a particular political party-coalition in all orders of government suppresses the political and policy diversity that is the hallmark of a genuinely federal polity. South Africa offers another point of comparison, because there is an effort to ensure that members of the Constitutional Court are "representative" but also to treat litigation as a last resort. Thus, members of the Court are appointed by the president from lists provided by a Judicial Service Commission composed of judges, lawyers, and national and provincial politicians from both major parties. However, the Constitution also requires all "spheres of government" and "all organs of state within each sphere" to interact in a respectful and cooperative manner, avoid legal proceedings, and make every effort to settle disputes before commencing such proceedings.

6. Court System and Jurisdiction

When Dicey said that federalism is a system of government in which "the ordinary powers of sovereignty are elaborately divided between the common or national government and the separate states,"[131] it seems he primarily had in mind the distribution of legislative power. But this idea of a division of sovereignty is not something he carried through into the analysis of judicial power within a federation. When he said that "the Bench of judges is not only the guardian but also at a given moment the master of the constitution,"[132] he was referring to the final authority of the highest court in the country to interpret and apply the constitutional distribution of powers. But are the courts of federal countries to be understood, fundamentally, in the singular or plural? Are they integrated into a single hierarchical court system, or are there dual (or multiple) systems of court hierarchies, each somewhat independent of the other? Most federal countries combine elements of both. There is usually a single supreme or constitutional court having final authority to determine constitutional cases and disputes among the federation

---

131 Albert Venn Dicey, *Introduction to the Study of the Law of the Constitution*, 8th ed. (London: Macmillan, 1915), 139.

132 Ibid., 170.

and/or the constituent polities, but the exact jurisdiction of this court varies from country to country, and systems of courts in the constituent polities and specialized courts often operate in conjunction with it.

The organization of the courts can be more or less federalist in design and structure considered across several dimensions. These dimensions include institutional features, such as the laws upon which they are established and the governments from which they receive funding, and jurisdictional features, such as the kinds of matters they are authorized to adjudicate and the relationships between courts established through various mechanisms of appeal and rules concerning the bindingness of their decisions. Thus, courts in federal countries may be established by combinations of federal and/or constituent-polity laws, which laws may be constitutional or statutory. The federal supreme or constitutional court, as well as other federal courts, is usually established by the federal constitution, but many of its institutional features are specified by ordinary federal law. Constituent-polity courts may be presupposed by the federation and thus established by state law (constitutional and/or statutory) or be provided for by the federal constitution and regulated by either federal or constituent-polity law. The extent to which this is the case often reflects the degree to which the federation is conceived as integrative or devolutionary.

The jurisdiction of federal and constituent-polity courts and the relations between them are also vitally important. Most federations confer constitutional jurisdiction in federalism-related matters upon the federal supreme or constitutional court. Such matters typically include the constitutionality, interpretation, and application of the federal constitution and federal laws, the constitutionality of constituent-polity laws, and disputes between the federation and a constituent polity or polities, or among the constituent polities themselves. Whether courts of the constituent polities have jurisdiction in such matters, however, varies. Federal countries that have distinct constitutional courts (usually within the civil-law tradition) ordinarily restrict jurisdiction in constitutional matters to those courts; countries that have a more general supreme court (usually common-law countries) affirm the jurisdiction of all courts of record, including constituent-polity courts, to determine any constitutional matters that might emerge in cases that come before them. Here, however, the jurisdiction of the federal supreme or constitutional court to hear appeals or references on points of constitutional law from constituent-polity courts is especially significant, as is the extent to which decisions of the federal supreme or constitutional court are authoritative and binding on the courts of the constituent polities. In common-law countries, such decisions are strictly binding as a matter of precedent (*stare decisis*); in civil-law countries, the authority of such decisions often varies. In some, constituent-polity courts tend to follow relevant decisions of superior federal courts lest their judgments be overturned on appeal; in others, there has developed a special doctrine that establishes the binding authority of constitutional court decisions, such as the *jurisprudencia* in Mexico and the *súmulas vinculantes* in Brazil.

The EU's judicial system provides an important example and contrast.[133] The European Court of Justice has limited jurisdiction, which is concerned largely with ensuring consistent interpretation and application of European community law within the member states and includes jurisdiction to determine whether European laws are within EU competence. Many such cases brought before the court are commenced by way of preliminary ruling on the initiative of the national courts of member states, and once the Court of Justice delivers its judgment, the matter returns to the national courts for resolution. Thus, enforcement of European community law often depends on the active cooperation of the member-state courts, both to refer questions of interpretation and validity to the Court of Justice and to enforce European community law in the disputed cases that come before them through the remedies available under their respective national systems of law.[134] Even the final authority of the Court of Justice in relation to the interpretation of the EU's treaties does not stand altogether unchallenged by some of the highest constitutional courts of the member states, such as the Federal Constitutional Court of Germany, which have insisted that the law that is implemented in their countries be consistent with their national constitutions as interpreted by national courts.[135] The EU's judicial system is thus highly dualistic.

---

133 Trevor C. Hartley, *The Foundations of European Community Law*, 7th ed. (Oxford: Oxford University Press, 2010), chaps 2 and 7.

134 Anne-Marie Slaughter, Alec Stone Sweet, and Joseph H.H. Weiler, eds., *The European Court and National Courts – Doctrine and Jurisprudence: Legal Change in Its Social Context* (Oxford: Hart, 1998).

135 E.g., *Maastricht Treaty* case (1993), BVerfGE 89; and *Lisbon Treaty* case (2009), BVerfGE 2 BvE 2/08. See Eric Stein, "Treaty-Based Federalism, A.D. 1979: A Gloss on Covey T. Oliver at the Hague Academy," *University of Pennsylvania Law Review* 127, no. 4 (April 1979): 897–908; and Trevor C. Hartley, "Federalism, Courts and Legal Systems: The Emerging Constitution of the European Community," *American Journal of Comparative Law* 34, no. 2 (April 1986): 229–47.

There have also been times in American history when the authority of the U.S. Supreme Court was challenged by the governing institutions, including courts of the constituent states. While, at least since the Civil War (1861–5), the authority and jurisdiction of the Supreme Court to make final determinations in constitutional matters have been generally accepted, the judicial system remains highly dualist, especially when compared to the judicial systems of many other federal countries. This is because the jurisdiction of the U.S. Supreme Court is limited to a specific range of matters, such as the interpretation of the Constitution and federal law, while state courts retain control over the development of the common law and the interpretation of state legislation in each state, including the interpretation of each state constitution. The U.S. Supreme Court did, for a time, contemplate the existence of a federal common law that it would apply as necessary in cases that came within its jurisdiction, but this idea was abandoned, and the Court applies the common law of the particular state applicable to the case before it.[136]

This is not so in Australia and Canada, largely because their supreme courts have general appellate jurisdiction to hear appeals from state and provincial courts.[137] This jurisdiction has supported the development in Australia of a "national" common law determined ultimately by the highest court of appeal operating within a "nationally integrated" system of courts.[138] In Canada, there is likewise a general common law throughout the country, except that Quebec has retained its civil code guaranteed to it through the provinces' exclusive jurisdiction over "property and civil rights."[139] As Halberstam and Reimann therefore observe, common-law federations tend to confer general appellate jurisdiction on a general court of appeal for the entire country, thus enabling that court to pronounce authoritatively on the interpretation of state statutory law and the common law generally.[140]

---

136 *Swift v. Tyson*, 41 U.S. 1 (1842), overruled in *Erie Railroad Co. v. Tompkins*, 304 U.S. 64 (1938). For a critique of the complications that have developed since *Erie*, see Diane P. Wood, "Back to the Basics of *Erie*," *Lewis & Clark Law Review* 18 (2014): 673–95.

137 Mark Leeming, "Common Law within Three Federations," *Public Law Review* 18 (2007): 186.

138 *Kable v. Director of Public Prosecutions for N.S.W.* (1996) 189 C.L.R. 51, 114–5 (McHugh J); *Lipohar v. The Queen* (1999) 200 C.L.R. 485, 505.

139 Canadian Constitution, s. 92(13).

140 Halberstam and Reimann, "Federalism and Legal Unification," 12–13.

One further important exception concerns the place of religious law in some common-law federations, such as India, Malaysia, and Nigeria. In India, the Supreme Court presides as a general court of appeal over a unitary system of courts, thus giving rise to a uniform common law across the country developed through the interpretation of a series of national statutes that in the second half of the nineteenth century codified the common law in a manner considered suitable for Indian conditions. However, there also remain distinct bodies of Anglo-Hindu and Anglo-Islamic religious and family law.[141] In Nigeria, as well as in Malaysia, there is likewise a unified appellate system for the whole country. However, in Nigeria, there are distinct sharia courts established by constituent states, and in both Nigeria and Malaysia, there are continuing disputes concerning the jurisdictional borders of religious and secular law.[142]

On first analysis, the civil-law federations appear to be significantly more unified, because national codes govern much of their private and criminal law. However, several of them display a different kind of judicial pluralism traceable to the division of the courts into specialized subsystems that deal separately with constitutional, administrative, civil, commercial, and criminal matters. This, together with the absence of a strict doctrine of precedent, can give rise to greater diversity in law and interpretation across the legal system, especially in Germany, for example.[143]

Despite these important differences between the common-law and civil-law federations, in all of the federations considered in this book except Australia, the existence of a federal constitutional bill of rights authoritatively enforced by the highest court has a general unifying effect on the entire body of law throughout the country. In some federal countries such as Brazil and the United States, judicial protections

---

141 Jayanth K. Krishman, "India," in *Legal Systems of the World: A Political, Social and Cultural Encyclopedia*, ed. Herbert M. Kritzer (Santa Barbara, CA: ABC-CLIO, 2002), 693.

142 Andrew Harding, "Sharia and National Law in Malaysia," in *Sharia Incorporated: A Comparative Overview of the Legal Systems of Twelve Muslim Countries in Past and Present*, ed. Jan Michiel Otto (Leiden: Leiden University Press, 2010), 491; J. Isawa Elaigwu and Habu Galadima, "The Shadow of Sharia over Nigerian Federalism," *Publius: The Journal of Federalism* 33, no. 3 (2003): 123–44; and M.H.A. Bolaji, "Shari'ah in Northern Nigeria in the Light of Asymmetrical Federalism," *Publius: The Journal of Federalism* 40, no. 1 (2010): 114–35.

143 Compare the chapters on Belgium, Germany, Mexico, and Spain in this volume.

of human rights have especially centralizing effects, because the constituent states are seen as having been historic rights violators.[144] The constituent polities in some federations also have sets of rights embedded in their constitutions, which are interpreted and enforced by state courts. In some countries, such as the United States and Switzerland,[145] this can give rise to greater human rights expectations being imposed on state/cantonal legislatures and governments than those that apply from the federal constitution. But the rule in all such federations is that the rights standards established by the federal constitution can only be augmented, not displaced.

In Mexico, the *amparos directos* procedure has emerged as a means by which decisions made by state courts are challenged on constitutional grounds. Federal circuit courts were created in order to reduce the mounting backlog of cases before the Supreme Court. Many cases were referred to these courts, and cases are now ordinarily heard at first instance. There has been, as a result, a corresponding exponential growth in the number of federal courts, with every Mexican state now having a resident federal circuit court. The decisions of the federal courts are published, and state courts are bound by them. State courts have little incentive to publish their own decisions, and the result, as Caballero Juárez points out, is that the state courts "have *de facto* lost their status as high courts in their respective states."

144 It might be argued that rights constraints imposed on constituent polities are less centralizing than judicial rulings that give more legislative power to the federal government, because rights constraints increase the autonomy of individuals and civil-society groups that might advocate decentralization. This is questionable, however, because autonomous civil-society groups have no inherent motivation to increase the power of constituent governments vis-à-vis the federal government; they might actually advocate centralization under the theory that is better to be governed by one 225-kilogram gorilla than many monkeys. Further, insofar as rights constraints are promulgated in the name of federation-wide equality, they will likely, as Alexis de Tocqueville argued in the case of the United States, have highly centralizing impacts. See *Democracy in America*, trans. and ed. Harvey C. Mansfield and Delba Winthrop (Chicago: University of Chicago Press, 2000), 640–50.

145 William J. Brennan Jr, "State Constitutions and the Protection of Individual Rights," *Harvard Law Review* 90 (1977): 489–504; John Kincaid, "Federalism and Rights: The Case of the United States with Comparative Perspectives," in *Human Rights: Current Issues and Controversies*, ed. Gordon DiGiacomo, 83–113 (Toronto: University of Toronto Press, 2016).

7. Political Parties

In 1901, an American journalist, Finley Peter Dunne, wrote through his comic character, Mr Dooley, that "th' Supreme Coort follows th' election returns."[146] The case studies in this volume show that high courts are sensitive to their country's general political trends, including trends emphasizing federalism or unitarism. Courts are sensitive also to their country's general political view of federalism. Courts follow these trends in part to enhance acceptance of their rulings. Although few courts follow political trends slavishly, they do vary in the extent to which they are constrained by politics, especially party politics.

Parties first developed in England, but they are intimately linked to federalism because they achieved their modern form in the United States.[147] The modern Democratic Party, organized in 1828, is the world's oldest continuing party. The party system stems partly from the contest between Federalists and Anti-Federalists over ratification of the U.S. Constitution. The party system emerged in the early 1800s in order to capture the U.S. presidency (beginning with the 1800 election) by generating electoral college votes from the states, organize the election system in each state to elect members of the U.S. House of Representatives, control state governments not only for self-government but also to make state legislative appointments of U.S. senators (from 1789 to 1913), and transmit state-based public opinion to federal officials. Until the mid-1960s, both parties were confederations of state and local party organizations substantially controlled by governors, mayors, and the like. As such, they often restrained federal policymaking that infringed on state and local powers they deemed important.

In 1960, Morton Grodzins predicted that if the political parties became more nationalized and disciplined, the "hallmarks of American decentralization might entirely disappear."[148] He was almost right. Beginning in the mid-1960s, the parties became significantly more nationalized, and members of Congress broke free from their traditional state and local party moorings, in part because the U.S. Supreme

---

146 Finley P. Dunne, "Mr Dooley Reviews the Supreme Court's Decision," *Sunday Chat*, 9 June 1901, 6.

147 John H. Aldrich, *Why Parties? A Second Look* (Chicago: University of Chicago Press, 2011).

148 Morton Grodzins, "The Federal System," in *Goals for Americans*, ed. President's Commission on National Goals (Englewood Cliffs, NJ: Prentice-Hall, 1960), 276.

Court under Chief Justice Earl Warren (1953–69) issued numerous rulings that overrode state powers and helped dismantle the confederated party system.[149] The federal system became more nationalized, and the U.S. Supreme Court has not significantly interfered with that nationalization, despite the fact that all three chief justices who followed Warren were appointed by Republican presidents who vowed to fashion a court that would, among other things, revive federalism.

Thus, the Supreme Court helped transform the party system, but its entry into the political process upped the ante for the more nationalized parties to assert more ideological control over judicial appointments. As a result, the court is polarized between conservatives and liberals such that virtually every federalism ruling has for several decades been a 5–4 decision.[150] Until about 2016, the Republican Party was more successful because federal court judges have been, on average, more conservative than the lawyers who argue before them.[151] Ideology is important because judicial discretion increases as one ascends the judicial hierarchy such that conservative votes increase from the federal district courts to appeals courts and then the Supreme Court.[152]

Political parties have important impacts on courts, because parties control the institutions that select judges, pay their salaries, fund court budgets, determine in some countries certain aspects of court organization and jurisdiction, bring cases to the courts, generate policies that trigger court cases, and enact laws and propose constitutional amendments that alter, augment, or diminish judicial decision-making. Key factors in the federations examined in this volume are whether the party system features a dominant federation-wide party, as in South Africa; multiple parties rooted in culturally or nationally distinct constituent polities, as in Belgium and India; two party systems, one in

149 E.g., *Brown v. Board of Education of Topeka*, 347 U.S. 483 (1954); *Cooper v. Aaron*, 358 U.S. 1 (1958); *Gideon v. Wainwright*, 372 U.S. 335 (1963); *Baker v. Carr*, 369 U.S. 186 (1962); and *Reynolds v. Sims*, 377 U.S. 533 (1964).

150 The 2016 death of Antonin Scalia will not change this division, because the division will remain 5:4 whether a liberal or conservative is appointed to the Court, until another justice leaves the Court.

151 Adam Bonica and Maya Sen, "The Politics of Selecting the Bench from the Bar: The Legal Profession and Partisan Incentives to Politicize the Judiciary," 2014, http://j.mp/11g7YJZ.

152 Lee Epstein, William M. Landes, and Richard A. Posner, *The Behavior of Federal Judges: A Theoretical and Empirical Study of Rational Choice* (Cambridge, MA: Harvard University Press, 2013).

constituent polities and one in the federation arena, as in Canada; and two or more parties that compete and govern in both the federation and constituent-polity arenas, as in the United States.

When there is a dominant federation-wide party, the high court tends to exhibit a unitarist orientation, as in South Africa and India (before 1989). South Africa might seem to be a partial exception, because the Constitutional Court has been friendly to local governments, but so is the ANC. The ANC opposed a federal system of provinces and then constitutionalized local governments as the third order of government in order to nurture its grassroots base, deliver services, and promote development.[153] The Constitutional Court's support of hourglass federalism comports with the ANC's position. In these monopolistic party systems, moreover, the high court is less likely to be asked to resolve federalism disputes because they are resolved within the party. The significance of party organization also is evident in Nigeria for long periods of its federal history, where a dominant national party system has reinforced centralization within the country. Similarly in Ethiopia, intergovernmental disputes are managed within the EPRDF rather than in the House of Federation.

Dominant party systems can seriously compromise the independence of the courts, which may even find themselves under attack by partisan political leaders. In 2015, for example, the chief justice of South Africa's Constitutional Court, feeling the stings of attacks by President Jacob Zuma and his ANC cohorts, held a press conference flanked by twenty-six other senior judges at which he defended the role of courts in maintaining the rule of law.[154] A year later, the Court ruled that Zuma violated the Constitution by refusing to repay the government for public money spent on improvements to his home.[155]

When parties are organized in culturally distinct constituent polities and those parties compete in the federation arena, the high court tends to be less unitarist, as in Belgium. In India, where states are organized along linguistic lines, the emergence of multiple state-based parties and national governing coalitions in 1989 created a climate more conducive

153 Jaap de Visser, "Republic of South Africa," in *Local Governments and Metropolitan Regions in Federal Systems*, ed. Nico Steytler, 268–97 (Montreal and Kingston: McGill-Queen's University Press, 2009).

154 "Judges Uncowed," *Economist*, 8 August 2015.

155 Norimitsu Onishi, "Zuma's Spending on Home Is Ruled Unconstitutional," *New York Times*, 1 April 2016.

to assertive and federalist Supreme Court rulings. This political climate also tends to present the high court with more federalism cases, including disputes that cannot be settled among the parties.

When a federation has two party systems, as in Canada and Spain, unitarist or federalist orientations hinge on the political philosophy of the governing federation party, the extent to which the federation parties are themselves centralized, and the ability of constituent-polity parties to influence the governing federation parties. Of the major federation parties in Spain, the Partido Popular, the governing party from 2011 to 2015, and the new Ciudadanos Party are centralist. The other new party, Podemos, opposes Catalan independence but appears to support regional autonomy.[156] The nationalist parties that are strong in some autonomous communities are weaker at the centre. In Canada, provincial influences on the federation parties have been sufficient to temper unitarist leanings.

When two or more parties compete and govern in both the federation and constituent-polities, as in Australia, Germany, and the United States, unitarist or federalist orientations hinge on the political philosophy of the governing federation party and the extent to which the federation parties are themselves centralized. Even if the constituent-polity branches of the federation party are relatively independent, they may be obliged to support, or not openly oppose, centralizing policies of their partisans in power in the federal government.

Generally, the high courts in developed federal democracies appear to be more independent and less directly controlled by political parties than courts in less-developed and less-democratic federations. Experiences in India and Mexico also suggest that transition from a monopolistic party system to a multi-party democracy allows more space for a federal high court to assert itself.

The judicialization of politics is evident in some of the federations examined in this book, especially the more developed federal democracies. Judicialization includes the willingness of courts to enter the political thicket and the willingness of parties to recruit the courts as a safety valve for conflict. Although federalism appears not to be a prominent subject of judicialization, several high courts have issued significant

---

156 In late 2014, a new federation party, *Podemos*, surged in public opinion polls and promised a Third Way, including changing the 1978 constitution to create a federal system or give more autonomy to autonomous communities such as Catalonia. *Podemos* also pledged to respect a Catalan independence vote.

federalism-relevant decisions. Canada's Supreme Court became the first court to authorize a procedure for a federation's dissolution while, at the same time, assuming authority to define the federation's core principles as federalism, democracy, constitutionalism and the rule of law, and protection of minorities.[157] The Court also had a major impact on health policy in Canada when it ruled that Quebec's limits on private health-care delivery violated the province's Charter of Human Rights and Freedoms.[158] In the United States, the Supreme Court's 1857 *Dred Scott* ruling played a significant role in precipitating the Civil War,[159] and in 2000, the Court vacated a state-law process, thus essentially deciding a presidential election.[160] South Africa's Constitutional Court was the first to reject a constitutional text written by a representative constitution-making body, although in negotiations leading up to the final constitution, it had been agreed that the Court could certify whether the final constitution adhered to the constitutional principles set forth in the interim constitution.[161] In the 1993 *Maastricht Case*, Germany's Constitutional Court decided the status of the newly unified federal republic in the EU.[162]

In summary, the countries examined in this volume demonstrate the importance of party politics for federal high courts and illustrate the tensions that can surround courts as they navigate political thickets.[163]

III. Conclusions

The Swiss and Ethiopian cases demonstrate that a federal system does not need a high court exercising constitutional judicial review over

---

157 *Reference re Secession of Quebec*, [1998] 2 S.C.R. 217.

158 *Chaoulli v. Quebec* (Att'y Gen.), [2005] 1 S.C.R. 791.

159 *Dred Scott v. Sandford*, 60 U.S. 393 (1857). Robert H. Bork headlined his analysis of *Dred Scott* with: "Chief Justice Taney and Dred Scott: The Court Invites a Civil War," in *The Tempting of America: The Political Seduction of the Law* (New York: Free Press, 1990), 28.

160 *Bush v. Gore*, 531 U.S. 98 (2000).

161 *Certification of the Amended Text of the Constitution of the Republic of S. Afr.* 1997 (2) SA 97 (CC); and *Certification of the Constitution of the Republic of S. Afr.* 1996 (4) SA 744 (CC).

162 *Maastricht Case*, BVerf GE 89, 155. Kommers, *Constitutional Jurisprudence of the Federal Republic of Germany*, 182–6.

163 See also Detterbeck, Renzsch, and Kincaid, *Political Parties and Civil Society in Federal Countries*.

federation law, although the viability and desirability of the Ethiopian model and the generalizability of the Swiss model are doubtful. Otherwise, judicial review appears to have become a permanent feature of modern constitutions, federal and non-federal. In federal systems, judicial review has the added tasks of policing the balance of power and umpiring disputes between the federation and its constituent polities. The high courts examined in this book display remarkable diversity in executing these tasks while also manifesting some underlying similarities.

Of course, a viable federation depends on more than judicial review. The internal boundaries of federal systems are best regulated by complementary safeguards – structural, political, and popular – in addition to judicial.[164] Each type of safeguard has strengths and weaknesses. One advantage of judicial review, compared to the others, is that it is ostensibly impartial and politically disinterested. Judges are usually meant to be independent of particular political interests, they are tasked with interpreting and applying the written text of the constitution, and they are expected to provide reasoned justifications of their decisions.[165] These supposed advantages, however, do not necessarily hold in practice. Consequently, framers of constitutions need to be aware of the multiple factors that shape judicial review.

Careful reflection on the historical circumstances surrounding the founding or re-founding of a federal system is important for designing a constitution to remedy past injustices or imperfections without being so reactive as to neglect transcendent principles and general practices of enduring importance. To some extent, constitution-makers can benefit from stepping behind a veil of ignorance[166] in order to make choices likely to benefit all parties to the federal covenant, especially when cultural and political heterogeneity can lead to mere interest aggregation. As such, defining who are the parties to the covenant is important and, ideally, needs to be inclusive.

For purposes of judicial review, it is useful to recognize the difficulties in trying to ground a constitution in a singular demos or plural

164 Jenna Bednar, *The Robust Federation: Principles of Design* (Cambridge: Cambridge University Press, 2007), chap. 4. Bednar also discusses the more extreme sanctions of secession and intergovernmental retaliation (11, 95) and the need for a "federal culture" that values federalism itself, 187–8.

165 See Madison, *Federalist* 39.

166 John Rawls, *A Theory of Justice* (Cambridge: Harvard University Press, 1999).

demoi. Is the conception of the constitutive authority homogeneous or heterogeneous? A problem, of course, is that there may be disagreement – for example, a majority community advocating a single demos against minority communities advocating plural demoi. Fudging this issue at the founding, which is sometimes the case, may require the federation's high court to confront the issue in the future and reach decisions that might aggravate rather than resolve the issue. And yet the issue is usually fudged in the first place because agreement about it cannot be reached.

To this end, the manner and extent to which federalism is to be construed as an intrinsic value that prizes, among other things, unity and diversity along with self-rule and shared rule might be clarified, if possible, in constitutional design. An eternity clause partially enshrines such a value in the constitution but is not sufficient, because it guarantees the structure and sometimes the integrity of the federation's constituent polities but not necessarily the spirit of federalism. The concept of *Bundestreue* might be one indicator for courts of the spirit of the federation.[167]

The case studies in this volume indicate that while the common-law and civil-law traditions each pose some specific issues for consideration in constitutional design, federations are equally viable under both traditions. Constitution-making needs to be attentive to the implications of the civil law's emphasis on a written code conceived as a systematic whole whereby reason and logic are deemed the basis of jurisprudence, and to the common-law's emphasis on a more diverse collection of discrete judicial decisions whereby experience is an important ground of jurisprudence.

The constitutional specification of the distribution of powers also is important. A federal constitution may provide guidance by setting out separate lists of competences for each order of government. While the idea that governments might be restricted to exclusive, watertight compartments is unrealistic, two lists of powers provide courts with a specific constitutional basis for assessing the content of one head of power in the light of another, giving rise to a kind of balance in that sense. However, many federations, especially integrative ones, presuppose the general powers of the constituent polities without particularizing

---

167 See also Michael Burgess, *In Search of the Federal Spirit: New Theoretical and Empirical Perspectives in Comparative Federalism* (Oxford: Oxford University Press, 2012).

them, and they specify only the federation's powers. Although intended to accord a temporal and logical priority to the constituent polities' powers, such approaches enable courts to interpret federal powers as widely as the language used can possibly convey, without regard for the powers reserved to the constituent polities. Consequently, one federal list without a counter list of constituent-polity powers may not be in the best interests of the constituent political communities.

At the heart of federalism-related arguments are not only distributive questions about which order of government is best placed to achieve a certain goal, but also questions about which order is best able to determine the goals that ought to be secured in the first place.[168] Much contemporary debate about federalism overlooks this second question, presupposing that such judgments should ultimately be made from the perspective of the "whole." Much of the reason for this seems to be the tacit assumption that in normative deliberation, an encompassing "universal" perspective is always to be preferred to a "parochial" one. But to think in that way is to overlook something fundamental about the nature of federalism, particularly in its original, integrative sense of a consensual coming together of political communities, each assessing the normative benefits of federation independently of the other.[169] The question posed by federalism is not only which polity should have responsibility for a particular matter, but which polity should decide *that* question. If federalism is only a "system of government," we might think the answer must be given by the system as a whole. But if federalism is also, more fundamentally, a "federation of polities," then perhaps the polities themselves ought to play this role, or at least have a say in its determination.

This points to the process of choosing judges for the federation's courts, especially its high court, and the criteria for their selection. The cases in this volume suggest that a more federalistic mode of selection in which the constituent polities have an influential voice is more likely to lead to judicial decision-making that seeks a balance between federalism and unitarism. Likewise, in heterogeneous federations, a high

168 Daniel Halberstam, "Federalism: Theory, Policy, Law," in *The Oxford Handbook of Comparative Constitutional Law*, ed. Michel Rosenfeld and András Sajó (Oxford: Oxford University Press, 2012), 576, 593–94.

169 Even devolutionary federations, as has been seen, are prompted by similar claims to an independent right to assess such matters on the part of sub-state groups.

court whose members are at least partially representative of the constituent polities is more likely to seek balance.

Constitution-making also needs to consider the role of political parties in relation to the judiciary and consider the extent to which courts can and cannot be shielded from partisan influences. As the cases examined in this volume suggest, different party systems can have substantial effects on the nature and direction of courts' jurisprudence.

The structure of the courts requires consideration as well, including the existence and authority of courts of the constituent polities. James Madison observed that[170] if the courts of the constituent polities decide their own interpretations of the federal distribution of powers, the federal constitution will be "different in every state," a result hardly conducive to sustaining a federation based on the rule of law. However, the idea that final authority should therefore be vested in the courts of the federation is liable to criticism for the corresponding reason that self-interest may incline federal judges to favour federal power. Indeed, Madison criticized the U.S. Supreme Court's tendency under Chief Justice John Marshall (1801–35) to extend its own jurisdiction and interpret federal legislative powers broadly.[171] The remedy for this, Madison thought, lay not in denying the final jurisdiction of the Supreme Court but in underscoring the ways in which it is to be restrained under the Constitution. "Trust" would have to be "vested in the Government representing the whole and exercised by its tribunals," he said, but this trust must be "controllable by the States who directly or indirectly appoint the Trustees." As the state courts grew in learning, ability, and stature, he added, "their decisions at once indicating and influencing the sense of their Constituents, and founded on united interpretations of constitutional points, could scarcely fail to frustrate an assumption of unconstitutional powers by the federal tribunals."[172]

In Madison's view, the jurisdiction, structure, composition, and mode of appointment of the courts are vital to the preservation of a balanced federal system. As noted above, federal courts composed of judges who have strong connections with the constituent polities of their federation tend to interpret their constitution in a more federalist manner, while

170 James Madison to Spencer Roane (a judge of the Virginia Supreme Court of Appeals), 29 June 1821.

171 Jack N. Rakove, "Judicial Power in the Constitutional Theory of James Madison," *William and Mary Law Review* 43 (2002): 1513–47.

172 Madison to Roane, 29 June 1821.

more centralist systems of judicial appointment are associated with more unitarist interpretations. Furthermore, the authority of courts of the constituent polities to develop bodies of jurisprudence independently of the federal courts extends the principle of the distribution of powers to the courts themselves and to their exercise of jurisdiction within the federation.

The life of a federal system depends, of course, on many factors, but the design decisions made by constitution-makers with respect to the judicial matters examined in this book can have enormous impacts over the years on the viability of the federation and its fundamentally federalist or unitarist orientation. The studies in this volume do not reveal one best set of decisions but do shed light on potential federalist or unitarist consequences of those decisions. As such, we hope this book serves as an invitation to further comparative research that can examine more cases and specify more precisely the findings presented in this volume.

Contributors

Elisenda Casanas Adam is a lecturer in public law and human rights and a member of the Centre for Constitutional Law at Edinburgh Law School. She was previously a lecturer in constitutional law at the Autonomous University of Barcelona (2009–11) and the University of Girona (2008–9). The dissertation title for her PhD at the European University Institute was "Judicial Federalism from a Comparative Perspective: Spain, the United States and the United Kingdom." Her main research interests lie in the comparative analysis of the organization and functioning of federal and devolved systems, focusing on the legal accommodation of national identity, the courts and the judiciary, and the protection of human rights. She has a special interest in the public law of Catalonia and Scotland.

Nicholas Aroney is professor of constitutional law at the University of Queensland. He has initiated and led several international research projects in constitutional law and legal theory, with particular emphasis on the theory and practice of federalism, the design and performance of bicameral parliamentary systems, and religious freedom in multicultural societies and the accommodation of Islamic law within Western democratic states. In 2011 he was awarded a four-year Australian Research Council fellowship to undertake research on comparative federalism. He has held visiting positions at Oxford, Paris, Edinburgh, Emory, and Sydney Universities and is the author of over 100 books, book chapters, and articles. His books include *The Constitution of a Federal Commonwealth: The Making and Meaning of the Australian Constitution* (Cambridge University Press, 2009), *Shari'a in the West* (Oxford University Press, 2010), *The Future of Australian Federalism* (Cambridge University

Press, 2012), and *The Constitution of the Commonwealth of Australia: History, Principle and Interpretation* (Cambridge University Press, 2015).

Arthur Benz is professor of political science at the Technische Universität Darmstadt, Germany. Before moving to Darmstadt in 2010, he worked as professor at the Universities of Konstanz, Halle, and Hagen, and as a visiting scholar at the Max-Planck-Institute of Social Science in Cologne and at Carleton University, Ottawa. Multi-level governance and comparative federalism are at the centre his research. His recent publications include *Federal Dynamics: Continuity, Change, and the Varieties of Federalism* (Oxford University Press, 2013, ed. with Jörg Broschek), and *Constitutional Change in Multilevel Government: The Art of Keeping the Balance* (Oxford University Press, 2016). His articles published, e.g., in *European Political Science Review, Publius: The Journal of Federalism, West European Politics, Regional and Federal Studies* contributed to empirical and theoretical research on the effectiveness and legitimacy in national and European multi-level governance.

Eugénie Brouillet is a full professor, lawyer, and dean of the Faculty of Law at Université Laval. Her research focuses on constitutional law, more specifically Canadian federalism and the comparative study of federalism in a pluri-national context, and on the protection of human rights and freedoms. She is the author of *La négation de la nation: L'identité culturelle québécoise et le fédéralisme canadien* (Septentrion 2005), which received the Prix Richard-Arès (2006) and the second Prix de la Présidence de la l'Assemblée nationale (2006). She has also written numerous articles and co-authored the treatise *Droit constitutionnel* (with Professors Henri Brun and Guy Tremblay, 6th ed., Yvon Blais, 2014). Ms Brouillet is a member of the Research Group on Pluri-national Societies (Groupe de recherche sur les sociétés plurinationales) and vice-chair of the Quebec constitutional law association (Association québécoise de droit constitutionnel). She also codirects the laws, institutions, and intercommunity relations research sector at the Centre for Interdisciplinary Research on Diversity and Democracy (Centre de recherche interdisciplinaire sur la diversité et la démocratie).

Jacques Bühler received his doctorate in law of the University of Lausanne (Switzerland) in 1993 (Otto Riese Price). Since 1986, Jacques Bühler has been an employee of the Swiss Federal Supreme Court. He is deputy general secretary and head of the scientific services (IT, legal documentation and library). He also is a delegate of Switzerland within the European Commission for the Efficiency of Justice (CEPEJ) of the Council of Europe and head of the Judicial Time Management working group of the CEPEJ. In 2015 he received the Pro Merito Medal of the Council of Europe in the light of widely recognized commitment and contribution to the work of the organization and specially of the CEPEJ.

Gedion T. Hessebon is an assistant professor at Addis Ababa University School of Law and a visiting professor at the Central European University in Budapest, Hungary. He graduated with an LLB from Addis Ababa University and an LLM. and SJD at the Central European University in comparative constitutional law. His research is in the fields of comparative constitutional law (with a focus on anglophone Sub-Saharan Africa), freedom of expression, and freedom of religion.

Abduletif K. Idris is a lecturer at the Center for Human Rights of the Addis Ababa University. He graduated with an LLB from Addis Ababa University and an LLM from the University of Alabama. He teaches courses on federalism and human rights. His research is in the fields of human rights, federalism, and administrative law.

José Antonio Caballero Juárez received his law degree from the Universidad Nacional Autónoma de México. He has a doctorate in law from the Universidad de Navarra and a master's degree in law from Stanford University. He is a researcher at the Centro de Investigación y Docencia Económica in Mexico City. He teaches constitutional procedure and criminal procedure. His work focuses on legal history, regulation, justice, judicial reform, and criminal justice reform. His most recent publications discuss criminal law reform, access to judicial information, judicial accountability, judicial federalism, and a book on due process in Latin America (2014). He has served as consultant to several national and international agencies in projects that involve regulation, judicial reform, and criminal law reform. He has also worked as a consultant for legislators for constitutional and legal reforms in Mexico. As a litigator he has represented public interest cases as well as private cases before the Mexican Supreme Court.

Daniel Kettiger studied law at the University of Bern (Switzerland). From 1988 to 2002 he worked in leading positions in public administration. In April 2000 he obtained a master's degree from the

German University of Administrative Science Speyer. Since January 2003 he has been an independent lawyer and consultant and a senior research fellow at the Center of Competence for Public Management of the University of Bern and teaches public management at the Bern University of Applied Sciences. He published on constitutional and administrative law, penal procedure, regional governance, court management, and new public management. From 2012 to 2016, he has co-managed the Swiss National Science Foundation project "Basic Research into Court Management in Switzerland."

John Kincaid is the Robert B. and Helen S. Meyner Professor of Government and Public Service and director of the Meyner Center for the Study of State and Local Government at Lafayette College, Easton, Pennsylvania. He is an elected fellow of the National Academy of Public Administration, recipient of the Distinguished Scholar Award from the Section on Federalism and Intergovernmental Relations of the American Political Science Association. He served as senior editor of the Global Dialogue on Federalism, a joint project of the Forum of Federations and International Association of Centers for Federal Studies (2001–15); editor of *Publius: The Journal of Federalism* (1981–2006); and executive director of the U.S. Advisory Commission on Intergovernmental Relations, Washington, DC (1988–1994). He is the author of various works on federalism and intergovernmental relations, co-editor most recently of *The Covenant Connection: From Federal Theology to Modern Federalism* (2000), *Constitutional Origins, Structure, and Change in Federal Countries* (2005), the *Routledge Handbook of Regionalism and Federalism* (2013), *Intergovernmental Relations in Federal Systems: Comparative Structures and Dynamics* (2015), and *Political Parties and Civil Society in Federal Countries* (2015) and editor of *Federalism* (4 vols., 2011).

Andreas Lienhard is professor of constitutional and administrative law at the Center of Competence for Public Management (managing director) and the Institute for Public Law at the University of Bern (Switzerland). He studied law at the University of Bern, qualifying as an attorney in the Canton of Bern in 1991. In 1994 he received his doctorate, and in 2002, his postdoctoral degree (Habilitation). His activities focus on constitutional and administrative reforms, public financial and economic law, and law-making processes. Since 2009 he has managed the Evaluation of Research into Law project, run by the Rectors' Conference of the Swiss Universities, and from 2012 to 2016, the Swiss National Science Foundation project Basic Research into Court Management in Switzerland. Andreas Lienhard was the leader of the Evaluation of the Effectiveness of the Reformed Federal Judicature project in Switzerland. He is a co-editor of the *International Journal for Court Administration (IJCA)* and a co-chair of the EGPA Permanent Study Group XVIII on Justice and Court Administration.

Marco Antonio Garcia Lopes Lorencini – PhD and MSc in procedural law (São Paulo University-USP) LLB (USP). He is professor of procedure law at the Paulista University, affiliated to the São Paulo Bar and responsible for the Litigation Department at the São Paulo office of L.O. Baptista, Schmidt, Valois, Miranda, Ferreira, and Agel. He is a researcher at the Brazilian Centre for Judicial Research, São Paulo, Brazil, core of studies involving conflict resolution mechanisms, State of São Paulo University, and expert in alternative dispute resolution. Co-author (Brazil chapter) of *International Arbitration*, a country-by-country look at alternative dispute resolution methods around the globe (Aspatore Books, 2005).

Loranne Mérillat is head of the Division for Migration at the Swiss Conference of Cantonal Ministers of Social Affairs. After passing her matura with a focus on economy in St Gallen, she studied law at the bilingual University of Fribourg (Switzerland) as well as at the Universidad Autónoma de Madrid (Spain). As part of her PhD thesis in the field of constitutional law at the University of Fribourg, she compared the decentralized state systems of Switzerland and Spain on the basis of constitutional principles. A scholarship from the Swiss National Science Foundation granted Mérillat a research visit at the Universidad Autónoma de Madrid. Apart from her research, she worked at the Institute of Public Law at the University of Bern (Switzerland) as well as at the Federal Department of Foreign Affairs of Switzerland.

Jens Mosselmans is attorney at law at the Brussels bar and partner at Portico, a boutique law firm specializing in public law. He is also secretary of the editorial board of *CDPK (Chroniques de droit public / Publiekrechtelijke Kronieken)*, one of Belgian's leading public law journals.

Patrick Peeters is professor at the Faculty of Law, Constitutional Law Department, University of Leuven (KU Leuven). He lectures on comparative federalism. He is also attorney at law at the Brussels bar and partner at NautaDutilh, a leading Benelux law firm. Peeters is country rapporteur for European Public Law and member of the editorial board of Chroniques de Droit Public / Publiekrechtelijke Kronieken. He is author of numerous publications on constitutional law, comparative federalism, and Belgian state reform. He is co-editor and co-author of *International Encyclopaedia of Constitutional Law: Belgium* (2013).

Gilberto Marcos Antonio Rodrigues – PhD in international relations (Pontifical Catholic University of São Paulo-PUC-SP), MSc in international relations (University for Peace, Costa Rica), and LLB (PUC-SP) – is adjunct professor at the International Relations Department at the Federal University of ABC, São Paulo, Brazil. He is also a researcher at the National Scientific and Research Council. He is rapporteur of the International Organizations Project at the Manchester International Law Centre, University of Manchester, UK (2016–17). He was a Fulbright Visiting Scholar at the Center for Civil and Human Rights, University of Notre Dame (2010). Co-author (Brazil chapter) of *Diversity and Unity in Federal Countries* (McGill-Queen's University Press, 2010).

Rekha Saxena is professor at the Department of Political Science, University of Delhi. She is also the honorary vice-chairperson of the Centre for Multilevel Federalism at New Delhi and honorary senior adviser to the Forum of Federations, Ottawa. She was appointed as a member of a Task Force of the Second Commission on Centre-State Relations set up by the Union Ministry of Home Affairs. She was recently appointed as a member of the International Advisory Board, Global Autonomy and Governance Forum 2016. She has published more than ten books. She edited *Varieties of Federal Governance: Major Contemporary Models* (2010) and *Mapping Canadian Federalism for India* (2002); wrote *Situating Federalism: Mechanisms of Intergovernmental Relations in Canada and India* (2006); and co-authored *India at the Polls: Parliamentary Elections in the Federal Phase* (2003), *Indian Politics: Constitutional Design and Institutional Functioning* (2011), and *Federalizing India in the Age of Globalization* (2013).

Ilya Somin is professor of law at George Mason University. His research focuses on constitutional law, property law, and the study of popular political participation and its implications for constitutional democracy. He is the author of *The Grasping Hand: Kelo v. City of New London and the Limits of Eminent Domain* (University of Chicago Press, 2015), and *Democracy and Political Ignorance: Why Smaller Government Is Smarter*

(Stanford University Press, 2013, revised and expanded second edition, 2016), co-author of *A Conspiracy against Obamacare: The Volokh Conspiracy and the Health Care Case* (Palgrave Macmillan, 2013), and co-editor of *Eminent Domain in Comparative Perspective* (Cambridge University Press, forthcoming). Somin's work has appeared in numerous scholarly journals, including the *Yale Law Journal*, *Stanford Law Review*, *Northwestern University Law Review*, and others. Somin has also published articles in a variety of popular press outlets, including the *Wall Street Journal*, *Los Angeles Times*, and the *New York Times*. He has served as a visiting professor at universities in Argentina, China, and Germany.

Nico Steytler holds the South African Research Chair in Multilevel Government, Law, and Policy at the Dullah Omar Institute of Constitutional Law, Governance, and Human Rights, University of the Western Cape, South Africa. He co-authored with Jaap de Visser *Local Government Law of South Africa* (8th rev. ed., 2014) and was the editor of the *Global Dialogue* volume in *Local Government and Metropolitan Regions in Federal Systems* (2009) and co-editor of *Kenya–South Africa Dialogue on Devolution* (2015). He was a member of the Municipal Demarcation Board (2004–14) and is a commissioner of the Financial and Fiscal Commission (2013–17).

Rotimi Suberu teaches politics and international relations at Bennington College, Vermont. Earlier, he taught political science at the University of Ibadan, Nigeria. He is the author of *Federalism and Ethnic Conflict in Nigeria* (United States Institute of Peace Press, 2001) and has written widely on Nigerian government and politics. He has held fellowships and visiting positions at the Woodrow Wilson International Center for Scholars, United States Institute of Peace, the University of Oxford, University of Pennsylvania, Northwestern University, National Institute for Legislative Studies, Abuja, Nigeria, and New Delhi's Centre for the Study of Developing Societies.

Manish Tewari is a practising lawyer in the Supreme Court of India. He has been a member of the Indian parliament (Lok Sabha) and was minister for information and broadcasting in the Government of India. He has also been a member and special invitee to the Cabinet Committee on Economic Affairs, Cabinet Committee on Parliamentary Affairs, and Cabinet Committee on Investments, and has been a member of numerous Empowered Group of Ministers and Group of Ministers dealing with a diverse array of policy issues. He has been a member of the Parliamentary Standing Committees of External Affairs, Law and Justice and Defence and served on the Parliamentary Consultative Committees of the Ministries of Defence and Law and Justice. He is the national spokesperson of the Indian National Congress and the secretary of the Foreign Affairs Department of the Indian National Congress. He is a prolific writer and is published both nationally and internationally.

Daniela Winkler received her master's degree in sociology and political science from the Universities of Basel and Zurich (Switzerland) in 2011. During her studies, she worked for five years as a research assistant at the Basel Institute on Governance (Switzerland), which included a three-month research period at the Institute for Democracy in South Africa (Idasa) in Cape Town (South Africa). Since December 2011, Daniela Winkler has worked as a research assistant at the Center of Competence for Public Management of the University of Bern (Switzerland). From 2012 to 2016, she was responsible for the coordination and management support of the Swiss National Science Foundation project "Basic Research into Court Management in Switzerland." She is also involved in judicial research and judicial consulting projects. She is writing her PhD thesis on the methodology of workload assessment in Swiss courts.

Augusto Zimmermann – LLB (Hon.), LLM cum laude, PhD (Monash) – is a commissioner with the Law Reform Commission of Western Australia and a professor of law (adjunct) at the University of Notre Dame Australia in Sydney. Dr Zimmermann is also postgraduate research director and former associate dean (Research) at Murdoch University's School of Law, where he teaches and coordinates the units Constitutional Law and Legal Theory. Dr Zimmermann is the founder and president of the Western Australian Legal Theory Association and editor-in-chief of the *Western Australian Jurist*, a blind peer review publication. His books include *Curso de Direito Constitutional* (Lumen Juris, 2006), *Direito Constitutional Brasileiro* (Lumen Juris, 2015), among several others. A prolific writer and the author of numerous articles and academic books, Dr Zimmermann was awarded the 2012 Vice Chancellor's Award for Excellence in Research, and two School Dean's Research Awards, in 2010 and 2011.

Index

Page numbers with (t) refer to tables. Legal cases are entered as a group under the name of the country.

www.ingramcontent.com/pod-product-compliance
Lightning Source LLC
LaVergne TN
LVHW020434080826
844660LV00033B/1287

* 9 7 8 1 4 8 7 5 2 2 8 9 6 *